'There is certainly no circumstance of landscape more interesting or beautiful than water and there can be no person so void of taste as not to feel the necessity of improving the valley at Normanton [now under Rutland Water] by enlarging the river, yet this is a subject attended with some difficulty and requires more management than may at first be conceived; for though it might be possible to make such a dam or head as would convert the whole valley into one vast lake, yet the expense of such a bank, and the waste of so much valuable land, is more than I would dare to advise . . . .'

Humphry Repton, 1797

The Heritage of Rutland Water

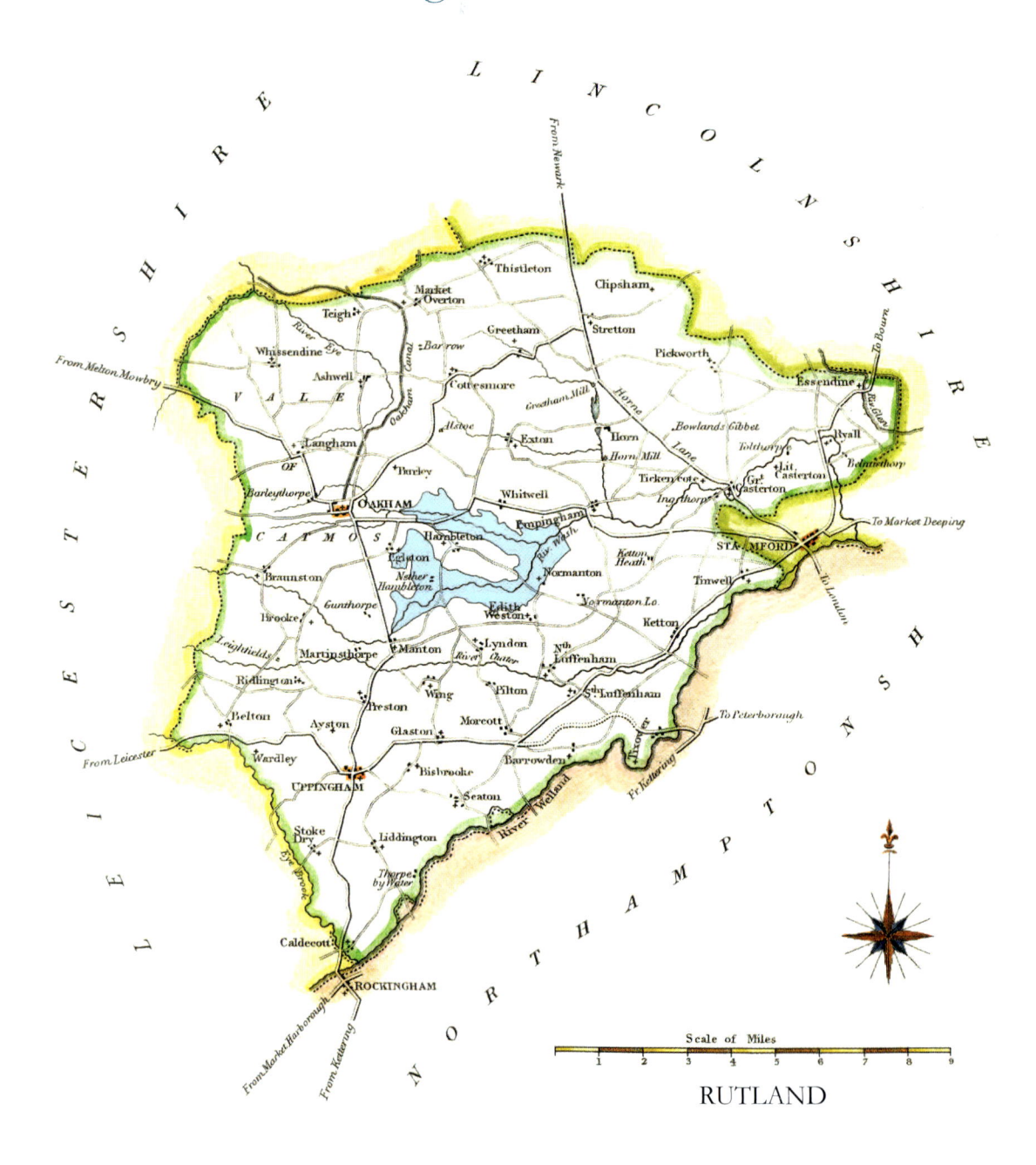

After J & C Walker's map of Rutland, circa 1840, with Rutland Water superimposed

The Heritage of Rutland Water

Compiled and Edited by

Robert Ovens & Sheila Sleath

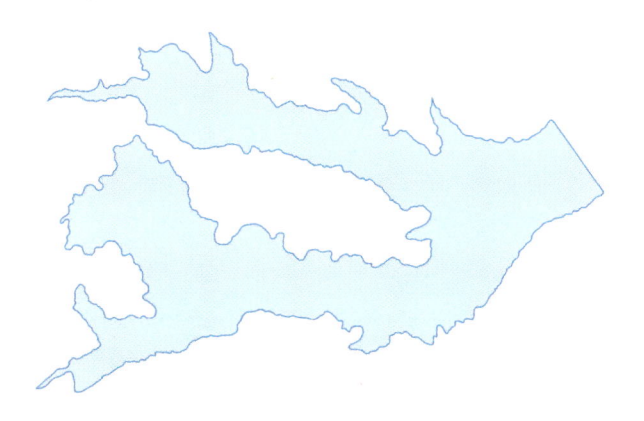

Supported by The National Lottery® through the Heritage Lottery Fund | Heritage Lottery Fund

anglianwater

Rutland Local History & Record Society
Rutland Record Series No 5
2007
Registered Charity No 700273

RLHRS Rutland Record Series No 5

First published in 2007 by the Rutland Local History & Record Society, Rutland County Museum, Catmose Street, Oakham, Rutland, LE15 6HW

The Society is grateful to the Heritage Lottery Fund for a generous grant towards the cost of producing this publication under the Local Heritage Initiative

Copyright © Rutland Local History & Record Society 2007

ISBN 978-0-907464-39-6

The rights of Robert Ovens and Sheila Sleath as editors of this work and those of all the individual authors have been asserted by them in accordance with the Copyright, Designs and Patents Act 1993

All rights reserved. No part of this publication may be reproduced, stored in a retrieval system, or transmitted in any form or by any means, electronic, mechanical, photocopying, recording or otherwise without the prior permission of the Rutland Local History & Record Society

British Library Cataloguing in Publication Data
A catalogue record for this book is available from the British Library

Edited for the Society by T H McK Clough

Designed by Dan and Phil Jarman,
philjarman@yahoo.co.uk
01778 343516

Printed and bound in Malta by Gutenberg Press Ltd

Museum, Alick Freer (OH), Kemmel Freestone (OH), Michael Frisby (SC), Lord Gainsborough (OH), Prince Gregory Galitzine, Barrie Galpin (A), Nick Giles, Peter Golden, Sam Gorin, Maggie Gover (OH), *Grantham Journal* ©, Tony Gray (A), staff and pupils of Great Casterton C of E Primary School, Denis Gregg, Dennis Gregory (OH), Marcus Gregory (OH), Dr Mike Griffin (Ed, A, OH), Jane Grylls, Mary Grylls, Dorothy Hackett, Lawrence Harris, Robert Hartley, Charles Hawarth (SC, OH), Tim Hawkins ©, Julie Healey, Angela Herbert (OH), Mr and Mrs John Hibbitt, John Hill, Raymond Hill, Brian Hollingshead, Martin Hollingshead, Sue Howlett (A, SC, OH), Pam Hubbard (OH), *Illustrated London News*, Institution of Civil Engineers ©, Dan Jarman (D), Phil Jarman (D), Mike Johnson, Dr Dorothy Johnston, Chris Jones, Dr Clive Jones (A), Elaine Jones, Philip Joyce (OH), Alan Jury, Marion Kelham, Jill Kimber, Brian Knight, Ron Knight, Vic Lambert, Marigold Lamin (OH), Peter Lane, Janet Lavender, Marion Lawrie (OH), Sylvia and Michael Leach (OH), Sue Lee (A), *Leicester Mercury* ©, the late Jim Levisohn ARPS, Joan Levisohn, Lincolnshire Archives ©, Edna Locke (OH), Madge Lombard (OH), David Lowe (A), Chris Lythall, Andrew Makey (OH), Sheila Manchester (OH), Manton Millennium Group, Manton Parish Council, John Matthews, Brenda May, Roland Meadows, Peter Meakin, Tony Melia, Diana Mellows (OH), Terry Mitcham (A), David Moore (A), National Monuments Record (English Heritage) ©, the Rev Brian Nicholls (OH), Brian and Elizabeth Nicholls Photography ©, Normanton Park Hotel, Northampton Libraries and Information Service, the Churchwardens of North Luffenham, staff and pupils of St Mary & St John C of E School at North Luffenham, *Nottingham Evening Post* ©, William Nourish, John Nowell – Zodiac Publishing ©, the staff at Oakham Library, Jim O'Connor, Jean Orpin (A), Jane Ostler, Robert Ovens (Ed, A, SC, Ph, Arc, OH), Robert Owen Smith, Mr and Mrs Eric Palmer (OH), Shirley Palmer, Mary and David Parkin (A), Risi Pasqualino, Janice Patient, Alan Peel Shaw, Jim Pickering, John W Pinder, Margaret and Laurence Plumb (OH), Brian Pollard (OH), Richard Pollard, Dr D A Postles, Canon John R H Prophet, Eileen Ray, Diana Read (OH), Record Office for Leicestershire, Leicester and Rutland (ROLLR) ©, the staff at ROLLR, Sally Redrup, Paul Reeve (Ed, A, SC, OH), Ruth and Christopher Renner (OH), Bob Roberts (OH), Mike Roberts, Robinson Library ©, Alison Rogers (OH), Philip Rudkin, Gerry Rudman, Rutland County Council ©, Rutland County Museum (RCM) ©, Simon Davies and the staff at RCM, the officers and committee members of Rutland Local History & Record Society, Rutland Natural History Society ©, Rutland Osprey Project ©, Rutland Radio, Rutland Sailability ©, Rutland Sailing Club, the staff at Rutland Sailing Club, *Rutland and Stamford Mercury* ©, *Rutland Times* ©, Dr Ian Ryder (A, SC), *Sailracer* ©, Vicky Sanderlin-McLoughlin (SC), Nigel Savage, Dorothy and Noel Sharp (OH), Shirley Design ©, Rovy Slater, Harold Sleath, Sheila Sleath (Ed, A, SC, Arc, OH), Adrian Smith, the late C Walter Smith, Gordon Smith (OH), Freda Smithson, the late Derek Spence, the staff at Stamford Library, Anthony Squires, Ian Starkey, *Sunday Express*, Steve Swan, Jane Theobald, Jane Thomas (OH), Auriol and David Thomson, Winifred Tibbert (OH), Malcolm Todd, Peter Tomalin, Phil Tomaszewski, Ann Tomlinson, Tony Traylen, *Trout Fisherman Magazine* ©, Malcolm G Underwood, University of Leicester Archaeological Services, Uppingham School Archives ©, John Wadham (A), Bryan Waites, Henry Wakerley (OH), Ben Walker, John Walker, Joan and Roy Walton, Cliff Waters Design ©, Barbara and Alex Watt (OH), Linda Watts, Mrs Weatherby, B West, May Wheatley, Janet Whittaker, Whitwell Hotel and Conference Centre, Wikipedia ©, Joan Wild (OH), Joan Willerton (OH), A J H Winder (OH), Rosemary Woodland, John Wright, R Wright.

The following abbreviations are used in the above:

A	Author
Arc	Scanning photographs & archival material
D	Designer
Ed	Editorial
OH	Interviewer, interviewee and/or transcriber
Ph	Photography
SC	Steering Committee
©	Institution granting permission to reproduce copyright photograph(s)

The majority of the photographs used in this publication are © The Rutland Local History & Record Society. Other illustrations have been reproduced with the kind permission of individual and institutional owners and whilst every care has been taken to trace copyright holders, if the Society has omitted anyone it apologises and will, if informed, make corrections in any future edition.

Dr Michael Tillbrook
Chairman
Rutland Local History & Record Society

Acknowledgements

The Heritage of Rutland Water is the culmination of a two-year community project involving a great deal of intensive research and this publication would not have been possible without the help, guidance and commitment of many individuals and organisations. Nor would it have been possible without the support of the National Lottery through the Heritage Lottery Fund, which awarded Rutland Local History & Record Society a substantial grant towards the cost of the project, including the production of this book.

The huge success of this project and the number of people involved means that it is virtually impossible to name everyone who has made a contribution. Without exception, those who were contacted willingly provided information, loaned photographs and archival material and gave valuable advice and support. The Society expresses its gratitude to all of them.

It is not the Society's intention to single out or to categorise the contribution made by every individual or group, but special mention must be made of the following: Tim Clough, Honorary Editor of the Rutland Local History & Record Society for editorial guidance and proofreading; Robert Ovens for his unstinting contribution in his roles as co-ordinator of the project, joint editor and official photographer; Sheila Sleath as joint editor and oral history convener; Dan and Phil Jarman as the ever-patient designers of this publication; Mike Griffin and Paul Reeve for their invaluable assistance with editing and proofreading; and Mike Frisby for his guidance on all matters relating to information technology. Those who attended the initial meetings and who became part of the Steering Committee must also be acknowledged. This includes Sue Howlett, one of the initial driving-forces behind the project, who not only found time to be secretary of the Group, but also organised a competition for school children.

One of the main tasks early in the project was to convene an oral history group. This resulted in many memories being recorded with specific reference to Rutland Water and also provided an insight into aspects of life as it used to be for people living in and around the Gwash valley. This collection will become a valuable resource for researchers in the future. It will be held by the Society at the Rutland County Museum and in the fullness of time transcripts will be freely accessible on request. The contribution of the interviewers and interviewees is of great merit and a special thank you is extended to them.

Without the contributions of the authors this publication would have been very difficult to complete. The Society is therefore particularly grateful to all of them for devoting their time to and for submitting such varied and well-researched material which will inevitably appeal to a very wide readership.

The number of photographs which were loaned or donated to the Society was overwhelming. We are particularly grateful to Anglian Water, Tony Traylen and Richard Adams, as well as many other individuals, for giving free access to their photographic collections, and to the Rev Brian and Elizabeth Nicholls (official photographers for the construction of the reservoir) who donated their complete collection of Rutland Water negatives to the Society. In addition, the Rutland County Museum kindly allowed the Society to make use of its collections, especially the Jack Hart Collection of Rutland postcards, an extensive and unparalleled source of early Rutland views. Most of the present-day digital photographs were taken by Robert Ovens, many of which are used to illustrate this publication. This vast archive will compliment other donated or loaned project material which has been digitised by the editors and which will be retained by the Society at the Rutland County Museum.

Overall public interest has been heartening and encouraging. One of the particular aims, and a particular condition of the Heritage Lottery Fund award, was to progress the project through community involvement. This has been admirably achieved, the involvement of local schools being particularly rewarding. Whilst it is impossible to acknowledge everyone who has made a contribution, the Society's gratitude is extended to the following:

Fred Adams, Richard Adams (SC), Dora Allibone, Angus Baker ©, aphotoflora.com ©, Tim Appleton, John Bailey, Edward Baines (A, SC), Dan Baker, John Ball, Barnsdale Hall Hotel, Michael Barsby (A), Hayley Bell, Mary Bell (OH), Jane Bews, Ray Biggs, Bobby Blackstock, David Bland (OH), Justin Boughey, Christine Brammal, John Branson, Liz Branson, Bridgeman Art Library ©, Noel Bridgeman, Elizabeth Bryan, Andrew Burns, Audrey Buxton (OH, SC), Cambridge Museum of Air Photography ©, Barbara Camp, David Carlin, Caroline Cartwright (SC), Lisa Cavenagh, Sue Cavanagh, the late Roger Chandler, R C Chatburn, Janet Christian, Robin Church (OH), Patrick Clay, Tim Clough (Ed, A, SC), Mary and the late Louis Cockerill (OH), Gwen Coggan (OH), Tom Coggan (OH), Edward Conant (OH), Sir John Conant (OH), Nick Cooper, Roger Corby (OH), Country Life Picture Library ©, David Cram, Peter Craven, Malcolm Croson (OH), Hilary Crowden (A, SC), Peter Diplock (SC), Kate Don (A, SC), Sheila and Peter Drake (OH), Betty Eaton, the late Jim Eaton, Roy Eaton Photography ©, Edith Weston Parish Council, staff and pupils of Edith Weston County Primary School, Daphne Elliott, Patrick Elliott, Empingham Parish Council, Sheila Ervin (OH), Betty and the late George Finch, Fotolia © (S Camp, S Chushkin, D Freer, J Gil, K Hewitt, ivp, M Kosmal, pdtnc, Stafford, D Zidar), Fox Talbot

The Middle Gwash Valley before and after Rutland Water

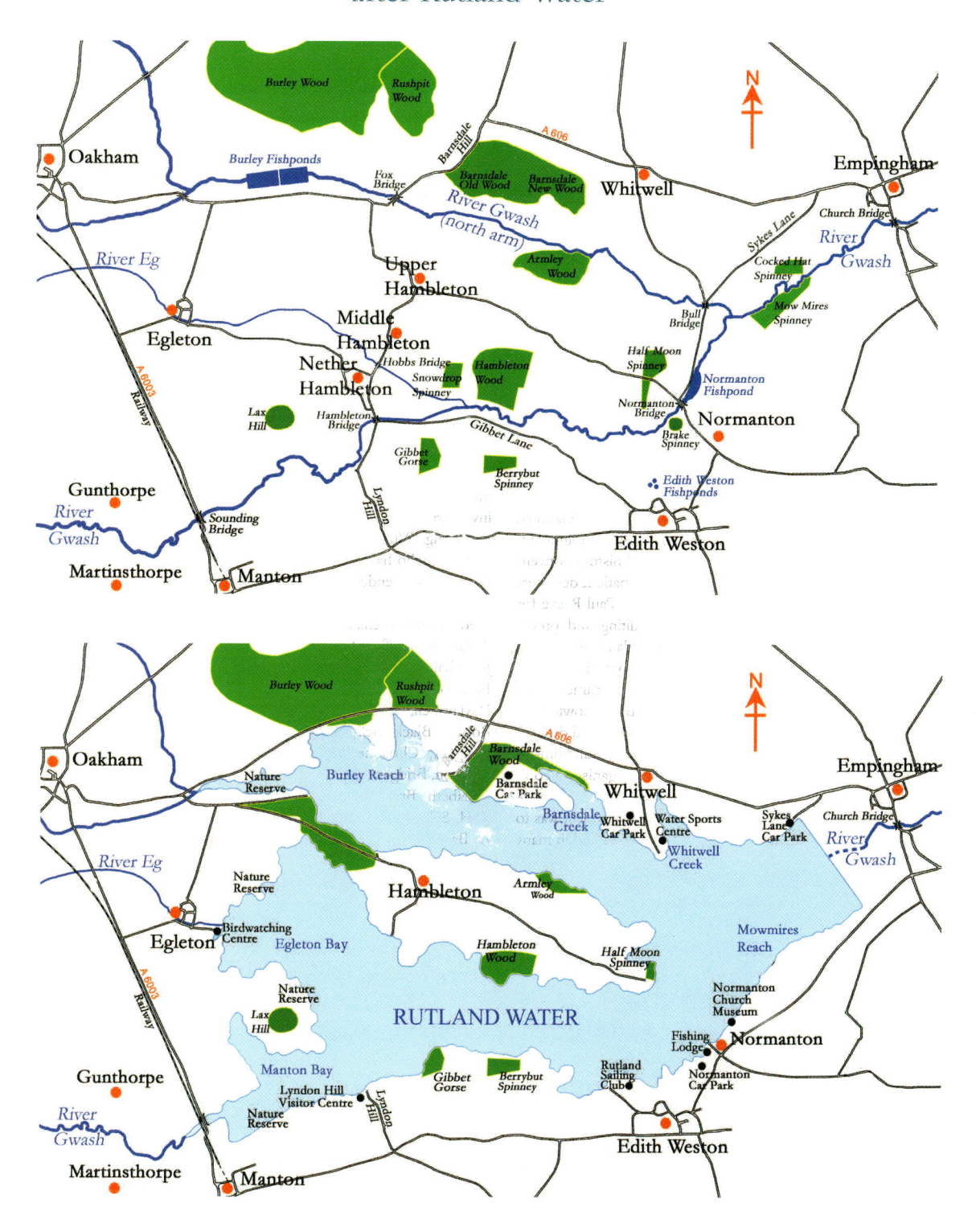

Foreword

Rutland Water occupies the heart of the county of Rutland: a small county, and a very big heart. Even so, when the Rutland Local History & Record Society first proposed that the reservoir area's extensive and varied heritage should be recorded and commemorated, I think no-one envisaged that the project would give birth to a publication on such a scale as this, nor that it would cover such a range of subject matter – from Rutland Water's underlying geology to the management of its nature reserves, from the history of families that once lived nearby to the types of boat that now sail its waters. Anyone who has an interest in Rutland, its history and its environment will find something in this book which will catch the imagination, and if its readers are inspired to talk about what they have read here, or to find out more, then one of the project's aims will have been fulfilled.

That this book has come to see the light of day is very largely due to the dedicated hard work of its two editors, Robert Ovens and Sheila Sleath. When they first asked me if I would contribute a Foreword, I demurred. As the publishing society's Honorary Editor, I was, I thought, too close to the project, and in any case I felt that such a Foreword should be contributed by someone whose name would lend more kudos to the book than would mine. However, I was persuaded that by my closeness, and through the knowledge of Rutland which I had accumulated during my time as Curator of the Rutland County Museum, I was suitably qualified to perform this task. Now, having seen at first hand the effort that has gone into the making of the book, it is a very pleasant duty for me to congratulate Robert and Sheila – not for the first time – on making a major, and probably unique, contribution to the study and recording of Rutland's heritage.

We should be enduringly grateful not only to Robert and Sheila, but also to the wide range of authors who were persuaded, encouraged, or – rarely, it should be said – cajoled into writing their many and varied chapters for this book. They and others are more fully acknowledged elsewhere, but without all their efforts the book could never have appeared. Nor could it have appeared without the support of the Rutland Local History & Record Society's members and the ambitions of its management committee: it is a small society, and the project has represented a major commitment on its part. We should also gladly acknowledge the generous recognition of the worth of the project by the Heritage Lottery Fund's Local Heritage Initiative and its sponsors, whose significant financial contribution to the cost of production has made possible the design and printing of this book. The LHI was designed to support local community projects, and there can be few such projects which have involved such a wide range of contributors and participants. This has been a community project *par excellence*, and the Rutland Local History & Record Society is now proud to present the results to the community for which it was prepared: not a large community, but big-hearted.

T H McK Clough

17	Planning and Constructing the Reservoir	Robert Ovens & Sheila Sleath	369
	Map of Archaeological Sites in the Middle Gwash Valley / Archaeological Timeline		402
18	Brooches, Bathhouses and Bones – Archaeology in the Gwash Valley	Kate Don	403
	Aspects of Topography: High Bridge Road		414
19	The Archaeologists	Sheila Sleath & Robert Ovens	415
20	Medieval Settlements at Nether Hambleton and Whitwell	Tim Clough	421
	Aspects of Topography: Gibbet Lane		444
21	Lost Homes	Sheila Sleath & Robert Ovens	445
	Aspects of Topography: The Stamford to Oakham Turnpike		480
22	Rutland Water: Planning and Developing a Water Supply Reservoir as a World-Class Leisure Venue	David Moore	481
23	Fauna and Flora before Rutland Water	Mike Griffin	499
	Aspects of Topography: Old Barnsdale Hill		528
24	Tim Appleton MBE – Thirty Years of Rutland Water Nature Reserve	Sue Howlett & Robert Ovens	529
25	The Birds of Rutland Water	Terry Mitcham	575
26	A New Home for the Osprey	Barrie Galpin	587
27	A Panorama of Activities at Rutland Water	Robert Ovens & Sheila Sleath	601
28	Rutland Water Fishing	John Wadham	611
29	Sailing on Rutland Water – Rutland Sailing Club	Tony Gray & Mike Barsby	625
	Aspects of Topography: New Barnsdale Hill		642
30	Extra, Extra, Read all about it!	Sheila Sleath & Robert Ovens	643
	Bibliography		665
	Index		668

Contents

	Map of Rutland, *circa* 1840, with Rutland Water superimposed		2
	Foreword		7
	The Middle Gwash Valley before and after Rutland Water		8
	Acknowledgements		9
	Introduction and Abbreviations		11
1	Working the Soil – the Generation of Wealth 1086 to 1800	Ian Ryder	13
2	The Agricultural Revolution and Beyond	Edward Baines	25
3	Barnsdale	Sue Howlett	45
4	Burley on the Hill	Sue Howlett	55
5	Edith Weston: A Queen's Dowry	Sue Howlett	93
6	Egleton: A Glimpse into the Past	Sheila Sleath & Robert Ovens	117
7	Empingham: An Entire Model Village	Sue Lee & Jean Orpin	133
8	Hambleton: The Settlement on the Crooked Hill	Sue Howlett	149
	Aspects of Topography: Lost Footpaths, Footbridges and Bridleways		192
9	Lower Hambleton in 1797	Sheila Sleath & Robert Ovens	193
	Aspects of Topography: An Ancient Ridgeway		210
10	Manton: A 'Town on a Rock'	Manton Millennium Group with Robert Ovens & Sheila Sleath	211
11	Normanton	Sheila Sleath & Robert Ovens	231
	Aspects of Topography: The Egleton to Nether Hambleton Road		282
12	Whitwell: A 'pretty little village'	Sue Howlett	283
13	Changing Communities	Paul Reeve	303
	Aspects of Topography: Normanton Park Road		314
14	Rutland Waters	Robert Ovens & Sheila Sleath	315
	Aspects of Topography: A New Wetland Habitat		348
15	Don't Dam Rutland	Hilary Crowden	349
	Aspects of Topography: Normanton Bridge		358
16	The Geology of the Middle Gwash Valley	Clive Jones	359
	Aspects of Topography: Bull Bridge		368

Introduction

Early in 2004 the management committee of Rutland Local History & Record Society agreed to a suggestion that it should set up a study group to research the local history of the area now covered by Rutland Water. More than thirty years had passed since people living in the mid-Gwash valley, particularly those who earned their living from the land, had fought a concerted, but unsuccessful campaign to prevent the valley from being permanently flooded. This research needed to be commissioned rather sooner than later if it was to be carried out within living memory of life before the reservoir.

Almost at the same time, the Society became aware of grants that were available from the Heritage Lottery Fund (HLF) for projects involving the community. So our local history project became a community project, and a small steering committee was set up to apply for a grant. Its scope was widened to include archaeology and natural history, and it became known as the Heritage of Rutland Water Project. In retrospect, filling in the HLF application forms was easy compared with what was to follow, although we did have to predict, for example, what equipment and specialist training would be required, and how many volunteer hours would be needed.

In no time at all, it seemed, we had been offered nearly £25,000 and within a week half of it was in the bank. Rather worryingly, we now realised that we were committed to performing and completing this major undertaking, by far the largest that the Society had ever been directly involved in.

From the outset we expected the project to be like a large flywheel – slow to get up to speed, and then difficult to stop. How right we were. In May 2004 there were lots of ideas but little action. Then someone had the very bright idea of hiring a stand at the imminent Rutland County Show. Armed only with a small display on Rutland Water and a few Society publications to sell, three of us had a most exciting day. We could not believe how many were interested in our project, and by the end of the day we had a long list of people to see and interview. This, combined with local press and radio coverage and a poster campaign, kick-started the project.

As well as local museums and record offices, we always envisaged that much of the information generated for our project would come from four main sources – local people with memories, old photographs, newspaper cuttings and local publications. We were very successful in all these areas.

Memories of living and working in the valley, the campaign against the reservoir and the impact of reservoir construction work were recorded by our oral history group. In all there were 50 recordings to transcribe, type and analyse, a major project in itself. A competition for local schoolchildren, devised and directed by Sue Howlett, ensured that this section of the community was involved. Following presentations at a number of schools by members of the steering committee, more than 50 children took part and the Galitzine Prize was presented to the winner Evie Smith, of North Luffenham Church of England School, in a ceremony at Oakham Castle in June 2005.

The *Stamford Mercury* was a mine of useful information, not only for its archive going back some 300 years, but also for the years leading up to and during the construction of Rutland Water. Other local newspapers also reported on aspects of Rutland Water and we were particularly fortunate to locate four collections of cuttings. Other rich veins were the often self-published local village histories, the *In Rutland* Series researched by Tony Traylen, the Society's own *Rutland Record*, the *Victoria County History*, and George Phillips' *Rutland Magazine*.

The most successful aspect of the whole project was photography. A new digital camera purchased for the project ensured that we were able to accumulate a huge archive of 'now' photographs, many of which are reproduced in this book. The important Jack Hart collection of early Rutland postcards in Rutland County Museum was another constant source of inspiration.

Before he was ordained, the Rev Brian Nicholls, and his wife Elizabeth, were the official photographers for the Empingham Reservoir Project. We were amazed and delighted when they offered all their negatives and slides to our project. Until this generous gesture, we were struggling for good quality photographs of the construction process. In fact we were overwhelmed by the generosity of the many individuals and organisations who contributed their photographs either as donations or for copying

So, at the end of the second year of what was intended to be a two-year project we had amassed a huge amount of material and information, all of which will be retained at Rutland County Museum. However, we were yet to achieve our major objectives.

One objective, that of involvement with the media, was achieved when members of the steering committee were invited to take part in 'Countryfile' and 'Castles in the Country' for BBC television. Another objective was to devise a guided historical walk based on the project, and this took place early in September 2006 at Normanton, on the south shore of Rutland Water. A third objective was achieved two weeks later with a major presentation and exhibition on the project at Empingham, the exhibition then being displayed at Rutland County Museum for the next two months.

However, the main objective, this book, was at this stage a long way from publication, and it was to be another year before it was ready to be sent to the printers. At the original meeting to decide on the content and layout it became clear that no one person could write it, and that the best plan would be to invite individual authors to write chapters on specific topics. This plan worked well and very few restrictions were placed on them as to content, style, length, or what images were to be included.

Originally it was planned to have 260 pages, but as time went on and contributions came forward to go through the editing, proof-reading and designing processes, the page count gradually crept up to nearly 700. However, thanks to our HLF grant, our designers and additional support by the Society, we were able to let this happen, particularly as it was a once-and-only opportunity.

We know that our volunteer group has produced a book to be proud of and we hope that it proves to be an interesting read as well as an inspiration for further research.

Robert Ovens and Sheila Sleath
Rutland Local History & Record Society
October 2007

Abbreviations

TA	Tim Appleton	ROLLR	Record Office for Leicestershire, Leicester and Rutland
AF	*Airfield Focus*	RCM	Rutland County Museum
AW	Anglian Water	RLHRS	Rutland Local History and Record Society
CSPD	*Calendar of State Papers, Domestic*	RNHS	Rutland Natural History Society
CIPM	*Calendar of Inquisitions Post Mortem*	RSC	Rutland Sailing Club
Hart	Jack Hart postcard collection in RCM	RO	Robert Ovens
HMP	Her Majesty's Prison	RAF	Royal Air Force
HLF	Heritage Lottery Fund	RCAF	Royal Canadian Air Force
IFDS	International Federation of Disabled Sailors	RYA	Royal Yachting Association
		RWFF	Rutland Water Fly Fishers
JHC	*Journal of the House of Commons*	snr	senior
JST	Jubilee Sailing Trust	SS	Sheila Sleath
jnr	junior	SSSI	Site of Special Scientific Interest
SH	Sue Howlett	SPA	Special Protection Area
LHI	Local Heritage Initiative	TWL	top water level
MNWB	Mid-Northamptonshire Water Board	UK	United Kingdom
NVQ	National Vocational Qualification	*VCH*	*Victoria County History*
NATO	North Atlantic Treaty Organisation	W&NRA	Welland & Nene River Authority
OD	Ordnance Datum (height above mean sea level)	WI	Women's Institute
OS	Ordnance Survey		

Chapter 1
Working the Soil – the Generation of Wealth 1086 to 1800
Ian Ryder

The earliest survey of Rutland was that ordered by William the Conqueror in 1086, part of the Domesday Survey of England. The aim of the survey was to list feudal holdings and detail their value and assets. Though the individual village entries were highly condensed, they provide a wealth of information on land and, how it was used and populated. A typical entry is that for Whitwell. A man called Herbert held the manor as a sub-tenant of the Countess Judith (William's niece). The entry informs us of the amounts of tax the village paid, the extent of land that could be used, and how much was worked. All three of these are expressed in numbers of ploughs. Three ploughs worked the village fields, one held by Herbert and the others by the villagers. The use of ploughs, or more correctly plough teams, for taxation and land measure, informs us that these were the main generators of wealth and that agriculture was primarily arable.

Whitwell in the Domesday Survey of 1086

In Witewelle Besi had 1 carucate of land taxable. Land for 3 ploughs. Herbert has from Countess Judith 1 plough and 6 villeins [bondmen or villagers] and 4 bordars [cottagers or smallholders] who have 2 ploughs. A church and a priest; meadow, 20 acres; 1 mill 12d; woodland, pasture in places, 6 furlongs and 6 perches in length and 3 furlongs and 13 perches in width.
Value before 1066, 20s now 40s.

So why did Domesday use the seemingly strange assessment of plough teams for measuring the arable land, and what did they constitute? At the time of Domesday measures such as acres were not standardised and the number of plough teams provided a simply-determined and standardised alternative. The standard was the amount of land ploughed by a team of eight oxen (the plough beast of the time) in a year and was known as a carucate or hide. Sub-divisions of this standard were also named: a quarter was called a virgate or yardland, while an eighth was a bovate. These terms had a long life. The yardland continued in common agricultural usage until the nineteenth century. At Ridlington yardlands varied from 22 to 32 acres (Ryder 2006, 13); this variation is perhaps not surprising as the amount of land that could be ploughed by a team depended on the nature of the soil. Whitwell, like most of the villages that surround Rutland Water, has two very different types of soil. In the area below the village, now covered in water, there are heavy clay soils which are difficult to plough and which influenced the choice of reservoir site, and in the area above the village there are limestone tilths which are easier to plough. In reality the number of animals actually used in a plough team varied considerably. Sometimes Domesday gives specific information – at Thistleton two villagers had three oxen in a team and at Oakham one villager had a team of five oxen.

While the importance given by Domesday to plough teams reflects the importance of arable agriculture, this does not mean that there was no pasturing of animals. In fact some pasture was needed simply to feed the plough beasts. The pastoral components of village agriculture are reflected in Domesday's recording of meadow, pasture and woodland. Meadow was the most productive and therefore most valuable pasture land, and even small quantities of it are listed. Besides plough beasts, these lands could also be used to support cattle and sheep, while woodland was sometimes measured by its capacity to support pigs. At a time when wood was the main fuel, maintenance of productive woodland was essential for the community, as was a mill to grind the corn produced by the villagers. This would have been a watermill, as windmills were not introduced until the twelfth century. A careful reading of Domesday therefore paints a picture of most Rutland village fields dedicated to growing arable crops, while on the remaining parts animals were pastured to provide dairy produce, wool and meat. Along Rutland's river and stream banks were water meadows and mills, and carefully managed woodlands nearby.

Ploughing with a team of four oxen (Luttrell Psalter, AD 1335-40)

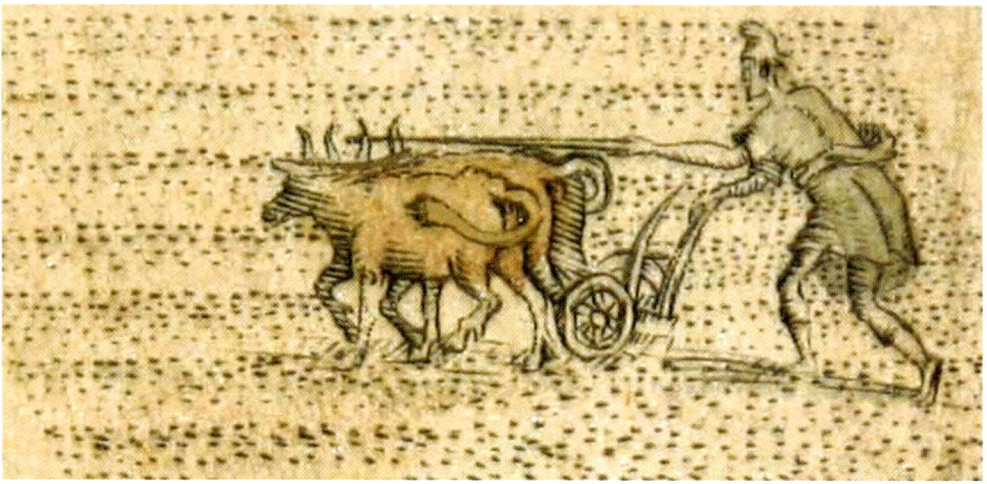

A medieval ploughman with two oxen (Speed's map of Rutland c1610)

Besides giving details of the agricultural assets of each village or manor, Domesday also groups its villagers by status. At Whitwell it records six villeins (bondmen) and four bordars (cottagers), but generally provides little information about individual holdings. However, this is provided in considerable detail in the 1305 survey of Oakham Lordshold (Chinnery 1988). What is clear from this survey is the regularity of land-holding for bondmen, generally either a full or half yardland, while the cottagers had little land. The 1305 survey also gives extensive detail about the onerous labour services that bondmen and cottagers provided to the lord. An indicator of how great these were for a bondman is that while his rental for his house and a yardland was 2s 4d per annum, the value of his services, should someone else be paid to undertake them, was almost nine times higher, at 20s 2d.

While Domesday and the 1305 survey reveal a highly structured society, they give few insights into the working of medieval agriculture, but the 1305 survey does mention the presence of three fields in Oakham: the North, South and West. What is their significance?

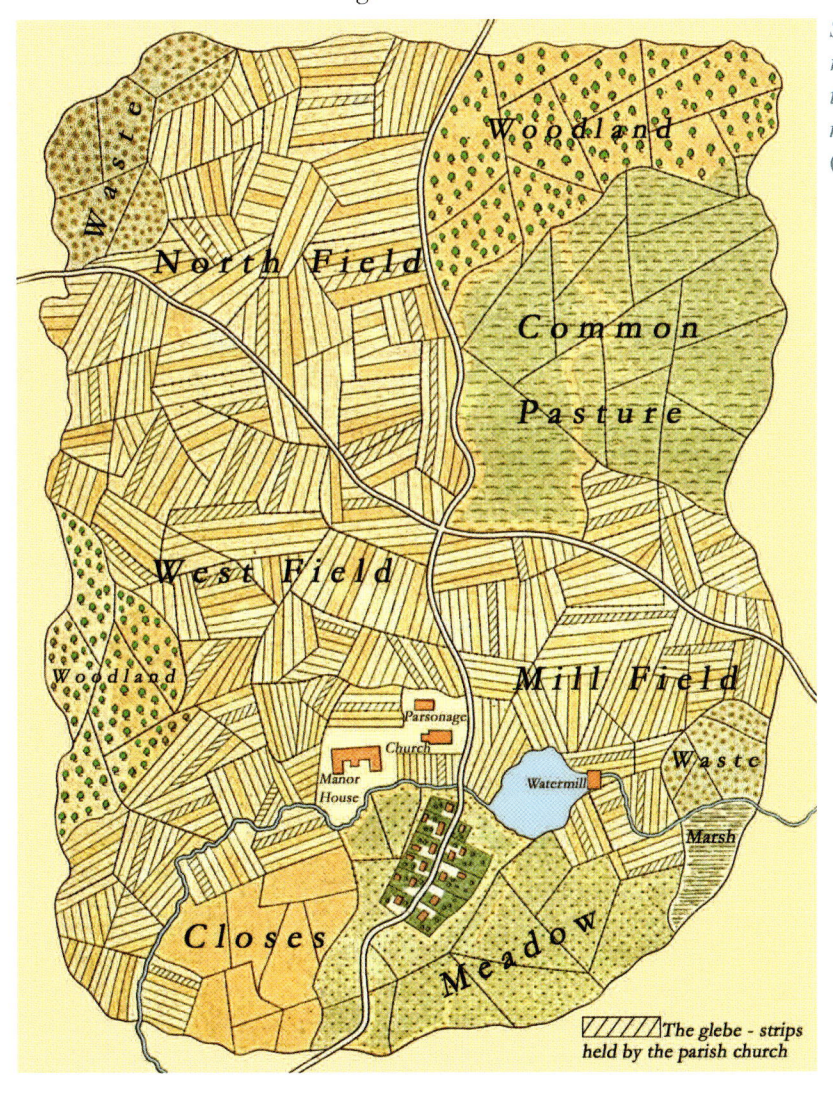

Schematic plan representing a typical medieval manor (RO)

A system of agriculture had developed in the Saxon period that divided land into strips. These strips were grouped into furlongs and the furlongs combined into great fields, such as the North, South and West Fields mentioned in the Oakham 1305 survey. Originally the land of the village had been divided into two great fields, with one used to grow arable crops while the other was left fallow to recuperate. Another feature of the system was that while the land was producing crops each strip was the sole right of an individual, but for a short period after harvest and during the fallow it was open to common use by others in the community. Hence the name 'common field system' or 'open field system' from the open appearance of the landscape it created.

The period between the Domesday and 1305 surveys was a period of almost continuous population growth that created increased demand for land. For a period this had been achieved by bringing excess pasture, woodland or waste under the plough, and by reorganising from two to three great fields. The creation of a third great field allowed for two crop years followed by a fallow year. This rotation reduced the amount of land fallowed each year from a half to a third. The common field system had a great longevity, lasting in some Rutland villages into the late nineteenth century. Its existence affected how Rutland's villages developed, and the vestigial remains of its old strips are still seen in many modern fields as ridge and furrow. A recent publication has examined the common fields of Rutland in detail (Ryder 2006).

So how did the common field system impact both on the bondmen working their yardlands and on the community? Unlike today, where individual fields usually have a single owner, the bondmen and their successors, working the common field system into the nineteenth century, had their strips scattered throughout the great fields, with equal shares of good and poor lands. There was also regularity in the sequence of neighbouring owners of strips, indicating that the distribution of strips was planned rather than random (Hall 1995, 120). A consequence of the villagers' land being scattered in strips was that a villager did not have a large block of contiguous land on which to build a homestead. Village farms and cottages were therefore drawn together, near a source of fresh water. As the common field system lasted in most villages for at least 700 years, this pattern persisted and created the Rutland village with its farms, houses and cottages clustered around the church. This is not to say there was no movement out of the village when the common fields were enclosed, but the inertia generated by an unwillingness to abandon existing buildings was too great for the majority. Only in recent years has the high value of older farm properties for conversion to homes, together with the need for larger farm buildings, propelled most farms out of the centre of villages.

The bondmen and their successors travelled out from the village each day to plough, tend and harvest their remote strips, but even these simple actions created the need for arbitration and regulation. The scattering of land in strips created a huge number of boundaries between neighbours that could be encroached upon. Similarly, they created a need for community agreement on, amongst other matters, what crops to plant and when, and how many beasts an individual could pasture on the commons and when. This was the province of the Manor Court, held under the authority of the Lord of the Manor. While the court was usually presided over by one of the lord's officials the villagers formed the court jury that met to amend old or create new regulations. The jury also decided the merits of cases brought before them. These were important duties and the requirement to attend court was an obligation imposed by the manor in the 1305 survey.

Westminster Abbey's Gross Income from its Oakham [Deanshold] Manor, 1275-1535

The relative importance of the various income sources generated from a medieval manor is illustrated by this table of income (in pounds) from Westminster Abbey's Oakham [Deanshold] Manor accounts (Donnelly 1985, 167):

Source of Income:	1275-76	1300-01	1317-18	1362-63	1399-1400	1499-1500	1516-17
Rents	21	22	21	24	30	29	30
Manor court profits	15	7	6	2	-	1	1
Sale of crops & grain tithes	73	94	1	90	78	48	57
Sale of livestock	3	4	-	-	-	7	-
Other income	4	1	36	3	-	-	-
Total	116	128	64	119	108	85	88
Rent arrears	5	9	13	-	83	52	-
Total with arrears	121	137	77	119	191	137	88

The accounts for the period nearest to the Oakham 1305 survey show that income for Westminster Abbey from its manor in the parish, known as Deanshold, peaked at this time. In fact this was the high water mark for the feudal economy as a whole. By far the largest income source at that time was sales of grain (73 per cent). This was generated both from the manorial demesne (land kept by the Abbey and not rented to villagers, but on which the villagers had to provide labour services) and from the tithe (a tenth of all the produce of the manor provided for the upkeep of the church). The dominance of this source of revenue compared to sales of livestock further illustrates the importance of arable farming at that period. Of secondary importance were the villagers' rents (17 per cent), with the manor court providing the bulk of the balance (5 per cent) through grants of licences, fines, and other feudal requirements. Compared to later years arrears were relatively low. This is not perhaps surprising as the period around 1300 saw the population of England reach a peak, a level that was not reached again until the eighteenth century. Demand for land was consequently at its highest, making it very easy for a lord of the manor to replace any defaulting tenant. However, within fifteen years manorial income had collapsed to half of its peak level in the face of a widespread famine caused by high population and a climatic change to cooler conditions that decreased crop production. This climate change was to last several centuries. The collapse in income is even greater if the exceptional £36 of other income is removed, as this comprised overdue rents from previous years that the monks had included as a way of massaging the income figure. In the period immediately after the famine, the

Abbey's income recovered quickly, but it never returned to the levels seen at the opening years of the fourteenth century. Within 30 years another more devastating calamity hit the community with the arrival of the Black Death. Its immediate effect was to kill about a third of the population. The effect of this catastrophe was recorded at Hambleton, where '11 tofts and 11 virgates of land [were] in the lord's hands for want of tenants, which paid £11 yearly before the pestilence' (Ryder 2006, 22). As the plague became endemic, continually revisiting communities, the population was kept at a low level. The effect of this dramatic change was seen both in the sales value of the Abbey's crops and in the large rent arrears in the century and a half following the onslaught of the Black Death. These figures demonstrate that the classic feudal economy was in serious trouble and new economic methods were needed to face the challenge.

When the Rector received tithes he needed a barn to store them in. This tithe barn at Empingham is one of the few surviving in Rutland (RO)

The massive decline in population brought on by the plague created problems for some, such as the Westminster Abbey monks, but for others it provided opportunities. The feudal world described by the 1305 survey was gradually changed by the new reality of excess of land and shortage of labour, and by 1485 bondage had virtually disappeared in the Midlands. In its place had evolved the capitalist system. However, because of the nature of evolution the new system contained many of the characteristics of the old one. Leasing land had been extensively practised in the medieval period. By the sixteenth century many tenancies were held on long leases for up to 99 years or three lives (mother, father and child), for which an entry fee was required. In addition, a new form of tenure had developed called copyhold. Copyhold still required a change in tenancy to be registered at the manor court and the tenants to pay an entry fine to the lord of the manor; the tenant was given a copy of the entry as proof of title (hence the name). Many of the new copyholders and leaseholders held yardlands as had the feudal bondmen, but the burdensome labour services had virtually disappeared.

Also, from the sixteenth century, the royal courts increasingly intervened to protect the rights of both leasehold and copyhold tenants from undue demands of landowners. These gave the copyholder an almost freehold right to pass or sell on his tenancy. Copyhold tenancies continued until 1925 when an Act of Parliament converted them into freeholds.

If the structure of landowner-tenant relations had dramatically altered in the centuries following the Black Death, the method of working the land survived almost intact in most Rutland villages. The tenant farmers and their agricultural labourers still worked the common field system to the old three-fold rotation of two crops and a fallow, while their beasts were still pastured together in common herds and flocks. However, the reduction in population had allowed an expansion of pasture, and these animals now represented a significant proportion of a farmer's wealth. Hoskins (1965, 236) showed, for Wigston, Leicestershire, that the livestock provided as much value as the crops, despite about 80 per cent of a seventeenth century farmer's land being in arable production. However, a few villages had seen dramatic change which presaged the eventual change in the agricultural system from common to enclosed fields.

An aerial view of Martinsthorpe in the 1950s, looking west, This settlement had been depopulated by 1550 as a result of the introduction of sheep farming. However, evidence of the medieval community survives in the form of house platforms, close boundaries, and ridge and furrow
(Cambridge Museum of Air Photography)

Landowners were not passive in the face of the changed circumstances following the Black Death. The value of livestock noted by Hoskins created a significant opportunity for landowners, one that could be achieved by clearing away tenants and turning the land over to sheep. Such action led to depopulation, and both Gunthorpe and Martinsthorpe were deserted and enclosed by the early sixteenth century (Cornwall 1980, 7 & 86). This kind of action also created great fear of and antagonism towards enclosure amongst the tenantry, and provoked sixteenth century governments into making it difficult to enclose and depopulate. Nevertheless, the economic pressure to convert to pasture was ever-present, and attempts to enclose usually small areas of land continued into the seventeenth century, together with consequent legal disputes. Even though Gunthorpe had been deserted and enclosed by 1520, challenges for the recovery of common right continued later into the century (*VCH* I, 222). Essentially these disputes were about competing rights, the right of the landowner to alter land use to whatever he saw fit, and the tenant's right to common over the land. If the latter was allowed to continue, this eliminated much of the benefit of enclosure; if common right was removed, it took away a major means of self-support. An observer in 1780 wrote, 'Strip the small farms of the benefit of the commons and they are at one stroke levelled to the ground' (Ryder 2006, 13).

With legal challenges to forced enclosure increasingly common, if land was to be enclosed this had to be achieved by agreement. An agreement appears to have been made between the major landowners at Burley, including Alsthorpe, for the enclosure of the majority of the fields and the creation of the park. However, disputes occurred later as not all the commoners had been party to the agreement (Ryder 2006, 39). Such legal difficulties

The Enclosure of Whitwell

Whitwell's West and North Fields were originally cultivated in strips according to the medieval system. In the 1630s parts were enclosed into smaller units of land when the lord of the manor decided to increase the efficiency of these great open fields. There were further enclosures later in the century, when the South Field was enclosed and the remaining parts of the West and North Fields were reorganised into three new fields, Nether, Middle and Clay (Ryder 2006, 8).

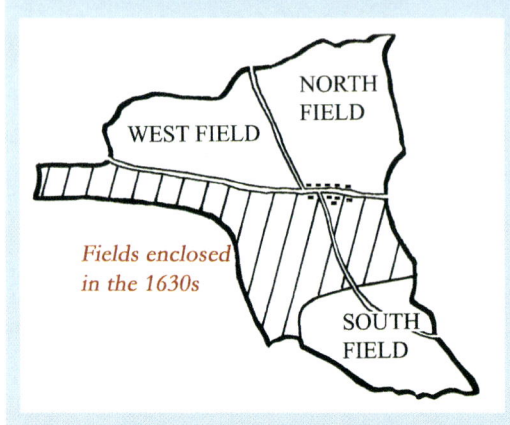

Map of Whitwell circa *1630 showing earlier enclosures* (ROLLR, DE 3214/601)

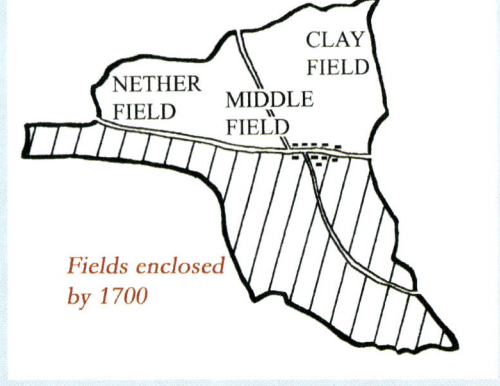

Map of Whitwell circa *1700* (ROLLR, DE 3214/M51)

and the presence of multiple landowners in many villages limited the number of complete enclosures up to the eighteenth century, although some partial enclosures were made; for example, one third of Whitwell was enclosed early in the sixteenth century (Ryder 2006, 10).

The rate of enclosure in any period was highly variable, being dependent on economic conditions. The periods prior to 1640 and after 1750 were economically generally good and both were marked by an increase in enclosure, while the period in between saw difficult times and there were relatively few enclosures. The most contentious enclosure of the seventeenth century was the forced enclosure of Hambleton during the Commonwealth (Ryder 2006, 39), the legal ramifications of which were to last another 40 years. In an attempt to deal with the complex situation he found after the Restoration, the Duke of Buckingham contrived a legal case before the Court of Chancery to confirm the enclosure. Although the court concurred, such

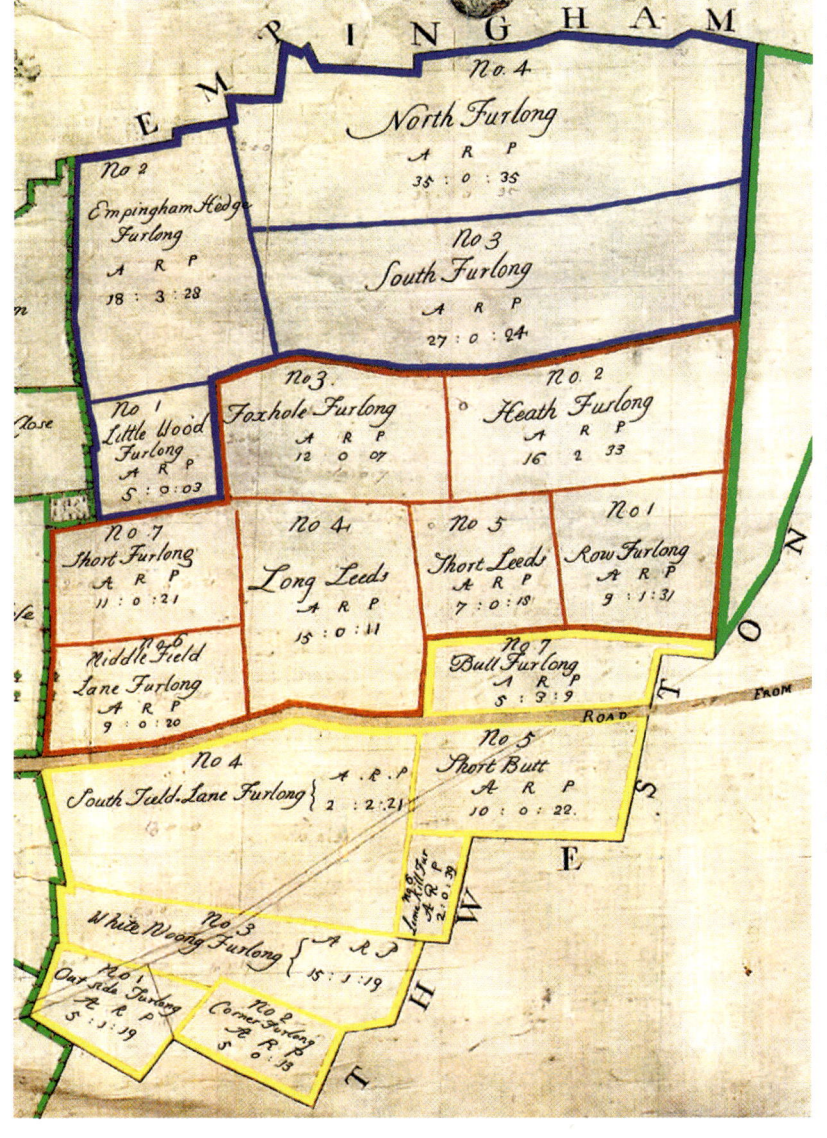

Left: From An Exact Survey of all Normanton and Part of Hambleton Lordships in the County of Rutland belonging to Charles Tryon Esq. Measured and Mapp'd in the year 1726 by Tycho Wing. *By this date most of Normanton had been enclosed, leaving only the open fields shown on this extract* (Lincolnshire Archives, 3 ANC 5/104/1)

verdicts were potentially open to challenge if all those who had interests in the fields were not involved, and often the commoners were left out. Eventually, to resolve the continuing legal uncertainty, resort had to be made to a specific Act of Parliament to confirm the enclosure, one of the first in the country. This set the pattern for the future. The landowners had found a legal method of enforcing an enclosure. Although Parliament usually required 80 per cent of the landowners to agree, no longer could a small minority of landowners or the commoners prevent an enclosure, and by 1806 only eight common fields remained in the county (Parkinson 1808, 5).

The explanation cartouche from Tycho Wing's map of 1726 (Lincolnshire Archives, 3 ANC 5/104/1)

A recent study (Ryder 2006, 54) has shown that the majority of Rutland enclosures that occurred before the middle of the eighteenth century were in villages towards the south and west of the county, in the clay lands best suited to pasture. In the light limestone soils to the north and east of the county, best suited to growing grain, the peak period for enclosure was the time of very high grain prices caused by the Napoleonic wars (1793-1815). Enclosure gave two benefits to the farmer compared to the common field system. It consolidated an individual's scattered strip holdings into more manageable blocks of land, and removed others' right of common over the land. In short it provided a farmer with complete control over his land. Initially this enabled conversion to pasture, and permitted the county to become a fattening area for servicing the increasingly important London market. Later, it also enabled an individual to take advantage of innovations in stockbreeding that were not possible in the common herds and flocks. Similarly, as the agricultural revolution of the eighteenth century developed, even in the grain areas, innovations such as the use of turnips and clover could be adopted in enclosed fields without needing the agreement of fellow commoners (Ryder 2006, 32).

Besides the benefits of new agricultural methods, and probably of more direct importance to the large landowner, was the ability to increase rents on enclosure. This also provided a good return on the high costs associated with obtaining an Act of Parliament. Generally rents in Rutland could be doubled on enclosure. In Lyndon in the mid seventeenth century it was recorded, 'Before the said lands were improved the rent of them was three score and ten pounds. Since the improvement [by enclosure] . . . the rent is a hundred and four score pounds' (Ryder 2006, 31). Similarly of the Oakham common fields it was recorded that enclosing 'would certainly double its present value' (Parkinson 1808, 40). While enclosure provided the large landowners with increased income from their tenants, its benefit to the small landowners was less tangible. On enclosure these individuals were usually left with significantly less land, as the tithe holders were allocated land in compensation for loss of their rights. In addition they had to fund their share of the cost of the enclosure and, if enclosure prompted a change to pasture, pay for extra animals. It is not surprising then that the process of enclosure saw a reduction in the number of landowners. During the period of the Uppingham, Caldecott and Lyddington enclosure (1802 to1804) the number of proprietors decreased from 192 to 179 (Ryder 2006, 50). An attrition of leaseholds had also been happening. While the average size of tenancy in the mid seventeenth century (15-30 acres) was similar to those described in the 1305 survey, by 1806 the average had increased to 200 acres (Ryder 2006, 36 & 38). Efficiency was the guiding principle of eighteenth-century farming gentry. One way in which it could be increased was through the consolidation of farms, whether common or enclosed, when long leases ran out. By the end of the eighteenth century there were very few long tenancies left in Rutland, and most tenancies were let from year to year at a rack rent.

A great deal of evidence of the early open field system of agriculture can still be found in Rutland. Here, ridge and furrow is exposed on the south side of Hambleton peninsula when Rutland Water was at low level in October 2006 (RO)

This aerial view of the area just south of Nether Hambleton was taken in 1968. It shows the extent of the then surviving ridge and furrow. Much of this area is now under Rutland Water (Anglian Water)

This has been a rapid journey through 700 years of agricultural and social change, one that started with the medieval bondsman required to work his own and his lord's land. However, the calamity of the Black Death created a shortage of labour that enabled him to break these feudal demands. By the sixteenth century the bondsman had evolved into a peasant farmer, still working the common fields of his predecessors to essentially the same rotations. The disaster of the plague had also forced the economic system to evolve from feudal to capitalist. Initially this caused some forced depopulations and village desertions, but by the late sixteenth and seventeenth century government and legal actions had left the peasant farmers in 'quiet enjoyment' of their holdings. Nevertheless by the eighteenth century a combination of increased wealth together with Acts of Parliament provided the gentry with the power to extract increased revenue from their estates. This they achieved through a combination of consolidating farms, enclosure, and the introduction of agricultural innovations, and the most tangible expression was in increased rents. The larger more efficient farms did not need as many workers, and at the end of our journey unwanted agricultural workers were left destitute or were compelled to migrate to expanding manufacturing cities.

Chapter 2
The Agricultural Revolution and Beyond
Edward Baines

The creation of Rutland Water coincided with, and locally accelerated, changes which were taking place in agriculture throughout the country. The age of small mixed farms (arable and livestock) worked by individual farmers, was over. In their place came large intensive and specialized units, often more reliant on politics than on good husbandry for their profits. At the time Rutland Water came into existence there was considerable and understandable regret for the loss of a traditional way of life in the area. In fact the parishes most affected had seen several radical changes in the previous 200 years. The difference in 1974 was the scale of the change, its rapidity, and in particular its visual impact. A patchwork of small fields stitched together by hedges and dotted with stone houses linked by winding lanes was transformed into a lake.

Looking from Hambleton towards Normanton. The stubble remains in the fields following the last harvest in this part of the Gwash valley (Richard Adams)

The landscape in 1800 had already been altered: quickthorn hedges enclosed the fields and Normanton Park had 'about two thousand large timber trees, principally oak, ash, beech and limes' (Laird 1818, 122). The parishes which surround and overlap with Rutland Water had been enclosed in the 1760s and 1770s and Normanton Park itself extended to about 400 acres at the same date. In *Beauties of England* (1818), Laird commented that he did not approve of cottagers and farmers being forcibly removed so that a great man (Heathcote of Normanton) could enjoy his 'lawns'. No doubt he would have been equally sympathetic to their successors in the 1970s who made way for sailors and fishermen.

In the immediate area around what was to become Rutland Water about three quarters of the land was grass, except for Empingham parish where the lighter soils favoured arable crops. There were 79 farmhouses in this area in 1808; the farms themselves varied in size from ten acres to well over a hundred. Fourteen thousand sheep, over 800 cattle and between 300 and 400 horses grazed the fields. At Normanton the cows in 1808 were 'very large' and 50 turkeys were reared each year (Parkinson 1808, 26-30 & 115-41).

A prize-winning Leicester ram from an engraving published in 1871 by Rogerson and Tuxford (Edward Baines)

Below: A flock of sheep in a field near Beehive Cottage, Nether Hambleton, in 1973. Lax Hill can be seen beyond. This area is now under Rutland Water (Jim Eaton)

Above: Sheep shearing in 1910, before the introduction of powered shears (Hart)

Right: Sheep have been reared in the Gwash valley for both wool and meat for over 500 years, and the tradition continues. This flock of sheep is grazing on the south shore of Hambleton peninsula in 2006 (RO)

Peasgood's Farm, Empingham, from the Normanton Estate Sale Catalogue *of 1924. It had 146 acres of pasture and 266 acres of arable land. This was one of eighteen tenanted mixed farms included in the sale. They varied in size from 50 to 500 acres* (Edward Baines)

Farms at Middle Hambleton before the flood. Beech Farm (left), a smallholding, was lost. Old Hall Farm (right) lost its farm buildings and most of its land, but Old Hall itself just survived. All the land in the foreground of this picture is now below Rutland Water (Richard Adams)

The landowners usually let their farms, but Richard Parkinson, who reported on the agriculture of Rutland in 1808, noted that an unusually large number of 'gentlemen farmers' were actively involved in day-to-day farming. Two hundred years ago the Gwash valley would have looked like every child's picture of the countryside. Green fields contained white-fleeced sheep and lambs, brown cows and placid carthorses, while in every farmyard poultry, 'kept for domestic use' as Parkinson noted, scratched in the dust.

This idyllic state of affairs continued for the next 150 years. Farming during that time went through several cycles of economic peaks and troughs, particularly during the great agricultural depression of the late nineteenth century, but the landscape remained largely unaltered until the 1940s.

The Farming Landscape in the Mid-Gwash Valley

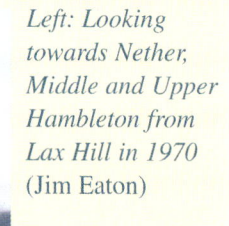

Left: Looking towards Nether, Middle and Upper Hambleton from Lax Hill in 1970 (Jim Eaton)

Above: Looking east along the Gwash valley towards Normanton in 1970 (Jim Eaton)

Above: Looking north towards Barnsdale from Upper Hambleton in 1968 (Joan Wild)

Left: Old meadow at Egleton in 1971 (Jim Eaton)

Willingham Fowler

Willingham Fowler initially farmed at Manton before becoming a tenant of the Earl of Gainsborough at Hall Farm, Exton. He left Manton in 1873 following the sale at auction by Messrs Royce of his beasts, horses, implements, carriages, and grass, hay and straw keeping (rented land). At Hall Farm, where he lived with his wife Ellen and three daughters, he became well known for his herd of pure-bred Short-horn cattle. His most famous young bull was 'Royal Windsor', whose offspring won many prizes at local shows, including the Cottesmore Hunt Prize at Oakham Show eight times in a period of nine years. He later sold this bull to HRH The Prince of Wales.

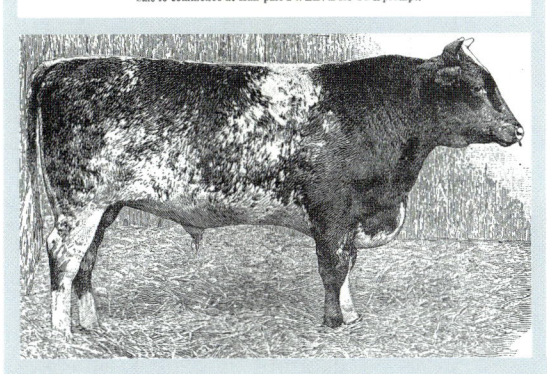

However, this success was not to last and the herd was sold at auction in 1899. The following extract from the auction catalogue makes the reason clear:

'Through the long continued agricultural depression, the owner has at last been forced to relinquish agricultural pursuits, and sell off his choicely-bred herd at short notice, and without the usual preparation, so that the cattle will be found only in breeding store condition, and will be absolutely sold, without any reservation whatever.'

Census returns show that Willingham Fowler and his family had left Hall Farm, Exton, by 1901.

Left: The sale particulars for Willingham Fowler's farm at Manton in 1873
(Edward Baines)

Right: Willingham Fowler outside Hall Farm, Exton
(Edward Baines)

Bottom Left: 'Eryholme Prince 35th', one of Willingham Fowler's prize-winning bulls
(Edward Baines)

Left: The catalogue title page for the auction of Willingham Fowler's Short-horn herd
(Edward Baines)

Even the effects of the 1914-18 War did not materially change the pattern of farming in the area, although there was a brief increase in the arable acreage towards the end of the war. Far more significant was the social and economic aftermath. Agriculture, like industry, suffered in the depression of the 1920s. The land in some cases reverted to a condition probably not seen since the Middle Ages: under-stocked and poorly cultivated, its rank pasture and untrimmed hedges provided an enjoyable cross country ride for huntsmen but a very scanty livelihood for those who worked on the land. Most of the Normanton estate was sold off in 1924 and the hall itself demolished in 1926.

In the latter part of the First World War the Food Ministry ordered 500 of these 35-horsepower 'chain rail' crawler tractors from Clayton and Shuttleworth of Lincoln to assist with the production of food. This example was photographed at the rear of Forsyth and Ferrier's garage in Main Street, Great Casterton (Hart)

The title page of the Normanton Estate Sale Catalogue of 1924 (Edward Baines)

Rutland

Between Stamford and Oakham, about 4 miles from Stamford Stations (L. & N.E. Rly.) and (L.M. & S. Rly.), 2 miles from North Luffenham (L.M. & S. Rly.) and 6 miles from Oakham (L.M. & S. Rly.)

Illustrated Particulars, Plans and Conditions of Sale
of the
VALUABLE FREEHOLD, RESIDENTIAL,
AGRICULTURAL & SPORTING ESTATE
known as the

NORMANTON ESTATE

including
AN IMPOSING AND HISTORICAL EARLY 18th CENTURY MANSION.

Occupying a beautiful position within its noble Park, and containing :—Hall, 9 Reception Rooms, 10 Principal Bed and Dressing Rooms, 5 Bathrooms. Ample Servants' Quarters. Excellent Stabling and Garage Accommodation.

Also

EIGHTEEN HIGH-CLASS MIXED FARMS (some with possession) varying in size from 90 acres to 500 acres, each equipped with exceptionally fine Farmhouses and Buildings.
NUMEROUS SMALL HOLDINGS.   ACCOMMODATION LANDS.
THE ENTIRE MODEL VILLAGE OF EMPINGHAM
including the Valuable Free and Fully Licensed Premises, known as
THE WHITE HORSE INN.

TWO SUPERIOR RESIDENCES.   PART OF THE VILLAGE OF EDITH WESTON.
BUILDING SITES AND WOODLANDS.

The whole extending to about

6,000 Acres

and producing an actual and estimated rental of about
per £8,000 annum.

Underlying the Estate are valuable beds of Ironstone.

Messrs. DUNCAN B. GRAY & PARTNERS
in conjunction with
Messrs. ROYCE

will offer the above for SALE BY AUCTION in Lots, on **Wednesday and Thursday, 17th and 18th September, 1924**, at 11.30 a.m. and 2.30 p.m. o'clock each day at the
STAMFORD HOTEL, STAMFORD, LINCS.
(unless previously disposed of privately)

The change in the actual ownership of land did not in itself result in a change in farming patterns. If Richard Parkinson in 1808 had stepped into a 'Tardis' and arrived at Whitwell in 1937, he would not have noticed dramatic differences.

It was in the early 1930s that Dudley Stamp, an eminent British geographer, instigated the First Land Utilisation Survey of Great Britain. He organised schools throughout Britain to map land use in their local area using a simple classification which included the main rural land uses of arable, grassland, woodland, heathland, water and built land. Survey work began in 1931 and was completed for most counties by 1935. The survey of Rutland was organised by Margaret Broughton and published as Part 53 of the *Land Utilisation Survey* in 1937.

In 1939 the most significant alteration of all had taken place. Allotment holders and gardeners were urged to 'dig for victory' and on the farms the plough, now usually pulled by a tractor, carved furrows across virgin turf. Over 70 per cent of the land had been pasture; now that proportion was needed to grow corn. The German U-Boat was the most influential agricultural implement of the century.

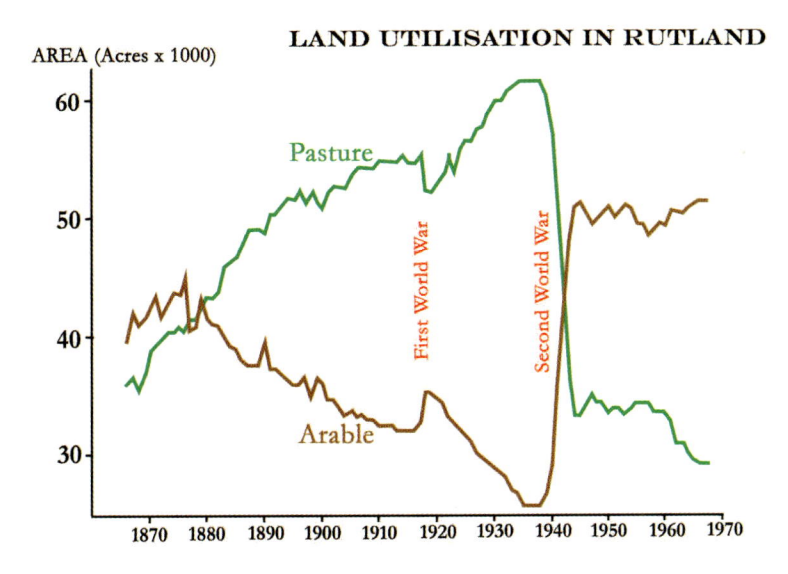

This chart highlights the dramatic change in land utilisation from pasture to arable in Rutland during the Second World War (Messenger 1971, 23)

Interesting aspects of history are to be found as often in footnotes as in headlines. The 1924 Normanton Estate Sale Catalogue stated that 'underlying the estate are valuable beds of Ironstone'. Had these been worked, Empingham might have been another Corby and open-cast mining would have pre-dated the excavations for the reservoir by 50 years. In the event, the nearest ironstone quarry was to be at Exton Park, some two miles to the north of Rutland Water, which was worked from 1957 until 1974.

In fact farmers and smallholders adapted to the need for increased production in order to make a living. The memories of those directly involved reveal a snapshot of rural life typical not only of Rutland but of the country as a whole.

In 1948 the Earl of Gainsborough gave the United Steel Company permission to quarry ironstone at Exton Park, approximately two miles to the north of the future Rutland Water. Sundew, the world's largest walking dragline worked here from 1957 until mining ceased in 1974. Sundew then walked to Spanhoe airfield, near Harringworth, Northamptonshire, its final resting place (Richard Adams)

The following example serves to illustrate this. In 1951, 85 acres of land at Whitwell were sold to a local farmer. He remembers that the 'War Ag' (War Agricultural Committee responsible for maximising food production from farmland) would inspect the farm annually and the mixed arable farm still worked in the traditional way. It was still labour intensive. Horse-drawn machinery was converted to tractor-drawn, but some practices were as old as farming itself. For instance, sowing seed:

'This was quite an art and we used to have a sling – hold a bucket in our left hand and sling between the thumb and pointing finger with a sort of half-closed hand and broadcast the seed five yards to the left and right' (Philip Joyce).

Harvest could take weeks and farming was financially precarious. Not surprisingly, when the acquisition of land for the reservoir took place, people who had invested time and money into the land felt aggrieved when the rewards of a lifetime's effort were snatched away by an arbitrary and inexorable process:

'They classed it as third-class agricultural land and I got up at a village meeting and stated that in future it would not be third-class agricultural land, it would be nothing but the Klondike and people would be selling property at a million pounds . . .' (Philip Joyce).

Undoubtedly at a time of economic inflation, the delay between valuation for compulsory purchase and the actual payment of compensation meant that the farmers could not afford to buy replacement land at the same price, so the bitterness felt at the construction of the reservoir was both understandable and justified.

This sense of the destruction of a way of life, which had played its part nationally by adapting to war-time requirements, was widespread. The farming families were an integral part of the local community and women as well as men were actively involved. Again, one voice – that of Joan Wild – speaks for many: 'My mother used to make butter and we sold cream'. This family also sold eggs, fruit and meat directly from the farm and, in common with most, kept and killed a pig. The bacon was home-cured in a lead salting trough, 'as long as a settee', and was then hung on hooks in the farmhouse kitchen.

Farming has always been seasonal, but the introduction of mechanisation accelerated the pace of change. Thus hay making and corn harvesting are now completed in days, but even in the 1950s were more drawn out:

'The grass was mown and each time they went around the field they called it a swathe of hay. If the weather was good it wasn't much trouble but if they had spells of rain . . . they had a swathe turner which allowed the air to dry it and then it was raked into rows and collected by a sweep into cobs (small heaps) before being carted to the stack yard and built into stacks which were then thatched' (Joan Wild).

Albert Wild of Home Farm, Hambleton, with his hay sweep
(Joan Wild)

Collecting hay on Home Farm, Hambleton in 1948
(Joan Wild)

Building haystacks in a Hambleton stack yard in 1910 (Hart)

The hay was used for winter fodder for cattle and sheep and cut from the stack using a large metal hay knife. The hay harvest in June and July was followed by the corn harvest in August and September. Before the combine harvester (a machine which combines cutting the corn and separating the grain from the straw, thus removing the need for threshing) was widely used, the process was carried out in stages. First the corn was reaped using a self-binding reaper, often referred to as a 'binder'. This Victorian invention cut the corn and automatically bound it into bundles, known as sheaves. These were then propped into stooks of six or eight. When they had dried in the field they were carted to the stack yard and built into stacks and then thatched. At some point during the winter, the threshing machine would arrive to separate the grain. This would be driven by a steam traction engine and this operation was usually contracted work.

Reaping with a horse-drawn self-binding reaper at Home Farm, Hambleton. Arthur Wild continued to use horses until well into the 1950s, but by this time many farmers had adapted their binders so that they could be drawn by a tractor. Others had been using combine harvesters since before the Second World War (Joan Wild)

Messrs Nourish of Langham were threshing contractors hired by many Rutland farmers. Threshing day was an important event – though not without danger from unguarded machinery. In common with many farming activities, it often involved neighbours helping out and doubled as a social occasion. During the winter, rats and mice would creep into the corn stack, and as the sheaves were removed the final layers would reveal scores of rodents, which would provide good sport for the workers who had brought their terriers especially for this hunt.

'The corn was put into big sacks which the men used to carry on their shoulders to the barn, where it was stacked up. Then my father would go off to the Melton or Peterborough corn exchange to sell it. Mother used to make small linen bags for the samples of corn, and when it was sold it was collected on lorries' (Joan Wild).

Above: Sheaves of corn propped into stooks to dry (RCM)

Left: Stooking sheaves of corn (RCM)

Left: A Deering horse drawn binder demonstrating that it is still in good working order (Noel Bridgeman)

Loading sheaves of corn ready to be carted to the stack yard at Stokes' farm, Normanton in August 1934 (Hart)

Neatly thatched stacks of corn sheaves in a stack yard. Thatching was necessary to keep the corn dry until it was time for threshing (RCM)

Below: Steam threshing from a Clayton and Shuttleworth of Lincoln advertising poster. This was a common sight in stack yards throughout Rutland until well after the First World War. Tractors replaced the steam engines until the late 1950s by which time the combine harvester had been universally adopted (RCM)

Above: This Massey Harris No 780 combine harvester, manufactured in 1950, was restored by Ron Knight of Great Casterton (Noel Bridgeman)

Right: Straw left behind by the combine harvester is compacted into large bales
(John Nowell, Zodiac Publishing)

Right: This huge stack of straw bales at Normanton is destined for a straw-burning electricity power station (RO)

Above: Harvesting the modern way. This New Holland combine harvester has an air-conditioned cab to protect the driver from dust and heat, and lights to allow work to carry on through the night. The corn is emptied into a huge trailer for carting to the farmer's grain bins
(John Nowell, Zodiac Publishing)

The age-old pattern of seasonal work, carried out on small family farms, was already altering in the decade before the arrival of the reservoir. Many of the skills of the farm worker – thatching, horsemanship – were becoming redundant and the economic viability of small mixed farms was under increased pressure. As well as the effect on farming practice, the demographic changes were profound. Mechanisation meant that fewer people were required to work the land. In turn, this drift away from the countryside meant that cottages previously 'tied' to farms (and usually occupied as part of the remuneration for work on the land) were increasingly sold off or let to people who regarded the countryside as a recreational amenity rather than a place of employment. The proposals for the reservoir and its immediate surroundings recognised this change in attitudes to the countryside. 'Rutland Water', as it was subsequently named, was seen from the outset as a rural retreat for the urban population of the Midlands.

As the generation of Rutland farmers who had experienced this great change from the slower-paced but more physically demanding horse-drawn age to that of universal mechanisation retired from farming, especially in the 1970s and 1980s, the old equipment they had used was often laid out in a field or farmyard to be auctioned off in farm sales. Not all was lost. Some made its way into the collections of the Rutland County Museum or into the hands of local enthusiasts. Today, through displays, recorded memories, photographs and working days, something of the flavour and character of that agricultural era can still be savoured.

Sharp's Tractors

Before Rutland Water, Frank and Noel Sharp farmed at Nether Hambleton. Frank lived with his sisters, Ivy and Mary, at Ivydene. Their brother Noel, his wife Dorothy and two daughters, Wendy and Christine occupied Red House (*see* Chapter 21 – Lost Homes).

By 1968 they were farming 363 acres, most of which was devoted to cereal crops. No root crops were grown on the farm and livestock included 400 sheep, 30 milking cows and 150 mixed cattle. By 1975 they had lost their homes and farm to the reservoir.

Noel Sharp's former 1941 Model N Fordson tractor at a Rutland ploughing match
(Ron Knight)

In 1941 Noel purchased FP 3804, a Model N Fordson tractor which he needed as part of the war effort to increase their acreage under plough. It was used on the farm for many years until it was sold for scrap. Ron Knight of Great Casterton subsequently acquired it from the scrap dealer and set about restoring it. Noel was not aware of this until some years later he recognised it at a ploughing match.

Noel also acquired a little McCormick Deering International W12 tractor during the Second World War. Again it was used on the farm for many years until it was put into storage in a barn on Lyndon Hill. Ron Knight also purchased and restored this tractor. Its moment of glory came, in 2000, when it took part in the late Queen Mother's 100th birthday procession in Birdcage Walk, London.

Left: Noel Sharp was reunited with his Model N Fordson at Tolethorpe Park in 2000 when this photograph was taken for the front cover of Farmer's Weekly *(Ron Knight)*

Above: Brian Knight driving Noel Sharp's former International W12 tractor in the late Queen Mother's 100th birthday procession (Ron Knight)

It is perhaps ironic that wildlife flourished in 1800 as a by-product of the agriculture practised at the time, and in the twenty-first century environmental conservation helps to sustain farming. At Rutland Water this has meant that Dexter cattle have been introduced to maintain a suitable habitat for some bird species: a change of emphasis producing the same results (*see* Chapter 24 – Tim Appleton MBE – Thirty Years of Rutland Water Nature Reserve). Similarly, one of the skills of the farm labourer – hedge cutting – is now utilised so that volunteers are taught how to 'lay' a hedge. In this method partly-cut and mature hedge stems are bent and layered in such a way that stakes (inserted vertically) and binders (plaited horizontally) produce a stock-proof boundary which also provides a rich habitat for wildlife.

There is increasing recognition of the importance of the environment and it is likely that the Gwash Valley would have changed in line with the English countryside generally. To some extent this change was anticipated and accelerated by the arrival of Rutland Water. It has also meant that it has preserved the surrounding landscape in a way that would have been unlikely had the reservoir not been there. The man-made lake of the twentieth century sits in a landscape formed by men in the eighteenth and nineteenth centuries.

The modern farmers on the shores of Rutland Water, like their predecessors, are custodians as well as cultivators. No one is better placed to be so. They know the land and make their livelihoods from it, but they are also aware of their wider responsibilities. Their ancestors ploughed the fields to provide food in wartime; they in turn have adapted their methods to meet modern requirements. The result is the landscape you see: not an artificial theme park but the result of sensible compromise between farming and conservation.

Pulling Power

The agricultural revolution has changed farming out of all recognition, and these changes are nowhere more apparent than in the methods used by farmers for traction – from two horses pulling a single furrow plough 150 years ago to the huge 500 horsepower (and more) tractors seen on some of the larger farms today. The following pictures, all taken in Rutland, demonstrate this revolution.

Rutland Ploughing Match, Empingham, 2006. The steel ploughshare was a big advance on its wooden predecessor, but it was still hard work for the ploughman, and the horses (RO)

Ploughing by steam using a single steam engine at Ridlington in October 1857 (Illustrated London News)

Ploughing by steam was an important part of the countryside for 75 years following the introduction of the first commercially successful engine in the 1850s. The balance plough, which was introduced soon after, was pulled backwards and forwards across the field by a steel rope attached to drums on traction engines either side of the field. Sometimes only one engine was used with a system of pulleys round the field. This avoided soil compaction by the heavy steam engines.

Such a system was featured in the *Illustrated London News* (No 883 – Vol **XXXI**, Saturday, 17th October 1857):

An '. . . important feature in the proceedings of Tuesday week was the exhibition of the power of Fowler's steam-plough, which was tried in a field upon Mr. Wortley's farm, at Ridlington. Very great interest was excited by this somewhat novel exhibition . . . Mr. Fowler, who was on the ground, stated . . . that the steam-plough was capable of ploughing, with an ordinary eight horse-power engine, ten acres per day . . . . The cost of the apparatus and engine would be about £750 . . . . It was indeed extraordinary to see a rather clumsy-looking implement sliding smoothly along the field at a speed of about 100 yards per minute, and turning up the ground with ease at a depth of nearly seven inches. There were about 600 persons present in the field. Amongst this number we observed Lord and Lady Aveland; Stafford O'Brien, Esq.; the Hon. H. Noel; General Fludyer; R. W. Baker, Esq.. . . .'

One of a pair of matched Fowler BB1 ploughing engines owned by Brian and Ron Knight of Great Casterton. They were made by John Fowler of Leeds (Brian Knight)

— 41 —

'Little Jim' at a Little Casterton Working Weekend. Smaller steam driven tractors like this one were later used for direct ploughing, but they were still very heavy and hardly overcame the soil compaction problem (RCM)

Brian and Ron Knight's engines are used to pull their anti-balance plough, which is similar to a balance plough except that it has a mechanism to change the point of balance as it is pulled in each direction. It is seen here a Little Casterton Working Weekend (Brian Knight)

Below Left: An 'Overtime' paraffin tractor, manufactured about 1917 by Deere & Company in the United States. It was one of the first tractors with an internal combustion engine in Rutland and was owned by E Nourish & Sons of Langham who were steam threshing contractors. John Nourish is driving and Ebenezer Nourish is on the mowing machine (William Nourish)

— 42 —

The Fordson N was by far the most numerous type of tractor used in the Second World War ploughing campaign. It enabled self-sufficiency in the darkest days when the U-Boat menace nearly brought the United Kingdom to its knees (RO)

It was Harry Ferguson's vision in 1917 to provide a completely new tractor and a full range of implements to integrate with it. This dream was achieved in 1946 when the grey 'Fergie' eventually went into production in Coventry, Warwickshire, and from then on thousands were manufactured for home and export markets. Farmers literally changed the way they farmed because of the 'Ferguson System' and the world's other tractor makers had to copy it or die.

One of Harry Ferguson's tractors at the 2006 Rutland Ploughing Match (RO)

Below Right: It could be said that most modern tractors are just big 'Fergies' with cabs, but this does no justice to the technology under the shell. This Case MXU 135 four-wheel-drive tractor was photographed during the 2006 Rutland Ploughing Match at Empingham (RO)

Ploughing is a thing of the past on some of the larger farms. This disc set pulled by a Claas Challenger crawler made short work of cultivating the field. Wide rubber tracks give good grip without compacting the soil. Some Rutland farmers are even experimenting with dispensing with this operation – they are direct-drilling seeds for cereals crops into uncultivated soil (RO)

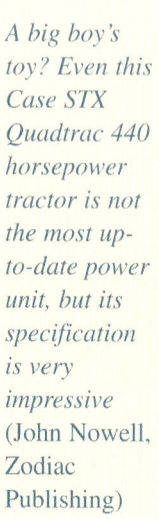

A big boy's toy? Even this Case STX Quadtrac 440 horsepower tractor is not the most up-to-date power unit, but its specification is very impressive (John Nowell, Zodiac Publishing)

Chapter 3
Barnsdale
Sue Howlett

For modern visitors to Rutland, the name of Barnsdale provides a regular source of confusion. Tourist information draws their attention to the horticultural pleasures of Barnsdale Gardens, or to the events, meals or accommodation offered by Barnsdale Lodge Hotel and Barnsdale Hall Hotel. They may follow signs to the impressively landscaped Barnsdale car park on the shores of Rutland Water. From here, on a May evening, they may wander delightedly along the bluebell-lined path through Barnsdale Wood.

And yet, Rutland has no village or parish of Barnsdale. An early form of the name appears in 1283, when Bernard de Brus of Exton made a generous donation to the monks and church of St Andrew, Northampton. This included the income from the church of Exton 'and all the Tithes of Hay, which in his Park of Bernardyshill, or elsewhere they have been accustomed to receive' (Wright 1684, 53). According to the *VCH* (II, 10) 'Bernardshill' is mentioned as early as 1207. It is 'Bernardeshul' in 1329 and 'Bernardeshilpark' in 1421.

These references confirm that Bernard's Hill, or Barnsdale, was a park, created for hunting, in the parish of Exton near its border with the parish of Whitwell. An area of woodland would be enclosed by earth banks and wooden palings not only to keep the deer in but also to provide cover for them. They would be hunted by the lord of the manor, providing valuable venison as well as sport. There were ten such parks in medieval Rutland, many of which were marked on various early county maps. In 1579, Christopher Saxton produced the first printed Atlas of the English and Welsh counties. His map of Rutland shows the encircling palings of 'barnesdalep[ar]k'. Thirty years later, John Speed's map of 1610 also shows the enclosed park at 'Barinsdale'.

From Speed's map of 1610 showing the enclosed park at Barnsdale

The boundaries of Barnsdale Park probably reached from 'Barnsdale Wood in the north to Armley Wood in the south . . . with a laund [grassy glade] between them. The park was typically elliptical in shape, and remained largely unaltered until recent replanting and the creation of Rutland Water' (Cantor 1980, 15-18). This area was investigated by R F Hartley for his 1983 publication, *The Medieval Earthworks of Rutland*. He notes that the open area between the two woods contained a small moated site known as 'Robin Hood's Cave', which he suggests might have surrounded a lodge for the keeper of the park. This feature was destroyed, along with much of Barnsdale and Armley Woods, in the creation of Rutland Water.

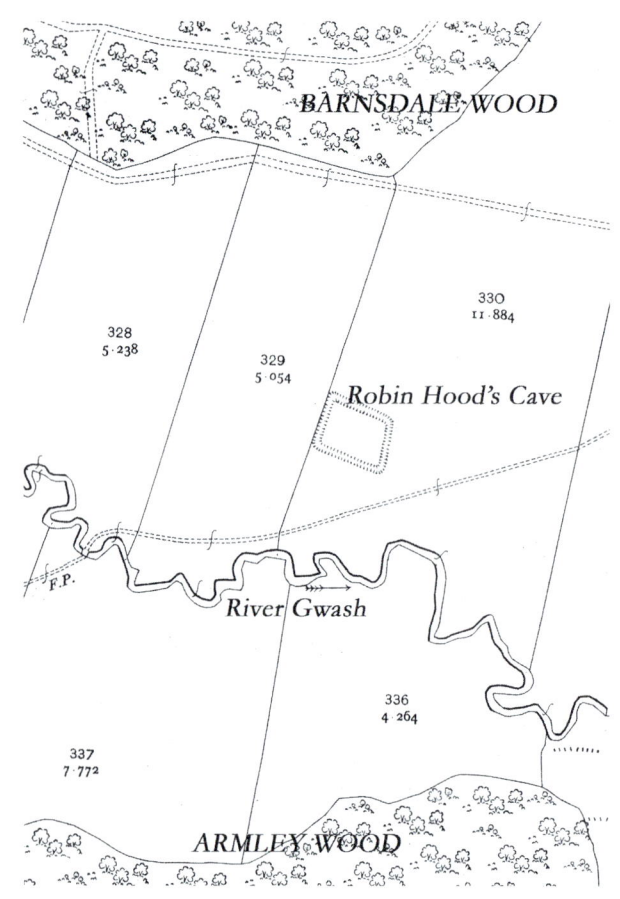

Barnsdale was maintained as a deer park by its various owners between 1206 and 1602 (Cantor 1980, 17). Twenty years later, Barnsdale and Exton came into the possession of Sir Edward Noel, 2nd Viscount Campden. When the countryside became more settled after the upheavals of civil war, the Noels, soon to become Earls of Gainsborough, set about enlarging and improving their greater park at Exton. It was transformed by laying out geometric areas of woodland divided by avenues, formal gardens close to the house and a lake, all enclosed by a hedge or fence (Cantor 1994, 158-61). Meanwhile Barnsdale Wood, having no resident owner, lost its importance as a deer park.

Left: The earthwork remains of 'Robin Hood's Cave', near the north arm of the River Gwash, highlighted on the OS 2nd ed 25" map 1904

Right: Looking north-west across the north arm of the Gwash valley towards Barnsdale Hill and Barnsdale Hall before this area was flooded to create Rutland Water (Joan Wild)

As an area of ancient woodland surviving into the twentieth century, Barnsdale Wood was designated as a Site of Special Scientific Interest, although sadly part of it had to be lost with the creation of the new reservoir. Trees were felled where required, their stumps providing forlorn testimony to their loss when the water level falls in dry weather.

In the winter of 1997, Clive and Elaine Jones carried out a survey of the boundaries of Barnsdale Wood, especially along the Rutland Water shoreline, as well as the state of the woodland and its rides. They found many rides overgrown and woodland neglected. However, evidence was found of a possibly medieval external ditch and internal earthen bank along the west side of the wood, parallel with the old Stamford Road which now leads down into the water at Barnsdale. There may have been a former entrance into the medieval deer park from the road near this point, indicated by surviving parallel ditches and banks, 15m apart, crossing the pasture field at the north-west corner of Barnsdale Wood.

Tree stumps on the shore of Rutland Water indicating the former extent of Barnsdale Wood (RO)

Elaine and Clive Jones also explored the eastern edge of Barnsdale Wood at the Exton/Whitwell parish boundary (SK 892093), where 'wave action had revealed the outer bank and ditch and inner stone wall'. The remains of an adjacent stone causeway or bridge can be seen entering the wood at low water level (*Rutland Record* 18, 366).

Barnsdale Wood, showing its location in relation to the parish boundary and Rutland Water (Elaine Jones)

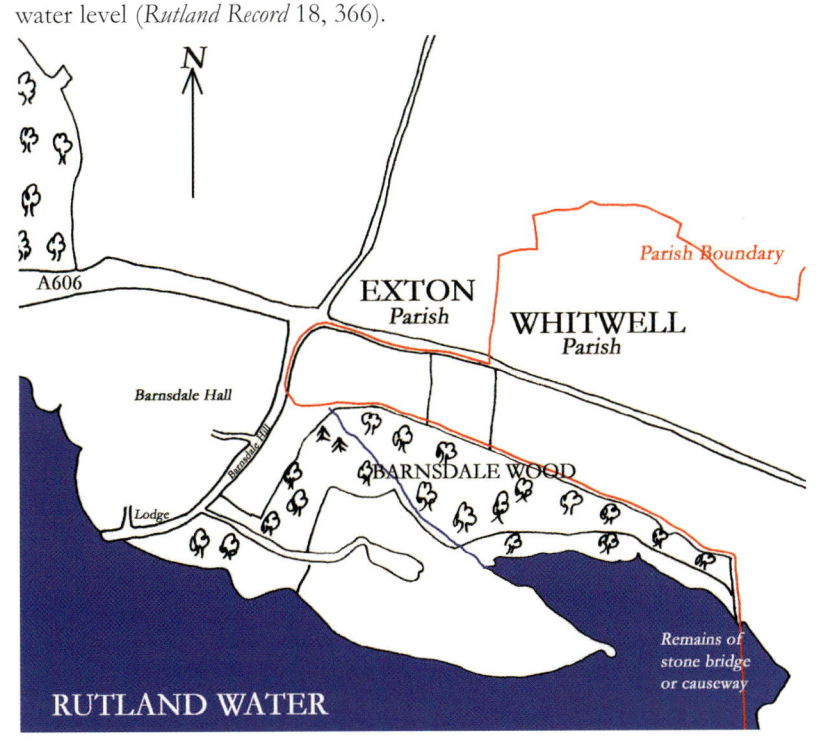

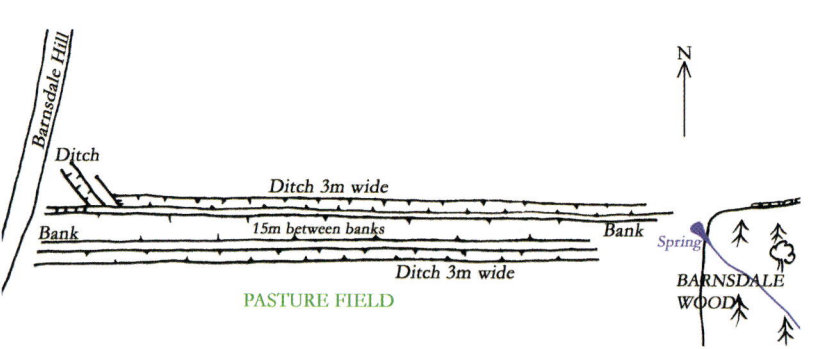

Two banks about 15m apart, flanked by 3m-wide ditches at the north-west corner of Barnsdale Wood (Elaine Jones)

Left: Earthworks at the north-west corner of Barnsdale Wood (SH)

Below: The eastern boundary of Barnsdale Wood and adjacent causeway exposed on the shore of Rutland Water (Elaine Jones)

During the nineteenth century, particularly with the coming of the railways, Rutland once again became a magnet for lovers of hunting. Now, however, huntsmen and hounds pursued foxes instead of deer, across enclosed fields and wooded coppices, rather than within the confines of a wooded deer park. Wealthy businessmen and aristocrats were attracted by the proximity of the Cottesmore, Belvoir and Quorn hunts to build hunting lodges around the county. These included Springfield and Catmose in Oakham, Hambleton Hall and the new Barnsdale Hall, built in 1890 for the Fitzwilliam family. The architect was E J May, who had been involved in designing Bedford Park, England's first garden suburb, in 1875. He adopted a neo-Tudor design 'with a canted two-storey bay and tiled roofs' (Pevsner 1984, 285).

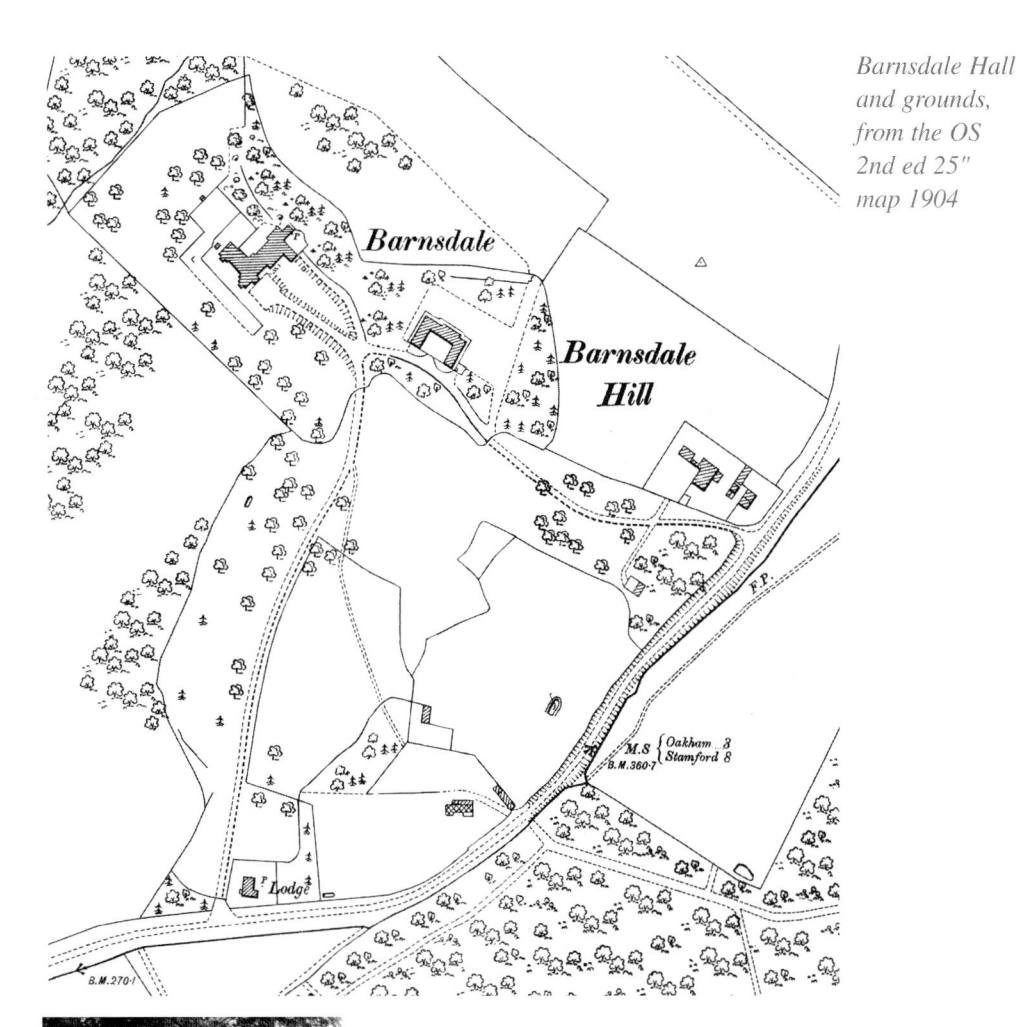

Barnsdale Hall and grounds, from the OS 2nd ed 25" map 1904

Barnsdale Hall from a picture postcard dated 23rd December 1907 (Hart)

— 49 —

The Fitzwilliam estates included Milton, near Cambridge (home of the Fitzwilliam Hunt) and Wentworth Woodhouse in Yorkshire. After 1857, the 6th Earl Fitzwilliam (1815-1902) resided in Yorkshire, while Milton Hall, with its 23,300 acre estate in the Nene Valley, became home to his brother, George Fitzwilliam. According to the 1901 Census, the Earl's nephew, George Fitzwilliam (1866-1935), a former Lieutenant in the Royal Horse Guards, was living at Milton Hall with his wife Evelyn and eighteen servants. In future years his son, William Wentworth-Fitzwilliam (1904-79), would become the 10th Earl Fitzwilliam (www.thepeerage.com).

Barnsdale Hall from the east in 2006 (SH)

When the 1901 Census was taken, Barnsdale Hall in Rutland was occupied only by two housemaids and a kitchen maid. Its stables provided accommodation for two stablemen and a coachman, while the stud groom and gamekeeper lived with their families on Barnsdale Hill. At Barnsdale Hall Gate (now a much enlarged guest house on the shores of Rutland Water) lived the gardener with his wife and twin babies. On the night of the census they were enjoying a visit from his sister-in-law, from Yorkshire, and her two small children.

Barnsdale Hall from the south in 2005 (RO)

By the late twentieth century, the world had changed. While hunting attracted a more democratic clientele, new purposes were found for the Victorian mansions built as hunting lodges. As was the case at nearby Hambleton Hall, Barnsdale Hall found its position greatly enhanced by the creation of Rutland Water. New money was coming into Rutland, and the hall was bought by Derek Penman, successful builder and founder of Penwise Properties.

The house referred to as Barnsdale Hall Gate in the 1901 Census (RO)

Outline planning permission had already been granted to convert Barnsdale Hall into a hotel and conference centre. Mr Penman then made a further application to create the Barnsdale Country Club, with luxurious health club and Scandinavian-style 'time-share' timber lodges, sited in landscaped parkland on the side of Barnsdale Hill. Despite opposition led by Rutland CPRE [Council for the Protection of Rural England], the proposal was accepted and the holiday complex took shape. Critics who had opposed the creation of the reservoir now feared an invasion of holiday-makers along its quiet shores. But careful planning and the exclusive character of the hotel and surrounding facilities have ensured that peace and tranquillity are retained, adding to the appeal of this upmarket holiday provision.

Modern time-share holiday lodges in the grounds of Barnsdale Hall Hotel (SH)

Attractions for visitors to the Barnsdale area of Rutland are not restricted to the former Barnsdale Hall. A seventeenth-century farmhouse, at the crossroads of Exton Avenue and the Stamford to Oakham Road, has now become the Barnsdale Lodge Hotel. It, too, offers accommodation, dining and conference facilities. Further along the tree-lined Exton Avenue, towards the imposing gates of the privately-owned Exton Park, the tourist will find Barnsdale Gardens, established by the television gardening presenter, Geoff Hamilton. Since his death in 1996, the gardens have been open to the public, who come from far afield. Many also visit the arboretum and drought garden designed by Geoff Hamilton beside the Barnsdale car park at Rutland Water.

The memorial to Geoff Hamilton at Barnsdale Gardens (SS)

Once famed for its hunting park, Barnsdale now offers a wider range of leisure activities. A road through the woodland brings visitors to the extensive landscaped car park which, divided into different levels, is skilfully screened from the reservoir and surrounding areas. Although huntsmen no longer gallop through the medieval deer park, on a fine Bank Holiday dozens of cyclists may speed through the woodland while walkers and dogs of all shapes and ages follow the shaded path at a more leisurely pace.

A corner of Barnsdale Gardens in June 2006 (SS)

Bird watchers may gaze over the lake from the wooded hide in Barnsdale Wood, while fishermen exercise their patient sport from boats in the bay, or along the lake shore. White and black Hebridean sheep may graze with their lambs on the adjacent hillsides. Sections of the surviving woods are now being maintained and coppiced by volunteers of the Leicestershire and Rutland Wildlife Trust. In the Spring, Barnsdale Wood becomes a misty, azure sea of bluebells veiling the hillside, while a chorus of birdsong enchants the ear.

Top to Bottom: A notice at Barnsdale Gardens (SS)

Bluebells in Barnsdale Wood, May 2006 (SH)

Megan and Jeffrey (two young researchers into the Heritage of Rutland Water) in Barnsdale Wood, 2005 (family photograph)

Sheepshearing, Or the Invitation
by Samuel Messing of Exton

1.

I'd a kind invitation to merry Barnsdale,
To meet an old friend, and be sure not to fail;
But, when I got there, what surprised me the more,
Instead of one friend, why I met half a score.

2.

June was the month, and all nature seemed gay,
While ripening the flowers and the produce of May;
Here friendship did revel on all that was good,
While the warblers of nature all sung round the wood.

3.

Our tent was with hawthorn and poplars intwin'd,
Where the wild rose and woodbine were wav'd by the wind;
Our carpet was nature, and green was the floor,
While daisies and cowslips all bow'd round the door.

4.

When clipping was done, and the table cloth laid,
(On the ground to be sure,) from the sun in the shade,
A profusion of pies with a ham and a tongue;
Then afterwards music and singing a song.

5.

The ale flow'd in goblets of silver with glee,
Beneath the green hedge and the breeze-stirring tree,
When I look'd at the tumblers, and thought of old Time.
It made it drink sweeter than Malaga wine.

6.

Just opposite us, t'other side of the wood,
There's a cave once belonging to old Robin Hood;
It puts me in mind of those days of romance,
For 'twas said in an evening they'd come out and dance.

7.

Now we have been dancing before the tent door,
In miniature just like those warriors of yore,
With two or three lasses both modest and trim;
Not like those marauders, we are true to the king.

8.

When the ev'ning was come they were all full of glee;
Then I begg'd they'd excuse being parted from me;
So I wish'd 'em good night for to finish the day;
Then I mounted my pony and canter'd away.

1819.

(Messing, S, *Poems on Various Subjects*, Stamford, 1821)

Chapter 4
Burley on the Hill
Sue Howlett

Distant view of Burley on the Hill with part of Burley Fishponds in the foreground (RO)

Burley in the Middle Ages

Even before the coming of Rutland Water, most visitors' overriding impression of Burley has always been the great house of Burley on the Hill. For centuries, that first sight has been one to take the breath away. In 1953 it was glimpsed by two lady travellers as 'mistily blue in the summer haze, like some fairy palace set in enchanted woods' (Stokes 1969, 37). Rutland's early historian, James Wright, summoned the Muse of Poetry to do justice to the awe-inspiring location:

'Hail Happy Fabrick, whose auspicious view
First sees the sun, and bids him last adieu!
Seated in Majesty, your eye commands
A Royal Prospect of the richest lands . . .' (Wright 1684, *Additions*, 5)

The origins of the settlement of Burley are obscure. Its name suggests a fortified place (perhaps an Iron Age hill fort) close to woods, and indeed the Domesday Book of 1086 records extensive woodland one league long by three furlongs (about three miles by three eighths of a mile). This part of Rutland had been settled by Danes, and Burley fell within the Danish-named 'Wapentake' (hundred or shire division) of Alstoe. The pre-Conquest meeting place may have been the mound, or motte, in what is now the deserted village of Alsthorp. Although listed as the separate manor of 'Awsthrup' in the Domesday Book, it now lies within the manor and parish of Burley.

At the time of the Domesday survey, Burley had 38 villagers and small-holders, working the land of their lord, Geoffrey, 'Gilbert of Ghent's man'. The manor descended through the same families until, at the end of the thirteenth century the heiress, Alice, married Sir Nicholas de Segrave (*VCH* II, 114).

Holy Cross Church, Burley, in 1927 (Hart)

Much of the early village of Burley was destroyed by fire in the 1370s, causing such impoverishment that the residents threatened to desert their holdings, and cease working on the lord's land. The Lord of the Manor, Sir Thomas le Despenser, was forced to relieve them of their debts, at the same time establishing an annual fair at Burley. When Sir Thomas died, the manor came into the hands of his brother, the Bishop of Norwich.

By the time of the Wars of the Roses in the late fifteenth century, Burley was in the hands of the Sapcote family, who were supporters of Richard of York and his son King Edward IV. During this period a carved octagonal font was given to Burley Church, and twenty marks (£13 6s 8d) left in the will of Isabel Sapcote, who wished to be buried in the Lady Chapel. But the most conspicuous survivals of this period are the damaged alabaster effigies probably representing Sir Thomas Sapcote and his wife, Joan (*VCH* II, 118).

According to the Military Survey of 1522 the 'Chieff lord' of Burley was Edward Sapcote, worth £60 in lands. In case of war, he possessed 'harness' (equipment) for himself and three men, plus three horses, two bills (pole-arms with a wide cutting blade), two bows and two sheaves of arrows. His Steward was William Overton, Gentleman, who was worth forty shillings in fees. The Vicar, Gilbert Urmeston, held a vicarage worth £12, the Prioress of Nuneaton held a parsonage worth ten marks (£6 13s 4d), while the parish priest of Burley, Thomas Crispe, had his stipend of five pounds and goods worth 26s 8d. Of the other 25 adult males able to serve as archers or bill men, most were tenants of Edward Sapcote. These worked mainly as 'husbandmen' (farmers), with one miller and one weaver (Cornwall 1980, 29).

John Harington

Following the death of Edward Sapcote in 1550 with no male heirs, the manors of Burley and Alsthorpe were bought by Sir James Harington of Exton, whose youngest son had married Frances Sapcote. Through steady acquisition of estates in Rutland and beyond, by the end of the sixteenth century the Haringtons had built up one of the largest landed fortunes in England, yielding an income of between £5,000 and £7,000 per year. As the lord of many estates, Sir James Harington made his chief home at Exton, where he rebuilt the manor house in splendid style.

In 1570 John, the son and heir of James Harington married the heiress Anne Kelway, who brought more estates into the family, including Coombe Abbey in Warwickshire. As a wedding gift, Sir James settled on his heir the manor of Burley. John inherited his father's estates in 1591, by which time it is likely that the mansion at Burley had been or was being totally rebuilt.

A great gathering of the Harington family and friends was held at Burley to celebrate the Christmas of 1595. This was vividly described by a French tutor, Jacques Petit, who travelled to Rutland with Sir John Harington's fourteen-year-old daughter, Lucy, and her new husband, the Earl of Bedford. He compared the scale of Harington hospitality over the twelve days of Christmas with that of the royal court. Two hundred private guests dined in the refectory, while daily banquets were provided in the hall for eight or nine hundred country men and women. These had to be arranged in two sittings, with four or five long tables, each 'decked with foodstuffs for eighty or a hundred persons at a time' (Ungerer 1987, 244).

When Queen Elizabeth I died in 1603 the new Stuart king, James VI of Scotland, began a leisurely progress south to claim his crown as James I of England. Sir John Harington and his brother James met the king in Yorkshire, offering their hospitality

King James VI of Scotland and I of England (Wikipedia)

when his journey brought him into Rutland. The king reached Belvoir Castle, Leicestershire, on Maunday Thursday 1603, then on Good Friday he slept at Burley on the Hill (then known as 'Burley-Harington' to distinguish it from Burghley, Stamford).

On Easter Saturday, after a morning's hunting in Exton Park, King James and his entourage made their way to Stamford, to stay with the Cecils at Burghley House. After celebrating Easter here, King James was determined to return to Rutland to enjoy further hunting, but this plan was prevented by a fall from his horse, after which the king had to continue his journey south by coach. However, he was to see much more of Sir John Harington and his family. On Coronation Day, Sir John was made Baron Harington of Exton, and he and his wife were appointed guardians of the young Princess Elizabeth. It seemed as if a golden age lay ahead for the foremost family of Rutland as well as for their royal patrons.

During the first decade of King James I's reign, Burley on the Hill saw little of its important owners. Lord and Lady Harington now made their chief home at Coombe Abbey, where Princess Elizabeth was kept safe from the conspiracy of the Gunpowder Plotters, continuing her education under the personal supervision of her guardian.

Princess Elizabeth, ward of Lord Harington – later the 'Winter Queen' of Bohemia (Bridgeman Art Library)

Coombe Abbey, Warwickshire, chief home of Lord Harington of Exton and Burley (SH)

Barely ten years after the accession of King James I, and the elevation of the Harington family, tragedy struck both families. England was preparing to celebrate the marriage of Princess Elizabeth, and her guardian no doubt looked forward to being relieved of his responsibilities. The royal bridegroom, Frederick, Elector Palatine, arrived in London in October 1612. But within three weeks Princess Elizabeth's brother, Prince Henry, was suddenly dead of typhoid, to be replaced as heir to the throne by his diffident brother, Charles.

The royal marriage was delayed until Valentine's Day, 1613, after which the final duty of Lord and Lady Harington was to escort the princess, at their own expense, to her new home in Heidelberg. By this time Lord Harington, now 73 years old, was exhausted and financially drained. He managed to deliver the princess safely to her new home where he was obliged to stay for three months. He was desperate to return home, but he died of fever in the German town of Worms, in August 1613.

Henry, Prince of Wales, with John Harington of Exton (Nichols 1824, i, 528)

Inheriting an estate encumbered with debts of £40,000, and in poor health since his return from a European tour, the 22 year-old John, now 2nd Lord Harington, drew up his own will. He gave to his heirs power to sell land as necessary to discharge the many inherited debts. Nine days later, he succumbed to smallpox and was buried at Exton. Shortly before his death the Exton estate was sold to Sir Baptist Hicks, a wealthy merchant who was later made Viscount Campden. As he had no sons, it passed to his daughter Juliana and her husband, Sir Edward Noel, who succeeded his father-in-law as 2nd Viscount Campden. Sir Edward Noel also hoped to buy Burley on the Hill, securing his power base in Rutland, but was beaten to that prize by the king's favourite, George Villiers. But Sir Edward's inheritance of Exton and Chipping Campden marked the beginning of the long rise of the Noel dynasty. The 4th Viscount Campden was created Earl of Gainsborough and to this day the Noel family occupies Exton Hall. This was built in the 1850s after a fire had destroyed the early seventeenth-century Exton Old Hall, in 1810.

The effigy of Sir John (later Lord) Harington from the Kelway Tomb in Exton Church (SH)

George Villiers

The man who bought Burley, as well as Hambleton, Greetham, Cottesmore and Oakham Lordshold and another Harington estate, Coombe Abbey in Warwickshire, in 1620, was George Villiers. The asking price was £28,000. George and his bride, Katherine (*née* Manners), moved into their new mansion in the summer of 1621, planning a great house-warming at which the king would be guest of honour. George Villiers was created 1st Duke of Buckingham in 1623.

Buckingham's house at Burley on the Hill has given rise to many questions. Any evidence on the ground was buried under the grand new house which was built in the 1690s. Most early writers described the house which Buckingham bought from the Haringtons as 'improved' by its new owner, although Hoskins and Pevsner in the twentieth century echoed James Wright's suggestion that Buckingham completely rebuilt the house during the 1620s. This seems to be unlikely, although Buckingham certainly improved the house, and made extensive improvements to the grounds and surrounding deer-park. New walls were built, nine feet high and three feet thick, with five stone gateways, of which two still stand. Other survivals are the bowling green and the great stable block, described by Thomas Fuller as so superior that its horses 'were the best accommodated in England'.

Katherine Manners, Duchess of Buckingham (Bridgeman Art Library)

A portrait by an unknown artist of George Villiers, later created the 1st Duke of Buckingham (Wikipedia)

The Stables built for the 1st Duke of Buckingham at Burley (Wright 1684, 55)

Left: The Buckingham Gate on the old Oakham to Stamford road (RO)

The 1st Duke of Buckingham and King Charles I

It was apparently his elegant legs that first brought George Villiers, soon to be Duke of Buckingham, to the adoring attention of King James I. Their close relationship lasted for the rest of James's reign, and Buckingham's influence was strongly felt in all aspects of royal policy.

In 1623 the king was attempting to secure for his heir, Prince Charles, marriage to the Spanish Infanta, but her father was proving reluctant. Buckingham and Prince Charles hatched a scheme to travel to Spain in disguise and sweep the princess off her feet. Things did not go to plan and the two young men spent several months kicking their heels at the Spanish court, refused access to the princess. However, this deepened the growing friendship between them, securing Buckingham's role as royal favourite to the second Stuart king as well as the first.

When James I died in 1625, courtiers eagerly observed the new king, Charles I, and the new regime. He proved to be a poor judge of men and policy, and Buckingham soon became an unpopular scapegoat. Ironically, it was Heneage Finch, grandfather of the future owner of Burley, who as Speaker of the House of Commons read out a call for Buckingham's removal in March 1626 (HMC Finch, 1913, i, 43-44).

Another person less than delighted with Buckingham's close attendance on the king was Henrietta Maria. Married to Prince Charles at 15, she saw Buckingham as a threat to her marriage. Skilfully, the Duke made efforts to win her friendship. His most original gift to her was the Rutland dwarf, Jeffrey Hudson. Sadly for Rutland historians, and contrary to tradition, the memorable presentation probably took place in London, since there was no royal visit to Burley at the relevant time.

Buckingham's ignominious end came as a result of his command, as Lord Admiral, of a naval expedition to relieve the siege of La Rochelle. With casualties of 5,000 men, the expedition was a total disaster and on his return he was greeted with hostile demonstrations, partly mitigated by the birth of his male heir, George, in January 1628. A second expedition, this time under the command of Buckingham's brother-in-law, the Earl of Denbigh, proved equally unsuccessful. By now the surviving sailors and troops were sick, unpaid and mutinous. In Portsmouth, rioting sailors were not to be placated with promises of wages from Buckingham's own pocket. One, John Felton, was determined to end what was widely seen as the Duke's tyranny and corruption, and assassinated him on 23rd August 1628.

The death of Buckingham left the king bereft of his dearest friend, and Burley without an adult owner. The grieving king paid the Duke's debts, while his estates and titles passed to his seven-month-old son. A second son was born to Duchess Katherine posthumously, and she and her young children, Mary, George and Francis, lived in York House, close to the court in London.

The 2nd Duke of Buckingham and the 1st Civil War (1642-46)

Throughout the eleven years while its owner, George Villiers the 2nd Duke of Buckingham, passed through childhood and King Charles ruled without parliament, Burley on the Hill was left to the management of stewards. The first Duke's ambitious plans for its gardens and deer park fell into abeyance and his fine horses no longer occupied their majestic stables.

In 1642, everything changed. On the anniversary of the 1st Duke of Buckingham's death, the king declared war on his parliament, and Rutland fell into the hands of parliamentarians. Sir Edward Harington, a nephew of Burley's former owner, seized Oakham Castle with its magazine of arms and ammunition, and a few weeks later assisted Lord Grey of Groby, Leicestershire, in the occupation of Burley House. With no resident owner, the servants put up little resistance and the magnificent mansion became the headquarters of the Rutland County Committee, governing the county in the name of Parliament.

George Villiers joined the royalist forces, and was with Prince Rupert at the storming of Lichfield, Staffordshire. His estates were now officially confiscated, and Burley became the property of Parliament. Trees were felled, horses commandeered for military use and fortifications dug around the house and stables.

For much of the war, Burley's garrison commander was Colonel Thomas Waite, who led frequent brutal raids on surrounding royalist strongholds. One of his most bitter opponents was Baptist Noel, 3rd Viscount Campden, whose Exton estate had also been commandeered by parliament, but who led his royalist cavalry in bold campaigns from their bases at Belvoir, Leicestershire, or Newark Castle, Nottinghamshire. Even between members of the Rutland County Committee there were constant disputes, and for a time Waite was replaced by Major Layfield in command of Burley House.

In 1645 the royalists captured Leicester, and there were fears that they might overrun Rutland. The garrison at Burley rushed to improve its defences, only to be reprimanded by the London-based Committee of Both Kingdoms:

'We are informed that in fortifying Burley House there has been more spoil and waste made of that house than is necessary.

George Villiers, 2nd Duke of Buckingham and his brother, Lord Francis Villiers in 1636, after Van Dyck. George inherited Burley on the Hill when only seven months old (Bridgeman Art Library)

We desire you will consider what is necessary to be done for the fortifying thereof, and that as little damage be done to the building as may be.'

However, with the king's defeat a year later bringing an end to the first civil war, Burley no longer needed to be maintained as a fortified garrison. The Rutland Committee was ordered to 'slight' the defences and dismantle the fortifications 'without making any further spoil of the house or stables' (CSPD 1644-5, 1646). However, at some stage during 1645-6, in defiance of the orders of Parliament, Buckingham's beautiful house of Burley on the Hill was '. . . utterly consumed by fire so that at present there remains nothing but certain ruinous parts and pieces of the walls' (ROLLR DG 7/1/70).

The 2nd Duke of Buckingham and the 2nd Civil War (1648-51)

During the second civil war the second Duke made his escape abroad. Most of his confiscated estates were granted to the parliamentary commander, General Lord Fairfax. Burley House was uninhabitable, but the 1652 survey reported that William Horton and Thomas Wing were living in the stables. In the same year Fairfax gave up Burley, and some of its assets were sold to Oliver Cromwell, Fairfax's successor as Lord General.

Unable to return to his estates, Buckingham accompanied the uncrowned future king, Charles II, fighting with him at the Battle of Worcester in 1651. Once again defeated and in exile, he planned and schemed. His opponent, the Earl of Clarendon, predicted with unconscious irony that Buckingham 'will no doubt marry Cromwell's daughter or be Cromwell's groom to save his estate'. He was only partly wrong. Buckingham had set his sights on the daughter of his past enemy, Lord Fairfax.

George Villiers, 2nd Duke of Buckingham (Finch 1901)

Lord and Lady Fairfax reluctantly agreed to the match, but despite their pleas for the freedom of their new son-in-law, Buckingham was imprisoned first on Jersey, then at Windsor, and finally in the Tower of London. Following Cromwell's death in 1658, Buckingham was released from the Tower the following year. With no capable ruler to take his place, King Charles II was recalled to his kingdom. His coronation was on 29th May 1660.

Restoration of the monarchy brought restitution of confiscated property, and with an income from land and rentals of £26,000 a year, the 2nd Duke of Buckingham was considered the richest man in England. Once again at the centre of court life, except during his frequent quarrels with the new king, Buckingham had little desire to lead a quiet life with his Duchess on their estates at Burley or elsewhere. With his extravagant tastes and love of gambling, it was not long before his great estates were once again encumbered with debt. The stables, all that remained of his house at Burley on the

Hill, were little used, except as accommodation for tenants or estate officials.

Even before the Duke's death, many of his debt-laden estates had been settled on trustees. Financial interest in Burley was claimed by his dubious relation, Lady Purbeck. At her request, a survey was made in 1683 of Burley and the Oakham Lordship. This report confirmed:

'The house was a very fair building of stone but burnt down in the Civill Warrs, nothing left but Walls . . . The stables very large and fair standing, but out of repair. The Park large reputed 7 mile round enclosed with a very high stone Wall, generally very good Land paled with a high pale, in the North part some woods & Timber and good hill-ground, & many both red & fallow Deer in it, The South part kept for Meadow & pasture, the deer do not come in it . . .'.

In 1687 Buckingham died, after hunting, in the house of one of his Yorkshire tenants. The estate he had squandered had once been one of the greatest in England. Moves were already under way for the sale of Burley, and in the absence of a legitimate Villiers heir, it was left to another, more reputable, owner to rebuild the once great house. The arrival of the Finch family was to challenge the local supremacy of the Noels of Exton and from the vision of Daniel Finch, 2nd Earl of Nottingham, the new mansion of Burley on the Hill was about to rise, phoenix-like, from the ashes of the old.

New Arrivals in Rutland

It was in 1689 that details of the Burley estate came into the hands of Daniel Finch, 2nd Earl of Nottingham (1647-1730), who was searching for a country seat in the Midlands. His father, Heneage Finch (named from the Essex family into which his grandfather had married), had risen to become Solicitor General and Lord Chancellor, before being created 1st Earl of Nottingham in 1681, a year before his death. He was buried at Ravenstone, Buckinghamshire, the family seat, where many members of the family continued to be buried.

Succeeding to the title in 1682, Daniel Finch married as his second wife Anne Hatton, of Kirby Hall, Northamptonshire, who brought a dowry of £10,000. He sold his London home, Kensington House, to the new king, William III, planning to move his household of 60 people to live near his wife's family.

The tradition which tells of Nottingham's first view of Burley on the Hill while riding to view, with the intention of purchasing, the late Duke of Buckingham's

Heneage Finch, 1st Earl of Nottingham, father of the builder of Burley (private collection)

The Effigies of the Lord Finch, Baron High Chancellor & Lords of the most to King Charles y. *Right Hon:ble Heneage of Daventry, Lord of England, & one of Hon:ble Privy Councell, second. Anno Dñi: 1676.*

estate at Helmsley, Yorkshire, is probably inaccurate: but after he first determined to buy Burley, he was able to begin negotiations, which were completed in 1694. As well as Burley, Lord Nottingham acquired the former Buckingham manors of Hambleton, Egleton, Greetham and Oakham Lordshold. The price was £50,000 for the estate, park and stables: all that was required was to build a suitable house.

As his political views proved less acceptable to the Whig administration of King William III, Nottingham was forced to resign his post as Secretary of State in 1693, resolving 'to go into the country, though I live in the stables at Burley'. Expressing his intentions to his sons in case he died before the new house was completed, Nottingham hoped that it would not cost much above £15,000: 'For I would not have my eldest son under the temptation of living in town for Want of an House nor of being too extravagant in building one' (Finch 1901, i, 26).

Impatient to see the house quickly completed according to his plans, Nottingham was able to obtain a lease on the Earl of Gainsborough's house at Exton, where the family lived until 1699. In that year they were able to move at least partially into the new house. Lady Nottingham wrote from Burley, 'I can't say we are more settled than when we first came for we still eat at Exton and I'm afraid must do so for some time.' Both the time-scale and building cost were greatly underestimated: the house was not finally completed until after 1710 and the cost was at least double Nottingham's original estimate (Habakkuk 1990, 348-352).

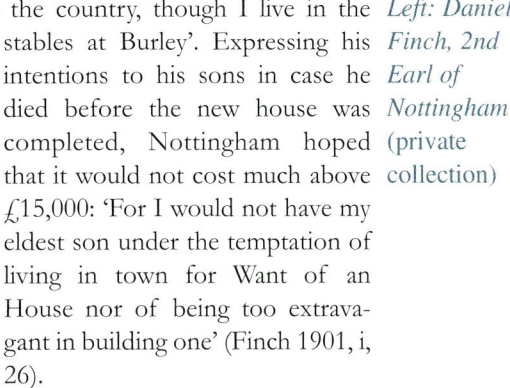

Above: The inscription on the Heneage Finch engraving (private collection)

Left: Daniel Finch, 2nd Earl of Nottingham (private collection)

The New House

All the evidence suggests that Daniel Finch, 2nd Earl of Nottingham, employed no architect for his grand new house at Burley. While travelling in Italy as a young man, he had observed the building of Bernini's colonnades in front of St Peter's in Rome, which might have influenced his desire for the striking pair of colonnades at Burley. He had apparently discussed house-building with Sir Christopher Wren, and sought other expert advice. When his ideas had taken shape, Nottingham commissioned a model of the proposed house from the joiner, Thomas Poulteney. When building began in 1694, it was superintended first by Henry Dormer and then by John Lumley of Northampton. The bailiff, Thomas Armstrong, who was paid a hundred pounds per year, lived in a house at the end of the stable which later became the Estate Office (Finch 1901, i, 27).

Bricks, made on the site, were used for the 'carcase' of the building, while the foundations, exterior facings and ornamentations were mainly of Clipsham stone. The stone for the colonnades came from Ketton. Many builders and masons were employed from local quarries but difficulties in maintaining prompt deliveries of the vast quantities of materials required, and a shortage of masons, caused many problems.

Burley House, from a nineteenth-century print drawn by J P Neale and engraved by H Winkles (private collection)

Desperate for skilled stone masons, Nottingham urged his father-in-law to recommend the work to men from Weldon, Northamptonshire, who would be paid between nine and twelve shillings a week. It is easy to sympathise with the view which Nottingham expressed in a letter of 1701, '[Building] is a pleasure your Lordship will not envy me once you have tried it' (Habakkuk 1990, 351).

A detailed account of the years of trials and tribulations, as revealed through the agreements, bills and letters between Lord Nottingham and his various agents, can be found in Pearl Finch's history of her family's home.

Much of the interior work was not completed until 1704, and the family found themselves living among painters and decorators for several years.

Everything was of the finest quality, personally chosen by Lord Nottingham. He ordered walls and ceilings to be painted by Gerard Lanscroon, the Flemish artist who had assisted Verrio in the decoration of Hampton Court. The main staircase was decorated in the baroque style with the history of Perseus and Andromeda, including the winged horse, Pegasus, which featured on the Finch family crest.

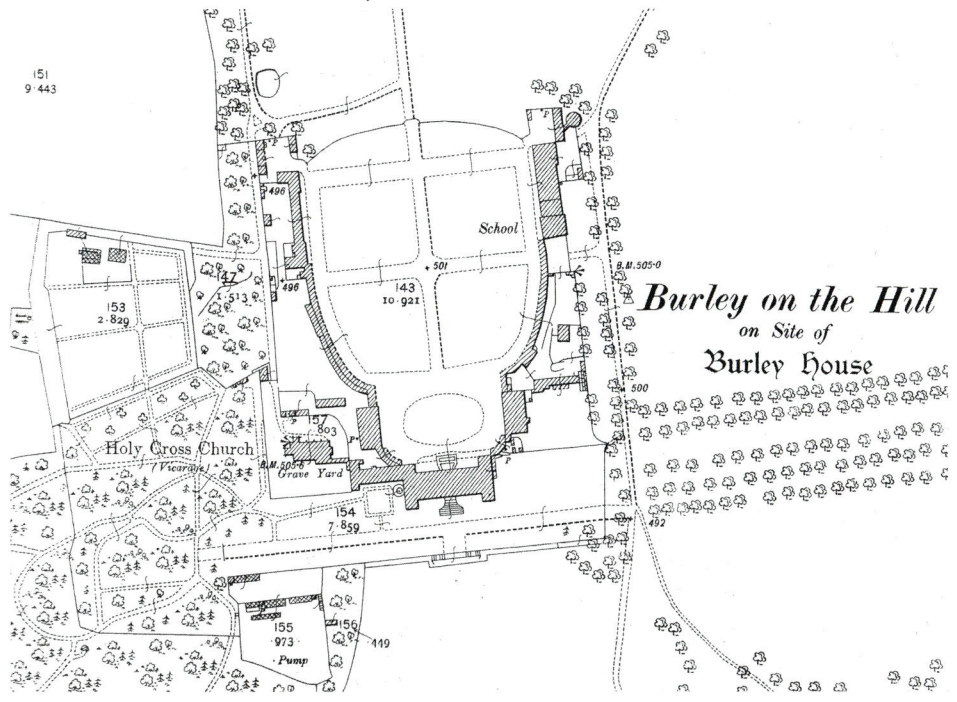

Burley on the Hill from the OS 2nd ed 25" map 1904

In 1901 Pearl Finch described a more human inclusion among the classical subjects depicted in the frescoes of the huge Painted Hall, 60 feet long by 40 feet broad, and half the height of the house. Near the door leading in from the grand staircase were two little figures of Lord Nottingham's children, Lord Finch and Lady Essex Finch, who had watched the artist at work. Sadly this magnificent room was destroyed in the fire of 1908. Following restoration, it became the great ballroom, commanding spectacular views which, as well as the distant Rockingham Castle, now include Rutland Water in the valley below.

Left: Burley House, main staircase (private collection)

Many walls within Burley House were hung with tapestries, commissioned by Lord Nottingham from workshops at Mortlake, London, or possibly Brussels. These included a series of The Months, copied from those at Windsor Castle but no longer hanging at Burley in 1901, and Hero and Leander, destroyed in the fire of 1908. Great chimney pieces and mirrors were also ordered from London, causing some concern over their safe delivery to Rutland.

> **Letter to Lord Nottingham concerning the delivery of mirrors to Burley, 27th September 1711:**
>
> My Lord
> I received your Lordship's letter as for ye wood frame it was made according to ye drafts and in order to fix ye glasses and borders and gilt frame. I have bin with ye Waginer and he says that in case the wagin should overturn or any other casolity should happin that he will not stand to ye loss of any glasses; therefore My lord my opinion is that t'will be ye safest way to bring ye glasses by Pon [the carrier] and it will be but labor more compleated, that it would be a great pity that it should come to any damage as for ye gilt frame I have made that in joynts so that I do design to send them in a box by ye Wagin. My Lord it was impossible for me to make ye chimneypiece without making ye wood frame first, I have sent ye wood frame by Pon ye carrier and your Lordships Coach glass in ye box that came with ye coach frame. My Lord I humbly desire your Lordships opinion by ye next post for it is all redy to send away and I design that it may be brought down before ye bad weather com, and this is all at present From
> Your Humble Sarvant
> Thomas Howcraft (Pearl Finch 1901, i, 78)

It is likely that the total cost of building Burley House, spread over 17 years, came to around £30,000 rather than the £80,000 later suggested (Habakkuk 1990, 352). This included the necessary rebuilding of the Buckingham stables, after a fire in 1705. However, once finished, the mansion was celebrated as a marvel by all who visited it. In a fulsome addition to his *History of Rutland*, James Wright extolled the newly completed house, claiming, 'There are not many in England that can equal, and few or none surpass Burley on the Hill; the very great Grace of this little County'.

> **From James Wright's poetic tribute to Burley:**
>
> Triumphant Structure! while you thus aspire
> From the dead Ruins of a Rebel fire;
> Methinks I see the genius of the Place
> Advance his Head, and with a smiling Face,
> Say, Kings have on this Spot made their Abodes;
> 'Tis fitted now to entertain the Gods! (Wright 1684, *Additions,* 5)

Drawing of Burley on the Hill (Wright 1684, *Additions*, 9)

The Finch Dynasty

With the completion of his majestic house, the 2nd Earl of Nottingham and his Countess made Burley their main residence, spending only the first three months of each year in London, where they rented a house before buying one in Bloomsbury Square. The younger members of the large Finch family probably remained in Rutland throughout the year. From the eight children of Lord Nottingham's first marriage, only one, Mary, survived. However, there were nine daughters and six sons surviving of his second marriage, to Anne Hatton. It is claimed that in total the 2nd Earl had 31 children (*VCH* II, 116)! His eldest son, Heneage, became blind following smallpox and died young, but was replaced as heir by the second son, Daniel.

In these early days of party politics, Lord Nottingham was a Tory supporter of the Stuart King James II, and of a 'High' Church of England. Rutland was represented in Parliament by two Whigs, John Noel and Philip Sherard, who supported the Protestant succession, constitutional monarchy and fewer privileges for the Church of England. Lord Nottingham was not happy with this situation, writing to one potential voter:

'I take for granted for I am sure you are persuaded that Mr. Noel and Mr. Sherard are by no means fitt to serve in Parl; to be trusted with all our civil & religious rights . . .' (ROLLR Finch MSS, Box 4969 Rut. 2 iii).

The Finch family crest (private collection)

Disqualified by his title from standing for Parliament, Lord Nottingham resolved to procure one of the Rutland seats for his heir, Lord Daniel Finch. In support of the campaign he followed the Whig precedent and created 300 new electors, in a total electorate of only 600, by helping them become 'forty shilling freeholders'. As Lord of the Manors of Oakham Lordshold, Hambleton, Egleton and Greetham, as well as Burley, Nottingham was well placed to influence voters in this period before the secret ballot. He was also a considerate landlord, arranging for cottages to be repaired and re-thatched when needed, not just before elections. The election expenses included the Bell-man, drums, horse hire and 'ten Ordinary's [pub meals] at the Bell' (Finch 1901, i, 275).

When the votes were counted, Lord Finch and his fellow Tory, Richard Halford, came second and third respectively. However, Halford petitioned for the removal of the winner, John Noel, on the grounds of 'corrupt and undue practices'. The following year Noel was expelled from the House of Commons, and Finch and Halford became the two Tory Members of Parliament for Rutland. Unhappy at the prospect of losing his seat, John Noel had sharp words with Lord Finch, and, according to the *Journal of the House of Commons*, 'they were required by the House to give their words and honours not to prosecute the matter any further' (Mitchell 1995, 207-12).

Watercolour of Burley House from the south-east (private collection)

Despite Lord Nottingham's Tory sympathies, by 1711 it was becoming clear that the last Stuart, Queen Anne, would die without an heir and that, with Whig support, the succession was likely to pass to the Protestant Hanoverian dynasty. For reasons that are not entirely clear, Nottingham changed his allegiance to support the Whigs in Parliament. When the next election came in 1713, Lord Finch was to stand in Rutland against his former party, in partnership with a new fellow-Whig, Bennet, Lord Sherard. Finch and Sherard were successful, against the national trend which was still largely Tory. It was likely that many who had supported Lord Finch when he campaigned for the Tories were prepared to transfer their party allegiance and continued to vote for him.

When Queen Anne died in 1714, Lord Nottingham continued in government under George I, serving as Lord President of the Council from 1714-16. Unpopular with long-serving Whigs and their leader, Robert Walpole, he acquired the nickname of 'Don Dismal' for his gloomy, swarthy complexion. He was finally dismissed for supporting the six Jacobite peers who plotted for the return of the Stuarts.

During her husband's absences in London, Lady Anne kept him supplied with news (and occasional game birds) from Burley. In November 1718 she wrote:

'They complain there are so many owls in the [Burley] Woods that they hinder their taking the few woodcocks that there are there, not without reason, you complain those I sent were lean w[hi]ch made me desire you to ask the Dr. (Charles Finch, DD) if there is a receipt to fatten them knowing he has a good many choice ones . . .' (Finch 1901, i, 208).

A New Title

There were several branches of the influential Finch family: Lord Nottingham's brother, Heneage, had been created 1st Earl of Aylesford, while his cousin, John Finch, was 6th Earl of Winchilsea. In 1729 John died, and the title of 7th Earl of Winchelsea now descended to his cousin Daniel, 2nd Earl of Nottingham. Rather than use only the new, superior title of Winchilsea, Daniel was resolved to maintain the title and dignity of his own branch of the family. He and his heirs continued to use both the Nottingham and Winchilsea titles. However, he did not live long to enjoy the new title, dying in January 1730. He was buried with his ancestors at the family manor of Ravenstone, Buckinghamshire (the family's estates there included the village of Middleton [Milton] Keynes).

The new 8th Earl of Winchilsea and 3rd Earl of Nottingham, Daniel Finch (1689-1769) had been born in Kensington Palace, in the year following the 'Glorious Revolution' which brought William and Mary to the throne in place of the Catholic James II. At the age of 21, as Lord Finch, he was elected to Parliament as a Tory member for the County of Rutland. Following his father into alliance with the Whigs, he was re-elected over the next two decades until, succeeding his father in 1730, he entered the House of Lords. By 1742 he had been appointed First Lord of the Admiralty, and the following year he was named as one of the Regents of the Realm when King George II led his troops into battle in Bavaria, in the War of the Austrian Succession (*VCH* II, 116).

Winchilsea later served as Lord President of the Council under the Whig Prime Minister, the Marquess of Rockingham. The general verdict on the career of this worthy Earl is summed up by his descendant Pearl Finch, 'He held many important posts in the State, but does not appear to have greatly distinguished himself' (Finch 1901, i, 282). His name survived for a period on the 'Winchelsea Arms', a wayside inn on his estate in Greetham, beside the Great North Road. However, since the late eighteenth century the inn has become better known as the Ram Jam Inn!

Despite following his father's wishes and serving above all the interests of the Finch family, the 8th Earl of Winchilsea left no son to inherit the titles on his death in 1769. His second wife, Mary Palmer, had produced four daughters, unusually named as Heneage, Essex, Hatton and Augusta (tradition holds that the youngest daughter was dressed for some years as a boy to supply the deficit!). The titles and estates were to pass to George Finch, son of Daniel's younger brother, William.

Lady Charlotte Finch

In Burley Church is a beautiful white marble figure, depicting a young, kneeling woman. The inscription informs us that she was 'Lady Charlotte Finch . . . relict [widow] of the Right Honourable William Finch . . . Mother of George Finch, 9th Earl of Winchilsea and 4th Earl of Nottingham'. Born Charlotte Fermor, she was married in 1746 to William, younger brother of Daniel, 8th Earl of Winchilsea and 3rd Earl of Nottingham. They had three daughters and one son, George, who was to succeed his uncle as 9th Earl of Winchilsea. Lady Charlotte Finch is best known for her appointment in 1762 as governess to the new-born George, Prince of Wales, son of King George III and Queen Charlotte. She died in 1813, having seen her son, George, succeed to his uncle's two earldoms and inherit the great house of Burley on the Hill. He erected this monument in her memory in Burley Church, by the sculptor Sir Francis Leggatt Chantrey, whose works include the statues of William IV and George IV in Trafalgar Square.

Above: Memorial to Lady Charlotte Finch in Burley Church (SH)

Left: An engraving of Charlotte Finch (private collection)

George Finch, 9th Earl of Winchilsea and 4th Earl of Nottingham (1752-1826)

As the only son many hopes were placed on the young George Finch, especially when it became clear that he would inherit his uncle's great titles. In 1761, the year before his mother, Lady Charlotte Finch, took up her appointment as royal governess, George was sent to Eton, where he became 'Captain of ye 1st form' and was much missed by his mother (Finch 1901, i, 325). At the age of seventeen he succeeded to the Earldoms of Winchilsea and Nottingham, and the great house of Burley on the Hill. He continued his studies, attending Christ Church, Oxford, where he enjoyed the pleasures of racing, balls and (when the season allowed) shooting.

After graduating in 1771, Lord Winchilsea left Oxford to tour Scotland before settling to life at Burley, interspersed with seasons in London and travels as far as Constantinople in 1775. He described the pleasures of country life, writing to his mother in 1774:

'Though Burley affords but little news, I sit down just to let you know that we are very well and very well entertained here, we have been very busy a hunting, and that tired me so much that in the evening I have had no courage to sit down and write, however to show that shooting is not quite deserted, we have packed off today a brace of woodcocks and a hare which I hope will prove good.'

His eagerness to hunt is confirmed in a letter from his sister, Henrietta, to their mother:

'[Lord Winchilsea] is at present quite provoked at Lord Gains[borou]gh being gone for a week to Lord Exeter's on a coursing and card-playing Party, as he says in ye very prime of ye Hunting season. He really cannot swallow it as you can easily imagine' (Finch 1901, i, 331 & 333).

The 9th Earl of Winchilsea (private collection)

Lord Winchilsea and Cricket

The 9th Earl of Winchilsea is probably best known today for his interest in cricket. He was the treasurer of a committee of 'Noblemen and Gentlemen' formed in 1784 to revise the laws of cricket. One important change was to instigate the six-ball over in place of the previous four-ball. As founder members of the MCC (Marylebone Cricket Club), Lord Winchilsea and a colleague prevailed on Thomas Lord to establish a cricket ground in Marylebone, London. MCC later moved to St John's Wood, London, where Thomas Lord is remembered in Lord's Cricket Ground. Winchilsea was a keen player, scoring 54 for MCC at Marylebone in 1792, and 56 on the same ground a year later. On 1st July 1793, the *Sporting Magazine* carried an illustration of a 'Grand Cricket Match played on Lord's Ground Mary-le-bone on June 20th and the

Cricket match played on 20th June 1793 at Lord's Ground, Marylebone (Raymond Hill)

following day between the Earl of Winchilsea and the Earl of Darnley for 1,000 guineas'.

In order to enjoy the noble game in Rutland as well as London, Lord Winchilsea ordered a cricket pitch to be laid out on the great forecourt of Burley on the Hill. According to Raymond Hill, it was christened in 1790 with a match between Hampshire and All-England. The site was used for cricket matches until the Second World War.

Burley cricket team in 1923 (Raymond Hill)

Fireworks at Burley

During the 1780s, following the traumatic loss of the American colonies, King George III suffered repeated episodes of what appeared to be mental illness (modern specialists have suggested that he was probably suffering from the inherited disease porphyria). On 17th April 1789, the *Stamford Mercury* carried the following report:

'The right hon. the earl of Winchilsea, lord lieutenant of the county of Rutland, appointed Monday last for a public rejoicing on his majesty's recovery, at his lordship's seat at Burley. An elegant entertainment was given on the occasion to the nobility, gentry, freeholders, and his lordship's tenants, all of whom received a general invitation.

'His lordship having engaged an eminent fire worker from London, a scene beautiful beyond description was exhibited in the large court in front of the house, at night. Amidst a variety of works was a pyramid 15 yards high, and a transparency, representing a medallion of his majesty suspended by two cherubs, bearing a crown, G III. Beneath, "Long live the King". The bust was in a glory; at top of the pyramid was a large crown, and a little below on each side, the letters G.R. which with the corresponding works around, surpassed any thing ever seen in this part of the country. At intervals rounds of cannon were fired, together with repeated shouts of the populace, producing a pleasing awful effect . . .

'The house and court yard was, literally speaking, like a fair, for many hours. It is supposed that near 4,000 people were entertained. In the left colonade was placed a very large quantity of ale, bread, &c. which was distributed to the populace so liberally, that near two hogsheads of liquor were obliged to be returned into the cellar. The whole entertainment was conducted in that true stile of English hospitality, which reflects the highest honor on the noble donor, and will ever be remembered by his guests . . . .'

Humphry Repton at Burley

During the 1780s, Lord Winchilsea made improvements to the house and estate buildings of Burley. He was concerned that his tenants and labourers were well treated and housed, publishing his views under the title *An Illustrious Example of Attention to the Condition of the Cottager* (Aston 1989, 312-17). According to Pearl Finch, the Earl was the first landowner to introduce a system allowing his cottagers 'to hire a small portion of land and to keep a cow' (Finch 1901, i, 336). He helped to found the Rutland Society for Industry in 1785, and advocated provision for the children of the poor to learn skills for employment (Broughton 1990, 363).

Seventy years after the grounds had been laid out to the Italianate plans of the 2nd Earl of Nottingham, Winchilsea decided that the time had come for a 'makeover'. Fashions in garden design were as mutable then as they are today. In the 1750s, the famous Lancelot 'Capability' Brown had been commissioned to redesign the grounds of the greater Burghley House, home of the Marquis of Exeter outside Stamford. The artificial, geometric formalities

Humphry Repton (RLHRS)

Burley south aspect before removal of terraces. From Repton's Red Book (private collection)

of knot gardens and parterres were to be swept away, and Brown aimed to create landscapes 'more natural than nature herself'. This frequently involved changing the contours and watercourses of the surrounding parkland.

By the time Lord Winchilsea turned his mind to a new garden, Capability Brown was dead and Humphry Repton was the rising star. Using the new term 'landscape gardener', Repton quickly acquired commissions with the help of his persuasive 'Red Books'. These gave the house-owner a collection of water-colour illustrations with folding flaps to show 'before' and 'after' his proposed changes. He retained formal garden features such as trellises and flower-beds close to the house, divided from the park beyond by balustraded terraces from which residents could view the glories of the landscaped parkland. Rather than building artificial ruins into the vista, Repton might include ordinary thatched cottages which would be of practical benefit.

When Lord Winchilsea invited Repton to Burley in 1795, he was the most important of Repton's clients to date. Repton observed the five sharply descending terraces to the south of the house, standing on what he called 'a table mountain'. He recommended leaving only the uppermost terrace, surmounted with an elegant balustrade, from which the gently sloping lawns (created by moving vast quantities of earth) could be observed. This major change was carried out according to the illustrations in the Burley Red Book.

Burley south aspect after removal of terraces as illustrated by Repton (private collection)

Repton's view of the replacement terrace (private collection)

Other proposals made by Repton for Burley on the Hill included enclosing the north forecourt by extending and linking up the colonnades with a central triumphal arch (Winchilsea had recently opened up this area by demolishing the enclosing wall, leaving only the ornate iron gates and two porters' lodges). He also proposed a new, curving approach from the east, removing the south avenue, significant thinning of the woodland and redesigning the fishponds at the foot of the slope. However, Lord Winchilsea had neither the funds nor inclination to carry out all Repton's suggested improvements. The fine entrance gates remain to this day (Aston 1989, 312-17).

Above: Repton's proposals for the north forecourt, which were never adopted (private collection)

Left: Entrance gates to Burley on the Hill (private collection)

Below: John Nash's design for the Home Farm, Burley (Raymond Hill)

Repton's designs cost £2,500. While they were being carried out, Lord Winchilsea also employed the well-known architect, John Nash, who had laid out two royal parks, Trafalgar Square and Regent Street in London. Nash designed the Home Farm at Burley, for which he was paid £1,500. Following his work on Burley, Humphry Repton continued to work in Rutland, producing a new Red Book with designs for the grounds of Normanton Park, now mostly under Rutland Water. Meanwhile, as a finishing touch to his grounds at Burley, Lord Winchilsea's personal contribution was to design the Hermitage, a reed-thatched 'folly', constructed in 1807 from tree trunks, which burned down in 1960 (Hill 2001, 34, 38 & 70).

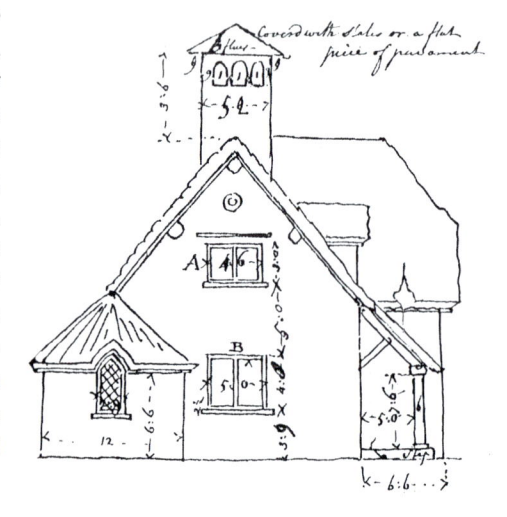

The End of an Era

No doubt influenced by his mother's position as royal governess, Winchilsea's career at court prospered. In 1804 he was appointed Groom of the Stole to King George III (far preferable to the similar-sounding post of Groom of the Stool!). This appointment required the courtier to array the monarch in his state robe, or stole, but would also involve handing him his shirt when he dressed. King George had now been on the throne for 40 years, and was suffering recurrences of the physical and mental illness that had afflicted him in the late 1780s.

Following the French Revolution, England was now engaged in war with Napoleonic France and there were widespread fears of invasion. During this and the earlier American War, Lord Winchilsea raised militia regiments in Rutland. But in addition to political problems at home and abroad, the king and queen were distraught at the scandals and debts incurred by their sons, particularly George, Prince of Wales. In 1811, with no hope of the king's recovery, this unpopular prince was declared Prince Regent to rule in his father's place before becoming king in his own right in 1820.

Burley on the Hill was honoured in 1814 by a royal visit of the Prince Regent and his brother, the Duke of York. Declining the grand bed prepared for him in the State Bedroom, Prince George chose to sleep instead in the large State Dressing Room.

In 1826 George Finch, 9th Earl of Winchilsea died, still unmarried, at the age of 73. In the absence of a legitimate heir, his two earldoms passed to his cousin, George William Finch-Hatton, who had taken the additional surname of his grandmother, Anne Hatton. Finch-Hatton became 10th Earl of Winchilsea (and famous for his duel with the Duke of Wellington!), and the titles descended through this branch of the family, whose home was in

The State Bedroom at Burley on the Hill (private collection)

Guildford, Surrey. From henceforth Burley on the Hill would no longer be the seat of a noble Earl of Nottingham or Winchilsea, but the home of an untitled commoner. The first of these was George Finch, natural son of the 9th Earl of Winchilsea.

George Finch (1794-1870)

Educated at Harrow and Cambridge, at the age of 26 Mr George Finch became Lord of the Manors held by his father, and owner of the beautiful mansion of Burley on the Hill. He had been granted the use of the Finch arms in 1809. In 1832, following the passing of the Reform Bill, Finch was elected as Member of Parliament for Stamford and later, for a short period, for Rutland. He combined evangelical Christianity with a love of hunting and cricket, encouraging his sons to hunt and his servants to join the estate cricket team.

George Finch's first wife, Jane Tollemache, had died aged 19 in childbirth, only two years after their marriage, and his second wife was Lady Louisa Somerset, daughter of the 6th Duke of Beaufort. She lived to the age of 86, and in 1892 was buried in the family vault in Burley churchyard. A vivid personal addition to the account of this event is recorded in pencilled marginal comments in the pages of Pearl Finch's *History of Burley on the Hill*, published 18 years later. A younger relative has added the intriguing note:

'Yes, & I was nearly buried there too. Being a bit inquisitive I went down the vault the day before she was buried & my cousin Somerset closed the door down' (Finch 1901, i, No. 15 of 200, 339-41).

A family group on the steps of Burley House, 1867 (private collection)

A family group inside Burley House, 1867 (private collection)

George Henry Finch (1835-1907)

In 1870 George Henry Finch, Conservative Member of Parliament for Rutland, County Councillor and Privy Councillor, inherited Burley on the Hill. Following in the family tradition, he was a keen huntsman, and his daughter, Pearl Finch, records his University tutor attempting to reduce his desire to hunt on six days a week down to two! His first wife died in 1865, leaving a son and two daughters, and in 1871 G H Finch married Edith Montgomery, daughter of an Inland Revenue Commissioner, who bore him seven further children. His parliamentary career lasted for 34 years, but after 1885 no further elections were contested, and Mr Finch was returned unopposed, becoming Father of the House in 1906.

Silver Wedding celebrations of George Henry and Edith Finch, 1896 (private collection)

The Twentieth Century

Pearl Finch's account of Burley on the Hill ended in 1901, six years before her father's death on 22nd May 1907. He was fortunate not to have seen the disastrous fire which caused such devastation at Burley a year later. The new owner of Burley, Alan George Finch (1863-1914), was the son of G H Finch by his first wife. In 1893, the year of the notorious Jameson Raid, he had been sent to fight in Matabeleland, South Africa, under General Carrington. On inheriting the estate, he rented it out temporarily to Freddie and Henry Guest.

Pearl Finch (right) and family members (private collection)

Frederick Guest was later to become a well-known politician, but in 1907 he had recently retired from active army service in order to serve as private secretary to his cousin, Winston Churchill, then a junior minister in the Liberal government. Guest had recently married an American heiress, Amy Phipps, while Churchill was about to become engaged to Clementine Hozier.

In the early hours of 9th August 1908, following a party, fire took hold of Burley on the Hill. Clemmie was then on the Isle of Wight, and on hearing reports, anxiously telegraphed Winston. Fortunately no-one was injured, and Churchill's reply gave a young man's view of the event, although it was probably not shared by his hosts, nor by the house's absent owner:

'The fire was great fun and we all enjoyed it thoroughly. It is a pity such jolly entertainments are so costly . . . The pictures were of small value, and many, with all the tapestries and about half the good furniture were saved . . . Whole rooms sprang into flame as by enchantment. Chairs and tables burnt up like matches. Floors collapsed and ceilings crashed down. The roof descended in a molten shower. Every window spouted fire, and from the centre of the house a volcano roared skyward in a whirlwind of sparks . . . ' (Hill 2001, 48).

— 82 —

Melton Mowbray Fire Brigade at Burley on the Hill following the fire on 9th August 1908 (Hart)

Despite the attentions of the Melton Mowbray fire brigade, estate workers and residents of the house – including Churchill directing retrieval operations with a coat over his pyjamas! – most of the interiors of the western half of the mansion were destroyed. These included Verrio's Painted Hall, subsequently restored as the Ballroom, although the painted Grand Staircase survived. The terrible effects of the fire were exacerbated by shortage of available water as well as the primitive fire-fighting equipment. Subsequently, a reservoir was built under the south terrace, supplied by rainwater from the roof and drains (Hill 2001, 53). A period of restoration ensued, which included the beautiful Adams Dining Room with its ornate ceiling and fireplace.

Burley on the Hill following the fire in 1908 (Hart)

Above: Part of the ceiling in the Dining Room at Burley on the Hill (private collection)

Left: The Dining Room at Burley on the Hill (private collection)

Below: A group of convalescing officers at Burley in 1918 (Raymond Hill)

Burley on the Hill during the Great War

During the First World War, Burley on the Hill was used as a hospital for officers recovering from trench warfare. One patient was 2nd Lieutenant Harry Howard, of the Royal Field Artillery, who stayed with the Skirth family at Home Farm, Burley, attending the hospital for daily treatment. Harry Howard recorded his time at Burley with a Brownie Box camera.

When Burley's owner, Alan George Finch, died in 1914, he was succeeded by his half-brother, Wilfred Henry Montgomery Finch (1883-1939). He also fought in the armed forces, reaching the rank of Lieutenant in the Royal Engineers. He never married, and died in 1939. At this point, parts of the Burley Estate, including the village of Egleton, were sold to meet death duties.

Burley on the Hill passed to a cousin, Colonel James Robert Hanbury, whose grandfather had married Gwendoline Finch. From 1945 he lived at Burley vicarage until he moved into Burley on the Hill in 1956. Following an uprising in Hungary that same year, refugees came to live in the mansion. One of these was Tibor Andres, a member of the Budapest Opera Orchestra, whose sole possession was a flute, which he practised in the bathroom at Burley, when not required to help shovel coal! He remained in touch with Raymond and Eunice Hill, returning to visit Burley in the 1990s (Hill 2001, 149).

During the 1950s the house was opened to the public for a period, and an illustrated guidebook was produced for visitors. Colonel Hanbury fully enjoyed the pleasures of country life. In true Burley tradition, he was a keen huntsman with the Belvoir, of which he was Master between 1947 and 1964 (Burke 107th edition, i, 380). However, he was described as 'not a good manager of assets', and by the time of his death the financial burden of maintaining the great house had become an insuperable problem (Duckers & Davies 1990, 172).

Wilfred Henry Montgomery Finch
(Raymond Hill)

Burley during the Second World War

From 1940-45, Burley on the Hill was once again used as a convalescent home for injured soldiers. Up to 150 patients were cared for under Matron Goodband and her nurses, many of whom attended a reunion in 1974. When the war ended, the mansion was occupied by the Red Cross as an orthopaedic rehabilitation centre for military personnel, and specialist diabetic hospital (Hill 2001, 60 & 118).

Matron Miss E Goodband MBE with members of her nursing staff at Burley, 1941 (Raymond Hill)

The last resident owner of Burley on the Hill was Evan Robert Hanbury, who succeeded his father, Colonel Hanbury, in 1971 at the age of twenty. For many years the great forecourt became the venue for the annual Rutland County Show, featuring livestock and equine events as well as popular stalls. But in 1990 everything changed. The mansion, parkland and wood were sold to the international tycoon, Asil Nadir, who proposed to turn Burley into 'the classiest Country House hotel and sporting estate', with two world-class golf courses, footmen and chambermaids in appropriate 'turn of the century' uniforms (Duckers & Davies 1990, 172). However, before the necessary planning enquiry could be held, Nadir's empire was in receivership and the owner of Burley on the Hill was in Cyprus, evading serious fraud charges.

Colonel James Robert Hanbury with his sons Evan and Tim, on the grand staircase of the mansion (Raymond Hill)

How could Mr Polly Peck let my house crumble?

PICTURE POWER IN THE SUNDAY EXPRESS

by Joanna Bale

THIS is the sorry state of a once-magnificent mansion belonging to fallen Polly Peck tycoon Asil Nadir.

It stands empty and decaying, a victim of the spectacular collapse of his £2 billion business empire.

The Grade I listed Burley House at Burley on the Hill, Leicestershire, is riddled with wet and dry rot.

Its walls are a mass of crumbling plaster and its once-immaculate gardens untidy and overgrown.

Beautiful tapestries and murals are left to disintegrate and fade away, long-forgotten by Mr Nadir who faces 18 charges of theft and false accounting.

Now the former owner of the house has spoken out for the first time, attacking him for letting it descend into dereliction.

Despair as farmer sees his heritage for sale at mere £3 million

FALLEN TYCOON: Nadir

Rescue came for the neglected mansion in the form of a partnership between the former owner, E R ('Joss') Hanbury and the architect, Kit Martin. While Joss Hanbury resumed management of the estate, Martin converted the Burley mansion and its outbuildings into a series of luxury houses and apartments. Now among the most desirable residences in Rutland, the homes look out over the south avenue to Rutland Water beyond, northward over the great courtyard, or across the wide expanse of the Vale of Catmose. No doubt the new inhabitants of Burley on the Hill rejoice to share this 'most beautiful and noble Edifice, with all those other requisite Imbellishments about it, that are suitable to so magnificent a building' (Wright 1684, *Additions*, 2).

This article appeared in the Sunday Express of 28th July 1991

Burley on the Hill from the north-west in 2005 (John Nowell, Zodiac Publishing)

— 87 —

The Estate Workers

The 1881 Census lists 21 indoor staff living at Burley on the Hill. The seven men named include a butler, 'boy' and footmen, while the women included a governess, housekeeper and various maids. In addition, the gardens, stables, workshops, sawmill and woods could not have been maintained without a small army of workers ranging from grooms to gardeners, living on or around the estate. Raymond Hill pays tribute to many of these in his book of 2001, *Burley on the Hill Mansion*. He recalls how estate workers were regularly called upon to clear snow off the leaded roof of the mansion, in case water leaked through the seams. It was cold, exposed work, with the one compensation that they could see all over Rutland!

Estate workers shovelling snow off the roof of the mansion in 1947 (Raymond Hill)

One such estate worker was Alick Freer, who began work at Burley in the 1950s. He was employed by Colonel Hanbury's agent, Mr Mellish, taking over his brother's former job as woodsman, for five pounds per week and a home at Rose Cottage. The basic woodland management included wood felling, coppicing, cutting stakes, binders and pen sticks, digging ditches and keeping the rides clear. Alick worked with the Wood Foreman, Jim Charity, to plant thousands of trees in place of those felled, on piece-work at seven shillings per hundred. Logs were cut in the steam-driven sawmill and sold by the sack for half a crown (12 $^{1}/_{2}$ pence), and all the fires in the mansion had to be supplied. As Alick recalls:

'Hunt Balls were the worst. We used to have logs then about two foot long and we used to have to carry them up flights of stairs to the big open fireplace for the Hunt Ball. Up and down, up and down . . . .'

When Alick began work in the woods at Burley, there were four full-time woodsmen and three full-time gamekeepers. But as others died or left the estate, Alick Freer was asked to take on more and more work. Eventually, 'there was only me left on the wood side of the estate, and I was woodman, gamekeeper and everything'. He used to trap vermin and hang them along the whole length of one of the rides. Alick retired in the 1990s having worked for the estate for 40 years.

Much of the Burley estate was directly farmed by tenants such as Jim Ellis of Home Farm, employed by Colonel Hanbury as farm foreman and in charge of all the stock. His wife, Sheilah Ellis, became locally renowned for her skill as a shepherd, appearing in 1982 on the TV programme 'One Man and his Dog' (Buxton & Martin 2001, 65).

Village Life

One important worker who lived in the village outside the gates was the blacksmith. In 1881 William Chambers, aged 29, lived at the forge with his wife, Lucy and two-year-old son, Rupert. Thirty years later, William Chambers was still shoeing farm horses, ponies and hunters at his forge. His smithy still stands today, 'under a spreading chestnut tree' (Longfellow), sufficiently picturesque to have featured in an advertisement for Cherry Blossom Boot Polish.

The Forge at Burley on the Hill (Hart)

Chestnut Farm, behind the Forge, was for almost three centuries the home of the Lane family, including James Lane, coachman to George Finch. For a time it was a public house known as the Horse and Groom, but in the early nineteenth century this was closed by the last Earl of Winchilsea, who moved the public licence to Hambleton. Chestnut Farmhouse continued as the village Post Office until 1939, when the postmistress, Fanny Lane, retired. In the early years of the century the Royal Mail van would change horses at Burley, and Mr Lane was paid ten pounds a month to deliver the mail for a radius of four and a half miles around Burley (Hill 2001, 91).

Until 1944, the children of villagers and estate workers attended Burley Village School, held in two rooms of the mansion's stable block. This school had been established by George Finch in the 1860s, with Miss Eliza Brown teaching the infants and the older children taught by Miss Martha Carr. In

Burley Village Feast Day, 1925 (Raymond Hill)

1922, Burley School won the Rutland Morris Dancing Competition, although by now the number of pupils had declined from over 60 to 24 (Traylen 1999, 54).

Raymond Hill remembers entering the fancy dress competition of Oakham Carnival in 1945, wearing costumes made by Miss Edith Lane of Chestnut Farm. Miss Lane was a loud singer and she was greatly missed if absent from church, as the congregation looked to her to lead the singing (Spelman 2000, 90). As well as the regular church services there would be celebrations such as Christmas, May Day and Harvest. The annual fête, which began as Burley Village Feast Day, would be held in the forecourt of Burley on the Hill, or occasionally at the Vicarage.

Burley Wood and Fishponds

As well as a valuable source of timber and a sporting facility, Burley Wood was a place of endless pleasure for the local children. They might be taken out on nature walks by their teacher, or play around the area known as the Lion's Den. Burley Wood's great rides, laid out by the Duke of Buckingham, survived the recommended 'improvements' of Humphry Repton, and still today provide magnificent vistas as well as convenient sectors for hunting and shooting.

As the largest tract of ancient woodland in Rutland, Burley Wood is rich in flora and fauna and was made a Site of Special Scientific Interest in 1992. Each spring brings spectacular displays of Bluebells, while there are rarer plants such as slender St John's Wort and woodrushes. Observations made by Rutland Natural History Society in 1989 recorded 73 species and varieties of mosses and liverworts, 154 different fungi and 80 lichens growing on bark, including eight lichens not previously recorded in Leicestershire and Rutland. Uncommon butterflies included Speckled Wood, Purple Hairstreak and Essex Skipper. There were 34 species of moth, 55 species of hoverfly, 41 of cranefly and 183 beetles. Two varieties of bush-cricket infrequent in Leicestershire and Rutland are commonly found in Burley Wood (Jeeves 1990, 68-70).

Even before the coming of Rutland Water, Burley Wood was well-known for its birdlife, including breeding Redstarts. A century ago, local landowners with an interest in birds shot as many varieties as possible, to add to their collections of stuffed birds or eggs. George Henry Finch, owner of Burley, was proud to provide notes on his impressive collection of stuffed birds for Haines' publication of 1907, *Notes on the Birds of Rutland*. In addition to specimens shot in the woods, many of the birds noted in the book were water fowl observed at Burley Fishponds, such as the Common Snipe which were reported as regularly breeding there.

It was not only bird-watchers, but also local fishermen and youths who knew the delights of the Burley Fishponds, which had lain for centuries at the foot of the wooded slopes of Burley on the Hill, at the end of the south avenue leading to the Buckingham gate on the old Stamford Road. Close by were the Cow Yard, Keeper's Cottage, former Toll Cottage and an unusual hovel, built into the dry stone wall. During many winters, the fishponds and flooded fields beyond would regularly freeze, and became a popular venue for ice skating. Eddie Butcher remembers how, in the 1930s, 'At night cars drove round the lake and shone their headlights on to it and skating went on all night' (Spelman 2000, 125).

Burley Fishponds are revealed when Rutland Water is at low level (RO)

An aerial view of Burley on the Hill from the south showing the now-flooded fishponds and the avenue leading to the house (John Nowell, Zodiac Publishing)

Today, at the beginning of the twenty-first century, both Burley Wood and the Fishponds provide valuable habitats for birds whose numbers and very survival have been under threat. Red Kites and Sparrowhawks fly above and the reintroduced Ospreys nest nearby. When the reservoir was built in the 1970s, the fishponds area fell inside its perimeter, and was to be flooded and incorporated into Rutland Water. Before this happened, quantities of reed and other plants were uprooted and replanted around the new lagoons of the Nature Reserve at Egleton. But the former fishponds in the north arm of the reservoir remain an important, secluded area of the Rutland Water Nature Reserve. Although for much of the year they are lost to view, during a dry season when the level of Rutland Water falls, the Burley Fishponds are once again revealed, their raised causeway at times now dense with Cormorants and other water birds (*see* Chapter 14 – Rutland Waters).

Chapter 5
Edith Weston: A Queen's Dowry
Sue Howlett

The Medieval Village

Although a significant settlement for nearly a thousand years, Edith Weston is not mentioned in Domesday Book, compiled by order of William the Conquerer in 1086. The seventeenth-century historian James Wright noted in his *History and Antiquities of the County of Rutland* (1684, 41), that the 'town' of 'Edyweston' had been one of the seven unnamed outliers, or hamlets, which belonged to the Church of Hambleton before the Norman Conquest. In the Anglo-Saxon estate which included Hambleton and its outliers, Queen Edith is recorded as having held four carucates (probably around 500 acres) before 1066. She had also been granted land in Oakham, Ridlington, Luffenham and the now deserted village of Sculthorpe, as well as property in the nearby town of Stamford, Lincolnshire.

The Church of St Mary, Edith Weston in 1839 (Uppingham School Archives)

So who was Queen Edith, remembered to this day in the village that bears her name? In 1066 there were two Ediths with royal connections. One, known as 'Edith of the Swan-neck' was the mistress of King Harold, killed at the Battle of Hastings. Tradition relates how she searched for his body and brought it for dignified burial at Waltham Abbey, Essex. But the Edith (or Ealdgyth) who gave her name to Edith Weston was an older woman who had been married to the previous Saxon king, Edward the Confessor.

The saintly King Edward, who reigned from 1042 to 1066, was persuaded by advisers to marry the daughter of his most powerful subject, Earl Godwin of Wessex (father of the future King Harold). This proved an unhappy marriage. Edith brought a valuable dowry to the king, and she received life interest in royal estates previously granted to Queen Emma, which included a large area of Rutland. This alliance between the king and his chief rival brought only temporary peace. Six years after the marriage, in 1051, King Edward sent Earl Godwin into exile and confined Edith to a nunnery at Wherwell, Hampshire. Edith's own account of her marriage, *Vita Edwardi Regis*, explains her lack of children as due to a religious vow of celibacy made by her husband. There were probably additional reasons!

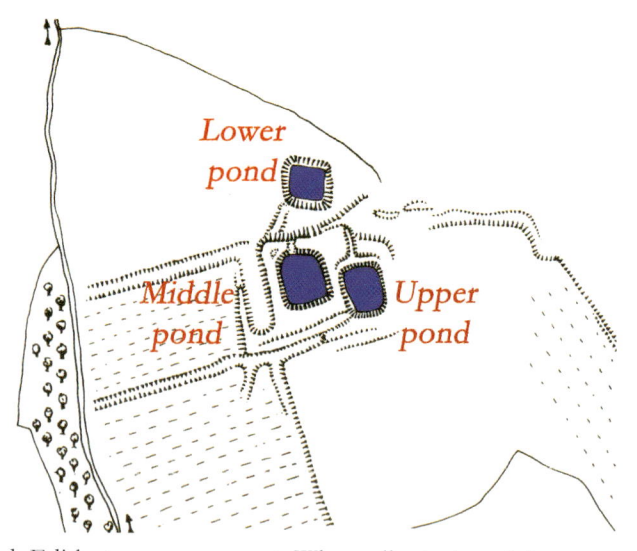

Among his religious benefactions, King Edward founded the new Abbey at Westminster, where he and Queen Edith were later buried. The Abbey required financial endowments, and Edward promised that after Queen Edith's death her estates in Rutland would pass to Westminster Abbey. In the event, Edith outlived her pious husband and was able to retain her Rutland landholdings until her death in 1075, when they passed to the new king, William I.

King Edward had hoped that his heir would be Duke William of Normandy, rather than Harold, son of his rival, Godwin, However, opposition to this choice forced Edward to recall Harold from exile and name him as heir to the throne. The resulting dispute led to the Battle of Hastings in 1066 and the establishment of the Norman royal dynasty.

William the Conqueror's son, William II ('Rufus'), was mysteriously killed in the New Forest in 1100, and quickly succeeded by his younger brother as King Henry I. Henry granted the manor of Edith Weston to his chamberlain, William de Tankerville, who in 1114 bestowed it on the Benedictine Abbey of St George de Boscherville, which he and his father had founded in Normandy (*VCH* II, 62). The monks of this abbey founded a small 'alien' priory

A plan of the fishponds and enclosure boundaries of Edith Weston Priory (after Hartley)

The upper of the three fishponds at Edith Weston in 2006. This and the middle pond survive but the lower fishpond is now below the high water level of Rutland Water (SS)

— 94 —

cell in Edith Weston, possibly housing only two or three monks. Their chief business was praying for the souls of the founder and collecting rents from their local tenants. During Lent and on Fridays they would consume fish from the nearby fishponds.

The church of St Mary in Edith Weston suffered major restoration in the nineteenth century, but some stonework supporting the chancel arch and north arcade survives from around 1170-95. A south aisle and arcade were built shortly afterwards, with the chancel and chancel arch being rebuilt later in the thirteenth century. In the fourteenth century the church was again extended, and the tower and spire built of Ketton stone between 1380 and 1400 (*VCH* II, 65).

The tower and spire of St Mary's Church, Edith Weston (SH)

Throughout the Middle Ages and beyond, monarchs received income partly in the form of regular lay subsidies, taxes imposed on their non-clerical subjects. The 1296 Lay Subsidy assessments for the Rutland parishes have been transcribed by Dr D A Postles, of Leicester University. The list for Edith Weston names forty heads of household, charged sums ranging from one shilling to 7s 5^3/$_4$d. One of these, William Fraunchhomme, appears to be a Frenchman, probably associated with the priory. Two men, Henry and Ralph, have the bynames '*ad crucem*'. This may indicate that they lived near the cross, Edith Weston's medieval market cross, of which only the base and a short section of shaft survive today.

The remains of Edith Weston's medieval market cross (SH)

Most of the medieval inhabitants of Edith Weston were peasants, labouring on the manorial land owned by the priory. This was divided into three open fields, known as West, South and East (or Mill) Fields, which, centuries later, were enclosed into smaller fields by an Act of Parliament of 1758 (Ryder 2006 Appendix II, 2). The eighteenth century hedgerows, planted by new landowners, were superimposed on an earlier pattern of strips and furlongs which remained visible for more than five centuries. These ancient field systems, to the north of Edith Weston, were finally obliterated by the creation of Rutland Water.

During periods of war with France, the English king occasionally took Edith Weston and its priory into his own hands. In the late thirteenth century it was seized by the officers of King Henry III because the prior was abroad, presumably in France (*VCH* II, 62). By 1357 there was only one monk in charge of Edith Weston Priory, who clearly abused his vocation:

Left: This aerial view, taken before the Gwash valley was flooded for Rutland Water, shows part of Edith Weston village and fields to the north and west with medieval ridge and furrow. The River Gwash meanders across the top of the picture and the three medieval fishponds (ringed) can be seen to the right of centre (Anglian Water)

'It was complained that he had laid aside the habit of religion and the tonsure, had neglected to say mass and the divine office, and had consumed the substance of the house in luxurious living. He had kept women in the priory, and maintained his illegitimate children from its revenues; he had cut down the trees and destroyed cottages, and driven out villeins from their homes with blows and other ill-usage' (*VCH* I, 163-4).

By 1394 ownership of the Edith Weston priory had passed from the Abbey of St George de Boscherville to the prior and Carthusian convent of St Mary and St Anne in Coventry. In 1404 a financial arrangement was made with William Dalby of Oakham for the priory of Edith Weston to pay rent of £20 per year to the warden of the newly-founded hospital of St John the Evangelist and St Anne, in Oakham (*VCH* II, 62).

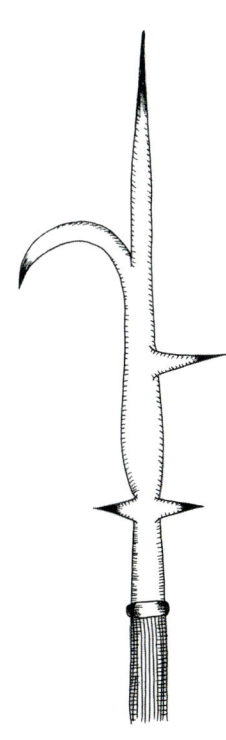

In addition to regular assessments for taxation, in 1522 King Henry VIII ordered a military survey of each county, produced in the form of muster books. These listed males over sixteen with their wealth in land and/or goods, and their potential military role in defence of the kingdom. The Rutland muster book, a rare survival, lists 30 men of 'Ediweston'. Heading the list, 'the Prior of the Charterhouse of Coventry is Chieff lord of the seid town', whose land was worth 40 marks. His goods were not valued since he is listed as '*q.e.*' [*quid extra*: non-resident]. The parson was Antony Bretton and the parish priest was John Richards. Virtually all the men listed were tenants 'to the seid prior', whether as labourers or husbandmen (small farmers). Two men were listed as able to fight if required as archers, and ten as billmen (soldiers armed with bills), although only one of these had his own weapon (Cornwall 1980, 66-7).

The Dissolution of the Monasteries, imposed by King Henry VIII, brought an end to the existence of the priory at Edith Weston. In 1550 his son, Edward VI, granted the manor to William Parr, Marquess of Northampton and brother of Queen Catherine Parr, on condition that he continued to pay the agreed yearly rent to the hospital of St John and St Anne in Oakham. Edith Weston then passed through various hands until it came into the possession of John Flore, or Flower. He was sued in the Court of Requests for failing to pay this annual rent, and was summoned before the Privy Council in 1582. The manor again changed hands, until in 1601 it was bought by Richard Halford. This family held Edith Weston until 1742, when it passed through a daughter into the Lucas family, lords of the manor until the end of the nineteenth century.

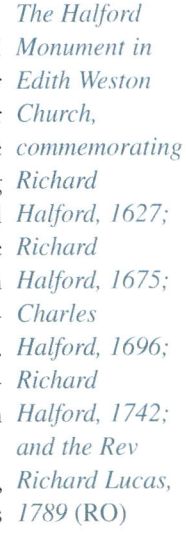

The bill was, in the fifteenth and sixteenth centuries, the main close combat weapon of the English infantry. Including its handle it was about 7 feet long (RO)

The Halford Monument in Edith Weston Church, commemorating Richard Halford, 1627; Richard Halford, 1675; Charles Halford, 1696; Richard Halford, 1742; and the Rev Richard Lucas, 1789 (RO)

The brass plaque on the Halford monument commemorating Richard Halford who died in 1627 (RO)

HIC SITVS EST RICARDVS HALFORD ARMIGER, PACIS FAVTOR: IDEOQ3 NON IMMERITO EI TRIBVERETVR NON SOLVM NOMEN, SED ETIAM LOCVS IVSTICIARIJ PACIS, SEPVLTVS VICESSIMO QVINTO DIE DECEMBRIS, ANNO DOMINI 1627.

Edith Weston Hall

The original Edith Weston Hall was probably built early in the seventeenth century by the first Richard Halford. A R Traylen, in *Villages of Rutland*, records the tradition that this building contained gothic doorways, which may have come from the abandoned priory. It was not unusual for purchasers of former monastic buildings to re-use the building materials in their new country houses. The first hall was built on the north side of the church, but after the new Edith Weston Hall was built in 1830, its remains were demolished to allow enlargement of the churchyard.

Richard Halford came to Edith Weston from Welham, Leicestershire, where his elder brother, William, continued to live. By his wife, Dorothy, Richard Halford had five daughters and five sons. When he died in 1627, Edith Weston Hall passed to his son, also Richard (1594-1675). The younger Richard Halford served as Justice of the Peace, and twice as Sheriff of Rutland, in 1619 and 1631 (Wright 1684, *Additions* XI, G). By his first wife, Anne, he had two sons, Charles and John.

The younger Richard Halford seems to have avoided active involvement in the Civil War. On 10th March 1660, shortly before the Restoration of King Charles II, his son Charles's name was added to the list of Commissioners for the Militia for the County of Rutland (*JHC 7, 1651-60*, (1802), 868-71). When the new king entered his kingdom in triumph, both Richard and Charles Halford added their names to the long list of loyal royalists, signing an address of 'Humble Congratulations' to the king, with their thankful acknowledgement of God's goodness 'in so great a Blessing accomplished without effusion of blood' (*VCH* I, 200-1).

The Halfords continued to prosper under the restored monarchy. When the villages of Rutland were assessed for hearth tax in 1665, the list for Edith Weston was headed by Richard Halford Esq with a house of eleven hearths. This was six more than the next largest house, that of the Rector, Mr Halford, probably his brother (Bourne & Goode 1991, 43). In the same year Richard's son, Charles, followed in his father's footsteps by serving as Sheriff of Rutland.

Charles Halford was an acute speculator, investing £5,000 in the scheme to make the River Welland navigable at Stamford. However, he may have regretted this as in 1696 he was petitioning Parliament against a new government tax on coal and other commodities carried by water. This had caused coal merchants, delivering 'sea-coal' from Newcastle to Stamford, to rely more on cheaper road transport, thus depriving Halford of valuable tonnage duty, the expected proceeds of his investment (13th January 1696, *JHC 11, 1693-7* (1803), 388-9). Charles Halford died in the same year, without seeing any resolution of his grievance.

Edith Weston Hall from the south-east in 1908 (Hart)

The new lord of the manor was Richard, son of Charles Halford. He is listed as one of Edith Weston's 22 voters in the poll book of 1710, and in 1712 was assessed for land tax of £23 5s 10d. This amount was nearly one-third of the total sum paid by the landowners of 'Edyweston' – the next highest assessment was the £7 7s 4¼d paid by Thomas Islip junior.

When Richard Halford died without a male heir in 1742, the manor of Edith Weston passed to Mary Halford and her husband, the Rev Richard Lucas. Confusingly, each succeeding heir to the estate was named Richard Lucas, three of whom were also Rectors of the parish. The Hall by this time was becoming dilapidated.

Edith Weston Hall from the north-west in 1912 (Hart)

In 1830 a new Edith Weston Hall was built for the Rev Richard Lucas (Rector of Edith Weston, 1827-46). It was designed in Tudor style by the fashionable architect, Lewis Vulliamy (1791-1871), whose commissions ranged from churches to country houses and workhouses. His work included Dorchester House (later replaced by the Dorchester Hotel) and Westonbirt, Gloucestershire, both built for the millionaire industrialist Robert Stayner Holford. At Chingford, in Essex, Vulliamy designed Friday Hill House in 1839 and the church of St Peter and St Paul in 1844 for the Rev Robert Boothby Heathcote, grandson of Sir John Heathcote, 2nd Baronet, of Normanton (www.leevalley-online.co.uk/towns/chingford; www.thepeerage.com). Since Mr Lucas would have been in frequent contact with the Heathcote family at neighbouring Normanton, he may well have recommended the architect to his fellow clergyman.

According to the 1841 Census, the Rev Richard Lucas was living in his new home of Edith Weston Hall with his wife, Mary. Five years later the Hall was inherited by another Richard Lucas. This namesake, however, was not a clergyman, being described as 'landowner', born in Tolethorpe thirty years previously. His wife was another Mary, and their fellow-resident at the Hall in 1851 was Richard's brother, Henry, a young officer born in Edith Weston. A tantalizing glimpse of the marriage of Richard and Mary Lucas is provided in a letter of 16th January 1849, from T K Arnold, Rector of Lyndon, to William Henry Fox Talbot, the Wiltshire polymath and early experimenter in photography.

The Lyndon clergyman writes from Hastings of his 'exile from Rutland' because of repeated bouts of asthma. As well as advising on suitable Latin lessons for his correspondent's small son, Mr Arnold reports on the well-being of a neighbouring Rutland cleric, Archdeacon T K Bonney, Rector of Normanton, and his unmarried sister, Henrietta:

Edith Weston from the OS 2nd ed 25" map 1904

'The Bonneys have both been ailing a little this year; they are seldom free from rheumatism. Mr Luces's [*sic*] disreputable marriage, which necessarily puts an end to all pleasant intercourse with their [Edith] Weston neighbours, is a great arrogance to them.' (Fox Talbot Museum/Lacock Abbey Collection 06204).

One wonders what was regarded as 'disreputable' about Richard Lucas's marriage, and why it made his presence unwelcome in the drawing rooms of disapproving neighbours! However, time may have mellowed these uneasy relationships, since when Archdeacon Bonney died in 1863, Richard Lucas attended the burial in Normanton churchyard.

The family name of Lucas died out in 1888, when Richard Lucas was succeeded by his brother George. The new heir had adopted the surname of Braithwaite, in order to claim an inheritance from Miss Braithwaite of Stock Park, Ulverston. George's son, Major Ernest Lucas Braithwaite, sold the Edith Weston estate, and some of the farms were purchased by the Earl of Ancaster to add to his Normanton Estate. Edith Weston Hall and Park passed through various hands, having to be rebuilt following a serious fire in 1921. At some stage an ice-house was constructed to help preserve perishable food through the summer months.

Finally, in 1927, the restored Hall became the home of Lieutenant-Colonel Francis Henry Hardy, JP, and his wife, Lady Cicely Hardy, who continued to live there after his death (*VCH* II, 63). As Lady of the Manor, she often provided soup for the village school children to eke out their lunches of bread and cheese.

Edith Weston Hall was demolished in 1957. All that remains is one of its buildings, now converted to a house named 'Old Hall Coach House', a reminder for future generations of the former grandeur of Edith Weston Hall.

The Old Hall Coach House, seen here, the ice house and the ha-ha are all that remain of Edith Weston Hall (SH)

The Village Community

The introduction of the national census in 1801 made it possible to record local populations at ten-year intervals. From this it can be seen that Edith Weston, in common with many rural communities, experienced a gradual increase throughout the nineteenth century. From 267 in 1801, Edith Weston's population rose to a high point of 399 in 1871. This was followed by a steady decline to 228 in 1931, as agriculture became less labour-intensive and young people moved to the towns to find work.

The 1901 Census shows that Edith Weston's population of 267 included six grazier/farmers employing 25 agricultural labourers, seven farm carters and four shepherds. The Hall provided considerable employment, with a gamekeeper, groom, coachman and seventeen domestic servants. Other occupations in the village included two road labourers, three quarry workers, three blacksmiths, four carpenters, four dressmakers, six laundresses and three teachers. Daily needs were provided by two bakers, two butchers, one grocer and two innkeepers.

The shop of C W Weaver, grocer, in 1908 (Hart)

Tibbert the butcher occupied the three-storey building, formerly the Old Hall laundry (Hart)

Traditional Customs of Edith Weston

As with other isolated rural communities, Edith Weston's inhabitants continued to observe several traditional customs, some dating to the seventeenth century and earlier. Readers of Thomas Hardy's *The Return of the Native* (1878) will remember the Christmas performance of an ancient Mummers' Play, with its unlikely collection of characters: the Turkish Knight, Saint George, the Doctor, the Saracen and Father Christmas. Edith Weston, too, had its very similar Morris-Dancers' Play. The text was recorded by V B Crowther-Beynon, in 'Notes on some Edith Weston Village Institutions' (*Rutland Magazine* II, 14 & 176-80). The characters who entertained Rutland villagers were King George, the Doctor, Albert Hart, the King of Prussia, First Man and Beelzebub. It is strange to speculate on the identity of 'Albert Hart', and to note the transformation of Saint George into King George. A flavour of the drama is provided by the following speech of 'King George':

'I am King George, this Champion bold,
With my blood and spear I won three crowns of gold,
I fought the fiery dragon and brought him to the slaughter
And by that means I won the King of Egypt's eldest daughter.
I hacked him and smacked him as small as flies
And sent him to Jamaica to make mince-pies.
Mince pies hot and mince pies cold,
Mince pies in the pot, nine days old.'

The Victorian residents of Edith Weston also revived on occasions a ritual described by Thomas Hardy in *The Mayor of Casterbridge* (1886), as the 'Skimmity' or 'Skimmington Ride'. Also widely known as 'Rough Music', this involved a procession through the village, led by a man wearing horns, denoting the cuckolded husband, to the door of anyone accused of adultery. Loud tin pans and trays were clashed, trumpets and whistles blown outside the offenders' windows, while their effigies might be subjected to burning or drowning. In Edith Weston the denouncement of sexual miscreants was known as 'Horn Fair' or 'Tin Panning'. For full details of this local tradition, *see* Chapter 30 – Extra, Extra, Read all about it!

A far-more widespread and edifying custom was the celebration of May Day, which Edith Weston regularly observed along with the majority of Rutland villages. Schoolchildren paraded round the village singing May songs at every house, finishing with a tea party which included bread and jam, plum cake and seedy cake.

Edith Weston School

In the second half of the nineteenth century, the Lucas family, as Lords of the Manor, had founded the first village school in 1852, the boys and girls being taught by separate teachers in two cottages. Twelve years later a purpose-built school was erected, and it was enlarged in 1893. In 1904 the Head Master was Mr Brown. In 1925 Miss Dolce Ellingworth moved from Empingham School to Edith Weston, which had now declined to about 40 pupils (from 55 in 1902). She taught the 'three Rs' in the morning, with history, geography, drawing, poetry and singing in the afternoon. The boys were allowed to play football or cricket, while the girls learned sewing, darning and knitting. By 1935 the number of pupils had shrunk to eleven and the school, then the smallest in Rutland, closed down.

Edith Weston school children in 1910 (Hart)

Edith Weston Band in 1916 (Hart)

RAF North Luffenham

The decline in population which brought Edith Weston down to 228 in 1931, leading to the closure of the village school, rapidly underwent a sudden dramatic reversal. In 1951 the population of the village was 920, and in the next ten years it shot up to 2,064. This was not due to a miraculous increase in the birthrate but to the creation of RAF North Luffenham. Although the airfield was closer to the village centre of Edith Weston, it took its name from the nearest railway station.

Built initially as a training airfield, RAF North Luffenham opened in December 1940, with new pilots flying mainly Tiger Moth aircraft from grass runways. When the training school moved to Peterborough in 1941, 61 and 144 Squadrons were brought into Luffenham from Hemswell (Lincolnshire), which had been selected as a base for Polish bomber squadrons. Both squadrons flew Hampdens and were fully operational, much of their work being mine-laying.

No 61 Squadron, now flying Manchesters, soon transferred to a new airfield with hard runways at Woolfox Lodge. Meanwhile No 144 Squadron continued to operate from North Luffenham, successfully attacking a ship carrying the German Anti-aircraft Defence Commander for North Germany, and taking part in raids on the Renault motor works near Paris. In April 1942, No 144 Squadron transferred from Bomber to Coastal Command and torpedo work, moving north to Scotland. RAF North Luffenham then became home to No 29 Operational Training Unit, formed to provide the final stage of training for bomber crews, mainly on Wellingtons, which remained until June 1943.

It was clear that new hard runways and expanded facilities were essential for the war effort. This work was carried out by George Wimpey & Co Ltd.

A Hampden bomber of 408 Squadron climbing out from North Luffenham (Airfield Focus)

New accommodation was also built to house a total of 2,118 males and 311 females. The station re-opened in March 1944, to be used for the first six months by No 21 Heavy Glider Conversion Unit. North Luffenham then went back to bomber crew training, flying Lancasters, until the end of the war. Other aircraft based at the airfield included Albemarles, Balliols, Spitfires, Hurricanes, Whitleys and Horsa gliders.

Between 1939-45, Bomber Command lost a total of 60 bombers, missing or crashed in the UK, on operational flights from North Luffenham. Fifty-six of these were Hampdens, three Manchesters and one a Wellington (www.raf.mod.uk/bombercommand).

The end of the Second World War and the years of Cold War brought a change of personnel to North Luffenham and Edith Weston. In 1951 the Royal Canadian Air Force (RCAF), under a NATO directive, established three Sabre-equipped fighter squadrons at North Luffenham. These remained for three years, until the RAF resumed control of the station in 1954 for operational training.

A Whitley bomber of 21 Heavy Glider Conversion Unit. This aircraft was used to tow Airspeed Horsa gliders at North Luffenham, some of which can be seen in the background (Airfield Focus)

A Lancaster from North Luffenham flying over Rutland (John Nowell, Zodiac Publishing)

— 105 —

A Stirling heavy bomber and its crew (John Nowell, Zodiac Publishing)

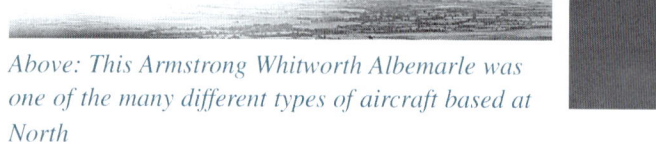

Above: This Armstrong Whitworth Albemarle was one of the many different types of aircraft based at North Luffenham during WWII. It was often used as a glider tug (Airfield Focus)

Above: An Airspeed Horsa glider returning from a training flight from North Luffenham, clearly showing the underside yellow and black striping (Airfield Focus)

One of the Hawker Hurricanes of the Battle of Britain Memorial Flight visiting North Luffenham (AF)

From the *Leicester Evening Mail*, 16th June 1952:

MORE CANADIAN JETS REACH NORTH LUFFENHAM

The high-pitched scream of five Sabre jet aircraft, circling North Luffenham airfield at 6.37 on Sunday evening [15th June 1952], was sweet music to a crowd of waiting watchers on the ground. They were the first flight of the remaining 16 aircraft of 439 Fighter Squadron, Royal Canadian Air Force, on the last lap of their 3,560-mile flight from Ottawa to Rutland.

This was a historic flight, for they were the first Canadian jets to fly the Atlantic. They were coming to join two other Sabre jet squadrons at North Luffenham that had been ferried across the Atlantic by *HMCS Magnificent*.

It was an exciting moment for those on the airstrip, who had long been scanning the horizon. Among the anxious spectators were RCAF officers, waiting to complete the official records of the long pioneer flight, a strong contingent of British and Canadian newspapermen, with a battery of Press photographers, and, most anxious of all, the wives, families and friends of the pilots.

It had been a successful but far from uneventful flight. The squadron took off from Uplands, near Ottawa, on May 30. With ideal weather all the way, they could have arrived at North Luffenham on June 2. But the weather was far from ideal. Another snag developed at Quebec, the first leg of the trip.

Weather delays:
Sqdn Ldr Cal Bricker, in command, was taken ill, and doctors diagnosed a grumbling appendix. Although an operation was not necessary, he could not undertake the jet flight, and was transferred to the North Star transport plane. Flt Lt Bill Bliss took over command.

Weather held up the flight for three days at Quebec and then they were off on the 580-mile hop to Goose Bay, Labrador, where, again, weather grounded them for eight days.

Then came 780 miles to Greenland (one day delay), a further 750 miles to Iceland and then the final 775-mile over-water trip to Kinloss, Scotland, where they arrived on Saturday.

They're off:
Weather again held them up, but the waiting crowd at Luffenham were cheered to hear on Sunday that the squadron hoped to arrive at about 3.30 pm. Another delay was announced, but at last, at about 6 pm Flt Lt. Marshall, Canadian PRO, announces 'They're off'.

There was a mad dash to the airstrip, for once airborne, the Sabres were expected to cover the last 379 miles in about 40 minutes. Horizons were scanned, and eager groups chatted impatiently. A loud roar made a group of newspapermen look round expectantly. It was not a Sabre, however, but a 350cc motorcycle that had just sprung into life under a Canadian 'Erk' learner-driver.

Aerobatics:
At about 6.30, four Sabres from the squadrons already at Luffenham, took off to act as a reception committee, and, a few minutes later roared overhead, leading in Flt Lt Bliss and four others. The remaining 16 came in, in groups of four, at five minute intervals while another flight from Luffenham gave the spectators a short, thrilling acrobatic display.

There were many happy family reunions as the pilots climbed weary, but cheerful, from the cockpits.

Mighty sore:
Although disappointed at missing the flight, Sqdn Ldr Bricker was also quite cheerful when he arrived in the North Star, with reserve pilots. He told *The Evening Mail* that he had already flown the Atlantic by jet when he was attached to the USAF. 'I'm mighty sore at this appendix of mine,' he commented.

The three squadrons, forming No 1 RCAF Fighter Wing, are the first of 11 being provided by Canada under the North Atlantic Treaty.

Left: Four RCAF Sabres in formation over North Luffenham (Airfield Focus)

Below: RCAF 439 Squadron Sabres at North Luffenham in June 1952 (Airfield Focus)

Above: F-86 Sabres of No 1 RCAF Fighter Wing arrive at North Luffenham on 15th June 1952 (Airfield Focus)

Far Left: RCAF pilots – Flying Officers Ruker and Wilson – in survival suits at North Luffenham (Airfield Focus)

A Canadian Airman Remembers

One Canadian who still remembers his time in Rutland is Jim O'Connor, now of Stratford, Ontario, Canada, who served in the Royal Canadian Air Force from 1946-66.

The RCAF Advance Party, sent to assist with the transfer of RAF North Luffenham to Canadian control, were accompanied by wives and families. However, it soon became clear that there was a serious shortage of housing in the area, so from then on any airman who wanted his family to join him in England had to pay for their travel and arrange suitable accommodation. Jim O'Connor, part of No 1 Fighter Wing, was desperate to see his new wife, Virginia, but short of the necessary funds. He recalls:

'Within a very few days of my arrival, I got into a card game much like "Blackjack" and before more than an hour was up I had won about two hundred pounds all in cash! I had never been so lucky in my life before (or since). That money was sufficient to rent a caravan for a month, stock it with groceries as well as pay Virginia's way to England. Virginia arrived by sea aboard the *Empress of Canada*, disembarking at Liverpool on 18th January 1952.

Above Left: Sabre pilot Flt Lt Dean Kelly (Airfield Focus)

Above Right: Jim O'Connor, formerly with No 1 Fighter Wing, RCAF, in June 2005 (Jim O'Connor)

'We moved out of our "large" caravan on January 1st 1953 and into the little row cottage at Edith Weston. It had one room up and one room down. There was no fireplace; the place was heated by a small, and very old, cook stove (coal fired). The floor of the lower room was made of brick which the landlady insisted be waxed and polished regularly with some rather hideous red wax. The result was that our baby's nappies became pink coloured from her scooting around the red floor on her bottom!

'The place was extremely damp and cold that January and coal was still on the ration list. We were able to supplement our rationed coal supply by obtaining additional coal from the Air Base. So after a while we were able to keep the place reasonably warm and comfortable. However the coal was of a very low grade, with stones embedded in it. Every so often one of those stones would explode from the heat of the fire. It scared the hell out of us the first couple of times that it happened. It also caused our landlady and her husband, who lived in the adjoining cottage, great curiosity as to what was going on in the O'Connor cottage. Who could blame them?

'Many of the buildings in Edith Weston had thatched roofs and were constructed primarily of Collyweston slate [*sic*]. As Canadians in England for the first time, we had never previously seen buildings that were constructed of such materials. It was all very much like a trip through a history book for us and we considered ourselves very privileged to be made welcome by the local people. It was a wonderful experience for us which we hold in our hearts and our minds to this very day.'

Although much has changed, the thatched cottages and public house, the Wheatsheaf, still survive. Perhaps fortunately, Edith Weston's village inn no longer lives up to the name of 'Smokey Joe's' bestowed on it by Canadian servicemen in the 1950s.

'It was just a wee pub with hardly enough room to swing a cat, but somehow there was always room for another Canadian Airman. The publican's first name was Alf, but I cannot recall what his surname was for the life of me. The place was called "Smokey's" because it being so small it didn't take many patrons smoking at the same time to sort of dim the vision in the place! I always liked the "Nut Brown Ale" in bottles best. Next to that it was those little tiny bottles of Bass's Ale. Great beer, great memories!' (Jim O'Connor)

The Wheatsheaf, Edith Weston. In the 1950s it was known as 'Smokey's' or 'Smokey Joe's' by the Canadian servicemen based at the nearby airfield (RO)

A bird's eye view of North Luffenham airfield in the 1950s (Airfield Focus)

Below: Meteors and their crews waiting for a scramble during Operation 'Mainbrace' in 1957 at North Luffenham (Airfield Focus)

The Royal Canadian Air Force left North Luffenham in 1955 and the station returned to the RAF, who continued to train air crews on Vampires and Meteors, one of which remained at the base entrance as a reminder of this era.

Above Left: A formation of Meteors over Rutland (Airfield Focus)

Above Right: This Meteor was one of the gate guardians at RAF North Luffenham (Peter Drake)

Left: The other gate guardian at RAF North Luffenham was this Bloodhound missile (Peter Drake)

The 1960s

In June 1958 RAF North Luffenham was selected for another mission, which brought it into the front line of international tensions in the years leading up to the Cuban Missile Crisis. Following negotiations between the governments of Macmillan and Eisenhower, Rutland became home to American 'Thor' strategic missiles, which carried nuclear warheads.

'The 1958 agreement led to the stationing of 60 Thor missiles in the United Kingdom. To be deployed under dual control and operated by the RAF, the missiles carried a 1.44 megaton warhead, and had a range of 1,500 miles. Thor was deployed at four main bases: Driffield, Hemswell, Feltwell and North Luffenham. Surrounding each main base were four satellite stations, with Bloodhound missiles deployed at each location in groups of three. All squadrons were fully manned by RAF personnel, with the warheads under the control of American custodial officers' (Twigge and Scott, www.history.ac.uk/ejournal/art3).

Above Left:
A Thor missile arrives at North Luffenham in 1960 (David Carlin)

Above Right:
A Thor missile being prepared for a practice launch at North Luffenham (Airfield Focus)

The Thor missiles arrived in 1960, along with a large colony of Americans from Douglas Aircraft and the US military. These were housed in 'Silver City', a complex of 60 caravans, 33ft long, each with a smaller adjoining side caravan, fitted out with all modern conveniences. This period is recalled by Alan Peel Shaw, a member of the RAF Police serving at North Luffenham from 1959-63. While most RAF personnel lived in married quarters in Edith Weston, he with his wife and two young boys 'first of all lived a hellish three or four months in a 22ft caravan at the missile site at Melton Mowbray, with no connected facilities and an Elsan toilet'. Fortunately they were then able to move into a 33ft caravan at Silver City, before obtaining married quarters in Edith Weston.

'The two boys attended school at Edith Weston, which was very close at hand, but I don't think my youngest son thought much of the idea, for on the first day of attendance, having had his lunch, he promptly came home, and when questioned by my wife, said it was going home time so he left . . . Entertainment wise, we were very lucky, we had a cinema on camp, there was a ten-pin bowling hall, we had all the usual functions in the various messes, such as tombola, whist, weekly dances etc, which were well attended by several hundreds at a time. I was very much involved with the RAF Motor Sport

Bloodhound missiles at Woolfox Lodge which were part of the defence ring of four satellite stations round North Luffenham (Airfield Focus)

Members of RAF Motor Sports Association Kart Club at RAF North Luffenham in 1962. Alan Peel Shaw centre row far left (Alan Peel Shaw)

Association, having formed a Kart Club, which eventually held racing events on a quarter-mile racing circuit which we built ourselves on the perimeter track, and involved National teams, including Bruno Ferrari, a National champion, and many other well-known kart racing drivers of that time. We considered ourselves extremely privileged, to be racing against such esteemed drivers and we were justifiably proud of our circuit' (Alan Peel Shaw).

The Thor missiles finally departed in 1964 and RAF North Luffenham became home to a succession of ground signals organisations. Edith Weston became home to many service families, including a young John Matthews, now of Gosport, who remembers:

'Life was spartan by today's standards, but we were very happy, enjoying the freedom to roam for miles around in complete safety. Fishing for minnows in the river Gwash and playing in the fields which are now flooded by the reservoir. We loved to play in the stubble in the wheat fields during harvest time. I remember the smell of the paraffin heater in Edith Weston post office, and the jolly laughter of the drinkers in the Wheatsheaf pub when sent by my mother on an errand for "20 Senior Service tipped, and a bottle of Mackeson please". Saturday morning was a real treat as we often attended the camp cinema for the matinee, tickets priced 1s 3d. We listened to the music of "The Shadows" while waiting for the red curtains to open for the performance. I attended the primary school on the camp for service children and children from the surrounding villages. I recall our English teacher, Mr Evans, and our weekly spelling test on Friday morning . . .

'I recall a very strange experience that I shared with my father. We were both out doors when we heard an unusual sounding aircraft above us. Dad looked up to the sky and said "It's a bomber". However, no aircraft was in sight. North Luffenham airfield was non-operational in those days. I have learned since that Lancaster aircraft operated out of North Luffenham during the war. I wonder if anybody has had a similar experience?'

The school attended by John Matthews and other children, both from the air base and from the village of Edith Weston, was headed from 1955 by John Starkey, who also became Church Warden and later President of Rutland Water Fly Fishers. His son, Ian, now of Norfolk, describes the school and their housing as being in 1940s pre-fab buildings, also used by the RAF as overflow accommodation. The site is now the Normanton Car Park for Rutland Water. Ian's vivid memories also include the joys of fishing in the Gwash:

'The river held several species of fish, namely Sticklebacks, Bullheads, Minnows, Gudgeon, Dace, Roach, Chub, Perch, Pike and Eels, which provided good sport for local anglers. After Normanton Fishpond was stocked in *circa* 1960, a few Trout could also be caught in the Edith Weston/Normanton stretch of the Gwash. The river supported a good selection of aquatic insects, birds and small mammals.'

The River Gwash from Normanton Bridge in 1972, looking east (Jim Eaton)

He also recalls the original post office, with 'room enough for one customer at a time . . . newspapers delivered on foot by Mrs Townsend . . . and meat by Ernie Tibbert. The circus came annually to the playing fields'. Ian Starkey is one of many former residents who regret the changes which have beset Edith Weston, now surrounded by the leisure attractions of the new reservoir: 'Let them enjoy Rutland Water, but they will never find the inner sense of well being and satisfaction that I did'.

In November 1963 the first of a succession of ground based units arrived and from this date on RAF North Luffenham was to be a non-operational airfield. The initial squadron was Radio Technical Publications. In 1964 the Station came under Signals Command, later transferring to the Maintenance Group in Logistics Command. Other units which moved to the Station included the Ground Radio Servicing Unit, which included the Civilian Aerial Erector Unit, the Training Unit Language School, the Aviation Medicine Training Centre, Midland Radar, the Rapier Missile Trials Unit, the Training Development Support Staff, the Armament Support Unit, a unit of the Bomb Disposal Squadron, and South Midlands Wing of the Air Training Corps. The Aerial Erector Unit mentioned above was involved in building a new bell frame and re-hanging the bells at North Luffenham Church.

By 1997, all these units had moved from the Station and a formal closing down ceremony was held on 23rd October 1997, when many ex-RAF personnel attended. The RAF ensign was lowered for the last time at 12.00 hours as three Tornadoes and a Nimrod flew over. RAF North Luffenham finally closed on 31st December. On 31st March 1998 the site was transferred to the British Army. It is now St George's Barracks and is currently occupied by the new Duke of Lancaster's Regiment.

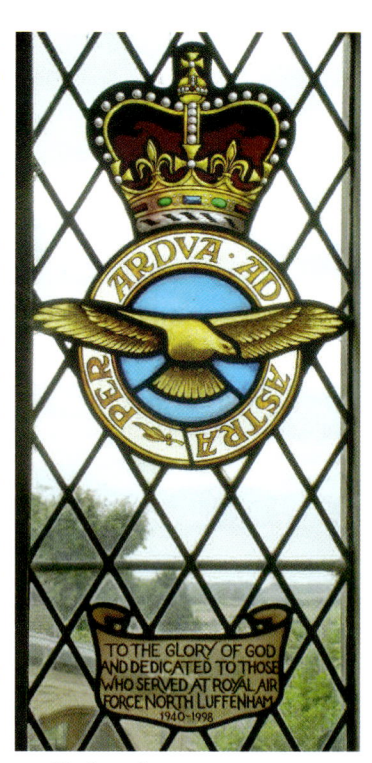

Above and right: RAF memorial windows at Edith Weston Church. There is another memorial window in North Luffenham Church (RO)

End of an era: The RAF standard is lowered as RAF North Luffenham is officially handed over to the Army.
Photo: E4907/30

Hand-over marks end of an RAF era

RAF North Luffenham was officially handed over to the Army in an emotional ceremony on Tuesday.

The base, which has been an operational RAF station for more than 50 years ,was formally closed in October last year.

It is now in the hands of the 1st Battalion the Royal Regiment of Fusiliers.

Personnel from the RAF and the Army watched as the ceremony started with the lowering of the RAF ensign and unit commander's pennant.

Wg Cdr Stewart Bolam, the RAF unit commander, handed over the keys to the main gate to Army camp commandant Maj Bob Broadbent.

The Army camp will now be formally known as St George's Barracks and will be home to 600 soldiers next year.

Maj Broadbent said: "It was an emotional day as some of the RAF personnel have been serving for a number of years. Everything went smoothly and the Army is now looking forward to life there."

Rutland Times reports the handover of RAF North Luffenham to the Army on 31st March 1998

— 114 —

The Impact of Rutland Water

The pace of life around the former Gwash Valley has changed out of all recognition, although many of these changes would have occurred without the building of the reservoir. Edith Weston has also been transformed by the construction and presence of the North Luffenham air base – now St George's Barracks. The post-war school, in its prefabricated buildings, has now been replaced by a bright, modern, purpose-built school, complete with its own heated swimming pool, on the shores of Rutland Water. It serves around 120 pupils, of whom two-thirds come from service families.

During 2005, many of the present-day pupils of the two local primary schools, St Mary & St John C of E School, North Luffenham, and Edith Weston Primary School, assisted with the project to produce this book. They carried out research into the local history of their area and the impact of Rutland Water. One group of children from Edith Weston, aged seven and eight, reported:

'It was easier and quicker to get to Whitwell and Oakham from Edith Weston before the reservoir was built. Some of the roads that linked these places went straight across the valley through Hambleton, and had to be flooded when the reservoir was filled . . . People in Edith Weston have had to get used to spending more time and petrol getting to Hambleton, Oakham and Whitwell.'

The children were told that, when the reservoir was planned, 'lots of people were worried about traffic jams because of extra visitors that would come to see the new reservoir'.

When the parishes around the Gwash Valley were confronted by firm proposals to build what was then to be the 'Empingham Reservoir', there were many doubts and reservations. As well as the obvious loss of land, residents had serious concerns about noise, disruption and increased traffic involving both heavy machinery and, later, visitors' cars. Manton Parish Council expressed concerns about loss of rights of way and the ignoring of 'No through road' signs in the village. Empingham was more adversely affected, and concerned by the noise, traffic and accommodation implications of the reservoir's construction. An unexpected concern of all the surrounding parishes was a plague of non-biting midges that bred around the reservoir in 1977-78. The hopes of the then Rutland District Council that

Pascal Risi, of St Mary & St John Church of England School, North Luffenham, who researched the construction of the dam (Pasqualino Risi)

this situation would resolve itself seem to have been fulfilled, as the issue then disappears from Parish Council minutes.

In addition to these concerns, Edith Weston Parish Council addressed the issue of leisure facilities. On 14th September 1978 they issued a statement recommending that 'any additional facilities should be confined to the present car parks and picnic areas, preferably away from Edith Weston. No additional attractions should be located in the Village to draw more visitors, as a Pursuit Centre, Sailing Club and Car Park-Picnic Area in the district was enough'. Although these wishes have been largely respected, the village and its surroundings have inevitably changed out of all recognition. Some of Edith Weston's more fortunate home-owners now find themselves with lakeside gardens and spectacular views, while residents and visitors alike can enjoy, for a price, the adjacent attractions of the Rutland Water Golf Course and the Rutland Sailing Club. On busy summer days, parked cars (and bicycles) are testimony to the many visitors who wish to explore the delights of this traditional Rutland village.

The spectacular views across the former Gwash Valley, now submerged under Rutland Water, have transformed this once sleepy rural backwater into a thriving centre of leisure and tourism. But despite the major changes brought by the reservoir, as well as by technical progress and new patterns of work and leisure, Edith Weston remains at heart a village community. The parish church, the primary school, the village shop and public house still serve the various needs of local people, while providing treasured memories for villagers and visitors alike, into the twenty first century.

Edith Weston on the south shore of Rutland Water in 2006. Rutland Sailing Club is just right of centre (John Nowell, Zodiac Publishing)

Chapter 6

Egleton: A Glimpse into the Past

Sheila Sleath and Robert Ovens
(with extracts from *Egleton, Rutland*
by Mary and David Parkin)

Historical Introduction

The name of Egleton is interpreted as Ecgwulf's *tun* or homestead, suggesting that it was originally an Anglo-Saxon settlement. It is not mentioned in the Domesday Book of 1086 but it may be one of the five berewicks which the survey attaches to Oakham. The first recorded use of the name, as 'Egiltun', is in the Forest Rolls of 1209. By then the church already existed, indicating an established settlement. The carved chancel arch, the south doorway, part of the south wall and the upper part of the font are all twelfth century. From its earliest days, the church, like those of Langham and Brooke, was a chapelry attached to Oakham, served by a curate appointed by the Vicar of Oakham who owned a third of the village tithes. Now it is a separate parish within the Oakham benefice. Baptisms, marriages and burials have been recorded in the church registers since 1538.

Egleton village sign stands on the green near the church (RO)

Egleton Church in 2006. It has undergone many structural changes in its long life (RO)

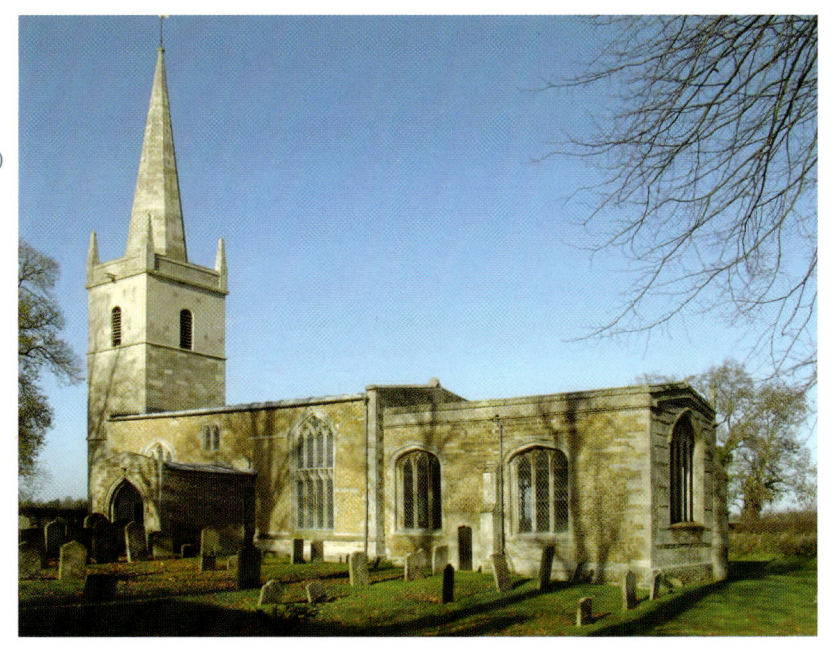

The twelfth-century south doorway at Egleton Church in 1910 (Hart)

The church has undergone many structural changes in its long life. A north aisle with a clerestory, the tower and the porch were added in the 1300s and the chancel was rebuilt in the fifteenth century. The north aisle has since been demolished and only the lower part of the original tower remains, the upper part, together with the spire and the porch, having been rebuilt in the nineteenth century.

In 1305, when most of Egleton belonged to Margaret, Countess of Cornwall, a survey of the taxes payable by the inhabitants indicates that there were then about 26 houses in the village. Egleton was also included in the military survey of 1522 when Henry VIII ordered his chancellor, Cardinal Wolsey, to devise a survey that would discover people's wealth. One purpose of the survey was to prepare subjects for war against France, but the main reason was to establish the level of forced loans which were to be demanded later. It names seventeen male heads of household in the village. Two years later the lay subsidy included nineteen heads of household.

Medieval guilds, like modern friendly societies, were associations of people who contributed money which was then used to help members in need. One such guild, dedicated to the Trinity, is recorded in Egleton in 1551. Its priest was Thomas Kelso and he lived in one of the four houses owned by the guild in the village. It also owned property in Oakham. All the guild's property had been confiscated by the Crown by 1553.

During the Civil War (1641-49), most of Egleton belonged to the Duke of Buckingham who was a supporter of the King. Consequently the Commonwealth considered him a traitor and confiscated his lands, but they were returned to him after the Restoration (1660). A survey at the time of the confiscation identifies fourteen farms in Egleton with acreages varying from 13 to 89. Some of the dwellings described were substantial, with a parlour, a hall, a kitchen, a buttery and lodging chambers as well as farm buildings. At the other end of the scale there were cottages with only two rooms. There were also two shops, one of them a butcher's.

The Hearth Tax Return of 1665 lists 31 heads of household in Egleton, which suggests that the population was probably about 140. Ten people were not taxable because they were considered too poor.

The Rent Rolls for the Duke of Buckingham's estate, compiled in 1686 and 1690 (ROLLR DG 7/1/13 & 56), list two cottages 'on the Lord's waste' occupied by William Corner and Austin Hubbard. These were probably the poorest households in the village as the annual rents for their cottages were only two shillings and one shilling respectively and they were excused from paying the Hearth Tax.

Wills made in the sixteenth and seventeenth centuries give a good idea of the villagers' possessions as household contents are often listed among the bequests. Faith Ward, who lived at what we know today as Home Farm, made her will in 1642 and left to her daughter:

'. . . the sealed bed [a four-poster bed with hangings] in the chamber and the furniture belonging to it, a fetherbed, two mattreces, fower pillows, one bolster, two blankits, one chest in the same chamber next a bed, ten pairs of sheetes, three pairs of pillow-boards [pillowcases], two board clothes [tablecloths], eighteen napkins, two boxes, three pannes, one brass pott, one posset [small cauldron], one dripping pan, one spit, one pair of cobirons [irons for supporting the spit in front of a fire], one salt box, one brazen candlestick, one pestell and mortar, the cupboard in the hall and the table and frame, three buffet stools, a joined chair at the cupboard end and one other chair, two linen wheels and one linen wheel, one rackiron, three hookes, one pair of tongs, one bolting tun [a container for sifting flour], an elting trough [for kneading dough], two tubs, three pales, one other little tubbe, a cheese presse and all the milk vessels, two little barrels and half the provisions that I have the house throughout, half the pullen [poultry] in the yard, one stock of bees, one bed more in the kitchen chamber, one churne, one henpen, one load of wood, one little board logge in the yard, one oatmeale skip, one strike [half a bushel] of oatmeale if it be to be had, one flax heckle [a comb for dressing flax], all the pewter and brass little and big that is about the house.'

The seventeenth-century dovecote in the farmyard of Home Farm, Egleton (RO)

In 1558 Robert Tymson left to Alice Tymson:

'. . . my best carte and ploughe and ploughe geares and six yearne [iron] harrowes, the hovel where the spares lie. She shall have all the other hovels of a reasonable pryse if she occupye the farme styll, half of all the plough tymber and board about the house abrode saving those over the millhouse.'

In 1598 Robert Longsett (or Longfoote), a mason, left to his daughter 'so much board as shall make her a framed table of joinery work with frames and stools needfull for the furnishings of tables', and Michael Dodgson, a weaver, buried in 1661, left a long list of textile bequests.

Some wills mention money owed to the testator. In 1627 Eliza Smith's will records that 'Old Black's wife ought me 10s. and I have forgiven her 2s. of it', and it was not unusual for people to leave two shillings to each of the four bearers at their funeral.

A terrier of 1566 lists holdings in the open fields and provides the names of many of the village farmers at that date. This and later documents show that a number of families were farming in Egleton for several generations and even longer.

Members of the Seaton family were living in Egleton almost continuously from the early sixteenth century, and possibly earlier, until the death of Ernest Seaton and his wife Sarah Elizabeth in 1950 and 1963. They lived and worked at what is now 11 Church Road.

Memorial inscriptions to the Tomsons, who lived at Brook Farm, can be seen in the church. Eleanor Tomson married Joseph Tirrell jun and continued to run the farm with Eleanor's mother, Catharine. Joseph's father, Joseph Tirrell sen, had come to the village in 1801, when he married Eleanor Meadows of Home Farm and farmed there with her. Father and son both lived into their nineties. The stained glass in the east window of the church is a memorial to Joseph sen and other members of the Tirrell family.

The east window in Egleton Church is a memorial to members of the Tirrell family (RO)

Members of the Towell family lived at what is now known as Barnett's Farm for more than a hundred years. They are recorded as living there in 1652. Nicholas set up a charity for the relief of the poor by his will dated 21st December 1774. Money for the same purpose was being provided by the Finch family of Burley in the 1770s and many village wills included bequests for the relief of the poor of Egleton. Nicholas Towell's charity has only recently been discontinued owing to lack of funds. Nicholas Towell's memorial is on the north wall of the nave of Egleton Church. He died on 23rd February 1776.

The Bradshaw family first appears in the census of 1881 when they were farming Longcroft Farm with 360 acres. At this time Robert and Elizabeth had nine children living with them, aged from six to twenty. The eldest son, Frederick, died in 1927, having taken over the farm. His widow continued to farm there, with her nephew, Rowland Hubbard, acting as farm manager. He took over the farm when she left the village and was followed by his son, Norman Hubbard. Another son, John Robert Bradshaw, farmed at Home Farm from the end of the nineteenth century for about 40 years. The youngest son, Robert Lee Bradshaw, farmed at Brook Farm until his death in 1934. Members of the Bradshaw family gave the oak gates and the pine vestry furniture to the village church.

The number of farms in the village had dwindled from fourteen smallholdings at the time of the Commonwealth survey to five at the end of the 1700s and to three by 1871. The acreages farmed increased to an average of over a hundred by 1790. Of the four farms listed in 1851, one had 350 acres, two 200 acres and one 100 acres.

The common fields of Egleton were enclosed by Act of Parliament in 1757. The implementation of the Act resulted in the stream which runs through the village being straightened and a windmill being demolished. The mill belonged to Thomas Carter of Egleton. The site of his mill became the property of George Finch (9th Earl of Winchilsea and 4th Earl of Nottingham) of Burley on the Hill, the lord of the manor. In return, he was given a site in Oakham field where there had formerly been a windmill and which the Commissioners claimed was a more suitable position. Until quite recently, there was a Mill Way in Egleton. After enclosure, there was still a common cow pasture where cottagers had the right to graze their cows. This

The map of Egleton in 1797. This image has been enhanced to improve clarity (ROLLR DG 7/4/27) right still existed after the Second World War but fell out of use as individual cottagers gave up their holdings.

Among the Finch family papers there is a notebook (ROLLRDE7/4/27) dated 1797, with later additions, prepared when John Crutchley was agent to the Burley estate. It includes a map of Egleton and descriptions of the residents, the first document to give such detail. Sadly, several of the villagers were in poor health or lame, two children suffered from fits and one resident was caring for a 'foolish sister'. Occupations mentioned include baker, cavalryman, exciseman, farmer, schoolmistress, servant, under-gamekeeper and weaver. One cottager spun stockings for Lady Charlotte Finch, one is described as 'cross, but a good woman', one woman is thought to have had 23 children and 'has taken to drink', one couple are 'not good people'. Others are praised as 'remarkably industrious'.

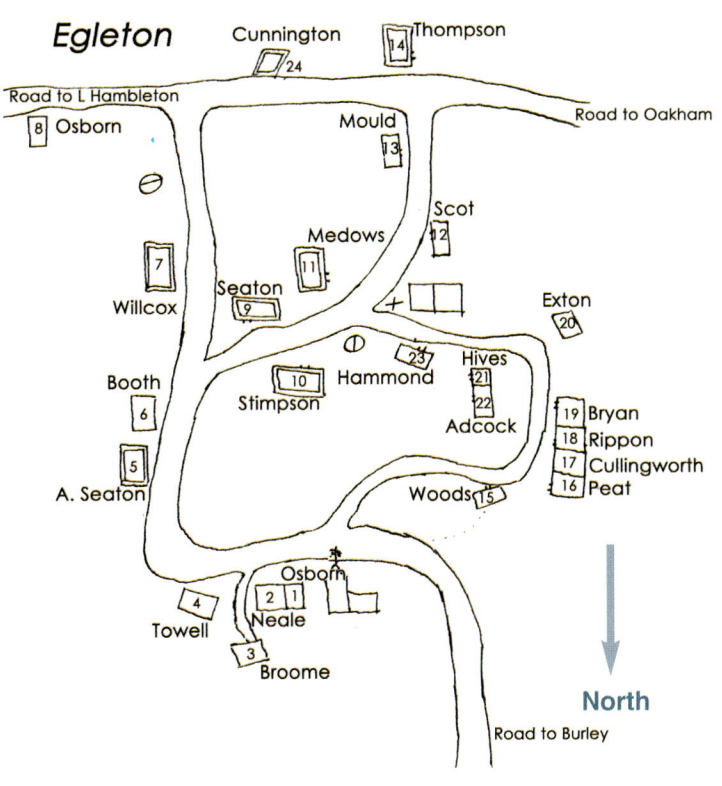

The nineteenth century is better documented. Detailed census returns are available at ten-yearly intervals from 1841. During this period there were 30 to 34 houses in occupation, and the population varied from 111 to 138. Many villagers were still employed in agriculture or in service. Trades include baker, blacksmith, brickmaker, builder, carpenter, dressmaker, milliner, nurse, schoolmistress, shoemaker, tailor, weaver and wheelwright.

Egleton Men who served in the Cavalry in 1797

In March 1794 the Government circulated its ideas for individual counties to raise auxiliary forces. These were to include mounted corps of 'Gentlemen and Yeomanry'. Through its Lord Lieutenant, the 9th Earl of Winchilsea, Rutland had already submitted a proposal to the Government to create its own 'Volunteer Troop of Cavalry'. Therefore it was not surprising that the first mounted Yeomanry corps to be raised under the new Act was from Rutland.

The Earl of Winchilsea initially offered the services of three troops of 50 men each. Originally nominated as one of the three captains, the Earl soon assumed command of this new corps with the rank of colonel. By 1797 each troop contained 73 men and by 1803 the county could muster four troops with a rank and file of 168.

The 1797 notebook names three men from Egleton who were in the cavalry. They were

Farmer Cunnington, who lived at what is now The Old Bakehouse in Hambleton Road (24 on the map), the son of Farmer Thompson (Tomson) who lived at what is now Brook Farm in Hambleton Road (14 on the map), and the son of Farmer Stimpson who lived at what is now Longcroft House in Main Street (10 on the map). It is assumed that these men were members of the Rutland Yeomanry rather than the Rutland Fencibles as they would no doubt be loyally bound to their landlord, the Earl of Winchilsea.

Another similar organisation was the Rutland Fencible Cavalry, raised in 1794 by Gerard Noel Edwards. It comprised part-time regulars for whom he had built a Riding School (now Rutland County Museum), complete with stables and quarters, opposite Catmose, his mansion in Oakham.

Wheelwrights and Carpenters at Forge Cottage, Hambleton Road

Forge Cottage almost certainly gets its name from the occupation of its tenant in 1881. He was William Henfrey, a wheelwright, and he was living here with his wife Catherine, and children Ida and Harry. Kelly's *Directory* of 1904 records that William was a wheelwright and carpenter. The business was taken over by Albert Ward and his son, also Albert, and it was still there in 1948 when the Finch estate at Egleton was sold to the Merchant Venturers of Bristol.

This workshop at the rear of Forge Cottage was used by Albert Ward for his wheelwright's business. Shown here, circa *1925, with a new dray are (left to right) Mr Guy, Frederick Shelton, Albert Ward jnr, Marmie Elliott, Albert Ward snr and two workmen* (May Wheatley)

The nineteenth century saw the coming of the railway, and the Syston & Peterborough Railway was the first line to pass through Rutland. It opened in 1848, and the railway still passes through the western side of Egleton parish. A railway gatehouse and a signal box were built at the side of the Oakham to Uppingham road, opposite the road leading to Egleton. The cottage had become uninhabited by 1968 and both cottage and signal box have now been demolished. There was also a toll gate in this vicinity prior to 1870. The gate was erected at 'Egleton Lane', having been ordered by the Trustees of the Turnpike on the 21st December 1825. It was to be 'at or near and on the North side of the entrance of the highway leading to Egleton, branching out of the said turnpike-road' (Traylen 1982, 74). The nineteenth century census returns record gatehouse keepers, a platelayer, a railwayman, and a toll collector among Egleton's residents.

Egleton signal box and crossing keeper's cottage circa 1930. Both have since been demolished (May Wheatley)

Egleton school, provided by George Finch, was opened in 1867, but children in the village were being taught long before this date. In 1773, Mrs Ann Adcock was paid three shillings per week by the Finch family for teaching here. She was succeeded by her daughter, Charlotte, who was still schoolmistress at the age of 73, when the 1851 census was taken. By 1871 she had been succeeded by Harriet Emma Elliott who was born in Markfield, Leicestershire. She lodged with the Gregory family in the cottage known today as 5 Church Road. The village school was closed in 1919. It reopened briefly during the Second World War to cater for both evacuees and village children. It is now the village hall.

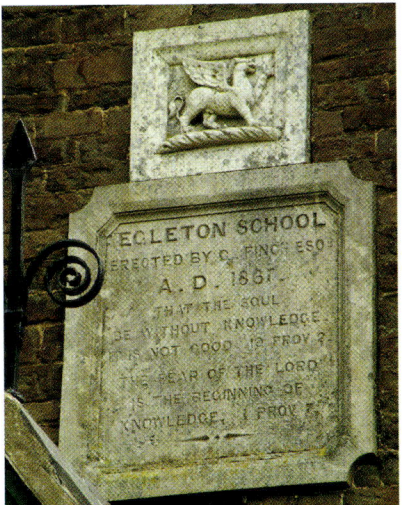

The plaque over the entrance porch to the former school (RO)

The former Egleton School is now the village hall (RO)

The Great War of 1914-18 affected every village community in Rutland, and Egleton was no exception. The parish chest contains a roll listing seventeen men from the village who served, including two who died in battle. Reuben Carpendale was an able seaman on *HMS Black Prince*, which went down with all hands at the Battle of Jutland. Chief Petty Officer Charles Throsby was in the Naval Brigade and was killed at Arras in August 1916. A third man, Thomas William Gregory, is listed as paying the ultimate sacrifice, but he actually returned safely from the war. During the Second World War, both Land Army girls and Italian prisoners of war worked on Egleton farms. Some of the prisoners cycled to work from Whissendine and others were housed in farm barns. There were also evacuees from Walthamstow, London, in the village. One bomb fell in a manure heap in Henry Griffin's farmyard at Home Farm, demolishing a poultry shed.

The connection with the Finch estate ended in 1948 when, with the exception of 14 Orchard Close, all the property in Egleton was sold to the Merchant Venturers of Bristol. Most of the houses have since been sold again and are now owner-occupied. Since 1948 new dwellings have been built and barns converted. When the mid-Gwash valley was flooded in the 1970s to form Rutland Water, Egleton gained a new perspective, being very close to the largest reservoir in the country. In 1975, Anglian Water established a nature reserve at this end of the reservoir and in 1992 the present bird-watching centre was officially opened on the old Hambleton Road at the south-east corner of the village. This, together with the annual Birdfair, attracts thousands of visitors from all over the world (*see* Chapter 24 – Tim Appleton MBE – Thirty Years of Rutland Water Nature Reserve). At the time of writing it seems almost certain that new lagoons will be built close to the village. The objective of the scheme is to protect the nature reserve from problems caused by lower water levels as a result of increased draw-down of the reservoir.

Since the break with the Burley estate, the nature of the village has changed dramatically. Though there are still three farms in the village, only a

An aerial view of Egleton and Rutland Water Nature Reserve. The birdwatching centre is at the end of Hambleton Road which runs from the lower right of this picture towards Rutland Water (John Nowell, Zodiac Publishing)

few of the residents now work in agriculture. Most earn their living outside the village or have chosen to retire here, and young people have to go elsewhere for their education and to work. Changes in residents are probably more frequent now than at any time in the village's history. Yet Egleton remains a close-knit community with a thriving village life. Many of those who have chosen to come here value the sense of community they find and are prepared to contribute to it. Egleton's older buildings are Grade II listed; they are treasured by their owners and are a permanent reminder, to an increasingly modern village, of its agricultural origins.

1797 Houses in Egleton Today

The 1797 notebook referred to earlier identifies the homes of Egleton families at that time. Twenty-four occupied dwellings belonging to the Finch estate are shown on the map. The accompanying notes indicate that there were a further two which were uninhabitable and awaiting repairs. Reference is also made to four non-estate properties. Five estate and three non-estate dwellings have since been demolished. The remainder, which have been modernised and some extended, have survived as desirable Grade II listed residences. The lost and surviving dwellings are shown on the annotated OS 2nd series 25" map of 1904. The following photographs illustrate these properties, and extracts from the 1797 notebook give details of the tenants. The number in parentheses, (22) for example, identifies the location of each property.

19 Church Road (4) in 1797 was home to Henry Towell, who was 'an old infirm cottager' who had 'built the Cottage himself' (RO)

In 1797 there were three cottages on the site of what are now 1 and 2 Meadow Way, to the north of Henry Towell's house. The occupants at (1) on the 1797 map were Mr and Mrs Osborn, who were cottagers. They were said to have had 23 children. Mr Osborn was of 'a remarkably good Character'. Of his wife, 'it is said the Woman drinks'. Peter Neale, wife and four young children lived at (2). He later moved to (12), now known as Woodbine Cottage, 11 Main Street. At (3) lived cottagers Mr and Mrs Broome and their family. Mrs Broome was lame.

It is probable that all of these houses remained when the village school was built in 1867, but they had all been demolished by 1961. Meadow Way was formerly called Tip Lane as it led to the village tip.

Surviving and demolished dwellings from the 1797 survey highlighted on the OS 2nd ed 25" map 1904

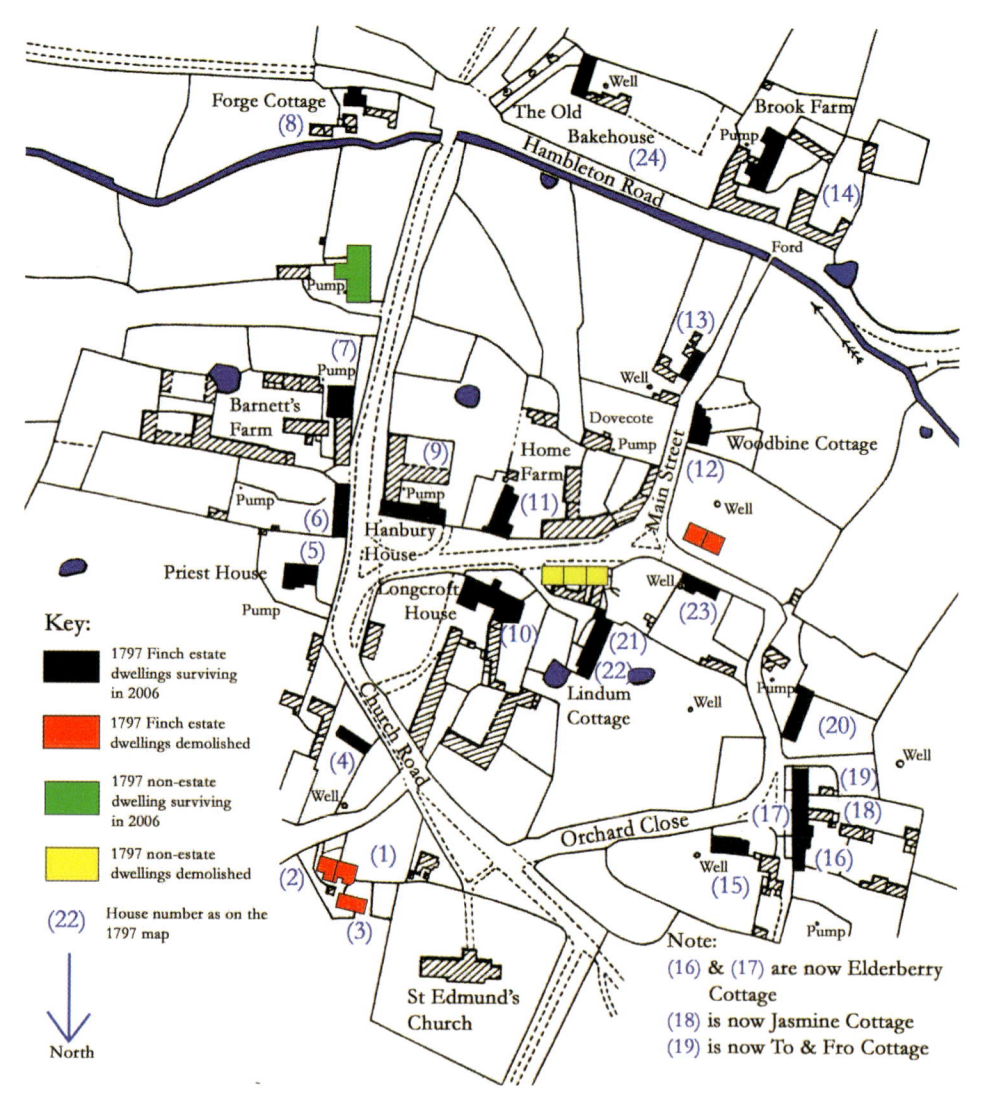

The Priest House, 11 Church Road (5). This is a modern name, and there is no evidence that it was ever occupied by a priest. The tenant in 1797 was Abraham Seaton, 'clerk of the Parish . . . has a [third wife] and a very good House' (RO)

Right: In 1797 The Cottage, 9 Church Road (6), was home to 'the Excise Man', William Booth (RO)

Below: 5 Church Road, Egleton, in about 1910. It was a non-estate property in 1797 located south of (7). It was the village Post Office until about 1954. Note the Post Office sign over the doorway (Hart)

Above: Barnett's Farm, 7 Church Road (7). In 1797 it was a 'good Farm House' and Farmer Wilcox farmed 115 acres, his farm being one of three large farms in the village (RO)

Left: Forge Cottage at 1 Hambleton Road (8). The original house of 1797, home of Thomas Osborn, is painted white (RO)

— 127 —

Hanbury House, 2 Main Street (9). In 1797 the occupants of this house were Farmer William Seaton and his wife, who were 'remarkably industrious' (RO)

In 1797 the occupants of Longcroft House were Farmer John Stimpson, his wife Frances, and their children. A survey of the Egleton estate in 1790 (ROLLR DG 7/1/86) shows that John was farming just over 140 acres. Farmer Stimpson may have also been a butcher.

'L^d W' is the 9th Earl of Winchilsea and 4th Earl of Nottingham who resided at Burley on the Hill, the landlord and employer of John Stimpson. John's eldest son is thought to be Thomas who was baptised in September 1774. 'Herring's Farm at Lower Hambleton' is almost certainly what was in 1970 The Limes at Middle Hambleton (*see* Chapter 21 – Lost Homes).

A non-estate property in 1797 was located between (10) Longcroft House and (23) 1 Orchard Close. It was on the site of present 5 Main Street. The agent for the Finch estate recorded in 1797 that this was: '. . . where there are five children & a neat woman & her husband. Cottagers, of the name of [John and Elizabeth] Needham & in part of their house lives that poor most dropsical Woman and her husband.' By 1828 this property had been converted into three cottages.

Upper: Longcroft House, 1 Main Street (10) (RO)

Lower: This group of three cottages in Main Street west of (10) was not part of the Finch estate in 1797. They were demolished about 1965 prior to the erection of the present bungalow (5 Main Street) on the site (Tony Traylen)

Right: Home Farm, 4 Main Street (11). A farmhouse in 1797 tenanted by Farmer Thomas Meadows and his wife Eleanor (RO)

Below: Woodbine Cottage, 11 Main Street (12). Home in 1797 to an elderly couple, Thomas Scott and his wife – 'a good spinner' – and one of their daughters (RO)

Below: 10 Main Street (13). William Mould was a weaver and in 1797 lived in this cottage with his wife and 'six fine children' (RO)

Right: Aerial view of Brook Farm (14). In 1797 it was tenanted by widow Eleanor Thompson (Tomson) and her two sons, Thomas and Kitt, one of whom was in the cavalry (John Nowell, Zodiac Publishing)

Egleton Post Office, 20 Orchard Close (15)

Harry and Louisa Sharpe (*née* Shelton) lived here from about 1895 until their respective deaths in 1939 and 1951. By 1954 the house was occupied by Florence Gregory and her sister Louisa and it was from here that Louisa ran the Post Office. Sometime later her sister Florence took over the position of post-mistress. Florence and Louisa were the daughters of Arthur and Sarah Gregory. The family had previously lived at 5 Church Road where Sarah and then her daughter Louisa had been postmistress.

20 Orchard Close (15) was in 1797 occupied by Thomas Woods, a cottager, his wife and '8 or 9 fine Children'. The left-hand part of this building was Egleton Post Office in the 1950s (RO)

The row of four terraced cottages in Orchard Close is now occupied as three dwellings. Cottages (16) & (17) have been converted into one dwelling known as Elderberry Cottage, (18) is now known as Jasmine Cottage and (19) is To and Fro Cottage. In 1797 the occupants of these terraced cottages were:

'Nº 16 [John and Elizabeth] Peat. Cottagers with Cows – 8 children – eldest boy at Burley under Game Keeper – keep a little shop – a very industrious family.'

'Nº 17 [William] Collingwood. an old infirm Cottager – his daughter & her husband & children live with him – his name is James Neale.'

'Nº 18 Alice Rippon an old maid – cross – but a good woman – had Lodgers last yr but they have left her & she lives alone – teaches children to read.'

'Nº 19 [John] Bryan. Married a Widow [Ann] Carter, who has children by both Husbands – not good people – some story last yr about stealing wood.'

The row of four cottages in Orchard Close (16, 17, 18 & 19) circa 1910 (Hart)

— 130 —

Anne Exton's brother-in-law and sister, Henry and Alice Beaver, were living at (20) on the 1797 map, now 10 Orchard Close. They were still living there in the early years of the nineteenth century. During this period the tenancy alternated between Anne and her brother-in-law. Henry was a baker and a bakehouse was recorded as being part of this tenancy in 1804.

There were two cottages in the field opposite 1 Orchard Close (23). Robert Pettifer sen occupied one and, in 1782, he was requesting 'wood to prop' his house. However it had become uninhabitable by 1797. The other cottage was rented by 'old Brown & his Wife', but by 1797 it was falling down. As a consequence they were lodging with Anne Exton. The Brown's cottage was supposed to be rebuilt but it never was.

10 Orchard Close (20) was tenanted by Anne Exton in 1797 (RO)

> No 20. Anne Exton
> an old Woman, unmarried & lame — her sister's Husband Beavor a Baker, lives with her — Brown & his Wife board with them till Cottage rebuilt.

Lindum Cottage, 3 Main Street (21 & 22) was two semi-detached cottages in 1797. The occupants were William and Mary Hives (21) and Ann Adcock, schoolmistress (22) (RO)

1 Orchard Close (23) home to Ralph and Mary Hammond in 1797. Both were elderly and infirm and their 'son & Daughter unhealthy' (RO)

The Old Bakehouse, Hambleton Road (24)

By 1743, this property was in the hands of the Cunnington family. In 1790 the house, yard and Home Close occupied an area of 1 acre 3 roods, and there was a barn and yard with an adjoining close of over one and a half acres. The total farm was just over 58 acres, and at that time it was the smallest of the five farms in Egleton.

By 1797, the farm had been taken over by James and Elizabeth Cunnington's son, Edward, who had married Elizabeth Preston of Burton Lazars, Leicestershire, in 1794. Edward's wife made Stilton cheese, thus placing Egleton on the list of local villages where this cheese was made in the eighteenth century. The three children recorded in the notebook were Elizabeth, Edward and Peter who were baptised at Egleton between 1795 and 1798.

Above: The Old Bakehouse, Hambleton Road (24). This property had been home to a baker from at least 1891 until well after the First World War (RO)

> No.24   Farmer Cunnington
> Young Man & Woman – 2 young Children – has in the Cavalry – she makes Stilton Cheeses – 5 Cows another Boy Peter born in 98 very industrious she comes from Leicestershire, her Name Preston milks 5 Cows keeps Poultry & has only One Maid to assist her.

Chapter 7
Empingham: An Entire Model Village
Sue Lee and Jean Orpin

'The Entire Model Village of Empingham' is how the village was described in the sale advertisement for the Normanton Estate of 1924. There were 149 separate lots, including eighteen farms, up for auction so it was clearly anticipated that ownership would be dispersed. This would bring a long era in the life of the village to an end.

The Beginnings

The village we see today is largely the legacy of the Heathcotes, who were the main landowners from 1729 to 1924. The family rose from ordinary beginnings, fulfilling all their dreams by achieving wealth, power and prestige. The foundation was laid by Gilbert Heathcote, a Richard Branson of his day. He was a man of considerable ability: the son of a Chesterfield merchant, brought up in a privileged but not upper class household who became a Merchant Adventurer and a Director of the East India Company, and rose to be Lord Mayor of London and Governor of the Bank of England. In 1729 he retired but he had never been ennobled. To enter the peerage it was almost always necessary to own land and an impressive house, and gain political influence. It was also essential to establish a county family by connections and making good marriages.

When Gilbert Heathcote was 70, he decided to buy a country estate. There was no large estate on the market so he bought the Normanton estate in Rutland with the intention of purchasing more land when it became available (*see* Chapter ? – Normanton). This estate had been owned by the Mackworths since the Middle Ages but Thomas Mackworth had had financial difficulties after the 1722 election. He sold it possibly in settlement of a debt to Charles Tryon, who then sold it to Gilbert Heathcote. Heathcote built a large imposing house, a house for show and a symbol of social and economic power, engaging an architect who was clerk of works at Blenheim. When the house was finished he was granted his baronetcy but did not live long enough to enjoy it as he died in January 1732, leaving £700,000.

Gilbert Heathcote, 1st Baronet

Although he was fabulously wealthy Gilbert Heathcote was not a generous man. In fact he was notorious for his meanness. A saying attributed to him was, 'A penny saved is a penny got'. He was satirised by Alexander Pope, the eminent essayist:

'The grave Sir Gilbert holds it for a rule
That every man in want is a fool.'

Empingham, the largest village on the Normanton estate, had houses situated round the church and along Main Street. Up to its enclosure by Act of Parliament in 1795 it had five great fields (Ryder 2006, 64). Each great field was divided into blocks, called furlongs, and the furlongs into strips. A farmer's land was inconveniently scattered in these strips throughout the parish. The process of enclosure consolidated these strips together into the hedged fields seen today. Some of the tenant farmers would be substantial gentlemen with large farmhouses and others were cottagers, often living in thatched cottages, with smallholdings. Most other villagers with no landholding would have been involved in agricultural labour. Blore's *Rutland*, published in 1811, described the village as remarkable for the neatness of its farms, houses and cottages.

This house in Main Street, Empingham was described as a 'Block of Three Cottages' in the Normanton Estate sale catologue of 1924 (Sue Lee)

The largest of these farmhouses was probably the house on Main Street now known as The Firs. Several other farmhouses pre-date the purchase of the estate. They can be identified by their stone chimney stacks, and one gable on the south side of Main Street displays a seventeenth century datestone.

The seventeenth century datestone in the gable of Syson's House, one of the substantial farmhouses purchased by Gilbert Heathcote in 1729 (RO)

The First Model Village

John Heathcote, who succeeded the first Gilbert as second baronet, was MP for Grantham, Lincolnshire, and Bodmin, Cornwall, and lived most of his life in London. When he retired from these duties in 1741 he settled in Rutland and concentrated on increasing the estate. Consequently, Gilbert, the third baronet, inherited in 1759 a larger estate with property in many Rutland villages. His house at Normanton now needed a suitable setting with uninterrupted views.

In the eighteenth century a common cause of deserted villages was the fashion for making landscape gardens in the Italianate style. Normanton had already been enclosed when the estate was bought and the third baronet decided to remove the villagers to Empingham in order to make his park, which was eventually to enclose 900 acres.

An Estate Village

From 'The Deserted Village' by Oliver Goldsmith:
 'But times are alter'd; trade's unfeeling train
 Usurp the land and dispossess the swain;
 Along the lawn, where scatter'd hamlets rose,
 Unwieldy wealth and cumbrous pomp repose,
 And every want to opulence allied,
 And every pang that folly pays to pride.'

The removal did not take place overnight but began shortly after he came into his inheritance, and over a few years the inhabitants of Normanton became the inhabitants of Empingham. The newcomers were probably housed in rows of thatched cottages. Some of the smallest have disappeared but there remain in Empingham a number of this type of cottage, now with the thatch heightened over second-storey windows, pretty porches and attractive gardens in front. They are highly desirable to twenty-first century residents and may well have been so to their first occupiers in the eighteenth century.

One of the thatched cottages in Main Street, Empingham (Sue Lee)

After the Empingham Enclosure Act in 1795 the village changed. Gilbert Heathcote, 4th Baronet, must have welcomed enclosure as the land could be improved and new machinery used. The farms could be fenced and the land drained if necessary. Smaller holdings were absorbed and the tenants encouraged to keep improved stock. The middle years of the nineteenth century saw a Golden Age in farming in England; millions were spent nationally on farming at this time and this is reflected in the number of people employed in agriculture and allied trades in Empingham in the 1841 census.

Empingham people employed in agriculture and allied trades in 1841:

Farmers	29
Cottagers	10
Agricultural labourers	177
Shepherds	4
Blacksmiths	7
Wheelwrights	5
Millers	2
Other occupations	42
Total	276

The Notebook of Charles Peach, Empingham Gamekeeper

This notebook was started in 1831 and Charles Peach records snippets of information – game shot, poachers apprehended, recipes for treating dogs (and a few for people) until his 'sudden departure' in 1868. It also notes important dates relating to the Heathcotes.

Charles Peach was born in Empingham in 1819. He was the eldest son of Thomas Peach, a gamekeeper, employed on the Normanton estate, who lived in a cottage near the vicarage in Empingham, with his wife Sarah and their eleven children.

In 1833, Thomas Peach was wounded by John Perkins, a 26-year-old from Ketton, who was subsequently hanged at Oakham. Perkins' two brothers, who were from Easton-on-the-Hill, Northamptonshire, were transported for life in connection with the same offence. It created much ill feeling among the residents of Easton when one of the gang was acquitted in return for giving the names of the other culprits. This episode is commemorated in a ballad entitled 'Oakham Poachers or The Lamentation of Young Perkins' which can be found in Matkin's *Oakham Almanack* of 1904.

The 1841 Census Return records that Charles Peach was a gamekeeper employed on the Normanton estate. In his journal he recorded notes regarding poachers:

'Caught Francis Buckworth night snaring. Went to prison 3 months in February 1842. Caught William Hill and Thomas Wade poaching Woolfox Oct 5th 1849. Convicted in the penalty of £5 each. Did not appear. Warrant granted for their apprehension.'

There were many navvies in the area building railways, including the Seaton Viaduct, and poaching by these men was a real problem. For example an entry in 1848 records, 'Caught 2 Railroad men 30th April John Lacy, William Nicholls'.

Weather is frequently mentioned in the book. In summer 1860 he records:

'. . . the wettest and worst . . . remembered by the oldest man living. Raised 340 pheasants many perished by the cold after turning out and many destroyed by the Greatest Enemy to game Foxes it being so wet that the pheasants could not fly to perch.'

Extremes of weather are noted particularly: 'Summer 1861 Severe frosts perished many of the early pheasant's eggs' and 'A very hot summer in 1868, the hottest I ever remember'.

He notes the date Gilbert Henry Heathcote, aged 21, commenced shooting in 1851 and his election as Member of Parliament for Boston in August 1852. In 1853 he obviously accompanied the family to Scotland for three weeks because he records the amounts paid to transport himself and the dogs.

The London addresses of several members of the Heathcote family are entered. He was clearly in the confidence of Lord Aveland (Gilbert Henry's father) at this time as he was asked to witness his will: '25th July 1861 Signed Lord Aveland's will or codicil in the presence of Lord Aveland and the said John Guy. Also saw Lord Aveland sign it'.

There are many cures for ailments in the notebook, including the following:

For dogs:
> 'For the inside of the ear. Put a lump of soft soap into the root of the ear and pour on a tablespoonful of Brandy. Rub in.
> The best Meddic for a dog is a lump of butter and salt mixed.
> When dogs feet are cut by flint and other accidents Friar's Balsam I have used for years and found excellent.'

For people:
> 'Medicine for a cough. Boil linseed and a stick of licquorice [sic] well together and when cold use as a common drink.
> A good smelling bottle for the headache. 1d of sal volatile, 1d of essence of bergamot, 1d of spirits of ammonia all put in a bottle and used if necessary.
> Half a pint of new milk warm from the cow made sweet with conserve of roses and two tablespoons of the very best rum. An excellent cordial.'

There was obviously some serious incidents in 1867. Charles Peach jnr, his son, broke his leg in the New Wood in February and Charles Peach snr met with a serious accident by 'a straining his ankle' in May 1867: 'the Doctors Newman and Scott said it were fractured. F Trolley a Bone-Setter say it were not broke.'

The end of his career as a gamekeeper seems to be related to these incidents although the connection is not clear:

> '1868 Charles Peach left Normanton park Saturday 28th March 1868 was not permitted to stop at Luffenham only one month although there were nothing against his character in any shape or form this were Lord Aveland's cruelty and tyranny Lord Aveland behaved very bad in this respect. Came to Barrowden April 23rd left Normanton through an accident in the ankle. Had been born in the service of the Heathcote Family and lived in their service up to the 49 year of my Age. C Peach.'

The last entry in the book records his father's death:

> 'Thomas Peach died on January 3rd 1870 leaving his 11 children £437 7s 5½ d each after all his expenses were paid which were trifling he being clear of debt Owe no man anything were his motto. Hope he is in Heaven.'

Charles went to live in Luffenham Road, Barrowden, with his family. He never worked as a gamekeeper again, presumably living on his inheritance. He is described in the 1871 Census as 'Gamekeeper unemployed' and in 1891 as 'Gamekeeper retired'. He died in 1895 aged 75.

Two pages from Charles Peach's notebook (Jean Orpin)

The Building Earl

The 5th Baronet, Gilbert John, was created Baron Aveland in 1856. As a widow, his wife Clementina unexpectedly inherited the Willoughby landholdings which included the Grimsthorpe estate. However she preferred to live in the mansion at Normanton. Their son Gilbert Henry inherited his father's title, Baron Aveland, in 1867 and on his mother's death in 1888, became the 25th Baron Willoughby d'Eresby. Soon after, in 1892, he was created Earl of Ancaster. He now moved in the highest social circles.

The Prince and Princess of Wales visit Normanton

The Prince and Princess of Wales visited Normanton in January 1881 and the following is quoted from *The Graphic*: 'On the Tuesday Lord Aveland and some of his guests, on their way to shoot over one of the preserves drove through the village of Empingham where triumphal arches and other decorations had been erected in honour of the Royal visitors, and the inhabitants greeted them with enthusiasm, 'God bless the Prince of Wales' being sung by a hundred schoolchildren as they passed the parish church . . .'

Left: A grand ceremonial arch was erected in Empingham for the visit by the Prince and Princess of Wales in 1881 (The Graphic, 22nd January 1881)

At the time Gilbert Henry inherited the Normanton estate in 1867, Empingham was far from being a 'model village'. It was described in the *Post Office Directory* of 1876 thus: 'The village is in a dilapidated state, many of the houses are in ruins.' However it was not to stay that way. By the end of the nineteenth century, Gilbert Henry was justifiably called 'The Building Earl'.

In 1860 the Poor Law Commission had investigated rural housing and like other landowners he obviously took note of their reports. The family owned 13,600 acres in Rutland in fifteen different parishes and Gilbert Henry set about modernising his properties all over the estate. A large workshop and woodyard was built at Normanton to serve the needs of the estate, and brickyards at Luffenham and Pilton provided bricks and tiles. Old farms were repaired and acquired red tiled roofs instead of thatch; brick extensions were added and both small and large properties alike gained tall brick chimneys, with decorative banding. Many of these remain.

Weed's farmhouse (Wisteria House) in Main Street acquired a new Ancaster roof to replace the old thatch (Sue Lee)

Below: Several properties have Ancaster style brick extensions (RO)

Right: Ancaster roofs and chimneys on the Old Post Office in Main Street (Sue Lee)

In the second half of the nineteenth century it became less common for agricultural labourers to be lodged in farmhouses so extra housing had to be provided. In due course new buildings, some of stone but mostly of brick, all with the characteristic red tiled roofs and tall decorative chimneys, appeared around the whole of the Rutland estate and most notably in Empingham, the model village.

An Ancaster cottage in Main Street (RO)

The earliest cottages were constructed before 1892 while Gilbert Henry was still a Baron and display his Baron's coronet. After 1892 the Earl's crown proudly adorns the front of all new Ancaster buildings. The style of these buildings is distinctive. It was the result of collaboration between Gilbert Henry Heathcote, his Surveyor and Agent, Edward Brett Binns and Joseph Newman, his Clerk of Works. Second-storey windows are small or non-existent and the most characteristic feature of the houses is the overhanging eaves. These were often decorated with wooden braces extending down below the eaves. A good example is Home Farm where it is easy to see the curve and overhanging eaves although there are no braces remaining (if there ever were any). The braces are very obvious on Normanton Cottages (actually in Empingham parish) and Mill Farm.

One of a number of semi-detached brick cottages in Empingham, all built to the Ancaster style. Note the absence of first floor windows on the front elevation (RO)

Two elevations of this pair of semi-detached cottages in Nook Lane are stone and the other two are brick (RO)

— 140 —

The Heathcote coat of arms, surmounted by a coronet or crown, is a feature on estate houses built by Gilbert Henry, the 6th Baronet (RO)

Right: Normanton Cottages, with wooden braces below the eaves (RO)

Walking around Empingham nearly a hundred years after the death of the 'Building Earl', the effect of his investment in the estate and the justification for the description in the sale catalogue can clearly be seen. However the influence of the Heathcote family did of course extend way beyond mere buildings.

Left: Mill Farm, near the former Empingham watermill. Note the curved wooden braces supporting the eaves (RO)

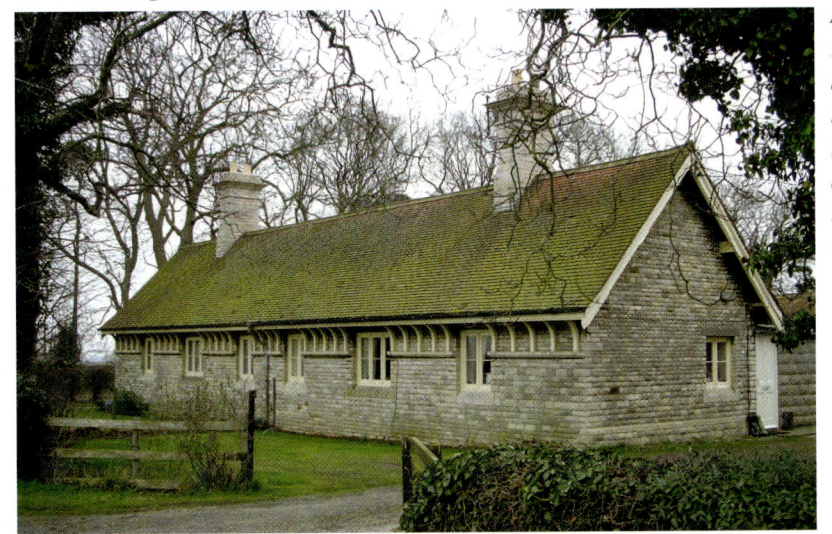

Above: Home Farm in Main Street. This house appears to have lost its curved wooden braces below the eaves (RO)

— 141 —

Management of the Estate

The Heathcotes employed an Agent or Steward to act on their behalf and manage the estate in their absence. These employees were very important and took charge completely, often fulfilling personal tasks as well as public duties for their employer. There are many stories told of the power of the Agent in Empingham, who was able to remove families from the village if he wished. The Land Agent in 1841 was Thomas Syson and the house where he lived in Main Street is now called Syson's House. Although it is now divided it was originally a substantial house and reflected the status of the position held by its occupant.

Syson's House, although now divided, is a substantial house reflecting the status of Thomas Syson, Land Agent to the Normanton Estate, one of its former occupants (RO)

The whole of the Normanton estate was managed from Empingham. As Lords of the Manor the Heathcotes would be responsible for the Court Baron, a local civil court to deal with all matters relating to tenancies and rentals. Leases were for one to five years and renewed on Lady Day or Michaelmas. Rent Days took place in the Audit Hall. The Steward would preside and keep records. Petty Sessions to deal with minor criminal matters were held every Monday at the White Horse Inn. More serious legal matters were referred to Assizes at Oakham.

Audit Hall, now Empingham village hall, is where tenants of the Normanton Estate paid their rents to the Steward (RO)

Social Responsibility

Before the Welfare State landowners were expected to care for their tenants. In 1794 Heathcote rented the house now known as the Wilderness as a House of Protection for the Poor and provided beds and bedding for them. In 1837 when the Union Workhouse at Oakham opened it took over some of those responsibilities and the Wilderness became the doctor's residence.

The Wilderness. Sir Gilbert Heathcote rented it in 1794 as a House of Protection for the Poor. Early in the twentieth century it was the residence of Edgar Steele Edwards, medical officer and public vaccinator for the Empingham district of the Oakham Union (RO)

In 1838 Gilbert Heathcote, 4th Baronet, built a new school, which was then let to the managers. It comprised a large room divided by a screen. He presented the school with chandeliers and gave £15 towards a salary for the schoolmaster whom he appointed. The 5th Baronet added an extra room in 1872. Members of the family would visit the school from time to time and the children were expected to show them due respect. When the Prince and Princess of Wales visited, the children were given an extra half hour at playtime in order to line the street.

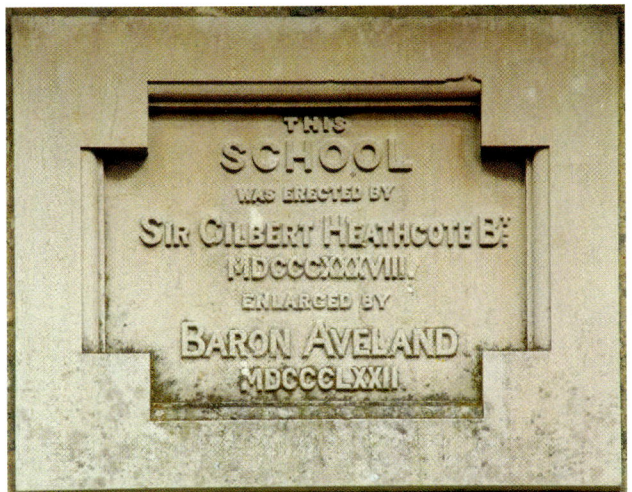

A plaque recording that members of the Heathcote family built and extended the village school. It is now a private residence (RO)

— 143 —

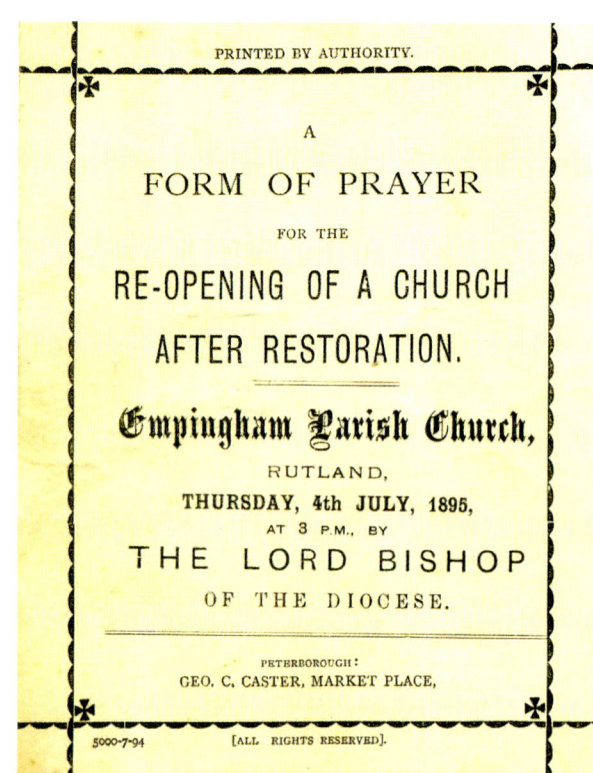

The front of the Service Sheet printed for the church re-opening following its restoration in 1894 (Jean Orpin)

In 1894, Empingham church was restored under the direction of J C Traylen, a Stamford architect. The Heathcotes personally paid £399 0s 10d for the recasting of the bells by Taylors of Loughborough and £47 for nave chairs, which were bought from Mr William Royce of Stamford. Lady Ancaster also held concerts to raise money for the appeal.

On Thursday 4th July 1895 the Bishop of Peterborough visited the parish to officiate at the re-opening of the church. The service began with verses from Psalm 118, 'Open me the gates of righteousness: that I may go into them, and give thanks to the Lord. This is the gate of the Lord: the righteous shall enter into it'.

Gilbert Henry allowed stone from the old Methodist Chapel on Crocket Lane to be sold to raise money for a new chapel and he also gave the land for it. Five hundred people attended the opening in 1899 and tea was provided in the Audit Hall.

The Heathcotes provided a water supply for the village and, as there were many thatched houses, they contributed half the cost of a fire engine and house. They also gave land for the Primrose Hall on Main Street, which was opened in 1899.

The Methodist Chapel in Main Street, Empingham, was opened in 1899. It was built on land donated by Gilbert Henry, 1st Earl of Ancaster (Sue Lee)

The Primrose League was an organisation for spreading Conservative principles in Great Britain. It was founded in 1883 in memory of Benjamin Disraeli (the primrose was reputedly his favourite flower) and active until the mid 1990s. It was finally wound up in December 2004. Membership of the League was open to women as well as men. In Empingham the Primrose Hall was also used as a Reading Room and for men to play billiards and cards.

Primrose League badges (Sue Lee)

Primrose Hall in Main Street, Empingham, was a meeting place for the Primrose League as well as a Reading Room (RO)

Employment

During the Heathcotes' ownership, the village was virtually self-contained with nearly everyone reliant on the estate for employment, making the whole community dependent on the Heathcotes. It did not 'do' to fall out with the Agent or fail to take notice when the Heathcote carriage stopped and its occupant complained about the state of one's garden.

A large majority of villagers were employed in agriculture either directly by the estate or by farmers who were all tenants of the estate. Up to the middle of the nineteenth century a number of labourers lived in the farm houses but the number of farm servants 'living in' fell steadily from 1861. This would have made agricultural labourers more dependent on seasonal work. Neither labourers nor tenant farmers had a great deal of stability of employment. Short leases were common and farms seem to have changed hands quite often.

Empingham remained an agricultural community throughout the nineteenth century although the number of farms reduced as they were consolidated into larger units. The farms were mixed arable and pasture with some grass near the farm, but each farm was required by the estate to have a share of the poorer grass. In the years of agricultural depression at the end of the nineteenth century farmers diversified and we find occupations listed in the census as 'Farmer and Butcher 'Farmer and Innkeeper,' Farmer and

Some estate employees recorded in the 1901 Census Return for Empingham:

Clerk of Works	1
Draughtsman	1
Bricklayers	5
Carpenters	5
Stonemasons	3
Thatcher	1
Forestry workers	9
Gamekeepers	5

Blacksmith'. Several farms were also taken 'in hand' and a Farm Foreman or Farm Bailiff put in charge.

Towards the end of the nineteenth century there was increasing variety in the employment of the villagers although the influence of the estate had not diminished. The works at Normanton (*see* Chapter 11 – Normanton) employed about 50 men, many of them from Empingham, and there were also estate workshops in Jubilee Yard (behind South View Farm). The occupations relating to the activities of the 'Building Earl' are easily identified – there is an estate thatcher, painters and decorators, carpenters, bricklayers and stonemasons. He was also a 'shooting man' so there are several gamekeepers, and forestry had become an important aspect of the estate with the Head Forester having up to ten men under him.

The village may have been dependent on the estate but it also reaped the rewards in terms of the duty of care the family undertook with regard to their estate. This included treats for the villagers and employees. The Heathcotes invited the children from the school up to the Hall once a year for a treat and also arranged outings for their workers.

Estate Outing

The *Rutland Churchman* of 1904 reports:

'On Saturday 10th Sept, the whole of the workmen on the Earl of Ancaster's Empingham and Normanton estates, with their wives, were taken, through the kindness of his lordship, to Yarmouth for an outing. The special train left Ketton at 5.15am. travelling via Saxby and Bourne, and stopping only at Luffenham, South Witham, and Bourne. Yarmouth was reached about ten o'clock and eight hours were spent at this popular sea-side resort: the party reached Ketton once more about eleven o'clock at night.'

Sale of the Estate

The fall in farming incomes, death duties and his wife's preference for Grimsthorpe resulted in the second Earl of Ancaster's decision to sell the Normanton estate and to dispose of the unwanted house. Most of the estate properties were sold prior to or after the auction, which took place in 1924, although some remained in Ancaster ownership until 1959. The Estate was not put up for sale as an entity and some families like the Hibbitts, Weeds and Corbys who had by then occupied farms for more than one generation were in a position to purchase them when the estate was sold. As reported in the *Stamford Mercury* of 19th September 1924: 'The vendors had arranged that the schools at Edith Weston and Empingham should not be offered, and a pleasing announcement was that they had also decided to present the Audit Hall at Empingham to the village.'

Above: The Empingham village sign has images which represent the community before and after the construction of Rutland Water (RO)

Left: This map of Empingham is from the OS 2nd ed 25" map 1904. The farmyards, large gardens and other open spaces have largely been filled with modern developments

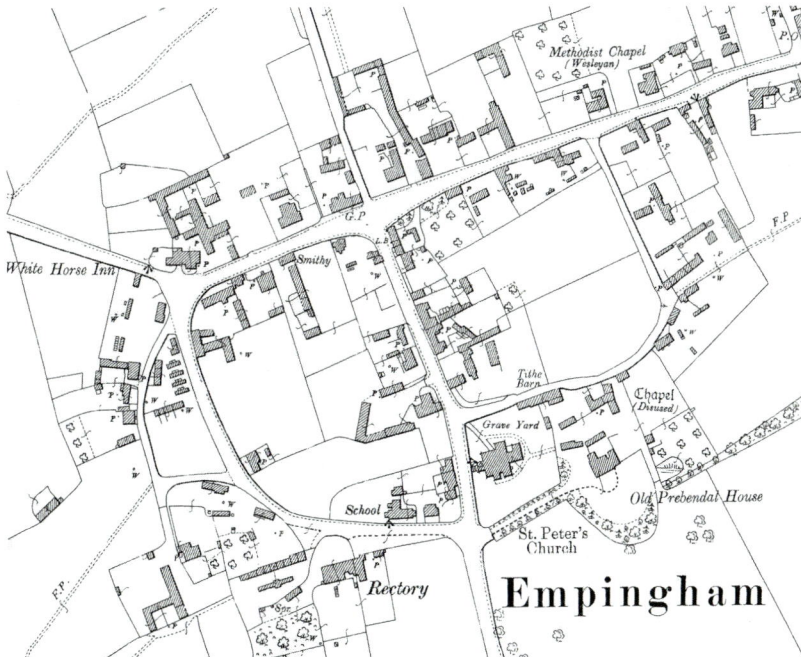

The Heathcote family owned Empingham for almost 200 years, and the village we see today is largely a legacy of that dynasty. However, in the last hundred years Empingham has changed from being a self-sufficient village mainly occupied by tenant farmers, farm workers and others employed by the Ancaster Estate. Now, most of the houses, farmhouses and farm buildings are private owner-occupied residences. The Ancaster style is still much in evidence throughout the village, but there has been a great deal of modern development which has taken over the farmyards, large gardens and other open spaces as seen on early twentieth-century maps.

Empingham village from the air in 2006. Its close proximity to Rutland Water is evident, but from ground level only the grassed embankment can be seen, and then only from the western end of the village (John Nowell, Zodiac Publishing)

The impact of Rutland Water on Empingham has much to do with increased tourism in the area and possibly the creation of a more desirable place to live. Although the reservoir is very close it is not visible, but the earth embankment, which holds back many millions of gallons of water, and which was the largest in the United Kingdom when it was built, can be seen, but only from the western end of the village. However, thanks to excellent landscaping, it is by no means an eyesore.

Chapter 8
Hambleton: The Settlement on the Crooked Hill
Sue Howlett

The western end of Hambleton peninsula from the air in 2006 (John Nowell, Zodiac Publishing)

The Medieval Village of Hambleton

Visible for miles on its high ridge above the Gwash Valley, Hambleton was always an important and valuable estate. Even before the Norman Conquest it had been part of the dower of Saxon queens, including the wife of Edward the Confessor, who gave her name to the village of Edith Weston. According to Domesday Book, compiled in 1086, the manor was extensive enough to contain three churches and seven hamlets, five of which afterwards became separate parishes. One of the churches belonging to Hambleton was St Peter's, Stamford, which with half a carucate (around 60 acres) of land at Hambleton was held by Albert of Lorraine, William the Conquerer's chaplain (Morris 1980, 19-21).

In addition to its arable lands, the manor of Hambleton contained 40 acres of meadow and more than three square miles of woodland. With male adults listed in 1086 as 140 villeins and thirteen bordars, the total population probably exceeded 500. Serfs toiled up and down the three great open fields, behind oxen pulling the 45 ploughs belonging to the king and the villagers. Today, nearly a millennium later, areas of former ridge and furrow strips can still be seen.

An 1839 drawing of Hambleton Church (Uppingham School Archives)

Some time after the Domesday survey, William the Conquerer granted Hambleton to the powerful Norman family of Umfraville, who sub-divided the large and sprawling manor into two: Great and Little Hambleton. In 1412, Little Hambleton was sold to the prosperous, wool-dealing Flore family whose town house in Oakham stands to this day (*VCH* II, 70). All that now remains of their manor is the faint trace of a moated site near Half Moon Spinney, at the north-eastern point of the present Hambleton peninsula, close to which sherds of medieval pottery have been found. The 1296 Lay Subsidy recorded five tax payers in Little Hambleton, and in 1588 there were still four houses. The tiny manor was probably deserted long before 1726 when it was included on the Estate Map of Normanton (Ryder 2006, Appendix II, 3).

Ancient ridge and furrow near Hambleton Old Hall revealed when the reservoir was at low level in November 2005 (RO)

Flore's House in High Street, Oakham, in 1908 before the wing projecting into the street was demolished for road widening (Hart)

    The Black Death of 1349 spread its deadly shadow over Rutland as elsewhere, and in Hambleton eleven small farms were 'in the lord's hand for want of tenants, which paid £11 yearly before the pestilence' (*CIPM*, 27, quoted in Ryder 2006, 22). Some of these may have been in the settlement of Nether Hambleton, which retained the earthworks of a deserted village until flooding of the valley obliterated both the lost and the living village (*see* Chapter 20 – Medieval Settlements at Nether Hambleton and Whitwell).

    By the time of the Wars of the Roses, the manor of Great Hambleton was held by the Duke of York and his victorious son, King Edward IV, who granted it to the Ferrers family. In the early sixteenth century there were between 30 and 40 households. In 1522 King Henry VIII's minister, Cardinal Wolsey, organised a Military Survey to assess the wealth and military potential of the nation. The Rutland survey, the most complete to survive, shows Sir Edward Ferris [Ferrers] as 'chief lord' of Hamyldon [Hambleton] with John Harington the elder as his steward. Both a parson and vicar are listed, while among the lord's tenants, fourteen are noted as archers or 'bill men' and several actually possessed the necessary weapons (Cornwall 1980, 67).

    Another Lay Subsidy granted to the king in 1524 assessed the 'goodes' or 'profyte of wages' of the seventeen husbandmen, fifteen labourers, one widow and 'Edward Burton, Gent.' of 'Hamyldon', whose wealth ranged from £30 to twenty shillings. Edward Ferris is no longer listed, presumably residing elsewhere, although still in possession of the manor of Great Hambleton. In 1601 Henry Ferrers sold the manor to Sir John Harington, whose family had by now accumulated many estates in Rutland including Exton and Burley. However, the sudden decline of that family, after the death of the first and second Lords Harington in 1613-14, brought the manors of Hambleton and Burley into the hands of the most powerful subject in England, the king's favourite, George Villiers, Duke of Buckingham.

With the new Stuart dynasty on the throne of England, it seemed that an era of peace, stability and prosperity was about to dawn, and Rutland was well placed to share in the benefits. In 1603 King James I passed through the county on the journey south to claim his new kingdom, staying at Burley to enjoy the hunting for which Rutland was becoming renowned. Further royal visits by James and his son, Charles I, brought the exciting presence of the court and royal entourage combined with a heavy demand for provisions of all kinds. While Buckingham was rarely in residence in his grand house at Burley, and following his assassination in 1628 was succeeded by an infant son, Hambleton saw little of its Lord of the Manor. But other residents of Hambleton were about to exploit the changing economic and political conditions of the age, and begin to climb the social ladder.

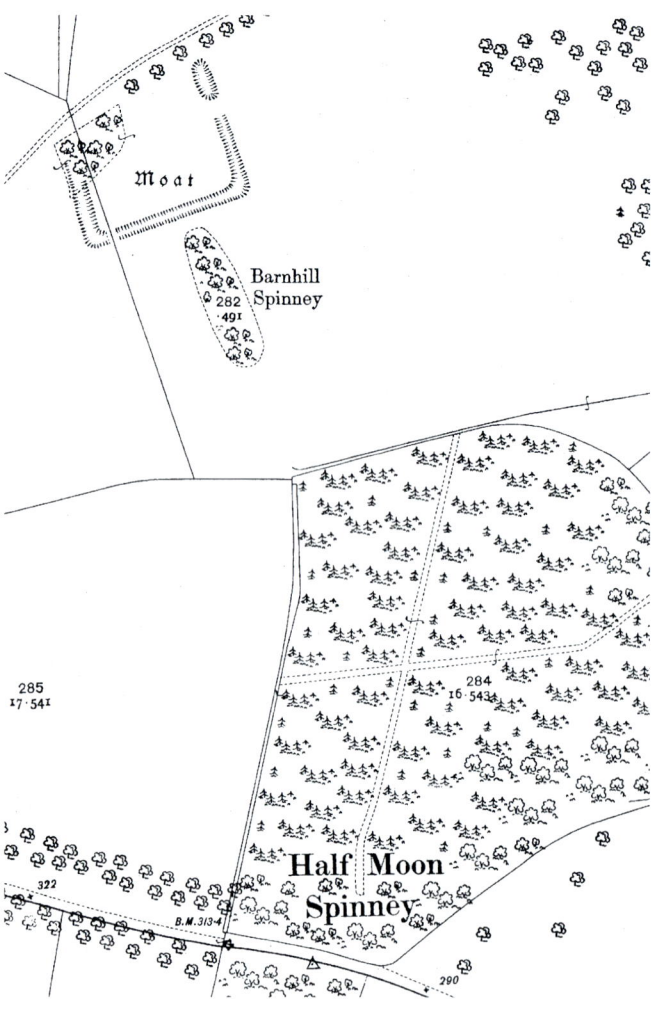

The former moated site of Flore's Manor at Little Hambleton from the OS 2nd ed 25" map 1904

The 1524 Lay Subsidy for Hambleton (Cornwall 1980, 104)

HAMYLDON

1524

Edward Burton Gent. in goodes	£30	Rafe Nutt laber. in lyke profyte		20s
John Atkyns husb. in goodes	£15	Robert Newell laber. in lyke profyte		20s
William Fowley husb. in goodes	£16	Robert Scott laber. in lyke profyte		20s
Robert Freman husb. in goodes	£13	Robert Fynne laber. in lyke profyte		20s
Thomas Fowler husb. in goodes	£10	Thomas Redhed laber. in lyke profyte		20s
Thomas Bradley husb. in goodes	£8	Robert Jacson laber in lyke profyte		20s
George More husb. in goodes	£6	Edward Richardson laber. in lyke profyte		20s
William Richardson husb. in goodes	£5	Thomas Broke laber. in goodes		40s
Symond Fowler husb. in goodes	£8	John Mathew laber. in goodes		40s
Richerd Aswell husb. in goodes	£5	Johne Fowler wedow in goodes		£5
John Whytwell husb. in goodes	£3	Henry Fowler laber. in profyte of wages		20s
John Baldoke husb. in goodes	£3	William Whytwell laber. in goodes	£3	
John Fynne husb. in goodes	40s	William Burges laber. in goodes		40s
Robert Aswell husb. in goodes	40s	Robert Wyles laber. in profyte of wages		20s
Robert Freman husb. in goodes	£3			
John Bell husb. in goodes	40s			
William Gunthorp husb. in goodes	£3			
John Gunthorp husb. in goodes	40s			
John Cole laber in profyte of wages	20s			
Thomas Walker laber. in lyke profyte	20s			

— 152 —

The Old Hall, Hambleton

Although not the actual Manor House of Hambleton, one of the most attractive buildings in the village to this day is the Jacobean farmhouse now known as 'The Old Hall'. It was built in the early seventeenth century by Christopher Loveday and sold soon afterwards to Roger Quarles. This 'delightful stone-built manor house' was described thus three centuries later in *Country Life*, 27th September 1930:

'For a seventeenth century yeoman's residence it possesses a surprising individuality, with its loggias back and front, its balustrade and galleries and its arcaded parapet; while, in addition to, and in spite of, these ornaments, there is a reticence and a conscious sense of design which are altogether modern in feeling.'

The south facade of Hambleton Old Hall in 2005 (RO)

Abel Barker, Father and Son

In the early years of the seventeenth century, as Christopher Loveday built his new house and James I enjoyed his new kingdom, a farmer named Baldwin Barker died at Hambleton. Baldwin had held a messuage (house) 'lying in Henbecke in the Lordship of Great Hamelton, co. Rutland, and one and a half yard lands of arable in the fields of Great Hamelton with meadows and pastures appertaining to the said messuage' (ROLLR DG/11/404). Baldwin Barker left his house and strips in the open fields to his eldest son Abel Barker, £150 to his youngest son Samuel, and five shillings each to his seven remaining children. His wife, Elizabeth, received £20 a year for five years plus accommodation, half a yardland, six cows and forty sheep as well as the right 'to grind her malt at one of the mills, and gather her herbs in the garden, and have room for hanging her clothes in the orchard' and 'a horse or mare to carry her to market or elsewhere' (ROLLR DG/11/989). However, the newly widowed Elizabeth encountered problems with her eldest son, beginning one letter to Abel in 1604 (ROLLR DE 730/1/1), 'Harp not so much upon my death . . .'.

Abel Barker proved a capable, ambitious farmer. He added to his inheritance by leasing additional strips from the new Lord Harington of Exton, so that by 1629 his holding in Hambleton was four yardlands, totalling about 120 acres. He also leased additional closes (small enclosed fields) outside Hambleton from Sir Kenelm Digby of Stoke Dry. By 1634, Abel Barker had amassed sufficient wealth to pay £1,010 for the Old Hall of Hambleton, together with one cottage, four yardlands in the open fields, 'Flowers Land' and all other fields in Hambleton formerly owned by the Quarles family (ROLLR DG/11/571). The new owner of the Old Hall had only three years to enjoy it before his death in 1637. His will shows the family's increased prosperity and social status over one generation. Whereas Baldwin Barker had been described as 'Yeoman' (farmer), Abel Barker was identified as 'Gentleman'. His wife, also Elizabeth, received £100 a year and a house for life; four of his children received over a thousand pounds each. In addition, the second son, another Abel, inherited the Old Hall and some of his father's leases, while the eldest son, John, the executor, inherited the freehold land with remaining property and leases (ROLLR DG/11/995).

Not content to remain a farmer and grazier, the younger Abel Barker seized every opportunity to extend his business interests. He served King Charles I in the provision of twenty good horses and riders to attend the royal entourage returning from the belated Scottish coronation of 1633, as they passed through Rutland along the Great North Road. John Barker's death in 1639 brought additional property into the possession of his brother Abel, who was by now sufficiently prosperous to employ a bailiff and expand his landholdings by entering into additional leases.

Civil War in Rutland

The second Stuart king was less adept than his father in managing recalcitrant parliaments. In 1642 the rumbling opposition to King Charles I's Personal Rule erupted into civil war.

Amid the deepening conflict, it became essential to protect investments in livestock and harvests, and Abel Barker instructed his bailiff, John Musson, to buy wheat 'and have it brined after the Lincolnshire fashion to avoid blasting'. He enquired anxiously about his own sheep and urged the collection of debts due to him. The proximity of the opposing armies was soon to cause more desperate concerns. In 1645, Abel Barker was seized and carried off to the Royalist stronghold of Belvoir Castle, Leicestershire, where he was forced to pay over to his captors rents which he had already paid to their enemy, Sir Edward Harington. Sir Edward was unsympathetic, expecting that Abel would also pay the taxes due to Parliament on his rented lands. For years, such disputes between tenant and landlord were a recurring topic in Abel Barker's letters. Rents could be confiscated, charged twice, or otherwise disrupted, during the turbulent times. Any moneys kept at home were vulnerable to plundering, and Abel wrote:

'If these times continue, landlords with us must expect little or no rent, or if any very slowly, neither do I for my own part expect to receive the one half of my rents due unto me' (HMC *Appendix to the Fifth Report*, 398).

In Rutland as in other counties, the long-standing social order, agricultural routines and economic relationships were disrupted for nearly two decades. Those leading families who supported the losing side were heavily fined and temporarily displaced, while others seized the opportunity to rise to new levels of wealth and influence, which in some cases survived the Restoration. One of these was Abel Barker. He supplemented his expanding farming and sheep-dealing interests by serving as agent and later treasurer to the Rutland County Committee.

King Charles I (1600-1649) by Sir Anthony Van Dyck (Bridgeman Art Library)

This group of local gentry, opposed to the king and headed by Sir Edward Harington, governed Rutland in the name of Parliament. Their headquarters were the magnificent mansion of Burley on the Hill, extended by the first Duke of Buckingham but largely neglected by his heir, who was living in London. The stables, grander than any in England, were occupied by the Parliamentary troopers, their horses and equipment. Regular supplies of food and fodder were required, as well as a constant replenishment of horses. These Abel Barker undertook to obtain. In the Barker archives, deposited by the Conant Family in the Record Office for Leicestershire, Leicester & Rutland, a large collection of receipts provides evidence of his tireless and no doubt profitable activities. As well as supplying large quantities of oats, horses and other commodities to Burley and the nearby garrison at Rockingham Castle, in 1644 Abel Barker 'lent upon the public faith' money and goods to the sum of £208 10s. Perhaps equally reluctantly, he was required to assist in the provision of 'quarter' (accommodation) for Parliamentarian troops, including those billeted at his own house and that of his landlord, Sir Edward Harington. He dealt with the complaints of householders such as Katherine Walcott of Uppingham, 'burdened with a soldier to whose maintenance I am weekly to pay half-a-crown, which far passeth my ability . . .' (ROLLR DE 730/1/30).

In 1645 Abel Barker's name was added to the Rutland County Committee, and in 1647 his devotion to Parliament's cause was rewarded by his election as High Sheriff of Rutland. Abel Barker was now a local figure of status and authority.

A New Bride at Hambleton

As his status and prospects steadily improved, Abel Barker made a significant improvement in his financial position. His ambitious mother negotiated her son's marriage with Anne Burton, daughter of a Royalist family of Stockerston, Leicestershire, who brought with her a dowry of £1,500 and lands in Lincolnshire. It seems to have been a marriage of affection as well as convenience, as Abel wrote in a letter to his intended:

'That you may not judge me oblivious of our forepassed amity, I have presumed to break the ice, in confidence that you will not disdain to wade after, and impart your present condition of your affairs. For change of place cannot alter the mind of yours you know who and how' (ROLLR DE 730/4/43).

For his new bride, Abel ordered a wooden clothes-press or cupboard to be built into the wall of the Old Hall's principal bedchamber, carved with '1646', the date of their marriage. Tragically, the marriage lasted less than two years. Anne died giving birth to Thomas, a much desired heir. Her clothes-press, with the carved wedding date, remains to this day.

Seventeenth-century gentlewoman by Wenceslaus Holler, 1640 (ROLLR DE 730/9)

Right: A wooden cupboard which was built into the wall of the main bedchamber at Hambleton Old Hall, carved with the date of Abel Barker's marriage to Anne Burton (SH)

Anne Barker's correspondence during her brief married life at Hambleton highlights many fascinating aspects of country life. Her sister in London was requested to buy and send to her by carrier, 'bone lace and satin for a gown and kirtle, and a laced handkerchief and cuffs made and starched, and a love hood'. Anne enquired of a relation in Oakham about the character of a possible maidservant: 'Send me word whether you think Mrs Ross's daughter of Edith Weston will be a fit chambermaid for me. I must put her to wash clothes'. For Twelfth Night, Anne sent her sister a traditional 'country cake', with sticks marking the pea and bean contained within, the finders of which would play King and Queen for the day. Yet in the same year, more serious concerns were caused by the upheaval of civil war:

'We . . . lived in daily expectation of troopers whom we have had already quartering with us almost these three weeks, and my maid having the green sickness and gone away we could no ways leave the house in safety . . .' (ROLLR DE 730/4).

Abel Barker's own correspondence identifies these troopers, billeted with their horses at the Old Hall, as Cornet William Ranze and Corporal William Petty in the regiment of Sir Robert Pye.

A letter written by Anne Barker to her cousin Henry Herne in 1646 (ROLLR DE 730/1)

Noble Cosen

I am sory that I coulde not see you at my weddinge for truely I wrote for you although I did not then know the certaine day, I chose rather to have had you lost your labour then to have wanted your sweete company. but now my suite is that you would be plesed to come to Hambleton and solemnize my weddinge there, pray doe me the favour to present my humble duty to my Lord Cobham & my Lady, and my service to your sisters when you see them, hopeing you will be pleased to honour with your presence in Rutlande

mr Barker presents his service unto you.

yor humble servant & kinswoman

Anne Barker.

— 157 —

The address on Anne Barker's letter to her cousin (ROLLR DE 730/1)

Hambleton, shown as 'Hamleyton', on John Speed's 1610 map of Rutland (private collection)

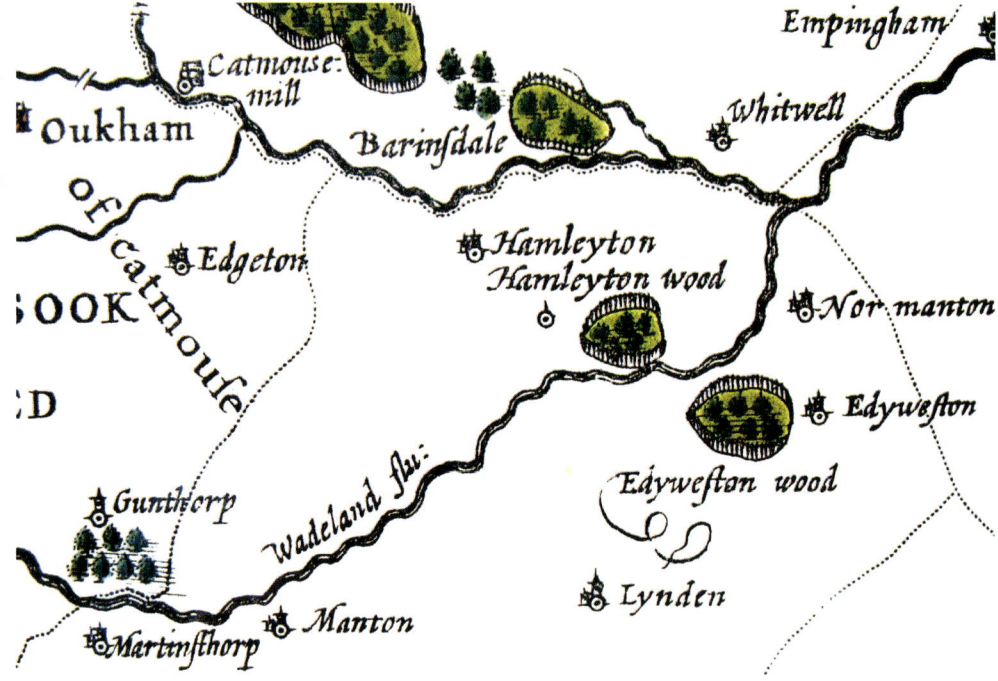

Changing Masters

The civil war brought dramatic changes in ownership to the parish of Hambleton. The Haringtons had sold it to George Villiers, first Duke of Buckingham, together with the manor and great house of Burley on the Hill. But following the assassination of the high and mighty duke, his young heir rarely visited Rutland, and his estates were confiscated by Parliament for his support of King Charles. The Parliamentarian commander who bought the sequestered manor of Hambleton, with its 2,244 acres, was Colonel Thomas Waite, a far more grasping local landlord. War had brought new opportunities to rise through the ranks, and Waite was now in a position to exert ruthless authority over his social superiors, subordinates and enemies. Elected to Parliament in 1646, Waite gained immortal infamy as a regicide when in 1649 he signed the death warrant of King Charles I

Thomas Waite who was quick to purchase this most desirable of sequestered estates took action to maximise his income. He persuaded the Hambleton tenants to support his purchase by promising to protect their interests. Yet once in possession, he ordered enclosure of the medieval open fields, pastures and springs. Rents were doubled and brooks diverted, so that villagers were cut off from water, and they could not reap corn without additional payment of ten shillings an acre. In desperation, they appealed directly to Oliver Cromwell, now Lord Protector:

'Through the oppression of Colonel Thomas Waite, by enclosing the town, and taking away the best of our lands . . . we were obliged, at great expense, to come up to town and petition the late Council of State . . . Colonel Waite offered an agreement which for peace's sake we accepted. But Parliament dissolving, he refuses to make it good, intending to prevent us by poverty from helping ourselves, so that we shall be ruined and the town depopulated' (*Calendar of State Papers Domestic*, 1653-4, 27).

Armley Wood and the northern arm of the Gwash Valley in 1972 (looking west), showing enclosed fields of Hambleton parish (Jim Eaton)

While Colonel Waite outraged Hambleton villagers by depriving them of their common rights, the ever-pragmatic Abel Barker corresponded regularly with his landlord, offering support and information. He was party to an agreement made in 1653 between Waite and his fellow landlords, John Poole of Hambleton, Richard Spell of Exton and George Andrews of Egleton, 'to inclose the open and common fields of Hambleton'. This involved transferring leases between the parties to allow the enclosure to take place, following which:

'The said John Poole and Richard Spell release unto the said Abell Barker all lands, meadows, pastures, etc., contained within the plots set out for the said Abell Barker, all of which the said Abell Barker stands seised by virtue of a lease made 1st April 1653' (ROLLR DG/11/672-678). A fine map, drawn up by Richard Daynes, confirmed Abel Barker's new landholdings at this time.

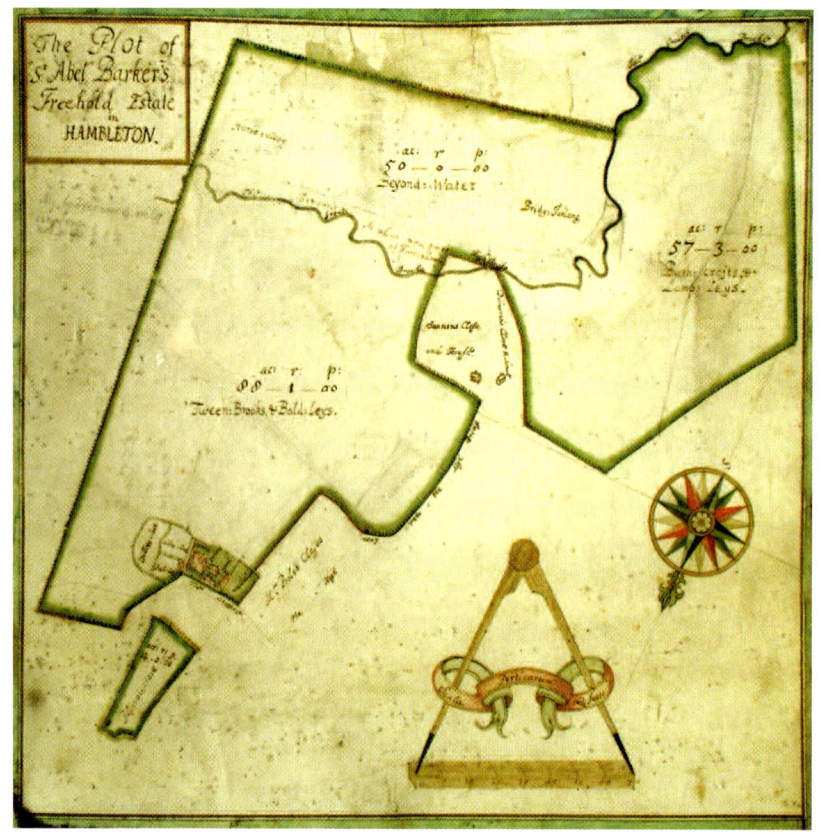

Abel Barker's landholdings following Enclosure of Hambleton 1653 (Edward Conant)

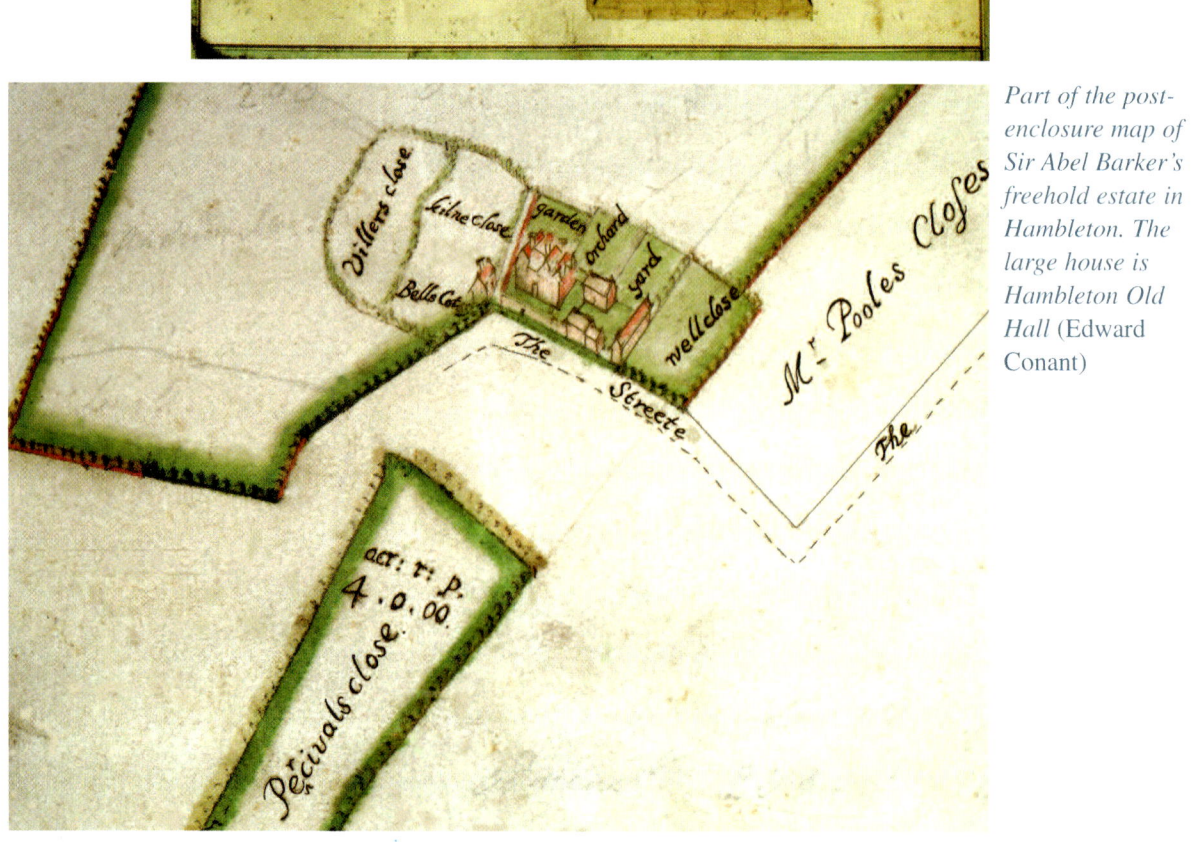

Part of the post-enclosure map of Sir Abel Barker's freehold estate in Hambleton. The large house is Hambleton Old Hall (Edward Conant)

Unlike Colonel Waite, Abel Barker never bore arms against the king, though sympathetic to Parliament's cause. Playing a safer, long-term game, he continued to serve Parliament's interests while expanding his lucrative sheep-dealing business. From the Old Hall at Hambleton he maintained a regular and wide-ranging correspondence with friends, relatives and business contacts, all carefully copied into his still surviving Letter Book. In November 1648, as plans were being laid for the king's trial in London, Abel Barker wrote that he was sending 350 tods of wool to weavers at Coggeshall, Essex. Each tod, or bundle, weighing around 28 pounds, was worth 29 shillings, and contained between seven and eight fleeces.

Rising Fortunes

As England adjusted to republican government and regional administration by Major-Generals, Abel Barker saw the steady increase of his wealth and local influence. Still an eligible widower, he looked for a second wife who would care for his growing son and perhaps bring influential connections. His successful choice fell on Mary, daughter of Alexander Noel of Whitwell. They were married at Ketton in a civil ceremony before Evers Armyn, Justice of the Peace.

By 1656 Abel Barker had achieved sufficient status to be elected as Member of Parliament for Rutland (*Journal of the House of Commons*, 19th September 1656). However, the Commonwealth which he had served so diligently could not survive the death of Oliver Cromwell. As competing republican interests struggled to fill the vacuum, General Monck moved decisively to recall the Stuart dynasty. Once again, Abel astutely seized a golden opportunity to secure his own interests. He was instrumental in arranging a monetary gift and declaration of loyalty by the gentlemen of Rutland to the new king, Charles II. The Royalist relations which his second marriage had brought to Abel Barker were to prove a sufficient counterweight to his record in supporting Parliament against the king, albeit as a non-combatant. His wife's uncle, Sir Geoffrey Palmer, was shortly appointed as Attorney General to the new king, a connection which can only have enhanced his prospects.

Pardoned by Charles II's Act of Oblivion for his support of the wrong side in the Civil War, Abel Barker saw his steady advancement continue under the new government. His undoubted talents

King Charles II, restored to the throne of England in 1660 (Wikipedia)

were employed as Deputy Lieutenant, Justice of the Peace and one of the Commissioners responsible for levying taxation, such as the 1665 Hearth Tax. The returns kept by his brother-in-law, Andrew Noel, show that in that year Abel Barker's property, the Old Hall, was the largest in Hambleton, with ten hearths. His widowed mother, Elizabeth, lived close by in a substantial house of five hearths. In the same year his brother, Thomas Barker, was recorded as having an even larger house of twelve hearths at Lyndon. It was in this neighbouring parish that the Barker brothers would both shortly begin building a grand new house.

In the early years of the Restoration, Abel Barker was frequently absent in London, sending regular letters by carrier to his anxious and fretful wife at Hambleton. As with her predecessor, Mary sent frequent requests of clothes and commodities, such as 'sherry of amber' or 'a satin mantle for my child to christen it in'.

One of Mary Barker's Letters to her Husband

'1673. June
My Dearest Heart,
I was in a greate perplexity when the carrer came, and had noe letter for me, I shall not bee well a gane this day or tow., I have resaied your letter from Mr Greane haws an nower after the carrerboy was come., truly I amin so great a disord I can hardly rite., I am sory you cannot com downe so soune as you intended., your bulding goos not on in the lest., for it is the sadist wether that ever was knone of man for this time of the yeare., the carpenders have doune what the can dow with in Dores, Mr Storges tels me, and all the masons was constraned to goo a wa, Sutons stayed the longest, but John sayed the deed more hort than good., heare hath bene such a flued in twine brookes as was never sene be fore., all your meadowes are flotten every wheare., I desire to know if Mr Hudson be found, for I am in great want of a goune, and would have those things I sent for all best, if posabell., all your corne is tharesed out, and the ould all sorte, I would know if you would sell any of that it ris is very much, it was seven grates a strik of fryday., thare is a grate many pepell desire to by, but I tell them I can not let them have it so with out your order., John wased but halfe his sheepe,. the rane beat them out, he mus was them a gane he sath, the weather is so un sertan hee can dow nothing to wasing your sheepe yet., one Thursday last John Bell coled at brake a day for same and tow or three more, to help him to get out all his cattell to save them from drouning, all the dikes meat., pray god send you a good Jorney doune, you will find durt innofe., the children present you with ther duty, by deare heart

thy truly loveing
Wife M Barker

Hambleton
22 Jun: 73'
(ROLLR DE 730/1)

It was apparent that Abel Barker was easily irritated by his wife, who expressed her fear of a chiding if she urged Abel to return from London before completing his business. In an undated letter, she confesses, 'I would be loth to have you angry at your return, as you was at your departure . . . Let us know if Lamples [fields named Upper and Nether Lampleys] are to be ploughed in your absence'. Mary was constantly anxious about the farm, for which she was often left responsible. In June 1673 she described a flood in Tween Brooks as had never been seen before. All the meadows were flooded, and the price of corn rose rapidly to seven groats a strike (2s 4d per bundle), so that Mary requested her husband's permission to sell in his absence (ROLLR DE 730/1).

Abel Barker's post-enclosure estate with field names and adjacent landholdings added to the OS 2nd ed 25" map 1904

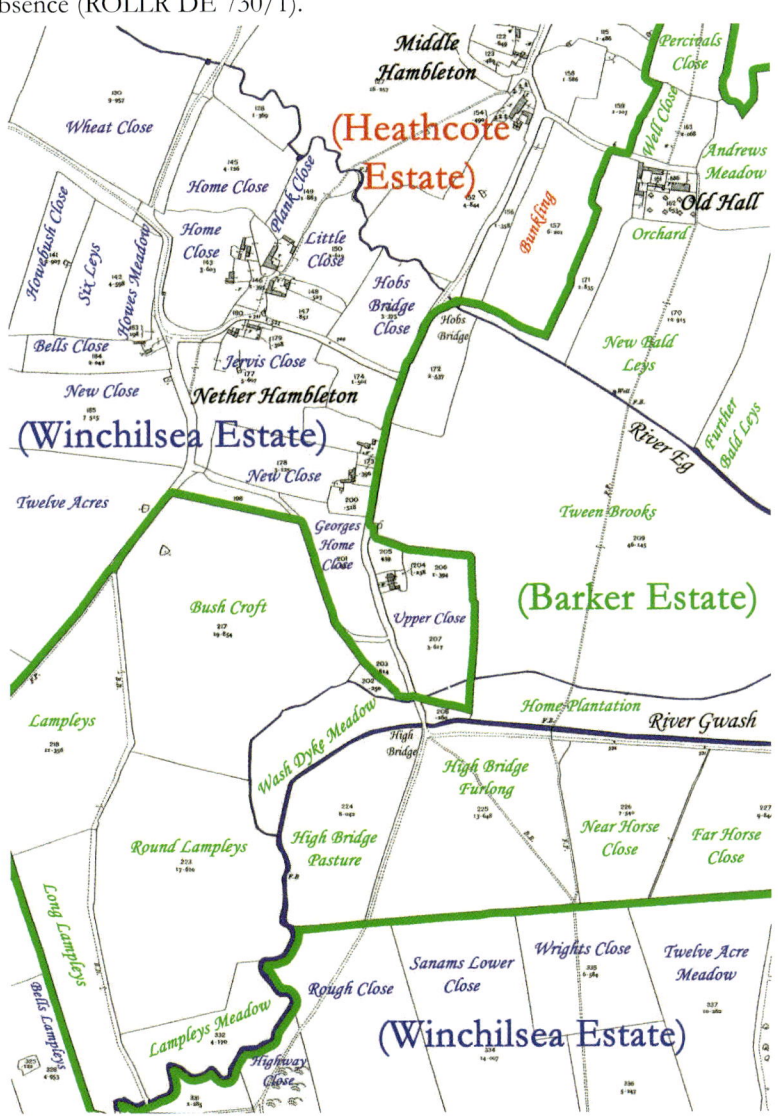

The enclosure of Hambleton's open fields, imposed on the reluctant tenants by the forceful Thomas Waite in 1652, continued to cause hardship and discontent. When the manor was returned to the Duke of Buckingham following the Restoration of King Charles II in 1660, the enclosures were confirmed by a deed of 1662. This described the Manor of Hambleton as comprising: '30 messuages, 30 cottages, a windmill, 60 gardens, 60 orchards, 800 acres of land, 200 acres of meadow, 1,000 acres of pasture, 100 acres of wood and 30 acres of furze and heath'. Disputes continued, however, until an Act of Parliament ratifying the enclosure was passed in 1692. This brought Hambleton the distinction of having one of the earliest Parliamentary Enclosures in England, few others taking place before the mid-eighteenth century.

The New Estate

In 1661, with his fortunes and prospects assured, Abel Barker felt sufficiently confident to negotiate with his brother, Thomas, to purchase the nearby estate of Lyndon from Hugh Audley. The purchase price was £9,400, of which Abel paid two thirds and Thomas one third. Mary's letters make clear that she was kept in the dark about this significant development, although she continued to assail her husband with reports from Hambleton of sickness, bad weather, and her own and her daughters' desperate need for new clothes (and dowries):

'I hear you're in a manner agreed about Lyndon, and that you're like to buy it. I wonder I should never hear anything from you of it. I much desire to know [if] it be so. Not that I shall desire anything therein for myself, but desire you to have a care of my children. You know what is best to prefer daughters. If you put all into land, I desire you will take care how they shall be provided for out of that, if God should cut off you and I before they are of age. This is all I desire. This day hath been so turbulent a wind that it hath done a great deal of hurt abroad, and us more than ever we had. All the rails are blown down in the court on both sides, and the out hovel down to the ground . . . and a great deal of hurt in the field. It is a great flood, it hath been the saddest weather for a day and a night that ever I knew in my life' (ROLLR DE 730/1).

Major events such as the Great Plague and Fire of London carry no mention in the collection of letters between Abel and Mary Barker. Nor is there reference in their surviving letters to what must have been a cause of great delight and satisfaction, when in 1665 Abel was made a baronet by King Charles II, as Sir Abel Barker. Abel and his brother had already, with the assistance of Sir Geoffrey Palmer, negotiated the purchase of the estate at Lyndon from Hugh Audley. The original gabled manor house was demolished in 1673 as Sir Abel's new house took shape.

In 1670, before his new house was built, Sir Abel Barker made his will. His body was to be buried in Hambleton Church and five pounds left to each parish for the poor of Hambleton and Lyndon. His 'dearly beloved Wife', Lady Mary, was amply provided for, while their three daughters would receive fifteen hundred pounds each on attaining the age of 21, or on their marriage. Sir Abel's brother, Thomas, was made sole executor, receiving lands in Lincolnshire as well as the profits of other Rutland properties for a term of 30 years. Meanwhile Abel's only son, Thomas, would inherit the baronetcy and the new house and estate at Lyndon (ROLLR DE 730/1/70).

As he grew to manhood, Thomas Barker shared the management of the Hambleton and Lyndon estates in his father's absence. In 1675 Lady Mary reported that, following in his father's footsteps:

'My son did sell ten sheep at nineteen shillings a piece to Ned Ward, I have given an account to you . . . I showed my son your letter of what you desired, and he said he did look to your grounds, and after the shepherds' (ROLLR DE 730/1).

In recognition of his father's importance, Thomas Barker, now aged 27, was seen as a desirable match in the marriage stakes, but Thomas Barker remained unmarried. After his death the wealth and grand house established by Sir Abel Barker passed to a cousin rather than a direct heir.

Lyndon Hall

Mindful of his enhanced status, Sir Abel Barker, Baronet, prepared to build a grand house more suited to his family's social position than their relatively humbler farmhouse at Hambleton. At about the same time that Abel was planning his new house at Lyndon, his brother, Thomas Barker, built Top Hall close by. Sir Abel kept detailed notes for his new mansion, still preserved at Lyndon. These show that Sir Abel had read intensively about architecture before planning his new house, particularly the newly translated, fashionable Palladio. By 1668 his ideas had been shown to his architect, John Sturges, whose work included contributions to Chatsworth (Derbyshire) and Belton House (Lincolnshire). Sturges was paid 30 shillings for advice by Sir Abel in 1672, and oversaw building work, as Mary Barker reported on 22nd June 1673:

'Your building goes not on in the least, for it is the saddest weather that ever was known to man for this time of the year. The carpenters have done what they can do within doors, Mr Sturgess tells me, and all the masons was constrained to go away. Suttons stayed the longest, but John said they did more hurt than good' (ROLLR DE 730/1).

'John' was Sir Abel's bailiff, John Musson, while John Sutton was the Stamford (Lincolnshire) builder contracted by Sir Abel to build some of the walls and all the chimneys of Lyndon. By 1674 the interior was begun and by 1677 the house was complete, having cost £1,690, excluding the internal painting.

The south front of Lyndon Hall in 1905, showing the original entrance (Hart)

Top Hall, Lyndon in 1910. It was built by Thomas Barker, Sir Abel Barker's son (Hart)

Sadly, Sir Abel Barker was only able to enjoy his elegant new home for two years. He and Philip Sherard were elected to Parliament as Rutland's two Knights of the Shire in 1678, but the following year Sir Abel died, leaving his son Thomas to inherit the baronetcy and Sir Thomas Mackworth to replace him as Member of Parliament. The inventory of Lyndon Hall, taken by Tobias Hippisley and his son after Sir Abel's death, listed 'Goods, chattels and Credits' worth £3,110 15s 2d. Fittingly for a man who made much of his fortune through sheep, Sir Abel Barker was buried in a woollen shroud, according to the law passed the previous year to protect England's wool industry.

Portrait of Sir Thomas Barker, 2nd Baronet (Sir John Conant)

Sir Abel Barker's son, Thomas, inherited his estate and baronetcy. However, after Sir Thomas Barker's death without direct heirs, Lyndon and Hambleton passed through the family of Sir Abel's cousin to Samuel Barker of South Luffenham. It was his son, another Thomas Barker, who compiled the celebrated *Weather Journals of a Rutland Squire*. By 1846 this branch of the Barker family had also died out and the estate passed to a nephew by marriage, Mr E N Conant. To this day the Conant family owns and farms the Lyndon estate, and still owns the Old Hall at Hambleton. Meanwhile the Manor of Hambleton, linked in ownership with Burley, was purchased by Daniel Finch, second Earl of Winchilsea. Hambleton's public house, the Finch's Arms, bears testimony to that family which remained in possession until the mid-twentieth century.

Left: Thomasina and Elizabeth Barker, twin daughters of Sir Abel Barker (Edward Conant)

Below: The Finch's Arms public house at Hambleton circa 1972 (Brian Hollingshead)

The Palmers of Hambleton

When Sir Abel Barker moved out of the Old Hall, Hambleton, to live in his grand new house at Lyndon, his former home no longer had a resident owner. It remained part of the Lyndon Estate, to be occupied by tenants for the next three and a quarter centuries. One such, in 1727, was Robert Ridlington of Edith Weston, who was to allow free liberty to Samuel Barker and his Lyndon tenants, 'for the time being to wash their sheep in the sheep-wash near the Bridge in Hambleton' (ROLLR DG/11/887). In 1735 Samuel Barker leased to Daniel Adcock, grazier, 'the capital messuage in Hambleton called the Hall House' with 133 acres which included Andrews Close, Well Close and Tween Brooks (ROLLR DG/11/895). However, by 1760, the Hall provided a home for Thomas Barker's three unmarried sisters, Sarah, Elizabeth and Anne Barker, provided as security for their loans to him of £1,200 each (ROLLR DG/11/910).

From the last quarter of the eighteenth century, one family leased the 'Hall House' and its associated fields, remaining in occupation for more than a century. These tenants were members of the Palmer family, whose papers survive in the ownership of a descendant now living in Essex. The collection contains no maps or photographs. However, the apparent dreariness of dozens of farm accounts is relieved by a pencil sketch of the Old Hall, unsigned and undated – evidence that at least one of the family felt a close affection for the Jacobean farmhouse.

The first surviving records of the Palmer family date from the time when Samuel Barker, the Hebrew scholar who inherited Sir Abel Barker's estate, was living at Lyndon Hall. Among the villagers of Lyndon were John Palmer (1700-72) and his wife, Elizabeth, with two infant sons. The earliest document suggests that John Palmer was involved in brewing as on 25th October 1749 he paid 12s 5d for the excise duty on three quarters of malt. Surprisingly, the collector of this tax must have been illiterate, since John Dimbleby acknowledged receipt only by making his mark. Two further receipts indicate that between 1753 and 1758 John Palmer was renting 'three nooks in peacks midow [three corner plots in Peak's Meadow]', from Abraham Sapcote, for the sum of 3s 6d per year, due each Lady Day [25th March].

A pencil sketch of Hambleton Old Hall in the Palmer family papers (Janet Lavender)

Thomas Barker of Lyndon Hall

The Palmer records become more detailed after 1759 when Thomas Barker, the naturalist, author and vegetarian, succeeded to the Lyndon estate. He had already begun to keep his now famous *Weather Journals*, which span a period of over 60 years. The new landlord seems to have been a most energetic and enquiring individual. Married in 1751 to Anne, sister of Gilbert White of Selborne (Hampshire), Thomas Barker was regarded as 'naturally prone [to] extreme Abstractedness and Speculativeness' (Kington 1988, 10).

As well as managing his estate, serving as Deputy Lieutenant of Rutland and Governor of the Oakham and Uppingham Schools, Thomas Barker found time throughout his life to record every aspect of the changing weather and natural phenomena. His detailed observations cast light on the farming environment on his new estate in 1759:

'Those who sow'd turneps early this year had great crops, but what were sown after midsummer lay dry in the ground till August, came up well then, but had not time to grow large. Harvest was I think hardly ever more plentiful than this year of almost all sorts, good in its kind and most of it well got yet some of the Barley was caught out in the rain towards the end of August. Wheat was about 3 Shillings, Barley scarce 2. Pease from 2 to 2s. 6d. and Oats about 16d a strike' (Kington 1988, 72). A strike was a measure of corn, normally equal to one bushel, weighing about 60 pounds.

William Whiston 1667-1752 (Edward Conant)

William Whiston, Thomas Barker and *Weather Journals*

With recent interest in global warming, the *Weather Journals* of the Squire of Lyndon, Thomas Barker (1722-1809), have proved a valuable record of past climate patterns. Thomas' grandfather was William Whiston who studied Mathematics at Cambridge before becoming a Church of England minister in Norfolk. In his *New Theory of the Earth* (1696) he expounded the view that Noah's flood was caused by a comet.

William later resigned his parish to become Sir Isaac Newton's deputy at Cambridge, succeeding him as Lucasian Professor of Mathematics. However, his unconventional religious views led to his expulsion from the university in 1710. For many years he attempted to solve the problem of longitude; he predicted that the world would end in 1736, and he also became a Baptist. William Whiston's later years were spent at Lyndon Hall, the home of his daughter, Sarah Barker and her family, where he died in 1752.

Sarah married Samuel Barker in 1715 and their first son, Thomas Barker, was born in 1722.

Influenced by his brother-in-law, Gilbert White of Selborne, Hampshire, Thomas kept meticulous notes of weather and seasonal changes over a continuous period of more than sixty years. These included the 'Great Frost' of 1739-40, the year when a 'Frost Fair' was held on the frozen River Thames. At the time, these records were recognised as being so important that from 1771 onwards they were published every year in the *Philosophical Transactions* of the Royal Society.

Right: Lyndon Hall in 2006 (RO)

Below: The agreement between Thomas Barker and John Palmer (Janet Lavender)

> Mar 29th 1774
> Grounds at Hambleton
>
> | | | £ s D |
> |---|---|---|
> | House garden &c 2 acres at 25 | | 2. 10. 0 |
> | Andrews close 8 | 25 | 10. 0. 0 |
> | Ball leys 28 | 25 | 35. 0. 0 |
> | Well close 2 | 25 | 2. 10. 0 |
> | Bushcroft 20 | 25 | 25. 0. 0 |
> | Long Lampleys 20 | 15 | 15. 0. 0 |
>
> The above to be enter'd on at old Martinmas next.
>
> Round Lampleys 20 acres at 15 — 15. 0. 0
>
> this to be enter'd on at Lady day 1775   105. 0. 0
>
> I pay the Land tax & tythe, John Palmer the Parish levies. I repair the house but J. Palmer to thatch and glaze, and fetch the materials for repairs.

The new landlord kept his own accounts, and several pages of notes and receipts in Thomas Barker's neat handwriting, retained among the Palmer papers, testify to his efficient oversight of his tenants. In listing some of the enclosed fields available for rent at Hambleton, he noted that the animal pens belonging to the closes had been in bad condition for several years. He therefore specified which corner posts, gates and bars should be repaired by the tenant of each close, presumably including members of the Palmer family.

The John Palmer who had rented meadowland from Abraham Sapcote had two sons: the elder, also John, was born and baptised at Lyndon in 1745, and the younger, William, four years later. At the age of 30 the elder son, also John, was married by licence to Jane Russell of Leigh Lodge, whose lack of education is shown by the fact that she signed the Lyndon parish register only with her mark.

The description of John Palmer junior as 'Grazier' indicates that he had become a successful sheep-farmer, and marriage proved an incentive for him to take on a more ambitious landholding in a neighbouring parish. While his brother, William, remained at Lyndon, John Palmer junior moved with his bride the few miles northward to Hambleton. There he entered into a formal agreement with Thomas Barker of Lyndon to become tenant of the [Old] Hall at Hambleton.

John Palmer's Tenancy

According to this agreement, John Palmer would enter into the property at Martinmas [11th November] 1774, while an additional field, Round Lampleys, was to be rented from the following Lady Day. Thomas Barker agreed to pay the Land Tax and tithes, while John Palmer was to pay the parish levies. House repairs would be the landlord's responsibility although the tenant agreed to thatch and glaze as necessary, and fetch the materials for repairs. For the Old Hall and fields at Hambleton totalling 80 acres, John Palmer's annual rent was to be £105.

Half yearly rental receipts signed by Thomas Barker (Janet Lavender)

John Palmer's accounts for his new farm were kept in a leather notebook which served him for the rest of his life. He also purchased and signed in 1784 a leather bound *Daily Journal or Gentleman's, Merchant's and Tradesman's Complete Annual Account Book for the pocket or desk*. Farming at Hambleton soon proved profitable, and John Palmer continued to expand his landholding, entering a joint tenancy with Robert Croden for Panks Ground and Meadows. The stock raised on this land was sold in November 1780 for £97 16s. His attentive landlord, Thomas Barker, continued to sign half-yearly receipts for his rents, which continued unchanged for twelve years.

In 1785, as Thomas Barker prepared to divide his estate with his son, Samuel, the farms at Hambleton were 'new arranged'. According to the new Estate List, John Palmer's holdings now included Great Wall Close, Great Wall Close Meadow and Watkin's Meadow (ROLLR DG 7/1/77). A year later, he was probably unsurprised to receive a letter from his landlord at Lyndon, raising his rental for Round Lamp Leys by a modest two pounds per year, since 'taxes are so very high, and all other things so very dear'. The rent on all the other lands remained the same.

In the fields around the Old Hall at Hambleton, sheep-rearing continued to be a lucrative business. John Palmer's sheep were normally sold by agents at Smithfield Market in London, for prices of around £1 10s per sheep.

Many receipts survive for his animals and crops sold during the 1780s and 1790s. This was a period when the population was rapidly increasing, there were several bad harvests and, towards the end of the century, fear of war following the French Revolution. While food shortages combined with high prices, many farmers prospered, although the landless poor inevitably suffered.

> Mr Palmer
>
> I have hitherto done less in raising my Rents than almost any body in the country, but taxes are so very high, and all other things so very dear, that I find it now necessary to do it, especially as I am going to divide my Estate with my Son: I shall however still be very moderate in it. The alteration I have determined to make in your rent is 17£ for Round Lamp Leys instead of 15, making 2£ increase in your rent from 105 to 107 to take place from Apr.5 next
>
> I have written a like letter to my several tenants where I have determined to make an alteration. and am
>
> Yours &
> T. Barker
>
> Lyndon June , 1786

Letter from Thomas Barker to John Palmer, his tenant at the Old Hall, Hambleton, in June 1786 (Janet Lavender)

Eighteenth Century Sheep Rearing

The eighteenth-century Agricultural Revolution saw many improvements in animal husbandry and crop cultivation, helping to increase productivity and hence profits. In neighbouring Leicestershire, Robert Bakewell experimented with sheep-breeding until he had produced the new Leicester Longwool sheep, which gave more and a better fleece. His prize rams were hired out to farmers so that they could improve their own stock. In 1786 Bakewell made 1,000 guineas from hiring twenty rams; three years later he made 1,200 guineas on just three rams. The breed was exported to far-flung colonies, and it is very likely that graziers of Rutland including John Palmer of Hambleton were affected by such developments.

Leicester Longwool sheep (Robinson Library)

A new shorn RAM of the improved LONG WOOLED BREED.

John Palmer served for around twenty years as churchwarden in Hambleton, recording the amounts 'due to me [for] Whitsunday Bread & wine'. He noted the publication in 1802 of Henry Clavering's useful new handbook, *The Complete Parish Officer, or, A Perfect Guide to Churchwardens, Overseers, Constables.* Along with his neighbour, Robert Croden, he also served as Executor for the Estate of Mrs Ward, who died in 1791, leaving him a legacy of five pounds. When the Archdeacon conducted his regular Visitation of Hambleton in 1821, it was the churchwardens, Mr Needham and Mr Palmer, who were summoned before him on Friday 1st June at St Martin's, Stamford.

Among the births and deaths listed in the Hambleton parish registers is a transcript of a valuation of the parish, dated 1792. Another copy survives among the Palmer family papers. It lists the major landowners as Lord Winchilsea of Burley on the Hill; Sir Gilbert Heathcote of Normanton; Tobias Hippisley of Hambleton and Thomas Barker of Lyndon. Among Thomas Barker's properties were listed all the fields, house and garden rented by John Palmer for the past eighteen years, totalling 94 acres. However, John and his wife had no children to inherit this prosperous tenancy – there are no entries in the parish register relating to the couple between their marriage in 1775 and John's death in 1807.

An extract from the Hambleton parish valuation of 1792 (Janet Lavender)

A Period of War

The momentous events of the 1790s, with the French Revolution leading to the rise of Napoleon, leave no mark in the *Weather Journals* of Thomas Barker nor in the account books of the Palmer family. However the repercussions of the resulting war with France reached the tranquil heart of England in 1804, when John Palmer of Lyndon, nephew of the tenant of Hambleton, was among those balloted to serve in the Additional Army, called up to defend the country from threatened invasion. As with many other gentlemen who preferred to pay for a substitute, rather than leave their property to risk life and limb, John Palmer paid Richard Case to take his place. History does not record whether Richard Case made a good bargain.

The uncertainties of war brought a steady rise in prices and profits for farmers. But the final accounts of John Palmer's life bear witness, not to profitable sales of stock, but to increased expenditure on fortifying spirits. An invoice sent by Mr Thomas Stimson shows that the farmer's regular order of one bottle of brandy per week, at six shillings per bottle, was supplemented in February and March 1807 by increasing quantities of sherry, port and wine. Then, on 16th April 1807, the Hambleton parish register records the burial of 'John Palmer, Grazier'. His heir was the nephew, who had avoided military service three years previously. A note in the parish register reads: 'John, the elder son of his brother, William Palmer of Lyndon. Now aged 33, John moved to Hambleton, where in 1816 he brought his new wife, Elizabeth Ormond of Little Bytham [Lincolnshire].' Their first son, yet another John, was born the following year, followed by a brother and two sisters. Once again a young family would grow up in the Old Hall.

John Palmer's Additional Army certificate of 1804 (Janet Lavender)

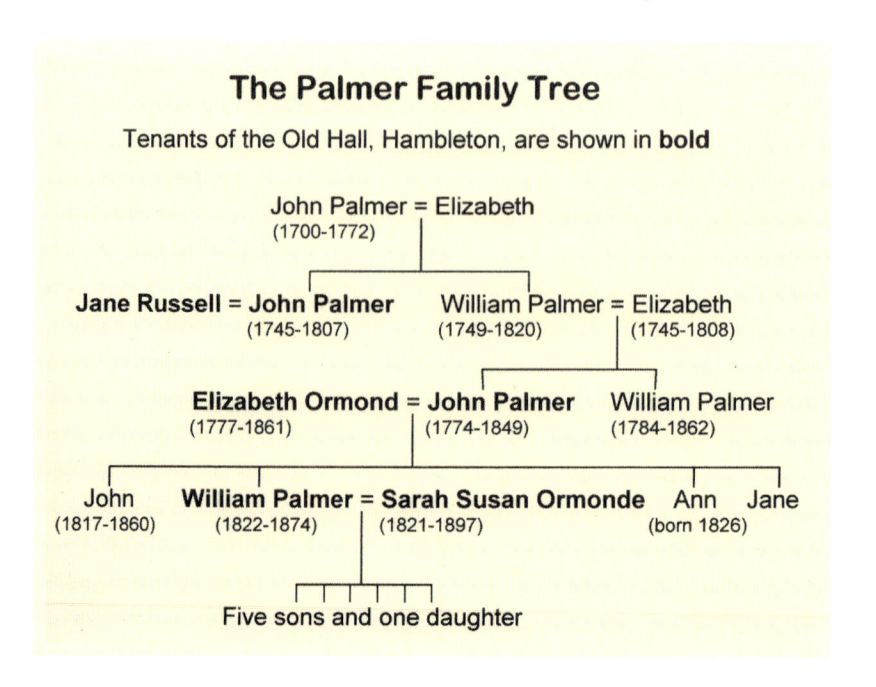

The Palmer Family Tree

Tenants of the Old Hall, Hambleton, are shown in **bold**

John Palmer = Elizabeth
(1700-1772)

Jane Russell = **John Palmer** (1745-1807)   William Palmer = Elizabeth (1749-1820) (1745-1808)

Elizabeth Ormond = **John Palmer** (1777-1861) (1774-1849)   William Palmer (1784-1862)

John (1817-1860)   **William Palmer** = **Sarah Susan Ormonde** (1822-1874) (1821-1897)   Ann (born 1826)   Jane

Five sons and one daughter

Taxation and Poverty

Shortly after the young John Palmer took up his uncle's tenancy at Hambleton, his landlord, Thomas Barker of Lyndon, compiler of the *Weather Journals*, died in 1809. He was succeeded by his son, Samuel Barker, who had already assumed responsibility for half the estate on his marriage to Mary Haggitt in 1786. Samuel Barker now moved his family from Whitwell to Lyndon Hall, taking on the management of the whole estate and collecting rents from his many tenants. After a long period of stability, these rents had seen more frequent increases – the £107 annual rent paid by the Palmers since the small increase of 1786 had risen by 1834 to £145 per annum for the same acreage. This was, as claimed by Thomas Barker, partly due to the increasing burden of taxation.

As with every rural village, Hambleton had its share of hungry, suffering poor. From 1785, Hambleton's Overseers of the Poor had been listed as having use of 'Two small Tenements upon the Waste and Two Houses in Andrew Close', with a total value of ten shillings (DG7/1/77). Spurred on by an Act of Parliament in 1819, the Churchwarden and Overseer of the Poor, Nicholas Needham, convened a meeting of Hambleton parishioners to elect a committee, or 'Select Vestry for the Concerns of the Poor', to deal with the problem. The elected group of 'substantial householders or occupiers' included John Palmer, tenant of the Old Hall. His landlord, Samuel Barker, counter-signed the election return in his role as Justice of the Peace.

A paid Overseer was empowered to provide 'outdoor relief' – food for the starving without the necessity of their going into a workhouse. While a few Rutland villages such as Exton and Empingham had their own parish workhouse, the system of poor relief became far more rigid after the Poor Law Amendment Act of 1834. From then on, Hambleton was included in the Oakham Union. The new Oakham Workhouse, still standing today, became the refuge of last resort for the destitute of all the surrounding villages.

Above: An early photograph of Sarah Susan Palmer (née Ormonde) standing at the door of her home, Hambleton Old Hall (Janet Lavender)

Right: Oakham Union Workhouse as depicted on the dial of the workhouse clock. The clock was commissioned by the Workhouse Guardians and made by Stephen Simpson of Oakham circa 1837 (RCM)

Victorian Hambleton

In 1846, the full extent of John Palmer's landholdings was once again listed when additional charges were calculated in lieu of tithes. These included 'The Old Hall, Courts, Farm building Yards Orchard and Gardens'. Out of thirteen fields, totalling over 100 acres, John Palmer kept twelve fields to grass, indicating the extent of his pasture and sheep rearing: there was a similar pattern for other tenants (DE 1381/514).

John Palmer, grazier, of Hambleton died, aged 75, in 1849. He was buried on 12th March and succeeded as tenant of the Old Hall by his son William, who died at the early age of 52, in 1874. A handwritten anonymous obituary describes William's 'manly appearance . . . long remembered by those frequenting the fairs of Oakham and Uppingham; he was very well known on account of his business abilities . . .'. An inventory of William's personal effects, signed by the solicitor John Royce of Oakham, lists personal and household goods valued at just over £343, but 'Farming Stock and Implements of Husbandry' worth £5,457 18s 4d. William's 'business abilities' had made for his family what in those days was a considerable fortune.

An Inventory and Valuation for Administration of the Personal Effects of the late Mr William Palmer of Hambleton in the County of Rutland deceased

	£	s	d
Household Goods and Furniture, Plate, Linen, China, Books, Wearing Apparel Trinkets &c	219	5	3
Wine and other Liquors	39	17	0
Horses and Carriages	84	10	0
Farming Stock and Implements of Husbandry	5,457	18	4
	5,801	10	7

Valued by us   Geo Wood, Teigh
                John Royce, Oakham

The Gwash Valley before flooding – looking towards Middle Hambleton on the road to Lyndon (Jim Levisohn ARPS)

> **Sarah Susan Ormonde's Poetic Description of the Gwash Valley**
>
> William Palmer's widow was Sarah Susan Ormonde, a relation of his mother, Elizabeth Ormonde. She lived on in the Old Hall for a quarter of a century, attending services in Hambleton Church at which she kept a note of the sermons, and copying out poetry which took her fancy. The following ditty, which she copied out on 1st July 1882, describes the view from Hambleton churchyard, long before the flooding of the Gwash Valley totally re-ordered the landscape:
>
> > 'Lo – the glorious landscape round;
> > Tread we not enchanted ground;
> > From this bold and breezy height;
> > The charm'd eye sends its magic flight
> > O'er the panoramic scene,
> > Undulating, rich and green;
> > And with varied pleasure roves
> > From hill and dale to field and groves,
> > Till the prospect mingling grey,
> > With the horizon fades away;
> > Shutting in the distant view,
> > By fainter lines of glimmering blue.'

For much of her widowhood, Sarah Susan Palmer continued to farm the rented fields around the Old Hall. She is described in the census of 1881 as 'Farmer of 360 acres employing five men and two boys'. Two of her sons had left home, but Charles and Edward, aged twenty-two and thirteen respectively, remained at home, along with their unmarried only sister, Susan. The family was served by three indoor servants, including a fourteen-year-old housemaid and her older brother. Meanwhile the eldest son, William Palmer, had moved into a nearby farm of his own at Hambleton, totalling 200 acres. Although only 24 years old he did sufficiently well to employ a housekeeper, labourer/horsekeeper, two other men and a boy.

Unlike his forebears, William Palmer did not spend the rest of his life farming in Rutland. According to his grand-daughter, Janet Lavender, he moved to London, possibly following his marriage. As the nineteenth century drew to its close, villagers of Hambleton, as elsewhere, celebrated the Diamond Jubilee of Queen Victoria in June 1897. A month later, Sarah Susan Palmer was dead, and more than a century of Palmer tenancy at the Old Hall, Hambleton, came to an end.

The New Hambleton Hall

The late nineteenth century saw increasing prosperity for the landowners of Rutland, as farms became more efficient. Fewer agricultural labourers were required, and Hambleton's population continued to decline. From 336 in 1801, it fell to 290 in 1851 and 244 in 1901 (*VCH* I, 231-2). By 1951 it had fallen still further, to 199. But 'new money' was coming into Rutland, as successful businessmen mingled with the old families of Finch, Noel, Conant and Heathcote. Rutland's many attractions, not least hunting with the Cottesmore, proved a magnet to the rich and titled.

Among those who recognised the delights of the area was Walter Gore Marshall, an unmarried brewing millionaire. His new mansion, built as a hunting lodge on the crest of Hambleton Hill in 1881, overlooked the scenic, tranquil Gwash valley. Now that the Victorian mansion was named Hambleton Hall, the Jacobean farmhouse lower down the hill, still part of the Lyndon Estate, became formally known as the Old Hall. Walter Marshall entertained lavishly in his grand new mansion, gaining a reputation for the excellence of his table and cellar and the 'raffishness' of his company. In 1884 he became High Sheriff of Rutland.

Hambleton Hall was ideally situated to meet its owner's taste for fox-hunting. The Cottesmore provided regular local meets, but not far away in Leicestershire were the equal attractions of the Quorn, Belvoir and Fernie Hunts. During the late nineteenth century, several aristocrats and business tycoons built or rented hunting lodges around Rutland and Melton Mowbray. Their elegant guests could arrive by steam train, to be safely delivered by carriage to the various house parties.

Much local life was arranged for the convenience of the hunters. One of the early benevolent acts of Mr Marshall, as the new 'Squire' of Hambleton, was to build a new village school in 1892. The new building was not on the original site in the centre of the village, but lower down the hill on the road to Middle Hambleton. His reputed reason for this magnanimous gesture was that 'the children were hindering hunting horses on their way to the Hall, and when assembling on the Green opposite the old school' (Traylen 1999, 120).

Hambleton Church and the old village school (Hart)

Evaline Astley Paston Cooper

When Walter Marshall died childless at the end of the nineteenth century, Hambleton Hall passed to his younger sister Evaline. She was married to Clement Astley Paston Cooper, a retired army officer, whose ancestor, Sir Astley Paston Cooper, was a pioneering surgeon who received a baronetcy for his successful treatment of King George IV. When the census enumerators arrived at Hambleton Hall in 1901, they found Mr and Mrs Astley Cooper in residence with their three daughters and seven indoor servants. Four grooms maintained the stables, while the family's German governess, footman and thirteen-year-old hall boy lodged with the Cole family nearby.

Following her husband's death, Mrs Astley Cooper became the centre of a fashionable circle, inviting many famous visitors to enjoy her celebrated house-parties at Hambleton. One was the Stamford-born conductor, Sir Malcolm Sargent, but probably the most glamorous was Noel Coward. First taken under her wing while still a boy, Coward quickly forgot his humble origins. The sophisticated milieu and luxurious lifestyle to which he quickly adapted provided fertile inspiration for his later comedies. Indeed, *Hay Fever* is reputed to have been written at Hambleton. Noel Coward described Mrs Astley Cooper in his autobiography, *Present Indicative* (1937): 'Mrs Cooper was gay company. Her principal pleasure was to lie flat on her back upon a mattress in front of the fire and shoot off witticisms in a sort of petulant wail'.

Hambleton Hall in 2006 (RO)

Mrs Astley Cooper's Hambleton Estate included Home Farm, which was rented out to the Wild family. Miss Joan Wild still recalls how, as a child, she was allowed to borrow, groom and ride a little Shetland pony belonging to Mrs Astley Cooper. She described the excitement of watching the hunt, which met at Hambleton once or twice a year. On one occasion, as a small child, she accidentally became caught up with the riders. Her little pony was swept along, trotting half-way down the hill with the hunters before coming to a halt in the farmyard, to her great relief.

Enjoying her role as 'Lady of the Village', Mrs Astley Cooper was a generous benefactor to the village children. She donated yards of red material to make winter cloaks, which became a colourful school uniform for the girls. Every two years, they were summoned to Hambleton Hall to be given cakes and milk in the nursery, before being presented with their cloaks by Mrs Astley Cooper in the drawing room (Traylen, *Rutland Villages*). Dorothy Westland, a contributor to *Rutland Voices* (Spelman, 2000), described how 'Mrs Cooper used to ride through the village in her carriage. The men were expected to doff their caps and the girls to curtsey. If they didn't then they were unlikely to get their bag of coal at Christmas!'

Village Life

Several older residents of Hambleton today remember the traditional highlights of the 1920s and 1930s, such as May Day. Joan Wild described how the May Queen was chosen, 'usually one of the pretty ones', while Joan served as groom, leading an old horse-drawn brougham from the Hall. The children got up early to gather flowers, decorate the vehicle and make garlands. The procession set out from the school or village green to go round all the houses. When they reached Hambleton Hall, Mrs Astley Cooper sniffed disapprovingly when they once made the mistake of using Arum lilies. People came out to admire the procession, and contributed pennies which went towards the annual village outing. This took the form of an annual coach trip to Skegness or Hunstanton, with food provided by Mrs Astley Cooper, packed up in biscuit tins.

May Day procession at Upper Hambleton in 1933 (Joan Wild)

Joan Wild with the May Day procession outside Ivydene farmhouse at Lower Hambleton in 1933 (Joan Wild)

Hambleton's school teacher from 1926 until 1935 was Miss Dolce Ellingworth, teaching between twenty and thirty pupils up to fourteen years old in one large room, with the infants taught by an assistant teacher in the smaller room. The fire needed regular stoking, but at times it was so cold that the ink froze in the ink pots! Miss Ellingworth recalled the importance of discipline and concentration: 'When you told the children to do a thing, they did it!' (Buxton & Martin 2001, 31).

There was no excuse for the children to be late to school. In 1898 Mr Marshall had provided the village with an impressive Post Office, complete with 'art nouveau' clock, similar in style to the clock and sundial he had installed at Hambleton Hall. For nearly 70 years the clock was wound weekly by George Bushell, whose wife received the British Empire Medal for fifty years' service as Postmistress, beginning in 1932 (Ovens & Sleath 2002, 200).

The pupils of Hambleton School with their teacher, Dolce Ellingworth, in 1935 (May Wheatley)

The Village Community

In the first half of the twentieth century, Hambleton, like so many rural villages, was able to call on the skills of many of its residents. According to the census of 1901, there were three dressmakers, two carpenters, a milliner, baker, mason and laundress. A blacksmith from Manton, Mr Tyler, visited Hambleton on two afternoons a week. Although at this time there was no village shop, many requirements could no doubt be obtained from the 'Higgler Hawk', presumably a pedlar prepared to haggle! The main occupation of the village was farming, with four farmers, ten graziers, eleven agricultural labourers, and other farm workers such as bailiff, shepherd and farm horseman.

Several of the graziers listed in 1901 probably had shares in the Hambleton cow pasture, lush meadows in the Gwash Valley. In the same year, it was described by Sir Henry Rider Haggard:

'The Hambleton cow pasture, which is 102 acres in extent, [is] divided into eighty cow-commons. Some holders occupy two or more small fields, but the general system has been for the tenants to graze large fields in common, and to have separate small fields reserved for mowing hay for the winter. In the fields which are grazed in common five roods [one and a quarter acres] have been taken as being sufficient to keep a cow' (Rider Haggard 1902, 260).

Top: Upper Hambleton Post Office, built in 1898 by Walter Gore Marshall (RO)

Above: The 'art nouveau' clock at Upper Hambleton Post Office (RO)

Hambleton Cow Pastures were to the north of Nether Hambleton (RO)

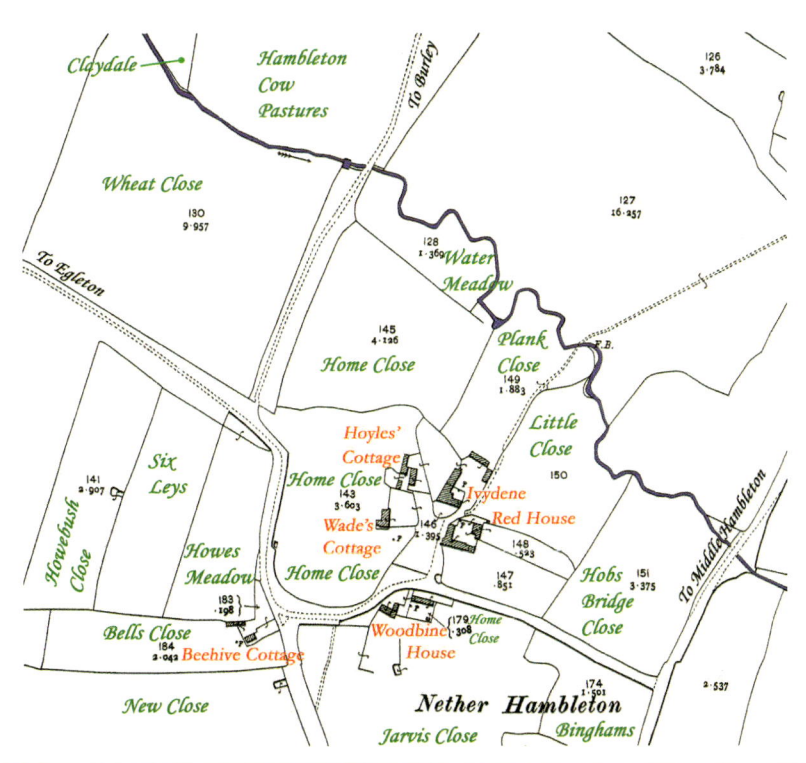

The Residents of Hambleton in 1938

Arnold, G
Bayliss, Miss M
Blackwell, Miss A
Bushell, G
Chamberlain, H C, grazier
Chappell, F
Charity, T E, labourer
Clark, H, grazier
Clements, W D, 'Finch's Arms'
Cooper, Mrs Astley, The Hall
Fowler, S B S, Crazy Cottage
Gregory, A
Gregory, J A, grazier
Halliday, W, grazier
Harvey, Mrs
Hibbitt, Mrs
Ireland, D W, wheelwright
Ireland, J A, grazier
Jenkins, Mrs
Jenkins, R, chauffeur
Johnson, H, keeper
Ludgrove, Mrs
Marriott, H
Mason, the Misses

Meadows, W
Noble, Mrs, shopkeeper
Orr-Ewing, Major, Hambleton Manor
Parker, J R & A, graziers
Parker, Miss A, Post Office
Parker, Miss M
Preston, J, gardener
Preston, C, gardener
Robinson, Mrs
Servante, Rev F A, The Vicarage
Sharp, T, farmer & grazier
Sharpe, T, Lodge Farm
Skellett, C H, gamekeeper, Burley Fishponds
Smith, A A, grazier
Taylor, H, waggoner
Tryon, Miss M, The Old Hall
Tween, W R, chauffeur
Wade, H, Lower Hambleton
Wakerley, G B, Grazier
Wild, A E, The Farm
Williamson, J T, grazier

(*Matkin's Oakham Almanack*, 1938)

Killing the Pig

Rural self-sufficiency in Hambleton, as elsewhere, included the centuries-old tradition of pig killing. Joan Wild described how most households would keep a pig, to be killed before Christmas by the local butcher. This annual ritual took place in the yard, after which the carcass was put in a long pig trough and scalded to remove the hair. Then began a busy time for the housewife. Joints of ham were cut up, rubbed with salt and soaked in the trough, before being hung from ceiling hooks until ready to be boiled or fried. A more immediate task was making pork pies and sausages, with sweetbreads and other remains being enjoyed as 'fries' for breakfast. In the absence of freezers, anything which could not be eaten or preserved by the family was passed on to relatives and neighbours, who would reciprocate when their own pig was killed. Similar exchanges took place with farm produce such as butter, cream, eggs and fruit.

Joan Wild's mother feeding the hens in the farmyard at Home Farm, Upper Hambleton, in 1932. Fresh 'free-range' eggs were then an important part of the near self-sufficient diet (Joan Wild)

Miss Tryon of the Old Hall

While the new Hambleton Hall at the top of the hill attracted well-heeled guests from London and beyond, down in Middle Hambleton, life at Old Hall Farm continued much as it had for the previous three centuries. Still owned by the Conant family of Lyndon Hall, it provided an attractive home for family members or other tenants. In 1910 it was let to an intrepid farmer, Miss Maud Tryon. Her cousin, Eva Mildred Tryon, of Bulwick Park, Northamptonshire, had in 1898 married Ernest William Proby Conant, High Sheriff of Rutland in 1907, and father of the first baronet. This marriage led to the eventual ownership of the Bulwick Estate by the Conants of Lyndon Hall.

Maud's father, Richard, was a younger son of the Tryons of Bulwick, and had moved in around 1874-75 from Loddington, Northamptonshire, to set up home with his growing family at The Lodge, Burley Road, Oakham. According to the 1881 Census, he was serving as Sheriff [of Rutland], while the 1901 Census identifies him as Justice of the Peace.

Among the Tryon family listed as residents of Oakham in 1901 were Richard and his wife Jane, five children (the youngest aged 22) and six female servants. Two of their sons, Captain Henry Tryon and Captain Richard Tryon, were later killed in the Great War. One daughter, Jane Matilda Tryon, born at Loddington in 1873, was generally known as Maud. A keen botanist, Miss Tryon found time in 1912 to help with the *Cambridge County Geographies – Rutland* by George Phillips. In the preface, the author expressed his thanks to 'Miss Tryon of Hambleton for botanical notes'. She was also an artist, having prepared 'reductions and copies of the original plans of the house' for *The History of Burley on the Hill* by Pearl Finch in 1901. Six years later she contributed two drawings of birds for Haines' *Notes on the Birds of Rutland*.

Compared with the ladylike Mrs Astley Cooper in the new Hall, Miss Tryon demonstrated a very different personality, particularly to the children visiting her home for Carol Singing or May Day. When the May Queen's procession reached the Old Hall one year, they had to traipse across the fields looking for Miss Tryon. When found, she demanded that the children sang 'The Farmer's Boy' for her, but was sufficiently approving to reward them with ten shillings towards their summer outing (Traylen 1999, 121).

Kemmel Freestone in 2005 (RO)

One of her farm workers in the 1930s was fourteen-year old Kemmel Freestone, who lived at Beehive Cottage with his mother and step-father, also employed at the Old Hall. Seventy years, later Kemmel recalled vivid memories of his employer:

'[I helped] Maud in general duties until the milkman left, then she said, "Would you like to take the cows over?" That was 44 cows and a machine and I said, "Yes". She said, "It'll mean starting early." I said, "What do you call early?" She said, "You'll start at half past four in the morning."'

When the cows had been washed down, Miss Tryon brought out a big mug of cocoa and a ham sandwich for Kemmel's breakfast. Then followed milking, after which the milk was put through the cooler into the churns, and lugged to a table to await collection by lorry, which would take the milk to Oakham Station. After calling home to Beehive Cottage for another breakfast, Kemmel had to clean out the milking parlour, or 'Nettas'. Then there were

The south front and garden of Hambleton Old Hall in 1930 (Country Life Picture Library)

calves and cows to be fed, and when all this was done: 'Maud used to say, "Come on Kemmel, we're going to mow the lawn". . . I used to pull, she used to push . . . and there was some lawn!'

Always a 'hands-on' farmer, Miss Tryon would say to Kemmel, 'We'll go to that field and haymake'. Kemmel recalled, 'We used to have this horse with the sweeper and sweep the hay into a heap and it used to be tossed and everything was shook up'. She was very methodical, making sure the hay had been well tossed and dry before being put into the stack. Water for the farm was provided by a wind pump, which was still in use until 1949. Miss Tryon checked this regularly, sending Kemmel to climb up the windmill if the blades needed oiling. His many regular jobs included 'helping the good lady' sweeping up the yard, or anything else that was required. There were two horses for farm duties, but Miss Tryon also had a van, 'an old pickup . . . a shackled old thing', in which her farm workers might be driven to their duties.

In 1930 Miss Tryon took a break from her farming duties to entertain Arthur Oswald, of *Country Life*. He was preparing an article on the Old Hall which appeared on 27th September that year, describing 'the care spent on the garden and the taste with which the house has been furnished' (*Country Life,* 27th September 1930). However, Maud seems to have been far more at home working the land rather than sitting at ease in her house or garden. Despite employing a foreman (Mr J T Wass from 1936), she would take decisions and deal with most of the problems herself. Most of the fields were kept to grass for sheep farming as they had been for centuries.

Wartime Hambleton

The Second World War changed lives for ever, and had a significant impact even on agricultural communities such as Hambleton. Farmers were ordered to plough up every possible acre of previously uncultivated grazing land, to produce grain and vegetables for the nation's needs. The Women's Land Army was recruited to work on farms in place of the young men now fighting for their country. In Rutland, Land Girls were issued with uniforms by Miss Brocklebank of Wing Grange, and paid one shilling per hour for a 48-hour week. A contingent of 60 to 70 was billeted at the Hambleton Hall Stables and travelled to various farms by bicycle. On the larger farms, girls were able to live in. For one, Dorothy Bailey, her new farming life at Home Farm brought romance, and she married Noel Sharp of Lower Hambleton.

In addition to the Land Girls, some farmers had German and, later Italian, prisoners of war to work on the farms. These would be transported from the prison camps at Ashwell or Normanton. Joan Wild recalled how the foreigners were treated:

'I think we were sensible enough to realise that they were people who didn't really wish to go to war. My mother used to do big sort of stews and things to give them a little bit of something to keep them going.'

At a later date, farm work was carried out by Latvian refugees, brought in from the camp at Woolfox. Joan Wild remembered three brothers, one named Arvitz, whom she described as 'nice men, very clever with wood'.

Other visitors to Hambleton during the war included servicemen from nearby airfields, especially North Luffenham. The landlord of the Finch's Arms since 1941, Doug Clements, recalled being besieged by thirsty Americans, desperate for more than their ration of six pints. When other needs prevailed, ardent servicemen attempted to climb the drainpipes of Hambleton Hall Stables, in pursuit of the closely chaperoned Land Girls! In addition to running the Finch's Arms for 40 years, Doug Clements was also a farmer, with a landholding of 160 acres before the coming of Rutland Water (Buxton & Martin 2001, 74-6).

Other wartime arrivals in Hambleton, whose lives must have been far more hidden and limited than those of the Land Girls, were a special class of evacuees who were brought into the parish between 1941-42, to 'Hamble Manor Residential Council School for Evacuated Physically Defective Children' (details of this little-known establishment are among the National Archives at Kew, in 'Special Schools Files' ED 32/661).

Post-War Changes

As England recovered after the war, it seemed that the rural tranquillity of England's smallest county had been restored. Tenants and landlords came and went: by 1950 Mrs Astley Cooper of Hambleton Hall had died, and the Hall and its estate were purchased by Lord Trent. John Campbell Boot, 2nd Baron Trent, was the son of the well-known Jesse Boot who established the chain of chemists. He was a philanthropist, keenly involved with the City of

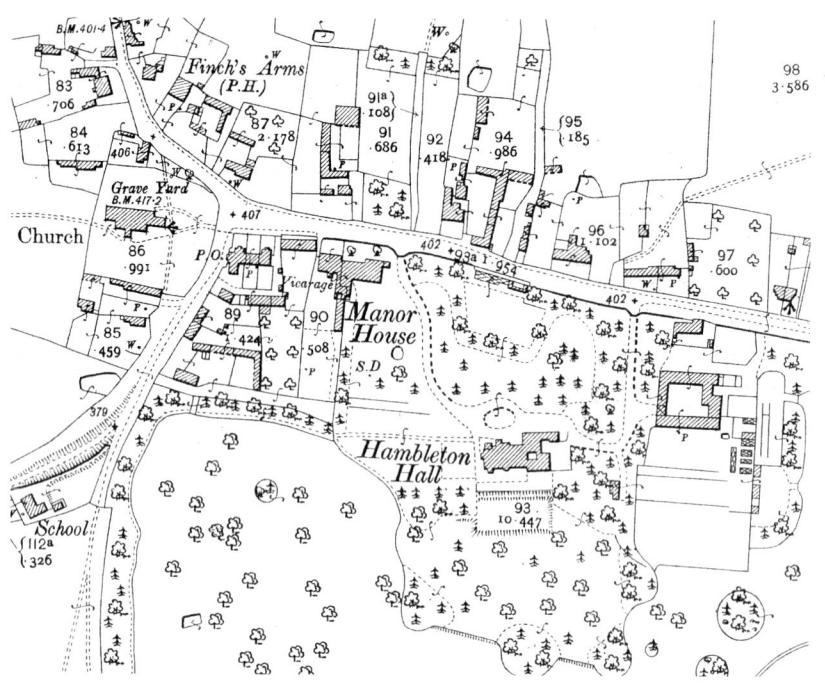

Upper Hambleton from the OS 2nd ed 25" map 1904 showing the Vicarage, and Hambleton Hall and its grounds

Nottingham, and the first Chancellor of the new University of Nottingham in 1948.

On arriving in Hambleton, Lord Trent did much to improve the lives of his tenants, with innovations such as installing electricity into all the farms and cottages. Joan Wild remembered how the new landlord arranged for one of the six bedrooms in Home Farm to be turned into a bathroom, with the wonders of hot running water. Previously, water had to be heated in a copper, poured into the bath tub by the fire in the back kitchen for the family bath night, and finally scooped out again into the drain.

In 1955, Hambleton's new vicar was the recently retired Post Office official, Hugh Westland. He brought his family to the beautiful vicarage with its Dutch gables and attics from which could be seen the whole Vale of Catmose. Dorothy Westland remembered the heavy housework for herself and her mother, since no girls were available in the village to help in the house: 'Mother used to alternate the rooms that had fires to keep the place aired . . . Coal, bread and milk were all delivered.' At this time Hambleton had no shop, although the Post Office was memorably decorated with Aggie Bushell's many little plants. Bread came from Mr Strickland's shop in Oakham, and on Wednesday afternoons a bus would take villagers the three miles into Oakham. Dorothy helped organise dances in the village hall, and joined her mother's working parties to provide products for the annual village fete, held in the gardens of Hambleton Hall.

Major Hoare became the new owner of Hambleton Hall following Lord Trent's death in 1956. Shortly before this, the estate was sold to Mr Bowley who divided it into six lots. At this time, Joan Wild's family moved out of Home Farm, which was sold along with the other farms. Major and Mrs Hoare had previously lived at Holywell Hall in Lincolnshire, while Major Hoare commanded a Home Guard unit during the war (V H Bettinson, bbc.co.uk/ww2peopleswar). Moving to Hambleton, the Major became Master of the Cottesmore Hunt. After his death in 1977, his widow sold Hambleton Hall to Tim Hart and his wife, who continued the hunting tradition. During the 1970s, the Rutland landscape changed beyond all recognition with the coming of the reservoir. Seizing the opportunities of their wonderful new lakeside location, the new owners converted the rambling Victorian house into a fifteen-bedroom luxury hotel, with what is now one of the country's finest restaurants.

Hambleton Hall from the north-west in 2006 (RO)

A Model Farm at Hambleton

After the war, changes had also taken place at Hambleton Old Hall. In 1949 Miss Maud Tryon retired to April Cottage, Lower Hambleton. The Old Hall became home to John Conant and, the following year, his new wife, Periwinkle. Having served with the Grenadier Guards during the war, John Conant began farming at the Old Hall while his father, Sir Roger, a keen politician who in 1954 was created 1st Baronet, lived at Lyndon Hall. Working hard to build up a profitable farm, the Conants gradually made significant improvements to The Old Hall and its gardens. The wind pump maintained by Miss Tryon proved an irregular supplier of water – either there was no wind and no water or strong winds damaged the equipment, so an electric pump was installed.

Sir John and Lady Periwinkle Conant (Audrey Buxton)

With only two men to help, John Conant worked Old Hall Farm, producing cereal crops or grass, the latter providing grazing and fodder for cattle and sheep. A new Ferguson tractor was bought in 1949, providing a sharp contrast with the fine Shire horses on Mr Wild's adjacent farm. Assisted by government grants and Irish labourers, many field drains were installed. These were sections of narrow pipe laid end to end, three feet underground, to drain the fields for arable crops. Half a century later, when Rutland Water is at low level, pipes can again be seen on areas of the exposed lake-bed.

The output per acre of Old Hall Farm in 1952-53 was £24. However, John Conant's innovative methods increased productivity to £72 per acre in 1956-57. These included more efficient use of fertilizer, which greatly increased the yield of wheat and barley. Grassland was managed more intensively, producing larger quantities of grass for silage and a significant increase in stock numbers. John Conant took early advantage of a government grant for the erection of silos, from which stock could feed without the normal waste. He also bred pigs and poultry, which in 1956 produced, together, 55 per cent of the farm income.

Gardens to the south of Hambleton Old Hall, now lost under Rutland Water (Sir John Conant)

The New Landscape

When the shock announcement came, the success of Old Hall Farm was no protection against the compulsory purchase of much of its acreage for the creation of Rutland Water. Many Hambleton villagers joined the protest movement against the new reservoir, which would affect many farms and change their landscape for ever. But the campaign proved unequal to the forces for change, and construction began in the early 1970s. At first it appeared as though Upper Hambleton would become an island, but according to Joan Wild: 'Someone said, "You may depend, they'll leave a road so that we can go and pay our rates!" and that's just what happened.'

With the demolition of Lower Hambleton and part of Middle Hambleton, the remaining Hambleton villagers were forced to accept a new way of life on what was now a peninsula. People adapted in their different ways. Jane Theobold recalled how her brothers worked on the dam while they were on university vacations, while she found herself unable to ride her pony in all the familiar places. 'I also remember taking my pony swimming in Rutland Water when they started filling it up – from the road at the end of Hambleton by Half Moon Spinney!'

Fortunately, unlike the neighbouring Beech Farm in Middle Hambleton, the Old Hall escaped inundation. By this time, Sir John Conant had inherited his father's baronetcy and moved back to Lyndon Hall. While the rising water lapped at the edge of the now shrunken gardens, Hambleton Old Hall was once again occupied by tenants. For most of the 1970s this included the glamorous fighter pilot, Air Vice Marshall Johnnie Johnson. But the view from the gardens and the south-facing windows had now changed beyond recognition. As the waters rose in the former valley of the River Gwash, fishing boats and yachts sailed above the foundations of Lower Hambleton and the fields once belonging to the Old Hall. No longer a farmhouse, it remains today one of the most attractive, unspoilt Jacobean houses in the Midlands and beyond.

The Old Hall as seen from Rutland Water (SH)

Aspects of Topography

Lost Footpaths, Footbridges and Bridleways

The earliest evidence of human presence in Rutland, so far, comes from an archaeological excavation in 2000 at Glaston, three miles due south of Rutland Water. Here, a worked flint was found amongst animal bones, including woolly rhinoceros, mammoth, reindeer and wolverine, which have been dated to about 30,000 years BC. This is the Upper Palaeolithic period, when this part of the world was in a warmer spell during the last Ice Age. The visitors were a party of hunter-gatherers who were exploring the area in search of food. The landscape would then have been lush grassland with outcrops of flat-topped sandstone boulders. However, over the next 20,000 years or so, oak forests became well established.

From the beginning of the Bronze Age (2000 BC), woodlands were being cleared for temporary settlements, and the tracks and ridgeways established then are no doubt the origins of some of the routes we walk and ride today. A great deal of evidence for Roman and Anglo-Saxon occupation was discovered before and during the construction of Rutland Water, indicating that the valley was then well occupied, and almost certainly by then, criss-crossed with tracks between settlements (*see* Chapter 18 – Brooches, Bathhouses and Bones – Archaeology in the Gwash Valley). However, the majority of Rutland's villages were established in the late Anglo-Saxon period when the routes of most of the present footpaths, bridleways and roads were first established.

Following the acquisition of land for Rutland Water, all the footpaths and bridleways inside this area were closed to public access and replaced by a concessionary perimeter track.

Above: The footbridge over the Gwash (X on the map) which was south-west of Brake Spinney (Jim Levisohn ARPS)

This map indicates the approximate locations of some of the more important public footpaths, footbridges and bridleways which existed prior to the construction of Rutland Water (RO)

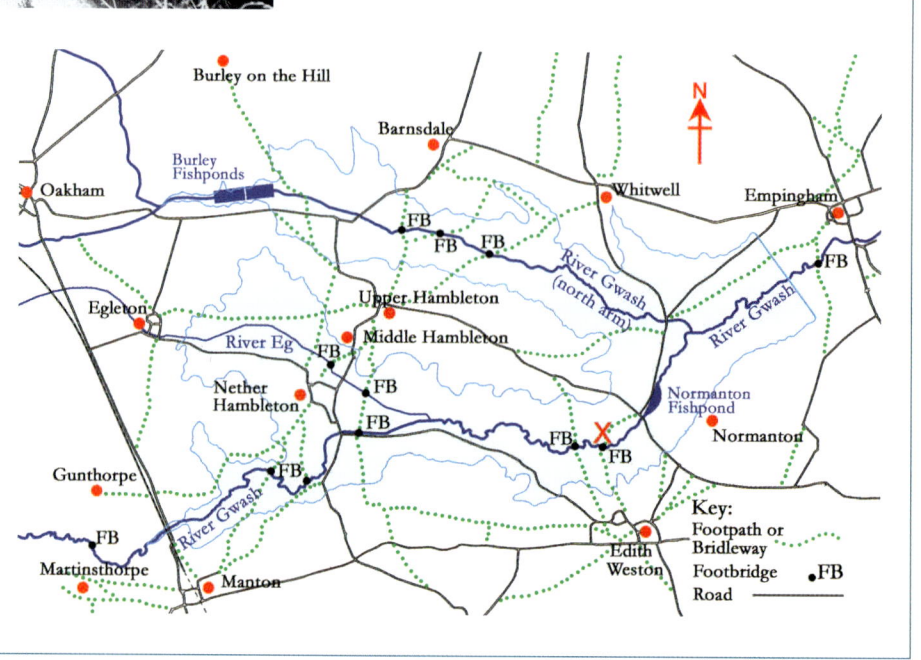

Chapter 9
Lower Hambleton in 1797
Sheila Sleath and Robert Ovens

A notebook amongst the Finch Papers (ROLLR DG 7/4/27) gives an intriguing insight into the lives of the 9th Earl of Winchilsea's tenants at Egleton and Lower (or Nether) Hambleton in 1797. It includes crudely drawn maps of both villages showing roads and houses belonging to the estate. Each house is numbered to correspond with comments on the occupants. These comments, together with information gleaned from parish registers, churchwardens' accounts, estate documents and charity records, provide more detail about these late eighteenth century families than is normally available.

The notebook also includes lists of tenants living at Upper, Middle and Lower Hambleton in 1798, Egleton in 1798 and 1801, Burley in 1798, and some general information on tenants at Greetham in 1798. It is the detail which provides the interest in this intriguing document. For example, a Mrs Bourne was given materials for use by girls at the Oakham Spinning School, and the names of six girls attending this school are listed. There are frequent references to hemp and flax, worsted, flannel and calico being given to the poor of the parish. These materials were used for spinning and weaving and for making clothing and bedding. They were supplied so that the poor could do such work as they were capable of performing as outworkers. The overall objective was to avoid future increases in the poor rate through the encouragement of industry among the poor.

The following account includes extracts from the notebook for Lower Hambleton. The names of the houses quoted are of twentieth century origin. All were demolished for the construction of Rutland Water.

The 9th Earl of Winchilsea of Burley on the Hill in his robes of the Order of the Garter. He was Lord Lieutenant of Rutland 1794-1826 and Groom of the Stole to George III 1812-20 (private collection)

The Earl of Winchilsea's tenants at Upper, Middle and Lower Hambleton in 1798. Later notes have been added in another hand (ROLLR DG 7/4/27)

Oakham Spinning School

The Earl of Winchilsea was involved in the promotion of the Rutland Society of Industry, founded in 1785. His account of the Spinning School, dated 16th March 1797, includes the following rules for attendance (*Reports of the Society* I, 42-6):

1. All inhabitants of the parish to be admitted.
2. No persons to receive relief from the parish upon account of their families, who refuse to send their children to the school unless they can prove, to the satisfaction of the overseers, that they can employ them to more advantage elsewhere.
3. They are to be instructed gratis in spinning jersey and linen and knitting, those who choose it, in reading, and those who can bring work with them, in sewing.
4. The hours of work to be from eight to one and from two to seven; from one to two, dinner and rest. No work after dinner on Saturdays.
5. A dinner to be provided for those, who choose to dine at the school on the working days; for which they are to pay each six-pence per week.
6. In case of illness, the dinner may be sent for to their homes.
7. The portions, if the dinner is sent out, to be as follows:
   One pint and a half of peas porridge
   One pint of rice milk
   One pint of rice broth
   One pound and a half of potato pudding.
   Those, who dine at the school, to have as much as they choose to eat, and a quarter of a pound of bread each; except on the pudding and rice milk days, when no bread is allowed.
8. The whole of the earnings to belong to the children.

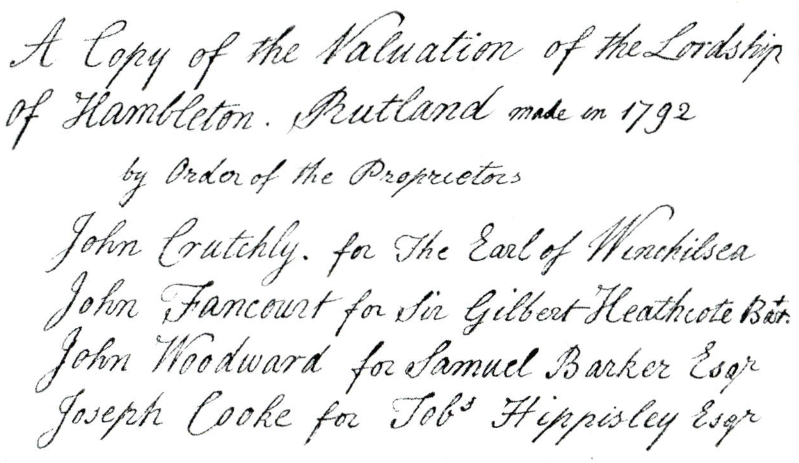

A Copy of the Valuation of the Lordship of Hambleton. Rutland made in 1792 by Order of the Proprietors

John Crutchly. for The Earl of Winchilsea
John Fancourt for Sir Gilbert Heathcote Bart.
John Woodward for Samuel Barker Esqr
Joseph Cooke for Jobs Hippisley Esqr

Title page of A Copy of the Valuation of the Lordship of Hambleton 1792 (Janet Lavender)

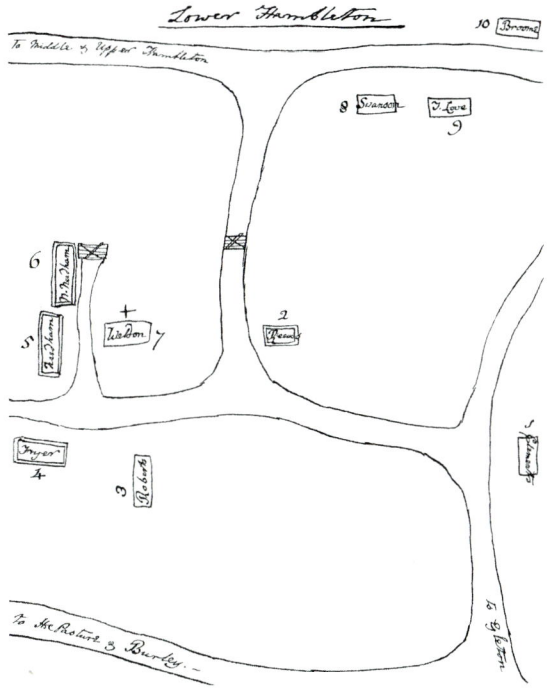

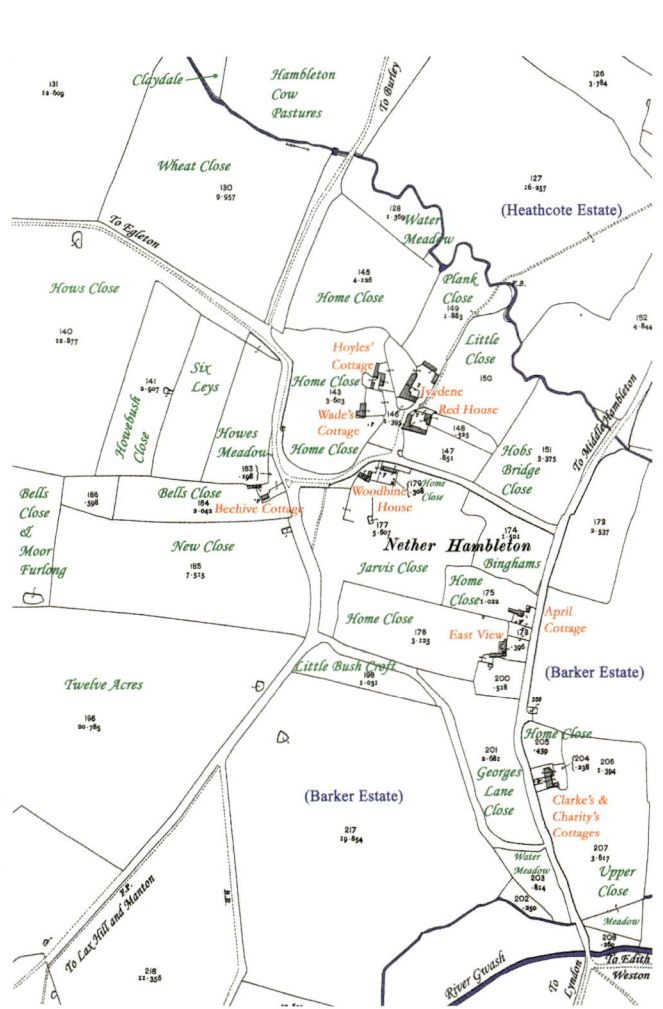

Above: The map of Lower Hambleton in 1797 included in the notebook (ROLLR DG 7/4/27)

Right: Dwellings (with modern names), closes and the majority of the fields rented by the inhabitants of Lower Hambleton in 1797 added to the OS 2nd ed 25" map 1904

— 195 —

George and Mary Clements

The occupiers of house number 1 were George and Mary Clements. George married Mary Andrews at Hambleton on 25th November 1779. Their children were George, John, Ann, Elizabeth, Mary and William and they were all baptised at Hambleton. Their ages in 1797 ranged from 2 to 17 years. William, the youngest, died on 11th March 1797, which probably accounts for the fact that only five children were recorded in the notebook.

George Clements became a tenant of the Earl of Winchilsea in 1785 when he rented a house and garden with an area of 3 perches. From 1797 until 1812 he rented part of Bells Close with a house and yard, the total area being 2 acres (ROLLR DG 7/1/100). This was field 184 adjacent to Beehive Cottage, as shown on early 1900s Ordnance Survey maps. As Beehive Cottage was undoubtedly built much earlier than 1797, 'new cottage' must refer to a change of accommodation for the tenant. George also rented one of fourteen gardens owned by the Earl and in 1812 he had the use of one common. The 100 acre cow pasture was located to the west of Middle and Upper Hambleton, shown as field 58 on the same maps.

Beehive Cottage from the south-east in 1974 (RLHRS)

Right: The possible route of George Clements' two and a half mile journey to work at Burley. It is superimposed on Letts' map of circa 1883

In 1797 George received three shillings twice yearly from Lady Ann Harington's Dole. This charity was set up by the wife of Sir John Harington of Exton in 1616. George continued to be a recipient until his death in 1829. In 1798 the Winchilsea Estate supplied the family with flax.

John and Martha Reeves

Farmer John Reeves married Martha Love on 25th October 1763 at Hambleton when he was described as a labourer. Eight of John and Martha's children were baptised at Hambleton between 1764 and 1776. Their daughters were Elizabeth, Sarah, Anne, Mary, Jane, Martha and Amy; their only son John died in infancy in 1774. Sarah, Anne and Jane were married by 1797. The family home was Woodbine House.

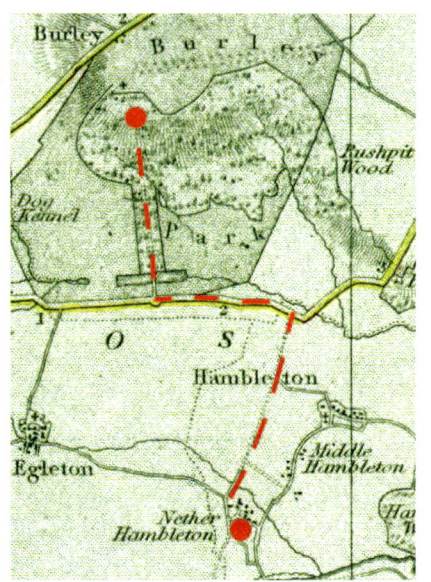

John received payments from Lady Ann Harington's Dole from 1775 until 1789. However, it seems that by 1797 he had become a successful farmer, able to support his family without the need for charitable assistance.

John was a tenant of the Earl of Winchilsea from 1773. Estate accounts between 1773 and 1788 show several payments to him for catching moles:

'1775　J: Reeve molecatcher to Christmas 1775 £2

1780　pd John Reeve for killing Moles in the park one year due Christmas 1780 £2'

This work had previously been carried out by Christopher Love snr, who died in 1773. A note in the rentals for 1788 stated that John required bricks for floors in his home.

In 1792 John was renting 'a house and Home Close', Binghams Close, part of Twelve Acres and Jarvis Close. The total area was 6 acres 3 roods 21 perches, which at this date had a rental value of £10 6s 1d. He was still renting these up to his death in 1813. His wife, Martha, died in 1804.

Right: The entry for Michaelmas 1788 from The Account Book of the Rt Hon Lady Ann Harington's Dole (ROLLR DE 3513) *for Hambleton. On this occasion, the second payment in the year, John Reeves received 3 shillings*

Richard and Mary Robarts

N.º 3.   Robarts

Cottagers — 2 Cows — seven Children all Girls — eldest in town with relations — 2? in service at Farmer Fryers — L.ʸ C. F. pnts two @ School at Vine's — very industrious working People. —

Richard Robarts (Roberts), labourer, married Mary Batts at Hambleton on 18th November 1776. Their seven daughters, Jane, Bridget, Mary, Frances, Alice, Sarah and Ann, were all baptised at Hambleton between 1782 and 1797. It would have been Jane 'in town with relatives' and Bridget in service at Farmer Fryers'. William Fryer was a very close neighbour. 'Lʸ C.F.' was Lady Charlotte Finch, who was supporting two other daughters at John Vine's school in Middle Hambleton. These would have been Mary and Frances who were of the appropriate age to attend.

> ### The First School in Hambleton
>
> In 1760 Mark and Mary Clayton assigned £10 worth of Old Sea annuities to Trustees to pay for a schoolmaster at Hambleton to instruct nine poor children. Those attending school were to be chosen by the Vicar and their ages were to be seven to eleven years. The subjects taught were reading, writing and 'Casting accounts'. As the first National School in Hambleton was not built until 1838 it is likely that the Roberts's daughters were taught by Mr Vine in his own house.

Richard was a tenant of the Earl of Winchilsea as early as 1779. His home in 1797 was that known as Wade's Cottage in the 1960s. It was possibly the same house he rented in 1792 together with a garden and home close as itemised in the valuation of that year. The total land area was 2 acres 1 rood 26 perches with a rental value of £4 1s 11d. A note in the rentals for 1787 reveals that Richard maintained the property 'well banked and neat' and other entries describe him as being 'a bright fellow' and 'good and industrious'.

In 1797 Richard received 3s 6d twice yearly from the Lady Ann Harington Dole. He had received money from this charity since 1787 and continued to do so until his death in 1807. In 1798 his family received six pounds of flax for spinning from the Burley Estate.

OLD THATCHED COTTAGE
NETHER HAMBLETON.

William and Ann Fryer

Farmer Fryer was William Fryer who originated from Pickwell, Leicestershire. He married Ann Nixon of Hambleton on 6th September 1784 and it was in this year that he first became a tenant of the Earl of Winchilsea. Of their eight children baptised at Hambleton up to 1797, six survived. They were William, Thomas, Joseph, John, Francis and Ann. Elizabeth, their eldest daughter, died in 1796, and Robert died in infancy in 1797. Three more of their children were baptised at Hambleton between 1799 and 1802.

Wade's Cottage from the south-east. It had a date stone inscribed 1729 (C Walter Smith)

No 4. — Farmer Fryer

he buys Cattle to sell again — & frequently goes to St Ives — & London to do so — they have ― Children — lost a fine Girl a year ago — & a little Infant since — They are only Cousins of the Fryers of Up. Hambleton. —

— 199 —

Two William Fryers are listed in the valuation of 1792. William, of the notebook, is described as a grazier and at that time he rented Furzy Close, Twelve Acres, Hill Close, Wrights Close, Lax Hill, Moor Furlong, Hows Close, Howebush Close, Six Leys, Howes Meadow, House Close, Bells Orchard and a dwelling house with the outbuildings, yards and gardens. The total area was 105 acres 28 perches with a rental value of £102 8s 2d. William had taken over William Bell's rentals in 1785 and it is interesting to note that one of the two houses he acquired was described as 'Dwelling house Sign of the Bull with the outbuildings Yard and Garden', suggesting that this building was a public house. This was probably on the site of Red House. The 1797 notebook reveals that William and his family were living in what was later known as Hoyles' Cottage.

Fryer Willm Grazier	A	R	P	Value	£	S	D
Furzy Close	10	..	5	12 6	..	..	4
Twelve Acres	10	1	13	18 9	6	..	..
Hill Close	20	3	33	19 19	18	..	4
Wrights Close	7	..	2	21 7	7	..	3
Lax Hill	25	2	16	14 17	18	..	4
Moor Furlong	7	2	18	26 9	18	..	..
Hows Close	12	2	18	26 16	8	..	..
Howebush Close	2	3	22	25 8	12	..	1
Six Leys & Howes Meadow	4	2	29	25 5	17	..	..
House yard & Garden &c	..	..	21	1 10	..	..	..
Home Close	1	..	3	28 1	8	..	6
Bells Orchard	2	1	8	28 3	4	..	4
	105		28		102	8	2

William Fryer's holding in the valuation of Hambleton of 1792
(Janet Lavender)

Hoyles' Cottage was between Wade's Cottage and Ivydene. It was the home of William and Ann Fryer in 1797 (Canon John R H Prophet)

Joseph and Dorothy Needham

No 5.   Farmer Needham

Men & his Wife — have 2 Sons — he is Uncle to Fryers Wife. —

Farmer Joseph Needham's farmhouse was almost certainly what was later known as Ivydene. It has been difficult to determine the exact identity of this farmer, but he was almost certainly the Joseph Needham who married Dorothy Lyne in 1773. Their sons, Thomas, Joseph and John were baptised at Hambleton between 1775 and 1779. John was buried in 1797.

Ivydene from the south circa 1970 (Edna Locke)

Joseph's father, Joseph snr, paid a half yearly rent of £52 6s 6d to Daniel Finch, Earl of Winchilsea in 1769, a large sum compared to rentals paid by other tenants. Joseph snr, according to the rent book, had greatly improved the land under his tenure and when he died in 1784 his son Joseph, Farmer Needham of 1797, was able to rent most of it. In addition he retained the use of three cow commons and continued to rent the farmhouse and the associated buildings. In 1785 Joseph was noted as keeping these 'in perfect repair'.

According to the valuation of 1792, Joseph rented a farmhouse with the outbuildings, yard, garden and orchard, Wheat Close, Northward and Southward Claydale Meadow, Upper Claydale, Plank Close, Home Close and Water Meadow. The total area rented was 75 acres 28 perches. The total rental value was £91 0s 11d. By 1812 the area he rented had increased to 103 acres.

The Needhams were a long established family in Hambleton. A Joseph had held the offices of Churchwarden and Overseer of the Poor at various dates during the 1700s.

Joseph Needham's entry in the 1792 valuation
(Janet Lavender)

Needham Joseph	A	R	P	Value Acres	£	s	D
Wheat Close	10	..	16	27	13	12	8
Northward Claydale Md	5	2	37	24	6	17	6
Southward do. Meadow	10	2	10	22	11	12	3
Upper Claydale	41	..	29	22	45	6	8
House yard Garden Orchard & Buildings		2	19	..	3	..	..
Plank Close	1	2	18	30	2	8	4
Home Close	4	..	19	30	6	3	6
Water Meadow	1	1	..	32	2	..	..
	75	..	28	..	91		11

Nicholas and Rachel Needham

N.º 6. Farmer Nic.s Needham

keeps the Publick House. —

There is some uncertainty as to Nicholas Needham's relationship with other Needham families living in Hambleton at this time. However, research suggests that he was the Nicholas baptised on 1st December 1754 at Manton, the son of Richard and Mary Needham, and cousin to Joseph Needham jnr of Lower Hambleton as described above.

A Richard Needham was renting land in Hambleton from the Earl of Winchilsea from 1769 to 1788, and on occasions, jointly with Joseph Needham snr between 1778 and 1784. Richard continued to be a tenant until 1793 and a note in the accounts states that his rental was taken over by his son Nicholas.

Nicholas married Rachel Woods of Brooke in 1776 and by 1794 at least seven of their children had been baptised at Hambleton, the earliest being 1785. Only three of their children survived. The notebook map shows that Nicholas Needham's home was next to, and just east of, Joseph Needham's farmhouse. It was later known as Red House, which in 1797 was only two years old, as confirmed by the date on the south gable.

A memorandum in the 1792 rentals confirms that the house on this site was 'considered as being a Public House'. As Nicholas Needham is described as keeper of the public house in 1797, the new house, built in 1795, obviously continued in this role. It was probably known as The Bull.

Red House from the south-east in 1973 (Richard Adams)

Nicholas Needham was a tenant of the Earl of Winchilsea from 1787. In the valuation of 1792 he is listed as renting a house and orchard with a yard and garden, Upper and Lower Rough Close, Hobs Bridge Close, part of Twelve Acres and Little Close. The area was 36 acres 7 perches, with a rental value of £41 17s 5d. By 1812, Nicholas Needham was renting considerably more land from the Burley Estate.

Hambleton Churchwardens' Accounts (ROLLR DE 2209/52) record payments made to Nicholas Needham for ale in 1797 and 1799. They substantiate the notebook comment that he 'keeps the Publick House'

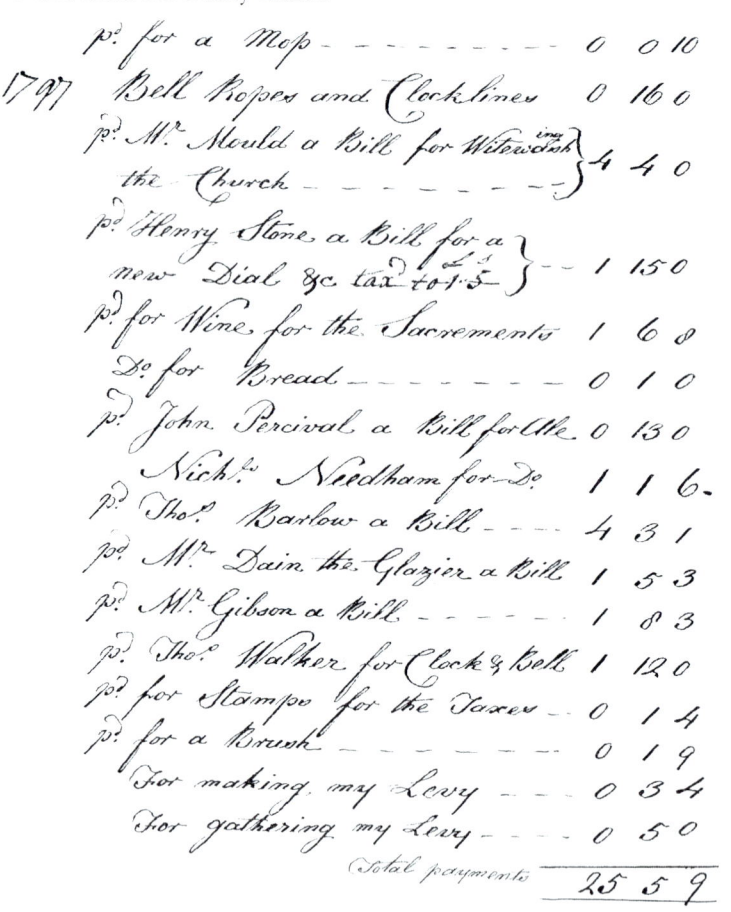

		£	s	d
	p:d for a Mop	0	0	10
1797	Bell Ropes and Clocklines	0	16	0
	p:d Mr Mould a Bill for Whitewashing the Church	4	4	0
	p:d Henry Stone a Bill for a new Dial &c. tax £1.5	1	15	0
	p:d for Wine for the Sacraments	1	6	8
	D:o for Bread	0	1	0
	p:d John Percival a Bill for Ale	0	13	0
	p:d Nich:s Needham for D:o	1	1	6
	p:d Tho:s Barlow a Bill	4	3	1
	p:d Mr Dain the Glazier a Bill	1	5	3
	p:d Mr Gibson a Bill	1	8	3
	p:d Tho:s Walker for Clock & Bell	1	12	0
	p:d for Stamps for the Taxes	0	1	4
	p:d for a Brush	0	1	9
	For making my Levy	0	3	4
	For gathering my Levy	0	5	0
	Total payments	25	5	9

Nicholas Needham held the offices of Churchwarden and Overseer of the Poor on several occasions. The following extract from *Victoria County History* (II, 72) regarding the charity John Mitchell's Gift indicates that he was a respected member of the community:

'John Mitchell, a native of Hambleton and a mariner, about the year 1800 sent the sum of £10 to Mr. Nicholas Needham to be applied for the benefit of John Mitchell's mother. His mother having died before the whole of the money had been expended, the balance of £3 13s 6d was paid over to the churchwardens and overseers for the use of the poor.'

A Mr Needham, either Joseph or Nicholas, was one of five Hambleton inhabitants that Richard Weldon of Lower Hambleton had intended to murder in 1788. He made this declaration prior to being hanged at Oakham in 1789. The sketch of Lower Hambleton in the notebook shows that the Weldon home was near to that of Nicholas Needham.

Richard and Mary Weldon

No 7. Weldon ✗

where you never go — Brother to the young Men that were hanged. —

Richard Weldon and Mary Walker were married at Hambleton on 9th June 1761. Eight of their children were baptised at Hambleton between 1761 and 1779. Of these, two sons were buried in 1780.

Two other sons, Richard and William, were 'very illiterate men'. When in their twenties, they were hanged in 1789 for the murder of John Freeman of Edith Weston and their gaoler, Henry Lumley. Their bodies were suspended on a gibbet within sight of the family home. William was employed as a shepherd just before the crime was committed. The Weldon home in 1797 was located in the centre of Lower Hambleton near Red House. It had been demolished by 1830, probably following the death of Richard Weldon snr.

House number 7 on the map and the notebook entry for the Weldon family are both marked with a cross, presumably to bring attention to the fact that this is 'where you never go'. Eight years after the crime it appears that the family home was to be avoided at all cost. However, the fact that in 1792 their daughter Mary had married near neighbour John Broome indicates that the family was not completely ostracised. This is again signified in 1801, when another of Richard's daughters, Elizabeth, married John Clements, who also lived in Lower Hambleton. The entry in the notebook seems to suggest that Mary was widowed by 1797, but this is not so, for Richard, her husband, was buried on 10th June 1824 at the age of 93. Mary Weldon died in 1806, her burial being on 27th April at Hambleton. Richard had been receiving regular payments from Lady Ann Harington's Dole until his death.

Richard Weldon was a tenant of the Earl of Winchilsea from 1786. In the 1790s he also tenanted one of the Earl's fourteen gardens. As he is not listed in the notebook as being one of the Earl's tenants in 1798, there may have been a period when he was not renting from the Burley Estate. In 1812 the rentals confirm that he was renting a house and yard with an area of 8 perches from the Earl of Winchilsea.

Susannah Swanson

No 8 — Swanson

Old Widow Swanson & her daughter — She is 84. — 3 lb. of meat every Saturday from J. C. T. — Faggots from L. W. ser.

Old widow Swanson was Susannah Swanson whose husband Thomas had died in January 1765. The couple had five children who were baptised at Hambleton. Of these, three had died by 1784. Hambleton Churchwardens' Accounts record that their son John was provided with an apprenticeship in 1758 at the expense of the parish. His clothing was also supplied, but there is no indication of his master or his trade. The daughter living with Susannah in 1797 was Mary, who was baptised at Hambleton on 29th September 1740.

Hambleton Churchwardens' Accounts for 1758 record that John Swanson's apprenticeship was being paid for by the parish (ROLLR DE 2209/51)

	£.s.d
pd. for flower for Swansons 7 Ws 7:7 for 14 Ws 14	1.1.7
May 4 pd. for ye. Indenture for Swansons Boy	0.1.6
6 pd. Mr. Sees a Bill for Jn. Swanson (viz, for 6¼ yd.) of Cloth 10: Drill 9 thread 4 Mohair 3: Canvis 2) tape 2 for 33 Buttons 1	0.11.6 0.1.2
6 pd. Mr. Pool for a pr. of Breaches for do.	0.2.6
18 pd. Wm. Meadows for making 1 Coat & 2 Waiscoats	0.4.0
22 pd. Wm. Tomlin for Jn. Swanson being put an Apprentice to Serve Whilst Martinmas 1765	3.3.0
22 pd. for 2 pr. of Stockins for do.	0.2.0
22 Charges when handed ye. Jordentures	0.1.0
pd. Thoms. Matthews for a pr. of Shoos for do.	0.3.6
pd. for 8 yds. of Hemp Cloth to make do. 4 Shirts	0.10.0
pd. for thread 3 pd. Mr. Scotney for filling ye Indentures 3: 3	
July 13 Charge: my self & Jn. Smith going to Oakham to hand Jn. Swanson's Indenture	0.1.2
Sept. 17 pd. for a pr. of Breaches & a Hat for do.	0.3.0
pd. Mary Broom for lodging Jn. Toone 8 p W: 55 Ws	1.16.8

Susannah was a tenant of the Winchilsea Estate for many years. Rental records reveal that her house needed thatching in 1787 and in the following year it was part thatched and banked around. Susannah's property was listed in the valuation of 1792. She rented a house and Home Close, the area being 1 acre 34 perches, and the rental value was assessed at £1 10s. Two years later her land was sublet to Francis Fryer and she was 'to have the benefit of it' and her 'house was to be repair'd at L'd W's [Lord Winchilsea's] expense'. Francis Fryer was a baker living in Hambleton. Susannah's home in Lower Hambleton was on the Lyndon road. It was known in the 1970s as April Cottage.

The Swanson family regularly received payments from Lady Ann Harington's Dole. During 1797 Sarah also received charitable gifts from the Burley Estate. On Saturdays she was given three pounds of meat from Lady Charlotte Finch and faggots from Lord Winchilsea. In 1798 she had two and a half pounds of flax for making a shift and her daughter received peppermint water, tea, sugar and one pound of worsted for making stockings. By the end of 1798 Susannah, and in 1800 her sixty-year-old daughter Mary, had been placed in a hospital, the location of which is indecipherable in the notebook. Susannah was buried at Hambleton on 13th December 1800.

Lady Charlotte Finch. She was the mother of the 9th Earl of Winchilsea and was well-known for her charitable deeds (private collection)

Thomas Bains Love

No 9 —

Thos. Love

Son of Christr. Love — he was once a Butcher in London — they are industrious, & in no distress — have 5 fine children, who read — work — & mark well —

Thomas Bains Love was baptised at Hambleton on 29th July 1747, the son of Christopher and Mary, *née* Bains. Thomas's father and grandfather, both named Christopher, were tenants of the Earl of Winchilsea. In his old age, and before his death in 1773, the Estate paid 'Chris: Love Senr for catching Moles'. Thomas's father, Christopher jnr, was a tenant of the Earl from 1773 until 1794.

Thomas Bains Love and his bride do not appear to have married in Rutland. The five children living with him at Lower Hambleton in 1797 were not baptised at Hambleton. Thomas first appears as a tenant of the Earl of Winchilsea in 1780 and in the rentals he was noted as being paid 'for thatching one of the Paddock stables'. For this he was paid £1 8s 4d. Thomas is listed in the valuation of 1792 and at that time he rented a house, yard, garden, Home Close, Water Meadow, Georges Lane Close and Little Bush Croft. He rented exactly the same in 1812, the total area being 8 acres 1 rood 27 perches. Thomas Love lived at East View in 1797.

Thomas Love's holding in the 1792 valuation of Hambleton (Janet Lavender)

Love Thomas	A	R	P	Value acre	£	S	D
Water Meadow	..	3	11				
Georges Lane Close	2	2	21	29	4	19	9
Little Bush Croft	1	..	11	29	1	11	..
An House yard &c	..	2	29	--	1	10	..
Home Close	3	..	35	29	4	13	..
	8	1	27		12	13	9

Henry and Sarah Broome

No. 10. Broome
Man – Wife almost blind – & one unmarried Daughter live in half the House — Their Son, & his Wife (who was a Weldon) young People & 4 young Children in the other part. —

House number 10 was a pair of semi-detached cottages known as Clarke's and Charity's Cottages in the 1970s. The occupants in 1797 were:

Cottage 1: Henry Broome who had married Sarah Taylor in April 1764 and their daughter Mary. Mary was baptised at Hambleton on 26th January 1772. The 1797 notebook entry implies that it was Sarah who was almost blind but the estate rentals state that it was Henry who had lost his sight.

Cottage 2: Henry and Sarah Broome's son John, his wife Mary and their four children Mary, Elizabeth, Sarah and Richard. All the children were baptised at Hambleton between 1792 and 1797. John had married Mary Weldon in 1792. She was sister to the two Weldon brothers who had committed murder just outside the village in 1788.

Henry was a tenant of the Earl of Winchilsea from 1774. In 1782 the rentals state, 'H^{se} in bad rep^r, not good for much' and in 1787 a note states, 'wants straw to thatch – notice to quit at Ladyday 1788 not hav^g repar^d ye end of his House – is doing it'.

Henry Broome's holding listed in the 1792 valuation states that he rented a house, Home Close, Upper Close and a meadow. The total area was 5 acres 2 roods 32 perches, with a rental value of £9 5s 4d. His wife Sarah died in October 1808. In 1812 his son John, eight years after Henry's death, was renting the same land and house. John also had the use of two commons.

Both Henry and his son John were regular recipients of Lady Ann Harington's Dole, and the family received flax from the Winchilsea Estate in 1798.

Clarke's and Charity's Cottages from the west, circa 1972
(Brian Hollingshead)

Aspects of Topography

An Ancient Ridgeway

The ancient ridgeway which follows the high ground between the rivers Chater and Gwash from east Leicestershire through Rutland towards Stamford is perhaps one of the oldest routes in the county, linking Lincolnshire and East Anglia with Leicestershire and the counties beyond. Until the end of the first millennium much of this ridgeway, particularly in east Leicestershire and west Rutland, was through forests. The high ground afforded greater safety from attack and avoided the often-flooded valleys. Part of this ridgeway, the bridleway through Martinsthorpe, is shown on an early nineteenth century estate map as an old coaching road, and today most of the ridgeway still exists as a combination of footpaths, bridleways and country roads.

Recent research by Joy Childs (*Leicestershire and Rutland Life*, March 2006, 27-29), has discovered that Mary Queen of Scots' last journey alive included passage through Rutland along this ancient ridgeway. Drawing on the journal of the French physician Dominique Bourgoing, who accompanied the Queen every step of the way, she was able to trace in some detail the route taken by Mary, then a prisoner under heavy armed guard, from her prison at Chartley, Staffordshire, through Leicestershire and Rutland, to Fotheringhay in Northamptonshire, a journey which took five days.

Mary Queen of Scots, who travelled by coach, and her huge escort, which included armed guards on horseback and carts laden with her belongings, entered Leicestershire from Burton on Trent, Staffordshire, on Thursday 22nd September 1586. She was accommodated overnight at Ashby Castle and The Angel Inn at Leicester. She left Leicester at 10am on Saturday 24th September, a very wet and miserable day, and travelled along the Gartree Road to join the start of the ancient ridgeway at Great Stretton. The royal cavalcade followed this route through Houghton on the Hill and Tilton on the Hill to arrive that evening at Withcote Hall, '. . . the house of a gentleman named Mr Roger Smith'.

Entering Rutland on Sunday 25th September, the route was now on the very narrow ridge between the Chater and the Gwash. The first settlement encountered was Martinsthorpe, by this time almost certainly a deserted village, although the Feilding family, later the Earls of Denbeigh, had a hunting lodge here by this date. The next part of the route was through Manton and Edith Weston, now overlooking the south shore of Rutland Water. Dominique Bourgoing mentions passing by the royal palace at Collyweston, just over the county border into Northamptonshire, suggesting that the entourage would have continued from Edith Weston towards Ketton where the River Chater would have been crossed. The medieval Collyweston Bridge would have provided a safe crossing of the Welland, leaving only seven miles before Fotheringhay Castle was reached.

On the orders of Elizabeth I, who saw her as a threat to the English throne, Mary Queen of Scots was beheaded there on 8th February 1587.

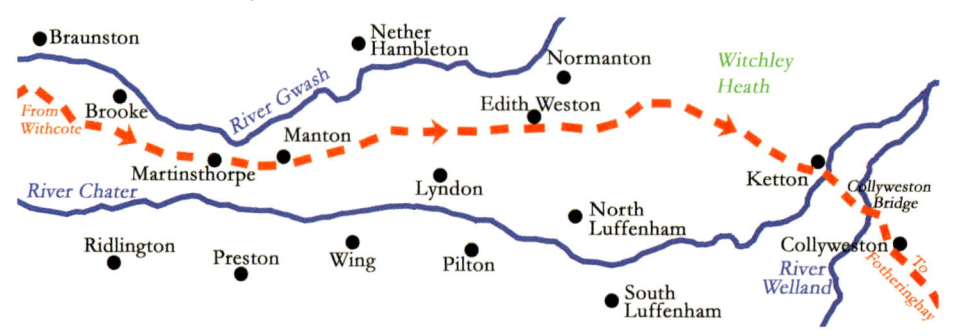

Mary Queen of Scots' final journey alive was through Rutland on Sunday 25th September 1586 (RO)

Chapter 10
Manton: A 'Town on a Rock'
Manton Millennium Group with
Robert Ovens and Sheila Sleath

Manton, from the Old English *maen* and *tun*, meaning 'town on a rock', is not recorded in the Domesday Survey of 1086, but it is probable that it was one of seven berewicks of the King's Manor of Hameldune Cherchesoch [Hambleton Churchsoke].

One of the earliest mentions of the manor in Manton occurs during the reign of Henry I, and for the next few centuries it was to be the dominating feature in the life and development of the village. The manor changed hands many times between the Abbots of Cluny, the English Kings, and those they rewarded, until it eventually ceased to exist in the early twentieth century.

The village of Manton stands on high ground with an underground water source running along the northern slope, where a line of wells still exists in the gardens of properties in St Mary's Road and Priory Road. Through the centuries, villagers have been able to observe on all sides rolling scenery of pastures grazed mainly by sheep, some cattle and a few horses, as well as fields cultivated for grass, wheat and other crops. Dramatic changes have occurred in more modern times, with the advance of road transport, the coming of the railways and the construction of Rutland Water. The central point of the village is still the tiny triangular village green with its three mature lime trees which were planted to commemorate the coronation of King George V in 1911.

The village green with its lime trees planted to commemorate the Coronation of King George V in 1911 (RO)

Manton railway tunnel passes directly below the village as shown on this OS 2nd ed 25" map 1904

Below: From Owen & Bowen's 1720 map of Rutland showing that the London road to Oakham (highlighted in red) then passed through Glaston, Wing and Manton

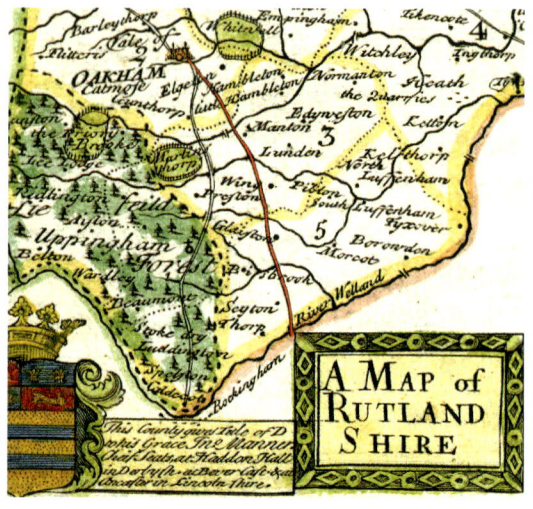

Owen & Bowen's 1720 map of Rutland, and other maps of this period, show that the main route from London to Oakham and beyond entered the county near Harringworth, Northamptonshire, and passed through Glaston, Wing and Manton. The constant flow of traffic, including pedestrians, those on horse-back, pack horses and horse-drawn carriages, must have been an interesting sight. Manton's location on such an important route probably contributed to the prosperity of the village. Evidence of this can be seen in the many well-built houses constructed in the seventeenth and eighteenth centuries. The Nottingham to Kettering Turnpike Act, passed on 6th April 1754, resulted in a new route through Rutland, with new roads between Caldecott and Uppingham, and between Preston and Manton. From then on Manton would have enjoyed the added spectacle of fast stage coaches, and later, mail coaches, all of which came to an end with the railway era.

In 1732 a severe fire swept through the village and caused such damage that a national appeal was set up. In spite of this disaster many of the earlier houses survived, particularly in Priory Road. These included Stonefield Farm, Manor Farm and The Hollies farmhouse, The Yews, Northfield, Blue Ball Inn and The Priory.

Above: Manton Priory (Hart)

Left: The Blue Ball Inn in 1905, now a private dwelling (Hart)

The arrival of the railway in 1848, with a station at Manton, offered rapid travel to London and other cities. This encouraged the nobility to build hunting lodges with stabling locally so that they could enjoy the fox-hunting that Rutland was so well known for. In Manton these included Manton Lodge Farm, The Grange and The Croft. The largest property was the Old Hall on Stocks Hill which, as well as stabling, had a coach house, an apple store, maltings and several cottages. It was built by the Heathcote family, and all these estate buildings are today much sought after residences.

Stocks Hill in 1908. Old Hall is seen right of centre behind railway cottages which were later demolished (Hart)

Left: The Croft in Lyndon Road in 1910 (Hart)

— 214 —

Manton Grange about 1910 (Hart)

These farms and hunting lodges set in Manton's 1,181 acres of land all generated employment for the villagers, either directly or in allied trades and occupations. The following are examples from nineteenth and early twentieth century directories:

Auctioneer	Chauffeur	Groom
Baker	Coachman	Mason
Blacksmith	Corn miller	Postmistress
Boot and shoe maker	Draper	Schoolmistress
Butcher	Gardener	Servant
Cake agent	General storekeeper	Victualler
Carpenter	Grazier	Wheelwright

The picture is very different today as, like the farmhouses and farm buildings, most of the premises of the tradespeople are now private dwellings. Other dwellings include the Thomas Fryer Almshouses (*see below*), the council houses, the first eight of which were built in 1934 on the south side of Lyndon Road, and modern detached and terraced houses built on infill sites.

The Horse and Jockey public house (RO)

The only surviving non-domestic dwellings are St Mary's Church, the Horse and Jockey public house, the Village Hall adapted from the old school, a residential home converted from Manton Hall on Lyndon Road, and an antiques shop, formerly cottages, on St Mary's Road.

Today, approximately 120 men, 130 women and some 35 children live in the 140 houses. The affairs and the needs of the village and its residents are currently looked after by St Mary's Church, the Parish Council established in 1894, the Parochial Church Council established in 1919, and the Village Hall Management Committee established in 1952.

With the coming of Rutland Water in the early 1970s the loss of some beautiful countryside to the north of the village was compensated for by new and splendid views over the water and the creation of the Lyndon Hill Nature Reserve. This western end of the reservoir is known as Manton Bay.

St Mary's Church and Rutland Water from the roof of Old Hall (Tony Melia)

Rutland Water was originally known as Empingham Reservoir and, until being granted Parliamentary approval in 1970, it was part of a scheme which included two new pumped storage reservoirs, the other being Manton Reservoir. This was to be in the Chater valley which is immediately south of Manton. The dam was to be constructed along the line of the Manton to Preston road (A6003), with the reservoir to the west of this line. In the event, two reservoirs so close together in Rutland was considered to be a step too far, and the Empingham Reservoir scheme was chosen because it was more cost effective (*see* Chapter 14 – Rutland Waters).

One hundred and sixty years earlier, in 1810, Thomas Telford proposed a new canal to link Oakham with Stamford, which would pass through Manton parish. It was to be called the Stamford Junction Canal, and the aim was to provide a link between the Melton Mowbray to Oakham canal and the Welland and Nene navigations beyond Stamford. The new canal was to follow a southerly route from Oakham to Martinsthorpe, and then turn eastwards through Manton parish to follow the Chater valley to Stamford. The scheme was considered again in 1815 and 1828 but never adopted.

Manton and the World Wars

The young men of Manton who gave their lives during the two World Wars are remembered on a memorial in the churchyard. It is in the form of a Celtic cross of rough-hewn Cornish granite. A Crusader's sword is carved on the cross, representing the old Crusader custom of striking the point of a sword into the ground and kneeling before it as if before a cross. The memorial was dedicated by the Archdeacon of Oakham, Canon Whittingham, on 11th April 1920. The men who lost their lives in the First World War were:

Captain William Stewart B Blackett	Leicestershire Yeomanry
Private W A Elliott	18th Yorkshire Regiment
Private Raymond Milner Bourne	29th Durham Light Infantry
Private Sidney Charles Corston	15th Sherwood Foresters
Private William Edward Taylor	Army Service Corps
Lance Corporal Robert Reeve	1st Canadian Division

(Information from *Rutland and the Great War* by G Phillips)

The men who lost their lives in the Second World War were:

F A E Lock	Royal Navy
J W Alexander	Royal Navy

Twenty other men from the village also served in the First World War, and a further three served as Special Constables. Unfortunately, a complete list of those from Manton who served their country in the Second World War is not available. There were a few bomb scares in and around the village and the Oakham sirens could be heard when raids were imminent. One large bomb was observed by the local Home Guard to fall on Lax Hill just to the north of the village, but it did not explode. People who lived nearby remember it being found and disarmed many years later. Anti-aircraft fire was audible during the bombing of Coventry.

The Church of St Mary

The picturesque church of St Mary stands in the centre of the old village on the site of a Saxon church. The present church is of Norman origin and has been extended throughout the centuries, resulting in the rather unusual appearance we observe today. Over the eastern end of the nave is a medieval Sanctus bellcote, one of only two surviving in Rutland. The bell has been missing for over 200 years.

Manton War Memorial (RO)

The porch with the little room above it and the south doorway were added in the fourteenth century. The room above the porch is separated from the main building, and the gap between the two is part of the distinctive look of the church.

St Mary's Church (RO)

The west front was rebuilt in the early thirteenth century. The small lancet windows, the two buttresses surmounted by unusual upright pillars and the double bellcote above give it a somewhat solid appearance. The double bellcote is a local characteristic, there being five others in Rutland. It holds two bells which were recast in 1920 by John Taylor of Loughborough, Leicestershire. Both bells retain earlier inscriptions. That on the treble reads 'CUM VOCO AD ECCLESIAM VENITE [When I call come to church] 1610 T.S.' [T S are probably the initials of Thomas Smythe who was Churchwarden at this time]. The tenor bell replaces a bell of *circa* 1550 and is inscribed 'ABCDEFGHI' (Ovens & Sleath 2002, 228).

The gravestones in the grassy churchyard are mainly of local limestone and slate. They are very weathered and lean at every angle, presenting a charming picture. A small area on the west side of the churchyard has several gravestones of people who lived in the nearby hamlet of Martinsthorpe. There is a more recent cemetery in Cemetery Lane on the west side of the village.

St Mary's Church and churchyard in 1908 (Hart)

— 218 —

The nave has typical late Norman pillars. The clerestory above it was added in the fourteenth century to give more light to the building. The nave houses a plain Norman drum-shaped font and an alms box dated 1637. The archway into the chancel is thirteenth century and bears the royal coat of arms probably dating from 1796 and restored in 1975. There is a small organ in the north transept.

The registers are lodged in the Record Office for Leicester, Leicestershire & Rutland. Baptisms are recorded from 1573, marriages from 1574 and burials from 1601. A complete list of 'Rectors and Vicars of Manton and of other Ministers to the Parish' is displayed in the church. The earliest is Helias de Berchampstead who was presented by Queen Eleanor in 1223.

Headstones in St Mary's churchyard in memory of Henry and Mary Green and their sons, John, Thomas and Bartin, who lived at Martinsthorpe in the eighteenth century (RO)

There are several interesting features in the development of Manton Church and the religious life of the parish, in particular its association with the Manton College of Chantry Priests. This college was founded within the parish church by Sir William Wade and others in 1356. Sir William, who is buried in the north transept, represented Rutland in Parliament. In 1548, around the time of the dissolution of the college and the appropriation of church income and property into secular hands, the commissioners pleaded that a vicar was necessary as there were 100 communicants in Manton. This recommendation does not seem to have had any effect, and from this time onwards Manton was without a vicar for long periods and permanently lost its vicarage.

In 1931 the parishes of Manton and Martinsthorpe were added to the parish of Lyndon and shared its Rector. The small civil parish of Gunthorpe was added in 1960, and joined by North Luffenham and Edith Weston in 1977. Today, although there are far fewer regular communicants than in the nineteenth century, the Church of St Mary Manton is still very well cared for.

Penelope Smith (1670-1727), an Extraordinary Woman

Little is known of this paragon, Penelope Smith, whose memorial tablet is in the north aisle of Manton Church. Penelope was buried on 13th September 1727, aged 57, and the monument to her memory states that she 'died exceedingly lamented . . . HER extraordinary Success in Physick and her *extensive* CHARITY to *thousands* of poor People, make her Loss universal to the BRITTISH Nation'. However it is known that she married Henry Smith Esq who was Sheriff of Rutland in 1708. Three of their children were baptized at Manton between 1689 and 1692, but the first-born did not survive infancy.

Despite a diligent search, no record of Penelope Smith's 'extraordinary Success in Physick' or her 'CHARITY to *thousands* of poor People' has been found.

James Wright, author of The History and Antiquities of the County of Rutland (1684), acquired the manor of Manton in 1683. The *Victoria County History of Rutland* suggests that the manor then passed to the Smith family, as Wright's heirs. Henry Smith died on 20th September 1716 and his body was interred two days later in the north aisle of Manton Church. His memorial tablet, which is adjacent to that of his wife, describes him as 'Lord of this Manour . . . Faithfull to his friend, Just to his Neighbour, and Devout and Pious towards GOD'.

Above: Penelope Smith's memorial tablet in Manton Church (RO)

Below: The title page of Wright's Rutland

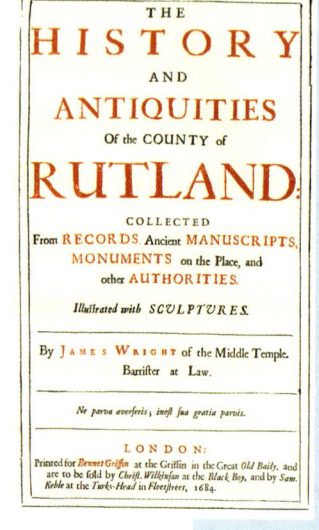

James Wright (1643-1716/17)

James Wright, antiquary and author, was Lord of the Manor of Manton from 1683 until about 1716. He was born at Yarnton, Oxfordshire, where he was baptized on 12th May 1644, the eldest son of Abraham Wright (1611-1690), Fellow of St John's College, Oxford, clergyman and author, and his wife, Jane.

Abraham Wright's career progressed under the patronage of Juxon, Bishop of London, who presented him to the vicarage of Oakham in 1645. However, because of the Civil War, he lived at Peckham, just outside London, until the Restoration in 1660 when he was finally able to claim the living of Oakham. He stayed there for the rest of his life.

Nothing is known of James Wright's boyhood and youth. He did not study at university but became a student of New Inn, London, in 1666, transferring to the Middle Temple in 1669. He was called to the bar on 14th May 1672.

Living and working as a lawyer in London, Wright loved the country and regularly visited his father at Oakham, as well as Manton where he acquired the manor in 1683. He enjoyed 'angling, and such like diversions of a country retreat', and probably fished the River Gwash and Burley Fishponds.

Wright's first published work appeared in 1668. It was an anonymous poem on the ruins of St Paul's after the Great Fire. Ironically, he lost his library of valuable books in a fire at the Middle Temple ten years later. His second publication was *The History and Antiquities of the County of Rutland* in 1684, and in his Preface he writes:

'As to this undertaking of mine, I must acquaint the Reader, that having been above twenty years past, for the most part, resident in the County of Rutland (tho' no Native of the same) I collected many years ago something of this nature, for my own private satisfaction. Which Notes tho' few and those imperfect, I have since been encouraged by several Persons of Honour to compleat into a just Volume as it is now publisht.'

The Collections of James Wright Concerning the County of Rutland and other Matters is a manuscript in the author's own hand, a facsimile copy of which is in the Rutland History Society collection. This most interesting volume of mainly unpublished material is sufficient to make a second volume to the author's *History of Rutland*.

James Wright never married and he died in his chambers in the Middle Temple in late December 1716 or early January 1717, leaving 'the comfortable sum of £1,600'.

Thomas Blore (1764-1818)

When the history of Rutland was next attempted, it was by Thomas Blore, another antiquary and author. He, like James Wright, was a lawyer of the Middle Temple, although he was never called to the bar. However, unlike James Wright, he did live in Manton for a time, before moving to Stamford.

Thomas Blore was born in Ashbourne, Derbyshire, in 1764, and educated at Queen Elizabeth's Grammar School in Ashbourne. He married Margaret, and their son, Edward, became a well known antiquarian artist and architect.

From at least 1791, Thomas was collecting materials for his intended history of Derbyshire. Later he transferred his attention to Hertfordshire while living at Benwick Hall, near Hertford, and collected historical notes which formed the nucleus of the history of the county. He then moved successively to Mansfield Woodhouse, Nottinghamshire, and Bakewell, Derbyshire, before settling for a short time in Manton.

In 1811 he produced the first instalment of a new history of Rutland, based on a more detailed investigation of the national records than James Wright. His vol I, part 2 of *The History and Antiquities of the County of Rutland,* illustrated with drawings made by his son Edward, covered the East Hundred of Rutland. This was the only part published. For this research he received a great deal of help and encouragement from the landed gentry of Rutland, especially Gerard Noel Edwards of Catmose House, Oakham, to whom he dedicated his work. For a short period he edited Drakard's *Stamford News*; he also produced an account of Stamford's charitable foundations in 1813, and a guide to Burghley House and its collections in 1815.

Thomas Blore died in London on 10th November 1818, and his memorial stone in Paddington Church, London, records that his 'days were embittered and [his] life was shortened by intense application'.

Manton Village School

The National School in Manton opened in October 1861, having been built on land given by E W Smith Esq, Lord of the Manor. The small stone-faced building cost £400 and was designed to accommodate 60 pupils.

In September 1863 an HMI [Her Majesty's Inspector] report states: 'not a single child in the 1st and 2nd standards has passed in reading, writing or arithmetic. My Lords of the Council House, Downing Street, therefore will deduct one tenth of the grant from Government. In addition attendance is so poor, that HMI suggests prepayment of fees by parents should include a discount for good attenders' (Traylen 1999, 142). The Managers, roused by this Report, suggested that some of the desks should be removed, and that a small gallery should be built on which the infants could sit. Seats would be supplied with back rails and it was hoped that this would result in less disturbance to the juniors. Like other Rutland villages, Manton at that time was very much a farming community and many of the children would have been expected to work on the land at certain times of the year instead of attending school.

The school was closed for three years from 1874 but the reason is not known. In 1895 Her Majesty's Inspectors suggested that a large, flat, open vessel containing water should be kept on top of the school stove. Presumably, this was to provide hot water for washing hands.

The school roll in February 1902 was 21 boys and 32 girls. There were no infants. Absenteeism was still a problem. One of the boys, eleven-year-old George Neal, was kept away from school to cart coal.

In November 1903 a report records that the playground supervisor was told that it was his duty to see that there was no rough play, and not to stand talking to the older girls!

By 1943 the roll had dropped to a total of 23 local pupils. In addition, thirteen evacuees were being taught at the school. Later in the Second World War, 50 or more children, mainly from London and Kent, were billeted with families in Manton and Gunthorpe. They were taught separately from the village children at the Old Hall, and The Croft was used for those who were ill or who had special problems.

Daphne Elliott, a former pupil of the school, became the new headmistress in 1946. The school was finally closed in 1948 and soon afterwards it was acquired for use as the village hall.

Headmistress Daphne Elliott with pupils of Manton School in 1947 (Daphne Ball, *née* Elliott)

The former school is now Manton Village Hall (RO)

— 222 —

Manton Village Hall

Before the present village hall was established in Manton, the malthouse, part of the Old Hall Estate owned by Col Heathcote, was used as a venue for social events. The George V and Queen Mary Jubilee celebrations were held here in 1935, as were many dances, fêtes and concerts. A stage was erected for performances by the village drama group directed by Mrs Street of The Priory.

The origins of Manton Village Hall lie in a Deed of Trust dated 10th October 1948, some two and a half years after the first committee had been formed to work towards the establishment of a community facility. The Trustees were Thomas Haywood of Gunthorpe Hall, Charles Cramp, William McKinn and George Sharp Smith. They undertook to erect a building known as Manton Village Hall to be used for '. . . the purpose of physical and mental training and recreational and social, moral and intellectual development through the medium of reading and recreational rooms, lectures and library classes, recreations and entertainments or otherwise, as may be found expedient for the benefit of the inhabitants of the Parish of Manton in the County of Rutland and its immediate vicinity, without distinction of sex or of political religious or other opinions'.

Funds for the project were raised through dances, fêtes, door-to-door collections, car rallies, interest-free loans and grants. When the village school closed at this time it was decided that it should become the new hall. The building and the land to the rear was acquired under trust from The Charity Commission. A large hall, two dressing rooms and a stage were added to the Victorian school building and this new village hall was officially opened on 1st November 1952 by W M Codrington, the Lord Lieutenant of Rutland.

Activities in the early days of the new village hall included the Cubs, the Girl Guides, the Youth Club, the Women's Institute, produce shows, badminton and dances. A representative of each user-group was entitled under the constitution to sit on the Village Hall Committee along with the elected members.

The hall almost closed in 1968 when it ceased to cover its costs. The situation was saved in 1969 when the main hall was let for a short time to Polytoy who employed about 25 women, mostly from local families, to pack Action Man toys, but the small hall was retained as a meeting room.

The last two decades of the twentieth century saw a marked increase in the number and popularity of activities in the village hall, both those organized by the committee as well as new user groups, particularly The Manton Players. Today visiting theatre companies, touring musicians, dance groups and live bands, as well as club events, ensure that it is a thriving village hall and one of the most active in the county.

Thomas Fryer Almshouses

Thomas, son of William and Ann Fryer, was born in Manton *circa* 1837. Like his father, Thomas was a grazier. By 1891 he had married Mary Hack, daughter of a near neighbour. In 1895, two years after the death of his wife,

Headstone of Thomas Fryer in Egleton churchyard (SS)

Thomas purchased Beech Farm at Middle Hambleton. He was living there in 1901 but died the following year.

The will of Thomas, dated 2nd August 1901 (private collection), gave two freehold cottages in Manton with gardens and premises at that time 'in the respective occupations of George Bellamy and John William Wade' to his Trustees upon trust, stating that immediately after his demise they were 'to establish and for ever after maintain' them as almshouses. The almshouses were to be called or known as Thomas Fryer Almshouses.

The occupants of the almshouses were to be chosen by the Trustees and the following rules were to apply. The 'inmates' were to be:

'. . . aged or infirm persons being inhabitants of the Parishes of Manton or Hambleton . . . of either sex, and either married or single . . . no able bodied person shall be elected, and no inmate shall without express permission be allowed to have any person whether a member of his or her family, or any other person to live with him or her in the almshouse, it being the express wish and intention to provide a home for aged or infirm persons who would otherwise probably be compelled to end their days in the Union Workhouse.'

The Trustees sold these original cottages in Priory Road but some of the garden was retained. In 1981 two bungalows were erected on this land and they still provide accommodation for aged or infirm persons in need.

The two cottages in Manton, owned by Thomas Fryer at the time of his death in 1902, have been converted in to one house. It has been named Fryers Cottage (SS)

These bungalows, built by the Thomas Fryer Charity in 1981, replaced the original almshouses (SS)

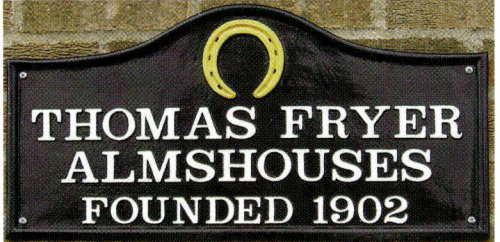

The Railway

The first railway through Rutland was the Midland Railway Company's Syston (Leicestershire) to Peterborough (then in Northamptonshire) line which opened for passenger traffic on 1st May 1848. Over the previous 23 years a number of railway companies had advertised their intentions to build lines linking the agricultural east and the east coast ports with the Midlands towns and coal fields, most of which passed through Rutland. The successful scheme received Parliamentary approval on 30th June 1845. From Syston, the line was to pass through Melton Mowbray (Leicestershire), Rutland stations at Whissendine, Ashwell, Oakham, Manton, South Luffenham and Ketton, and then on to Stamford (Lincolnshire) and Peterborough. However, the construction was not without its problems, particularly the section between Melton Mowbray and Stamford. The Earl of Harborough objected to the line passing through his Stapleford Park (Leicestershire), and a tunnel was proposed. However, he eventually agreed to a cutting, saving the railway company £35,000. Another major challenge was to excavate a tunnel under Manton, the most onerous component of the whole project. This led to more opposition in the village, particularly from local landowners. Col Robert Heathcote lived at the Old Hall on Stocks Hill in Manton at the time of the railway expansion. It was to him that an approach was made to cross his land and build a tunnel under the village. He gave his approval on condition that the railway company build him a new home to avoid any possible disturbance from trains running under his property. New Hall was built as a result. It is now Manton Hall Residential Home.

Manton Hall, often referred to as New Hall, in 1910. It was built for Col Robert Heathcote at the cost of the Midland Railway Company (Hart)

St Mary's Road Manton, about 1907. The railway tunnel passes under the village approximately where the man (ringed) is standing on the pavement on the left. An air-shaft (also ringed) is visible on the right of this picture. Behind the air-shaft is Old Hall (Hart)

Within two months of the railway company receiving approval, the first navvies were working on the line, and within a year there was completed track between Syston and Melton Mowbray, and Stamford and Peterborough. Work on Manton tunnel had also started and by November 1846 it was half completed. The hundreds of navvies working on the tunnel and living in a nearby temporary hutted encampment inevitably caused problems. Poaching and theft were rife, and there were complaints of a 'free trade' economy whereby beer and spirits were being sold without licence from certain huts. One more legitimate and prosperous business was that of William Robinson of Preston who, having set up as a boot maker in 1846, eventually employed eleven men making boots for the local railway navvies.

The navvies also had their own problems. There were many complaints that their pay was being withheld for trifling and unjust pretexts, and working conditions were such that there were many accidents. A typical example is that of William Tomlinson who was descending one of the tunnel access shafts when the basket he was standing in turned over and he fell 40 feet into the works below. His body was taken to the Horse and Jockey public house in Manton where it was left pending a Coroner's inquest.

In August 1847 the contract for building the station at Manton, as well as those at Ashwell and Oakham, was let to Norman Coleman Waterfield and Jarrom of Leicester. An innovation, considered to be expensive at the time, was the use of galvanised corrugated iron for covering the platforms.

By November 1847 there was concern that problems in constructing Manton tunnel were delaying the opening of the line and many more navvies were brought in to ensure that it was completed on time. By March 1848 the first coal trains were running along the whole route, and after five weeks of testing the track was considered to be ready for opening to passenger traffic on 1st May. Peak traffic in 1911 comprised 33 passenger trains and many goods trains running on each weekday.

The opening of the line was somewhat marred by the excessive prices of the tickets. A second class ticket from Melton Mowbray to Stamford was 4s 9d. At $2^{1}/_{2}$d per mile it was more than twice the rate for a ticket from Stamford to London.

Within less than 30 years Manton was to be affected again by the Victorian railway boom. This time the Midland Railway Company proposed a direct route from Nottingham to London by building new lines between Nottingham and Melton Mowbray, and between Manton and Kettering (Northamptonshire), utilising the existing Melton Mowbray to Manton line to link the two. Permission was given in the Midland Railway Bill of 1874 and work had started on the Manton to Kettering section by July 1875. The $15^{1}/_{2}$-mile route crossing the hills and valleys of south Rutland was to prove to be an immense engineering challenge. However, this section of the project was completed and ready for traffic by July 1879. It opened for passenger traffic in March 1880 and had sixteen cuttings, twelve embankments, four tunnels and five viaducts, including the impressive Welland Valley viaduct of 82 arches, each with a span of 40ft. The interesting story of the building of this line and the lives of the navvies who worked on it is given in *3000 Strangers* by J Anne Paul.

Manton station looking south-east in 1908. The line to Peterborough is on the left and that to Kettering on the right. The original (1848) station building is in front of the tall grain store. The second station building (of circa 1878) is immediately behind the long footbridge (Hart)

The original 1848 station building is now an office and the station site is now a small industrial estate (RO)

Manton now became an important junction with a new station building. As well as encouraging the nobility to travel to Rutland to enjoy the fox-hunting, it was a popular embarkation point for journeys to London St Pancras on the 'Robin Hood' which took little over one hour. Day trips were popular and easily managed.

Travel to Nottingham in the north, Leicester to the west and Peterborough, Cambridge or Norwich to the east was also possible directly from Manton Station. Employment was provided for the villagers as porters, platelayers and signalmen, as well as stationmaster. Several cottages were built for railway employees on St Mary's Road, formerly Middle Street, and on Stocks Hill opposite The Forge. All have now been demolished. Manton Station closed on 6th June 1966.

The second station building, of circa *1878, has seen better days* (RO)

Oakham is now the only remaining operational railway station in Rutland. Most of the elegant station buildings have survived at Manton and the site is now a small industrial estate. The tunnel, which passes directly under the village, and the railway lines are, however, still in use, having both survived the 'Beeching Axe'. The Syston to Peterborough line, although much quieter than in its heyday, remains an important link between Birmingham, Leicester and East Anglia. The Kettering branch is now used mainly for freight traffic, but occasional 'steam specials', and trains diverted to avoid engineering works on the Kettering to Leicester line, are popular with passengers who want the experience of crossing the Welland Valley viaduct.

The Manton Bus

Originally it was not intended for the Syston to Peterborough line to pass near Manton, but pressure from Uppingham residents persuaded the company to re-route and build a station at Manton, conveniently only three and a half miles from the town. From its opening until the 1950s the station was listed as 'Manton for Uppingham'.

Tiny Thorpe, of Uppingham, ran a horse-drawn bus between the Falcon Hotel, Uppingham, and Manton station from about 1900 to 1928. In the following poem, author John Perkins, whose family, before World War I, had a clothing shop in Oakham, and another in Uppingham next to the Falcon Hotel, recounts the story of the last journey:

The Passing of the Manton Bus.
(Scene – Manton Station)

I was travelling from London to Manton,
On the old Midland line as of yore,
T'was a journey I'd often repeated,
And hoped to complete it once more.

As far as the Railway conveyed me,
I had nothing to fear, you'll admit,
But what of the rest of the journey?
The puzzle was, how about it?

I hurried along the dim platform,
Climbed the steps, and crossed o'er the line,
To gain the box seat was my objective,
Should I do it ere others could climb?

How well I remember the picture,
The Hall, dimly lighted and bare,
Ah yes, I had gained my objective,
The notorious Busman was there.

With a touch of his hand to his forehead,
And a musical ring in his voice,
'Good evening Sir, any more luggage?'
I knew I'd the seat of my choice.

The familiar old bus was there waiting,
And so was a crowd of twelve more,
Could he do it? 'Why bless you Sir, easy,
I have brought up fully a score.'

I walked round the steeds, and appraised them,
Then glanced at the crowd waiting there,
To convey all that lot to Upp-ham,
There are very few others who dare.

'Come along Sir, we're ready', he shouted,
I clamber'd up into my place,
Gripped the cold iron rail, and we started,
Preparing the bleak wind to face.

We meandered our way by the Coal yard,
Thro' the gate and under the Arch,
When I noticed a weary pedestrian,
Bravely starting his four miles to march.

With a jerk at the brake, and a 'Whoa Pet,
Come Master, I've room for one more',
Good heavens, where will he place him?
On top, at the back, over the door.

With a click and a laugh we restarted,
The patient steeds heaving a sigh
'You're amused Sir, why bless you this
   aint nothing,
To what we have done years gone by.'

'You must know that our town is Scholastic,
And the boys at the end of the term,
Did perform many tricks quite gymnastic,
And a seat on the Bus did not spurn.'

The inside was full to o'er flowing,
On the top it was even so more,
Round the rail their long legs limply hanging,
The young rascals enjoyed it the more.

'My loads they are varied and numerous,
Blocks of ice, fish, bananas, and fruit,
Traveller's luggage, bikes, prams, very various,
And a lot of things stored in the boot.'

'This corner we're coming to now Sir,
Is a horrible turn, you'll admit,
Now my lads, click, click, come get at it,
Steady on, catch your wind just a bit.'

'My horses, they're not very fast Sir,
But they manage their work very well,
Never judge by appearance in Horse flesh,
It's blood, bone and muscle that tell.'

We crept by the Pond and the New Inn,
Threw the paper roll down to the door,
Nor stayed e'en a moment to lubricate,
More hill climbing yet was in store.

So you've heard that this Bus has
been running,
How many long years? eighty-four,
But we're told it is now antiquated,
That new schemes and ideas are in store.

Yes, this is the very last journey,
On the coach that is driven by two steeds,
A Motor Bus quickly will follow,
To meet all our present day needs.

'Old customs and ways seem to please you,
And a liking for things that are gone,
Would you buy the old Bus at a price,
Sir? If I put it in for you at a song.'

'No harm Sir, I'm sure you'll excuse me,
For trying to get on with "biz",
If I can't have a chat and a deal Sir,
Well, my name is not what it is.'

'I feel rather sad at the parting,
Bless my life, we are here at the gate,
Drive straight in without any slackening,
Or else they will think we are late.'

Well, Good night my friend, here's your shilling
And another one, added as well,
It is worth a bob more, every copper,
To hear all the tales that you tell.

'Thank you Sir, should you e're need a
   Coachman,
Don't forget for yours truly to send.
My address, wire "Tiny, Uppingham",
I'm very well known at this end.'

Tiny Thorpe's horse-drawn bus at Manton station (RCM)

Chapter 11
Normanton
Sheila Sleath and Robert Ovens

Normanton Park, looking south from Sykes Spinney in 1820 (Mary Grylls)

The Heathcote family acquired the Normanton Estate about 1729 and, by the end of the eighteenth century, had created a park in the small parish of Normanton. Within the bounds of the park were Normanton House, the parsonage, and a few houses. There were no other habitations in the parish outside the park. The house, now referred to as Normanton Hall, eventually became, by succession, the seat of the Earls of Ancaster.

In 1924-25, the bulk of the Normanton Estate was sold and the mansion was demolished in 1926. The Gwash valley, home to Normanton Park for two centuries, might have continued as fertile farmland for perpetuity had not Royal Assent been given in 1970 for a large reservoir to be built there. Little remains of the former park, but the church, now Normanton Church Museum, stands at the edge of the water as a very visible and treasured memorial to the past.

The Early Village of Normanton

Before Rutland Water was created, surviving earthworks identified the location of the medieval village of Normanton (after Hartley)

For many centuries before the creation of Rutland Water, there was a village at Normanton. Evidence existed in the form of earthworks to the north-west of the present church consisting of a hollow way, closes and building platforms. Records show that there were 29 taxpayers in 1377 giving an estimated village population of 150. The Military Survey of 1522 suggests a population of about 90.

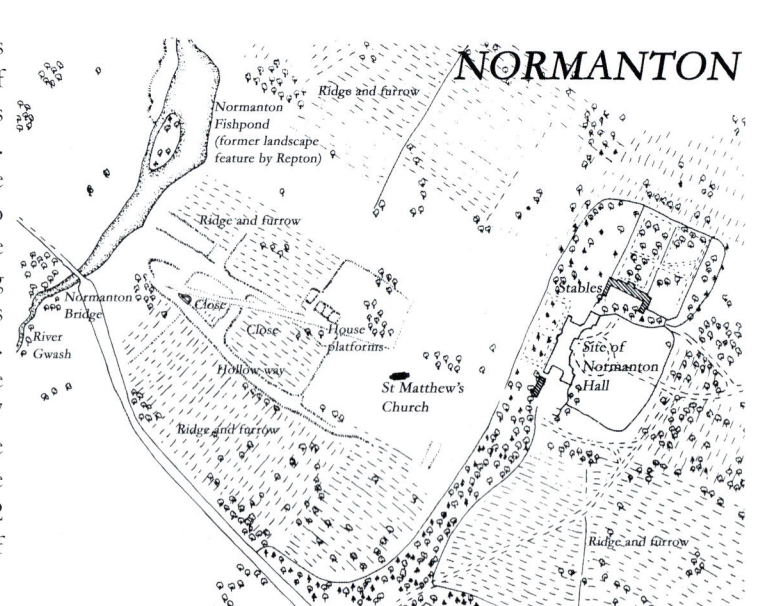

The Military Survey of Normanton in 1522

King Henry VIII ordered his chancellor, Cardinal Wolsey, to devise a survey that would discover people's wealth. The ostensible purpose of the survey was to muster and ready the King's subjects for war against France. However, there was also a fiscal reason behind the survey and it formed the basis of loans demanded later in 1522 and early 1523, and also the basis of the Lay Subsidy of 1524-25.

In 1522 Commissioners were sent out, ordering a survey of landowners' wealth and possessions and also of armour and arms. Everyone, whether clerical or lay, was required to state on oath the value of his goods and, where appropriate, the annual value of his lands, benefice or stipend. All males over the age of 16 were listed.

Many of these documents survive and they are acknowledged to be a valuable source of economic and social history. The following names are taken from the return for Normanton. From this list, historians can deduce that the population of Normanton in 1522 was about 90.

	George Mackworth Esquire is chief lord of the Town *
	William Ouerton is Steward of the Town *
	Thomas Walker is parson of the Town
	Peter Stevyn is parish priest of the Town
	Thomas Greneham the younger, gent and farmer to the parson
Bill man	John Naillour husbandman ✤
	William Sherwood husbandman ✤
	Richard Smyth husbandman ✤
Bill man	George Swetbon husbandman ✤
	Thomas Hoston husbandman ✤
	Thomas Meryll husbandman ✤
	Issabell Sherwood widow ✤
	Thomas Tilton husbandman ✤
	Simon Swaffeld gentleman has land at Normanton *
	Thomas Sherrard Esquire has land at Normanton *
	John Smyth labourer and tenant to Simon Swaffeld
	William Sherwood the younger labourer
Archer	Robert Walker servant, young man & poor
Bill man	John Taillor labourer, young man & poor
Bill man	John Meryll labourer, young man & poor
Bill man	John Sherwood servant, young man & poor

* non-residents ✤ tenants of George Mackworth

It is possible to trace the manor of Normanton back to the twelfth century when it was held by the Umfravilles. It later passed to the Normanville family, then to William de Basing in 1315 and eventually to the Mackworth family of Derbyshire in the fifteenth century. On inheriting the estate, Thomas Mackworth made Normanton his main residence.

Archbishops' Visitations at the end of the sixteenth and in the early part of the seventeenth centuries show that there were problems in the parish of Normanton. The low morals of Henry Tampion, Rector from 1572 to 1629, and his curate led to their respective suspensions in 1590 and 1591. Tampion also frequently declined to wear his surplice and failed to hold regular prayers and services.

Normanton Visitations

Visitations were regular and formal visits by an Archbishop, Bishop or Archdeacon to the parishes under his control, or to a convenient central meeting place, usually in conjunction with a fact-finding exercise. The records of many visitations have survived and they provide a unique insight into the condition of the church and the behaviour of those connected with the church.

The visitations to Normanton at the end of the sixteenth century show the church was neglected and in poor condition, much of it, no doubt, being due to the attitude of the incumbent, Henry Tampion, who was Rector from 1572 to 1629:

1589: Tampion was reported as being a common gamester and haunter of alehouses.
1590: Tampion had not received the Communion for more than twelve months; his maidservant was a lewd woman and not fit to be in his house; he had allowed the chancel windows to fall into decay.
1593: There was brawling in the church, and a Thomas Pope was presented for being a common swearer and a notorious sleeper during divine service.
1604: Instead of reading prayers one Sunday Tampion played at the tables with the schoolmaster at Hambleton.
1605: The church windows were daubed up with mortar; the pulpit was unfit to use, the communion table in a very bad condition and the seats broken and out of repair.

Several descendants of the Mackworth family became sheriffs and Members of Parliament for Rutland. In the second quarter of the seventeenth century, Sir Henry Mackworth rebuilt the manor house and this is illustrated in Wright's *Rutland*, published in 1684. In 1723 Sir Thomas Mackworth sold the manor of Empingham with Normanton and his other estates in Rutland to Charles Tryon of Bulwick, Northamptonshire. Within six years Gilbert Heathcote, the eldest son of an alderman of Chesterfield, had become the new owner.

The Heathcote coat of arms. Ermine three roundels vert each charged with a cross or (RO)

Normanton Hearth Tax Return, 1665

The tax on hearths was introduced in 1662 to help pay off the huge national debt inherited from the Commonwealth period (1649-60). All householders were liable to pay two shillings per year for every hearth, but some were exempt on grounds of poverty and low rent.

The surviving hearth tax returns can be used to estimate levels of population, prosperity and poverty. In the following, the Lady Hartoppe was responsible for Normanton House which was then in the ownership of Sir Thomas Mackworth. She had to pay for 23 hearths at two shillings, a total of £2 6s.

The Lady Hartoppe	23
Mr. Heaton	4
Edward Malson	2
Peregrine Moles	1
Mary Freere	1
John Harrison	1
John Bloodworth	1
William Woodard	1
Francis Charter	1
Curbert Bridges	1
Abel Vine	1 Not chargeable
Widdow Tailor	1 Not chargeable

Peregrine Moles (Constable)

Normanton House from a plate engraved at the cost of Sir Thomas Mackworth (Wright 1684, 94)

The Heathcotes of Normanton

Sir Gilbert Heathcote retired to Normanton after a distinguished career as a merchant. He had been a director of the East India Company, founder and Governor of the Bank of England, Member of Parliament for the City of London on four occasions, and Lord Mayor of London. Without doubt he was a remarkable man. He was knighted by Queen Anne in 1702 and created a baronet just eight days before his death on 25th January 1732. He was reputed to be 'the richest commoner in England' and he left a huge fortune (£700,000) including many large estates. He was interred in the crypt at Normanton Church and a memorial by Rysbrack was erected to his memory. The following is an extract from this memorial:

'A Person of Great Natural Endowments, improved by long Experience, Ready to Apprehend, slow to Determine, Resolute to Act . . . In his Character unblemished, in his *Extensive* Trade without a *Lawsuit*.'

Above left: From a portrait at Grimsthorpe Castle of Sir Gilbert Heathcote, 1st Baronet (Grimsthorpe & Drummond Castle Trust)

Above: Rysbrack's memorial to Sir Gilbert Heathcote. It was removed from Normanton Church and is now in the north aisle of Edith Weston Church. The crossed sword and mace and cap are symbols of the Lord Mayor of London (RO)

Left: The inscriptions on Sir Gilbert Heathcote's memorial (RO)

The Coming of Age of Sir Gilbert Heathcote

The following account from *The Gentleman's Magazine* (vol 64, 949), describes the festivities on Empingham Heath to celebrate the coming of age of Sir Gilbert Heathcote in 1794. He was only 12 years of age when his father, the third baronet, died in 1785:

'*Oct. 4.* A very elegant fête was given by Sir Gilbert Heathcote, on the occasion of coming of age, to all the nobility and gentry of the neighbourhood, and to near 820 of his *Lincoln* and *Rutland* tenantry. The assembled multitude was so great, that it appeared as if the whole of the surrounding country had joined in a general sentiment of congratulation to the heir of the hospitable mansion of Normanton.

'An encampment was formed in a commanding situation on Empingham heath, about seven hundred feet in length and two hundred in breadth. At the top was a pavilion for the ladies in which a table was spread with the most luxurious viands, and elegantly decorated. On each side down the lawn were covered booths, extending the whole length of the encampment, containing a profusion of generous cheer, placed on tables, sufficient for the accommodation of three thousand people.

'On the wings at each end of the pavilion, were the depots of provision. Six oxen, thirty sheep, and eight waggon-loads of bread, formed part of the immense quantity consumed, and these were diluted with forty buts [sic] of wine, punch, and old ale. An ox and several sheep were roasted whole before the encampment, and distributed to the populace, with very copious showers of bread. The order of the entertainment was admirably preserved.

'The company began to assemble at twelve o'clock, the carriages entering at the lower end of the encampment, passing up the line, and delivering their bright charge at the pavilion, where they were received by the elegant and accomplished Lady Heathcote. To describe the manly and attentive conduct of the worthy host, and the beauty and courtesy of the fair hostess, might appear to strangers to be the dictate of adulation; but all who were present will allow that the language of panegyric would be only the simple voice of truth.

'When the ladies were assembled, the pavilion displayed a most captivating scene of fashion and of grace. On a sudden was descried, on the road from Empingham, a long line of cavalry, as far as the eye could reach: they were the patriot bands of Lincoln and Rutland Yeomanry, in complete uniform, except their arms; those were useless at a festival of peace. The compliment of precedence was politely yielded to the former by Lord Winchelsea, and a most animating spectacle it was to see them enter; preceded by their regimental bands, they marched up the encampment in double files, parading in front of the pavilion, and saluting as they passed, the Stamford band receiving them with "Britons strike home."

'Having disposed of their horses at pickets, provided for the purpose, they marched back on foot to the encampment, and took their seats at tables, the Lincoln on the right, and the Rutland on the left of the pavilion. The tenantry were seated next to them, accompanied by their numerous families and friends; and the glass and brown jug had a brisk circulation, and powerful effect. When the dinner was over, a circle of vast size was formed by the Yeomanry, linking their arms together, and surrounded by the tenants.

'Within the circle the ladies and gentlemen assembled, with the different bands of music and bugle horns. Several excellent songs, in allusion to the families of Rutland and Heathcote, and complimentary to the corps, were sung on the occasion. Various races, and other sports to which prizes were affixed, were proclaimed for the entertainment of the company; but the day was too short for the performance of them all. At sun-set, magnificent fire-works were displayed, and a vast bonfire closed the whole of this noble and delightful entertainment.'

Sir Gilbert Heathcote's son, Sir John Heathcote, was also a director of the East India Company and a trustee of the British Museum. Sir John was succeeded by his son, Gilbert, in 1759 and by his grandson, another Gilbert, in 1785. This latter Gilbert, the fourth baronet, administered Normanton until 1851, a period of sixty-six years. During this time many changes were made to the Hall and the estate. He was Member of Parliament for Rutland in nine Parliaments between 1812 and 1841. This Sir Gilbert was a great sporting man; he was a patron of the turf and maintained a large racing establishment purely for the love of racing. He ran for fame, not money. When he won, his prize was always shared with those less fortunate than himself. He was also Master of the Cottesmore Hunt from 1802 to 1806.

In succeeding years the heirs to Normanton acquired the titles of Baron Aveland (1856), Lord Willoughby de Eresby (1888) and Earl of Ancaster (1892). All these titles related to their Lincolnshire estates. The barony of Willoughby de Eresby is an ancient title brought to the family by marriage, and, unusually, is inherited through the female line. The other titles are elevations of the family.

Although Grimsthorpe Castle, near Bourne, Lincolnshire, was inherited in 1892, the 1st Earl of Ancaster used Normanton as his main country residence until the marriage in 1905 of his son, Lord Willoughby de Eresby, who became the 2nd Earl. It was then that Normanton became the latter's home, and the 1st Earl resided at Grimsthorpe Castle. The 2nd Earl of Ancaster sold the bulk of the Normanton Estate in 1924-25. However, the site of the demolished Normanton Hall, along with some adjoining land and buildings, was not sold until the early 1950s.

From a portrait at Grimsthorpe Castle of the 1st Earl of Ancaster (Grimsthorpe & Drummond Castle Trust)

The Death of the 1st Earl of Ancaster

The 1st Earl's death (24th December 1910) was announced in the 30th December's edition of the *Stamford Mercury*.

'As a landlord, he was always generous and considerate, and extremely popular with his tenantry. It is not yet forgotten how, in the agricultural hard times of 1904, the Earl made his tenants a welcome Christmas present by remitting a considerable portion of their rent.'

His funeral held at Edenham Church, near to Grimsthorpe, Lincolnshire, was fully reported in the following edition. Also reported:

'At Empingham a memorial service was held at the parish church . . . while the funeral was taking place at Edenham. The service was conducted by the Rev. T. W. Owen (Rector) and was most impressive. In the evening a half-muffled peal was rung on the church bells and after the evening's service on Sunday the "Dead March" in Saul was played by the organist, Miss Dawson.'

From a portrait at Grimsthorpe Castle of the 2nd Earl of Ancaster (Grimsthorpe & Drummond Castle Trust)

Family Tree of the Heathcotes of Normanton Hall

Gilbert Heathcote (1625-1690) of Chesterfield
    = **Ann Dickins**
Eight sons, all bar one being merchant adventurers.
He was succeeded by his eldest son:

Sir Gilbert Heathcote (1651-1732) 1st Baronet
    = **Hester Rayner** (died 1714)
Governor of the Bank of England, Mayor of London and MP.
Purchased the estate of Empingham with Normanton from Charles Tryon of Bulwick *circa* 1729.
He was succeeded by his eldest son:

Sir John Heathcote (1689-1759) 2nd Baronet
    = **Bridget White** (died 1772)
He was succeeded by his eldest son:

Sir Gilbert Heathcote (1722-1785) 3rd Baronet
    = (1) **Marguerite Yorke** (died 1796)
    = (2) **Elizabeth Hudson** (died 1813)
He was succeeded by his eldest son:

Sir Gilbert Heathcote (1773-1851) 4th Baronet
    = (1) **Katherine Sophia Manners** (died 1825)
    = (2) **Mrs Eldon** (died 1842)
He was succeeded by his eldest son:

Sir Gilbert John Heathcote (1795-1867) 1st Baron Aveland of Aveland, 5th Baronet
    = **Clementina Elizabeth Drummond-Burrell**
    Baroness Willoughby de Eresby (died 1888)
He was succeeded by:

Sir Gilbert Henry Heathcote-Drummond-Willoughby (1830-1910)
1st Earl of Ancaster, 25th Lord Willoughby de Eresby, 2nd Lord Aveland of Aveland, 6th Baronet
    = **Evelyn Elizabeth Gordon** (died 1921)
He was succeeded by:

Sir Gilbert Heathcote-Drummond-Willoughby (1867-1951)
2nd Earl of Ancaster, 26th Lord Willoughby de Eresby, 3rd Lord Aveland of Aveland, 7th Baronet
    = **Eloise Breese** (died 1953)
Following the death of the Dowager Countess of Ancaster, the bulk of the Normanton Estate was sold and by 1926 the house had been demolished. Grimsthorpe Castle, Lincolnshire, then became the family home.
He was succeeded by:

Sir Gilbert James Heathcote-Drummond-Willoughby (1907-1983)
3rd Earl of Ancaster, 27th Lord Willoughby de Eresby, 4th Lord Aveland of Aveland, 8th Baronet
    = **Nancy Phyllis Louise Astor** (died 1975)

Normanton Hall in the 1901 Census

The Census Return of 1901 for Normanton includes Normanton Hall. It shows that Gilbert Heathcote-Drummond-Willoughby, 1st Earl of Ancaster, and his wife Evelyn, had a household of 27 servants living at the Hall. It is interesting to note that only one of these, Walter Stone, was born in Rutland. Four of the Earl's daughters were still living at home and the family had five visitors on the night of the Census, making the total occupancy 39. A further fourteen of the Earl's staff, mainly grooms and gardeners, were living in the stables and elsewhere in the Hall grounds. The total number of people in the parish on the night of the Census was 80.

NAME	RELATIONSHIP TO HEAD	AGE	OCCUPATION	PLACE OF BIRTH
Ancaster Gilbert H D Willoughby	Head	70	Peer of United Kingdom	Portman Lane, London
Ancaster Evelyn E H D Willoughby	Wife	55		Overton Longville, Hunts
Margaret M H D Willoughby	Daughter	35		Belgrave Lane, London
Nina H D Willoughby	Daughter	31		Belgrave Square, London
Alice H D Willoughby	Daughter	24		Belgrave Square, London
Mary A H D Willoughby	Daughter	22		Belgrave Square, London
Robert Heathcote	Visitor	57	Living on own means	Aix la Chapelle
Edith Heathcote	Visitor	45		Eaton Square, London
Robert E M Heathcote	Visitor	16		Manton, Rutland
Sibyl B W Heathcote	Visitor	22		Queen's Gate Tce, London
George G Aston	Visitor	39	Major, Royal Artillery	Cape Town, Cape Colony
Mary Ross	Servant	36	Laundry Maid (Domestic)	Lesswade, Scotland
Emily Muirhead	Servant	26	Laundry Maid (Domestic)	Edinburgh, Scotland
Caroline Busby	Servant	25	Laundry Maid (Domestic)	Liverpool, Lancs
Alice Mandeville	Servant	22	Laundry Maid (Domestic)	Hungerford, Berks
Jane Dewar	Servant	20	Laundry Maid (Domestic)	Crieff, Scotland
Maria Davies	Servant	44	Housemaid	Bishop's Frome, Hereford
Nora Rolfe	Servant	36	Housemaid	Chelmsford, Essex
Alice Forbes	Servant	22	Housemaid	Chelsea, London, Middlx
Edith Rainbow	Servant	18	Housemaid	Kenilworth, Warwick
Hannah Reeves	Servant	30	Kitchenmaid	East Dean, Sussex
Agnes C S Bussell	Servant	21	Kitchenmaid	Churchstanton, Somerset
Jane Prince	Servant	21	Kitchenmaid	Tarrant Gunville, Dorset
Annie M L Walker	Servant	21	Still-room maid	Edinburgh, Scotland
Agnes French	Servant	40	Housekeeper	Lamington, Scotland
Alexandrina Coghill	Servant	49	Lady's maid	Wick, Scotland
Rose Louisa Canfield	Servant	23	Lady's maid	Knebworth, Herts
Fanny Crouch	Servant	29	Lady's maid	Penshurst, Kent
Selina M Ream	Servant	39	Lady's maid	Caythorpe, Lincs
Edward Gallop	Servant	55	Butler	Blagdon, Somerset
Francis Bessow	Servant	37	Cook	Foreign Subject, France
James Newhaven	Servant	27	Groom of Chamber	Melton Mowbray, Leics
Henry Davies	Servant	25	Footman	Beacon, Brecknockshire
Percy Blow	Servant	20	Footman, Domestic	Milford, Hampshire
George Dennis	Servant	24	Footman, Domestic	Winderton, Norfolk
Arthur Pile	Servant	20	Steward's Roomboy	Newbiggin, Northum
William Laurant	Servant	22	Odd Man	Edenham, Lincs
Walter Stone	Servant	23	Scullion	Edith Weston, Rutland
George Bletchley	Visitor	27	Butler	Sussex

The Village Disappears

Estate records give an excellent picture of Normanton village as it was laid out in the eighteenth century. A map dated 1726, prepared by Tycho Wing (Lincolnshire Archives, 3 ANC 5/104/1), reveals that the estate had been partly enclosed. It also pinpoints the location of the manor house in relation to the village along the main street. This street led down to a bridge over the River Gwash. Other roads are shown along with the names of tenants who rented the fields.

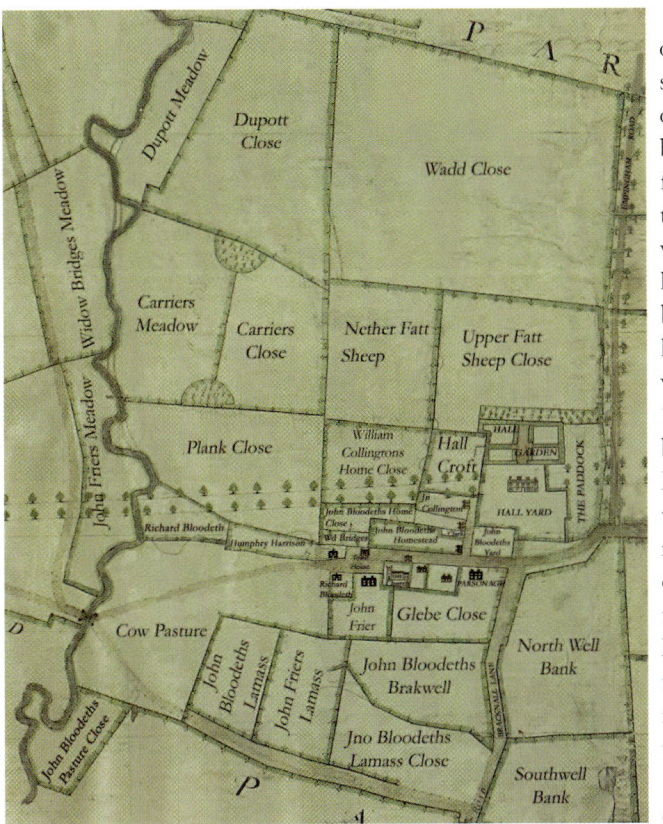

A mid-eighteenth century map of the village (ROLLR PP400/2) shows some changes, the principal one being that the mansion has been altered to include wings flanking the central block. It is thought that the new house, of which the stone alone is said to have cost £10,000, was completed between 1730 and 1740, and it is known that some re-modelling was carried out between 1763 and 1767. 1764 is often quoted as being the date when Sir Gilbert Heathcote, 3rd Baronet, removed the villagers of Normanton to his model village of Empingham in order to create a park. The relocation must have continued over a long period because records show that the estate was still receiving rents from Normanton tenants thirty years later.

The village was completely depopulated by 1796, the year that

Above: Part of Tycho Wing's map of 1726 showing Normanton village and the surrounding fields. This image has been enhanced to improve clarity (Lincolnshire Archives, 3 ANC 5/104/1)

Right: From a mid-eighteenth century map of Normanton (ROLLR PP400/2)

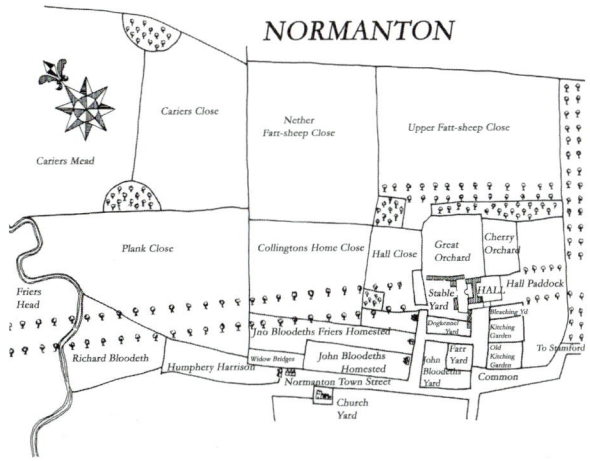

the landscape architect Humphry Repton visited Normanton. The following year he produced one of his Red Books in which there is no mention of the village. His illustrations give an excellent picture of the house and park and he recommended:

'The elegance and magnificence of the house are not at present sufficiently supported by the original size of the park ... and therefore its extension or enlargement was a very natural object of improvement.'

He made many suggestions and some of his improvements were carried out. Amongst these were the removal of old fences and the creation of new approaches, terraces and 'Pleasure Grounds' with walks. A larger kitchen garden and a lake in the Gwash Valley below the house were also created.

Humphry Repton

Humphry Repton was born in Bury St Edmunds, Suffolk, in 1752, the son of a tax collector. He was expected to become a merchant but his real interests of botany and gardening eventually dictated his career. When he moved to Essex in 1788 at the age of 36 with four children and no secure income, he had the idea of combining his sketching and gardening skills to become a landscape gardener. By sending circulars round his wealthy contacts he soon obtained his first paid commission at Catton Park, Derbyshire.

Repton's ideal was natural beauty enhanced by art, and his success was his vision of a house and how it should be placed in relation to the landscape surrounding it. Repton prepared a book bound in red leather for every client, detailing proposals for changes, maps, plans, drawings, watercolour paintings, and before and after sketches. These became known as his Red Books. In his 30-year career, he undertook over 400 commissions, including Normanton and nearby Burley on the Hill.

In 1811, Repton was involved in a serious carriage accident which left him disabled. He died in 1818 and is buried in the churchyard at Aylsham, Norfolk.

The south-east front of Normanton House as illustrated by Repton (Grimsthorpe & Drummond Castle Trust)

Brewer in *Beauties of England & Wales* (1813) wrote:

'NORMANTON . . . is now completely depopulated, nothing remaining but its venerable little church which stands separate from all other buildings in the grounds of Normanton House . . . The modern residence of NORMANTON HOUSE stands in a park containing about 400 acres . . . The mansion is an elegant modern edifice of white stone, with a centre of fine elevation and two wings; both fronts being in style of great architectural beauty, and the interior presenting a rich scene of modern elegance throughout. From the *Hall*, which is light and airy . . . we proceed to the *Library*, an elegant room fitted up with sofas, and the books so covered with handsome chintz curtains that it has more the appearance of a dressing room, than an apartment occupied for purposes of study. Passing through the *Small Drawing Room*, which is fitted up with studied elegance, we enter a *Dressing Room*, in a simple style of ornament . . . The *Dining Room* is a very superb apartment, with a vaulted and stuccoed ceiling, in compartments. Over the fire-place is the original painting of the present Lady Heathcote, in the character of Hebe, the engraved copies of which have been so much admired in the London print-shops. The *Drawing Room* is a most brilliant apartment, fitted up with embossed gold paper, with gilt borders and mouldings; the chairs are of light blue satin, with white flowers; and the whole is extremely light and elegant, without being gaudy. The *State Bed Room* is in a style of simple magnificence; the bed of white and gold, with the furniture and ornaments of the walls to correspond; the *Dressing Room* belonging to it is also a handsome specimen of modern taste, and the ceiling in particular is very fine, being elegantly painted in treillage and foliage. The *Back Drawing Room* has a pleasant bow-recess, and is fitted up with spotted Chinese paper, with crimson pannels [*sic*] on which are laughing and sporting Cupids in chiaro scuro, and interspersed with pannel [*sic*] slips of plate-glass. Each suite of apartments, on both floors, has doors which throw open a vista from end to end; and as there are large plate-glass mirrors at each extremity, the reduplicated effect is extremely fine.'

A visionary plan! Repton's plan for improvements in the park included a lake in the Gwash valley (Grimsthorpe & Drummond Castle Trust)

Normanton Park and Estate

White's *Directory* (1846) records:

'NORMANTON... has in its parish only 28 inhabitants, and about 2000 acres of land, all the property of *Sir Gilbert Heathcote, Bart.*, of NORMANTON HOUSE, which stands near the Church and Rectory, in a beautiful *Park* of about 500 acres, which was considerably enlarged about sixty years ago, when the village was swept away, and its inhabitants removed to Empingham... The gardens are modern; and the grounds are tastefully laid out, and command beautiful prospects. The park is well wooded, and contains many very large timber trees, principally oak, ash, beech, and limes, whose shade and foliage have a very fine effect, especially near the river [Gwash], which crosses it about half a mile west of the house. Among other rare plants found here, is the *Gentiana autumnalis fugax*, or later autumnal Gentian. The woods and plantations in the parish comprise about 200 acres.'

Normanton Park in 1822 from the north-west. The church is the only survivor of the old village of Normanton (RLHRS)

Normanton Gardens

Lord Aveland opened his gardens at Normanton to the public in 1863. It was reported in the *Stamford Mercury* on 2nd October:

'*The Gardens at Normanton*. The mansion stands on the north west declivity of one of those great ridges which intersect Rutland in different directions, and which add so much to the beauty of the county. The site could not have been more happily chosen, commanding as it does several extensive and pleasing prospects into the wooded vale of Catmos. The park here is very picturesque: great taste has been displayed in arranging and planting the different groups and single specimens of trees which now adorn the landscape. The gardens belonging to this interesting place were opened to the public on Sunday last, through the kind permission of Lord Aveland, who is pleased at all times that they may be shown to visitors. On entering the pleasure grounds the first objects to attract the attention are the magnificent Portugal laurels, forming great globes and huge obtuse cones: probably their equal is not to be found in this or any other country. Further on is a stone basket or basin, called Lady Chetwynd's basin, filled with flowers, which has a very pretty effect. We next arrive at the principal parterre, which is now most excellent for its gorgeous display of flora and its beauty of arrangement. The primary colours are those chiefly used here, and when seen over each other from different points of view blend together, and give it a softness which cannot but be pleasing to every eye of taste. The geraniums appear to have flowered extremely well this season. The beds of the dwarf chrysanthemum-flowered aster are very beautiful. Also the beds of *Verbena venosa*, the gem of all the verbenas, and without doubt the best bedding plant in existence for autumn gardening. The mixed borders are also very effective: these are planted according to heights, forming slopes of flowers, with a background of evergreens. We observed, in passing along, a very fine plant of the gigantic "Wellingtonia" from the now called Mammoth Tree Valley in the district of Calaveras, California . . . the ribbon borders in the kitchen garden are all that can be desired, and only require to be seen to be appreciated. Here, again, the *Verbena venosa* shows its qualities to perfection. The gardens in every way exhibited the best of keeping, and we went away highly delighted with one hour's ramble in the grounds at Normanton, as did also many others, who equally seemed to enjoy the scene.'

Normanton House from the south-east in 1822 (RLHRS)

During the nineteenth century there were many changes to the house. Interior decorations were renewed, in the same manner as they were in 1813, in time for the visit of the Prince and Princess of Wales in 1881. This Royal visit was fully reported in the *Stamford Mercury*, the *Graphic* and the *Illustrated London News*. In the 15th January 1881 edition of the *Illustrated London News*, correspondent 'Cuthbert Bede' described the house in the following way:

'The whole of the exterior of the mansion is remarkable for the beauty of the stonework and carving, and important additions and improvements have been made by the present noble owner [the 2nd Lord Aveland]. On the first floor, communicating with the spacious hall by a fine double stone staircase, are the suite of three handsome drawing-rooms and other rooms, from which beautiful views are obtained of the park and surrounding country. These rooms, as well as the library and dining-rooms on the ground floor, were originally decorated by Adams. Within the last few years the interior has been entirely redecorated, keeping to the same style, and is furnished with great taste, and with due regard to domestic comfort.'

Normanton House from the north-west in 1881 (Illustrated London News). It was drawn by local correspondent the Rev Edward Bradley, incumbent at Stretton (1871-83). He wrote under the name of 'Cuthbert Bede'

Normanton Park was featured in the 8th February 1913 issue of *Country Life*. By this time, the mansion was more often referred to as Normanton Hall by local people. A ground floor plan and both interior and exterior views of the house were illustrated, along with items of furniture that had been in the house for over a century. Garden ornaments were also shown. The article noted:

'The main building exhibits the exquisite sense of proportion which marks the best work of the period [eighteenth century]. Ornament is sparingly used, but what there is, is of extreme refinement. The contrast between the square wings of the west front and the semi-circular bay is charming, and the whole effect is a source of delight to all who appreciate the delicate handling of architecture. The interior decorations, put up when the house was first built, have given place almost everywhere to the "elegance" of the latter years of the century; but several ceilings, as well as the chimney pieces in the state bedroom and in the Chinese room or dressing room are original.'

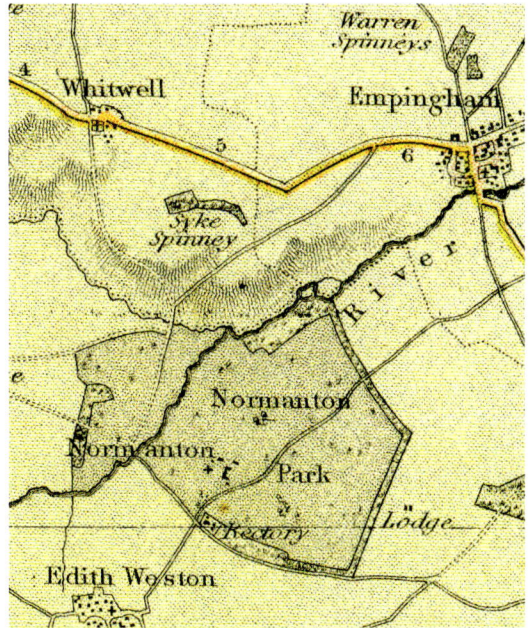

Above: Another drawing by 'Cuthbert Bede' showing 'a view on the lawn' at Normanton House in 1881 (Illustrated London News). *The dining room at the centre of this picture was a later addition to the house. A ball in honour of the Prince and Princess of Wales was held here in January 1881*

Left: Normanton Park from Letts' map of 1883. Kelly's Directory *of 1877 records that the park 'was well wooded and stocked with about 200 head of deer'*

Normanton Hall from the north-west in 1913 (Country Life Picture Library)

The terracotta chimney-piece was a prominent feature in the hall at Normanton (Country Life Picture Library)

The latticed bookcases in the library at Normanton were divided by narrow grisaille panels which were decorated with goddesses, fauns, animals and scrollwork (Country Life Picture Library)

The back drawing-room at Normanton Hall in 1913. The 'spotted Chinese paper' which decorated this room in 1813 had disappeared, but the panels with 'laughing and sporting Cupids in chiaro scuro' still remained. The panels were of crimson and grey, the family racing colours (Country Life Picture Library)

A bedroom at Normanton Hall in 1913 (Country Life Picture Library)

The cost of maintaining Normanton Hall was immense and, by 1924, the 2nd Earl of Ancaster had decided to sell the Normanton Estate and reside at Grimsthorpe Castle. The Heathcote family portraits, some items of furniture, tapestries and various garden ornaments from Normanton Hall were retained by the Earl of Ancaster and transferred to Grimsthorpe Castle. A number of these can be seen by visitors to the Castle today.

An eighteenth century table sundial stood in the circular lawn at the south front of Normanton Hall. It was illustrated as No 20 in a series of 25 cigarette cards of Old Sundials published by W D & H O Wills in 1928 (RO)

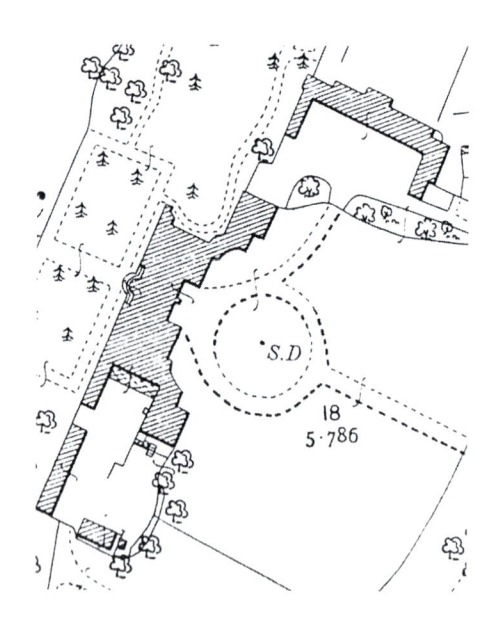

Above: The table sundial (SD) at Normanton Hall is marked on the OS 2nd ed 25" map 1904

The state bedroom in 1913 (Country Life Picture Library). This was hung with yellow decorative tapestry upon which parrots perched upon 'fantastic scrollwork' supporting a vase of flowers. The tapestries can be seen in The Tapestry Room at Grimsthorpe Castle. The white marble mantelpiece, with its white and gilt over-mantel enclosing a flower picture, is in The Gothic Bedroom at Grimsthorpe

Many of the statues removed from Normanton now grace the arcaded courtyard and garden at Grimsthorpe Castle (RO)

A garden urn removed from Normanton Hall to Grimsthorpe Castle (RO)

The Sale of Normanton Estate

An 'Important notice of sale of the valuable freehold residential, agricultural and sporting estate known as the Normanton Estate' appeared in the *Stamford Mercury* on 15th August 1924. For sale was the mansion, 'occupying a beautiful position within its noble Park, and containing hall, 9 reception-rooms, 11 principal bedrooms, ample servants' accommodation, 5 bathrooms, good domestic offices, excellent Stabling, Garage Accommodation' and eighteen high class mixed farms varying from 90 to 450 acres, 'each equipped with exceptionally fine Farmhouses and Buildings'. Also up for auction were numerous smallholdings, accommodation lands, the entire model village of Empingham, part of Edith Weston, building sites and woodlands. The whole area extended to some 6,000 acres.

The peach house from Normanton Hall is now at Grimsthorpe Castle (Grimsthorpe & Drummond Castle Trust)

— 251 —

Top Right: This announcement was published in the Stamford Mercury *on 15th August 1924*

Bottom Right: The last page of the Normanton Park 'Fixtures and Fittings' auction catalogue showing prices realised (Grimsthorpe & Drummond Castle Trust)

The sale was held at the 'Stamford Hotel,' Stamford, Lincolnshire on 17th and 18th September 1924. The *Stamford Mercury* reported in the following day's issue that 'Bidding was not very brisk, and only a few sales were effected, the majority of the lots offered on Wednesday not reaching the reserve figure. A considerable number of lots had been disposed of previously to the tenants'. Lot 9, Normanton Hall with gardens and grounds, and Lot 10, part of Normanton Park offered as one lot, were withdrawn from the sale. As the mansion could not be sold intact a decision was made to demolish it. Most of the land had been privately sold by 10th April 1925.

An auction for the interior and exterior fixtures and fittings of Normanton Hall and for 'The Remaining Shell of the MANSION' was held over three days from 24th February 1925. This auction also included the kitchen garden, stables, garages, the site of the mansion, 'pleasure grounds' and two cottages. A separate auction sale of the standing timber in Normanton Park and the adjoining Belt Plantations, which included oak, lime, beech, elm, larch and sycamore, had taken place on 20th February.

Interior fittings for sale included: oak and pine flooring, 150 sash and casement windows, store cupboards, dressers, a massive stone double staircase with mahogany hand-rail and brass balustrades, 53 carved marble, stone and wood mantelpieces with polished steel grates, bathroom and lavatory fittings, ranges, hot plates and coppers. Exterior fittings listed in the sale catalogue included: stone paving, stone vases and urns, lead rain-water heads and pipes, fencing and iron gates. The fittings and fixtures were sold at 'excellent prices' and the shell of the building realized a total of

---

RUTLAND.
Between Stamford and Oakham, about 4 miles from Stamford Station (L. and N.E. Railway) and (L.M. and S. Railway), 2 miles from North Luffenham (L.M. and S.R.), and 6 miles from Oakham (L.M. and S. Railway).
IMPORTANT NOTICE of SALE of the VALUABLE FREEHOLD RESIDENTIAL AGRICULTURAL and SPORTING ESTATE,
known as the
NORMANTON ESTATE,
including
An IMPOSING and HISTORICAL EARLY 18th CENTURY MANSION,
occupying a beautiful position within its noble Park, and containing hall, 9 reception-rooms, 11 principal bedrooms, ample servants' accommodation, 5 bath-rooms, good domestic offices, excellent Stabling, Garage Accommodation Also 19 HIGH-CLASS MIXED FARMS, some with possession,
Varying in size from 90 Acre to 450 Acres, each equipped with exceptionally fine Farmhouses and Buildings;
NUMEROUS SMALL HOLDINGS, ACCOMMODATION LANDS,
The ENTIRE MODEL VILLAGE of EMPINGHAM,
Including the Valuable Free and Fully-licensed Premises, known as
THE WHITE HORSE INN;
Two Superior Residences,
PART of the Village of EDITHWESTON, BUILDING SITES and WOODLANDS,
the whole extending to about
6000 ACRES.

64

The Remaining Shell of the MANSION,

As it will stand after the Sale of the FIXTURES AND FITTINGS, as Catalogued, which includes:—

The whole of the Roofing Slate, the Roofing Timbers and the Deal Linings to the Roof (all in most excellent order). The whole of the Stone and Brick Work, the Stone Carved Window Frames, and the massive stone pillars in the Hall.

The whole of the Floor Joists, all the Beams and other Timbers in the Mansion, all the Landing Floors, Pitch Pine Ceiling in the Servants' Hall.

£1900 · 0 · 0

The whole of the Valuable Piping in the Building (except any of which may have been sold with the Fittings), including the Heating Pipes, the Hot and Cold Water Supply Pipes, Copper Pipes from Circulating Boiler to Baths, the Lead and Iron Soil and Waste Pipes. Two Stone Staircases.

Also the Enormous Quantity of Lead and Zinc on the Roof, Flats, Ridges, Gutters and Valleys. A quantity of Glass Partitions and Glazed Roofs. Fire Hydrants and Force Pump.

The Enormous Quantity of Bricks and Stone Work in the Cellars. In fact everything in the Mansion and Buildings that has not been Lotted and Sold.

THE EXCELLENT WALLED
KITCHEN GARDEN WITH STABLES AND GARAGES
adjoining; together with the
SITE OF THE MANSION AND PLEASURE GROUNDS,
With Greenhouses, Vineries, Forcing Pits, Fruit Room, Potting Shed, Heated Frames;
TWO COTTAGES,

£960 · 0 · 0

Bothey and Open Shed; also all Fruit Trees as planted, comprising an area of
22.197 ACRES OR THEREABOUTS
will be offered as a whole AFTER THE SALE OF THE FABRIC OF THE MANSION.

ALL TIMBER, other than Fruit Trees and Ornamental Shrubs, have been Sold, and are not included in the Sale.

A PLAN of the Property may be inspected at the Auctioneers' Offices, and will be produced at the time of Sale.

The Conditions of Sale under which this Property is Sold may be had on application to MESSRS. CLAYHILLS, SON AND FEETHAM, Darlington, or THE AUCTIONEERS, Bridgnorth.

END OF SALE.

£160 · 0 · 0   Brew House Range of Buildings

SOLD IN PORTIONS.

PENDING DEMOLITION OF NORMANTON HALL.

A demolition sale took place at Normanton Hall last week. Messrs. Perry and Phillips, of Bridgnorth, being the auctioneers. A large company was present each day. buyers being represented from practically all the large centres in the Midlands, in addition to the local ladies and gentlemen who were anxious to secure some of the items as mementoes of the mansion. Considerably more than 900 lots were catalogued.

The following are the more important items with the prices they made:— Mantelpieces, £45. £40. £37. £31, £25, and several others from £10 to £16; grates, £32. £28. £26. £18 to £10: oak floors. £40 and £20: weather vanes. £19 10s. and £21: stone vases and flower beds. £20. £17 10s., £17 10s.: smaller vases and urns (about 40), £93; open shed. £53; terrace and other walls. £48. £30, £19; pair of iron gates, £30 and £18.

£1,900. The house had to be demolished before March 1926.

A further notice regarding the demolition of Normanton Hall was published in the 24th April 1925 edition of the *Stamford Mercury*. This announced the future sale of 'an enormous quantity of Ketton stone, comprising handsomely carved Cornices, Doorways and Windows, also Ashlar, Quoins, Jambs, copings, etc., all in perfect condition. Practically no re-working required. The whole is a perfect specimen of this beautiful Stone, the quarries of which have been practically worked out. Therefore an exceptional opportunity arises for architects, builders and others to secure this supply at an exceptionally low price'. Also advertised was 'a large quantity of Oak Beams, Joists, Battens, Scantlings, etc., in perfect condition, and in suitable lots'. The sale, to which 'estate owners, building contractors, antique furniture manufacturers and others' were invited, took place on 28th May 1925.

Top Left: A brief account of the auction of the fixtures and fittings at Normanton from the Stamford Mercury *of 6th March 1925*

Bottom Left: A sketch by Harry Kelham who visited Normanton Hall whilst it was being demolished (Marion Kelham)

Normanton Reclamation

When Normanton Hall was dismantled and sold at auction, many of the lots were purchased by local people. Some examples are given below showing the diverse uses to which the stone, fixtures and fittings were put:

The White House

Much of the stone from the demolished Normanton Hall was purchased by Thomas Henry Crumbie, who owned a printing business in Leicester and who was secretary of the Leicester Tigers Rugby Football Club from 1895 until his death in 1928. The stone was numbered and transported to Scraptoft, Leicestershire, where it remained on the site for nearly three years. Much of it was used to build a family home incorporating many of Normanton Hall's internal features, including panelling and fireplaces. However, he only enjoyed living in it for a month before he died. For many years after this the house was occupied by the Harrison family who were important seed merchants. Later, the house was purchased by a brewery and now it is known as The White House, a public house and restaurant.

Above: The White House, Scraptoft, Leicestershire (RO)

Below Left: Footpaths in the garden of The White House are made from dressed stones recovered from Normanton Hall (RO)

Below Right: The main entrance to The White House was formerly the porch to the south-east front at Normanton Hall (RO)

Left: This lantern was recovered from Normanton Hall and was for many years in the garden behind Hallstones at Empingham. When the neighbouring surgery was extended it was purchased by a local builder (Sylvia & Michael Leach)

Right: This bungalow in Main Street, Empingham, was built using stone from Normanton Hall. It was built by Mr J J Healey and is known locally as Hallstones. Mr Healey also erected a workshop adjacent to the bungalow, again using stone from Normanton (RO)

Normanton Stone at Knossington

Mr Charles Spence, a Knossington builder, purchased stone, doors and other fittings at the Normanton sale. A cottage conversion in the village is believed to have internal doors and staircases from the former mansion. A detached house to the east of this cottage was built on the site of The Greyhound, a former public house. It was constructed using ironstone from the demolished inn and Normanton stone for the front elevation. Some of the windows were originally in the nursery at Normanton Hall.

Left: Reclaimed stone and windows from Normanton Hall were used when this house at Knossington, Leicestershire, was built (RO)

Left: The southern boundary wall of Empingham cemetery was constructed using stone which came from Normanton. A plaque on the wall records that it was built in 1946 (RO)

Right: Stone balustrading from Normanton was used for an ornamental bridge and a patio surround at Preston Lodge, Withcote, Leicestershire. It was sold in separate lots in the Fixtures and Fittings Sale held in 1925 (RO)

10.0.0	834	THE STONE PALISADING, 75ft., AS FIXED OVER HOUSEKEEPER'S ROOM AND STUDY ON LEFT-HAND SIDE OF THE HOUSE, TOGETHER WITH 16 STONE BALLS
10 0.0	835	A similar lot over smoke room on the right-hand side of the house
6.18.0	836	THREE CARVED STONE VASES OVER NURSERY WING
5.10.0	837	FOUR DITTO OVER ENTRANCE DOOR
4 4 0	838	THE STONE PALISADING, AS FIXED OVER FRONT DOOR, ABOUT 45ft.

Left: Palisading and other stone ornaments included in the Normanton Park fixtures and fittings sale catalogue (Grimsthorpe & Drummond Castle Trust)

A contemporary view of the south-east elevation of Normanton Hall showing the stone balustrading and ornaments included in the auction catalogue (Hart)

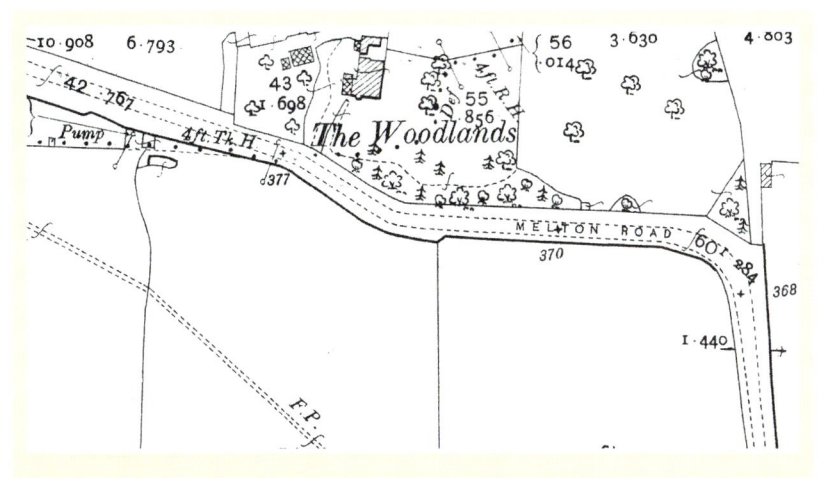

Right: The Woodlands in Melton Road, Oakham, as shown on the OS 2nd ed 25" map 1904

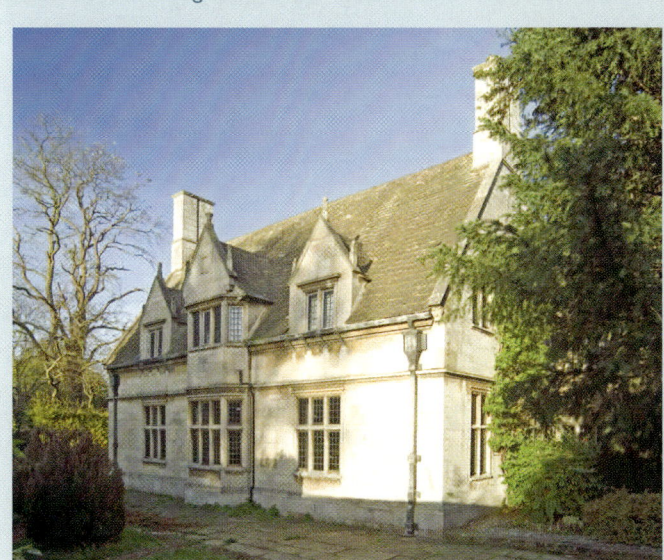

Below Left: The west wing of Langham Old Hall (Mike Frisby)

Below: A staircase from Normanton Hall, now at Langham Old Hall (RO)

Bottom Right: The new west wall to Langham Old Hall was built using stone from Normanton (RO)

Road Improvements

Originally there was a sharp corner near The Woodlands in Melton Road, Oakham. It is now the junction with Pillings Road. In 1926 a decision was made to widen the road and to make the bend less severe. A large quantity of stone was required and this came from the recently demolished Normanton Hall.

Langham Old Hall

Langham Old Hall has a core of 1665, but it was extensively altered between 1925 and 1930 by Owen Hugh Smith. A new wall to close off the old carriage entrance, a new west wing, a staircase in the main building, and possibly the summer house, were all built using recovered materials from Normanton Hall.

Top Right: The south-east entrance to Normanton Hall in 1881. Note the decorative wrought-iron gate posts (Illustrated London News)

Today there is little to see of the former mansion. The stable block, now Normanton Park Hotel, the gun room and brew house, now Park House, and the kitchen gardens remain on the site. The pasture between the hotel and Park House identifies the site of Normanton Hall and the gate posts to the former south-east entrance can be seen here. Part of the garden terrace wall remains near the Rutland Water perimeter path. Much of the parkland is now under Rutland Water but the former St Matthew's Church, albeit much altered, has been saved as a memorial to the lost village and estate of Normanton.

Above Left: Normanton Hall stables before being converted to an hotel circa 1984 (Richard Adams)

Above Right: The gate posts can still be seen at Normanton today (RO)

Left: The ornamental top to one of the gate posts (RO)

Right: The site of Normanton Hall. To the left is Park House, the former brew house, gun room and store rooms of the mansion (RO)

Park House, Normanton

Mike Griffin talks about his home which was once part of Normanton Hall:

'My home, Park House, was part of Normanton Hall but was not physically connected to it. It was separated by probably five to ten yards of space. It used to serve the main house as a brew house and part of it was a gun room and various store rooms. I think that was what the building was originally designed for, but in later years the Ancasters used some of the rooms as a sanatorium for when the staff in the hall were ill.

'In terms of the layout of the house, and starting at the bottom end of the slope, there was a large area which was the brew house and, although you don't see any remains of it now other than in the loft, on top of the roof there was a fairly large, square structure which, I think, housed a hoist and also provided ventilation. If you then rise up on to the next level up the slope you come to the former gun room which had five very large pinewood cupboards, each of which held three guns.

'Moving into the top two rooms, these were variously stores, mess rooms and, I think later, one of them was a sanatorium. Outside of the house there is a very large and substantially built barn. In fact, that barn on the old plans is shown as a faggot shed where faggots, being lengths of wood, were stored for providing fuel for the laundry boilers. There are also two fairly large tunnels opposite the house which were coal bunkers for the laundry. On top of these tunnels is a fairly large area about the size of a badminton court which was a drying area for the laundry.

'There were also some ruins there which were part of some more brewing activity. On the other side of the house, on the reservoir side, there are some trees in the gardens which were there during the time of Normanton Hall. We also have a view across to Normanton Church or what was Normanton Church, now a museum and owned by Anglian Water. You also get a view straight across to Burley on the Hill.

'In old photographs of Normanton Hall, the cedar tree which is now in the grounds of Normanton Park Hotel can clearly be seen. In one of the small paddocks, you can see evidence of the original road which went down to the back of Normanton Hall and also the gate posts at the entrance to the hall grounds. The road came down and then swept round into a circle which provided access to the back of the house.

'The hotel used to be the stables which became our farm yard and about 1942 part of it was commandeered to house Italian and later German prisoners of war. They worked on farms, some for my father on the farm here at Normanton, and others worked on farms nearby. They lived at the stables and did their own cooking. There was a guard there with responsibility for looking after them but as far as I know there were never any break-outs.'

Left: Mike Griffin (Marigold Lamin)

Right:
A caricature of Edward, Prince of Wales which appeared in Vanity Fair in 1878 (RLHRS)

Below:
Luffenham Station (Hart)

The Prince and Princess of Wales visit Normanton

On Monday 10th January 1881 the Prince [the future Edward VII] and Princess of Wales visited Rutland. They were the guests of Lord and Lady Aveland and the visit was fully reported in the *Stamford Mercury* on 14th January 1881.

On arrival at Luffenham Station, the Royal party were received by Lord Aveland who then accompanied them to his carriage outside the station. On their appearance, loud cheers were sent up by the waiting crowd. They proceeded to Normanton Park, passing under several triumphal arches decorated with evergreens and festooned with flags and banners. One had the message 'Welcome' upon it and 'was made brilliant with lighted lanterns formed of huge Rutland turnips'. The Prince and Princess were received at Normanton Park by Lady

Left: A caricature of the 2nd Lord Aveland as featured in Vanity Fair, *30th July 1881 (RLHRS)*

Aveland, members of her family and the company staying in the house.

The estate village of Empingham observed the royal visit 'with the utmost respect and enthusiasm', being decorated in the best possible taste, and 'nowhere was the tawdry element to be met with'. It is reported that the decorations made a wonderful sight both during the day and at night. The local newspaper continued to report:

'On Tuesday Lord Aveland entertained the Prince and some of his other distinguished guests with a day's shooting on the Rutland estate. About 11 o'clock his Lordship, driving a four-in-hand, took the party through Empingham village (where a hundred of the school children assembled and sang 'God bless the Prince of Wales') on to the Exton road, in the fields skirting which sport was opened with eight guns . . . Returning to Empingham the party worked the fields near the Whitwell road, and then bore down towards the thickets known as Cocked Hat Spinny [*sic*], where pheasants are generally plentiful. Thence they proceeded to Normanton Park. At 1 o'clock the Princess, accompanied by Lady Aveland and the Hon. Margaret Willoughby, drove to see the shooting at Mowmires, and afterwards with the ladies joined the gentlemen at luncheon, which was laid out in a spacious and comfortable tent near the Lodges. After the repast the battue recommenced. Near the lodge gates the sport was really excellent: guns flashed and crackled, pheasants went up with a whirr-r-r-r and fell with a thud, and hares rolled over in their death throes with the greatest rapidity.'

Above: Lady Evelyn, wife of the 2nd Lord Aveland. From a portrait at Grimsthorpe Castle (Grimsthorpe & Drummond Castle Trust)

The south-east entrance to Normanton Hall in 1881. This was one of three sketches published in the Illustrated London News *to accompany the report on the Royal Visit*

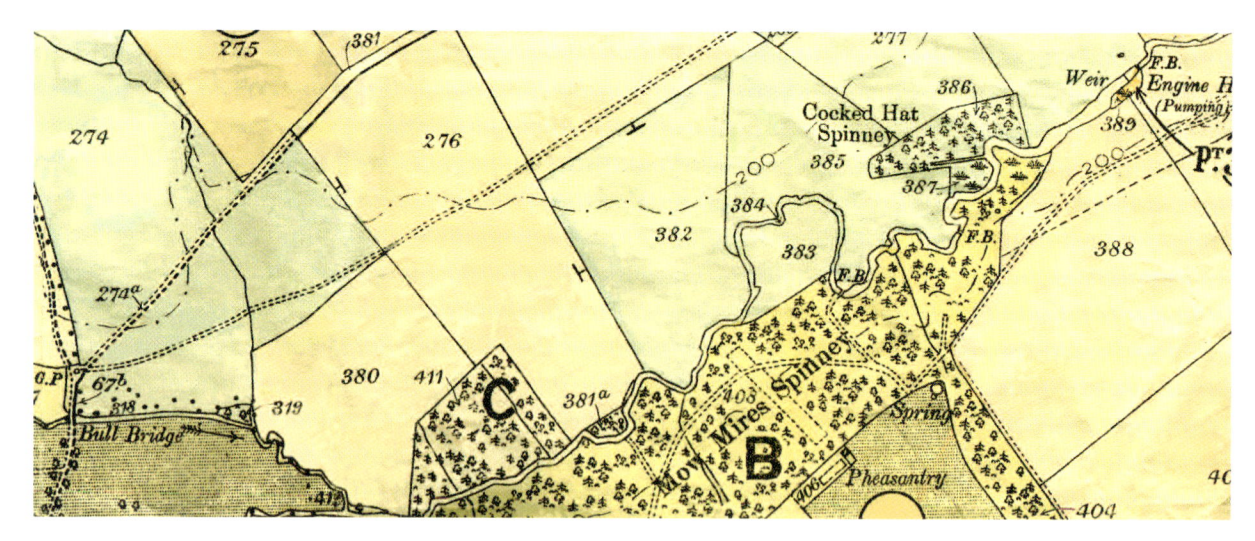

On the Wednesday the Prince, with the same shooting party, visited Grimsthorpe Castle, the seat of the Baroness Willoughby de Eresby. More shooting was enjoyed on the Rutland estate on the Thursday whilst a visit was made to Oakham Castle by the Princess. As it was her first visit to Oakham, custom demanded that the Princess should present a horseshoe to the town. At the castle she located a suitable position for the horseshoe to be fixed but it could not be presented to the dignitaries on this occasion. It was being made in the works of Lord Aveland but was not quite finished. A lawn meet of the Cottesmore hounds was arranged on the Friday with luncheon at Burley on the Hill. A ball was held at Normanton Park in the evening and the Royal couple left for Stamford the following day.

The festivities at Normanton were brought to a happy termination on the following Tuesday when Lord Aveland entertained about 400 of his workmen, their families and others employed on the estate. The estate workshops were cleared and a sumptuous supper provided – a band was provided for dancing and the party continued until 4am on Wednesday. Before separating, the company gave 'three times three' cheers for Lord and Lady Aveland.

Above: The area to the east of Bull Bridge, near Mow Mires Spinney, which was visited by the Royal shooting party. From the map accompanying the Normanton Estate Sale Catalogue of 1924

Left: One of the workshops at Normanton Works where Lord Aveland entertained his workforce and their families in 1881 (RO)

— 262 —

Normanton Works

White's *Directory* (1877) records:

'... just on the outskirts of [the park] Lord Aveland has established large workshops with wood-working machinery driven by steam. Here upwards of 100 workmen are employed, who, under the able superintendence of Mr. Newman, clerk of the works, execute all the building operations which are undertaken on the extensive estates both in Rutland and Lincolnshire.'

Normanton Works, now known as Normanton Lodge Farm, is located about two kilometres to the north-east of Edith Weston in Normanton Parish. The precise date for the construction of these Victorian workshops is not known, but they were certainly built between 1861 and 1871.

There is no mention of Normanton Works in the 1861 Census but a Joseph Newman was recorded as Clerk of Works in 1871. The return for that year states that he was 48 years of age and born in Norfolk. He was living with his wife Elizabeth, their two sons and two daughters. His eldest son Miles, aged 21 years, was an office clerk.

Joseph was still Clerk of Works in 1881 and he and his wife and four children are recorded as living at The Lodge. His son, Miles, was at this time farm bailiff for the Ancaster Estate. It is understood that The Lodge was built specifically for Joseph Newman, it being located almost opposite the farm and estate works. Joseph continued to be Clerk of Works until at least 1891. At this date he was living with his wife and a servant. A heavy burden must have fallen on the shoulders of Joseph and Miles when they made preparations to host Lord Aveland's festivities for the tenantry at the Normanton Works in January 1881.

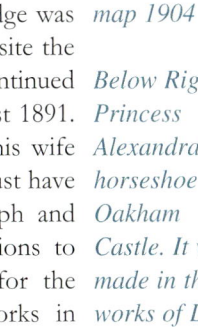

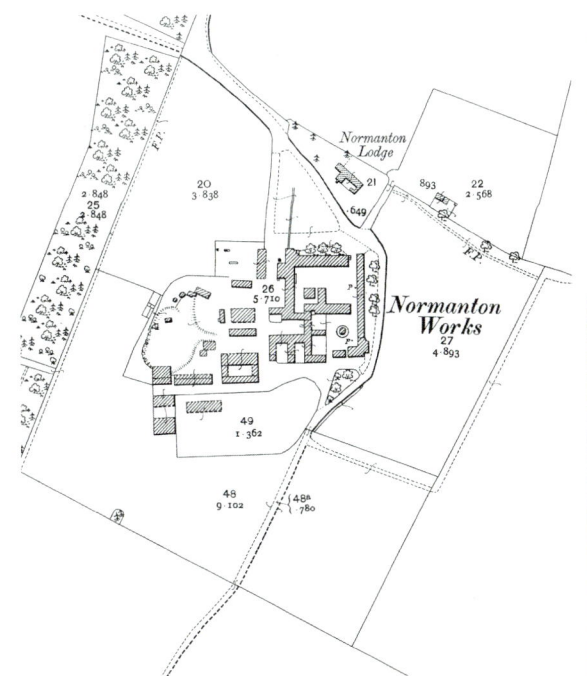

Above: Normanton Works as illustrated in the 1924 sale catalogue (RCM)

Below Left: Normanton Works from the OS 2nd ed 25" map 1904

Below Right: Princess Alexandra's horseshoe in Oakham Castle. It was made in the works of Lord Aveland in 1881

Right: From a drawing of Normanton Works in 1874 showing the blacksmith's and stonemason's workshops (Christopher Renner)

By 1901 Robert Yates had become 'Estate Clerk of the Works'. He was 49 years of age and living with him was his wife Anne, daughter Cecily and a female servant. Kelly's *Directory* (1904) records, under 'Normanton Works Office': 'Edward Brett Binns, agent; Alfred Schofield, sub-agent'. Edward Binns was Agent for three Earls of Ancaster, a highly responsible job. He introduced a distinctive style of architecture, known as 'The Ancaster Style', which is particularly evident in Empingham. In 1904 the workshops employed about 50 hands.

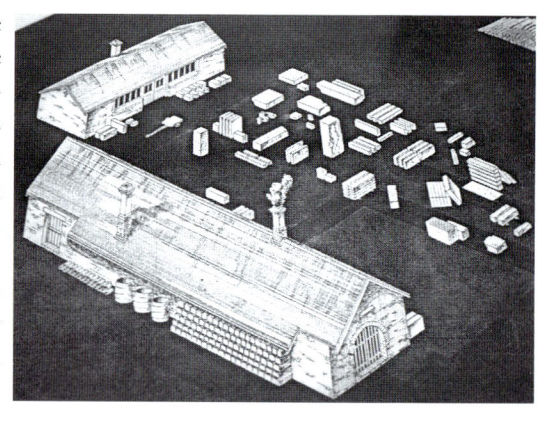

Above Left: Semi-detached Ancaster cottages in Main Street, Empingham. Note that the bedroom windows are placed in the gable ends. Tradition states that this was because Lady Willoughby did not want her tenants to look down on her as she rode by in her carriage (RO)

Above Right: The blacksmith's workshop at Normanton Lodge Farm today (RO)

Right: A late nineteenth century photograph of craftsmen and labourers at Normanton Works (Roger Corby)

— 264 —

A Normanton Works Timesheet

'An Account of the Time of Workmen employed by the Right Hon LORD AVELAND, on the Normanton Estate for the week ending Friday December 21st 1883.' (Christopher Renner)

This account, in the form of what would now be called a spreadsheet, lists all 139 workmen employed during the six-day working week starting on Saturday 15th December. Workmen are grouped together according to their trades and details are given of each man's employment for every day of the week. The last three columns give the employee's hours worked, his hourly rate of pay and his total pay for this week.

In general, pay rates vary between 10d per hour for senior skilled tradesmen to 3½d per hour for labourers. The lowest rate of pay is 1½d per hour and this is assumed to be for young apprentices. Most men worked a 54-hour week. The total wages for the week were £164 6s 10d, including a total of £10 18s 6d for expenses such as accommodation and travelling.

All the men listed on the account were based at Normanton Works, but many were engaged on projects elsewhere on the estates in Rutland and Lincolnshire. Plumbers, painters, joiners, masons and bricklayers, slaters and labourers were busy working on new buildings or carrying out maintenance work on estate property. The carters would be collecting and transporting building materials between the Works, local railway stations, local suppliers, the estate brickworks at Pilton, the estate quarries, and building sites. Other men carried on their trade at the Works. Sawyers converted seasoned timbers for the joiners and carpenters in the sawmill, and the blacksmiths, banker stonemasons and wheelwright all had spacious and well equipped workshops. Motive power for the sawmill and other workshops was provided by a central steam engine which powered a system of rotating shafts throughout the Works. All this machinery was overseen by the engineers.

The following analysis provides examples of the wide variety of work carried out on the Normanton Estate:

Trade	Number	Work
Engineers	4 men	Attending to working of machinery; sharpening saws; driving stationary engine.
Blacksmiths	3 men	Shoeing horses; making and repairing ironwork; assisting other blacksmiths.
Iron Fencer	1 man	Repairs to iron fencing at Stretton.
Plumbers	3 men	Working at the Hall; repairing church window; making lights for mills; glazing at late Bloodworth's cottage.
Painters	7 men	Painting at Knight's house and distempering; priming woodwork at late Bloodworth's cottage.
Joiners	20 men	Making desk for Estate Office; making door frames; repairing pheasant pens; hanging doors.
Carpenters	2 men	Supervising work at sawmill; making gates.
Wheelwright	1 man	Repairing trucks.
Sawyers	4 men	Cleaning machinery; sawing for stock; preparing wood for sawmill.
Masons/Bricklayers	24 men	Superintending masons; brick layout work at Shelton's house; repairing 2 roofs at Bulby.
Banker Masons	3 men	Making chimney piece for Shelton's house; working stone for Normanton Hall.
Slaters	2 men	Repairing slating at Empingham School; repairing roof of house in North Luffenham.
Mason Labourers	25 men	Assisting masons at Shelton's house; working at Knight's; levelling and excavating drains at Ingoldsby.
Labourers	32 men	Excavating at Works; cleaning up at Works; with traction engine; thatching at Mr Weed's premises.
Carters	8 men	Carting leaves off Coach road; carting materials from Corby [Glen] Station; to Stretton with Iron Fencer.

Left: The fowl house at Normanton Lodge Farm today (RO)

When the Normanton Estate was offered for sale in September 1924, Normanton Park Works was divided into two lots: Lot 29, Normanton Lodge Farm with a house, buildings, a pair of bungalow cottages and another pair of cottages, and Lot 30, Normanton Home Farm with a house, buildings, foreman's cottage and four bungalow cottages. Details of these buildings, which had 'originally formed part of Normanton Park Works', were included in the sale catalogue.

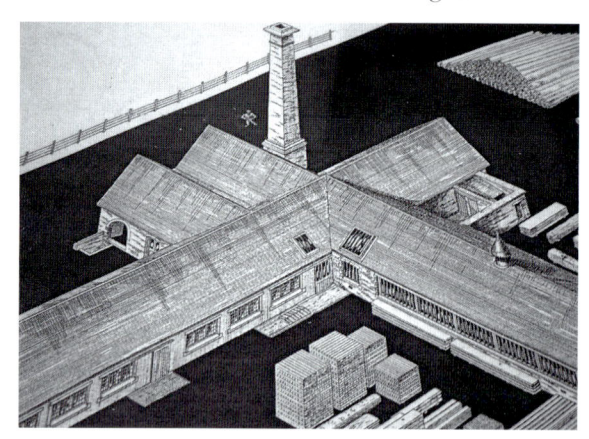

Above: Former 'Normanton Park Works' from the south in 2005 (RO)

Above: From a drawing of 1874 showing the sawmills and associated workshops at Normanton Works (Christopher Renner)

Above Right: From a drawing of 1874 showing the fowl house behind 'Home Farm' at Normanton Works (Christopher Renner)

Right: Normanton Lodge Farm from the Normanton Estate Sale Catalogue of 1924 (RCM)

NORMANTON LODGE

is pleasantly situate overlooking Normanton Park, and is in excellent condition and order. It is of stone and tile construction, and the accommodation, which is exceptionally well planned, includes:—

On the Ground Floor: Entrance Hall, Dining Room, Drawing Room, with bay windows, Breakfast Room, Kitchen with range and copper, Pantry, Cellars, Cloak Room and W.C.

On the Upper Floor: Five Bedrooms, Bathroom, fitted Bath (h. & c.).

Outside: Gardener's Hovel and E.C.

Pretty Gardens with Lawn, Kitchen Garden with Flower Beds and Borders, etc.

The Farm Buildings

which comprise part of Normanton Park Works, include:—Loose Box, Blacksmith's Shop, with two Forges, Shoeing Yard, Elaborate Implement Shed, Tractor & Threshing Machine House, newly-erected Brick and Tile Piggery, with sixteen pens opening on to large yard, two-bay open Cart Shed, Men's Room, three-bay Covered Implement Shed, Small Dutch Barn, four-bay Waggon Shed, Foldyard, having two-bay Shelters at either end, six Piggeries, six Large Boxes with tying for nineteen Cows, Trap House, ten-bay lean-to Implement Shed, Cart Horse Stable for twelve, two Chaff Houses, Harness Room, Large Enclosed Stackyard with ten double-bay Dutch Barn, with slate roof, match lined with iron supports, three-bay Shed with concrete floor used for Shearing and Lambing Pens, Barn, Large Partly Covered Foldyard with tying for twenty Cows, five-bay Large lean-to Implement Shed with corrugated roof.

NORMANTON HOME FARM

Situate about one mile from the Village of Empingham, being about two miles from North Luffenham Station (L.M. & S. Rly.), and convenient for Stamford and Oakham.
It is well roaded, and the land is farmed by the late owner, the Right Hon. the Earl of Ancaster, in conjunction with Normanton Lodge Farm (Lot 29).
The Buildings are extensive and in the finest state of repair.

The Farm Residence

is in excellent condition, is of stone and tile construction, and contains:—Seven Bedrooms, two Sitting Rooms, two Kitchens, Pantry, Scullery, Larder and Cellar.
Outside: Wash House fitted Copper, Coal House, Stick House, and two E.C.s.
Adjoining is a well-fitted Dairy.
The House is at present used as two Cottages, but could be readily converted into an excellent Farm House.

The Farm Buildings

which originally formed part of Normanton Park Works, include

A Group of Stone and Tile Buildings

Comprising:—Joiners' Shop, two Large Store Rooms and Offices, Garage with sliding door and fireplace, communicating with Saddle Room, two-stall Stable and Loose Box, Garage with sliding door, Paint Shop fitted cupboards and drawers, Trap House having cemented floor and communicating by sliding door with Store Room, 20ft. by 18ft., having fireplace.
Adjoining is a range of similarly constructed buildings, consisting of Forage Room, Granary, 33ft. by 16ft., with stone floor and loft over, Brick and Tile Carpenter's Shed, 39ft. by 21ft., Brick and Tile Large Implement Shed, range of Stone Slate and Tile Buildings, comprising Cake House with loft over, and Barn.

No. 1 FOLDYARD
is of Brick and Tile, with three-bay Shelter and Pigstye.

No. 2 FOLDYARD
of Brick and Tile, with four Pigstyes, Hay Store, four-stall Cow House, ditto for six, ditto for six, with feeding passage, and twelve-stall Cow House, also with feeding passage.

No. 3 FOLDYARD
having three-bay Cattle Shelter and Incubator House.

No. 4 FOLDYARD
with two-bay Cattle Shelter and Open Boxes, Cart Horse Stabling for twelve, and Harness Room, Tool Shed, Barn with Loft over, three Bull Boxes, opening on to Small Yard, Engine Room communicating with Cake House, measuring 24ft. by 45ft., and having water laid on.

Above: From the sale details for Lot 29, the sale of Normanton Lodge Farm. It is described as an 'Excellent Agricultural Holding', the lands being 'in the very highest state of cultivation, and the Farm Buildings . . . described as being probably the finest and best equipped in the County of Rutland' (RCM)

Normanton Bailiffs

The Normanton Estate was evidently very well managed. Census Returns and Directories provide names of the farm bailiffs who helped to accomplish this:

1851	John Clementson
1861	John Healey
1871	John Stacey
1881	Miles Newman
1891	George Culpin
1901	Joseph Harris
1904-25	Edwin Nichols

Above Right: From the sale details for Lot 30, 'The Exceedingly Valuable Mixed Farm' known as Normanton Home Farm. The land was farmed in conjunction with Normanton Lodge Farm (Lot 29), the buildings of which were 'extensive and in the finest state of repair' (RCM)

Both lots were withdrawn from the sale and although Normanton Works ceased to exist both units continued to function as one compact farm, known as Normanton Lodge Farm. Edwin Nichols continued as farm bailiff until the farm was taken over by W Robertson in 1927. W G Wakefield took over Normanton Lodge in 1928. Mr Irvine Renner began farming with his father-in-law, William Wakefield, in 1947 and took over the farm of 850 acres in 1961. Today, the farm continues to be run by his son and grandson, Christopher and George Renner.

Right: William Wakefield was the first family farmer at Normanton Lodge Farm (Christopher Renner)

— 267 —

Working at Normanton Lodge Farm

Kemmel Freestone (*see* Chapter 21 – Lost Homes) and his stepfather, Mr Bert West, worked for William Wakefield from about 1938. They lived in an Ancaster style semi-detached cottage on the Normanton to Ketton road. Kemmel lived here later with his wife, Margaret and their two daughters. He has fond memories of working at Normanton Lodge Farm:

'I went there as a labourer. There were about six or seven lads working on the farm; we took more looking after than a cart load of monkeys. When the tractor driver, who used to live next door to us, left Lodge Farm, Mr Wakefield, the boss, asked me if I would like to take over his job. I said that I would; at that time we had one tractor for 1000 acres. During the war we had more than three tractors; they had no cover on them so they were open to the elements . . . I used to be out there ploughing when they were bombing Coventry. I could see the flashes from the bombs. When ploughing at night I had a bicycle torch to show me where to go. I used to shine the torch down, hope and pray, and then lock the wheels into the furrow; you can do if you're good enough at it . . . we'd be ploughing the fields until 10 or 11 o'clock at night . . . Mr Wakefield was a good boss but if he caught you in the farm buildings smoking he'd say, "If the Good Lord wanted you to smoke he'd have put a chimney on your head". Every Christmas the boss used to kill two pigs and give everybody on the farm a pig's fry and a bit of pork; the pig's fry was a bit of liver, a bit of skirt [animal membrane], a bit of kidney and a chop.'

Above Left: William Wakefield and his daughter Mary with Kemmel Freestone at Normanton in 1946. Mary married Irvine Renner who continued to run the farm (Christopher Renner)

Left: Kemmel Freestone, on the tractor, talking to William Wakefield during the beet harvest in February 1946 (Christopher Renner)

Normanton Church Museum on a stormy day (Tim Hawkins)

St Matthew's Church

Perhaps the most prominent landmark at Rutland Water is the former church of St Matthew at Normanton. Its style is distinctive, looking more like a city church, its position at the edge of the reservoir giving the appearance, at a distance, of a moored ship. It seemed likely that this building would be demolished with the birth of the new reservoir but fortunately it was saved and Normanton Church Museum, as it is now known, is enhanced by its new surroundings.

The first permanent church at Normanton was probably built towards the end of the fourteenth century. Nothing is known of an earlier building. The earliest recorded Rector is Hugo de Novo Castro (1227-35). In 1579 the church was described as being in a very ruinous condition and 50 years later the chancel 'much decayed'. Sir Gilbert Heathcote, the 3rd baronet, rebuilt the church in 1764 as a plain building with a square chancel and aisleless nave, but the existing tower was left intact.

Above: The plaque in Normanton Tower recording that the church was rebuilt in 1764 (RO)

Left: A view of Normanton Church based on Repton's illustration of 1796 (Canon John R H Prophet)

Below: Normanton Church about 1839 with its new tower. Normanton House can be seen in the background (Uppingham School Archives)

Throughout the latter part of the eighteenth century the church was used less as a village church and more as a private chapel for the occupants of Normanton House. Brewer in *Beauties of England & Wales* (1813) describes it as a 'venerable little church, which stands separate from all other buildings in the grounds of *Normanton House*. Its appearance is interesting, its little Gothic turret peeping out from a shrubbery'.

In 1826 the fourth baronet commissioned a new tower featuring a portico. It had a vestibule forming the entrance and contained a double staircase which led to a gallery at the west end of the nave. This new work was designed by Thomas Cundy of London, architect to the Grosvenor estates, and the tower is said to be modelled on that of St John's Church, in Smith Square, Westminster.

The Funeral of the 1st Lord Aveland

The 1st Lord Aveland died at his London home on 6th September 1867 and his funeral was reported in detail by the *Stamford Mercury* on 20th September:

'The mortal remains of Gilbert John, 1st Lord Aveland, Lord Lieutenant and Custos Rotulorum of the county of Lincoln, Honorary Colonel of the South Lincoln militia, F.S.A. etc who died at his town residence, 12, Belgrave–square, were interred at Normanton church on Friday last.

'The corpse as stated last week, arrived at Normanton Park on the previous Tuesday, having been conveyed by the Great Northern Railway to Stamford. It was deposited in a lower room of the north wing of the mansion, which had been draped with black cloth . . .'

The hearse left the house on the Friday followed by six coaches carrying the chief mourners, the private carriage of the deceased and that of the newly created Lord Aveland, and four of the head servants.

'Next came 200 of the tenantry, two-and-two, wearing rich silk scarves and hatbands and gloves . . . The cortège slowly proceeded for some distance along the serpentine carriage road in an easterly direction, and before the mutes and lid of feathers had reached the screen of noble trees it had an imposing but unostentatious appearance, the effect being heightened by a brilliant meridian sun. On arriving at the semi-circular Grecian portico . . . the corpse was met by the Rev. T. B. Brown, Rector of the parish, and domestic chaplain to the deceased.

A baron's coronet ornament removed from the coffin of the 1st Lord Aveland (RCM)

'It was carried to the nave and placed on a bier, immediately after which the burial service was commenced, and after the lesson . . . the body was taken to the vestibule and deposited in a vault, where the burial service was concluded . . . The coffin was covered with rich Genoa crimson velvet, and studded with gilt nails, with four pair of handsome massive handles, and near each handle a baron's coronet. On the lid was a beautifully engraved plate with the family arms, and this inscription: "The Right Hon. Gilbert John, Baron Aveland, eldest son of Sir Gilbert Heathcote, 4th Baronet. Born 16th January, 1795. Died 6th September, 1867".

'There was a very large attendance of the inhabitants of Empingham and other adjacent villages, who lined the palisades enclosing the small church and cemetery until the return of the cortège, when they were admitted to take a farewell look at the coffin. Their behaviour throughout was becoming the solemn occasion. Mr Mitchell, chief constable, and several of the constabulary assisted to prevent any interruption to the arrangements. A hatchment was placed over the entrance to the mansion immediately after the funeral . . . .'

In 1911 the nave and chancel were rebuilt in a similar style to the tower of 1826 as a memorial to the 1st Earl of Ancaster. The staircase and gallery were removed and replaced by a wide archway on coupled Doric columns.

When Normanton Hall was demolished in 1926 the church, although left isolated in a field, was still used. Surviving Parish Registers are held at the Record Office for Leicestershire, Leicester and Rutland. The living was eventually amalgamated with Edith Weston and the Rectory became a private dwelling known as Bracknell House.

Below: Normanton Church before being rebuilt in 1911 (RLHRS)

Near Right: Normanton Church after being rebuilt in 1911 (© Crown Copyright.NMR)
Far Right: Normanton Church interior before 1911, showing the gallery (RLHRS)

Normanton Rectory, now Bracknell House. It became the home of Lady Alice, the daughter of the 1st Earl of Ancaster (Hart)

When the decision was made to construct a reservoir in the Gwash Valley, plans revealed that St Matthew's Church stood below the eventual high water line. The church was destined to be demolished and in 1970 it was deconsecrated by the Bishop of Peterborough.

Alex Watt, assistant sidesman at Normanton Church for a few years prior to its closure, remembers:

'My mother [Ella Watt] was the last person buried in the churchyard and that was in December 1966. Our eldest son Stephen . . . I think was one of the last christened in the church before it was closed. Services were held in the church once a month in the Summer months only. It was too cold in the winter. There was no heating and lighting was by oil lamps. Electricity wasn't put in until after the reservoir was there when it was made into a tourist attraction.'

After deconsecration, all the memorials, glass, fittings, graves and gravestones were removed from the church and churchyard. The altar slab and memorial tablets to the Heathcote family from inside the church were placed in the north aisle of Edith Weston Church. Other tablets went to Grimsthorpe Castle and Edenham Church. In 1972 two vaults were discovered beneath the church floor. The larger vault contained seventeen coffins. These were dated from 1710 to 1829 and belonged to thirteen adults and four children, all members of the Heathcote family. Four of these, dated 1710, 1714, 1719 and 1727, had been transferred in 1734 from the church at Low Leyton, now Leytonstone, Essex. Forest House, Low Leyton, was the home of Sir Gilbert Heathcote before he moved to Normanton *circa* 1729. In every case the inner lead coffins were exposed, the outer timber having decayed. The smaller of the vaults contained four coffins in much better condition. They dated from 1842 to 1888. The contents of both vaults were removed and the remains cremated along with those of 107 bodies exhumed from the churchyard. Two caskets of ashes from the churchyard were also removed for re-burial.

Above: The nave at Normanton Church after 1911, viewed from the altar (© Crown Copyright.NMR)

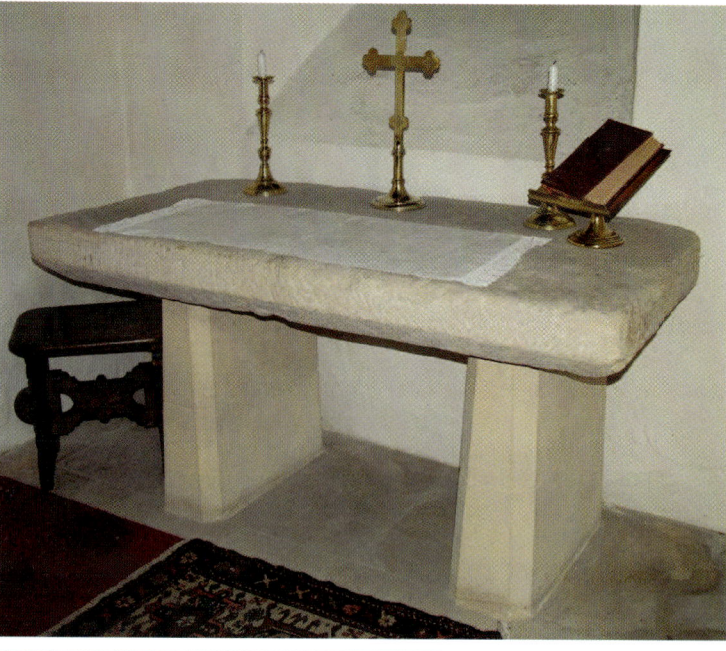

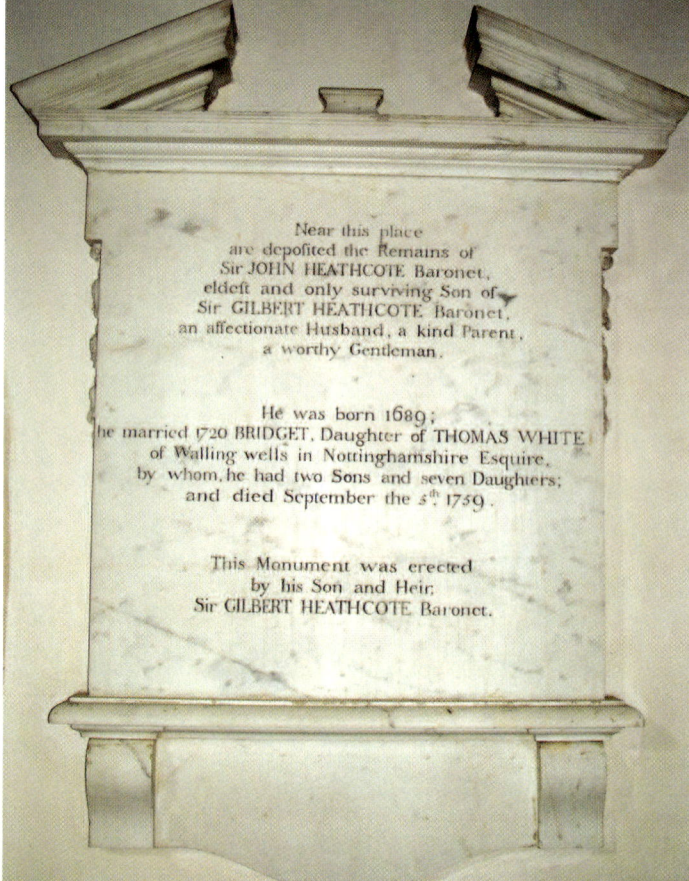

Above Left: The brass pulpit from Normanton Church was presented to Emmanuel Church, Western Flavell, Northampton, when it was built in 1973. It has now been returned and is displayed in Normanton Church Museum (© Crown Copyright.NMR)

Above Right: The altar from Normanton Church, now in the north aisle of Edith Weston Church (RO)

Left: Memorial to John, the son of the first Sir Gilbert Heathcote. This is one of six memorial tablets to the Heathcote family now in the north aisle of Edith Weston Church (RO)

> Near this place
> are deposited the Remains of
> Sir JOHN HEATHCOTE Baronet,
> eldest and only surviving Son of
> Sir GILBERT HEATHCOTE Baronet,
> an affectionate Husband, a kind Parent,
> a worthy Gentleman.
>
> He was born 1689;
> he married 1720 BRIDGET, Daughter of THOMAS WHITE
> of Walling wells in Nottinghamshire Esquire,
> by whom, he had two Sons and seven Daughters;
> and died September the 5th 1759.
>
> This Monument was erected
> by his Son and Heir,
> Sir GILBERT HEATHCOTE Baronet.

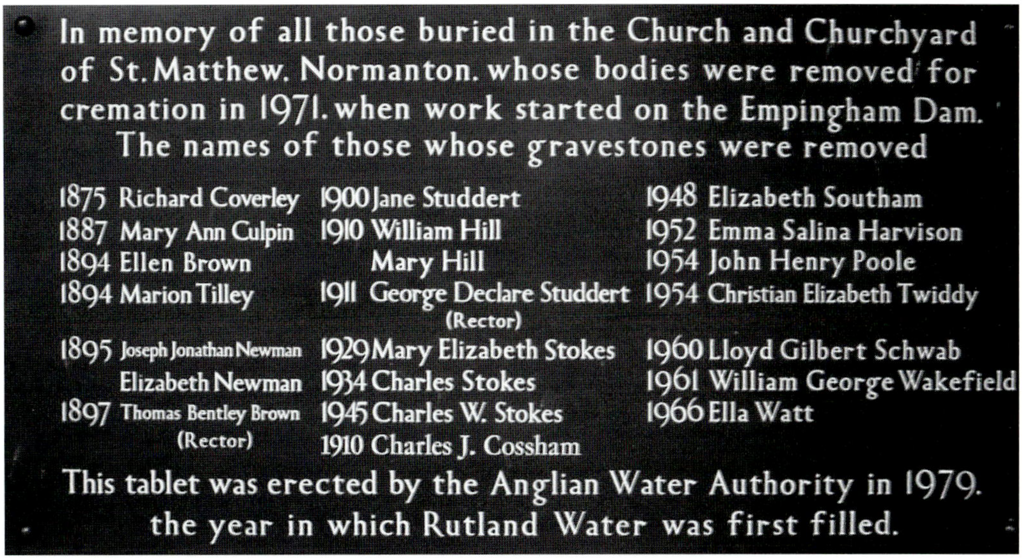

The tablet in the north aisle of Edith Weston Church to the memory of those who were buried at Normanton (RO)

> In memory of all those buried in the Church and Churchyard of St. Matthew. Normanton. whose bodies were removed for cremation in 1971. when work started on the Empingham Dam. The names of those whose gravestones were removed
>
> | | | |
> |---|---|---|
> | 1875 Richard Coverley | 1900 Jane Studdert | 1948 Elizabeth Southam |
> | 1887 Mary Ann Culpin | 1910 William Hill | 1952 Emma Salina Harvison |
> | 1894 Ellen Brown | Mary Hill | 1954 John Henry Poole |
> | 1894 Marion Tilley | 1911 George Declare Studdert (Rector) | 1954 Christian Elizabeth Twiddy |
> | 1895 Joseph Jonathan Newman | 1929 Mary Elizabeth Stokes | 1960 Lloyd Gilbert Schwab |
> | Elizabeth Newman | 1934 Charles Stokes | 1961 William George Wakefield |
> | 1897 Thomas Bentley Brown (Rector) | 1945 Charles W. Stokes | 1966 Ella Watt |
> | | 1910 Charles J. Cossham | |
>
> This tablet was erected by the Anglian Water Authority in 1979. the year in which Rutland Water was first filled.

Above: Some of the headstones from Normanton in the churchyard at Edith Weston (RO)

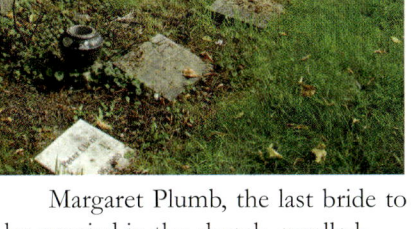

Left: The bell and window glass from Normanton Church were installed in the new church of St Jude's in Peterborough. Following the installation of three other bells in a new tower in 1984, this bell is again redundant. The bell is dated 1766 and was cast by Joseph Eayre of St Neots (RO)

Margaret Plumb, the last bride to be married in the church, recalled:

'I can remember when they were taking everything from the church ... they had to remove all the coffins and the tombstones ... they found a lot of coffins in the crypt that were made of solid lead. It really wasn't a very nice job for anyone but all the tombstones were moved to Edith Weston Church and they are now standing in the churchyard propped up against the wall.'

In 1972 a group of volunteers, known as the Normanton Tower Trust, began to raise money to preserve this local landmark. The final scheme adopted was to raise the internal floor level and to build a surrounding bank and a causeway to give protection and access. The main west door was sealed and a new door was inserted in place of a window on the north side. In 1983 it became a museum in the care of Anglian Water. It houses a fascinating display portraying the construction of Rutland Water.

Sylvia Leach (*née* Demaid), who was born and brought up in Empingham, has fond memories of the church: 'We always called it the Pineapple Chapel because of the pineapple at the top . . . we liked to walk down Sykes Lane, where the water is now, over to Edith Weston and you could see it. It was just part of our landscape really and we wanted it to be saved.'

Above: Normanton Church in the process of being saved (Anglian Water)

Below Right: An early internal picture of Normanton Church Museum (Anglian Water)

Below: Sylvia Leach who has fond memories of Normanton Church (RO)

Below: Normanton Church waits for Rutland Water like a ship in dry dock (Anglian Water)

A Remarkable Discovery

The efforts of the Normanton Tower Trust secured the preservation of Normanton Church. This building is now considered to be one of Rutland Water's most dominant and important landscape features.

When the Heathcote family vault was opened on 6th September 1972 in order to remove the coffins, this presented an opportunity to examine and photograph the only known fully documented Chippendale coffin.

Although many eighteenth century cabinet-makers were also undertakers, it is understood that the most eminent firms seldom performed funerals. There was therefore a great deal of interest shown when a bill, submitted to 'Sir Gilbert Heathcote Bart' from 'Chippendale Haig & Co' was discovered in Lincoln Record Office in the late 1960s (Lincolnshire Archives, 2 Anc 12/D/29). The bill, dated 12th May 1772, was Thomas Chippendale's account for furnishing and directing the Dowager Lady Bridget Heathcote's funeral. She was the widow of John Heathcote, the second baronet. The bill, which was for £121 15s 11d, was presented to her son and it clearly reveals that Lady Bridget's body had been brought from London to be buried at Normanton.

Alex Watt, former sidesman at Normanton Church recalls:

'When the church was deconsecrated all of the bodies were removed from the graveyard and the vaults. There were two vaults under the church. Access was gained through a stone man-hole in the floor of the church building and in the square shaped vault, on each of the four walls, there were recesses and in these recesses coffins were placed . . . I can't remember exactly how many . . . but they were very ornate. Most of the other coffins in the second chamber were lead-lined and all the timber on the outside of the coffins had rotted away. When I say lead-lined, they were actually sealed lead boxes and the names were engraved in lead on the top of the boxes. Some of them you could just read and make out the names . . . it upset me a little bit because in this chamber there were two tiny coffins, obviously children, and I thought that was very sad. All these coffins were removed from the vaults.'

Alex Watt with his wife Barbara. Alex was a sidesman at Normanton Church
(Alex Watt)

Normanton Church Vaults

Before his ordination, the Rev Brian Nicholls and his wife Liz were professional photographers, and they were appointed by the water authority as official photographers for the construction of Rutland Water. In 2005 Brian recalled 'a very interesting experience' when he entered the Heathcote family vault:

'Liz didn't come down with me, but they took up one flagstone from the floor of the church and put a ladder down where we discovered there were two crypts. The one facing what is now the Water, which would probably be the west end, was more modern, in fact, and the coffins were on shelves and the woodwork was intact and they all were of the Ancaster ancestors. But going into the main crypt there were – I couldn't guess how many now because it was such a long time ago, but it was absolutely full of coffins that had been made of wood or coated with wood, but the wood had disappeared and left the lead inner lining which regrettably had leaked over the years and so before I was allowed to go in they had to put down powdered disinfectant and so on. Fortunately for me, there was the curator of Temple Newsam House in Leeds who'd found an account from Chippendale for a burial at Normanton and he came down when they said they were opening it up. We went down together and we found the particular coffin he was interested in. It was good for me as he was able to hold the torch while I focused on the coffin plate with the name and then gave him the flash instead of the torch and reproduced the photograph. I understand that he was allowed to take out the coffin furniture – the handles and so forth back to match up with this burial invoice from Chippendale. This was totally secret – the opening up – because being nobility they thought that there'd be the possibility of people coming to try and break in, in case there was any valuable jewellery. In the event there were only wedding rings and, with the permission of the Ancaster family, the remains were then put into common wood coffins and taken off to the crematorium.'

Top Left:
The entrance to the Heathcote vaults at Normanton Church
(Alex Watt)

Below Left: Heathcote family coffins in the smaller of the vaults beneath Normanton Church. It was possible to remove these through the ceiling of the vault (Brian & Elizabeth Nicholls Photography)

Below Right: Heathcote family coffins in the larger vault beneath Normanton Church. These coffins had to be removed through a hole cut through the wall of the vault below ground level (Brian & Elizabeth Nicholls Photography)

A description of the Heathcote coffins and details of Lady Bridget's funeral are recorded in *Thomas Chippendale as Undertaker* by Christopher Gilbert:

'The chamber contained sixteen [seventeen recorded by Anglian Water] coffins, all dating from the Georgian period: the lead caskets, lined inside with timber, were well preserved, but the outer elm cases covered with black velvet enriched with nail patterns, fine brass handles, plaques and inscription tablets were in a decrepit state. The boards of the Chippendale coffin had unluckily completely decayed, although the woodwork of several ranged along the opposite wall was reasonably sound – conveying an impression of their original splendour.

> The Hon[ll]. S[r] Gilbert Heathcote Knight & Baronett Member of Parli[nt] & Senior Alderman of the City of London President of S[t] Thomas Hospitall & of the Artillery Company one of the Directors of the Bank of England Governor of the Eastland Company & Collo[l] of the Blen Regiment of trained Bands in the City of London Departed this Life January the 25th 1732 In the 82[d] Year of his Age

From the coffin plate of the Hon Sir Gilbert Heathcote, 1st Baronet (RCM)

'Chippendale's bill included charges for "a large strong Lead Coffin and soldering up with Inscription", the boldly incised legend ensured correct identification, confirmed by the presence of a second tablet resting on the lid itemized as "A Brass plate of Inscription with the Coat of Arms neatly Engrav'd and Gilt £4". This elegant plaque had, of course, originally graced the outer coffin, described in the invoice as ". . . cover'd with black velvett & finish'd with 2 rows best brass nails & 4 pair of large strong chas'd brass handles gilt". The handles – three on either side and one at each end – were found where they had fallen, buried in decomposed wood. Chippendale also supplied "a large Atchievment of Arms painted in oil, the outer frame cover'd with Cloath & fixing £5", but this hatchment, presumably subcontracted to a professional heraldic painter, has not been traced.

'The partner's account shows that Thomas Haig accompanied the cortège on its journey from London to the family's country seat at Normanton, suggesting that the Heathcotes were respected customers . . . Chippendale provided cloaks, scarves, silk hatbands and gloves for the mourners; ostrich feathers and velvet drapes for the hearse and paid all incidental expenses. One entry "the best Pall the journey £2.2" implies that this item was available for hire.

'It is difficult to assess what proportion of the furnishings Chippendale actually made for the funeral – his joiners and upholsterers were obviously competent to produce the outside coffin, cover it and add the brasses, but the lead casket and decorative features could well have come from the stock of specialist tradesmen. His main responsibility was apparently ensuring that the coffin was elegantly styled and the funeral performed with dignity. The detailed schedule indicates the complexity of the undertaking and if, as appears increasingly likely, administrative flair was not one of Chippendale's assets he displayed prudence in leaving the arrangements to his partner.'

Far Left: Inside the larger of the two vaults at Normanton Church. Lady Bridget's coffin is at the centre of the rear row (Brian & Elizabeth Nicholls Photography)

Left: Lady Bridget Heathcote's coffin plate (RCM)

Chippendale's Account

Selected extracts from Chippendale's account for directing and furnishing the funeral of the Dowager Lady Bridget Heathcote in 1772 (Lincolnshire Archives, 2 Anc 12/D/29):

							£	s	d
To 26 Silk Hatbands for Tennat as under @ 8/-							10	8	0
viz.	1st	Messrs Bunning	10th	Christian	19	Wyles			
	2d	Fancourt	11	Broadsworth	20	Parker			
	3	Springthorp	12	Mathw Stubbs	21	Burchnell			
	4	Collington Senr	13	Henry Stubbs	22	Allen			
	5	Do Junr.	14	Jno Skillington	23	Grant			
	6	Sutton Senr	15	Storey Senr	24	Ward			
	7	Do Junr	16	Do Junr	25	Chamberlain			
	8	Stephens Senr	17	Saxton	26	Stephen Skillington			
	9	Do Junr	18	Hill					
26 pair Gloves for Ditto @ 2/-							2	12	0
6 Silk Hatbands as under @ 8/-							2	8	0
	1st	the Gardener	4	Thos Cotton					
	2d	the Keeper	5	Christn Barrett					
	3d	Thos Bludworth	6	Sam'l Allen					
6 pair Gloves for Do @ 2/-							2	12	0
11 Silk Hatbands for the under Bearers including the Clerk at Normanton @ 8/-							4	8	0
11 pair Gloves for Ditto							1	2	0
1 Pair Lac'd Gloves Mrs Smith								5	0
3 pair of Kid for the Servants at Stoker								6	9
2 pair ditto for Servants at Normanton @ 2/3							4	6	
8 pair do for Tennants Wives that were present								18	0
21 pr of Women's Gloves for the Servants in Town									
& at Fulham including 3 Women at Wicherley Warren									
& 2 pair Extra: for the Women who Travelled @ 2/3							2	7	3
A Crape Hatband & Gloves, the Buttler								6	3

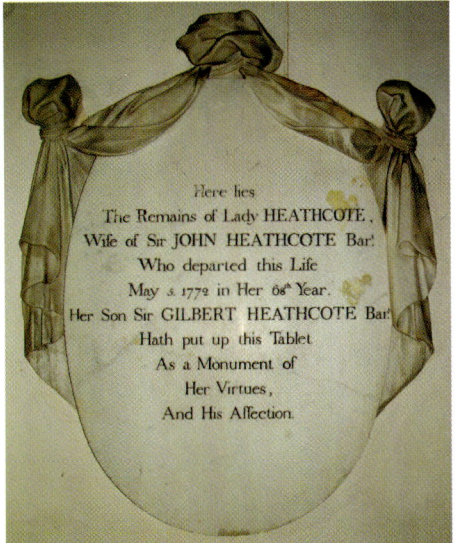

The Last Wedding at Normanton

Above Left: The memorial to Lady Bridget Heathcote, removed from Normanton Church, is now in Edith Weston Church (RO)

Above Right: The lane leading down to St Matthews Church, Normanton in 1954 (© Crown Copyright. NMR)

The bride and groom, Margaret and Laurence Plumb, were the last couple to be married at Normanton Church (Margaret & Laurence Plumb)

Margaret Hart and her parents moved to Rutland in February 1946. They lived at Park House, near Normanton Church. Margaret has happy memories of her time there:

'Living at Park House was very pleasant. My bedroom looked out over the fields down to the river and in the middle of the river there was a little island. There were lovely trees on this island and you could tell the passing seasons by the different colours of the trees. It was really a beautiful view along the valley to Oakham . . . .'

Margaret and Laurence Plumb were married at Normanton in 1954. It was to be the last wedding at the church:

'We had a service at Normanton Church every Sunday afternoon at half past three. My mother played the organ and my father was a sidesman and we had a short service lasting about half an hour. The Rev Beaumont from Edith Weston took the service. We usually had a congregation of ten people. I can remember we used to walk down the path from home to the church which was surrounded with an iron railing . . . It was always very cold in the church, there was no heating of any description except a small round paraffin heater in the winter. When we got married there . . . the church was quite full . . . I walked down to the church. I can remember it was very, very windy. When I walked in the church my mother was playing the organ and I saw Laurence standing at the end. Although it wasn't a very long church it seemed a long walk up to the altar. After the wedding we stood outside to take photographs in the doorway which now faces the water . . . and I can remember the photographer saying, "I can't take it yet", because the wind was blowing my veil up in the air. Then we walked and ran up from the church to a taxi that was waiting at the top of the path. We had the reception at Edith Weston Village Hall.'

Aspects of Topography

The Egleton to Nether Hambleton Road

Hambleton Road in Egleton no longer leads to the Hambletons. Now it is the access road to the Anglian Water Bird Watching Centre. But, for the nostalgic, a short stretch can be seen between the lagoons through the Centre windows.

Among the last people to travel this road were Philip Ennis and his imaginary friend 'Ganwick' who recorded the following in *Rutland Rides* Volume I:

'Alongside the stream [in Egleton], which months of dry had parched, grew the tall Hairy Willowherb, topped with its remnants of bright pink flowers . . . We come to this hamlet often, cycling through its narrow lanes to admire its gardens and thatched cottages. Out we went towards the Hambletons, pedalling easily past the barrier that says: "No through way" – to motor traffic. Into what desolation!

'Over the years we have enjoyed this ride, but for how much longer? Only the slow in-fill of water into the new reservoir gives us a brief respite, because soon this road will be flooded. In preparation for that day the contractors have flattened all that stands; the hedges have been uprooted, the trees felled, the houses demolished . . . Nether Hambleton is no more, is dead, is erased. Save for the occasional gatepost or remnant of fencing, nothing remains to testify that only brief months ago men lived and laboured and loved in the cottages just here.'

Towards Nether Hambleton from Egleton in July 1975 (Tim Clough)

Below: Hambleton Road in Egleton only leads to the Bird Watching Centre now (RO)

Left: A short section of the Egleton to Nether Hambleton road can be seen from the Bird Watching Centre (RO)

Chapter 12
Whitwell: A 'pretty little village'
Sue Howlett

Described in the *Victoria County History of Rutland* (II, 165) as a 'pretty little village' of 84 inhabitants, Whitwell is one of the smallest settlements in Rutland. Today, however, it is one of the busiest locations on the shores of Rutland Water. Hundreds of visitors regularly throng its two extensive car parks, taking advantage of Cycle Hire, 'Rock Blok' climbing, cruises on the *Rutland Belle*, sailing, windsurfing and canoeing. On a summer weekend, cars queue to turn off the A606 road, following the re-routed Bull Brigg Lane which once linked Whitwell with the villages of Normanton and Edith Weston, via Bull Bridge.

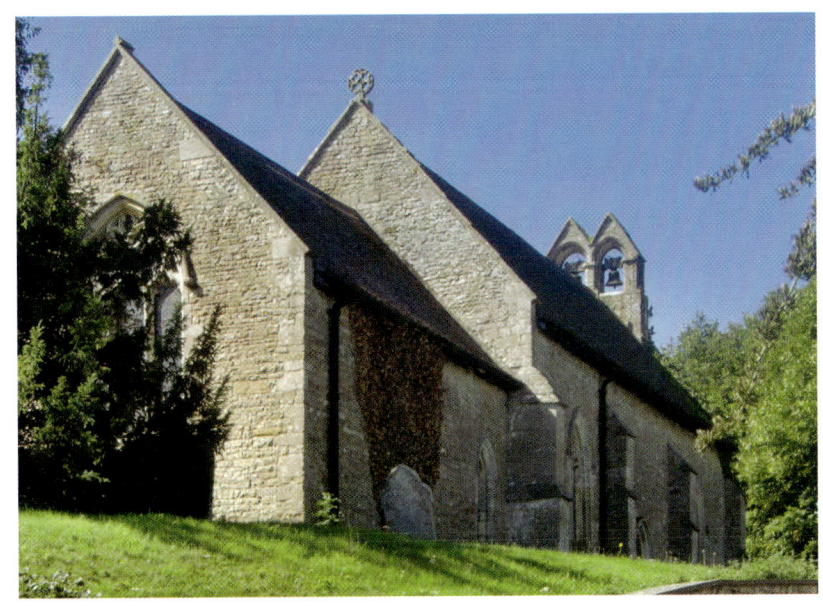

St Michael's Church, Whitwell (SH)

Bull Bridge in 1971 (Jim Eaton)

Before Rutland Water, Bull Brigg Lane linked Whitwell with Normanton and Edith Weston, via Bull Bridge (SH)

Human activity at Whitwell goes back at least two thousand years. In 1976-77 evidence of a small community living near to the present sailors' car park was discovered when archaeologists uncovered Iron Age post-holes, pits and ditches dating from the first and second centuries BC. Although this settlement was then abandoned, the area was re-occupied by a Romano-British farming community in the centuries following the Roman conquest of 43AD (*see* Chapter 18 – Brooches, Bathhouses and Bones – Archaeology in the Gwash Valley).

The Whitwell Coin Hoard

In 1991, a dramatic discovery was made at Whitwell. Four metal detectorists, searching with the landowner's permission, found a gold finger-ring, two gold coins [*solidi*] and 784 silver coins [*siliquae*], scattered across a fifteen-acre ploughed field. The discovery was reported to the police and analysed by experts at the British Museum, who identified the objects as Roman, dating mainly from the late fourth century AD. The find-spot was not far from the site of an Iron Age and Romano-British settlement at Whitwell, which had been excavated in advance of the construction of Rutland Water (*see* Chapter 18 – Brooches, Bathhouses and Bones – Archaeology in the Gwash Valley).

An inquest was held at Oakham Castle in May 1992 at which, according to legislation then in force, the find was declared to be Treasure Trove. This meant that when the ring and some coins were acquired by Leicestershire Museums and the British Museum, the finders received a reward equivalent to their full market value. Later that year, more silver coins were found, bringing the total number of these to 870.

Most of the coins were minted in Italy and Germany, and dating evidence indicated that the hoard must have been buried after 400 AD. Three-quarters of the *siliquae* had been clipped and 42 were forgeries, suggesting that they may have been used after the breakdown of Roman authority, as the legions were returning to Rome.

The most vivid and valuable item of the collection was the gold finger-ring, decorated with male and female busts facing each other. It was probably given to celebrate a betrothal, and is now in the collections of the Rutland County Museum (Bland & Johns 1994, 151-7).

The gold Roman betrothal ring found at Whitwell (RCM)

After the Roman legions departed from Britain, Whitwell eventually became an Anglo-Saxon village. In 1066 the estate was owned by 'Besi' and was worth the modest sum of twenty shillings. It had its own church on the steep knoll close to the crossroads. In common with many churches on high ground, this was dedicated to St Michael and All Angels.

The village took its name from the 'White Well', a spring rising in the hillside behind the church. Its water supplied a well in a nearby farmyard and emerged in the Rectory garden. In 1858 a parish conduit was built into a wall in the Rectory grounds, allowing villagers to obtain water from a tap in a round-arched recess. One local archaeologist has suggested that holy water was formerly supplied from Whitwell to other churches in the area (Adams 1980, 45). At the beginning of the twentieth century, when heavy rain fell, the waters of the spring could be heard beneath the church and on rare occasions rose through a floor drain close to the chancel arch (Harvey & Crowther-Beynon 1912, 218).

The floor drain in Whitwell Church (SH)

Whitwell parish conduit (SH)

When William of Normandy conquered England in 1066, Anglo-Saxon estates were redistributed to his relatives and followers. Whitwell was granted to his niece, Countess Judith, widow of the Saxon Earl Waltheof. Twenty years later it was visited by surveyors who were riding the length and breadth of England to compile the Domesday Book of 1086. They noted that, under her tenant Herbert, the estate's value had now doubled to 40 shillings. Ten villagers and smallholders tilled the land with three ox-drawn ploughs. By 1329 there were eighteen householders, including one woman, 'Isabel ad Fontem', who probably lived by the spring. There were two priests, Ralph and Henry, and another Ralph, the chaplain. Other occupations included Elias the carpenter and William the smith (www.le.ac.uk/english/pot/ruthome).

Early in the thirteenth century, Whitwell had passed to the Priory of St John of Jerusalem (the Knights Hospitaller). It was probably under their ownership that the church was extended, with the addition of a south aisle and double bellcote. According to Nikolaus Pevsner in *The Buildings of England*, this is probably the earliest example of the traditional Rutland double bellcote. Further alterations were made in the fourteenth century, with a window inserted in the south aisle. A stone slab, once used as the medieval altar, was reused in the seventeenth century as a gravestone for the Rev Daniel Nailer, one of Whitwell's Rectors.

In 1345 Richard de Whitwell, the prebendary of Empingham in the church of St Mary, Lincoln, founded a chantry, and the rent of lands in Hambleton and Whitwell was used to pay a chaplain to sing daily masses in the Lady Chapel at Whitwell for the souls of Richard, his parents and 'all faithful dead' (National Archives, *Chancery Inquisitions*, c 143/273/11). A few decades later the chantry chaplain was William of Whitwell.

The last of a succession of chantry priests was Robert Suckling, made redundant by Henry VIII's Chantry Act of 1547. The visiting commissioners described him as aged 46 years, 'of honest conversation and hath always heretofore been exercised in the Education of Youth in learning yet unable to serve a Cure [parish] by reason he is purblind [totally blind]' (Wright 1684, 137). His daily duties are remembered in the name of 'Chantry Cottage', one of Whitwell's most picturesque cottages. According to tradition, stones from the original Chantry House may have been used in rebuilding the manor house (later known as Old Hall).

Chantry Cottage, Whitwell (SH)

This window and some of the surrounding stonework at the former Old Hall, Whitwell, are thought to be from the medieval chantry (SH)

Today the village of Whitwell straddles the busy Stamford to Oakham road. In the Middle Ages, however, it also extended along Bull Brigg Lane to the south. There are traces of earthworks to the east of this road although the stone-faced mill dam was obliterated by Rutland Water. When this particular land was acquired for the construction of the reservoir, an excavation was carried out by the Rutland Field Research Group for Archaeology and History. Among the building foundations of this shrunken medieval village, they found sherds of pottery dating from the eleventh to the seventeenth century, and other finds including a thirteenth century halfpenny (*see* Chapter 20 – Medieval Settlements at Nether Hambleton and Whitwell).

The Prior of St John of Jerusalem continued to hold Whitwell until the 1540s, when ecclesiastical properties were confiscated as part of Henry VIII's Dissolution of the Monasteries. Before this date the manor of Whitwell was leased out by the Prior of St John for a rent of six shillings and a pound of pepper. In the fifteenth century it was held by members of the powerful Flower (Flore) family, whose properties included the surviving Flore's House in Oakham.

Sketch plan of the village and medieval earthworks of Whitwell (after Hartley 1983, 48)

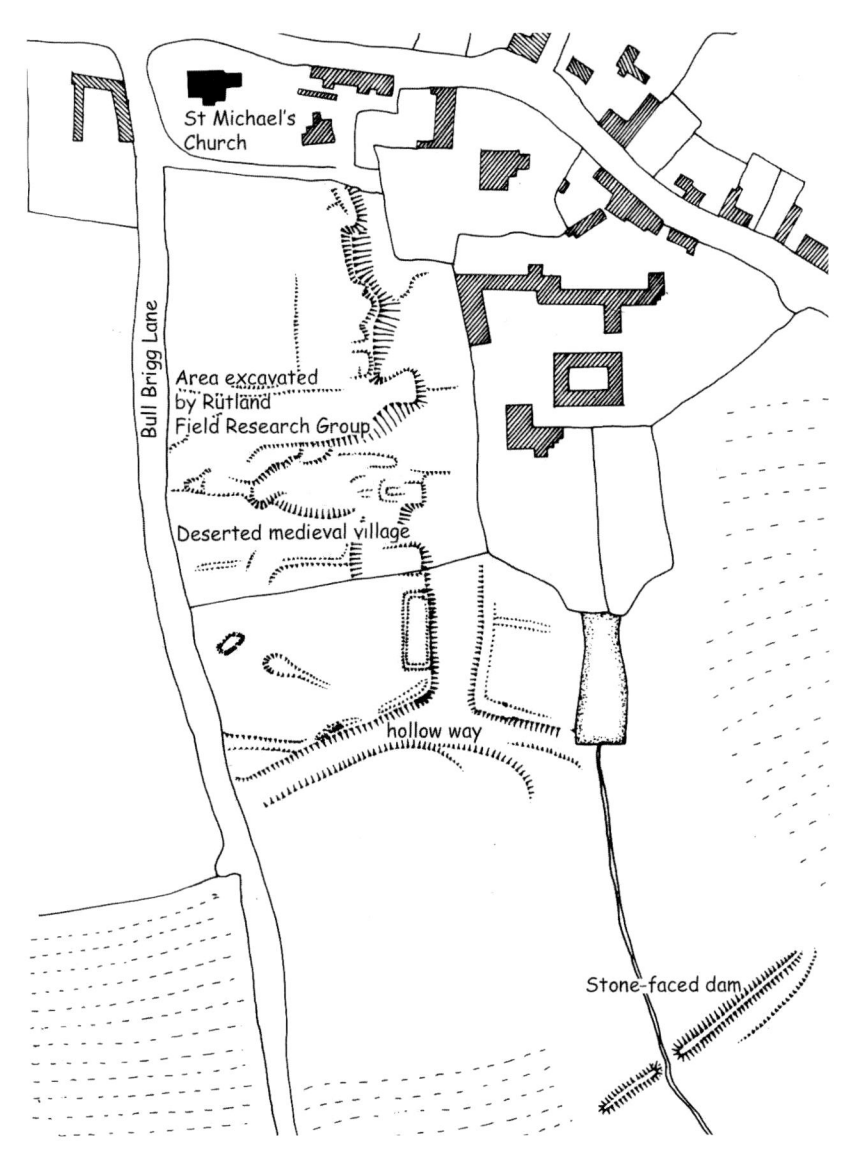

In 1523 Richard Flower died 'seised of lands and a watermill in Whitwell', but after his death his widow was quick to sue her stepson, the heir Roger Flower, for the watermill, land and 'a capital messuage' (house with land and outbuildings) (*VCH* II, 165).

The value of Richard Flower's property in Whitwell, an impressive £80 per year, is confirmed by the Military Survey of 1522. This assessment of every community's wealth, and ability to defend the kingdom, provides a snapshot of Whitwell on the eve of the Reformation. The Prior of St John of Jerusalem was represented by a steward, Henry Wykley, whose personal land was worth six shillings and eight pence but whose goods were exempt from assessment. The chantry priest, John Reynolds, continued to sing daily masses for the souls of the dead, receiving an annual stipend of six marks, one more than that of the parson, Henry Hasley. The landlord with the largest landholding, Richard Flower, was listed as having 'horse & harnesse for vj [6] men', ready to ride to the defence of the kingdom. Far smaller landholdings were held by Thomas Sherrard, receiving £4 13s 4d per year in rent, and John and William Haryngton (Harington), receiving six shillings and twenty shillings respectively. The remaining nine adult males living in Whitwell were either tenants of one of the landowners or labourers, 'yong men & pore', owning no land or rents but with wages of 20s (£1) per year (Cornwall 1980, 24-5, 114).

A damaged gravestone of about 1545 in the chancel of Whitwell Church. It is inscribed 'Filius [son of] Roger Flore' (SH)

The Flower and Harington families were connected by marriage when Richard Flower married Alice Harington of Exton. Richard's early death in 1540 left their five-year-old son, John, to inherit the manor of Whitwell. The last of the Flower family to hold Whitwell was another John, born in 1571, and his wife Jane, who were described in 1621 as recusants (Roman Catholics).

In 1620 the manor of Whitwell was sold to Sir Baptist Hicks, 1st Viscount Campden, who also bought Exton and other Rutland estates. His heirs, the Noel family of Exton, continued to hold Whitwell as Lords of the Manor until the twentieth century. They appointed Rectors to the parish church and provided them with a substantial Rectory, dating back to the sixteenth century, though subsequently much rebuilt and extended.

'Resurgam' [I will rise again] on the gravestone of Maria, wife of Thomas Frere, Rector of Whitwell (SH)

Whitwell's Rector from 1627 was Thomas Frere. When divisions between Puritans and high-church Anglicans led to the bitter tensions and civil war in the 1640s, the ministers of Rutland were equally divided. The two schools of Uppingham and Oakham spread puritanism across the county, although some parish priests such as Uppingham's Rector, Jeremy Taylor, remained loyal to the king with his Anglo-Catholic 'innovations'. Thomas Frere, appointed as Rector of Whitwell by the Royalist Noels was 'ejected' by the dominant Parliamentarians in 1650. In his later appeal to King Charles II, he stated that he had been 'imprisoned & plundered for loyalty', having seven children unprovided for (Walker 1948, 301). Thomas Frere died, re-instated as Rector of Whitwell, in 1667. His tomb lies beneath the chancel floor with those of his two wives, Prudence, who died in 1635, and Maria (Mary) who died in 1658.

Although the lords of the manor of Whitwell were members of the Noel family, the family's main seat was nearby Exton Hall. The eldest Noel sons, succeeding to the titles of Viscount Campden and later Earl of Gainsborough, took up residence at Exton where the family still lives today. Meanwhile the rebuilt manor house of Whitwell (Old Hall) became home to Alexander Noel, youngest brother of the 2nd Viscount Campden, with his new wife, Mary Palmer. She was sister to Sir Geoffrey Palmer, 1st Baronet, later to be appointed Attorney-General by King Charles II (www.thepeerage.com). This influential connection would in later years confirm Alexander Noel as a leading figure on the Rutland county scene.

Left: The area around Whitwell village showing ridge and furrow, evidence of the medieval strip farming system, surviving into the twentieth century, as well as the Barnsdale deer park (Hartley 1983, 58)

Below: The new manor house (later known as Old Hall, then Old Hall Farm) at Whitwell (SH)

During the 1630s, the new lord of the manor of Whitwell turned his mind to increasing the efficiency and output of the three great open fields, which were cultivated in strips according to the medieval system. Parts of Whitwell's West and North Fields were enclosed into smaller units of land, although, in the process, poorer villagers inevitably lost out. Further enclosures followed later in the century, when the South Field was enclosed and the remaining parts of the West and North Fields reorganised into three new fields, Nether, Middle and Clay (Ryder 2006, 8). The name of Clay Field was to prove highly significant three centuries later, when the geology of the area was an important factor in the decision to build Rutland Water.

The tranquil cycles of rural life were brutally disrupted in the 1640s by the outbreak of civil war with the gentry of Rutland equally divided in their choice of allegiance. The Noels were staunch Royalists. Baptist Noel, 3rd Viscount Campden, led his cavalry troop of 'Camdeners' in daring raids across Rutland and beyond, even confronting Oliver Cromwell at the siege of Burghley House, outside Stamford, Lincolnshire. Although Lord Campden was heavily fined and briefly imprisoned during the years of conflict, his uncle, Alexander Noel, seems to have led a quieter life at Whitwell, maintaining cordial relations with his Parliamentarian neighbours. Indeed, he was pragmatic enough to negotiate the marriage of his daughter, Mary, to Abel Barker of Hambleton, an active member of the County Committee which governed Rutland in the name of Parliament. As with most such alliances, money played an important role: Alexander Noel agreed to provide £1,500 to obtain a suitable husband for his daughter.

Restored to his kingdom in 1660 amid popular rejoicing, King Charles II found himself beset by debt and financial problems. New taxes were introduced, including the famous Hearth Tax, which became law in 1662. County receivers worked with local constables to count the hearths in every home, each to be taxed at two shillings per annum, one shilling to be paid on Lady Day and one shilling to be paid at Michaelmas. The officer appointed to administer the Hearth Tax in Rutland was Andrew Noel, son of Alexander Noel of Whitwell. In Whitwell, Alexander Noel's manor house was the largest building, with eight hearths, although his nephew, the 3rd Viscount Campden, had an impressive 32 hearths at Exton. Whitwell Rectory, where Thomas Frere was enjoying his reinstatement after the upheavals of the Commonwealth period, had six hearths, while each of the remaining 19 properties had no more than one taxable hearth. The parish constable, Clement Gregory, had a one-hearth home of his own but also owned a second cottage which was temporarily empty (Bourne & Goode 1991, 32).

The inefficiency of the Hearth Tax led to further experimental taxes. In the decades which followed, a variety of new taxes included the Window Tax which remained on the statute books from 1696 to 1851, leading to the many

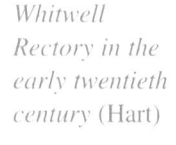

Whitwell Rectory in the early twentieth century (Hart)

blocked-up windows still seen today. However, the most successful, before the introduction of Income Tax, was the Land Tax introduced in 1692. The assessments for this tax allow researchers to compare the list of taxpayers in Whitwell and other parishes with those of earlier generations. Alexander Noel had died in 1667 and his son, Andrew, left no male heirs. Without a resident lord of the manor, Old Hall became a farmhouse and the manor of Whitwell became part of the Exton estate. When a Land Tax assessment was made for Whitwell in 1712, the Earl of Gainsborough was charged £10 5s 4d for land in the parish, and the Hon Lady Noel, probably his mother, was charged £9 13s 3d. However, the Rectory was worth more, with Mr John Chapman assessed at £13 9s 0d (*The 1712 Land Tax Assessments* 2005, 57).

A few years later, Whitwell had a new Rector, John Isaac. In 1719 Isaac married Mary White, who would become the aunt of the famous naturalist, Gilbert White of Selborne, Hampshire. A memorial in the church records the death of Mary Isaac, daughter of the Rector and his wife, 'taken to the angels in heaven', aged 10. In contrast, another daughter, Katherine Susanna Isaac, died at the age of 83 in 1803.

Whitwell Rectory provided hospitality for the fifteen-year-old Gilbert White, when he travelled from Selborne, Hampshire, to visit his aunt and uncle in 1736. Here he made the acquaintance of Thomas Barker of Lyndon, who was already beginning to keep his detailed weather journals. Six years later, Gilbert White stayed at Whitwell for three months. His younger sister, Anne White, born in 1731, also visited her aunt and uncle at Whitwell, meeting Thomas Barker whom she married in 1751. It is possibly due to his friendship with Thomas Barker that Gilbert White began his own more famous natural history journals (Kington 1988, 8-10).

Whitwell remained a tiny village and sleepy rural backwater for the following two centuries. In 1801 the population was only 80 and, although it increased to 139 in 1841, had declined again to 104 by 1861, possibly due to improved farming methods requiring fewer labourers. By the end of the century the population had continued to decline: the census of 1901 records 20 households and a total of 81 residents. The heads of four families were described as farmers, tenants of the Earl of Gainsborough, while Thomas Hall, possibly occupying Old Hall Farm (formerly known as Old Hall), was described as 'Grazier'.

The Old Rectory, which is now part of Whitwell Hotel and Conference Centre (SH)

Three homes in 1901 were occupied by different branches of the Springthorpe family. In one cottage lived William Springthorpe, still described as 'Labourer' although aged 74. Close by, were households headed by two distant cousins, both aged 43. One was Elijah Needham Springthorpe, 'Boot and Shoe Maker', who also served as Churchwarden, with his wife, two children and a boarder from Nottingham. Elijah

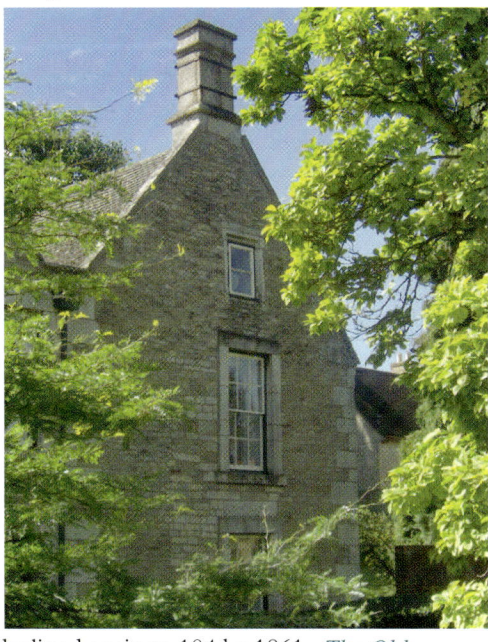

Springthorpe's earlier life was recalled by Lizzie Pinder, who grew up at Old Hall Farm in the 1870s and 1880s: 'rather lame; he used to spend Sunday evenings in our lower kitchen, sitting on the dresser between the sink and the steamer, accompanied by the cook [Hannah Andrew of Ketton], whom he afterwards married.' In the neighbouring cottage was Thomas William Springthorpe, a 'Road Labourer', whose two teenage sons were each described as 'Farm Labourer (Horseman)'. The younger, Herbert Cecil, was one of six men of Whitwell killed in the First World War.

Left: Whitwell Main Street about 1908. Note the postman, who walked to Whitwell from Oakham via Egleton and Hambleton. He returned to Oakham with the collected mail by the same route in the evening (Hart)

Right: Elijah and Hannah Springthorpe outside their cottage in Whitwell (Liz Branson)

Lance-Corporal Herbert Cecil Springthorpe, 1887-1915

'Lance-Corporal Herbert Cecil Springthorpe, 2nd Battalion the Lincolnshire Regiment, was the son of Mr and Mrs Thomas William Springthorpe of Whitwell and was born there on 30th May 1887. He was married. Private Springthorpe enlisted in the Regulars in 1903. Two years later his regiment was ordered to India where he completed his three years service. On his return to England he obtained a position as porter at Skipton station and after about five years he went to Canada. On the outbreak of war he returned from Vancouver, being still on the Reserve, and rejoined his old regiment in September 1914. They were drafted to France in November and on 12th March 1915 he was killed in action in Neuve Chappelle [sic]. Prior to leaving Vancouver in 1914 a memento with an address, signed by a number of his neighbours, was presented to Mr Springthorpe in which the following sentiments were expressed: "We appreciate the fact that you are to be our representative in the defence of our country, flag and honour. As a neighbour we shall miss your cheerful outlook on life, but when duty calls, manhood must respond"' (Phillips 1920, 90).

The Pinder Family of Whitwell

In 1951 John W Pinder recalled:

'Robert Pinder's name appears for the first time in 1866, when he signed his name on the Churchwardens' Accounts. He was a wealthy farmer and lived at Old Hall Farm. He must have been a comparative newcomer to the village because he did not appear on the 1851 Census. By 1870 he was appointed churchwarden and continued to serve until 1896. Although the Rector had proposed him as Churchwarden in April 1870, Robert did not hesitate to suggest that the Rector should pay the same parish rate as the rest of the parish. In that year it was three pence in the pound. Robert Pinder died in 1898 at the age of 61 and was buried with other family members at Whitwell. A brass memorial plate near the chancel arch records his and his wife's death. The remaining family then left Whitwell.

'Mr and Mrs Pinder's son, Robert, was accidentally shot and killed by his native manservant at Navua in the Fiji Islands. He was a sugar planter and died in 1908 at the age of thirty.'

Above: Herbert Cecil Springthorpe (Phillips 1920, plate viii)

During the late 1860s and 1870s Whitwell had as its Rector Charles Spencer Ellicott. His son was Charles John Ellicott (1819-1905), who became Bishop of Gloucester in 1863. Bishop Ellicott was a respected author and theologian, appointed in 1870 as chairman of the committee translating the New Testament for the Revised Version of the Bible. One of his unusual privileges was that of free travel on the Great Eastern Railway, awarded for his role in a railway accident, where despite severe injuries he exerted himself heroically to administer spiritual consolation to the dying victims of the disaster. Bishop Ellicott visited Whitwell for the funerals of his parents. Lizzie Pinder, looking back in 1950 on her childhood, remembered the Sunday evening after one of the funerals, 'four or five robed figures sitting in one of the pews. Our governess told us that people always came to Church the Sunday after they had buried someone they loved'.

Charles Ellicott, Bishop of Gloucester, was often to be seen on his tricycle (Liz Branson)

Charles John Ellicott, Bishop of Gloucester, son of the Rector of Whitwell (Vanity Fair 18th July 1885)

In 1881 Whitwell Church underwent restoration, at a cost of £1,600, paid for by a former Curate, the Rev R V C Kinleside. Lizzie Pinder, born in 1871, described how before this date she had been taken into her family's box pew, which was very comfortable, with 'thick cushions, very high hassocks, a thick carpet, and in the winter foot warmers'. She could hear voices but not see anyone until allowed to stand on the seat for the psalms. As the family grew in size, with thirteen children plus relations and servants, Lizzie and her siblings sat with their governess in the ordinary pew behind the box pew. While the restoration of the church was carried out, services were held in a stone barn owned by her family. 'That barn made a really good little church, it was much wider than the church itself, for I remember how very small the little Holy Table looked, which had been brought from the church – the harmonium too was brought.' The harmonium was played by Mrs Beecham, the wife of the new Rector, with Teddy Springthorpe, 'a weedy little boy with very poor eyes', blowing it.

The Pinder household at Old Hall made up the majority of the congregation, in addition to the 'Beecham boys', the Rector's sons, and the Sexton, Elijah Springthorpe. One regular churchgoer, remembered by Lizzie, was 'old John (or Tom) Allen with a withered hand and an iron hooked fixed up his sleeve. I heard often that he was found dead by his bed on his knees'. The congregation was greatly increased for Evensong on Good Friday, when Robert Pinder would give his farm workers 'a full day's wages, and a free day to spend in their own fashion, mostly on their allotments, provided they came back to church; the service was in the evening for their convenience'. The labourers earned about twelve shillings (60p) a week, and Lizzie describes them wearing 'coarse dark brown corduroy trousers tied below the knee', or in some cases, such as the shepherd, wearing smocks.

The Village Feast, celebrating the patron saint, was held at Michaelmas (29th September). 'There used to be gypsy stalls set up near the village inn, and a good deal of fun of sorts kept up for about a week I believe, but of course we [the Pinder children] took no part in it; our maids were allowed out those days.' By the mid-twentieth century, however, the autumn Feast Week was no longer celebrated and villagers would travel to Empingham to share in theirs.

Christmas was the time when everyone could celebrate. The church would be heavily decorated with evergreens until it 'turned into a big shrubbery'. Late on Christmas Eve, about fourteen men and boys gathered in the top kitchen of Old Hall, around a table covered in a thick brown cloth. They brought out fourteen shiny hand-bells and proceeded to play 'jingly' tunes such as 'Pop goes the Weasel'. If the children had already gone to bed they were allowed back down again, being sent back upstairs while the men enjoyed their beer and cake! Another highlight was the visit of the Mummers, 'five or six big lads who performed in the lower kitchen, with corked faces, sticks and bludgeons, giving Beelzebub the worst of it!' (*see* Chapter 5 – Edith Weston: A Queen's Dowry).

While Lizzie Pinder and her sisters had lessons with their governess at home in Old Hall, and their two brothers went away to school, local children had lessons in the village school. Unlike most neighbouring villages, Whitwell had no purpose-built school, but lessons were held in Chantry Cottage from the 1860s to about 1890. After the school was closed children had to walk or later travel by bus to Exton or Empingham. The village was also too small to have its own butcher or blacksmith, with tradesmen calling from Empingham or elsewhere. Until about 1900, the blacksmith from Greetham came once a week, using premises at High Moor Farm, which also had a bakehouse which was used by many villagers for baking bread and roasting their Sunday joints.

Interior of St Michael's Church, Whitwell (Liz Branson)

Lizzie Pinder, also known as 'Betty' Pinder, grew up to become an Anglican nun, taking the new name 'Sister Lisette'. She always felt that she had been blessed in her mother's womb when her parents attended the Roman Catholic funeral of the Earl of Gainsborough. In 1909 she joined the Community of St Mary the Virgin at Wantage, Oxfordshire, an active monastic order caring for the poor in the slums of East London. She revisited Whitwell only once, in 1947, to see once more the graves of her parents. Writing to her nephew, Robert, in July 1950, Sister Lisette recalled with love and gratitude the 'heaven-light' bestowed on her by the happy childhood days at Whitwell.

Elijah Springthorpe, bootmaker and churchwarden, lived to the age of 79. In their cottage at the west end of the village, he and Hannah brought up two children, John Hugh and Elizabeth Anne. Elizabeth's son, John Branson, who grew up in Empingham, has vivid memories of visiting his grandparents at Whitwell in the 1930s.

Elijah Springthorpe and Life at Whitwell in the 1930s

'My grandfather was Elijah Needham Springthorpe who lived in the house at the top of the hill on the right hand side of the Oakham road. He was a boot and shoemaker by profession, but also ran the village post office from his home. Like most other rural post offices he stocked a small selection of general goods, sweets, whips and tops and marbles. The room given over to the postal and sundry sales was to the front of the house, but service was through an opening onto the corridor that led from the main door on the western wall of the house. One wall of the room was totally occupied by a large glass-fronted cabinet containing dozens of pairs of wooden lasts on which the boots or shoes were made. Each customer had a last that was an exact replica of their feet, thus ensuring a snug fit when the footwear was completed. Each boot or shoe was made from leather and the smell of leather pervaded the house, but not unpleasantly. He was patronised by the aristocracy of that time. I remember the fine finish that he made even for a farm labourer. Taking pride in what you did was normal in those days.

'In 1936 Whitwell had no electricity. Every day, water had to be fetched from the tap in the middle of the village. For the men folk, beer was the everyday, drink. Elijah had his beer delivered in a barrel by dray from Oakham.

'Lavatory arrangements were primitive. There were no water closets, just a wooden framework concealing a steel pan into which the body waste products fell. The frame was often two stepped, providing seating at different heights to suit the stature of the user. The pan was exchanged for an empty one every week, usually very early in the morning, and the contents were taken and spread over fields as manure. Toilet paper as we know it today was rare in 1936 and use was made of cut-up newspaper. Deep sewerage and indoor lavatories were introduced long after the war.

'The nearest doctor was at Empingham, but only available to those that could pay. There was a "Sick and Dividend Club" at Empingham which would have been open to Whitwell residents. Families paid two pence per week per family member into this fund, which then gave them access to the doctor whose bill the fund paid. However some villagers were so poor that they were unable to join the club.

'The horse and cart era, the mainstay of rural transportation, only came to an end at the end of the war. Public transport was by United Counties omnibuses, but for people going to work, cycling was the only way since the first bus arrived, far too late, at 8.30am. Whitwell was served by a variety of local tradesmen selling from the backs of vans. The visit was usually once per week and was well patronised by the villagers. Paraffin was a popular fuel for cooking and lighting, brought by the Harrison and Dunn hardware van [from Stamford] or by Ellis and Everard [from Oakham]. Another vendor had fish and chips for two pence and found many takers at around 7pm on his day, as did the wet fish man on Friday morning. Butchers and bakers also made the rounds. Milk was totally local to Whitwell and delivered by jug. The coalman delivered coal from a horse and cart. Each bag contained one hundredweight (50kg) and cost 1s 9d. Everyone had open fires, burning wood and coal. The fire was lit first thing in the morning and burned all day. Often the fire was flanked by a hot water boiler on one side and an oven on the other. Elijah's fireplace was like this and it had a spit above it which was a rotating mechanism used in roasting meat' (John Branson, 2006).

Elijah Needham Springthorpe (Liz Branson)

Whitwell Main Street in the 1930s (Hart)

The villagers of Whitwell, as elsewhere in Britain, would have heard by wireless the news of the declaration of war in 1939. When local men went off to fight, much of the agricultural work in the valley was carried out by prisoners of war and the Women's Land Army. These anxious times were relieved by dances and whist drives at the Village Hall, a surplus Great War army hut, erected in 1921 and opened by Lady Gainsborough. The last function held there was probably the wedding reception of Harold Land and Violet Springthorpe in 1954. The hall gradually fell into disrepair and was finally demolished around 1970.

One young woman growing up in the village was Dorothy Hackett (*née* Brudenell), born in 1917 at Home Farm. On the outbreak of war she left Whitwell to join the Auxiliary Territorial Service (women's army service). She met a 'dashing' Cornishman and married him in Whitwell Church in 1943, before leaving for her new life in Cornwall, only returning to Whitwell much later in life. She remembers her mother's annoyance that, even during the wedding service, the church was made gloomy by blackout curtains.

The village of Whitwell from the OS 2nd ed 25" map 1904

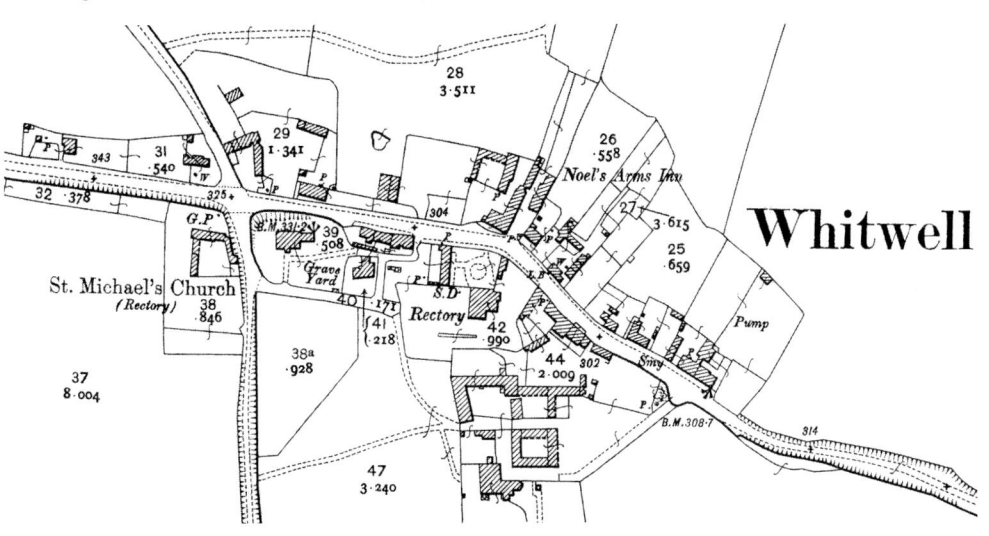

For a couple of decades after the war, Whitwell remained an estate village, with most residents, including farmers, paying rent to the Gainsborough Estate. There were four substantial farms, employing workers who lived in the surrounding cottages. High Moor Farm was the childhood home of Jane Thomas (*née* Bottomley), a typical mixed farm at the eastern end of the High Street. Jane remembers being expected to work hard on the farm from an early age. Even as a child she would drive tractors that pulled trailers, allowing her to feed the animals. Although local children came to play, there was little spare time, but 'no one knew any different'.

When news came that a reservoir was to be built in the Gwash valley, Jane's father, along with most other farmers, was devastated. He and others paid as much as they could into a fighting fund to try to prevent it, but all in vain: 'To start with we thought, no, it could never happen, then it started to get a bit more serious and the next thing we knew, yes, it was going to happen.' Tragically, her father died in a farm accident in the early 1970s, and later, the loss of land to the reservoir meant that there was not enough left for the farm to be viable. Jane remembered walks from Whitwell to Edith Weston, and sitting on one of the bridges, fishing in the stream in that beautiful valley. 'Many farms ended and families moved out. Nothing was ever the same again' (Jane Thomas, 2005).

High Moor Farm in 2006 (SH)

The largest farm in Whitwell was Old Hall Farm, formerly Old Hall, which included much land now submerged by Rutland Water. In the 1950s and 1960s it was owned by Brigadier Cavenagh, who employed Bert and Bet Jardine to manage the farm. The Brigadier's colourful career had included riding in the Grand National, for which he regularly had to lose weight in the sauna, and declining to accept a medal at Buckingham Palace, for which he received an official rebuke (information from Lisa Cavenagh). According to his daughter, the late Mrs Bridget Senior, the first he heard of the coming of the reservoir was when he looked out of his window and saw two men apparently surveying his field. He went out to question them. They said, 'Oh, didn't you know? All this' – with an expansive gesture of the arm – 'is going to be part of a new reservoir. Bought by compulsory purchase. You'll get compensation.' He said, 'Money can never compensate me for my own land'. His daughter reported that he never recovered from this loss and died before the reservoir was completed. No longer viable as a farmhouse, the Old Hall Farm was sold to Anglian Water and has more recently become part of the Whitwell Hotel and Conference Centre.

Following completion of the reservoir, a lighter episode in the history of Old Hall Farm is struck by a story recounted by Robin Church of Whitwell. About eighteen months after the waters of the reservoir started to rise, it began to be stocked with trout, and, by then, the new Whitwell Creek had been created on the former land of the Old Hall:

Brigadier Cavenagh, the owner of Old Hall Farm at Whitwell (Lisa Cavenagh)

'The stream that runs through the gardens of the Rectory ran straight into the creek and in spring, fish spawning go up running water. Well, the stream in the [Old Hall] garden is probably only four or five feet wide and 18 inches deep, and the trout got up there. Jam-packed full of trout, and we used to go down there in the morning . . . and we used to hoick these out with our bare hands. No tickling, we didn't need to. We had buckets, everybody's freezer was full. People used to come with baskets . . . great big linen baskets. Unfortunately, Anglian Water got wise to this because, if you look now, there's a big storm drain door over it with a big metal door that's mounted vertically and swings so that the water can get out and the fish can't get up.'

The stream in the grounds of Whitwell Rectory in 2006 (SH)

— 299 —

Woodlands Farm, opposite the church, was farmed for 30 years after the war by Mr and Mrs Ratcliffe, and when her husband died, Mrs Ratcliffe lived there alone until 1994. She had apparently been a keen cricketer and wicket keeper, and in later life would watch every Test Match on television. Mr Ratcliffe's father had been the railway crossing keeper at Ashwell, working on the railways for many years. In the First World War he worked at Melton Mowbray (Leicestershire) station where there were truckloads of boots sent back by the troops fighting on the front lines. He used to collect some of these off the train and take them home where he would repair them during the evening. On retirement, he moved with his son and daughter-in-law to Whitwell. Later, the tools of his trade were donated to Rutland County Museum by Mrs Ratcliffe.

When Whitwell's Postmaster, Elijah Springthorpe, died in 1936, the Post Office moved elsewhere. At first it was in an old cottage, now demolished, close to the church, where Jane Thomas remembers going with her mother, down four or five steps into a small general store. Then in 1961, a wooden extension was built to the north side of a pair of semi-detached council houses on the road to Edith Weston, now Bull Brigg Lane. This was operated by Hilda Bell, as recounted by her daughter, Mary:

'From the days of selling a few cigarettes along with her Post Office duties, Mum grew the business to sell groceries, confectionery, soft drinks and souvenirs of Rutland Water. Once the reservoir opened the shop became seven days a week, catering for the early morning fishermen who were looking to buy their bacon and eggs to cook Sunday morning breakfast after a few hours out on the water. It was not unusual for me to receive a call at work to pick up something in town for someone who had forgotten to bring it with them and Mum did not sell it. By the 1980s it became harder and harder to compete with the supermarkets, with the relaxing of the Sunday trading laws, and the opening up of the car parks for more businesses. The Post Office and shop was finally closed in 1994, three years after the death of Mum, Hilda.'

The tranquil village life of Whitwell was never the same after the building of Rutland Water, coming at the same time as other changes which totally altered the countryside. As churches were less well attended, parishes were amalgamated and lost their resident priests. Whitwell had been united with the benefice of Exton with Horn as far back as 1926, but in 1986 this group was united with Empingham, and Whitwell Rectory was no longer required. The building was sold and, in 1991, 'The Old Rectory' was offered for sale, 'completely renovated to provide two very large spacious properties on large plots close to Rutland Water'. Soon afterwards it became offices for Anglian Water and is now part of the Whitwell Hotel and Conference Centre. The conversion of the Rectory and of several former farm buildings was an indicator of new money, and new people, coming into Rutland. Although land to the north of Whitwell is still farmed, the farmhouses along the village High Street no longer hum with agricultural activity or the sound of animals in the yards.

Rutland Water also had a great impact on the prosperity of Whitwell's public house, The Noel, formerly the Noel Arms. Built as a farmhouse in the seventeenth century, it became one of two village inns, the other being the Three Steps Inn, on the corner where the telephone box now stands. This inn was demolished soon after the war.

When Jane grew up, she worked at the Noel Arms during the early days of Rutland Water, and remembers the atmosphere of the first season as being 'quite manic'.

The new owners of the Noel Arms, who bought it at auction in 1979, were Sam and Julie Healey. The inn buzzed with new energy and, while catering for the influx of fishermen and tourists to the new reservoir, it became the centre of a lively village community. The most audacious enterprise which took place at this time was to 'twin' the village with somewhere abroad, but this would not be just a tiny foreign hamlet. Two villagers wrote to the Mayor of Paris, Jacques Chirac, announcing that they intended to link Whitwell with Paris and inviting him to the ceremony. The letter was a masterpiece of tongue-in-cheek, schoolboy French:

The Noel, Whitwell, formerly the Noel Arms (SH)

'As you know, these days it is very chic, even *de rigeur* to twin towns having a common interest. Doubtless you know Whitwell-on-the-water, chief fishing port of the Midlands. When we have visited Paris we have noticed that there are many fish in the Seine. It is for that reason that we have thought to twin Whitwell-on-the-water with Paris. We hope you can participate . . . (*entente cordiale, mains à travers la mer et tout cela*). We would have wished to offer to pay your expenses, but thanks to Mrs Thatcher we are unfortunately too poor . . .'

The date set for the twinning ceremony scarcely allowed time for any reply. Nevertheless, on the day before, 13th June 1980, a response was received from the Mayor's office: 'Monsieur Jacques Chirac, who is appreciative of your attention, has asked me to let you know that it was unfortunately impossible to give a favourable answer to your request.' The polite reason given was that Paris was officially twinned with Rome, thus excluding any other twinning arrangements. The ceremonies went ahead regardless. A procession started at Exton with an open car containing the French master from Oakham School as a substitute for the Paris Mayor. As one resident remembers:

'Needless to say, there were plenty of onion sellers and ladies in French dress and split skirts and all that. You see, it was a good do. There were various ceremonies and the "Mayor of Paris" officially opened the booze and that sort of thing. Television people turned up and in the end they were supposed to go on to a couple of other things but they never left, they just stayed on all evening . . . It must have been Friday night, and on the Monday it was all on Central Television News. They interviewed Nick "the Thatcher", as they do, and it was in the Sunday papers . . . So that's why we have "Twinned with Paris" signs and, occasionally, I have had letters from people, mostly children, wanting to know what it's all about' (Robin Church).

Today, life in the village of Whitwell may have settled into a calmer routine, but a few hundred metres to the south, the newly created Whitwell Creek resounds with the happy sounds of children learning to sail. There, windsurfers improve their skills, yachtsmen launch their craft and families canoe or queue to cruise on the *Rutland Belle*. On the other side of Bull Brigg Lane, near the old Edith Weston road which now leads down into the waters of the reservoir, further energetic activities are on offer. Children may no longer roam the fields of Whitwell Parish, seeking their own amusements, or play in the near-deserted main street of the village, but people of all ages from much further afield can run, play, cycle or climb, and explore the beauties of this man-made landscape, or simply enjoy their leisure, with as much delight and enthusiasm as the carefree, rural children of centuries past.

The late Geoff Hamilton with two 'Parisiennes' on the day of the Twinning Ceremony (Julie Healey)

Whitwell village and Whitwell Creek from the air in 2006 (John Nowell, Zodiac Publishing)

Chapter 13
Changing Communities
Paul Reeve

This chapter takes a brief look at the way life has changed in the villages close to Rutland Water: Burley, Edith Weston, Egleton, Empingham, Gunthorpe, The Hambletons, Lyndon, Manton, Normanton and Whitwell.

Church Street, Manton, in 1905 (Hart)

Rutland's population has more than doubled over the last two hundred years, from just over 16,000 in 1801 to 34,563 at the 2001 Census. However, for the villages around Rutland Water, population has grown more slowly. At 2,069 their 1901 population was little changed from the 2,132 of 1801. The increase in the first half of the nineteenth century was offset by stagnation in the 1850s and 1860s and by a decline in the 1870s, 1880s and 1890s. Rutland's agriculture in these final decades of the nineteenth century was affected by a combination of low prices, a shift in emphasis from arable to pasture, and a big decline in the number of small farms.

By 2001 the population for these same villages was only 3,183. But for service personnel living at Edith Weston and the resident population of Ashwell Prison in the far corner of Burley parish, the figure would be even lower.

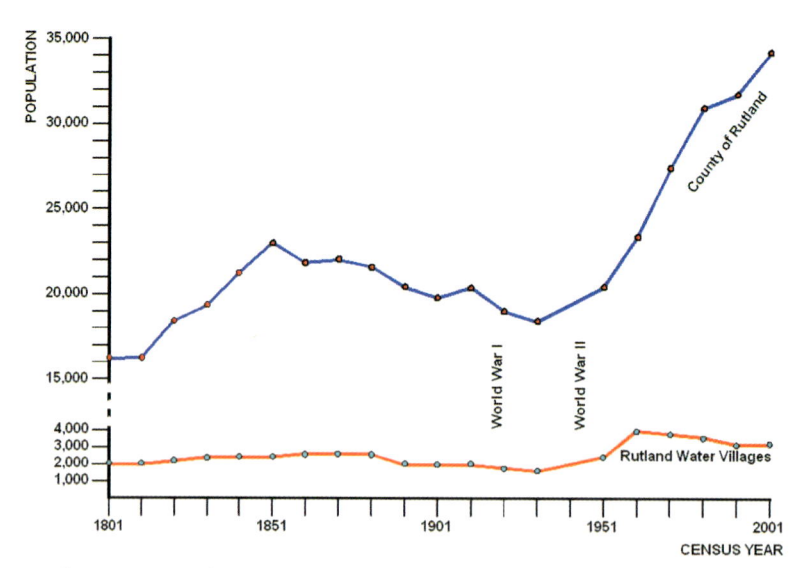

The variation in population of the Rutland Water villages between 1801 and 2001 compared to that of the whole of Rutland (RO)

The creation of Rutland Water displaced approximately twenty families, as recorded by the *Stamford Mercury* of 19th June 1970. Subsequent building on land within the reservoir planning area has been subject to strict control and this has helped to contain population growth.

At the close of the nineteenth century these villages evoked a world more traditional than modern. True, the railway at Manton gave access to the national network and more than twenty people from Manton were employed in connection with the railway. Telegraph wires had reached Empingham as early as 1871 and from 1898 cables could also be sent from Upper Hambleton. But overwhelmingly these were small agricultural communities, self-sufficient in many ways. The majority of those working had been born within the county.

More than 40 per cent of those employed worked in agriculture or related occupations, as labourers, horsemen, cowmen, shepherds, graziers and

Families looking for new homes

THE EXODUS of 20 Rutland families, whose homes will be submerged under 27 million gallons of water in the Empingham reservoir, is underway.

Above: Headlines from the Stamford Mercury *of 19th June 1970*

Right: Manton Station in 1905. More than twenty people from the village were employed on the railway at this time (Hart)

— 304 —

gardeners. More than a quarter of the total were in domestic or family service, from boot boys and grooms to cooks and housekeepers, to butlers and governesses. Many more affluent families and households would have had more than one servant. The larger halls carried sizeable domestic staffs, ten, twenty and sometimes more.

Beyond this, there were all the trades to support the rural economy, from carpenters to blacksmiths, from wheelwrights to harness makers. Others worked as cobblers, in village shops – particularly as grocers, bakers and butchers – on the railway and as labourers. Teachers, men of the Church, clerks and other professionals help to complete the picture. For young girls and women looking for work, domestic service beckoned, alongside dressmaker, tailoress, laundress or charwoman.

Bringing in the harvest – a postcard of 1911 by S Cooke of Upper Hambleton (Hart)

The Old Bakehouse, Egleton

Visitors to Egleton today may notice the house called The Old Bakehouse and draw the obvious conclusion. Looking more closely, they can see that the house nameplate was formerly the door to a baking oven. Further research would reveal that Egleton was one of several villages in the area where residents could take their Sunday joints to the baker for roasting in his oven.

The nameplate to The Old Bakehouse, Egleton, was taken from a former baking oven (RO)

The blacksmith's forge at Burley in 1908. At this time William Chambers was the blacksmith (Hart)

It was quite common for boys to start work at thirteen. Girls would start work a year or two later but there were exceptions. Mabel Baines, aged thirteen, was living away from home in 1901 and working as a domestic servant in Manton. She was one of thirteen or more children, with eight brothers and sisters still living at home with her parents in Hambleton. It is understandable that she was working away while so young.

There was no state pension at this time and many breadwinners would continue to work for as long as they were physically able. The 1901 Census gives many examples of men continuing with labouring or other manual work into their late sixties, seventies and even their eighties. John Chamberlain of Burley was a wood faggot maker at the age of 79 and Thomas Whitehouse of Empingham was an agricultural labourer, aged 81. For men in their seventies and beyond, unable to find other employment, work on the parish roads and in all weathers was one of the last refuges. John Berridge of Empingham, aged 81, is recorded as a road labourer.

Not all lived to these ages. Shortly after arriving in 1889 the Rector of Lyndon reviewed the church records for his village. For the period 1814-91 he calculated the average age at death as just below 50.

If all else failed, including family help, there remained the workhouse. The Union Workhouse at Oakham, opened in 1837, did not close until after the First World War. Its 1901 residents included a number of older poor born in Edith Weston, Empingham and Hambleton, aged from their late fifties to their eighties. George Topps was also there. He was born in Burley and only 12 years old.

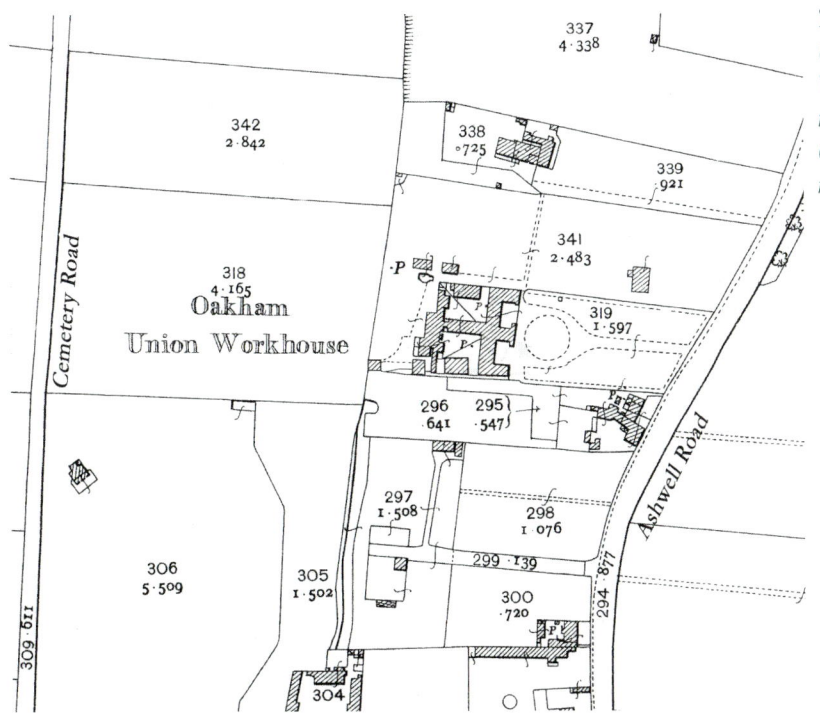

The Oakham Union Workhouse taken from the OS 2nd ed 25" map 1904

At this time there were great concentrations of landownership and wealth. In the 1870s the Earl of Derby promoted a government report on landownership, *Return of Owners of Land 1873*. For Rutland this established that around half the county was owned by just four landowners, including Lord Aveland of Normanton Park with 13,633 acres and Mr G H Finch of Burley on the Hill with 9,181 acres. This landownership and wealth entailed considerable power and influence. The landowner could expect and receive deference from those who worked on or dealt with his estates but he could also enjoy power and influence within the county. In 1900 Mr Finch was a long serving Member of Parliament, magistrate and Rutland County Councillor, holding many other civic positions. His kinsman Henry Randolph Finch chaired Oakham Rural District Council.

The former Oakham Workhouse is now The Schanschieff Site, providing boarding accommodation for Oakham School (RO)

Normanton Hall in 1905, the home of Gilbert Henry Heathcote-Drummond-Willoughby (1830-1910), 2nd Lord Aveland, created Earl of Ancaster in 1892 (Hart)

Edward Nathaniel Conant of Lyndon Hall owned 1,471 acres in Rutland in the 1870s and was not in the same landowning league as Mr Finch or Lord Aveland. Nevertheless, after he died in 1901 his gross estate was in excess of £450,000. The *Victoria County History* estimated the average wages of a Rutland worker in 1901 as about fifteen shillings per week. On this basis, it would have taken him over 10,000 years to earn an equivalent sum.

A wealthy landowner or squire had obvious power over the working lives of tenants, workers and the local community but this power could also extend to their private lives. Unmarried girls working in domestic service could lose their positions if they became pregnant. Without family or other help, they might find themselves in the workhouse. Offending behaviour could deprive a labourer of both employment and the house provided with it. Even the estate steward had great authority. In his book *Empingham Remembered* Ernest Mills recounts how his father was forced to leave the village. His father and a friend met two girls outside Empingham Church after Sunday evening service and walked along the road with them. They were seen by the Steward of the Ancaster Estate who employed the girls as maids and was unhappy at the possibility of losing them. The Steward let it be known that the two men should 'leave the village immediately or he would turn their parents on to the street'. Unwilling to cause difficulty in the village for his family, Ernest Mills' father left Empingham and set out to find work in Leicester.

To point out the disparity between the wealth of the few and the earnings of the many is not to deny the recurring generosity of squires to their local communities. The village hall in Egleton, originally erected as a school

Mr G H Finch (centre) of Burley on the Hill (private collection)

in 1867, is visible testimony to the benevolence of the Finch family. The old school in Empingham, now a private residence, was erected by Sir Gilbert Heathcote in 1838 and enlarged by Lord Aveland in 1872. The village hall in Lyndon was given by Mrs Conant in 1922 in memory of Mr E W P Conant, her late husband.

This nostalgic view of rural life has a less happy side. These were also times when people trapped blackbirds and thrushes for food, when they collected the eggs of wild birds, when poaching was not uncommon, and when women and children gleaned in the fields.

By their very nature, these informal activities leave few written records but they are occasionally recorded in some detail. The *Stamford Mercury* of Friday 14th November 1884 devoted a lengthy article on page four to a 'Fatal Poaching Affray'. The previous Saturday night a group of poachers had been on land adjacent to Burley Wood, on the estate of Mr G H Finch. From within the wood they were spotted by the head gamekeeper and six others who had been warned to expect poachers. A fracas ensued and one of the poachers, Robert Baker of Melton Mowbray, was struck on the head with a stick by William Collier and collapsed. He was carried to the head gamekeeper's house and died there. Mr Norman, medical practitioner from Oakham, was called and confirmed death shortly after 1.00 on Sunday morning. Two other poachers were apprehended.

The village hall in Egleton, originally erected in 1867 as the village school (RO)

The old school in Empingham, now a private residence (RO)

The next day, Monday, the Coroner held an inquest at the gamekeeper's house. There was disagreement about the number of poachers involved, one side saying three and the other six or seven. William Collier was represented by a Stamford solicitor, Mr Atter. Collier stated that he had struck back at Robert Baker after himself receiving a heavy blow to the head. The poachers were also said to have thrown large pieces of ironstone at the gamekeepers. The solicitor argued reasonable self-defence and the jury returned a verdict of justifiable homicide.

Two days later, on Wednesday, the two arrested poachers were tried at Oakham Castle. They had been found with 300 yards of netting and 54 rabbits so there was no easy defence to the charge that they had taken and destroyed a quantity of rabbits which belonged to George H Finch of Burley. Richard Tallis of Oakham and James Elenor of Upper Broughton, Nottinghamshire, pleaded guilty and were sentenced to three months imprisonment. They also had to find a surety of five shillings each not to offend again for one year.

Gleaning, the gathering of corn left by reapers, was a more legitimate activity, normally involving women and children. In some villages a Gleaning Bell would be rung, indicating the allowed time for gleaning, usually between 8am and 6pm. In 1880 the Gleaning Bell was being rung in Hambleton, Egleton, Empingham and Whitwell. It continued to be rung at Empingham into the early twentieth century.

The former gamekeeper's house to the Burley Estate on the old road from Oakham to Stamford (RO)

Not all was dearth and deference in the villages around Rutland Water at the end of the nineteenth century. Several villages kept on until the early 1900s the tradition of the annual Village Feast. This was a day for celebration, for former residents to visit friends and family, and for itinerant traders to come to the village. However by this time, the annual celebration of Plough Monday, on the first Monday after Epiphany, was dying out.

For small villages, it is not clear that these traditional village celebrations had survived so long. The Rector of Lyndon from 1889-1909, the Rev T K B Nevinson, kept a notebook and scrapbook covering that period. With little over one hundred souls to care for, he took a keen interest in village life. He records for 16th November 1890 a special ringing of the church bells, 'this being Lyndon Feast', but does not mention any accompanying fête or gala. Ringing the bells on the first Sunday after 11th November, Martinmas or St Martin's Day, had a special resonance for the church of St Martin at Lyndon.

Lyndon village hall was given by Mrs Conant to the village in 1922 (RO)

At that time, there was no public house in the village – nor is there now! – and no village hall. Concerts and meetings could take place in the laundry of Lyndon Hall. It must have been a sizeable laundry as more than 50 people came to a lecture in 1895 and 92 attended a concert in 1904. When the Peterborough No 1 Church Army Van visited the village and held several meetings in 1903, the average attendance was 48.

Mr Nevinson recorded the start of a choral society and a Mothers' Union branch. He opened a Reading Room in the Old Rectory which closed after four years for lack of demand. He noted a jumble sale and fête with an excellent tea in the Rectory garden and evening dancing to the Collyweston Band, on payment of a modest charge. He reported occasional celebrations and anniversaries where the squire entertained a combination of parishioners, tenants and tradesmen. These might include cricket and other games, fireworks and dancing.

The quiet pace of rural life was interrupted by a slight earthquake in the winter of 1896. Four years later there was a partial eclipse of the sun, when the Rector and his son carried pieces of smoked glass around the village. International affairs forced themselves on the village the same year when Church Lads' Brigade forces advanced on Lyndon from the direction of Oakham and Stamford. They fought the engagement of 'Lyndonsmith', recalling the recent Siege and Relief of Ladysmith in the Second Boer War. They adjourned for what was described as a 'sumptuous tea' provided by the Rector and his wife. Eventually, they fell in on the Rectory lawn and left in a procession, headed by the 'Stamford drum and fife band' and the 'Oakham bugle band'. A humorous article in *The Stamford Post* of 20th April 1900 reported on the military activities.

Events took a more sober turn when news reached the village in the summer of 1902 that Mr Frederick L Wright had died in South Africa after falling from his horse. He was accidentally killed while on duty with the South African Constabulary. Like his father and grandfather, he had been born in the village where his father was employed as head gardener. In 1889, shortly after the Rector's arrival, he had travelled from Lyndon to the

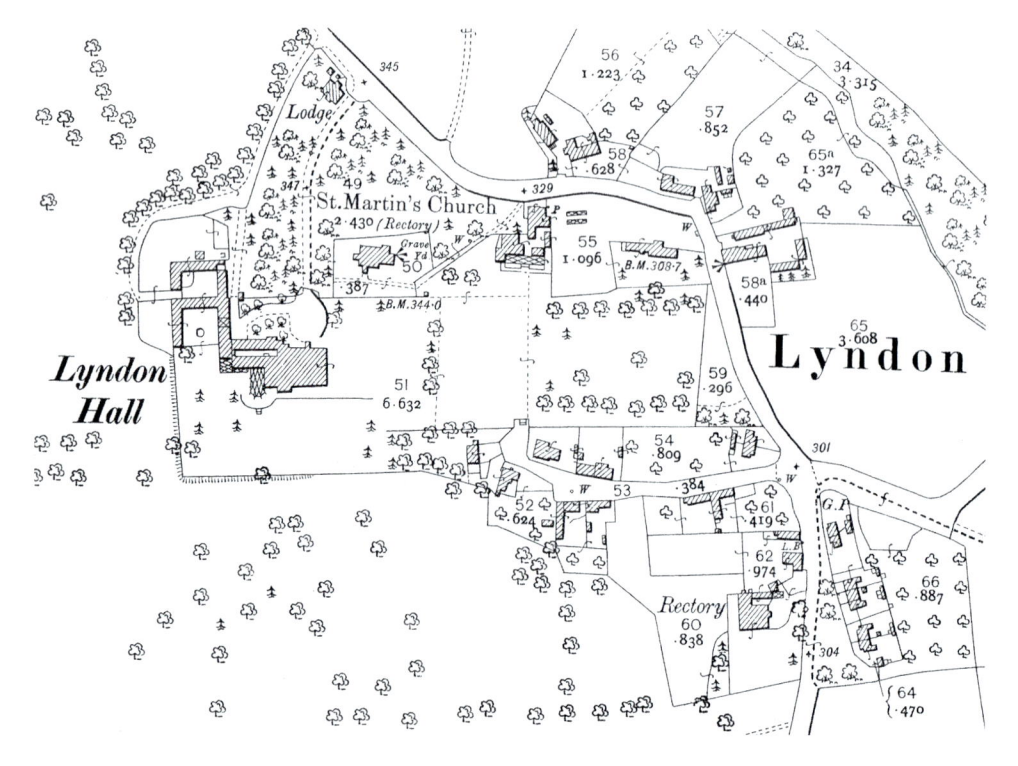

Lyndon from the OS 2nd ed 25" map 1904

An extract from Lyndon Churchwardens' Accounts for 1899 (ROLLR DE 1938/14)

		Expenditure.	£	s	d
1899		W Sidney Churchwarden			
April 14		Visitation & Expenses		1	4
May 15		Cox. Sweeping Wall. extra		3	6
Oct 7		Medwell putting coal in			1
10		S. Smiths salary		15	
		Coal. Bill	1	14	3
00 Jan 19		Sweeping Flues			4
		Coltmans Bill	1	17	6
April 6		V. Foster Washing Surplices		10	
10		Medwells salary	2	10	
11		Smiths J. "	2	12	
		Smiths. S "		15	
			£ 12	6	3

Examined & allowed
17 April 1900.
Thos. H. B. Nevinson
(Chairman)

neighbouring village of Wing for Confirmation at the age of fourteen. A tablet was erected in the church in his memory.

The Churchwardens' Accounts are a more local affair, simple and meticulous. They itemize regular purchases of coal and kindling, payments for washing surplices, cleaning windows and sweeping flues. Beeswax and turpentine were ordered. Spoutings were cleared and gutters tarred. Annual expenses are totalled and set against contributions and subscriptions. Frequently, there was not enough money to pay the expenses in full. Mr Conant of Lyndon Hall and other members of the family regularly made good the difference.

A record was kept of proceeds from collections at church services and of how they were used each year. Although a small village, Lyndon made regular gifts to worthy causes: Stamford Infirmary, Lincolnshire; St Mary's Church, Plaistow, London; The Royal Agricultural Benevolent Institution; The Church Missionary Society and similar organisations. Gifts were made to the local Coal Club and to the sick and needy but also in 1897 for the relief of famine in India.

In 1891 the Rector married in Stamford and brought his bride home to Lyndon. The carriage was met on the edge of the village where local men took over the task of pulling it to the Rectory. When he left the village, the *Stamford Mercury* of 6th August 1909 described a Farewell Party on the Rectory lawn. Guests enjoyed a meat tea. There were games and dancing to Mr Barnett's band. How times have changed!

Aspects of Topography

Normanton Park Road

Normanton Park Road was the first of the three new roads which were built during the construction of Rutland Water. Running from Normanton cross-roads to Bunkers Hill, Empingham, its initial role was to provide access for lorries carrying heavy equipment and materials to the nearby dam construction site. For most of its length it was built along the line of a farm track, which before 1925 was a coach road passing through an avenue of trees and open parkland. Margaret Plumb (*née* Hart) remembers: 'We used to walk through the park from Empingham where the road is now, it was just a cart track and sometimes it was very muddy.'

The coach road was originally the east entrance to Normanton Hall, and the route taken by the Prince and Princess of Wales when travelling to Stamford following their visit in 1881. The Rev Edward Bradley, in reporting the visit for *The Illustrated London News* on 15th January, recorded: 'On leaving the lodges at this [the east] side of the park the coach-road passes through a long avenue of beech and sycamores.'

The lodges were either side of the east entrance gates to Normanton Park, where the coach road passed through The Belt, narrow woodland on three sides of the park. To the north-west of the lodges was Mow Mires farmhouse and Mow Mires Spinney, both of which were lost when the reservoir was built (*see* Chapter 11 – Normanton).

The former coach road in 1970 looking towards Normanton (Jim Levisohn ARPS) Below: From the OS 2nd ed 25" map 1904 showing The Avenue, The Belt and the lodges which were either side of the east entrance gates to Normanton Hall

The east coach road highlighted on the OS 2nd ed 1" map 1906

The Avenue section of the old coach road was a long ride of beech and sycamore trees. Only a short section survives today (Hart)

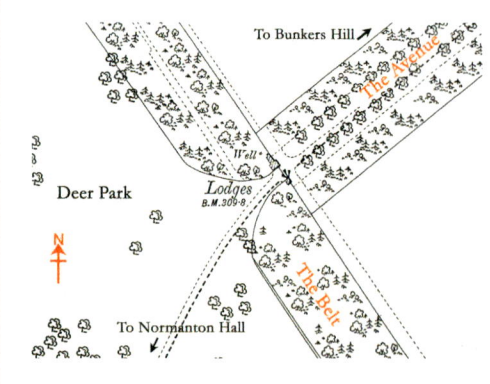

— 314 —

Chapter 14
Rutland Waters
Robert Ovens and Sheila Sleath

Rutland is in the driest region of the United Kingdom, receiving on average 600mm or 23.6 inches of rain a year, which is two thirds of the average for England and Wales. This equates to nearly 234 million cubic metres (51,520 million gallons) of water – sufficient to fill Rutland Water nearly twice over. Although a great deal of this is utilised directly by plant and crop growth, and some evaporates, this still leaves a staggering 58 million cubic metres (12,760 million gallons) or so to be drained away by the county's surface watercourses and underground aquifers.

Rutland Watercourses

A cursory inspection of the county map will soon establish that many of the natural surface watercourses, especially in the southern half of Rutland, flow generally eastwards, and these are often through steep-sided valleys. This will certainly be confirmed by the traveller crossing Rutland in a northerly direction, say along the A6003 from Caldecott towards Oakham. The roller-coaster nature of the road will definitely be noticed, and it is why the area was so carefully scrutinised when the search was on for new reservoir sites.

The county's only river of any significant size is the Welland, which is never wholly in Rutland as it forms the majority of its south-eastern boundary. At least 85 per cent of the county is in the drainage basin of this river, which has its source near Husbands Bosworth in Leicestershire. Its journey past Rutland begins at its confluence with the Eye Brook, near the former Rockingham Station, just south of Caldecott. It then flows past Thorpe by

The Welland in flood near Seaton Viaduct in November 2006 (RO)

Water and Seaton Mill, under the Seaton Viaduct and on to Barrowden and Tixover Church before skirting the Northamptonshire village of Duddington. Near Ketton it passes under Collyweston Bridge and on to Tinwell, which is the river's abstraction point for the Rutland Water aqueduct. It finally leaves the Rutland boundary at Broadeng Bridge. Its onward journey takes it through Stamford and Spalding in Lincolnshire and across the Fens to discharge finally into the Wash. It is navigable from Hudds Mill, just below Stamford, down to Fosdyke Bridge near its outfall into the Wash, a distance of 56km (35 miles).

The Eye Brook, sometimes shown on old maps as the Little Eye, rises near Skeffington in Leicestershire and, for some miles, forms the south-west boundary of Rutland with Leicestershire, beginning at Finchley Bridge near Belton in Rutland. It passes south of Belton, and north of Allexton and Stockerston in Leicestershire before flowing into the Eyebrook reservoir south of Beaumont Chase and Stoke Dry. From the reservoir it follows the valley for a short distance to join the Welland near Caldecott. It has a number of streams as tributaries, including West Brook which joins it from the north near Belton in Rutland.

The River Chater rises near Whatborough Hill in Leicestershire, and then flows east, past the site of Sauvey Castle, and Launde Abbey, before crossing the county boundary with Rutland at Leighfield. It continues its sinuous course north of Ridlington and Preston, and then to the south of Manton. Between North and South Luffenham, it meets a stream that rises south of Ridlington. It continues in a north-easterly direction, going through Ketton, before meeting the River Welland near Tinwell, the end of its 24-km (15-mile) journey.

The Welland in a quiet mood at Tixover, looking west (John Nowell, Zodiac Publishing)

The Chater at Ketton in the early 1940s (RCM)

The River Gwash, which appears on early printed maps as the Wash River, also rises in Leicestershire, near Owston. It takes an easterly course, passing through Braunston and south of the former Oakham Waterworks to Brooke, then between Gunthorpe and Martinsthorpe before running under the railway line and Sounding Bridge north of Manton. Here, it flows into Rutland Water to emerge from under the dam some five miles later, just before Church Bridge, Empingham. (Prior to the construction of the reservoir, the river followed a meandering course past Hambleton Wood, through Brake Spinney and on to Normanton Fishpond.) Just before entering Mow Mires Spinney, it was joined by its northern arm which passed through Burley Fishponds. Just beyond Empingham, near the former Empingham Mill, its volume of water is again increased by the North Brook, and at Wild's Lodge by water from the springs in Shacklewell Spinney. Continuing its course through Tickencote, the river crosses the Great North Road (A1) under Roman Bridge at Great Casterton. After passing close to Little Casterton and Tolethorpe it nearly encircles Ryhall, where it runs down the side of the street, and passing through Belmesthorpe, finally discharges into the Welland near Newstead Mill to the east of Stamford. Its total course is about 40km (25 miles).

The North Brook sources near Cottesmore and after flowing in an easterly direction through Greetham turns south past the site of the former Greetham Mill to flow through a deep gully into Exton Park and Fort Henry lakes. Just after the lower of the two lakes it passes on its eastern side the site of the deserted medieval village of Horn, before flowing under the remains of the Exton Park wall. A little later it is joined by a small tributary which flows through Ry Gate Lake in the grounds of Exton Hall, and later through the bed of a drained lake near Cuckoo Spinney. The North Brook continues in a southerly direction by Horn Mill, now a Trout hatchery, to Empingham where it joins the Gwash near the site of the former Empingham Mill.

The Gwash following its serpentine path through meadows between Braunston and Brooke (RO)

The North Brook flows under the remains of Exton Park wall near the deserted medieval village of Horn (RO)

The River Glen flows for a short distance through the north-eastern corner of Rutland, during which it skirts Essendine church and the adjacent castle mound. It eventually joins the Welland in the Fens.

The River Eye, not to be confused with the Eye Brook, sourcing to the east of Cold Overton in Leicestershire and running through Langham, leaves the county, after almost encircling Ashwell, in a north-westerly direction and eventually drains this part of Rutland towards the River Trent. Its tributary, Whissendine Brook, also runs from near Cold Overton, through Cold Overton Lake and Whissendine to join the Eye just before it enters Stapleford Park in Leicestershire.

There are many other streams in Rutland which, although shown, are rarely named on maps. However, they often have local names. Two examples are the River Eg, originally a tributary of the River Gwash, which flows through Egleton and into the nature reserve lagoons at the western end of Rutland Water, and the River Hlyde which flows past Lyddington fishponds, eventually joining the River Welland upstream of Thorpe by Water. In each case, the name of the river is associated with the name of the settlement through which it flows.

The watercourses of Rutland (RO)

Watermills in Rutland

The main function of most watercourses is to drain excess water from the landscape. Secondary uses include water supply for human and animal consumption, for irrigation, and for commercial and industrial applications. For centuries, larger rivers and canals have also been used for transport. Until the beginning of the twentieth century, another important use was a means of storing energy.

For over 1,000 years, until the introduction of the windmill in the twelfth century, the watermill was the only form of mechanical power available. The watermill and windmill were then the unrivalled providers of power until the steam engine was introduced in the eighteenth century.

The Domesday survey shows that there were some 5,624 mills in England in 1086, mainly in the south and east of the country. Thirty-nine of these were in Rutland, of which seventeen were on the River Gwash or on one of its tributaries. Six were located at Empingham.

For several hundred years after Domesday, the lord of the manor dominated mill life. These owners of ancient manorial mills possessed 'soke rights', which meant that all corn was ground in the lord of the manor's mill.

A good supply of water was essential in this highly profitable trade, and many lawsuits resulted from disputes between mill owners concerning the flow of water between watermills.

After Domesday, watermills were put to an increasingly diverse range of uses including grinding iron ore, driving tilt hammers, pumping bellows, and crushing bark for tanning. There were also sawmills, paper mills, gunpowder mills, boring mills, water-pumping mills, silk mills, and cotton-spinning mills. However, Rutland watermills were almost exclusively corn mills, grinding corn to produce flour.

At the beginning of the nineteenth century steam-driven mills, followed closely by steel roller mills, resulted in the eventual demise of watermills. Along the River Gwash and its tributaries in Rutland, there were eighteenth-century watermills at Brooke, Whitwell, Empingham, Tickencote, Tolethorpe and Ryhall, together with Greetham and Horn on the North Brook, most of which were able to continue as working mills until the end of the nineteenth century. There were other watermills at this time at Ketton and South Luffenham on the Chater, Caldecott on the Eye Brook, and Thorpe by Water, Seaton, Barrowden and Tinwell on the Welland. Today there are no working watermills in the county. However, some of the buildings survive, most having been converted into private dwellings. The OS Second Edition 25" map of 1904 shows the mills then surviving in Rutland. Particularly interesting are their water systems, including the leets, mill ponds, mill dams, weirs, sluices, mill races and tail races. The only watermill site known to have been lost to Rutland Water was at Whitwell. The stone-faced embankment of its mill dam can be seen to the south of the village on pre-Rutland Water aerial photographs. Its water supply was the stream which flows in a southerly direction through Whitwell, a tributary of the northern arm of the Gwash (*see* Chapter 20 – Medieval Settlements at Nether Hambleton and Whitwell).

Horn mill from the OS 2nd ed 25" map 1904. Although the mill house survives, many of the other buildings were demolished when the Trout hatchery for Rutland Water was built here in the 1970s

Horn Mill and mill pond about 1905 (Canon J R H Prophet)

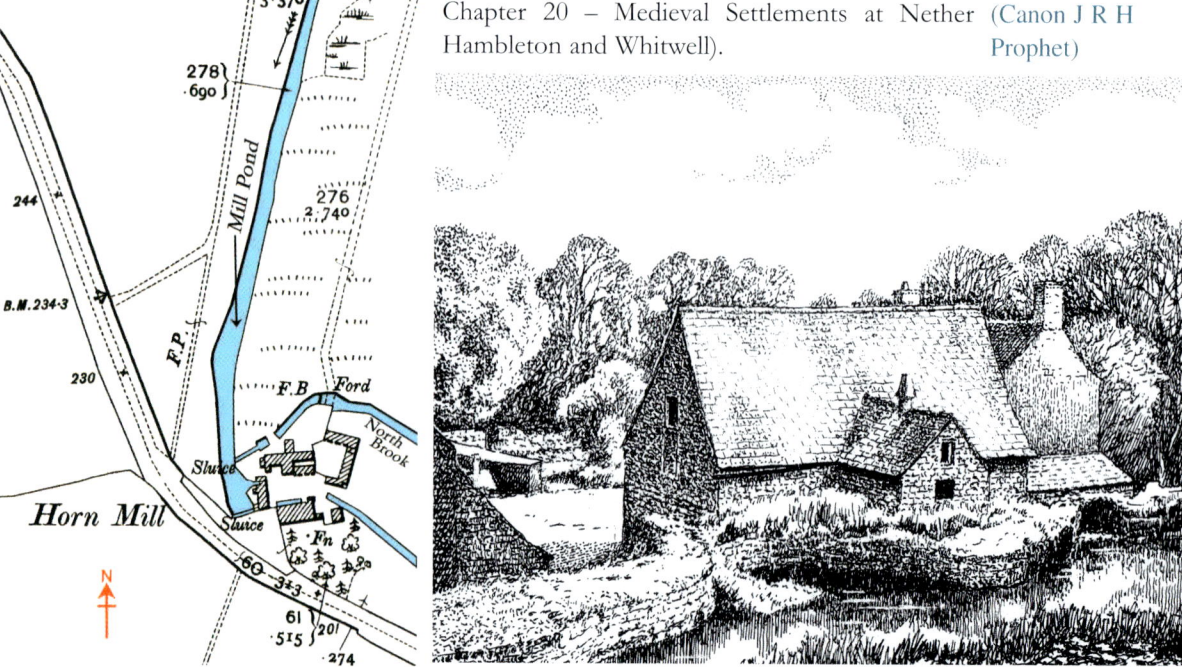

Barrowden Mill and mill pond on the River Welland, about 1908 (Hart)

Ryhall Mill in 1925, now demolished (Hart)

Empingham and Manton Reservoirs

Following the Water Resources Act of 1963, the local water authorities, the Welland & Nene River Authority and the Mid-Northamptonshire Water Board, the forerunners of Anglian Water, had reviewed the probable future requirements for water, and investigated various ways and means of supplying the estimated demands. In the area being considered the growth rate was predicted to be well above the national average, mainly due to new housing in developing Northamptonshire towns. It was considered that the only practical solution was to establish a large reservoir to store water pumped from two or more rivers as no single river in the area had sufficient flow.

Some 64 valleys with possible potential for water storage were investigated in what is now the Anglian Water area. In many cases the storage capacity was too small to be worth consideration, and many others were too remote from watercourses from which water could be transferred in adequate quantities for a pumped-storage scheme. In the majority of cases the geology of the valley was unsuitable. Only two sites were considered to be worth further investigation, the Chater valley to the west of the main road between Preston and Manton (the Manton reservoir), and the Gwash valley upstream of Empingham (the Empingham reservoir). These are adjacent valleys in the heart of Rutland and the reservoirs together would have covered some 4.5 per cent of the county.

Looking at water sources, the River Authority had also reached the conclusion by 1966 that the River Nene, with a catchment area of 1,554 square kilometres (600 square miles) and the River Welland, with a catchment area of 518 square kilometres (200 square miles), should be fully developed as constituting the only practicable way of meeting the required demand. Fortunately, they were close enough to the identified storage valleys for the planners to consider a full pumped-storage project. Records of water flow from the previous 27 years, which included two periods of severe drought, indicated that up to 900,000 cubic metres (200 million gallons) of water per day could be extracted from the Nene at Wansford, Cambridgeshire, leaving 140,000 cubic metres (30 million gallons) per day to flow down the river. Similarly, up to 450,000 cubic metres (100 million gallons) per day could be taken from the Welland at Tinwell, leaving 70,000 cubic metres (15 million gallons) per day to carry on down the river. The River Gwash, upstream of the dam, with a catchment area of 78 square kilometres (30 square miles), would supply only 5 per cent of the reservoir water.

Much of the investigative work to reach this stage had been carried out by T & C Hawksley, Consultant Civil Engineers of Whitehall, London, in conjunction with the two water authorities. In 1967 it was decided to seek Parliamentary approval for constructing the whole of the works described here and T & C Hawksley were engaged to prepare a report on the project, dealing in particular with the sequence in which the reservoirs, pumping stations and treatment works were to be built.

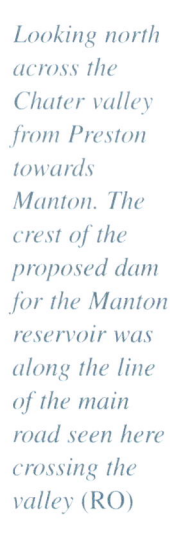

Looking north across the Chater valley from Preston towards Manton. The crest of the proposed dam for the Manton reservoir was along the line of the main road seen here crossing the valley (RO)

The geology of both valleys was investigated by drilling a series of boreholes. Both were found to have problems, but nothing was found that was considered to be insurmountable. The earth dam across the Gwash valley near Empingham was to be 37m high, 1,200m long and 810m wide on the Upper Lias Clay in which the valley has been formed. This would mean very gentle slopes and a very high volume of banking material. The resulting reservoir would have a top water level of 83.82m OD, would impound 124 million cubic metres (27,300 million gallons) of water, and would have a surface area of 1,260 hectares (3,114 acres). The village of Lower Hambleton and part of Middle Hambleton would be lost, together with three other isolated properties. Three new roads would be required: from near Burley Fishponds to Hambleton, from the east of Oakham to the top of Barnsdale Hill, and from Normanton to the top of Bunker's Hill near Empingham.

Drilling one of the many boreholes in order to establish the exact geology of the valleys (Brian and Elizabeth Nicholls Photography)

Looking across the Gwash valley from Hambleton towards Burley and Barnsdale in 1972 (Brian and Elizabeth Nicholls Photography)

For the Chater valley reservoir, the earth embankment near Manton was to be 42.67m high, and this was considered to be the maximum for this type of dam. It would cover the main road which crosses the valley south of Manton, and would therefore have to be wider at the top to accommodate the 37m necessary for a new road. Again the slopes would have to be very gentle and a very high volume of banking material would be required. The top water level of 114.2m OD, 30.5m higher than the Empingham reservoir, would impound 98 million cubic metres (21,560 million gallons) with a surface area of 595 hectares (1,470 acres). Only two properties were threatened: Jubilee Lodge on the road between Ridlington and Brooke, and Leigh Lodge in Leighfield, both being farm houses with adjacent farm buildings. Both could be saved by slightly lowering the top water level. Part of the Ridlington to Brooke road would be lost, but it seemed obvious that this could be replaced by a new road along the line of the old coaching road through Martinsthorpe, on the ridge between Brooke and Manton. A 132,000 volt electricity transmission line would also have to be realigned.

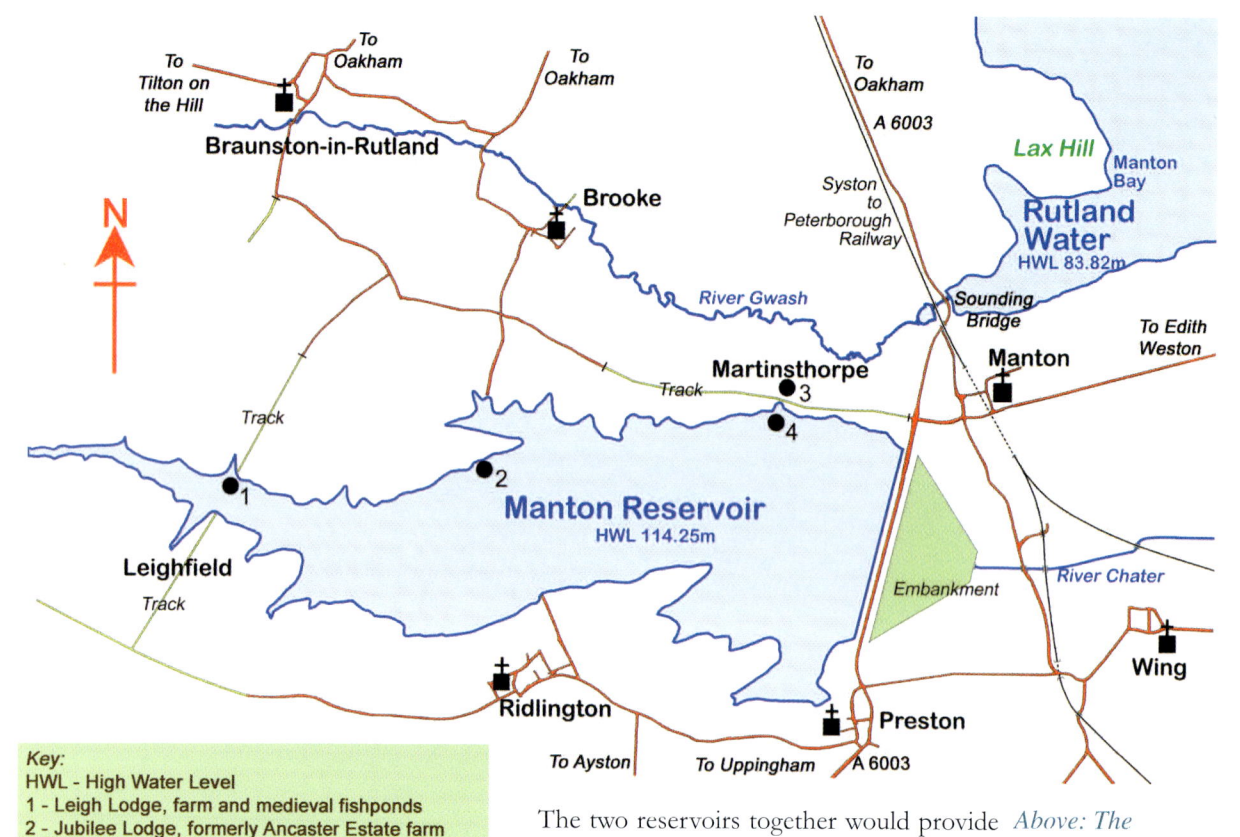

Above: The proposed Manton and Empingham reservoirs were in adjacent valleys and together would have covered 4.5 per cent of the land area of Rutland (RO)

Key:
HWL - High Water Level
1 - Leigh Lodge, farm and medieval fishponds
2 - Jubilee Lodge, formerly Ancaster Estate farm
3 - Martinsthorpe Deserted Medieval Village (Scheduled Ancient Monument)
4 - Martinsthorpe Park
5 - Old coaching road
6 - Grade II listed packhorse bridge over the Chater

The two reservoirs together would provide a maximum storage capacity of 222 million cubic metres (48,860 million gallons). This would ensure 82 days supply without top-up water being added.

As well as the reservoirs, the other works necessary included the installation of pumping stations at the abstraction points on the Nene at Wansford, and the Welland at Tinwell, a water treatment works at Wing, and aqueducts linking the pumping stations to the reservoirs and the reservoirs to the treatment works.

Left: Jubilee Lodge, built by the Ancaster Estate, was a potential victim of the Manton reservoir (RO)

— 324 —

Leigh Lodge, on the upper reaches of the proposed Manton Reservoir, was another possible victim. This aerial photograph, taken in 2006, shows that the Chater has now been dammed locally to create an ornamental lake (John Nowell, Zodiac Publishing)

The consultants considered a range of options. The main discussion was whether they should build Empingham reservoir or Manton reservoir first. Other considerations included different methods of constructing the aqueducts, various regimes for pumping and the effects on pumping costs. A further option was to consider a truncated reservoir at Empingham with two dams, mainly as a gesture to reduce the area of farming land lost. However, this was dismissed on the grounds of cost and feasibility.

Hawksley's recommendations were to construct the whole of the works, including both reservoirs for the long term scheme. This would ensure the maximum utilisation of the water available from the Welland and Nene rivers. However, in the shorter term, they recommended that Empingham Reservoir should be built first. This would save £3 million and provide 20 per cent more storage capacity compared to building Manton Reservoir.

These recommendations were adopted and Parliamentary approval was received in May 1970. Work commenced in June 1970 and the scheme was essentially complete, although not yet ready to supply water, by the summer of 1975 when water from the diverted River Gwash was allowed to flow into the new reservoir basin. At the end of a protracted campaign, Empingham Reservoir was renamed Rutland Water in 1976. It was 1979 before the new reservoir was full to capacity for the first time. There has been little mention of the need for Manton reservoir since (*see* Chapter 15 – Don't Dam Rutland, and Chapter 17 – Planning and Constructing the Reservoir).

At the time of writing plans have been agreed to increase the output of Wing water treatment works. These involve extracting larger volumes of water from Rutland Water and reducing water levels considerably below those experienced in the past. A new pipeline will be installed between Empingham and Wing, and between Wing and Hannington in Northamptonshire. In order to protect the nature reserve at the western end of the reservoir from low water levels, it is proposed to construct dams across Manton Bay in the south arm and across the western end of the north arm near the former Burley Fishponds. These will retain the water in the nature reserve area. Additional lagoons will also be created (*see* Aspects of Topography: A New Wetland Habitat). This work is due to commence in 2008.

> **From the *Stamford Mercury*, 22nd April 1977:**
>
> **Huge reservoir plan – go-ahead unlikely**
>
> A reservoir three-quarters the size of Rutland Water could be built at Manton if there is an 'enormous population growth' by the year 2000. The lake, three miles south of Oakham and four miles south-west of Empingham, would hold 18,000 million gallons, pump out 29,000 gallons a day and cover 6.1 square kilometres.
>
> But there is doubt whether it would ever go ahead.
>
> Mr Peter Doble, Anglian Water Authority spokesman, said: 'Whether the reservoir is ever built or not depends on future demand. It would need an enormous population growth or a higher industrial growth in the area.'
>
> Mr Doble said Manton was first thought about ten years ago as one of the original alternatives to Rutland Water. 'It was a bit of a toss-up between Manton and Empingham,' he said.
>
> Mr Doble said the reservoir could serve areas as far away as Grimsby and Essex if it were built.
>
> The 1975 cost of a reservoir at Manton was £23.8 million, 'but it would cost twice or even ten times that amount by the year 2000,' said Mr Doble. 'At the present growth rate of population we won't need another scheme anyway,' he added.
>
> Mr Richard Adams, Rutland council planning officer, said: 'As we understand it at the moment, we have been informed by the water authority that the proposed second reservoir is highly unlikely to proceed, particularly in the period covered by the Rutland Structure Plan, which runs out in 1991. But one gets the feeling that this is more in the future than that,' he added.
>
> Mr Doble said a reservoir at Manton would be against the plan. 'We would lose the character of the area; we would lose a lot of agricultural land, and almost certainly the presence of a second reservoir would lose a lot of development area,' he said.

Normanton Fishpond

Normanton Fishpond was originally an ornamental lake, almost certainly influenced, if not created, by the landscape architect Humphry Repton (1752-1818) who visited and surveyed Normanton in 1796. The following year he produced one of his Red Books detailing his proposals, illustrated with before and after watercolour views and a map. The views had fold-down flaps so that his client, Sir Gilbert Heathcote, 4th Baronet (1773-1851), could immediately see the proposed transformation. Repton's ideal was natural beauty enhanced by art, and the secret of his success was his vision of a house and how it should be placed in relation to the landscape surrounding it. In his Normanton Red Book he made many suggestions, and some of these were implemented. In particular he recommended the construction of a reservoir, or lake, as a feature to enhance the landscape on the north side of Normanton Hall. The following extract from the Normanton Red Book is particularly interesting in view of the changes which were taking place in this part of the Gwash valley some 175 years later:

'There is certainly no circumstance of landscape more interesting or beautiful than water and there can be no person so void of taste as not to feel the necessity of improving the valley at Normanton by enlarging the river, yet this is a subject attended with some difficulty and requires more management than may at first be conceived; for though it might be possible to make such a dam or head as would convert the whole valley into one vast lake, yet the expense of such a bank, and the waste of so much valuable land, is more than I would dare to advise especially as an effect equally pleasing may be produced by the more simple process which I shall now describe:

'I propose making a dam a little below the present head, and out of sight from the house, of sufficient height to flow the water to the bridge [Normanton Bridge] of an ample breadth, but to render the surface more considerable in the view from the house. I propose digging a channel or reach to supply materials for the head and also disguise the termination of the water. At the end of this bay I have supposed a boathouse with a fishing room over it, because from hence there will be the best view of the water. It is from this spot (now a gravel pit) that I have taken the sketch No XI showing the effect of the water, the bridge and the alteration suggested to the church of Normanton, but the house will not be seen from hence and of course this boathouse, tho' seen from the church, will be hid from the house, a circumstance to be studiously attended to, lest the landscape should become crowded by a multiplicity of artificial objects.'

He went on to describe how he would create a second channel, or lake, to the north-east of the first. This would be a widening of the river as before with a second dam, the second lake being lower than the first. The river would be 'the union between the two waters' and this 'union' would be disguised, when viewed from the house, by a small plantation. The deception would, in Repton's view, fool the eye into thinking that there was one vast lake.

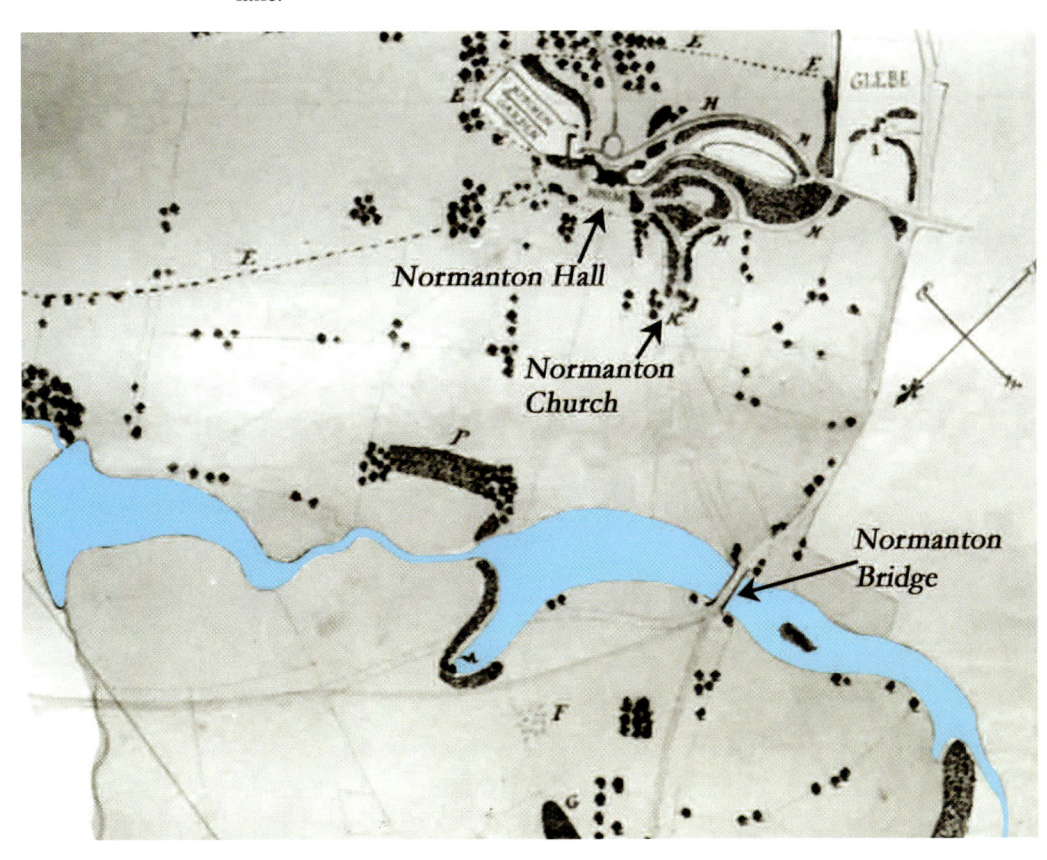

From Repton's plan of his proposals for Normanton with the lakes highlighted in blue (The Grimsthorpe and Drummond Castle Trust)

Repton's sketch No IX looking northwards along the proposed upper pool towards the boathouse (The Grimsthorpe and Drummond Castle Trust)

Repton's sketch No XI showing his proposals for the upper pool which extended under Normanton Bridge. His suggestion for the re-modelling of Normanton Church is to the left. Edith Weston Church can be seen in the background (The Grimsthorpe and Drummond Castle Trust)

Part of Repton's lake is shown in the foreground of this 1822 engraving of Normanton House and Park from the north-west (RLHRS)

Humphry Repton's proposals for the two pools described here were not adopted, but it seems that a lake, with an island, was created as a result of his report. An engraving of 1822 showing Normanton House and Park from the north-west shows part of the lake in the foreground.

On 15th January 1881 *The Illustrated London News* featured an account by the Rev Edward Bradley (who wrote under the name of 'Cuthbert Bede'), the then incumbent at Stretton, of the visit to Normanton by the Prince and Princess of Wales. In this he included: 'At the foot of the hill, on the slope of which the mansion is built, the road is carried by a bridge over a stream, which has been artificially widened into a small lake, with an island in the midst for the water-fowl.'

Thatched Village by James Buchan is an account of his life as a young boy in 'Overton' [Exton] in the 1920s when his widowed mother, Helen Buchan, was schoolmistress at the Catholic village school. The following extract describes a visit to the lake at 'Saxford' [Normanton]:

'When we were out for a picnic one day we found a lake up a narrow, overgrown road near Blackwell [Whitwell]. Bushes grew round most of it, but in the gaps between them you could see that the water was covered with lily pads with their yellow flowers scattered among them. Where the lake ended there were two iron plates set in concrete. They had cog wheels above them and a metal handle. My mother said that they were sluice gates which could be raised or lowered to control the level of the water. "Look," she said, pointing to where the top of a wall showed above the grass round the bank, "this lake has been made by people. It's an artificial one. I wonder why they put it here miles from anywhere." '

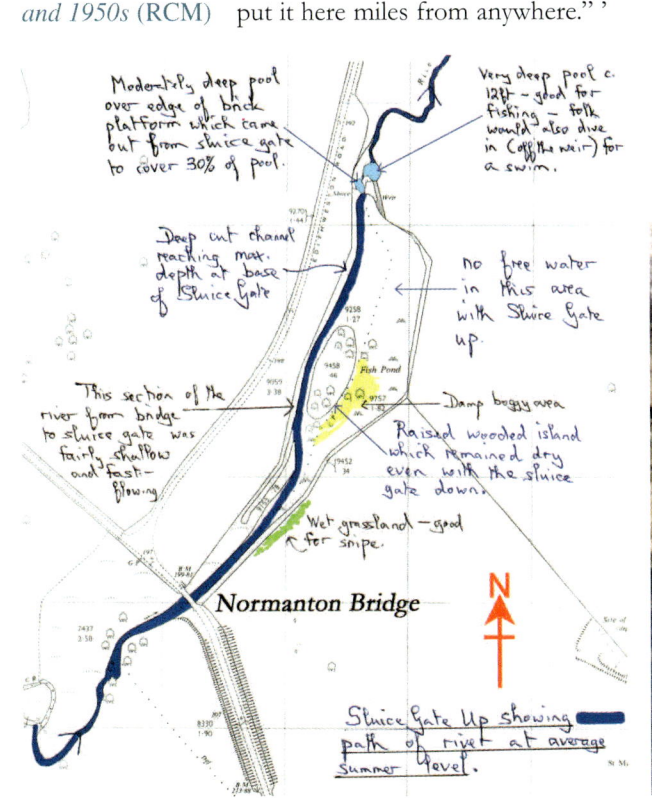

Mike Griffin's family farmed the land that was Normanton Park. In notes on the OS 2nd ed 25" map 1904, he records his memories of Normanton Fishpond as it was in the late 1940s and 1950s (RCM)

Water running down the weir at the north end of Normanton Fishpond in the 1960s. Normanton Church can be seen in the field beyond (Mike Griffin)

— 329 —

The ornamental lake at Normanton became known as Normanton Fishpond, and it is shown in detail on the OS Second Edition 25" map of 1904. During the second World War, the fishpond had to be drained and so the sluice gates were raised. Normanton Fishpond then remained 'dry' for about 20 years, except during occasional short periods of natural flooding. During this period, the course of the River Gwash was down a cutting which ran along the west side of the island and on to the sluice gates. Several trees and bushes became established in the fishpond area. In *circa* 1960, the sluice gates were closed to re-fill the fishpond which was subsequently stocked with Trout. The outlet for water was then over the weir. Normanton Fishpond remained as such until *circa* 1970 when it was drained as part of the construction process for the new reservoir.

An aerial photograph of the River Gwash and Normanton Fishpond at high water level circa 1969. Note some flooding over the margins of adjacent fields (Fred Adams)

Looking down from Normanton Bridge to Normanton Fishpond in 1970. Note the dense growth of vegetation (Jim Eaton)

Looking downstream from Normanton Bridge towards Normanton Fishpond in 1972 after clearance of trees for the new reservoir (Jim Levisohn ARPS)

Early Fishponds in Rutland

The surviving earthworks of medieval and post-medieval fishponds can be found in or near at least eighteen of Rutland's settlements (*see* Chapter 5 – Edith Weston: A Queen's Dowry), and others may have been lost as a result of land drainage, and agricultural and building development. Most of those that remain are protected as Scheduled Ancient Monuments. Fish rearing in purpose-built stews was a valuable

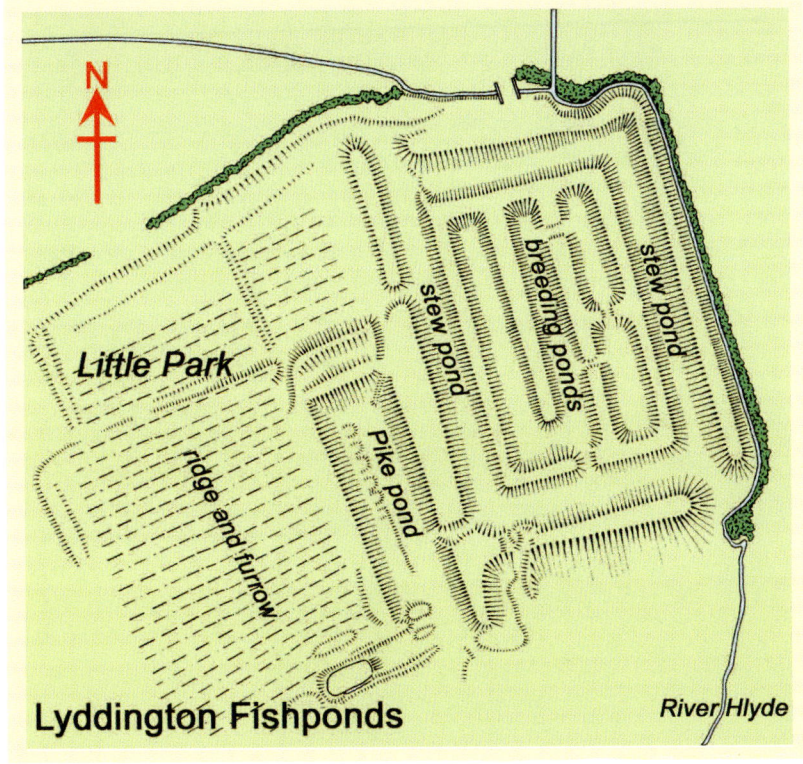

The surviving earthworks of the medieval fishponds in the Little Park, Lyddington (after Hartley)

source of food. Consequently, fishponds, some of a considerable size, were desirable additions to monastic sites, manor houses, castles and settlements. The aim was to maintain and breed a readily accessible and plentiful supply of freshwater fish, usually Bream, Pike and Tench. Carp were also introduced in the sixteenth century.

An aerial view of Lyddington showing the earthworks of the medieval fishponds in the Little Park to the east of the church. The Bede House is immediately adjacent to the church tower (John Nowell, Zodiac Publishing)

Probably the best preserved of all the fishpond sites in Rutland is at Lyddington. Lyddington Palace was, until 1547, a seat of ecclesiastical administration for the Bishops of Lincoln, and the nearby Little Park was part of the estate. Here, the large complex of fish breeding and rearing ponds was built about 1330, probably by Bishop Henry Burghersh. These ponds survive today as major earthworks and are sufficiently well preserved to enable an understanding of the main principles of their use. They consisted of a number of individual inner breeding ponds, surrounded by an outer rearing, or stew pond. This outer pond helped to protect the interior ponds from predators and the inner ponds were long and narrow to provide the maximum area of shallow edge for the spawn and fry. The ponds were interconnected by channels with wooden sluices which enabled individual ponds to be isolated. There would also have been a dam with a sluice across the south-east corner which controlled the water level in the outer pond. A further, much deeper pond, sometimes called the jack pond, was reserved for rearing the carnivorous Pike, a tasty and favoured game fish.

Looking west from just inside the south-east corner of Lyddington medieval fishponds (RO)

The fishpond earthworks and the nearby Bede House, the surviving part of Lyddington Palace, now administered by English Heritage, are open to the public and well worth a visit.

Burley Fishponds

Until 1940, when the Eyebrook Reservoir was first flooded, Burley Fishponds and Fort Henry Lakes were the largest stretches of open water in Rutland. Until Rutland Water, the fishponds at Burley were a familiar landmark to those who regularly travelled the road between Oakham and Barnsdale Hill and particularly popular with anglers. They are located at the bottom of the south avenue to Burley on the Hill, near the Buckingham Gate, and are fed by the north arm of the River Gwash. Little is known of their early history but it is thought that they were created in the 1620s when George Villiers, Duke of Buckingham, purchased, improved and beautified the Burley Estate. It is possible, though not confirmed by documentary evidence, that they are on the site of former medieval fishponds.

Burley Fishponds are mentioned in a survey, *A Particular of the Manor of Burleigh on the Hill in the County of Rutland and of the Park therein being the Estate of His Grace the late Duke of Buckingham* (ROLLR DG 7/1/56/1). The great house at Burley had been destroyed in 1646 by Parliamentary troops who had been garrisoned there during the Civil War, and this survey was commissioned by Daniel Finch, the new owner, about 1690. As a result, work started on building the present house in 1694. The survey mentioned the 'little brook' running through the park to the fishponds, saying that there were 'two fair fishponds' containing about 15 acres, with a 'cottage house' by the second pond; this was Keeper's Cottage adjacent to Buckingham Gate.

In 1795, the 9th Earl of Winchilsea commissioned Humphry Repton to remodel the Burley landscape. Repton was impressed with what he found: '. . . few places can vie with Burley in magnificence, both natural and artificial.' He presented his proposals in one of his Red Books, and the 9th Earl decided to adopt them, but in abbreviated form, excluding the ponds and proposals for the southern side of the Park. Repton wanted to make the fishponds more attractive and give them more prominence. He proposed a longer curved area of water which was to include a narrow section where there was to be a bridge, or a dam in the shape of a bridge, which would be visible from the house.

This plan is from Repton's Red Book for Burley on the Hill and shows his proposals for the fishponds (private collection)

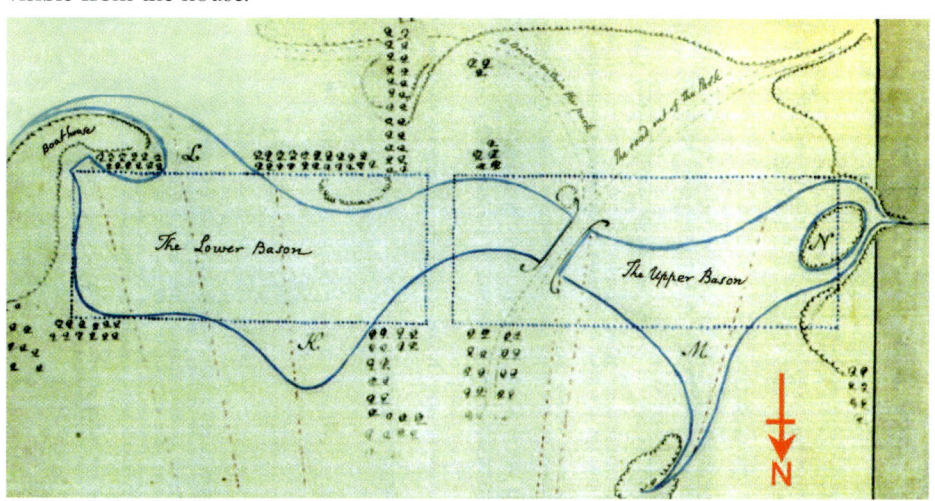

Repton's perspective of his proposals for Burley Fishponds (private collection)

Burley Fishponds from the OS 2nd ed 25" map 1904

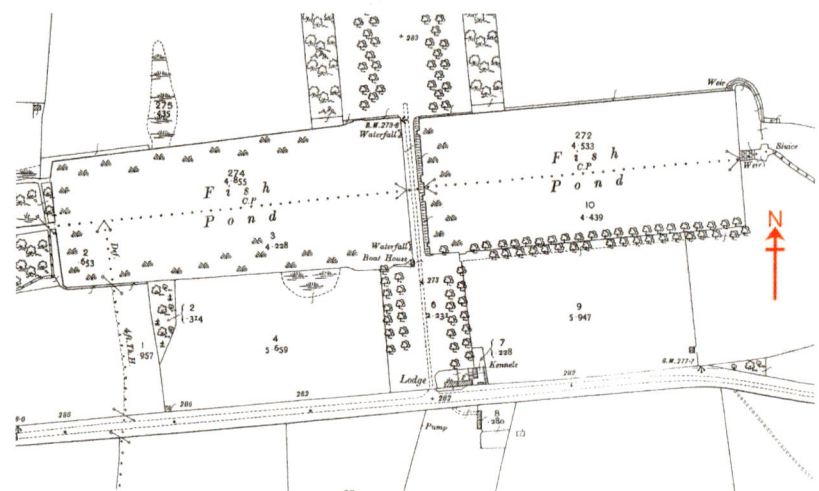

The causeway at Burley Fishponds in 1905 (Hart)

Fishing at Burley Fishponds. From an eighteenth-century oil painting (private collection)

It seems that the ponds have always been a venue for recreational fishing, being a particularly good spot to catch Pike, and a haven for bird watchers. C Reginald Haines refers frequently to 'Burley Ponds' in his *Notes on the Birds of Rutland* of 1907, for example:

'26. BEARDED TIT, *Panurus biarmicus*.

For the first recorded time, on January 18, 1905, two of these most beautiful little birds were seen in Rutland, selecting for their visit Burley Ponds, the most suitable spot in the county . . . .'

Immediately to the west of the ponds are Burley Water Meadows, once used to grow reeds for thatching.

Today, Burley Fishponds stand at the west end of the north arm of Rutland Water, and are part of the nature reserve, although not open for public access. At low water level the remains of the causeway between the two ponds can still be seen.

The causeway at Burley Fishponds and the ride to Burley on the Hill in 2006 (RO)

Charles Masters

Charles William Masters, gamekeeper to the Burley Estate from about 1877 until 1908, lived at the Keeper's Cottage which is adjacent to the Buckingham Gate on the old Oakham to Stamford road. From here he could see the great mansion of Burley on the Hill at the top of the ride which crossed the causeway between Burley Fishponds, as well as observe the great variety of birds that were attracted to this part of Rutland. Many of his observations were reported in Haines's *Notes on the Birds of Rutland* (1907), including, for example: 'C. Masters tells me he has seen the Ringed Plover again "this spring" [1906] at Burley Ponds.'

Exton Lakes

The ornamental lakes in Exton Park, usually referred to as Fort Henry Lakes, and owned by the Earl of Gainsborough of Exton Hall, stand adjacent to the deserted medieval village of Horn. They are fed by the North Brook, flowing down from Greetham, and a smaller unnamed stream which enters the lake from the west. It is this junction of two small valleys which gives the upper lake its unusual shape. Little is known of the early history of the lakes, particularly when they were created. They are shown in their present form on Thomas Badeslade's *Prospect of Exton Park* of *circa* 1730. Exton Park is a post-medieval park, originally enclosed by a stone wall and extending to the Great North Road.

A photograph of 1905 shows that there were once cascades at the southern end of the lower lake. These were designed by Stephen Switzer and built about 1760. He had been working for Sir John Vanbrugh and alongside Lancelot 'Capability' Brown at Blenheim Palace, and The Cascades at Exton was one of his first commissions after he started working on his own. The Cascades have long since gone, but otherwise the lakes remain much as they were and still attract bird watchers and fishermen.

Badeslade's *Prospect of Exton Park* also shows a third lake, which on J & C Walker's map of *circa* 1840 is located outside the Park, on the south side. This lake, which was near Cuckoo Spinney, has been drained for many years. It was fed by the stream which passes through Ry Gate Lake in the grounds of Exton Hall, and which eventually joins the North Brook just upstream of Horn Mill. It is possible to walk down the valley of this tributary from Exton where the remains of the old dam are easily seen.

Fort Henry Lakes in Exton Park from the OS 2nd ed 25" map 1904

The three lakes at Exton shown on J & C Walker's map of Rutland of circa 1840

The Cascades at the southern end of the lower lake at Exton Park in 1905 (Hart)

Fort Henry and the Bark Temple

Fort Henry is on the western shore of the upper lake in Exton Park. It was built for Henry Noel, 6th Earl of Gainsborough, after whom the building is named, by William Legg of Stamford between 1786 and 1789. The Earl had instructed him to design and build 'a gothic building by the pond' to replace an existing structure. Legg commissioned and supervised all the craftsmen who worked on the project, many of whom were local men. The principal mason was George Beaver who worked with Legg on other major projects. Most materials were also locally sourced, including stone from Clipsham quarry and bricks from Lord Winchilsea at Burley. Accounts show that William Legg made 116 journeys to Exton Park from Stamford whilst Fort Henry was being built. The overall building cost, calculated by totalling the various craftsmen's vouchers, was £1,426 4s 5d on which Legg took a commission of £71 6s 0d. He was also commissioned to carry out other work for the Noel family, including the dovecote by Ry Gate Lake near Exton Hall in 1792-93.

Records show that, even before the construction of Fort Henry, the lake was well used for boating activities, including the re-enactment of great sea battles. In 1761 Lord Gainsborough paid for a boat to be brought from London to Stamford via Spalding, and in 1778, a 'gunning' boat was purchased as well as another new boat which was transported from Peterborough to Wansford.

Fifty years or so after William Legg built Fort Henry, a rustic building was constructed a little way up the bank behind. In a report describing the preparations for Lady Louisa Noel's marriage to Andrew Agnew in 1846 there is a reference to '. . . the fairy temple now in the course of erection'. This was the 'Bark Temple', so called because it was constructed of wood and covered with bark and moss.

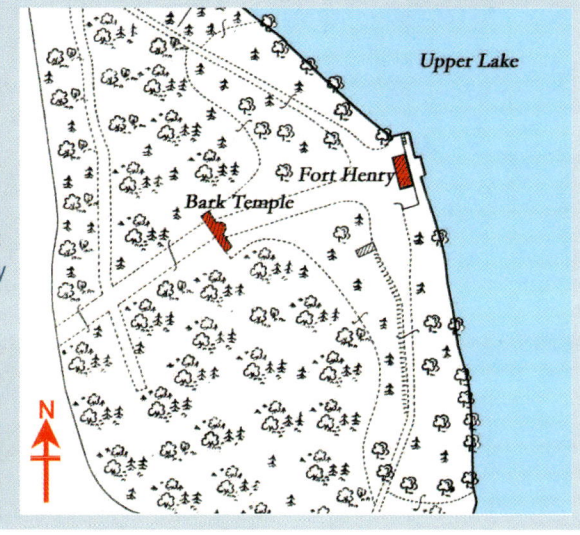

Right: Fort Henry and the Bark Temple based on the OS 2nd ed 25" map 1904

Fort Henry and the rustic Bark Temple provided an ideal venue for celebrating the births, birthdays and marriages of the Earl of Gainsborough's family. Lady Louisa's wedding celebrations included dinner by the lake for the Earl's 250 tenants the day before, and another meal for estate labourers and their families on the afternoon of the wedding.

Although Fort Henry has been fully restored it is rarely used. The Grade II listed Bark Temple was in a perilous condition by the mid 1990s. English Heritage did pay for a detailed drawing to be made but they were unwilling to fund its restoration. Sadly, it finally collapsed in the winter of 1997/98.

A side view of the surviving structure of the Bark Temple in April 1993. It finally collapsed during the winter of 1997/98 (SS)

Fort Henry on the western shore of Fort Henry Lake in 1908. At this time the Bark Temple, seen on the higher ground behind, was still in good condition (Hart)

Fort Henry upper lake in 2007 (RO)

— 338 —

Eyebrook Reservoir

The only other substantial area of water in Rutland is the Eyebrook Reservoir. It was formed by the construction of an earth dam across the valley of the Eye Brook, a tributary of the River Welland, to the north-west of Caldecott. It straddles the south-western county boundary with Leicestershire which follows the course of the old river down its centre.

The reservoir was built for Stewarts and Lloyds, now part of the Corus Group, to supply water for the former iron, steel and tube works at Corby, Northamptonshire. It was designed to provide 27,300 cubic metres (6 million gallons) of water a day, but since the closure of the iron and steel works in 1980 the remaining tube works only require 1,600 cubic metres (350,000 gallons) a day.

Construction started in 1937 and it was completed by early 1940. Like Rutland Water, the clay for the earth dam, which stretches about one third of a mile across the valley, was excavated from borrow pits in the floor of the valley. The reservoir was full by the autumn of 1940 and the first water was being pumped to Corby by the end of the year.

The design high water level was 68.5m OD, but this was increased in 1955 by raising the level of the overflow by approximately 750mm. This increased the reservoir capacity by seventeen and a half per cent to 8 million cubic metres (1,781 million gallons). It now covers an area of approximately 162 hectares (400 acres), being 2.8km long and 1.2km wide at its broadest. Compared to other reservoirs, it is relatively shallow, the average depth being only 5.2m. The maximum depth is 16.5m.

The reservoir is managed by Corby Water Company, a subsidiary of Corus. Until 1957, when the new Pitsford Reservoir was commissioned, this company was also responsible for distributing water from the Eyebrook Reservoir for domestic use in the Corby and Wellingborough areas. As well as the industrial requirement, 3,200 cubic metres (700,000 gallons) of water per day are released back into the Eye Brook to maintain its flow below the dam to where it joins the River Welland near Caldecott. Interestingly, some of this water is later transferred into Rutland Water via the abstraction pumps near Tinwell.

The new Eyebrook reservoir played an important role in the Second World War. Steel from the works in Corby which it served was vital to the war effort, and this included the pipe which carried fuel for the D-Day landings under the sea (PLUTO: pipe line under the ocean). The reservoir was also used to practise low-level bombing runs by the Lancasters of 617 Squadron, perhaps better known as the Dambusters, prior to the raids on the Eder and Mohne dams in Germany in 1943. This is commemorated by plaques on the dam wall and a display in the Fishing Lodge.

Today, the reservoir is a much quieter place, with recreational activities which are mainly confined to bird-watching and fishing for Rainbow and Brown Trout. In fact, as soon as it was built it very quickly became a haven for wildlife, particularly wintering wildfowl, to the extent that it was designated a Site of Special Scientific Interest (SSSI) in 1956.

An aerial view of the Eyebrook reservoir in 2005, looking north-west (John Nowell, Zodiac Publishing)

A Lost Opportunity

In 1907, C Reginald Haines published his *Notes on the Birds of Rutland*. In this he commented:

'The only artificial waters of any size, and those not considerable, are the Burley-on-[the-] Hill and Exton Ponds. A great opportunity was lost of making a big reservoir between Preston and Uppingham, when a water supply was required for Uppingham School. This would have answered every purpose, and besides being an ornament to the county, such as it sorely lacks, it would have been, ornithologically speaking, the greatest possible boon. Such sheets of water as the reservoirs at Naseby [Northamptonshire], Saddington [Leicestershire] and Kettering [Northamptonshire] have already had a marked effect upon the avifauna of their respective neighbourhoods.'

No details relating to this proposed reservoir for Uppingham School have been located, but inspection of the current OS 'Explorer 15' map (Rutland Water and Stamford) suggests that the most likely location for the proposal was in the valley located between the Preston to Uppingham and Ridlington to Ayston roads where it would have been fed by an unnamed stream, a tributary of the River Chater, which has its source to the south-west of Ridlington.

Rutland Canals

Other reservoirs have been proposed for Rutland. Two are shown on the plans for the Oakham to Stamford Navigation, an extension of the Melton Mowbray, Leicestershire, to Oakham canal.

Construction of the canal, which was to link Oakham with Melton Mowbray and the River Soar Navigation, was started in 1794 and the first canal barge with a cargo of coal reached Oakham in December 1802. Its route from Melton Mowbray to Oakham wharf took it by Brentingby, Wyfordby and Edmondthorpe in Leicestershire, and then between Teigh and Market Overton in Rutland. It had eighteen locks. From a very shaky start the canal gradually became more prosperous and better equipped, but by 1845 the Oakham Canal Committee had recognised that the proposed Syston to Peterborough railway was a significant threat to its prospects. In 1847 the committee eventually sold the canal to the Midland Railway Company who wanted to use part of the route for their new line.

In 1810, however, a proposal to build a new canal to link Oakham with Stamford and the Welland and Nene systems beyond was being considered. This was to be called the Stamford Junction Canal but the scheme was rejected by Parliament. The design for the new canal had been prepared by Thomas Telford and the accompanying plans show the route to follow a southerly path from Oakham wharf to Martinsthorpe, and then to turn eastwards to follow the Chater valley to Stamford. Top-up water was to be supplied by twin reservoirs which were to be constructed in the valley to the north-east of Braunston, and connected to the canal by a culvert which terminated below Gunthorpe. The scheme was considered again in 1815 and 1828, but it had been abandoned long before the Melton Mowbray to Oakham canal was closed.

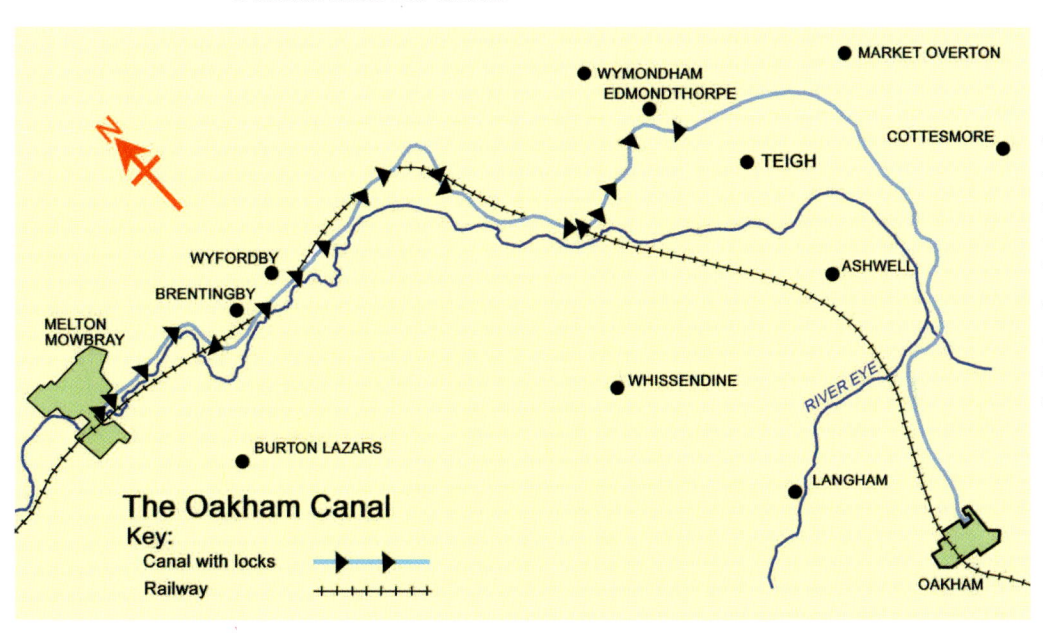

The route of the Oakham Canal, showing the locks and the line of the railway which was the eventual reason for its closure (David Tew)

Detail from the plan for the proposed Stamford Junction Canal designed by Thomas Telford. It was to connect Oakham with Stamford, then branch in one direction to Peterborough (then in Northampton-shire) and in the other to Boston, Lincolnshire (ROLLR DE 470/106)

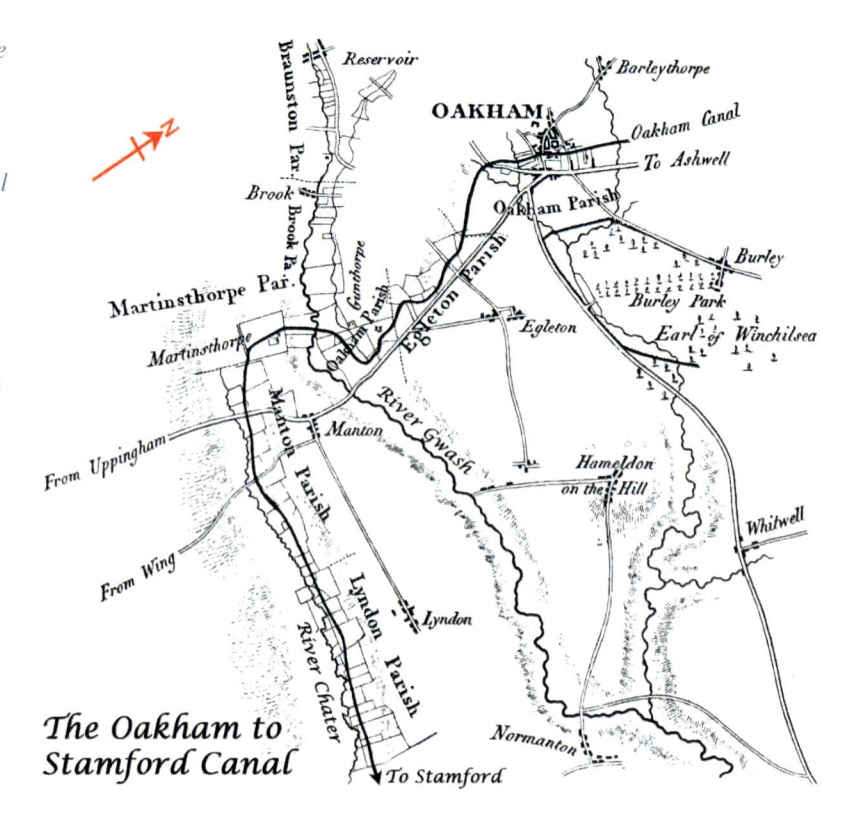

Domestic Water Supplies

John Judd, in *The Geology of Rutland*, published in 1875, makes some interesting observations on the use of springs and wells for the provision of water for human consumption:

'The frequent alternations, within the district under description, of pervious beds of limestone and sand with impervious clays, gives rise to numerous springs . . . . The constant outflow of these along the base of the harder beds, by causing a broken condition of the surface and imparting a freshness to the verdure, sometimes makes the division of the formations very distinct, and enables the eye to trace them even at a considerable distance.

'It is interesting to notice the manner in which the presence of springs has determined the sites of the towns, villages, and even isolated habitations of the district . . . .

'The question of the water supply of the area has, in modern times [late nineteenth century], assumed great importance, and an entirely new aspect. Although springs are so abundant in the district, yet as population has increased it has been found necessary, either for the purpose of supplementing the supply of water or for obtaining it in the most convenient situations, to open numerous wells. These have been for the most part of no great depth, passing merely through the first pervious bed into an impervious one, and thence obtaining, in almost every instance, an abundant supply. But the facility with which the refuse matter of a considerable population can be got rid of, where there is a substratum of porous material, has led to openings in these same rocks of innumerable cesspools and drains. Hence the water supply of the population is often poisoned at its source; wells and cesspools existing in the same rock and at no great distance from one another. Now it has been shown that waters from such a tainted source, though bright and clear to the eye and not unpleasant to the taste, may, nevertheless, be the means of propagating the worst forms of epidemic disease. Fortunately, in the district under notice, there generally exists a remedy, and it is in most cases easy of application; it is in fact only necessary to carry down the wells to the next impervious stratum, and to protect them from infiltration in their upper parts . . . The district being an almost purely agricultural one, the civil engineer is not called upon to make provision for large and closely packed populations, like those which demand such great works for procuring and storage of water supplies in manufacturing districts. In very few cases are the towns of sufficient size probably to need deep artesian wells . . . .'

Between 1831 and 1866 there were four major cholera epidemics, accounting nationally for over 55,000 deaths, and the realisation that polluted drinking water could lead to such serious diseases and epidemics resulted in the Sanitary Act of 1866. The Act required local authorities to undertake sanitary regulation, and set out powers for the provision of water supplies, for sewage disposal and for the abatement of 'nuisances'. Each local community elected a 'Nuisance Committee' or 'Board of Health' which had the power to inspect 'nuisances' and serve formal notices on offenders. At Belton in Rutland, for example, a meeting of the 'Board of Health' on 25th November 1870 decided to establish a uniform course of action. It was agreed that cesspools and refuse places be made dry, that drains be taken direct into the main sewer, and that pigsties, manure heaps and holes be removed from the fronts of houses, and elsewhere if found to be a 'nuisance' (ROLLR DE 1815/15).

Ernest Mills, in *Empingham Remembered* published in 1984, describes how piped water was taken to Empingham properties:

'Empingham has always been noted for its water supply. There were wells, some with pumps on them and springs to supply most houses in the village. The first I remember of a piped water supply was a brick built reservoir in the field above [to the north of] the Chapel, with a windpump over a well nearby to fill this reservoir when the wind blew, which was not often. However, sometimes it was too much which would blow the sails off and the supply would give out. This proved useless and a water ram was installed near Gunnel Spring to keep the supply going. These water rams were gaining in popularity, working on the principle of a large quantity of water in one pipe forcing a small quantity in another pipe up hill and down dale and they proved their worth. The installation entailed digging a trench from Gunnel Spring to the reservoir across two fields, under Loves Lane and across the field where the Council houses are now built. This trench was dug out by one man, the [Ancaster] Estate drainer Bob Downes who lived in Church Street . . . We youngsters would often go to see how it was progressing as he was the only one working on it.

'The reservoir was perhaps six feet deep in water and the brick wall was continued about four feet above ground level. This was very convenient for the farmer's cows in the adjoining field to rub their bottoms on, and who knows, perhaps they did two jobs at one time. I remember seeing some suspicious looking patches floating on the water that definitely did not come through the pipe. Whether this was the fact or not, a few years later a corrugated iron fence was erected round it. The water was piped down to Main Street, (I never heard of it being filtered, but we were a hardy lot in those days) and then into two branches, one down and one up street. The stop cocks for these two pipes were in the road near the village notice board and may be seen today.

'The stand pipes for the extraction of water for domestic use were huge ugly iron pipes surmounted by a man's face and hat; the water coming out of a pipe in this mouth. Well it may have been worse! The handle to turn him on was a knob-like affair on the side which one turned round to get water, holding tight until the bucket was full. On release it unwound and was ready to use again. It required a strong arm to turn it on; one never saw kids playing with it. The five places where these stands were fixed may be seen in recesses in the fence outside the Olive Branch and Hallstones and other places. Farm houses were connected up with a cold tap over the sink at a charge of £1 per year if the occupier wished it. The pipe was taken down street as far as Canada Lane and a solid oak plug was bunged in to cut it off. No one seemed to remember this and the water pressure was always low, until about 1925 when some one had the bright idea to dig the pipe out and found the wooden plug had nearly rotted away and the water was running into the limestone out of site [sic]. This leakage was stopped and the village water supply was later taken over by Rutland County Council.'

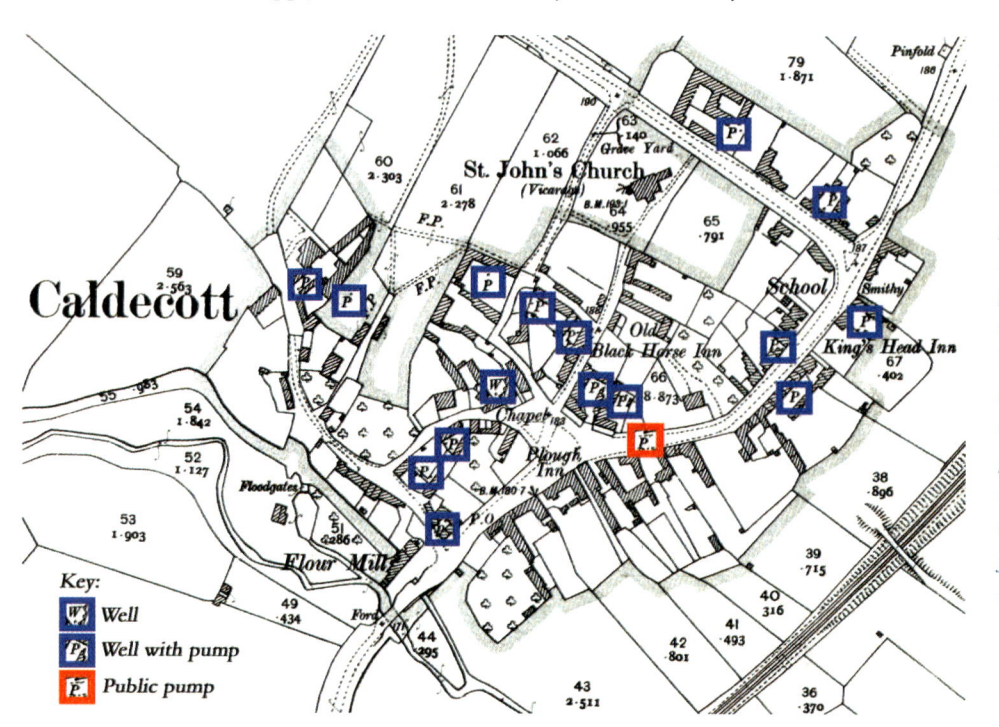

Caldecott was typical of most Rutland villages in that its inhabitants relied totally on wells for their potable water supplies until piped water came to the village. Those who did not have a private well could use the public pump, highlighted in red on this extract from the OS 2nd ed 25" map 1904

However, Empingham was somewhat unusual in having a piped water supply at this time, although there was a similar system at Exton which was installed about 1900 by the Earl of Gainsborough. Previously, in Exton, public drinking water had only been available from the village pump. The new system consisted of stand pipes installed throughout the village to which water was pumped from the Hawkswell Spring by a ram pump.

Most other Rutland villages continued to rely on wells and hand pumps for another 60 years or so, until the Dove Water Scheme was extended from Leicestershire into Rutland, thus bringing piped water to all but the most remote communities.

In the towns of Oakham and Uppingham piped water was available much earlier. At Oakham, water came from a 12m borehole near Braunston, in the Gwash valley, where a new waterworks was established just after the turn of the twentieth century. Uppingham suffered repeated outbreaks of typhoid between 1875 and 1877, centred on Uppingham School. Faced with ruin if nothing was done, the Rev Edward Thring, headmaster, removed the school to Borth, on the Welsh coast, for an entire year. The town's shopkeepers were heavily dependent on the school and they forced the local sanitary authority to improve the drainage system. Thring was a leading player in the group which set up a private company to supply water to the town (Richardson 2007, 195-213). Within a year new main water pipes had been laid in every street, and in 1880 it was agreed to install hydrants throughout the town for extinguishing fires, flushing drains and watering the streets. In 1882 a new large well was sunk by the water company to a depth of 32m, and at a cost of £500, but no water was found. A new Uppingham Waterworks was established about 1906 in the Welland valley, just south of Lyddington and about 4 miles from Uppingham.

The new Uppingham Waterworks, near Lyddington, in 1910 (Hart)

Rutland Ponds

Village ponds were considered to be valuable assets to the community. In this category we can include horse ponds, cart ponds, fire ponds, dew ponds, washdykes and sheep dips. Most of those located within villages have now been drained or filled in for safety reasons, and because they no longer serve a useful purpose.

In 1960 the old horse pond at Exton was filled in. It was situated in the dip on Oakham Road below the old school. A horse-shoe shape, it was used for washing horses' feet when they came off the fields – this would prevent their hooves from cracking, and for swelling the wood of the cart wheels in dry weather. Sheep were also washed here. Similarly, at Glaston, there is a cart pond with stone walls on three sides which has been dated as *circa* 1740. The now restored pond was used to soak cart wheels to expand them into their metal tyres. The much larger pond at Barrowden also survives, enjoyed today more by ducks and visitors to the village. Preston also still has its village pond, which was deepened during the Second World War as a reserve water supply in case of fires.

Out in the fields there are more ponds, some of which are dew ponds, although most are associated with a nearby spring. They were mainly created many years ago for cattle, sheep and horse watering, and some were no doubt used as cart ponds. Also amongst these are a number of ponds created by bombs dropped during the Second World War. At Braunston, a spring opened up by a bomb dropped in the Second World War was thereafter known as 'Hitler's Spring'.

There were many sheepdykes and washdykes for washing sheep before shearing. These were often created by temporarily damming a stream. There were more permanent washdykes at Cottesmore, Ryhall and Burley Fishponds for example, but all have now disappeared.

Today, there are new types of pond to be discovered, mainly in the countryside. Large ornamental ponds are popular as a landscape feature in private gardens, and farmers are creating fishponds for leisure fishing in order to generate alternative sources of income, often as part of a farm diversification programme.

A flock of sheep at Barrowden pond in the 1920s (Hart)

The sheepdyke at Cottesmore was filled in during the 1950s (Hart)

Left: The Earl of Winchilsea's washdyke at Burley fishponds in 1860. It was at the north-east corner of the east pond (private collection)

Below: Ryhall washdyke at the side of the Gwash in 1906. It was filled in many years ago (Hart)

And Finally . . . .

In this short survey of Rutland Waters – what was, what might have been and what is – there has only been space for a brief look at some of the more interesting and significant aspects. Personal observation and the study of, for example, aerial photographs, large scale maps, estate surveys, enclosure maps and awards, and old documents would no doubt reveal many other ideas for research.

Aspects of Topography

A New Wetland Habitat

Anglian Water has determined that it needs to find additional water supplies in order to be able to meet the increasing demand from new homes in its region. Since Rutland Water has never been used to its authorised capacity, it has been decided that the predicted shortfall can be satisfied by increasing the volume of water pumped out of the reservoir and processed by Wing Water Treatment Works. This is likely to cause the water level in the reservoir to be drawn down more often and for longer periods, thus decreasing the habitat for the large numbers of water birds that are attracted to the reservoir. Rutland Water is an internationally important nature conservation site, and strict legislation states that bird numbers must not be allowed to decrease through habitat loss.

In order to ensure that there is adequate wetland habitat even when the reservoir water level is low, additional lagoons and wetlands will be created at the western end of the reservoir, within and adjacent to the present nature reserve area. The additional amount of wetland habitat required has been determined from data on the densities of birds using the three existing lagoons (1, 2 and 3 on the map). This will be created by building dams and by excavating a series of new wetland areas.

The new dams across Manton Bay and Fishponds Bay will create new lagoons (A, D1 and D2 on the map) by preventing these areas from drying out when the rest of the reservoir is drawn down. The dams will be under water when the reservoir is full and will become visible only when it is below 85 per cent of its full capacity, and then only from the reservoir side.

The new shallow lagoons and improved wetland areas (B1 and C1 to C5 on the map) will be created on existing agricultural land and within the reserve. Water will be piped into these and the existing lagoons to maintain water levels, even during drought periods, and the new lagoons will be screened by hedges, trees and banks to ensure that birds are not disturbed by human activity. New walking and cycling routes will be created round and through this area.

Additional civil engineering works will be required to install a new raw water pipeline between Empingham pumping station and Wing Water Treatment Works, and a new treated water pipeline between Wing and the Hannington service reservoir in Northamptonshire.

This work is due to commence in 2008 with construction work on the new wetland habitats taking place during the spring and summer over a three-year period (*see* Chapter 24 – Tim Appleton MBE – Thirty Years of Rutland Water Nature Reserve).

The new wetland habitat, based on information provided by Anglian Water (RO)

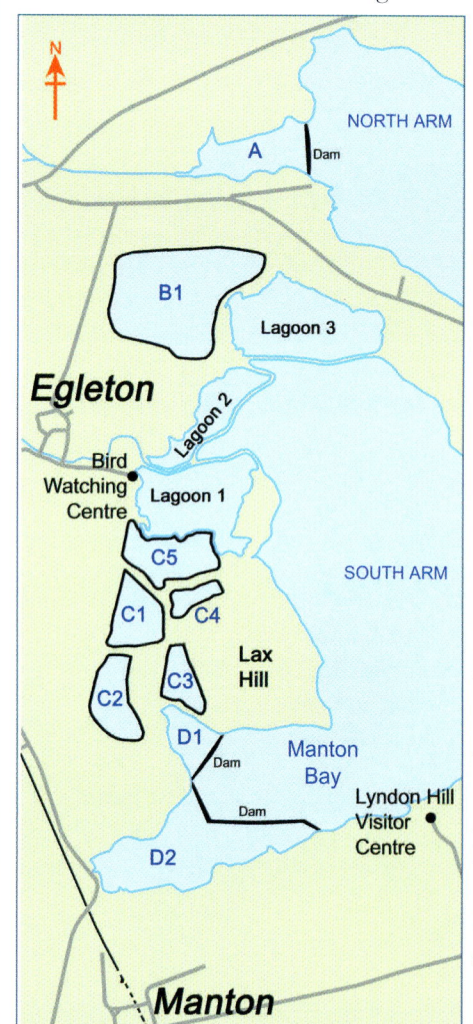

Chapter 15
Don't Dam Rutland
Hilary Crowden

The signs that went up across Rutland in 1968 with the exhortations 'Don't dam Rutland' or 'Don't flood Rutland' were indications of a titanic struggle by the small county. Placing a weak local argument against a national need, the arguments were imbalanced. With limited scope for compromise, Rutland's loss of this battle highlighted the conflict between rural resources and urban expansion and changed the physical face of Rutland forever.

> **DON'T DAM RUTLAND**
>
> Issued by the Rutland County and Stamford Branch of The National Farmers' Union in the interests of Food Production

A sticker for the anti-reservoir campaigners and supporters (Sir John Conant)

The origins of the decision to build a large pumped storage reservoir in the Gwash valley, with a dam at Empingham, lay in two pieces of legislation enacted in the early 1960s. The New Towns Act 1965 allowed for three New Town Development Corporations at Peterborough, Northampton and Corby and two expanded town schemes at Daventry and Wellingborough. These were all in the area covered by the Welland and Nene River Authority, set up by the Water Resources Act 1963. This Act empowered the Authority to assess the need for water into the next century. The search for a location for a large reservoir to serve this expanding population extended to 64 sites. The mid-Gwash valley was the site chosen because it achieved the criteria set out by Leonard Brown, the Authority's engineer. It had the right shape with the right geology to support the weight of a dam; sufficient local material to build the dam; a river reasonably near to fill the reservoir; and a location near the new centres of population, to minimise pumping costs. Because of the potential cost, detailed secret planning was requried before the private Bill could be put before Parliament by the Welland and Nene River Authority, the promoter, for consideration in Select Committee. Manton Reservoir in the adjoining Chater valley was the second choice. At one stage, both were to be built, with Manton coming second because of its marginally higher operation costs and lower yield. However, common sense prevailed at the Parliamentary stage when Manton was thrown out as being 'a step too far'.

The Welland and Nene (Empingham Reservoir) and Mid-Northamptonshire Water Bill went to Westminster in late 1968.

The promoter's case was simple and convincing. Regional planning policy depended on increasing the water supply, and *per capita* consumption was expected to rise at twice the national average within the Authority's area before the twenty-first century. Alternatives to Empingham, such as a Wash barrage, desalination and the use of the south Lincolnshire aquifers, were not available in the time limit required and would give insufficient yield.

The petitioners against the Bill, Rutland County Council, Oakham Rural District Council, The Country Landowners Association, The National Farmers Union and the Council for the Protection of Rural England, could not match the promoters in time, money or technical skills employed in their case. Their opposition was based around the claimed lack of adequate exploration of alternative solutions, the loss of agricultural land, and the disruption to local life and the landscape. Forty-eight agricultural holdings, twenty of which would become uneconomic, seven occupied cottages and gardens and seven 'miscellaneous units' would be affected, concerning nineteen owner-occupiers and 29 agricultural tenancies. Seven farmhouses and seven occupied cottages would be lost to the proposed reservoir.

Ivydene Farm at Lower Hambleton, lost to the flood (Canon John R H Prophet)

Rutland levied a threepenny (3d) rate to help pay for the defence but was unable to match the financial resources of the promoter, and eventually the fighting fund was exhausted. It was with resignation that in the end the petitioners fought for the best deal. 'We took it as far as we could but it was just no good,' said Idris Evans, County Treasurer and one of the campaigners. The figures to support the need for water came from local authority development plans and had to be accepted by both sides. The promoter showed some willingness to explore other options, even considering a truncated reservoir at Empingham with two dams. However, this was found not to be feasible, economic or practical.

In the second reading in the Commons, Tom Bradley, MP for Leicester North-east, claimed the reservoir would 'enhance the attractiveness of and in no way desecrate that delightful county', but he acknowledged 'the passion and fury' over this 'hydrological Stansted'. Kenneth Lewis, Member of Parliament for Rutland and Stamford, high on rhetoric, if weak on argument, argued against this 'massive and expensive miscalculation' and its 'exaggerated demand forecasts'. He had 'no wish for another Windermere in Rutland ... we do not wish to be a kind of towpath around a lake'. He was supported by many rural MPs in a town *versus* countryside division of opinion. The government declared itself regretfully in favour of the reservoir. The Bill spent nine days in Commons Select Committee, before it reported 'a deplorable and regrettable necessity' to build the reservoir in the Gwash valley, 'one of the melancholy consequences of the relentless demands of the urban dweller', said Keith Robinson MP. However, the Commons called for further investigations of a Wash barrage, to avoid further large shallow reservoirs, and emphasised the need for a national water grid. These misgivings helped in the creation of ten regional water authorities in 1973, Anglian Water Authority incorporating the Welland and Nene River Authority within its domain, but failed to stop the creation of Carsington Reservoir (Derbyshire) or Kielder Water (Northumberland).

Mow Mires at Normanton in 1970. It was one of the first casualties of Rutland Water (Jim Levisohn ARPS)

The House of Lords went to the unusual step of putting the Bill into Select Committee to ensure that, in the petitioners' absence, the Bill received detailed scrutiny. As with the Commons, the compelling case prevailed. Later, the talk in the 1980s of 'surplus capacity' in the water industry was to give way by 2000 to further talk of water shortages in the south-east. However, everyone vastly underestimated the cost of pumping the water.

The fact that the petitioners could only obtain broad assurances from the promoter at this stage over disruption, recreational provision, landscaping and restraints on commercialism at the reservoir gave rise to a lot of local scepticism and fuelled opposition to the reservoir. The promoter appointed Frank Knights to be a link with the local community in a public relations offensive of exhibitions and meetings. More than 3,000 acres of Rutland countryside were taken for the reservoir, and over £30 million spent on the project. Frank Knights ensured that some local labour was employed and that disruption to roads and services was kept to a minimum. Such was the faith of the local community in him that when he moved house, from a cottage beneath the dam at Empingham to a house further downstream in Ryhall, questions were asked at Empingham Parish Council as to whether he knew something about the safety of the dam that they didn't!

After inevitable delays, and the 1976 drought, Empingham Reservoir, originally known as 'Empingham Pumped Water Storage Project' and renamed 'Rutland Water' following an emotive campaign led by a local student, opened in May 1977. It flooded 3% of the county and could hold 27,300 million gallons at full capacity, which was not reached until 1979. What Bryan Matthews called in his *Book of Rutland* 'latent indignation' towards Anglian Water Authority was reflected in the actions of one man who avoided the obstacles and drove across the valley on his accustomed route to Hambleton despite the roads being 'closed' and water washing around his car wheels. This was the last vehicle to make the crossing. He and many other 'locals' refused to pay any charges at the reservoir car parks.

Apart from those who lost their homes and livelihoods, many other local people were affected by the construction works, which extended far beyond the four years of noise and dust which were an inevitable consequence of building the largest ever earth dam. As well as road closures across the twin

The Gwash Valley from Bull Brigg Lane, Whitwell, before flooding (Jim Levisohn ARPS)

valleys, new roads were built to bypass Barnsdale Hill, to connect Hambleton back to the Oakham to Stamford road, and to link Edith Weston, via Normanton, to Empingham. Extraction works were built at Wansford and Tinwell to pump water from the rivers Nene and Welland to the reservoir, and this involved driving long tunnels and laying massive pipes. More large pipes were laid between Empingham and Wing where a large water treatment works was constructed on the outskirts of the village. Further pipe-laying became necessary as a result of the 1976 drought when the reservoir was linked to Grantham, and some years later the Wing to Whatborough pipeline was laid across the western side of Rutland. At the time of writing a proposal to increase the output capacity of Wing Treatment Works is being considered. Although the area covered by the reservoir will not be increased, the draw-down will result in much lower water levels during the summer months. In order to protect the nature reserve habitat at the west end of the reservoir, new lagoons are proposed on farmland around Egleton, and bunds are proposed across Manton Bay and below the Burley Fishponds area.

As Dame Sylvia Crowe said '... the water would prove an enhancement to the surroundings' (RO)

There was undisguised mirth in the late 1970s when the reservoir, which by then was almost full to capacity, was found to be 'leaking' thousands of gallons a day under the hill and out into the Chater valley, this water then flowing into the Welland ready to be pumped back into the reservoir. Local legend has it that 'someone forgot to fill in the wells of the submerged farms at Hambleton properly'. Fly swarms in 1977 and toxic blue-green algae in 1989 were both endured as many people recognised the irony in the statement of Dame Sylvia Crowe, the landscape architect employed by the water authority, when she said she '... believed that the water would prove an enhancement to the surroundings'.

Rutland lost its independence in 1974 and became a district of Leicestershire. Rutland Water and the new post-1974 local authorities ushered in an era of planning for recreation and amenities, village conservation areas, 'settlement planning', 'local needs' and 'restraint villages'. There was, and in some areas still is, considerable resistance to tourism. 'Empingham to be the £700,000 playground for the East Midlands' warned a headline in the *Stamford Mercury*. Sailing, fishing, cycling and walking have all been accepted, but motorboats, other than those used by anglers and the nature reserve, and for safety and rescue purposes, are not permitted.

Sailing is now a natural part of the scene at Rutland Water (Richard Adams)

'Alexander', the bronze-cast sculpture on the North Shore of Rutland Water at Sykes Lane, Empingham (Richard Adams)

The nature reserves and their management were welcomed but it took fifteen years for the local community to accept a passenger cruiser on the reservoir and even longer for refreshment kiosks to be tolerated. Caravan parks, camping and golf courses are still contentious issues and the erection of 'The Great Tower', then the largest single bronze-cast sculpture in the world at Sykes Lane, Empingham, caused an uproar at the time. The unveiling ceremony, which took place on 9th October 1980, was boycotted by the Empingham Parish Council, while the Australian sculptor, Alexander, was absent suffering from influenza.

The reservoir has not resulted directly in any great increase in employment, but attractions such as Barnsdale Gardens, the Bird Watching Centre and the Nature Reserve, the annual Birdfair, the Falconry Centre, the Butterfly Centre, Normanton Church Museum, trout fishing, sailing, windsurfing, cycle hire, tracks for walking and running, time-share holiday accommodation, picnic areas, cafés, and a Tourist Information Centre, as well as public houses and hotels which have been developed around the reservoir, have made tourism a substantial contributor to the local economy, eclipsing that of farming. Despite the assurances in Parliament, 'a lot of farmers had a rough deal . . .', stated Frank Knights.

Compensation was set at 1970 values, woefully inadequate by the time it came to be paid in 1977. No allowance was made for inflation. Some farmers retired, some diversified, only to have to fight planning regulations stopping them fully exploiting their land. It was no longer considered 'their' land, 'their' barns or 'their' property. It belonged to the community. The agricultural interest no longer ran the county. There were strong feelings at a public meeting and one farmer asked the 'invaders' what they knew about rearing hamsters. When asked what he meant, he declared that with the amount of land left to him by the invading water authority 'hamsters are all I can reasonably put out to pasture!'

Frank Knights also had his public relations work cut out when 1,500 trout fishermen turned up on the first day of the fishing season, causing 'great consternation'. One lady had to wait two hours in her car to gain access to her driveway. It wasn't helped by the fact she was a local magistrate!

Idris Evans summed up local feeling: 'It put us on the map, there's no doubt of that, but did we really want to be on the map?' In the early 1970s Rutland County Council did not object to the name 'Empingham Reservoir', which had been adopted by the Welland and Nene River Authority for the new reservoir, although other names such as Rutland Water and perhaps less seriously 'Ruddle's Puddle' were discussed. 'Ruddle's Puddle' is a reference to Sir Kenneth Ruddle of Langham who was a leading light in the campaign against the local government reorganisation which was to

Sailors and bird lovers — and now the anglers

THE sailing enthusiasts and bird watchers have already flocked to Rutland Water.

And now this, the largest man-made water in Western Europe, stands poised for the greatest invasion of them all — that of the fly fisherman.

The water opens for fishing at 4.30 am on Friday, May 6. And, like all great events, be it an Oval Test Match or Wembley Cup Final, that first weekend will be all-ticket only.

Quarry

Well over 1,000 anglers will fish from bank and boat on each of the opening three days. They will come from all parts of Britain — and overseas too. Many will spend those last pre-dawn hours sleeping in cars or hastily-erected tents as they wait to snatch the favoured hotspots.

Some will stay for the three days. Others have already booked summer holidays locally so that they can tackle not only Rutland Water, but nearby Eye Brook and popular Grafham Water, which is little more than an hour's run down the A1.

The quarry of these enthusiasts? Brown and rainbow trout, the game, leaping fighters of all our reservoirs.

At Empingham, they will be hunted with imitation fly and aquatic life patterns which go by such exotic names as black and peacock spider, whisky fly, amber nymph, invicta, Mrs Palmer Lure, appetiser and baby doll!

Above: Stamford Mercury 7th April 1977

BRITAIN'S biggest man-made lake opens to anglers this week with the promise of 200 trout to each of the 3,000 acres of water.

Rutland Water, the size of Lake Windermere, has been the target of 90 phone calls a day and over 4,000 letters asking for permission to fish.

But as happy and lucky anglers flocked from all over the country, many through the night ready for an early start, hundreds have been disappointed.

Reservoir managers have again confirmed that their allocation for bank anglers is full over this weekend and that boats have been booked solidly throughout May.

Above: Stamford Mercury 5th May 1977

Right: Stamford Mercury 1st July 1977

RESERVOIR TROUT FISHING COURSES

RUTLAND WATER

Three One Day Introductory Courses will be held on 28th May 12th June and 26th July 1977 Cost £5

Week-End Residential Course will be held on 4th to 6th August 1977

Accommodation will be provided at Oakham Public School Cost £25 (including full board, accommodation and tuition

For futher details contact:—
J. J. Inglesant,
Recreation Officer,
RUTLAND WATER

20599   195pb20-5

Big bed hunt starts as anglers pack village inns

ANGLERS who raced to Rutland Water for the start of the fishing have brought a headache for residents.

More than 3,000 anglers from all over Europe converged on the reservoir within three days of its opening for fishing.

The problem is where to put them all. Some enthusiasts have had to book hotels as far away as Bourne and Peterborough.

The real worry is for campers and caravan anglers, for whom there are few official sites near the water.

Left: Stamford Mercury 5th May 1977

Right: Stamford Mercury *29th August 1975*

Centre: Stamford Mercury *15th October 1976*

Far right: Stamford Mercury *8th October 1976*

Or just a puddle?

SIR — With reference to your article last week about a name for the Empingham Reservoir, I would like to suggest naming it after Sir Kenneth Ruddle. Why not call it "Ruddle's Puddle"?

I hope this contribution to your list will add a little variety.

SALLY CRABB
Waggon Cottage,
Manor Court,
Morcott.

Rutland Water victory

SIR, — I should like to express through the medium of your newspaper my great thanks to all those people who helped with the "Rutland Water" petition campaign.

I would never have collected so many signatures if people from all over Rutland and Leicestershire, and indeed the rest of England, had not written to give their support and volunteer their services to help collect signatures.

To all those people I say a big 'thank you'.

Thanks to them the effort has all proved worthwhile. "Rutland Water" is official.

P. JANE MERRITT
Organiser 'Rutland Water' Petition.
101 Brooke Road,
Oakham.

'Rutland Water' victory

RUTLAND people have won their fight to rename the Empingham reservoir "Rutland Water" instead of "Empingham Water".

Members of the Anglian Water Authority's water committee, on Wednesday, decided overwhelmingly that they should back down in the face of a strong protest from the public.

The Anglian Water Authority is expected to make its decision on November 10, following the water committee's recommendation that the reservoir should now be called "Rutland Water".

result in Rutland becoming a district of Leicestershire in 1974. In 1975, the popular mood had changed. There was considerable discussion in the local press and a consensus emerged in favour of renaming the reservoir 'Rutland Water' to perpetuate the county name. Major R Hoare of Hambleton stated, in a letter to the editor of the *Stamford Mercury* in September 1976:

'Surely it would be the wish of a vast majority of the inhabitants of what was our county, that this bit of water . . . which is going to be very beautiful, should be called "Rutland Water" to remind posterity of what used to be a happy and prosperous county before the planners stepped in.'

Anglian Water Authority refused, partly to be consistent, partly because it felt the water itself came from the region and did not 'belong to the county'. They underestimated the support for the name change in the local community. Those outside found the campaign for a change 'ridiculous . . . tiresome . . . compounding an unimportant issue'. Those inside Rutland were incensed how an un-elected board with no representatives from Rutland could obstruct the popular will. They were considered 'meddlesome upstarts'. Mr Lustig of Whissendine, chairman of Rutland District Society of Ratepayers and Residents, threatened to throw any member of the authority who came to Rutland into the reservoir!

Jane Merritt, a Rutland Sixth Form College student and a prominent member of the East Midlands Young Liberals, organised a petition which raised more than 4,000 signatures in support of renaming the reservoir 'Rutland Water'. Kenneth Lewis MP threatened to boycott the opening. Councils, organisations, groups and

Below: Jane Merritt (centre) organised a successful petition which raised more than 4,000 signatures in support of renaming the reservoir 'Rutland Water' (Sylvia Leach)

Stamford Mercury 1st November 1976

Petition story

EIGHTEEN-year-old Rutland Sixth Form College student, Jane Merritt, faced a television camera on the bank of the Empingham reservoir on Monday morning for a recorded interview concerning her petition to try to persuade the Anglian Water Authority to call the reservoir Rutland Water instead of Empingham Water.

Also interviewed for next Tuesday's "Midland Today" programme was Rutland District Council's Chief Executive, Mr Ralph Francis.

The council, together with Leicestershire County Council and Oakham Town Council have strongly requested that the name be Rutland Water.

Jane's petition has received widespread support and it is hoped it will have around 4,000 signatures on it by this weekend.

She will present it at the Anglian Water Authority headquarters at Huntingdon next Tuesday afternoon and hopes to be back home, at 101 Brooke Road, Oakham, in time to see herself "on the box".

---

individuals within Rutland were unanimous for the change. Clearly, Anglian Water Authority, confusingly referred to as 'Anglican Warter Authority' in one Parish Council's minuted protests, had a potential major public relations disaster on their hands. Eventually, after a year's debate, wiser counsels prevailed. Mr T Hall, a member of the Anglian Water Authority, said at a meeting on 6th October 1976:

'I do feel that public opinion shows we can't steamroller all the little people and it would be a good exercise in public relations, if we went along with them.'

The full board of the authority endorsed the majority opinion of the Water Committee on 10th November 1976. One wonders whether public opinion would have been so agitated about this issue had popular feeling against local government reorganisation the year previously, and the loss of the battle against the reservoir, not been so much in the forefront of community politics. It proved that 'the little people' could still fight back.

Stamford Mercury 12th November 1976

'Rutland Water' — official

THE Anglian Water Authority have accepted the name of "Rutland Water" for the reservoir at Empingham.

The recommendation that the name of Rutland Water be used instead of Empingham Water was accepted without debate at the authority's meeting on Wednesday.

The change of name will take effect immediately.

Stamford Mercury 5th November 1976

Victory on 'Rutland Water'

RUTLAND residents have won a victory in their long campaign to name the Empingham reservoir "Rutland Water".

Aspects of Topography

Normanton Bridge

Normanton Bridge, now under Rutland Water, crossed the River Gwash just upstream of Normanton Fishpond. It was a Victorian iron girder bridge, often referred to as 'Iron Bridge'. The only road bridge in Normanton Park, it linked the former Normanton Park, a deer park, with New Park on the north-west side of the river (*see* Chapter 11 – Normanton and Chapter 14 – Rutland Waters).

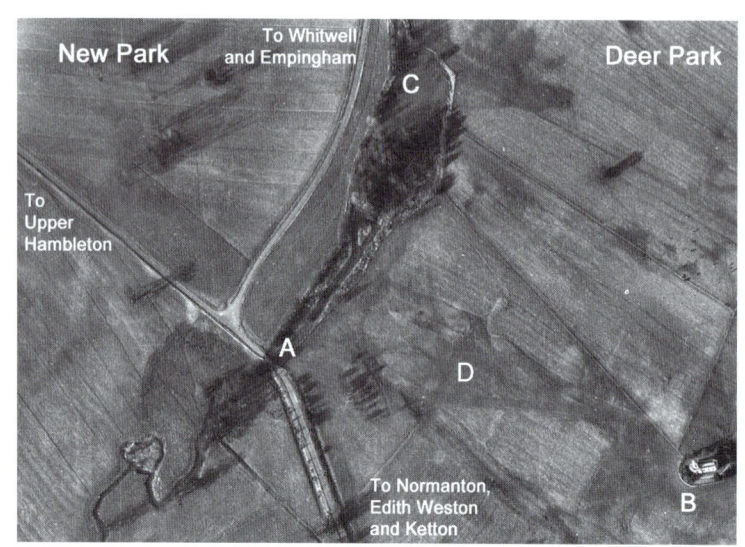

Left: An aerial view of the Gwash Valley at Normanton in 1967 showing: A – Normanton Bridge, B – Normanton Church, C – Normanton Fishpond, D – Normanton deserted village earthworks (Anglian Water)

Below: The upstream side of Normanton Bridge during flood conditions in 1968 (Anglian Water)

Below: Looking towards Normanton Bridge from the Hambleton Road, near Half Moon Spinney, in 1971, when most of the trees had been removed from this part of the valley. The stone pillars (arrowed) are the remains of a former Normanton Park gate (Richard Adams)

Chapter 16
The Geology of the Middle Gwash Valley
Clive Jones

Introduction

The Rutland landscape has an individual and distinctive character. Modestly hilly and rolling, it is dissected by long wide and deep valleys draining east towards the fenlands. The largest of these valleys is occupied by the River Gwash which rises near the highest point in east Leicestershire – Whatborough Hill at 230m OD (OD, or Ordnance Datum, is the height above the mean level of the sea at Newlyn, Cornwall. This level was established between May 1915 and April 1921). Flowing into Rutland the Gwash passes to the south of Oakham and, prior to the flooding of Rutland Water, it was joined by its northern arm just downstream of Bull Bridge. This stream drains the wide Vale of Catmose around and to the north of Oakham. The construction of the Empingham Dam in 1974 at a point where the riverbed is 48m OD led to the flooding of both valleys to a height of 84m OD at top water level, thus creating the present north and south bays which are separated by the high Hambleton interfluve.

Above: The Gwash valley looking north from Normanton in 1974
(Richard Adams)

Left: The River Gwash due north of Edith Weston, near Brake Spinney
(Jim Levisohn ARPS)

— 359 —

Above: The River Gwash south of Nether Hambleton in 1972, looking downstream (Jim Levisohn ARPS)

Left: Building the dam for Rutland Water in 1973 (Richard Adams)

The overall geology of Rutland is fairly simple. It was first surveyed systematically by J W Judd of the Geological Survey between 1867 and 1871 (Judd 1875). Interesting new information has accrued initially from the evaluation of the iron ore resources of the area (Hollingworth *et al* 1944) and remapping by the Geological Survey (Sheet 157, 1957), and more recently from urban development, road realignment and the construction of the Empingham Dam (Horswill & Horton 1976; Horton & Coleman 1977).

Rutland's geology comprises a succession of sedimentary formations or mapable rock units of Lower and Middle Jurassic age (150-200 million years old). These bedrock strata are gently inclined to the south-east at an average

4°. They consist of soft plastic sediments, mainly clays and muddy siltstones, forming incompetent beds, alternating with harder brittle rocks, mainly sandstones and limestones, forming competent beds. Lying irregularly over this bedrock are spreads of poorly consolidated material of Quaternary (a million years ago) to Recent age. These superficial deposits consist of glacial boulder clay, landslip debris and other hillwash and, in the valley bottoms, river gravels and sands (alluvium) including older river terraces.

The classification of the bedrock and superficial formations is shown in the table below. The table overleaf gives the names which geologists have given to the bedrock formations and it shows their respective ages within the Lias Group of the Lower Jurassic and the Inferior Oolite Group of the Middle Jurassic. With the recent adoption of the principles of lithostratigraphic mapping by the Geological Survey (mapping based on rock type rather than fossil content), the old and familiar unit names have been replaced. The table gives both the new and former names.

An aerial view of Rutland Water, looking east (John Nowell, Zodiac Publishing)

Succession of Strata

The succession of bedrock strata cropping out in the middle Gwash valley ranges upwards from the oldest unit, the Dyrham Siltstone Formation of Middle Lias age, to the youngest unit, the Lincolnshire Limestone Formation of Middle Jurassic Inferior Oolite age (*see* Table). Most of the valley however is underlain by the dark-grey mudstones of the Upper Lias Whitby Mudstone Formation. Because of the regional south-east tilt of the strata the oldest (lowest) occur in the west around and immediately below Oakham (Map A). Much of Oakham is in fact underlain by Middle Lias strata – the sandy, iron-rich limestone of the Marlstone Rock Formation and the underlying grey, muddy siltstones of the Dyrham Siltstone Formation. These strata extend down-valley almost as far as the Hambleton Peninsula. The flanks of the valley here are formed of the Whitby Mudstone Formation, the top of which slowly descends to the valley floor at Empingham. The harder sandstones and limestones of the overlying Northampton Sand and Lincolnshire Limestone Formations now occur on the lower valley flanks, their outcrop having dropped eastwards from the high ground around Burley, Manton and Upper Hambleton in the west (Map B). Because of this and due also to their relative hardness the valley becomes markedly narrowed. The dam wall of Rutland Water was therefore sited at this narrow point 1km south-west of Empingham. At this position the outcrop of the Northampton Sand Formation and the lower beds of the Lincolnshire

Limestone Formation lie beneath the dam wall. Designs for the dam had therefore to deal with the problem of leaking permeable strata overlying the impervious clays along the valley bottom. The solution was to install clay-filled cut-off trenches along the outcrop of the permeable strata.

The lithologies (rock types) composing the bedrock formations are summarised in the table. Because of the widespread occurrence and engineering importance of the Whitby Mudstone Formation at the dam site these strata have received particular attention (Horton & Coleman 1977). The unit is 63m thick and comprises mainly medium to dark grey mudstone with occasional limestone lenses and bands with nodules of calcareous, phosphatic and iron-rich material. Various subdivisions (Members) have been recognised. These include the Fish Bed Member at the base followed upwards by the richly fossiliferous Cephalopod Limestones Member, the Pisolite Bed, the Ammonite Nodule Bed and the undifferentiated silty mudstones which make up the rest of the sequence.

Of the superficial deposits Boulder Clay of glacial origin (the debris dropped from melting ice sheets) is the most widespread and occurs as thin spreads of sticky mottled grey-brown clay usually carrying many rounded

Table of bedrock strata and superficial deposits underlying the lower Gwash valley
(Clive Jones)

AGE	GROUP	FORMATION NAME AND FORMER NAME	NATURE OF DEPOSIT
QUATERNARY TO RECENT		**SUPERFICIAL DEPOSITS**	
		ALLUVIUM	RIVER GRAVELS, SANDS AND SILTS AND SIMILAR TERRACE DEPOSITS
		LANDSLIP	DISTURBED SOILS AND SUBSOILS
		BOULDER CLAY	PEBBLY AND NON-PEBBLY GLACIAL DRIFT
MIDDLE JURASSIC	INFERIOR OOLITE GROUP	**BEDROCK FORMATIONS**	
		LINCOLNSHIRE LIMESTONE FORMATION (LLF) formerly Lincolnshire Limestone	HARD CREAM-GREY OOLITIC AND NON-OOLITIC LIMESTONE
		GRANTHAM FORMATION (GF) formerly Lower Estuarine Series	LOOSE WHITE-YELLOW SANDS AND CLAYS
		NORTHAMPTON SAND FORMATION (NSF) formerly Northampton Sand	HARD BROWN IRON-RICH SANDSTONE
LOWER JURASSIC	LIAS GROUP (UPPER)	WHITBY MUDSTONE FORMATION (WMF) formerly Upper Lias Clay	DARK GREY MUDSTONE AND CLAYS
	LIAS GROUP (MIDDLE)	MARLSTONE ROCK FORMATION (MRF) formerly Marlstone Bed Rock	HARD GREY-BROWN IRON-RICH SANDY LIMESTONE
		DYRHAM SILTSTONE FORMATION (DSF) formerly Middle Lias Siltstone	DARK-GREY SILTY MUDSTONE AND CLAYS

pebbles on the high ground of the interfluves. The pebbles vary greatly in size and rock type. They include Cretaceous flint and chalk, various Jurassic limestones and hard quartzite derived from Triassic conglomerates. Landslip and related hillwash material occurs commonly along the lower valley slopes where the Lias mudstones outcrop. In this disturbed clayey ground there may be some admixture of material which has slumped down the hillsides from the overlying formations. This can include blocks of sandstone and limestones, sand and pelletal iron-oxide. Along the valley bottoms the unconsolidated gravels, sands, silts and muds of the Gwash and North Tributary floodplains now mostly lie submerged beneath Rutland Water.

Structure

As described above, the structure of the bedrock formations is simply that of a conformable, alternating sequence of hard and soft formations tilted at a low angle to the south-east, disturbed only by the occasional fault. The movements which raised the sediments from the sea floor to form a landmass took place during the mid-Tertiary, around 30 million years ago. By contrast, much more recent structural movement and deformation involving the stability of hillsides, valley bottoms and ridge crests dates only from the Quaternary, about 0.5 million years ago. The processes responsible for these structures are still operating.

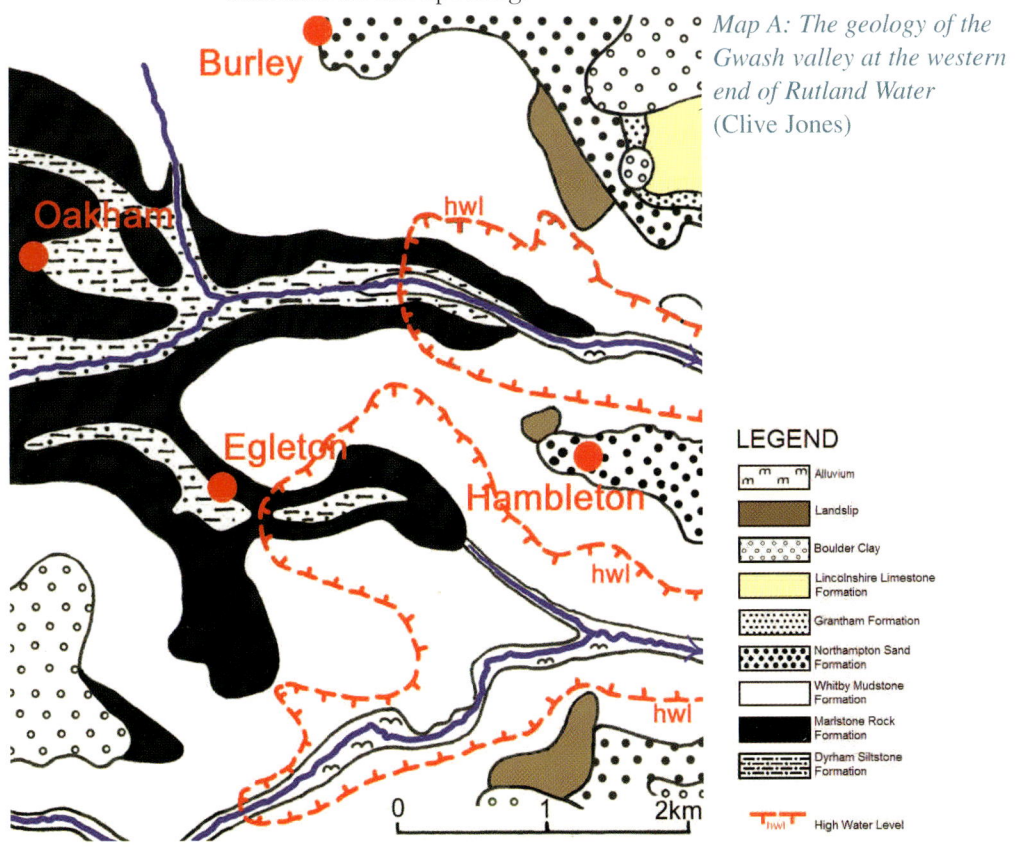

Map A: The geology of the Gwash valley at the western end of Rutland Water (Clive Jones)

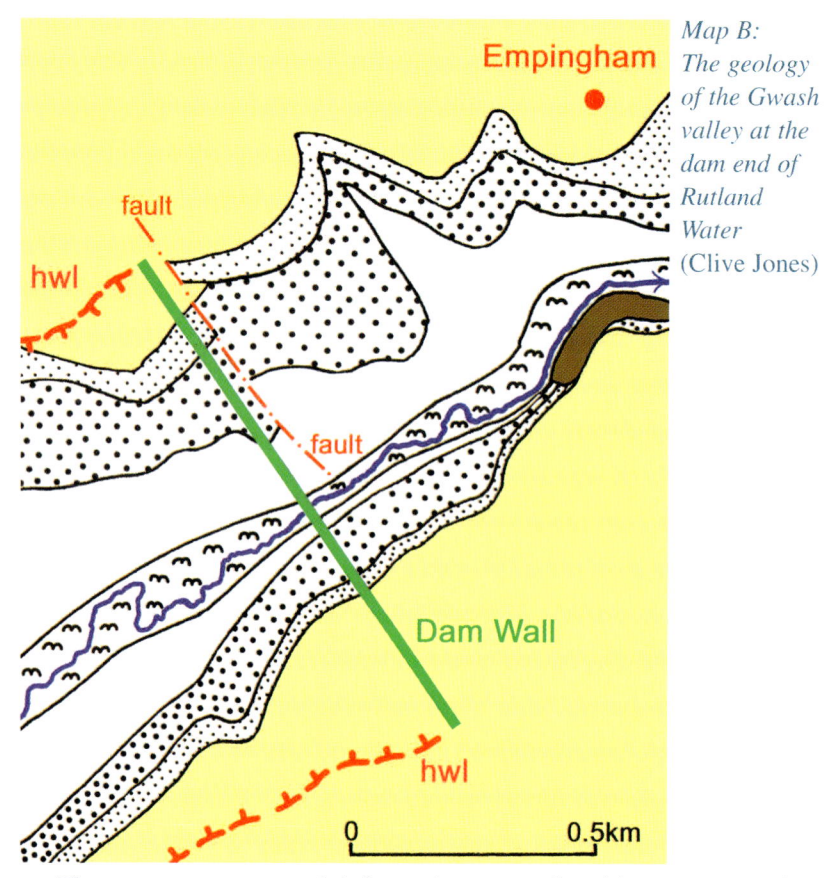

Map B: The geology of the Gwash valley at the dam end of Rutland Water (Clive Jones)

The recent structures and deformation are attributable to gravity and to the extensional stress caused by the lateral squeezing of plastic clays under the weight of superincumbent competent strata. These vectors have produced a variety of structures which are illustrated in Map C. Although the weight of overlying competent strata has been mainly responsible for the squeezing out of the underlying clays onto the hillslopes, it is likely that the process was facilitated, if not initiated, by the added weight of ice caps which remained on the ridge tops towards the end of the main (Anglian) glaciation. Melt-water and the effects of permafrost would also have assisted in the extrusion process.

On the upper valley sides extrusion mounds are the most obvious signs of clay squeeze. Downhill creep of these mounds leads to actual slope failure and the production of landslides. Arcuate failure planes are often exposed as gaping cracks and small faults with throws of about a metre which are best seen in mature pastures. Large landslides are preserved near Barnsdale and Upper Hambleton where slippage along old interglacial erosion surfaces has been recorded (Chandler 1976).

Loss of volume below ridges and the adjacent valley shoulders caused by clay extrusion results in the arching of the competent strata capping the interfluves. Along the shoulders the beds of hard sandstone and limestone bend down and fracture in a process known as cambering. At first, cracks appear which produce surface grooves known as gulls. These develop into small faults (camber faults) and finally the blocks become detached and begin creeping valley-wards. The lowering of beds of sandstone and limestone by an estimated 10m due to cambering has contributed to the narrowing of the Gwash valley at the Empingham dam site (Horton & Coleman 1977).

Along the ridge crests gravity and extensional stress have promoted axial trough faulting in the competent strata. This has resulted in blocks of younger strata falling down into position against older strata at the top of the interfluves, a feature spectacularly exposed in the working faces at Ketton Quarry.

Gravity-induced movements have also been responsible for axial doming of the bedrock beneath the valley floor in a process described as valley bulge. Site investigations before the construction of the Empingham Dam disclosed the presence of a narrow zone of deformation and arching in the Lias strata below the valley bottom (Horton & Coleman 1977). The Marlstone Rock Formation was found to be updomed by 2m and the overlying mudstones were fractured. The upward artesian groundwater pressure in this structural upwarp created a problem at the dam site which was solved by sinking relief wells down-valley from the dam.

Map C: The structural instability of the lower Gwash valley floor, sides and adjacent ridge tops
(Clive Jones)

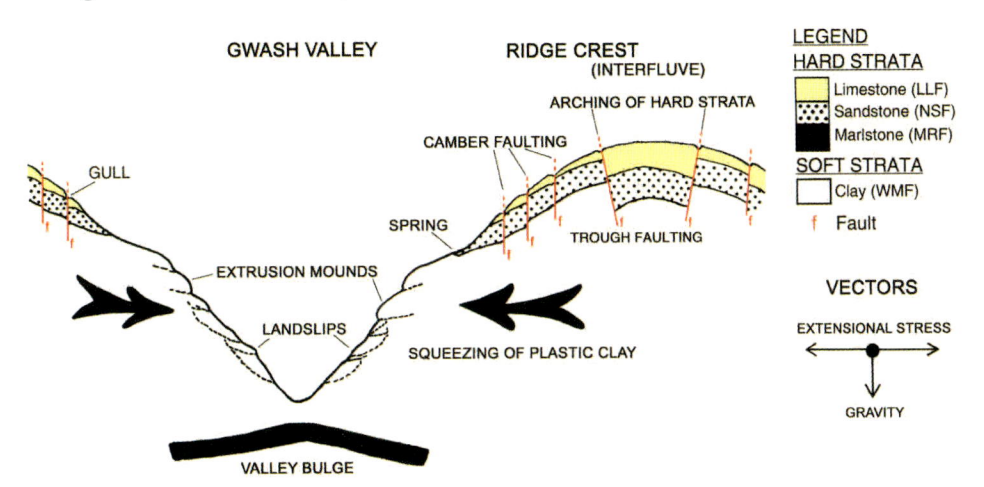

Fossils

Fossils occur in varying amounts in all the bedrock formations. Representative examples from the different units are shown on the following pages. A collection is also on display at the Normanton Church Museum.

Ammonites are particularly well distributed throughout the Jurassic and because they underwent rapid evolution in shell form they have been used to zone or classify the Jurassic. Full dimensional forms such as *Amaltheus* can be found washed out of the Middle Lias siltstones in drainage ditches running into the upper end of Rutland Water. Similarly preserved species of *Dactyloceras*, *Harpoceras* and *Hildoceras* are abundant in the Cephalopod Limestones Member of the Whitby Mudstone Formation. Elsewhere in the Upper Lias fossils are rarer and when they do occur they are usually squashed flat though occasional specimens in full relief, mineralised by

Below Top: Fossils from the Inferior Oolite Formation (©The Natural History Museum, London)

Below Bottom: Fossils from the Upper Lias Formation (©The Natural History Museum, London)

sulphide, phosphate or iron-oxide, can be found. Commonest are perhaps bivalves (seashells), of which *Pholadomya* and *Posidonia* are representative.

Although the dark colour of the Lias mudstones and siltstones is attributable mainly to finely disseminated iron sulphide, carbonaceous (plant) matter does occur and the fossilised trunks of large trees were found in the Marlstone Rock Formation in an archaeological excavation east of Oakham. Also in the marlstone occur conspicuous nests of brachiopod shells (Lantern Shells) belonging to two distinct species: *Tetrarhynchia tetraedra* and *Lobothyris punctata*.

Inferior Oolite fossils are common both in the Northampton Sand Formation and the Lincolnshire Limestone Formation. The lower beds of the former unit are hard and limey, and are full of both complete and broken bivalves commonly belonging to the scallop and mussel families (*Entolium* and *Modiola* repectively). Ammonites are rarer than in the Lias formations but are occasionally encountered in the Lincolnshire Limestone Formation. The limestone contains much broken shelly matter but complete shells in full relief of the gastropod (snail) *Nerinea* and bivalves like *Trigonia* can be found.

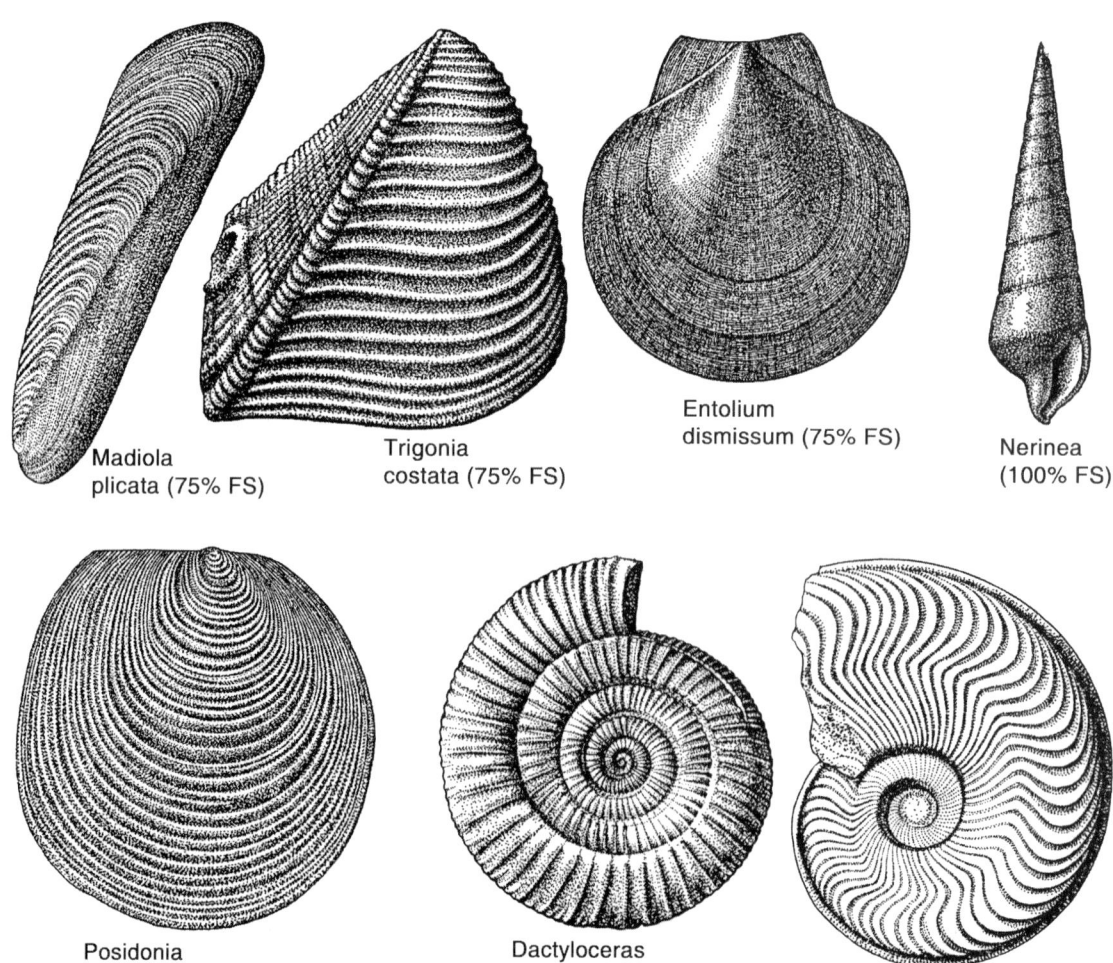

Madiola plicata (75% FS)

Trigonia costata (75% FS)

Entolium dismissum (75% FS)

Nerinea (100% FS)

Posidonia bronni (100% FS)

Dactyloceras commune (75% FS)

Harpoceras falciferum (75% FS)

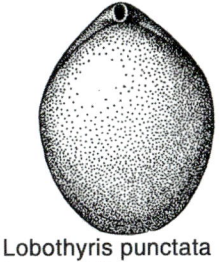

Lobothyris punctata (100% FS)

Tetrarhnchia tetraedra (100% FS)

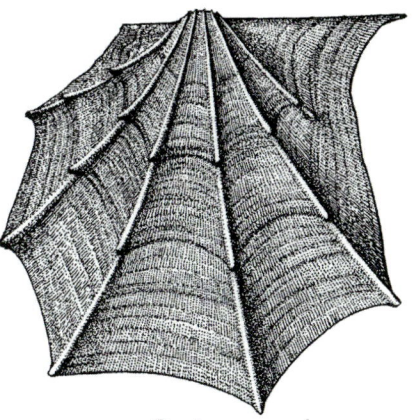

Oxytoma cygnipes (100% FS)

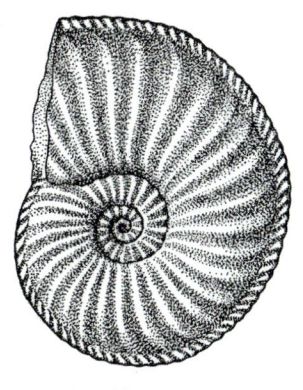

Amaltheus margartatus (75% FS)

Above: Fossils from the Middle Lias Formation (© The Natural History Museum, London)

Left: Rutland Water dam (RO)

Conclusions

The middle Gwash valley and its bordering interfluves are underlain by a sequence of alternating Lower and Middle Jurassic plastic clays and hard sandstones and limestones. The valley sides are composed mainly of the clays which have been squeezed out onto the hill slopes under the weight of the overlying hard beds which cap the ridges. This situation has produced unstable conditions not only along the valley sides but also beneath the valley floor and on the ridge tops. Empingham Dam was sited where the valley narrows as the hard strata dip eastwards towards the valley bottom. Structural problems caused by cambering, landslip, valley bulge and bedrock permeability were encountered during the planning and construction stages of the dam. Remedial design work was necessary to address these problems in order to secure the viability of the dam.

Aspects of Topography

Bull Bridge

The eighteenth-century Bull Bridge still exists, but it is now some 20m beneath the surface of Rutland Water, near the limnological tower. The origins of its name have not been established, but it is remembered today in 'Bull Brigg Lane', the access road to Whitwell Water Sports Centre and car park on the north shore of Rutland Water. 'Brig' is an old term for 'bridge', sometimes shown in old documents as 'brigg'. The lane, which was known as 'Edith Weston Road' before the reservoir, was renamed because it '. . . no longer went anywhere' (Mary Bell). However, it can still be followed along the Whitwell peninsula to the shore of Rutland Water, and more is revealed when the reservoir is at low level. The road originally led to Normanton and Edith Weston, Bull Bridge being its crossing-point over the north arm of the River Gwash.

The old Whitwell to Edith Weston road can still be followed to the shore of Rutland Water (SS)

Above: The eighteenth-century Bull Bridge in 1970 (Jim Levisohn ARPS)

Bull Bridge is adjacent to the north arm draw-off pipe, near the limnological tower seen here under construction in 1974 (Jim Eaton)

— 368 —

Chapter 17
Planning and Constructing the Reservoir
Robert Ovens and Sheila Sleath

This chapter is primarily based, with full permission, on the personal recollections of John Winder, and The Empingham Reservoir Project (Rutland Water) by A J H Winder MA FICE (formerly Chief Resident Engineer, Empingham Reservoir Project), R G Cole FICE (formerly Project Manager, Empingham Reservoir Project), and G E Bowyer BSc FICE (Director of Operations, Anglian Water) which was presented to the Institution of Civil Engineers on 14th May 1985 and published in the Proceedings of the Institution of Civil Engineers, *Volume 78, April 1985.*

The project to build Rutland Water was originally known as the 'Empingham Reservoir Project', or more correctly, the 'Empingham Pumped Storage Project'. It was completed in 1976, being one of the largest water supply schemes undertaken in the United Kingdom, and certainly the largest civil engineering project in Rutland. It involved the construction of an earthfill dam to form an impounding and pumped storage reservoir with a capacity of 124 million cubic metres in the valley of the River Gwash. The reservoir is filled partly by impounding water from the Gwash, but mainly by pumping water from the much larger Welland and Nene. The pumped supply system to the reservoir required river intakes, pumping stations, 14km of tunnelling in Upper Lias clay, and large-diameter pipelines. More pipelines were laid to connect the reservoir to a new water treatment works at Wing, and one major and two minor roads were constructed to replace those lost to the flood. Finally, a great deal of trouble was taken over the landscaping in order to make the reservoir worthy of its setting and suitable for a range of water-based and other outdoor leisure activities.

Large reservoir schemes have a reputation for long gestation periods before their final commissioning, and Empingham was no exception. After completion of the Pitsford Reservoir Scheme in Northamptonshire in 1956, Leonard Brown, then Engineer to the Mid-Northamptonshire Water Board (MNWB), and Thomas Hawksley, a consultant civil engineer, started searching for a suitable site for the next major water development that, in their opinion, would undoubtedly be needed in the area. The need arose from a steady increase in demand for water in the East Midlands in the 1960s, accelerated by the expected requirements of the five planned expansion areas of Corby, Daventry, Northampton, Peterborough and Wellingborough.

Leonard Brown set out the criteria for the new reservoir site:

'The valley must have a suitable shape, so that the reservoir will hold plenty of water, the ground must be strong enough to bear the weight of the dam, and the dam of course mustn't leak so the geology must be right. There must be plenty of local material from which to build the dam, there must be a river reasonably near so that a large quantity of water can be obtained to fill the reservoir, and lastly of course the site must be sufficiently near the centres of population where the water is wanted, so that the pumping costs are not too high.'

By 1967 the Gwash valley upstream of Empingham and the nearby Chater valley to the south-west of Manton had been selected as the most suitable sites for storage reservoirs to provide for the predicted demand, estimated at that time to exceed the capacity of available resources by over 300 million litres per day in the year 2001 (*see* Chapter 14 – Rutland Waters).

The Preliminaries

Preliminary geological investigations proved that both the Empingham and Manton sites were suitable for dam construction, and in 1968 a decision was made to proceed with promotion of the reservoir scheme. The original proposal was to promote both reservoirs, but it was eventually decided to proceed only with the Empingham Reservoir, in the knowledge that Manton Reservoir could be developed in the future, as a second stage, if required. The Welland and Nene River Authority (WNRA) took the lead in the joint promotion of the scheme with the Mid-Northamptonshire Water Board. During the construction of the reservoir they were replaced by the Anglian Water Authority, which came into existence as a result of the 1973 Water Act. In 1983 this Authority was renamed Anglian Water.

Despite a concerted campaign by local groups, including Rutland County Council, the National Farmers Union, the Country Landowners Association, the Council for the Preservation of Rural England and Oakham Rural District Council (*see* Chapter 15 – Don't Dam Rutland), the Welland and Nene (Empingham Reservoir) and Mid-Northamptonshire Water Board Bill received Parliamentary approval in May 1970.

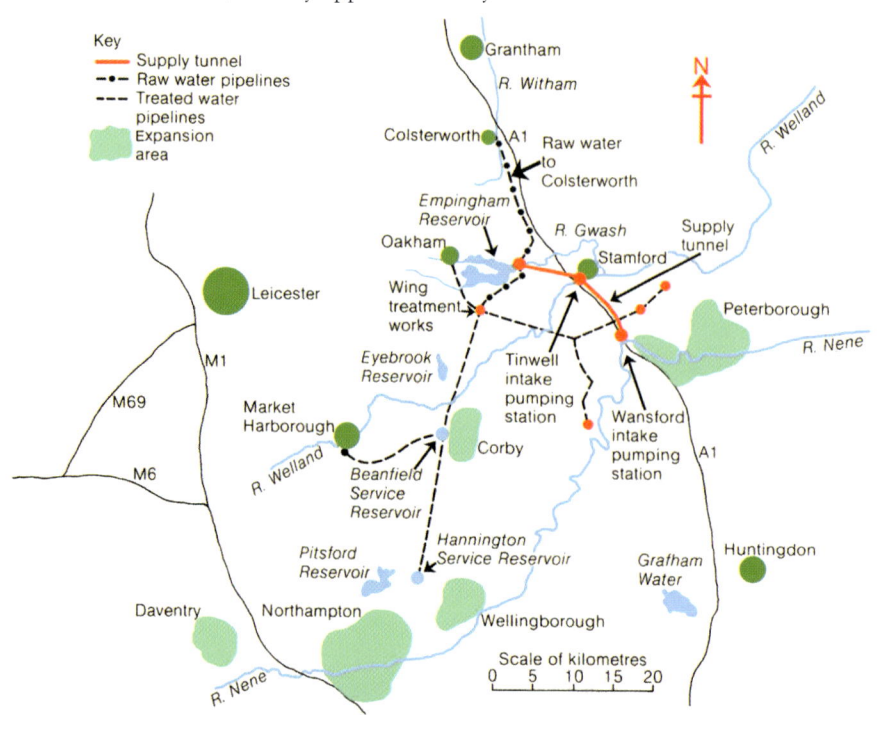

The Empingham Pumped Storage Project (after the Institution of Civil Engineers)

1. Dam
2. North borrow pit
3. South borrow pit
4. Supply tunnel from Tinwell
5. Pumping stations
6. Inlet pipelines
7. Inlet jets
8. Outlet shaft
9. Overflow shaft
10. Upstream diversion and draw-off tunnel
11. Downstream diversion and outlet tunnel
12. Raw water pipeline to Wing treatment works
13. Raw water pipeline to Colsterworth
14. Secondary outlet pipeline
15. Secondary outlet tower
16. Limnological tower
17. Picnic areas
18. Nature reserves
19. Sailing club
20. Sailing centre Fishing Lodge

An overall plan of the reservoir. Note that a new fishing lodge and restaurant has been built at Normanton since this plan was prepared. The original fishing lodge at Whitwell is now a café (after the Institution of Civil Engineers)

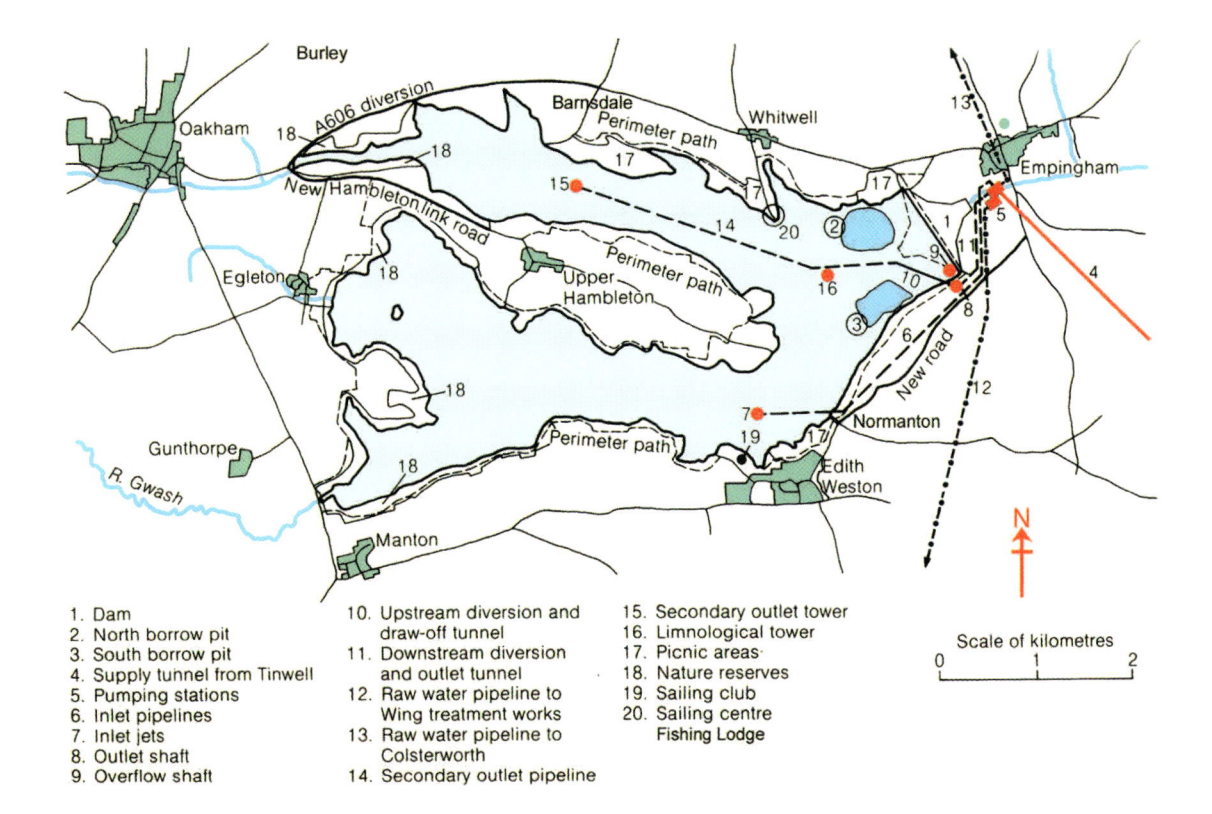

Project Organization

Responsibility for the design and construction of the reservoir was divided between the Welland and Nene River Authority and the Mid-Northamptonshire Water Board, the joint promoters of the scheme, and T & C Hawksley, the appointed consulting engineers. The organization of all aspects of the project was under the control of the Empingham Project Committee appointed by the River Authority. This committee was closely involved with the progress of the work and was charged with taking quick and positive decisions. Liaison between all the organizations and contractors involved was provided by regular meetings attended by all parties. Such close co-operation was essential to ensure that the overall project programme was maintained and that technical matters were not overlooked or duplicated.

Project Design

Because of uncertainties regarding the precise geology of the area near the dam and along the line of the supply aqueduct, final designs could not be completed until after construction had commenced. The successful design was to rely heavily on test results and other data from boreholes and a trial embankment which were to be completed in the first year of the project.

Monthly design and construction meetings chaired by John Winder, Chief Resident Engineer, and attended by his team, design staff, and geotechnical and soils consultants, reviewed instrumentation and test results, decided upon further investigation work, and made design decisions and modifications. Any construction instructions or implications resulting from the meetings were conveyed to the contractors within 24 hours.

John (A J H) Winder – Chief Resident Engineer for Rutland Water

John Winder spent the first five years of his life in Poona, India, where his father was an Army Medical Officer. Returning to the UK (United Kingdom) in 1927, his family lived at Folkestone, Kent, until his father was posted abroad again in 1932. He then attended boarding schools and from 1935 he was at Shrewsbury. On leaving, he enlisted in the Royal Signals and spent some time on a short course at Oxford on electronics and mathematics. Little did he know it at the time, but a contact made on this course was to have an important effect on the direction of his future career.

After passing out at Catterick, North Yorkshire, in 1941, he joined the Royal Signals and was appointed Signals Officer to 90th (City of London) Field Regiment Royal Artillery. The Regiment was sent in turn to India, Northern Iraq, Palestine and Egypt, where he was transferred to the 'Desert Rats' (the 50th Northumberland Division). He also took part in the
invasion of Sicily before returning to the UK in January 1944. 5th June 1944 saw him on a landing craft on his way to land on 'Sword' Beach as part of the D Day landings.

By the end of hostilities the Royal Signals were very busy restoring communications in Germany. This important work meant that he was unlikely to get early release from the army. However he managed to obtain 48 hours leave, and made his way to Oxford University where he visited A H Smith, Warden of New College, whom he knew from his course there in 1940. On his return to Germany, he received a telegram from the War Office giving him immediate release from the Army and instructing him to report to New College at the beginning of October.

In 1949, at the age of 28, he graduated with an honours degree in Engineering Science, but opportunities for young engineers in the UK were very few at that time, and salaries were low. So he looked abroad and early in 1949 he joined the Colonial Engineering Service as a junior engineer in Northern Rhodesia, now Zambia. Here he worked on water supply schemes, roads and bridges before resigning and returning to the UK in 1954.

John now joined consulting engineers Binnie, Deacon and Gourley in London who specialised in water supplies and dams. Until 1957 he served as a Senior Assistant Resident Engineer on the Tai Lam Chung Water Supply Scheme in Hong Kong, building a large concrete dam and three smaller earth dams.

Following his return to London, he married Cherry Lewis in May 1959, and later that month, he left for Nigeria to supervise water supply projects as a relief engineer. In 1960, he again returned to London and his next project was Diddington Dam, now known as Grafham Water (Cambridgeshire), where he was Chief Resident Engineer, living with his family in the village of Brampton, near Huntingdon, a few miles away from the project.

His next move was to Herbert Lapworth and Partners in Westminster who wanted him as their resident engineer for the construction of Scammonden Dam, high in the Pennines, near Huddersfield, West Yorkshire. Again he and his family moved to be near the job, this time to an old vicarage in a remote Yorkshire valley.

The project involved working closely with the County Council, who were building the M62 motorway, Britain's first mountain highway, which was to cross the valley on the crest of the dam. It was to be one of the highest dams in the UK, and was constructed using rock fill removed from the bottom of the valley. The M62 and reservoir were formally opened by the Queen on 14th October 1971, by which time John had moved to a new project in Rutland.

In December 1969 he was interviewed by T & C Hawksley (later Watson Hawksley), a small but much respected firm of consulting engineers. He was appointed as Chief Resident Engineer, to be in charge of the construction of a large earth dam and water supply scheme at Empingham – the future Rutland Water. On 13th October 1970 he started his new job, living at a hotel in Oakham, by which time there was already a great deal of activity on the site. Again, wishing to have his family with him, they moved to 'Stone House' in Wing in 1970.

The story of the building of Rutland Water is told in this chapter. John says, referring to Rutland Water and Grafham Water, '. . . I am proud to have played a part in both these projects'. His last day at Empingham was 31st January 1975, but he returned for a ceremony at the outlet shaft on 6th February 1975 for the closing of the scour (outlet) valve and the start of impounding water in the reservoir. For him '. . . it was a moment to remember . . . something important had just taken place, after years of effort by hundreds of people'.

One special aspect of the project that he was pleased to be involved with was the saving of Normanton Church. 'This was due to be demolished, but several local people wanted it to be preserved and I was one of them, and undertook to look into how it might be saved. We formed the Normanton Tower Trust, to put proposals before the Water Authority which firmly maintained that it must be demolished, and there was no money available to preserve it.

'We considered excavation all round it, and jacking it up, and moving it bodily, foundations and all, to a higher level. I contacted a firm which specialised in moving historic or important buildings, and they submitted outline plans for how it could be done, and a price for doing it – but the cost was way beyond what might be available.

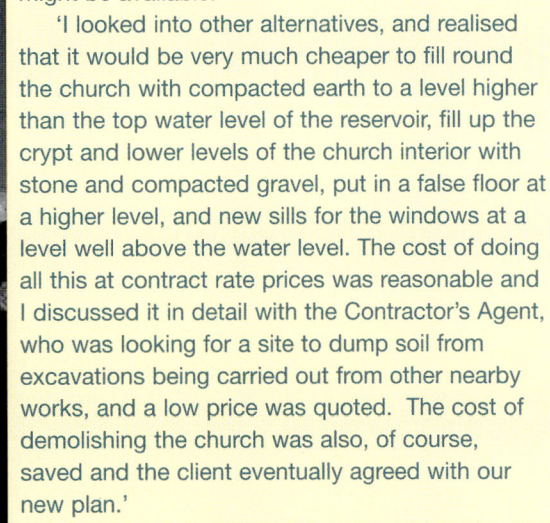

'I looked into other alternatives, and realised that it would be very much cheaper to fill round the church with compacted earth to a level higher than the top water level of the reservoir, fill up the crypt and lower levels of the church interior with stone and compacted gravel, put in a false floor at a higher level, and new sills for the windows at a level well above the water level. The cost of doing all this at contract rate prices was reasonable and I discussed it in detail with the Contractor's Agent, who was looking for a site to dump soil from excavations being carried out from other nearby works, and a low price was quoted. The cost of demolishing the church was also, of course, saved and the client eventually agreed with our new plan.'

The Normanton Tower Trust raised the money to cover the cost of saving the church building which has become a prominent landmark on the shores of Rutland Water.

After Rutland Water, John was offered a partnership with Watson Hawksley at their new offices in High Wycombe, and continued to work on water supply and reservoir projects. On 30th April 1985, he retired, but continued working as an Inspecting Engineer under the Reservoir Act for a few more years.

Above Left: John Winder at the scour valve closing ceremony on 6th February 1975 to mark the start of impounding water in the reservoir (Brian and Elizabeth Nicholls)
Left: John Winder near Normanton Church (John Winder)

Geology

Boreholes were drilled to prove the sequence of strata shown on Geological Survey maps and to provide more localised detail. The most significant geological components are the Upper Lias clay and the Marlstone Rock Bed. The Marlstone Rock Bed is a confined aquifer 22m below the valley floor in the vicinity of the dam, and extends under the whole of the reservoir area. It is covered by Upper Lias clay which gradually reduces in thickness along the twin Gwash valleys until the Marlstone eventually outcrops at the head of the reservoir near Oakham. The Marlstone Rock Bed also underlies the route of the tunnels. A 'valley bulge', which runs approximately along the line of the Gwash, results in considerable localised disturbance to the strata above the Marlstone Rock Bed (*see* Chapter 16 – The Geology of the Middle Gwash Valley). This was to result in some serious problems for the dam builders.

The layer of Upper Lias clay was to provide most of the material for building the earth embankment which was to form the dam and also offered a fairly easy excavation route for the supply aqueduct tunnels.

Right: Drilling one of the test boreholes (Brian and Elizabeth Nicholls)

Below: The geological section at the dam site, looking upstream. The Marlstone Rock Bed is too deep to be affected by the valley bulge at this point, but the Upper Lias Clay is severely disturbed (after the Institution of Civil Engineers)

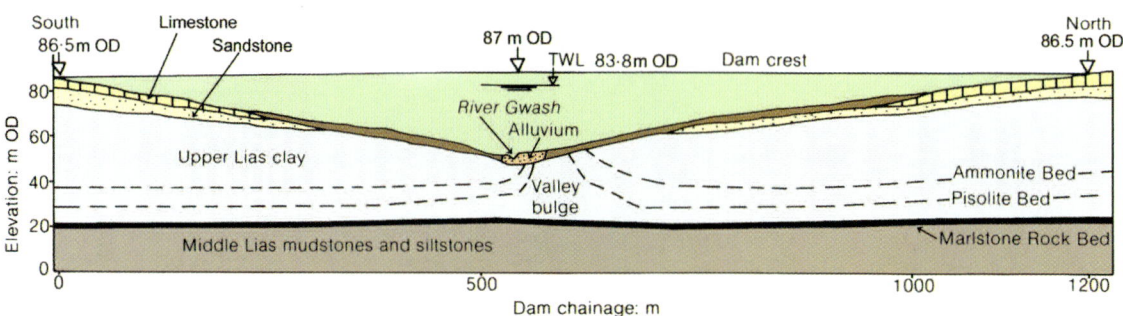

The Work Begins

A very rapid start on the construction was necessary because there was a predicted shortfall in water supply by 1976. Consequently, detailed site investigations and site clearance started in June 1970, only a month after Parliamentary approval, and the first major contract, for the River Gwash diversion tunnels, was let in December 1970.

Site Clearance

Below: Site clearance begins in June 1970 near Empingham on day one of the construction of Rutland Water (Brian and Elizabeth Nicholls Photography)

By far the greatest task in the site clearance programme was the removal of trees, hedges, shrubs and fences. This started in the dam area near Empingham, and continued along what was to become the south arm of the reservoir. It included the complete removal of Mow Mires Spinney, Cocked Hat Spinney, Brake Spinney and Snowdrop Spinney, and the partial removal of Hambleton Wood, Gibbet Gorse and Half Moon Spinney. Much of this had been completed by mid-1973. Within the next twelve months much of Armley Wood and Barnsdale Wood in the future north arm of the reservoir had been removed, as well as part of Burley Wood for the A606 Barnsdale Hill diversion (*see* Chapter 23 – Fauna and Flora before Rutland Water).

Right: The landscape cleared of hedges and trees near Nether Hambleton (Richard Adams)

Above: One of the many lorry-loads of timber felled during the reservoir clearance programme (Richard Adams)

Clearing trees near Burley Wood for the A606 Barnsdale Hill diversion (Brian and Elizabeth Nicholls Photography)

Another aspect of site clearance was the demolition of all the dwellings and farm buildings in Nether Hambleton, eight dwellings and numerous farm buildings in Middle Hambleton which were below the high water level, two dwellings at the foot of Barnsdale Hill, and Mow Mires farmhouse in Normanton Park. Some of the demolition rubble was used to create the Nature Reserve lagoons at the western end of the reservoir (*see* Chapter 21 – Lost Homes and Chapter 24 – Tim Appleton MBE – Thirty Years of Rutland Water Nature Reserve).

The end of the day and the end of an era for Red House at Nether Hambleton (Richard Adams)

The Diversion Tunnels

In order to start work in the bottom of the valleys it was first necessary to divert the River Gwash round the dam construction site. For this purpose a tunnel, which would later become a part of the permanent works, was driven from near the upstream toe of the embankment into the hillside on the south side of the valley at the reservoir outlet shaft location. A second tunnel was then driven back from the outlet shaft to the river near the downstream toe. The work was carried out by Edmund Nuttall Ltd before work on the main embankment had started. It also allowed removal of the surface material down to the Upper Lias clay on the embankment site immediately at the start of the main contract.

The outlet shaft, which is 10.7m internal diameter, was sunk first, followed by the two tunnel drives, all three being lined with concrete segments. The upstream and downstream tunnels are 3.7m and 4.4m internal diameter respectively. The upstream tunnel was lined with concrete infill panels and sprayed with an epoxy paint to provide protection against anaerobic water lying for long periods in this section of the tunnel.

Above: Excavating the reservoir outlet shaft. It is 10.7m in diameter and over 30m deep (Brian and Elizabeth Nicholls Photography)

Lowering the tunnelling machine into the outlet shaft (Brian and Elizabeth Nicholls Photography)

Right: Looking along the lined upstream diversion tunnel, now the reservoir bottom draw-off tunnel (Brian and Elizabeth Nicholls Photography)

Left: The entrance to the top half of the downstream diversion tunnel (Brian and Elizabeth Nicholls Photography)

Above: The downstream diversion tunnel before the dividing platform was installed. It now carries the overflow water and other services (Brian and Elizabeth Nicholls Photography)

The downstream tunnel, which was completed later under the main contract, is divided by a platform. In the top half, a 1.2m diameter steel pipe delivers the raw reservoir water to the outlet pumping station from where it is pumped to the water treatment works at Wing, or to Colsterworth, Lincolnshire. The remaining space is used as an access walkway, for power and control cables, and for other services. The bottom half of the tunnel carries the overflow from the reservoir and also any additional water necessary to maintain the minimum downstream flow of the River Gwash, known as the regulation water. It also carries water discharged through the scour pipe. The scour valve can be opened to let water out of the reservoir very quickly. For example, it can be used in an emergency if the dam is damaged or if it is necessary to lower the water level for any reason. The scour valve is also opened to flush sediment out of the reservoir when too much has collected behind the dam. The fast flowing water carries the sediment through the scour and downstream.

At the tunnel exit, there is a stilling basin and tailbay which incorporates a weir for measuring the river regulation water and the overflow water. Water is also discharged here from the Marlstone relief wells. A new river channel has also been constructed downstream from the tailbay to Church Bridge, Empingham, where the total water released is measured.

An early artist's impression of Empingham pumping station and the realigned River Gwash. The horizon is the crest of the dam (Anglian Water)

Empingham Dam – The Embankment

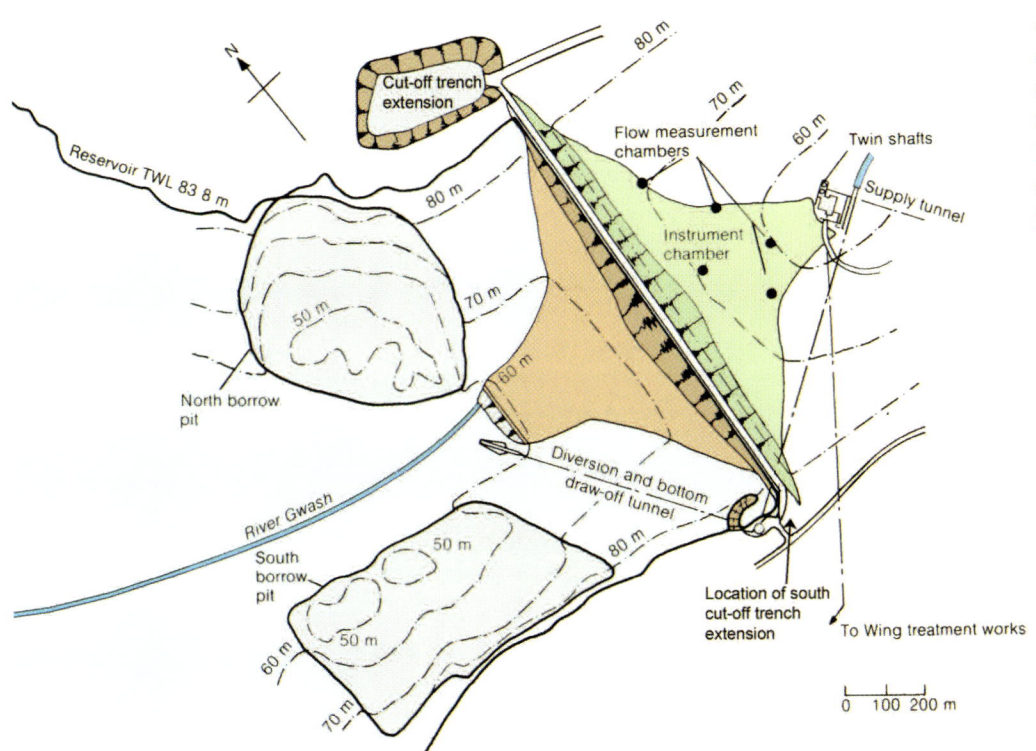

Plan of the dam and borrow pits (after the Institution of Civil Engineers)

Empingham Dam, an earthfill embankment 37m high, 1,200m long, and 810m wide at its foundation level, is an important component of the Empingham Reservoir Project. The main geological features of the valley were established before Parliamentary approval by a preliminary site investigation. The Upper Lias clay was the controlling geological factor and it was known that the valley sides were extensively disturbed (*see* Chapter 16 – The Geology of the Middle Gwash Valley). It was also expected that the Upper Lias clay in the valley floor would be affected by valley bulging. The strength of the clay foundation was known to be inadequate to support the weight of an embankment of the specified height. This was the controlling factor in its design and resulted in a wide cross-section with extensive slopes.

It was a planning stipulation that the majority of the material needed for building the dam must be excavated from inside the reservoir area. The Upper Lias clay would therefore be used to build the embankment. At 37m high it would be one of the highest ever built of clay on a clay foundation. If the Manton Reservoir project had gone ahead, the earth embankment there would have been 43m high, and this was considered to be the absolute maximum for this type of dam. It would also have to have been wider at the top to accommodate the 37m necessary for the A6003 which crosses the Chater valley at this point, resulting in a very high volume of clay being required (*see* Chapter 14 – Rutland Waters).

A feasibility study for the Empingham Dam indicated that, even with long slopes, sand drains would be required to ensure the stability of the clay foundation. The sand drains would collect water forced out of the pores of the clay by the weight of the dam above and drain via the drainage blankets within the dam structure.

Before the dam could be designed in detail a site investigation was necessary to gain a detailed understanding of the geology. This had to be completed within the twelve months before the set date for the start of the construction. It was carried out by Soil Mechanics Ltd between August and December 1970 and included drilling boreholes to investigate the structure and properties of the clay foundation beneath the sites of the dam and borrow pits, as well as consolidation and bearing tests. Core samples were initially tested off site, but a well-equipped site laboratory, commissioned during this period, allowed very quick analysis of samples.

While the site investigation was taking place, the availability of suitable materials for drainage, filters and rip-rap was investigated. Rip-rap is rock used on the dam face to reduce erosion by dissipating wave energy.

An understanding of the geology of the valley developed progressively during the investigation. The Institute of Geological Sciences carried out a fossil study of the core samples in order to establish a zoning system within the clay. This enabled the identification of the different types of clay required for the embankment.

It was established at an early stage that, although the valley bulge penetrated 20m below the valley floor, the Marlstone Rock Bed at the dam site was not affected. This was an important discovery as, in this area, it is a confined aquifer containing water under pressure. If a rupture was exposed it would behave as an artesian well and flood the area very quickly. In order to reduce this pressure it was necessary to install relief wells on the downstream side of the dam to control the uplift pressure.

The test results enabled the design of the dam to progress, although considerable uncertainty remained concerning the strength of the foundation clay and the behaviour of the embankment fill material under heavy loading. The solution was to build a trial embankment, but the tight programme meant that this could not be done until after the construction start date. The aim at this stage was, therefore, to progress the design sufficiently to enable tenders to go out for the selection of a main contractor for the construction of the dam and ancillary works.

To enable tenders to be made on a reasonably firm basis, it was decided that the contract should include provisional elements to cater for the uncertainties, with dates by which final decisions must be made. These elements were: the extent of the slopes, the number of drainage layers within the dam, and the spacing of the sand drains. Tenders were invited in May 1971 and Gleeson Civil Engineering Ltd was appointed as the main contractor on 14th September 1971.

A major feature of the contract was the construction of the large trial embankment within the upstream slope and this was to be retained as part of the final embankment. By using steep slopes, a shear stress in excess of that imposed by the final embankment could be imposed on the foundation clay. The trial was to be carried out during the first year of construction, and the slope design was to be fixed four months after its completion.

The trial embankment was built near the south side of the valley floor to avoid the main valley bulge. A trench was excavated into the valley side to ensure that it had a constant height over a length of about 70m, and calculations proved that the stress imposed on the foundation clay would be well in excess of that imposed by the final embankment.

Three failures of temporary steep clay embankments in the borrow pits occurred while the trial embankment was under construction. Data from these failures reduced the need to take the trial bank to failure, and construction ceased when the mean height was 21m. The dynamic performance of the bank and underlying strata was then observed for the next four months.

The trial bank can be seen upper left in this photograph (Brian and Elizabeth Nicholls Photography)

After excavation of the soft alluvium in the valley floor down to the Upper Lias clay, the material being taken to spoil heaps or used to make up the lower part of the slopes, the dam site was ready for the installation of sand drains. It is interesting to note here that the engineers were able to map in detail some of the shear surfaces apparent on the face of the newly exposed Upper Lias Clay. Peter Horswill, the site geologist, realised that this had occurred at the end of the last Ice Age, some 100,000 years ago, due to the bottom of the valley bulging upwards as a result of the immense pressure from the weight of the thick ice on the shoulders of the valley.

The sand drains were installed by Soil Mechanics Ltd who commenced work in January 1972. They drilled 10,873 600mm diameter drains to a maximum depth of 18m, using crane mounted augers, within the six-month contract period, a rate of approximately 60 sand drains per day. The drains were filled with sand and the area was flooded between clay bunds or saturated by spray irrigation to ensure consolidation. The drains were made up with additional sand before embankment fill placing started.

Installing sand drains in the foundation of the dam (Brian and Elizabeth Nicholls Photography)

A crawler crane-mounted auger drilling a sand drain (Brian and Elizabeth Nicholls Photography)

The final design for the dam was decided early in 1973. It incorporated extra information obtained from the trial embankment and borrow pit slips, and the observations of sand drain performance. The slopes needed were found to be smaller than those predicted by the initial design assumptions. More importantly, construction could be completed with much less uncertainty.

Material for the main embankment (dam) was placed using 12 Terex TS24 16 cubic metre twin-engined motor scrapers, ideal for the terrain and short-haul distances between the borrow pits and the embankment site. Bulldozers were used as pushers for the motor scrapers when collecting clay in the borrow pits.

Cut-off trenches, to prevent water leakage round the ends of the embankment, were excavated into the valley sides until the top of the Upper Lias clay was 1.7m above the reservoir top water level. These were then filled with clay to 2.2m above this level. Above this, the excavated surface material was replaced.

Above: Filling a sand drain (Brian and Elizabeth Nicholls Photography)

Left: A heavily loaded Terex motor scraper gets a push from a bulldozer (Brian and Elizabeth Nicholls Photography)

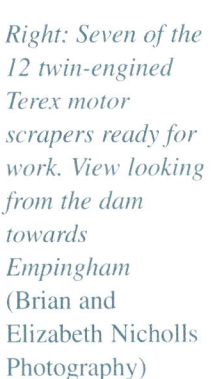

Right: Seven of the 12 twin-engined Terex motor scrapers ready for work. View looking from the dam towards Empingham (Brian and Elizabeth Nicholls Photography)

One of the Terex motor scrapers emerging from a borrow pit near the dam site (Brian and Elizabeth Nicholls Photography)

The south cut-off trench (Brian and Elizabeth Nicholls Photography)

Natural gravels from pits in the Fens were used as filters and drainage materials within the embankment, and because of sporadic high demand these were stockpiled on site.

The Upper Lias clay used for the embankment construction was extracted from borrow pits located below top water level upstream of the dam. They were excavated to full depth in sections, surface material being placed in worked-out areas. The drainage of the underlying Marlstone Rock Bed (*see* later) allowed the borrow pits to be deepened without risk of uplift through artesian pressure. However, a section brought upwards by valley bulging was unexpectedly exposed in the south borrow pit. It was subsequently blanketed with clay to prevent leakage from the reservoir.

The north cut-off trench after being filled (Brian and Elizabeth Nicholls Photography)

An aerial view of the borrow pits and the embankment, looking east towards Empingham (RCM)

Dam construction commenced with the placing of clay in the downstream slope. At first, excavation was restricted to the south borrow pit to increase the supply of deeper and drier clay. Fill placing for the upstream slope was restricted in 1972 by the construction of the trial bank. In 1973 the surface materials from the north borrow pit were placed on this slope and thereafter both borrow pits were used.

As the construction progressed, it was found necessary to adjust the water content of the clay. A section of the embankment was marked out and the requisite number of TS24 scraper loads was placed to give an uncompacted layer thickness of about 200mm. This was graded with a bulldozer and the clay was broken up by several passes of a heavy tine harrowing unit. This brought up claystones from the fill which were removed by hand by a gang of six men – claystone is fully-hardened clay material which does not break down when wetted. The contractor then quickly measured the water content using a microwave oven. The amount of water to be added was assessed and then placed using water bowsers equipped with sprays. The clay was then rotavated. Further watering and rotavating was carried out as required and the layer finally compacted.

Spreading and compacting the clay at the south end of the embankment (Richard Adams)

Watering the clay prior to harrowing and further compacting (Brian and Elizabeth Nicholls Photography)

The embankment was divided into zones using different classes of fill, the classes being decided by the shear strength of the material used. These were established during the preliminary site investigation:

Fill class	Fill type	Shear strength (relative to class A fill)	Where used
A	Upper Lias clay	1.0	Shoulders
A1	Weathered Upper Lias clay	0.6	Slopes
B	Upper Lias clay	0.5	Core zone
C	Upper Lias clay	1.1	Centre
D	Alluvium	Not measured	Slope toes

Control of the moisture content proved very difficult as drying-out occurred in sunny or windy weather. During spells of hot summer weather evaporation losses became so great that night working was adopted, the fill being placed late in the afternoon and treated, watered and compacted during the night. The fill was tested the following morning and any areas that did not meet the specification were re-treated the same day.

The specification called for construction to a minimum height of 60m OD by the end of 1972 to ensure early loading of the sand drain zone. To ensure adequate consolidation by the end of construction, a level of 80m OD by the end of 1973 and completion in June 1974 were specified. These targets were met in three periods with winter breaks. The maximum rate of earthmoving achieved was 470,000 cubic metres in August 1973. The total volume of the dam is about 5 million cubic metres.

In order to monitor the condition of the dam continuously, the embankment was furnished with devices to measure water pressure (twin-tube hydraulic piezometers) and movement (inclinometers, settlement gauges and wire extensometers). The installation of these was the responsibility of the Resident Engineer's staff and much of this work was carried out during winter breaks in earthmoving. An extensive system of permanent survey points was also installed, including twelve points on the dam crest, and others on the reservoir shore line near the embankment. Measurements are processed by computer in such a way as to indicate movements relative to the framework of the overall grid of survey points.

Protection against wave action on the dam was provided by rip-rap and for this purpose Carboniferous Limestone from Crich in Derbyshire was used. It was hauled and dumped by articulated dump trucks and spread by a bulldozer. Final adjustments to produce a dense uniform layer were made by hand. The lower upstream slopes were protected by beaching consisting of limestone and ironstone from site excavations. The rip-rap was extended above the crest of the dam and the inner face was hand-packed to form a dry stone wall on the upstream side of the crest roadway. The downstream slopes were grassed, the topsoil being placed over a layer of granular material to give soil drainage and conditions similar to those on the natural valley sides.

Below: Sections through the completed embankment: (a) full section (b) centre detail (after the Institution of Civil Engineers)

Placing the limestone and ironstone beaching on the upstream face of the embankment (Brian and Elizabeth Nicholls Photography)

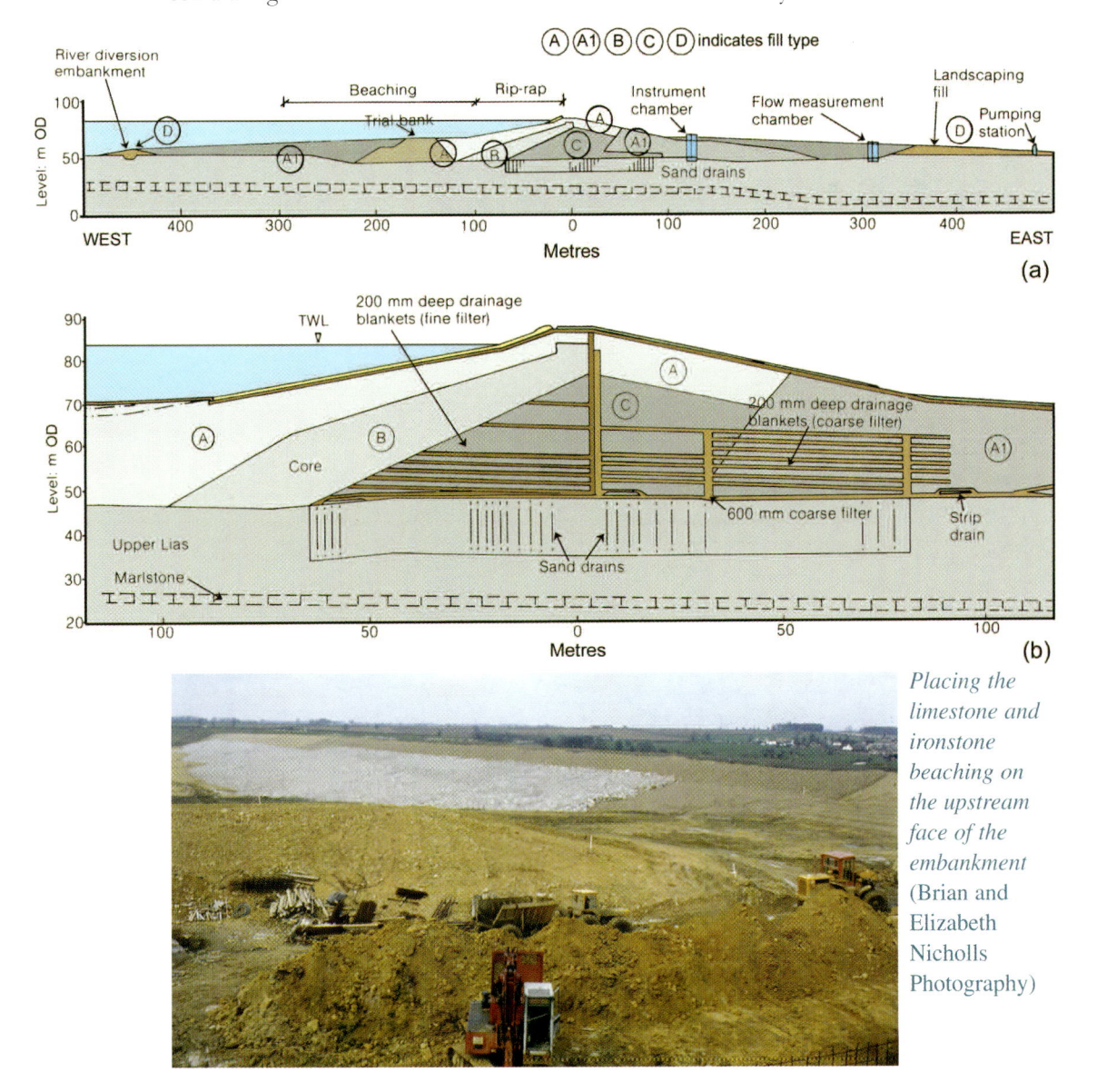

The Aqueduct System – Supply Tunnels, Pipelines and Pumping Stations

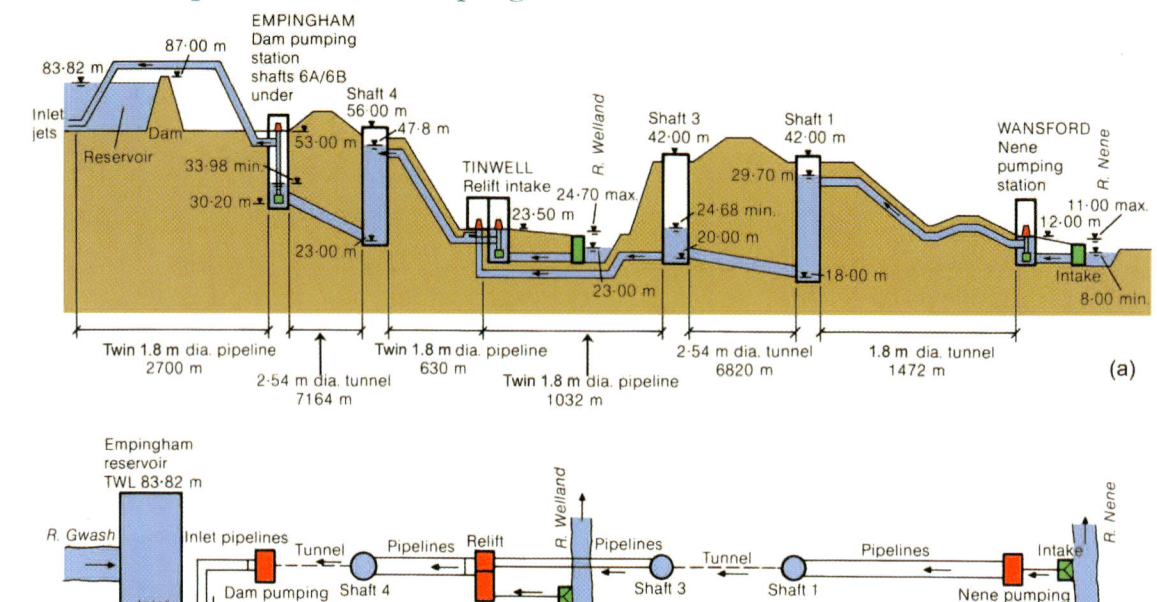

Water from the rivers Nene and Welland is delivered to the reservoir through a supply system of three pumping stations, two tunnels and connecting pipelines. The overall length of the aqueduct system, from the pumping station at Wansford on the River Nene to the inlet jets in the reservoir, is 21km. The design capacity of the system was 1,140 million litres per day, which allowed for the possibility of Manton Reservoir being constructed in the future.

Above: The schematic diagrams of the water flow system to the reservoir: (a) section, (b) plan (after the Institution of Civil Engineers)

Right: Building the River Welland abstraction point at Tinwell (Brian and Elizabeth Nicholls Photography)

The pumping station at Wansford intake on the River Nene pumps up to 518 million litres per day along twin 1.8m diameter steel pipelines into shaft 1 at the head of the first tunnel. The water then gravitates along the 2.54m diameter concrete-lined tunnel to shaft 3, from which twin 1.8m diameter pipelines cross the geologically faulted and disturbed Welland valley to the Tinwell intake and pumping station. From here, water from the River Welland can be abstracted at up to 363 million litres per day and pumped, together with the Nene water, along twin 1.8m diameter pipelines to shaft 4 at the head of the second tunnel. The water again gravitates along this concrete-lined tunnel to the twin terminal shafts (6A and 6B) located at the toe of the downstream embankment at Empingham. The level of the tunnels was dictated by the hydraulic gradient, the top of the Upper Lias clay, and the location of the Marlstone Rock Bed.

The final lift pumping station is located over the top of these terminal shafts. From here water is pumped via steel pipelines to the inlet jet control valves, followed by four lines of pre-stressed concrete pipes laid on the bed of the reservoir to the inlet jets located in, and pointing up, the south arm of the reservoir.

Preliminary site investigations in 1967 had indicated that it would be possible to drive tunnels between the River Nene at Wansford and the reservoir site at Empingham, except for the Welland Valley crossing where the strata was heavily faulted. By careful choice of levels and route it was also possible to keep the tunnels entirely within the Upper Lias clay, thus enabling soft-ground tunnelling techniques to be used. Tunnel A connecting Wansford to Tinwell was to be 6,820m long, and tunnel B connecting Tinwell to Empingham was to be 7,164m long. The contract for the supply tunnels was let to Edmund Nuttall Ltd in June 1972.

The 2.54m internal diameter tunnels were constructed using the expanding wedge block system developed by the Metropolitan Water Board. The lining ring consists of 140mm thick concrete segments which are expanded against the clay face by a wedge block driven in at the top of the ring by a ram operating from the tunnelling shield.

Below: Tunnel and steel pipe details (after the Institution of Civil Engineers)

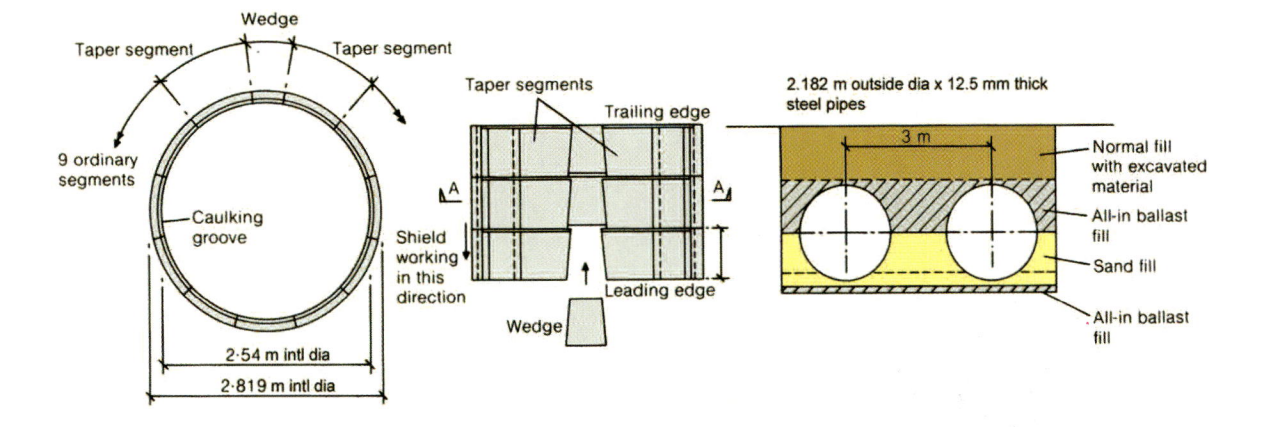

The tunnelling machine consisted of a shield about 3m long with a rotating cutting face on the front and equipment for erecting the lining at the rear. The shield formed an accurate profile in the clay to receive the linings. Behind the shield were sledges with conveyor belts, winches, electric generators, a transformer, pneumatic equipment, segment wagons and spoil wagons. The overall length of this plant was about 44m, and it was operated by a gang of four miners.

The concrete segments for the tunnel lining were cast in moulds on site. After 24 hours in the moulds the segments were kept in the casting shed for a further two days to consolidate, followed by 42 days in outside storage. This was to ensure that they were up to full strength before being used in the tunnel.

At each end of tunnel A, in the Wansford to Tinwell aqueduct, there is a 10.7m diameter shaft (1 and 3), with platforms and staircases for access, made up from bolted reinforced concrete segments. This size was required to cater for the mass oscillation surge that occurs on pump start-up, shut-down, or sudden power failure. At the start of tunnel B, in the Tinwell to Empingham aqueduct, there is a similar shaft (4), and at the Empingham end there are twin shafts (6A and 6B), again of similar size. The twin shafts are connected by a cross tunnel into which tunnel B was driven.

The twin shafts (6A and 6B) at Empingham, situated in the valley bottom, were started ahead of the main tunnel contract to allow for the pumping station above them to be completed according to the contract programme. The shafts were sunk simultaneously, one progressing slightly in advance of the other. One shaft had reached a level of 3m above bottom level when it started to flood, with water eventually overflowing at the top. The second shaft was then deliberately flooded as a safeguard. This water was from the Marlstone Rock Bed, even though it was 14m below the level

Steel pipes being installed near Wansford pumping station (Brian and Elizabeth Nicholls Photography)

The shield of one of the tunnelling machines (Brian and Elizabeth Nicholls Photography)

of the bottom of the shaft. In order to solve this problem it was necessary to reduce the water pressure by boring a total of eighteen 450mm diameter relief wells to a depth of 40m around the shafts.

When excavation restarted in the twin shafts and connecting tunnel, it was found from the attitude of the Pisolite Bed (a narrow band of coarse-grained limestone within and at the lower level of the Upper Lias clay) that the bottom of the excavation had penetrated the edge of the valley bulge. The steep bedding and disturbed condition of the material had allowed easy access for the water from the Marlstone Rock Bed into the base of the shaft.

The twin shafts were completed satisfactorily, and advantage was taken of the lowered water level to drive about 200m of bolted lining tunnel out from the connecting tunnel. This took the tunnel clear of the area of valley bulging, which would have caused problems as the main tunnel approached Empingham.

The twin shafts can be seen at the lower left of this picture, which also includes part of Empingham and its medieval manorial earthworks (Fred Adams)

It was originally intended to drive both tunnels using only one machine, starting with tunnel A from shaft 3. Progress was good for the first 1.5km, until the Pisolite Bed was encountered. It was immediately apparent that it was too hard for the machine to cope with and the contractor had to resort to hand excavation. However, after about 20m a fault was encountered which lowered the bed 2m below the tunnel base, and machine tunnelling could continue once again.

Empingham pumping station from the dam in 2007 (SS)

However, a new problem now arose which was to slow progress. This was 'overbreak'. The expanding wedge block system relies on the tunnelling machine being able to form an accurate profile in the clay to receive the tunnel lining. If the profile is not circular, then the ring will not be self-supporting. This problem may only become apparent when the tunnel is pressurised. The 'overbreak' was caused by blocks of clay being torn from the face by the tunnelling machine teeth instead of being cut to a neat profile. It was found by trial and error that making up the voids with softened clay provided a satisfactory but slow solution.

Because of these delays, a second tunnelling machine was brought in to excavate tunnel B instead of waiting for the first machine to become available. With two machines at work and with better ground conditions, progress greatly improved. Tunnel A was completed in 54 weeks, and tunnel B in 53 weeks, giving an average rate of progress of approximately 130m per week. The highest output achieved was 51 lining rings, each consisting of 12 segments, covering a distance of 35m in a ten-hour shift. The sheer physical achievement by the tunnel gangs is impressive, especially when it is realised that they lifted and placed each 83kg concrete segment by hand in cramped and confined conditions for ten hours at a stretch, giving a total of 20,000 tonnes lifted in the two tunnels.

Left: Miners at the Empingham end of the Tinwell to Empingham tunnel celebrating a successful breakthrough (Brian and Elizabeth Nicholls Photography)

Because of faulting and valley bulging, the tunnels were replaced by pipelines across the Nene and Welland valleys. Twin 1.8m diameter pipelines were laid from Wansford pumping station to shaft 1 and also across the Welland Valley to link shafts 3 and 4.

There were two other problems to contend with in crossing the Welland Valley – the river itself, and the railway line between Leicester and Peterborough. In order to cross the River Welland it was first necessary to de-water the gravels near the river crossing point. The twin pipelines were then laid in a sheet-piled cofferdam taken half-way across the river channel. This allowed the normal flow in the river to continue while the pipes were encased in concrete below river bed level. The sheet piles were then withdrawn and the whole process was then repeated for the other half of the river.

Crossing the railway line with minimal disruption to traffic was another challenge for the engineers. It was decided to route the pipelines through two lengths of bolted tunnel driven under the railway embankment, accessed by drop shafts on either side of the line.

Above: Pipes were encased in concrete below the bed level of the River Welland (Brian and Elizabeth Nicholls Photography)

Right: Crossing the River Welland at Tinwell (Brian and Elizabeth Nicholls Photography)

Reservoir Inlet Pipelines

Raw water from the rivers Nene and Welland starts the final part of its journey at the final lift pumping station located over the twin shafts (6A and 6B) near the downstream toe of the embankment at Empingham. From here twin reservoir inlet pipelines run along the southern shore of the reservoir for about 2.7km to the inlet jet control valves at Howells Inlet, near Normanton Church Museum. Four lines of pre-stressed concrete pipes carry the inlet water down into the reservoir from where it is discharged by four jets pointing up the south arm.

Installing the twin reservoir inlet pipes near Normanton (Brian and Elizabeth Nicholls Photography)

The four pipes to the inlet jets being installed across the valley floor near Normanton (Brian and Elizabeth Nicholls Photography)

The four inlet jets pointing up the south arm of the reservoir (Brian and Elizabeth Nicholls Photography)

Outlet and Overflow Works

The outlet shaft was sunk early in the project to serve as an access point when the River Gwash diversion tunnels were being driven. At the reservoir outlet, the shaft contains two 1.2m diameter cast iron standpipes with isolating valves, so that water for direct supply to the treatment works and river regulation can be drawn off from different levels, simultaneously if required, to overcome variations in quality. There are four outlet levels. The bottom outlet is through the river diversion tunnel, and the upper three through concrete tunnels, driven from the shaft to concrete forebays.

Water abstracted from the reservoir is piped to the raw water pumping station located alongside the river water final-lift pumping station. From here the raw water is pumped directly to Wing treatment works for treatment and distribution.

The reservoir overflow spillway is adjacent to the outlet shaft. It consists of a concrete-lined shaft with a 12m diameter bellmouth weir. The top level of the weir is 83.82m OD, and this sets the TWL (top water level) of the reservoir. Any water flowing over the weir free-falls to the base of the shaft. It then flows along a short length of overflow tunnel to the bottom half of the downstream tunnel. A breakwater was installed to shield the overflow bellmouth from reservoir wave action and hence prevent surges in the downstream tunnel. In order to avoid flooding problems at the head of the reservoir, the overflow weir was sized so that the water level would not rise more than 150mm above the weir. The system was designed to handle a flow of 18,000 litres per second.

A plan of the outlet and overflow area at the south end of the embankment (after the Institution of Civil Engineers)

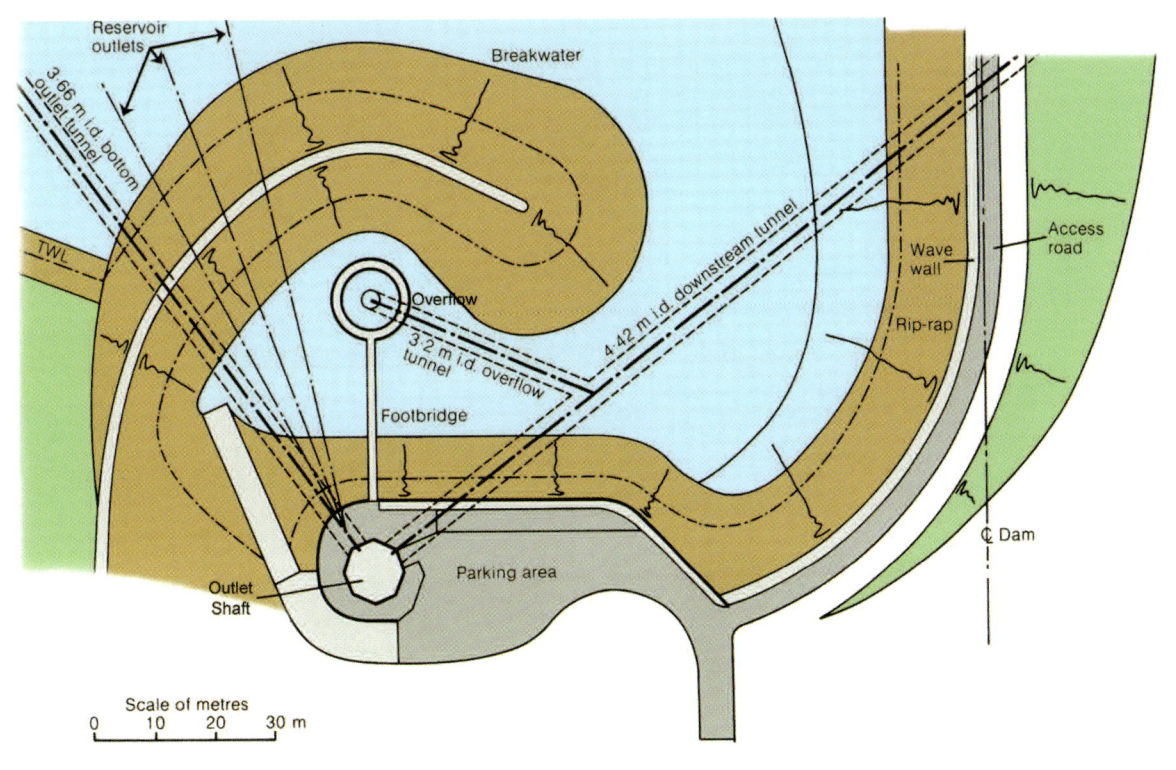

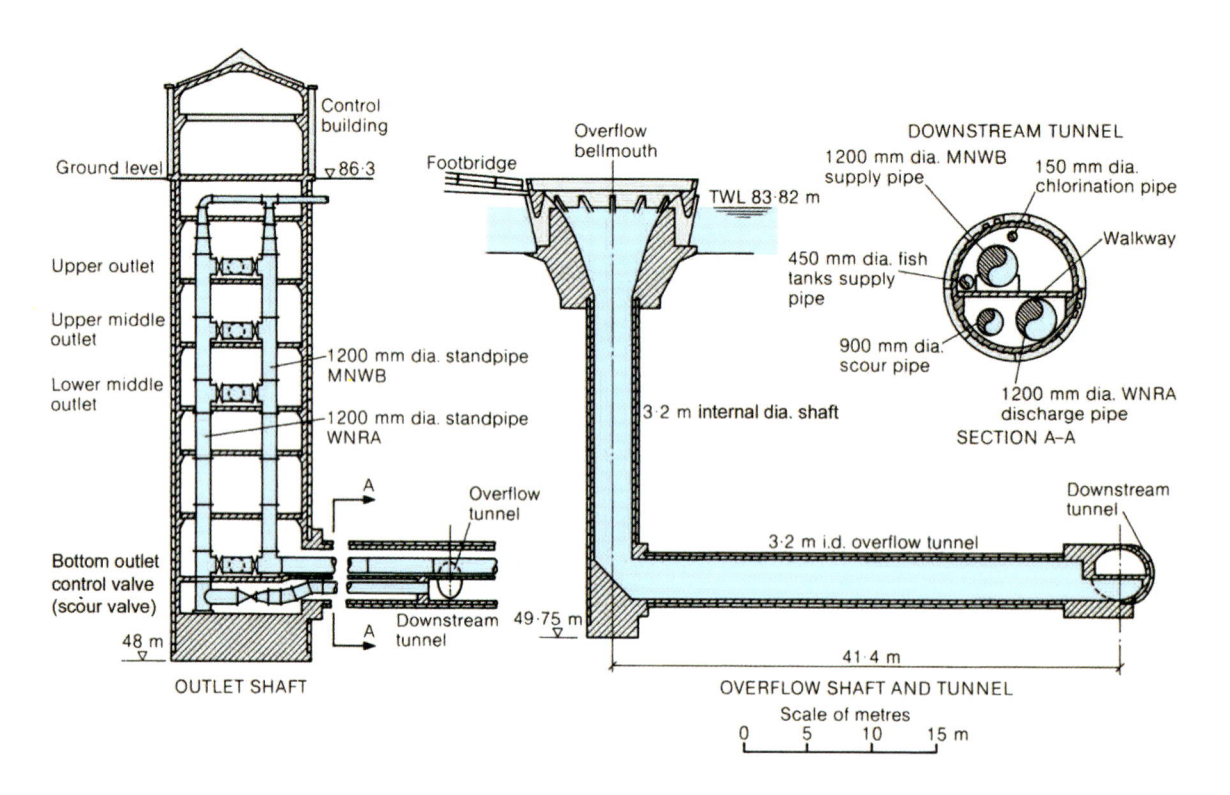

OUTLET SHAFT

- Ground level ▽ 86.3
- Control building
- Upper outlet
- Upper middle outlet
- Lower middle outlet
- 1200 mm dia. standpipe MNWB
- 1200 mm dia. standpipe WNRA
- Bottom outlet control valve (scour valve)
- Overflow tunnel
- Downstream tunnel
- 48 m

OVERFLOW SHAFT AND TUNNEL

- Footbridge
- Overflow bellmouth
- TWL 83.82 m
- 3.2 m internal dia. shaft
- 3.2 m i.d. overflow tunnel
- Downstream tunnel
- 49.75 m
- 41.4 m

DOWNSTREAM TUNNEL SECTION A–A

- 1200 mm dia. MNWB supply pipe
- 150 mm dia. chlorination pipe
- 450 mm dia. fish tanks supply pipe
- Walkway
- 900 mm dia. scour pipe
- 1200 mm dia. WNRA discharge pipe

Scale of metres: 0 5 10 15 m

Above: Outlet shaft and overflow sections (after the Institution of Civil Engineers)

Right: Building the outlet shaft (Brian & Elizabeth Nicholls Photography)

Right: Working on the overflow shaft (Brian & Elizabeth Nicholls Photography)

Above: Inside the overflow bay during construction (Brian & Elizabeth Nicholls Photography)

A secondary outlet tower was constructed in the north arm of the reservoir, with a 1.35m diameter pre-stressed concrete pipeline laid in the bed of the reservoir to the main outlet shaft.

Above: The secondary outlet tower in the north arm of the reservoir near Barnsdale (Andrew Burns)

Above Right: Looking along the secondary outlet pipe towards the limnological tower (Andrew Burns)

Reservoir Operation, Inlet Works and Secondary Outlet Shaft

Problems of algal blooms and of reservoir thermal stratification leading to the bottom water becoming starved of oxygen (anaerobic) were anticipated at the design stage of the reservoir. In order to overcome the algal problem, it was proposed that the north arm of the reservoir should be operated as a second reservoir, and a model of the reservoir was constructed by the River Authority to prove the feasibility of this proposal. Various combinations of inlet and outlet arrangements were tried using tracer dye to identify and record the different circulation patterns produced. It was found that the most effective scheme was to discharge all the water into the mouth of the south arm through an inlet jet system in the bottom of the reservoir, the four jets pointing up the arm of the reservoir. The normal water outlet is through the main outlet shaft, drawing water from the main body of the reservoir. In this way, the water that enters the north arm of the reservoir will have been subjected to a longer period of retention, and will be of different biological and chemical characteristics from that in the main body. When algal growth is experienced in the main body, it is unlikely to occur at the same time in the north arm and vice versa. To take advantage of this, a secondary outlet shaft and pipeline in the north arm allows water to be drawn from there during periods of bad algal growth in the main body, except at low water levels in the reservoir. In the unlikely case that algal growth affects the whole reservoir, river water can be pumped directly to the treatment works.

To prevent anaerobic conditions through stagnation, Helixor air-guns were installed. These consist of a vertical pipe into which compressed air is introduced at the base. The resulting air bubbles rise in the pipe, drawing water in behind. On exit from the pipe the spiralling cloud of air bubbles entrains a considerable quantity of water, producing a gradual overturn and mixing of water in the reservoir.

A permanent limnological tower was constructed in the main body of the reservoir to monitor biological, chemical and physical characteristics of the water, the results being used to control the operation of the air-guns. Limnology is the study of inland waters and the word derives from the Greek *limne* (lake) and *logos* (knowledge).

The two outlet shafts, together with the limnological tower, the inlet jets in the south arm, the Helixor air-gun installation to prevent stratification, and the diversion of the treated sewage effluent discharge from the Oakham area into one of the nature reserve lagoons, combine to give an overall reservoir operational system which will allow good quality water to be available for both direct supply and river regulation at all times of the year.

Building the limnological tower near Bull Bridge (Richard Adams)

Wing Water Treatment Works

The Wing treatment works receives raw water pumped from the pumping station at Empingham via a single 1.1m steel pipeline. It was designed and constructed by Degremont Laing Ltd and commissioned in June 1977. It can treat up to 285 million litres of raw water per day. From here drinkable water is distributed to both Anglian Water and Severn-Trent Water consumers.

Seepage Problems

The Marlstone Rock Bed is an aquifer up to 2.5m thick underlying the Upper Lias clay forming the bed of the reservoir, and it provides a potential seepage path for water from Rutland Water. It has been affected by valley bulging, resulting in some outcropping along the valley floor.

Investigations into potential seepage paths were carried out before construction of the reservoir started. These included the cataloguing of old well records, sinking boreholes, analysing river-water chemistry and carrying out field seepage trials. More data were obtained after de-watering of the aquifer following the rupture, early in the construction period, of the base of one of the shafts at Empingham, caused by uplift from the water pressure in the Marlstone. The investigations revealed that the pre-reservoir behaviour of the Marlstone aquifer was controlled largely by an outlet into the adjoining Chater valley, and that changes in groundwater levels there might result in land-slipping. It was therefore concluded that the water pressure in the area near the outlet should not be allowed to exceed pre-Rutland Water levels.

Various means of preventing seepage were considered but the most appropriate solution was to install relief wells downstream of the dam to release the additional water. Soon after the first filling of the reservoir a sudden rise in levels and discharges occurred. Extra relief wells were installed whilst unsuccessful searches were made for connections through the reservoir floor into the Marlstone Rock Bed. In particular, divers inspected the sites of known old wells, including those already backfilled with clay as part of the reservoir clearance works.

Research was also undertaken to locate any possible unrecorded wells, by interviewing local people and inspecting previously unseen records and maps, including those of the Ordnance Survey for 1886. This revealed that four old wells which might have penetrated the Marlstone remained unfilled in the reservoir floor. The largest was 1m square and 8.8m deep but no downward flow could be detected. All four wells were filled and capped between December 1977 and January 1978.

Various other causes were considered but the mechanism is not fully understood. However, the seepages soon stabilized to acceptable values and the behaviour of the aquifer continues to be satisfactory, with a steady discharge from the relief wells of about 185 litres per second.

Other Works

The new landscape. Trees planted at Whitwell car park in 1974 (Jim Eaton)

There are number of other aspects of the construction of Rutland Water which are covered in other chapters:

For landscaping and the creation of leisure facilities, *see* Chapter 22 – Rutland Water – Planning and Developing a Water Supply Reservoir as a World-Class Leisure Venue, Chapter 29 – Sailing on Rutland Water – Rutland Sailing Club, and Chapter 28 – Rutland Water Fishing.

For details of the project to save Normanton Church and its conversion into a museum, *see* Chapter 11 – Normanton.

For an account of the work involved in establishing the Nature Reserve, *see* Chapter 24 – Tim Appleton MBE – Thirty Years of Rutland Water Nature Reserve.

For accounts of archaeological excavations in the Gwash valley, *see* Chapter 18 – Brooches, Bathhouses and Bones – Archaeology in the Gwash Valley, Chapter 19 – The Archaeologists and Chapter 20 – Medieval Settlements at Nether Hambleton and Whitwell.

Filling and Commissioning

The pumps at Wansford, Tinwell and Empingham were first switched on by Dennis Howell, Minister of State at the Department of the Environment, on 15th September 1975. However, due to the severe drought in 1976, only limited pumping was possible for most of the year because of very low flows in the rivers. Filling of the reservoir commenced officially with the closing of the scour valve by A F Skinner, Chairman of the Anglian Water Authority on 6th February 1975 and continued steadily up to April 1979, when the water level first reached the crest of the spillway at 83.82m OD.

Filling of the reservoir officially commenced with the closing of the scour valve at a ceremony on 6th February 1975. In this picture are (left to right) Barry Gooding (Hydrologist), Harry Crowe (Reservoir Manager), Roland Field (Chief Scientist), Frank Knights (Reservoir Engineer), George Oglanby (Divisional Engineer), John Tindall (Finance Officer), and Peter Langford (Divisional Manager), all Anglian Water Authority employees (Brian & Elizabeth Nicholls Photography)

Right: Dennis Howell switching on the Wansford, Tinwell and Empingham pumps at what is now Howells Inlet near Normanton on 15th September 1975 (Brian & Elizabeth Nicholls Photography)

Below: Aerial view of Rutland Water looking north-east towards the dam and Empingham in 2006 (John Nowell, Zodiac Publishing)

Archaeological Sites in the Middle Gwash Valley

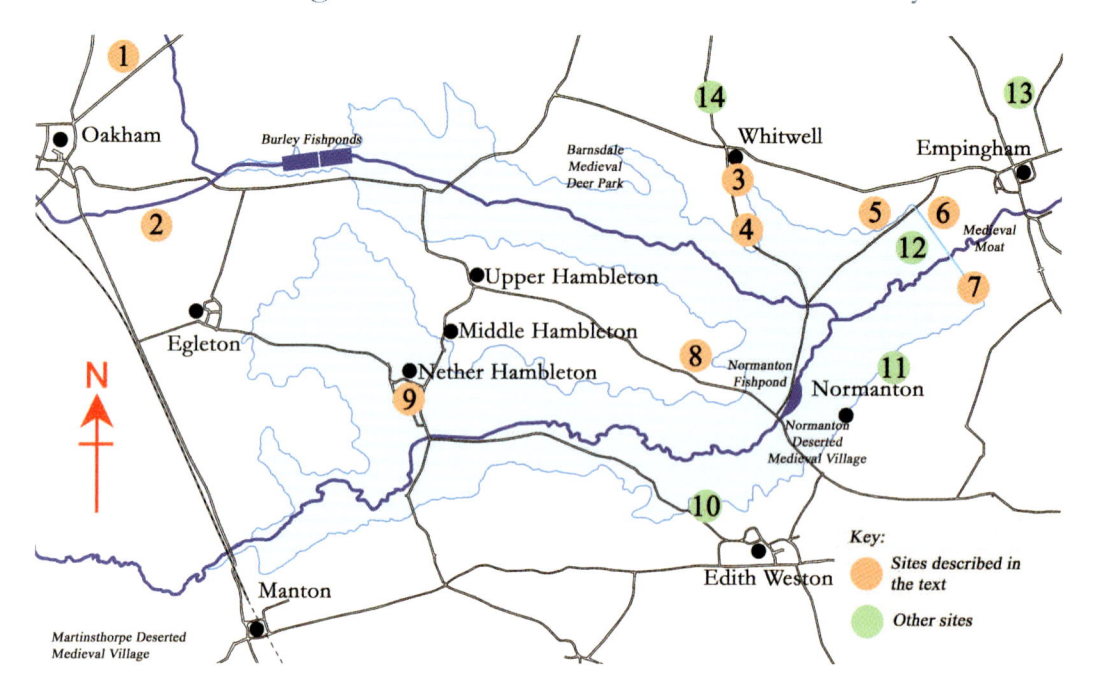

1. Burley Road, Oakham – Neolithic (New Stone Age) pit circle, Bronze age burial and Iron Age enclosure.
2. Oakham bypass route – Bronze Age male burial, ditches and line of pits.
3. Whitwell – Medieval settlement.
4. Whitwell – Iron Age and Romano-British site.
5. Sykes Lane, Empingham – Anglo-Saxon cemetery.
6. Empingham – Romano-British farmstead.
7. Empingham – Romano-British farmstead and Anglo-Saxon cemetery.
8. Hambleton peninsula – Iron Age and Romano-British site.
9. Nether Hambleton – Medieval settlement.
10. Rutland Sailing Club, Edith Weston – Romano-British burial.
11. Renner's Park, Normanton – Romano-British site including a corn drier.
12. Empingham – Iron Age and early Anglo-Saxon settlement.
13. Loves Lane, Empingham - Romano-British site.
14. Whitwell – Roman coin hoard.

The Archaeological Timeline

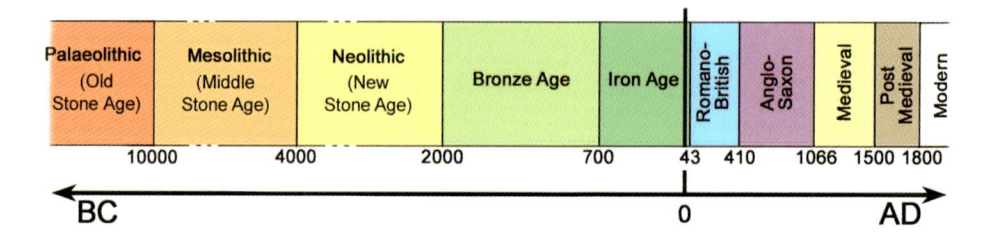

Chapter 18
Brooches, Bathhouses and Bones – Archaeology in the Gwash Valley
Kate Don

In January 1967 Shirley Palmer began to write a diary:

'Seven years ago an employee of Mr Eric Palmer of Church Farm, Empingham, whilst working in the fields, picked up a cruciform [cross-shaped] brooch in the ploughed field. No more was said about the archaeological find until 1967 when, while ploughing, Mr Palmer picked up a piece of bronze. This aroused his curiosity and then he decided to dig where he found the bronze piece and found a small drinking bucket and remains of a black pot.

'Mr Malcolm Dean, an archaeologist of Nottingham, was informed and he came down to Empingham with another archaeologist Miss Hilary Healey. He examined the finds and decided there must be a body there. It called for an excavation. Every Sunday onwards, Mr Dean and Miss Healey came and excavated the land.'

This excavation took place where the dam at Empingham would eventually be built. Up to that time very little was known about the archaeology of the Gwash Valley. The construction of Rutland Water would destroy any archaeology that was found, but, as topsoil was removed, a golden opportunity arose to see and record the ancient history of parts of the valley. No money had been set aside for this task, nor had any plans been made for archaeological investigation in advance of this major project. Grants from the Ministry of Public Building and Works, and later the Department of the Environment, were made as and when archaeology was uncovered. Professional archaeologists, students and volunteers worked against the clock to bring us the stories of the people who lived in this part of Rutland. The dam at Empingham, the visitor centres and car parks at Whitwell and Sykes Lane, and the now-drowned hamlet of Nether Hambleton were some of the main sites of excavation. Farmsteads, cemeteries and other buildings were found together with some very exciting objects, some of which are on display at Rutland County Museum.

Above: Two Anglo-Saxon cruciform brooches (RCM)

— 403 —

Empingham

Above: A male Anglo-Saxon skeleton with a spearhead, to the right, and a pot, to the left, of the skull (Shirley Palmer)

Shirley Palmer describes the first 'dig' at Empingham as 'a small excavation'. Mr Dean and Miss Healey uncovered two Anglo-Saxon skeletons during the early part of 1967, one male and one female. Both were buried with personal possessions, the man with an iron spear and a knife and the woman with beads, a shoulder-clasp and a square-headed brooch. This practice was typical of the early pagan Anglo-Saxons and demonstrated wealth and status. Waves of such Germanic migrants arrived to settle in Britain and through their possessions it is estimated that they arrived in Rutland around AD 500. Place names can often give clues to the origins of a settlement. The last three letters of Empingham, '-ham', meaning a village, estate or homestead, are typically Anglo-Saxon. '-inga' means 'the people of', so 'Empingham' is 'the village of Empa's people'.

The Ministry of Public Building and Works granted £450 for further excavation in March and April 1967. Students from Newark, Nottingham, Grantham and Bourne were paid the sum of ten shillings a day and lived in tents close to the site. Prisoners from HMP Ashwell were also brought in on a daily basis to act as labourers.

Students take a meal in their tented camp at Empingham (Shirley Palmer)

It became clear as the number of skeletons rose to fourteen that this was a cemetery. Two distinct groups of burials were found, the first with many grave goods including brooches, beads, buckles, spearheads and knives. These people were clearly pagan and their possessions were dated to AD 425-550. The second group were probably early Christians. There were very few grave goods and the burials were neatly laid out. Life was evidently hard. Some of the skeletons showed signs of arthritis, tuberculosis, tooth abscesses and anaemia. A hearth and post-holes (for posts which held up thatched roofs) pointed to dwellings. Articles used for weaving were found including a spindle whorl, a bone needle and a bone pin beater used to push back loose threads. Furnace bases and slag indicated metalworking. Romano-British and Anglo-Saxon pottery was recovered and a section of Roman road was revealed which suggested that there might be a Romano-British settlement nearby.

Above: Malcolm Dean, Director of Excavations, and student Elizabeth Sharman reconstruct Romano-British pots (Grantham Journal)

A row of reconstructed Romano-British pots (Shirley Palmer)

Further excavations took place in August 1969 and 1970, by which time the pay had risen to £1 a day, although a deduction of £2 10s a week was made for food! An exciting discovery was that of a Romano-British farmstead in an adjacent field. The valley side had been terraced to provide construction platforms for three buildings, one of them with an aisled barn, a cobbled farmyard and a well. The well had been filled with rubbish about AD 270 and an unusual wooden shoe was recovered from the bottom. The leather straps had rotted away and it had broken into three pieces.

Above: The upper part of the Romano-British wooden shoe recovered from the well at Empingham. The leather straps had perished (Sam Gorin)

Above: The underside of the shoe (Sam Gorin)

Many items of personal adornment were found including brooches, hairpins, rings, pendants and belt fittings. Bone needles and loom weights indicated weaving. Gaming counters made of bone attest to the Roman fondness for games. A well-preserved corn drier was also uncovered together with a metal working hearth. These people were not just farming but also making farm implements. Iron nails, a hammer head and a chisel were amongst the tools unearthed.

(Left to right): Graham Parkes, Joe Bach, Mary Harman and Jim Neville (in the well) excavate the Romano-British well (Stamford Mercury)

Just 400m to the north, on the north side of the River Gwash, a second Romano-British farmstead was found in 1971. There was an aisled building with evidence of an underfloor hot-air heating system, a bathhouse and painted wall plaster. This appears to have been a fairly comfortable place to live and rather grander than the first farmstead. Items of jewellery were also found including bone, copper and brass pins and blue glass beads. Five

— 406 —

A Romano-British zoomorphic brooch decorated with the head of a dog (RCM)

A Romano-British coin of the reign of Carausius, mid-third century AD (Shirley Palmer)

middle Anglo-Saxon period Christian burials were cut through the floor of the Roman building, a practice that has been seen elsewhere in Europe. A gravedigger would not go to the trouble of digging through a floor unless there was a good reason, especially when there was soft earth nearby. The building may have been remodelled into a church or chapel and this is the most likely reason.

These two farmsteads seem to be linked. A striking find was made of two stone coffins on opposite sides of the Gwash, roughly at where the ends of the dam stand today. The coffins were facing each other with the feet pointing to the river. Both were of Barnack stone; both had two pots, one inside the other, placed outside the coffin at the foot of the grave; and both were on the same north-northwest alignment. The grave to the north contained a man aged over 45, and that to the south held the remains of a woman with a child placed between her legs. Some kind of relationship must surely have existed between these people. What that might have been we will never know.

Four miles to the east of the farmsteads and also standing on the River Gwash was the Roman fort and town at Great Casterton. It seems very unlikely that the river was navigable at that time, but there would certainly have been trackways running along the valley floor to the town and its markets. Great Casterton stood on Ermine Street, the main Roman road from London to the northeast. The A1 closely follows the same route today. In addition to local produce and wares the Empingham farmers would have had access to fine pottery, foods and wine imported from the Mediterranean and the Continent. Stamford, Lincolnshire, which is only a few miles from Great Casterton, stands on the River Welland and this was almost certainly navigable to the east coast at this time. It may have provided another route for imports from the Continent.

A Romano-British belt buckle (Shirley Palmer)

Sykes Lane, Empingham

At what is now the visitor centre at Sykes Lane near Empingham a remarkable find was made. As the topsoil was stripped away a large pagan Anglo-Saxon cemetery was revealed. In total there were 132 graves containing 150 skeletons, three-quarters of them buried with grave goods. This was a wealthy society. Men were buried with spears, buckles, belt fittings and shields made of leather or wood, the iron fittings being the only parts to survive. Warriors were held in high esteem and the large number of weapons found here suggests that warfare, or the threat of it, was rife. Communities were constantly battling to increase their territories and thus their power. Women of high status were interred with finely-worked brooches, necklaces of glass and amber, rings, bone combs and sometimes domestic articles such as buckets, bowls and keys.

An Anglo-Saxon bucket (RCM)

An Anglo-Saxon skeleton under excavation at Sykes Lane (Brian & Elizabeth Nicholls Photography)

These possessions allow the cemetery to be dated to the late sixth or early seventh centuries AD. It is possible that the graves were marked in some way as very few graves cut into another, although a number of multiple graves were found. For many, life was short. About half of the population had died under the age of twenty-five, although some survived to middle age. The height range was much as it is today with men between 5ft 3in and 6ft 1in and women 4ft 10in and 5ft 11in. A curious find was the cremated remains of a twelve-month-old child. Why the infant was cremated and not buried like the rest of the population is a puzzle.

An Anglo-Saxon bone comb (RCM)

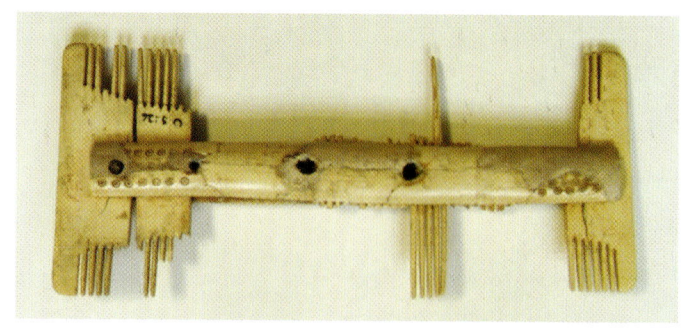

Whitwell

Right: The Iron Age section of the Whitwell excavation. Sherds of Iron Age pottery, post-holes and pits were found inside the ditch enclosure and beneath the foundations of the Roman farmstead (after Malcolm Todd)

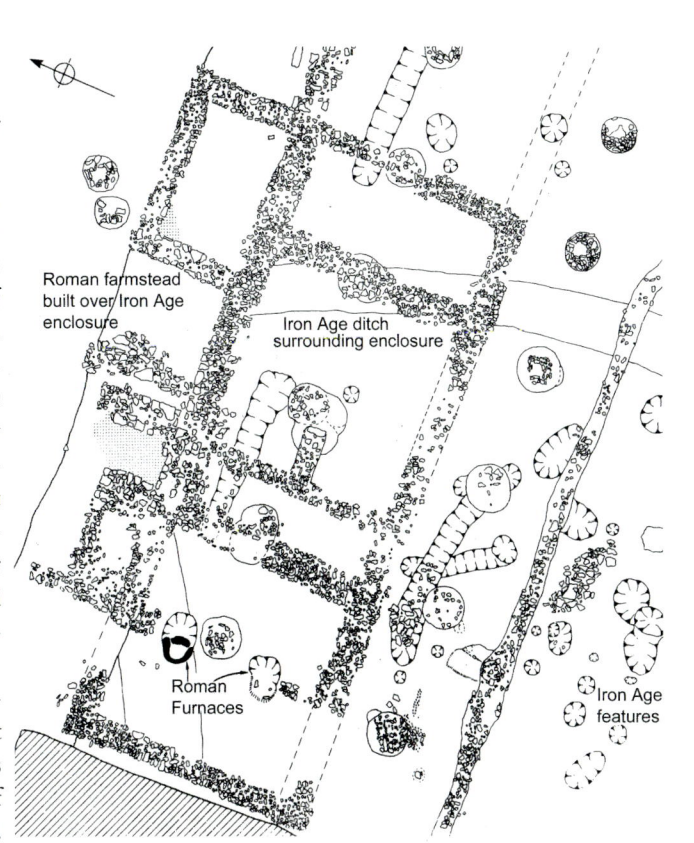

Below: A Romano-British corn drier (Shirley Palmer)

Ground clearance ahead of the construction of an office building for Anglian Water, the fishing lodge, sailing lodge and car parks resulted in the discovery of a wide scatter of Iron Age and Romano-British pottery. There were also signs of ditches, pits and stone buildings. This was totally unexpected. A team of excavators was quickly brought together and worked throughout August and September 1976, December 1976 and January 1977 under the direction of Malcolm Todd.

Post-holes, pits and ditches of an Iron Age settlement were identified and this was the first significant find of Iron Age material in Rutland. No certain evidence of buildings was found, but it is likely that a number of round houses would have formed a homestead, possibly in an enclosure.

The site was abandoned about a hundred years before the Roman conquest of AD 43 and was re-occupied by around AD 50. Over the centuries of Roman occupation there were successive phases of construction. A timber aisled building was replaced in the third century by a rectangular structure with stone foundations. This seems to have been at the heart of the settlement. Corn-drying ovens were found together with evidence of metal working. As at Empingham, this was a farming community that made at least some of the tools they needed.

A notable find was that of a large strap junction, part of a horse harness, dating from the days before Roman occupation. The site was finally abandoned in the mid-fourth century and the fields used as pasture for many years. The lack of ploughing helps to explain why no ancient finds had been made here in the past.

Below: Part of a late Iron Age horse harness (RCM)

— 409 —

Another site in Whitwell was investigated by Rutland Field Research Group between 1976 and 1996. On this site the building foundations of a shrunken medieval village complex were excavated and pottery sherds ranging from early Stamford ware to Midland Purple and Cistercian wares were found, together with a silver circular halfpenny of about AD 1280. Charcoal, smelted iron and slag were also found. It appears that the buildings were occupied from the eleventh to the seventeenth century.

Nether Hambleton

Nether Hambleton was destined to sink beneath the waves of Rutland Water. Before it did, members of the Rutland Field Research Group, under the guidance of Miss Christine Mahany of Stamford, undertook an excavation between 1973 and 1976. As turf was removed pottery was found ranging in date from the eleventh to the fifteenth centuries. A substantial rectangular medieval building was uncovered. In one corner, ash and charcoal led to the discovery of a large oven.

Below: Excavation site at Nether Hambleton (Tim Clough)

Over four and a half thousand sherds (or pieces) of pottery were recovered and it was possible to reconstruct some pots. Much of the pottery was made locally at Stamford and Bourne (Lincolnshire) and Lyveden (Northamptonshire). Some coins were also found. It is possible that such coins resulted from Baltic trade with east coast ports like Boston and Spalding (Lincolnshire) or Lynn (Norfolk), all of which would have served merchants for example in Stamford which is less than ten miles east of Nether Hambleton.

A total of 250 'small finds' was made including pegs and hooks, horseshoe fragments, knife blades, a mason's chisel, whetstones, buckles and belt decorations. The large number of nails found on the floor of the building showed where roof beams had collapsed. Bones and teeth from many species were found including sheep, cattle, ox, pig, and horse. It seems that the diet was quite varied. The decline of Nether Hambleton in the late fourteenth and early fifteenth centuries was probably due, in part, to waves of plague.

For a more detailed account of the Nether Hambleton and Whitwell projects *see* Chapter 20 – Medieval Settlements of Nether Hambleton and Whitwell.

Working on the south-west corner of the medieval house at Nether Hambleton in June 1973 (Fred Adams)

Hambleton Peninsula

Aerial photographs can provide excellent evidence of settlement sites and farming activity. Differences in crop height, and sometimes colour, may show the outline of buildings, ditches and other features.

A photograph of the Hambleton peninsula illustrates how effective 'aerials' can be. A large rectangular Iron Age enclosure measuring 120m x 80m is clearly visible. Inside it are two circular features, the smaller thought to be a dwelling and the larger an animal enclosure. Dating of the site was confirmed by fieldwalking in 1992 when Iron Age pottery was found along with a large amount of Romano-British pottery. As at Whitwell this site was occupied for many years, although not necessarily continuously, possibly from as early as the fourth century BC to the fourth century AD.

An Iron Age enclosure on Hambleton peninsula (Jim Pickering, National Monuments Record)

The Gwash Valley in Prehistoric Times

There is ample evidence that man was living in and around the valley from Middle Stone Age times, around seven thousand years ago. Fieldwalking by Rutland Field Research Group and Leicester University resulted in the collection of many hundreds of worked flint tools. Some were also found at the excavation sites mentioned previously.

These ancient Rutlanders led a 'hunting and gathering' lifestyle, following the herds of red deer, wild ox and wild pig for meat and harvesting fruits and plants from the countryside and

Right: A worked flint from the shoreline at Sykes Lane (RO)

forests around them. Flint was used to craft arrowheads, spearheads and cutting tools capable of killing and butchering even large animals. Particularly large concentrations of flint were found on top of the Hambleton peninsula and high above the valley floor at Normanton. It is probable that these were amongst the first areas of the valley to be cleared of woodland. Worked flints can still be found today along the shoreline between Whitwell and Sykes Lane where the land was not disturbed by construction work.

In February 2006 archaeologists excavating along the route of the Oakham bypass not far from Egleton came across the remains of what may prove to be a Bronze Age man. Estimated to be up to 4,500 years old, the body was buried between two ditches. This practice is thought to have had some kind of ritual significance. It is not yet clear what that might have been. The man, of about twenty years of age, was placed in a crouched position, the usual practice at that time. Several fragments of pottery and flint were also found which may help to date the burial more accurately.

The crouched body of what is believed to be a Bronze Age man, found on the route of the Oakham bypass (Rutland County Council)

The ditches and a line of pits may be evidence of the earliest ways in which the land was divided. Environmental samples were taken, including pollen, which may give an indication of the species which grew in the area and how the landscape looked. At the time of writing the remains and other finds are subject to scientific analysis and archaeological work is ongoing, but the site is certain to complement the evidence from another prehistoric site not far away on the north-eastern outskirts of Oakham, near Burley Road. Here a salvage excavation under the direction of Patrick Clay prior to the construction of a new road and housing estate discovered a New Stone Age pit circle, a Bronze Age burial and an Iron Age enclosure containing three hearths for iron smelting. People had evidently been active on this site from around 6,000 years ago to the Roman conquest in AD 43.

An alignment of pits found on the site of the Oakham bypass. They are thought to be Bronze Age (Rutland County Council)

Without Rutland Water, and more recently the Oakham bypass, we would probably still know little about the archaeology of the Gwash Valley. What we do know is very much dictated by where construction of the dam and visitor facilities took place and the current building works along the route of the new road. Much of the ancient history of the drowned valley will remain hidden from us. It is likely that there would have been other Romano-British farmsteads alongside the river which flows to the Roman town at Great Casterton. If so, they now rest beneath the waves. However, detailed reports on many of the sites in the Gwash valley that were investigated have been published, including the Empingham cemeteries and Whitwell Iron Age and Roman settlement (*see* Bibliography). There are also records of the Archaeological watching briefs that were carried out along the routes of the pipelines linking Rutland Water to the Welland, the Nene and the Wing treatment works and those taking the treated water to its far-off destinations.

If Rutland Water was proposed today, professional archaeologists would be consulted before any construction work took place and a programme of archaeological investigation would be agreed with the developer. In the case of the Oakham bypass this has, of course, taken place. Rutland County Council, Archaeological Project Services and Alfred McAlpine are working closely together to ensure that any archaeology that is uncovered during the works is thoroughly investigated and recorded. However, we cannot turn the clock back. A debt of gratitude is owed to those professionals and amateurs who worked hard, and often under great time constraints, to tell us at least part of the story of this corner of Rutland.

Aspects of Topography

High Bridge Road

High Bridge, also known as Hambleton Bridge, was across the River Gwash on the Lyndon to Upper Hambleton Road. This road was joined from the east by Gibbet Lane just before High Bridge. From here it passed through Nether Hambleton, over the River Eg at Hobbs Bridge, and on to Middle Hambleton. Most of this area is now under Rutland Water.

In *Just Rutland*, published in 1953, J and A E Stokes described this route in one of their journeys:

'After crossing two flat grass fields, the road twisted sharply into a fiercely steep and narrow track, bordered by big old gorse bushes whose golden fires were swiftly dying. Ahead and far below lay the valley of the Gwash . . .

'Rutland at its very best is here, gorgeous scenery on the Rutland scale, serene and dignified, aloof, independent, and utterly unspoiled. No motor coaches travel this wild little road; probably no motor coach could make it, and would certainly be unwise to try . . .

'The gated way ended with an old stone bridge over the Gwash . . . There are quite big fish in the little river; we stood watching them darting in the shadow of the bridge . . . .'

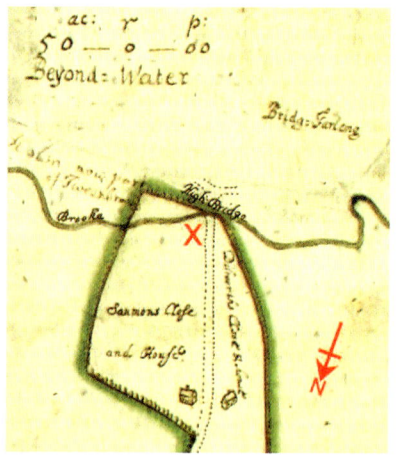

High Bridge (at X) on a map prepared following the enclosure of Hambleton in 1653 (Edward Conant)

High Bridge road looking north towards Middle Hambleton from Nether Hambleton in 1972. The turn to Egleton is on the left (Richard Adams)

Above: Hobbs Bridge over the River Eg (Fred Adams)
Right: High Bridge in 1970, looking north (Jim Eaton)

Chapter 19
The Archaeologists
Sheila Sleath and Robert Ovens

Today, planning to build the largest reservoir in the United Kingdom would entail a full-scale investigation by professional archaeologists before any construction work could start. In the late 1960s there was no such planning requirement, and in any case commercial archaeological units capable of undertaking investigations of this magnitude did not then exist. Only the Ministry of Public Building and Works through its Inspectorate of Ancient Monuments (the forerunner of English Heritage), some university archaeology departments, a few local authority museums or, rarely, local archaeological societies had the resources to initiate this kind of work. Locally, the Rutland County Museum had only just come into being, and it was the archaeology department of the University of Nottingham that initially took up, and continued to maintain, an interest in the archaeological potential of the reservoir area. Consequently, most of the excavation work was carried out by trained volunteers, including members of the newly-formed Rutland Field Research Group, supervised by a few professionals and encouraged by Anthea Diver, first Curator of the Rutland County Museum.

In the knowledge that the reservoir was on its way, early investigations were concentrated on previously identified sites, but as work on the reservoir progressed and new discoveries of Romano-British and Anglo-Saxon sites were made, particularly near the eastern end, rescue excavations became the norm. In 1968, Anthea Diver was in charge of the excavation of a Roman building near the future line of the dam, and other early excavations were directed by Nottingham archaeologists Hilary Healey and Malcolm Dean, until he was tragically killed in a car accident in May 1970. From the summer of 1971, Sam Gorin of Newark (Nottinghamshire), one of Malcolm Dean's students, directed archaeological activities at the reservoir site, and this included organising watching briefs where topsoil was being removed by contractors' machinery. Archaeologist Christine Mahany of Stamford (Lincolnshire) guided the work of the Rutland Field Research Group at Nether Hambleton, which began in early 1973.

In 1974, when Rutland County Museum became part of the enlarged Leicestershire Museums, Arts & Records Service following local government reorganisation, Tim Clough, himself an archaeologist, became involved as Keeper of the museum. The discovery of a second Anglo-Saxon cemetery, at Sykes Lane, led to the involvement of the Ancient Monuments Inspectorate, and when the remains of Romano-British buildings and Iron Age occupation sites came to light near Whitwell in 1976 it was Professor Malcolm Todd and the University of Nottingham that led the investigations. In subsequent years, archaeologists from Leicestershire Museums and from the University of Leicester have also made major contributions to archaeological and historical studies of the Gwash valley. Detailed archaeological reports on many of these sites have been published (*see* Bibliography).

The following newspaper articles and a volunteer's personal memories illustrate those exciting early times.

From the *Nottingham Evening Post*, Friday 2nd August 1974 by David Lowe:

Into the Past
Before the Waters come to Drown it

The East Midlands will soon have its own Great Lake at Empingham Reservoir, halfway between Oakham and Stamford. But before the water rushes in, archaeologists are working against the clock to discover as much as possible about Iron Age, Roman and Anglo-Saxon settlements on the site. *The Post* has talked to some of the people who are spending their summer holidays on the 'dig with a difference . . .'

Nottinghamshire archaeologist Sam Gorin is a down-to-earth chap. But the blood really stirred in his veins when the driver of a giant excavator reported, 'We've found eight Saxon warriors – and they've still got their helmets on'. That was just a few weeks ago. Now skeletons are uncovered almost daily on the site of what will be Britain's biggest man-made lake at Empingham.

If that name means nothing to you it soon will. By 1978 the lovely Gwash Valley in rural Rutland (few people here accept the merger with Leicestershire) will house a huge reservoir almost the size of Windermere with recreation facilities to match.

The 'little Lake District' is something for the future. Meanwhile women like Mrs Anita Brown are much more interested in stepping back into the past. And as one of Mr Gorin's voluntary diggers – all working against the clock – she takes along one-year-old baby Daniel too. 'He's as good as gold in his pram', says Mrs Brown, who has wanted to go on a dig ever since she was a little girl – and is now getting the chance, along with local villagers, students and an evening class from Radcliffe-on-Trent.

Sam Gorin, in charge of the Empingham excavation, looks down on an Anglo-Saxon skeleton (Nottingham Evening Post)

'Found anything, Mum?' Baby Daniel peers round his pram while his mother Mrs Anita Brown sifts through soil on the Empingham excavation site (Nottingham Evening Post)

In the Blood

But surely it's a bit grisly picking away at a pile of bones? 'Not at all,' she insists. 'It gets in the blood. When we pack up I can't wait to get back next morning. It's like starting a new chapter – except this is more exciting than any history book.' Mrs Brown, her husband Alan and their 14-year-old son Sam are getting St Tropez standard tans by spending part of their summer holiday at Empingham. All have made interesting finds. Mrs Brown has discovered a gilded cruciform brooch, a comb made out of bone and beads 'so beautiful they might have just come out of the shop today'. And the floor of the site caravan is filled with boxes of remains – jewellery, knives and spears. Enough to keep Oakham Museum [Rutland County Museum] busy for years.

Snobs . . .

The site is so rich because it was Saxon snobbishness to bury their dead with their most cherished possessions. 'We didn't find the helmets on the warriors,' says Mr Gorin, a 28-year-old lecturer in archaeology at Newark Technical College. They turned out to be the remains of shields.

But it shows how keen local lorry drivers have become to assist the archaeologists. So too have the Welland and Nene River Authority, who own the land, the engineers, architects and contractors all working on the £25,000,000 project. The Department of the Environment have even weighed in with a £1,000 grant to help the dig.

Enthusiasm

It all started in 1967 when a farmer's plough unearthed a Saxon cruciform brooch. Since then an Iron Age settlement, a Roman farmyard and buildings and three Saxon huts have been excavated. The Saxon cemetery now being dug dates from 500 to 600 AD and so far more than 80 skeletons have been found. The haul is expected to top 100 by the time the dig ends in a few weeks.

Of course there have been one or two wild goose chases. For instance a Roman wall turned out to be old field drains. But the enthusiasm is there, which is the main thing says Sam's chief assistant,

Mr Bill Thomas, an Empingham laboratory assistant who has been with the dig throughout.

Recently a rumour swept the site that the excavation was short of diggers. So one weekend a carload of people arrived with picks and shovels asking: 'Where do we start?' In fact, for safety's sake, the site is strictly supervised and parties of sightseers are shown round only on Sunday afternoons.

A Race

The entire dig has been what Mr Gorin calls real rescue archaeology, trowelling away while the giant earth moving machines almost work round them. It's a race against time because the huge clay dam is now complete and next April they begin filling the great horseshoe-shaped reservoir.

The project means the demolition of a hamlet and the diversion of the A606 road, plus the building of massive aqueducts – a major engineering feat. But the public have much to gain, besides an additional and urgently needed water supply for much of the East Midlands, including Leicester, Peterborough New Town and parts of Lincolnshire. For the Welland and Nene River Authority intend to develop it as a beauty spot and a waterman's delight with sailing marinas, canoe courses, picnic areas, fishing rights and a wildlife sanctuary with prepared observation posts.

Preserved

The Saxon cemetery being excavated will eventually become a car park, screened from the road by trees. But not all archaeological treasures will be lost to the bulldozer. Two skeletons are being lifted and after examination by bone specialists they will be preserved in a car park display.

My Skeleton

Brenda May was another of the many volunteer archaeologists who took part in excavations before and during the construction of Rutland Water. Here she recounts some of her memories:

'I had always been interested in archaeology and jumped at the chance to enrol in a class in Radcliffe on Trent, Nottinghamshire, on archaeology for beginners. The tutor was Sam Gorin who was responsible for any archaeological finds made at what would become Rutland Water. There was real excitement when he had a message to say that a possible Anglo-Saxon cemetery had been found at Empingham and he asked if any of us could help to excavate it. The site was at what is now the visitor centre at Sykes Lane near Empingham.

'So for most of that early summer of 1974, I drove the thirty miles to Empingham several days a week loaded down with food, spare clothes, pushchair and my two-year-old daughter Catherine. Joy Baptie and Kathleen

Hardy, two of my friends from Radcliffe, also came with me. We had to park at the side of the road between Whitwell and Empingham, climb through the hedge and then trudge across to the site. This was fenced off with barbed wire and was about 40 square metres.

'The site proved to be a large pagan Anglo-Saxon cemetery. The ground was very dry and stony and the graves had been damaged by the heavy machinery passing over them. The weather was kind to us and we soon got into the swing of it. It was just so exciting and we were so keen to get back there each day. In total we found 150 skeletons in 132 graves.

Brenda May excavates a skeleton, watched by daughter Catherine (Brenda May)

'Most of the skeletons had jewellery and ornaments, notably bronze shoulder brooches, pendants, and red and blue glass beads. Some of the skeletons had also been buried with pots. I found a small ammonite fossil in the neck area of one grave. When we cleaned it we discovered that it had a small hole drilled through the middle and that it had been painted red. It had obviously been used as a necklace. One skeleton was of a female, and she was holding a new-born baby. It was a bit unnerving to find two skulls. Another skeleton I excavated was later taken away to be preserved. First a shallow trench was dug round it and this was then filled with plaster. When the plaster had set the soil was scraped away from underneath before the skeleton was removed from the site. It is now in Normanton Church Museum.

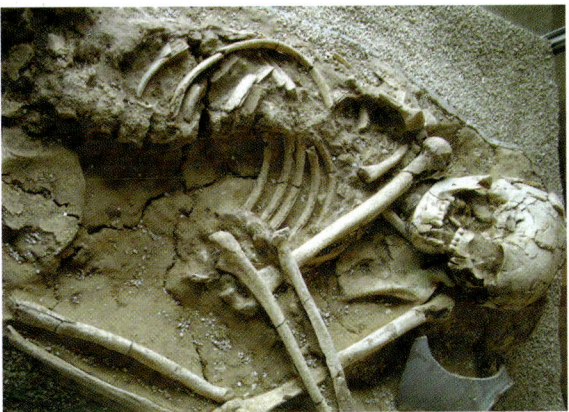

The female skeleton excavated by Brenda May, now in Normanton Church Museum (RO)

Roger Sandford of Rutland County Museum preparing the female skeleton for removal (Brenda May)

'For me, the Empingham dig was the achievement of a life-time's ambition to get into archaeology. I continued to dig in and around Nottingham, and later in Colchester where I now live. I recently returned to Rutland Water for the first time in 32 years. What a wonderful place it is now. Of course, the highlight for me was being reunited with my skeleton. We sailed across to Normanton Church Museum on the Rutland Belle. I was first off the boat and first in the museum. I was thrilled to see her looking much the same as when I last saw her, chuffed to bits in fact.'

From the *Leicester Mercury*, Thursday 4th May 1972:
Empingham Exhibition

A wooden Roman sandal, thought to be the only one ever found in England, was the star attraction last night at a show of relics unearthed at the Empingham reservoir site. The sandal, a size seven and fitting the left foot, was brought along to an open meeting of the W.I. in the Empingham Audit Hall by archaeology lecturer Mr Sam Gorin (25), who has been involved in digs at Empingham since 1969. He recalled that archaeological work began at Empingham following the lucky find of a Saxon brooch in the mid-60s by farmer Mr. Eric Palmer, of Church Farm, Empingham.

The find led to the first dig at Empingham, where an Anglo-Saxon burial ground was unearthed. Among the finds was the skeleton of a six foot seven inch man who had been buried along with his spear and vessels to hold food and drink for him in the afterlife. The next exciting discovery was the site of a Roman farmyard on which a well was found. It appeared that something had happened to stop the Romans using the water from the well and it had become a sort of dustbin. Into the well had been thrown the sandal together with items of wood, leather, clothing and the remains of 17 sheep, which had probably been slaughtered nearby. Later a Roman farmhouse was revealed. The occupants had lived in fairly comfortable accommodation as the building had an elaborate system of underfloor heating.

Another first which marks the Empingham site as being of unusual interest was the finding of a square well in the farmhouse area. This was a stone structure, explained Mr. Gorin, who added that normally square wells of this period were made in wood and as far as he knows this is the only one found of its type in England.

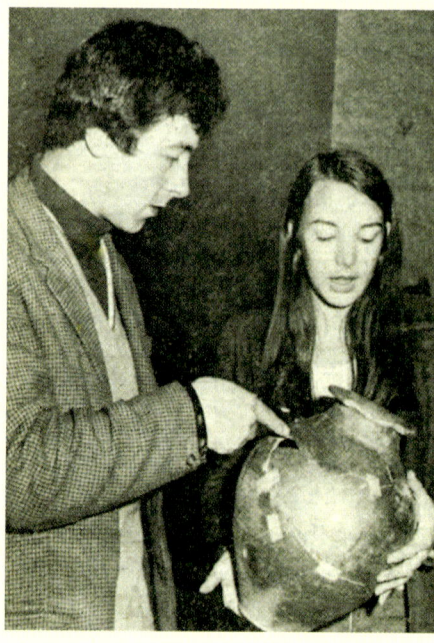

Sam Gorin, who had been involved with archaeological digs at the new Empingham reservoir site since 1969, shows a Roman water jug to Miss Elizabeth Dalby of Exton, one of the visitors to the exhibition of finds held at Audit Hall, Empingham 3rd May 1972 (Leicester Mercury)

Chapter 20
Medieval Settlements at Nether Hambleton and Whitwell
Tim Clough

Following the acquisition of land for the construction of Rutland Water in the early 1970s, a programme of archaeological fieldwalking was begun by the newly-formed Rutland Field Research Group for Archaeology and History, based at the Rutland County Museum. At Nether Hambleton this revealed earthworks which seem not to have been noticed previously, centred on OS plot no 177 (National Grid reference SK 894067), part of the land to be inundated; these were identified as the site of a medieval settlement. The earthworks continued into two small adjoining fields, a total extent of less than ten acres. The area was flanked to the north-west and south-east by four farmhouses and six cottages, five of which were thatched. These were all examined prior to their demolition.

It was decided in 1972 that a training excavation on a 'rescue' basis should be attempted, to be continued until reservoir construction and flooding precluded any further work. Permission was given by Mrs Gregory, the sitting tenant of the small farm at Woodbine House overlooking the site, to excavate a small area which appeared to enclose one house platform. Archaeologist Christine Mahany of Stamford agreed to supervise the work, which began in early 1973. The professional guidance and direction given helped considerably to expand the limited experience of Group members and to maintain their enthusiasm. The Group's Chairman was Les Emmerson, the excavation was led by Sqn Ldr Fred Adams, and the main participants were Jo Ecob, Jack and Maureen Dodds, and Olive Adams. Additional assistance was provided by staff and pupils of schools in the area and staff and men from Ashwell Prison near Oakham. Eventually, the rising level of Rutland Water meant that the excavation, which had continued part-time for three years, had to end, and the Group's activities continued elsewhere. A summary of the results of this work, identifying a medieval house site that went through several phases of development, was published in a multi-disciplinary volume covering many aspects of research carried out during the construction of Rutland Water (Adams *et al* 1982, 64 and fig 5). A programme of historical research was also initiated, using the resources of Leicester University Library, the Record Office for Leicestershire, Leicester & Rutland, and Lincolnshire Archives.

Several years on, in 1976, the construction of the reservoir was nearing completion, and action had been taken to clear higher ground south of Whitwell village for the building of the planned Fishing Lodge, Rescue Centre and other buildings. Part of the work included bull-dozing land adjacent to Whitwell Old Hall, OS plot nos 47 and 58 (National Grid reference SK 924087), where a proposal to erect cottages for reservoir staff south of a dividing hedge led to some turf and soil clearance. The exposure of large stone building blocks led to postponement of the work and called for a full archaeological investigation, which took place with the permission of Mrs Senior and Captain Cavenagh, who then owned the Old Hall building complex and adjoining paddocks.

Members of the Rutland Field Research Group and others were transferred from assisting on the Romano-British site which had been discovered on the Whitwell peninsula (*see* Chapter 18 – Brooches, Bathhouses and Bones – Archaeology in the Gwash Valley) and set to work on the new area, at first under the direction of Malcolm Todd of Nottingham University. It became clear that the paddock west of the Old Hall was the site of medieval buildings at the southern end of Whitwell village, lying between the Old Hall and Bull Brig (Brigg) Lane, which led to Edith Weston. The exposed stonework was interpreted as part of a substantial complex; excavation of its remains, again led by Fred Adams, continued part-time and was later extended into the adjacent field. However, only part of the complex could be investigated with the limited resources available and the results were less well defined than at Nether Hambleton.

Members of the project team on site at Nether Hambleton in August 1975, with Allen Chinnery of Leicestershire Museums (seated) looking on (Fred Adams)

Neither excavation could have taken place without the permission and generous assistance of Anglian Water Authority and the respective landowners. The Group's willing volunteers not only gave their time in the field but also spent many hours on the mundane washing and labelling of thousands of sherds of pottery and small finds; thanks are due to them, to Fred Adams, on whose excavation records this chapter has drawn so extensively, and to those who provided the specialist reports which form the basis of the accounts that follow. The full excavation records are retained by the Rutland Local History & Record Society, with which the Group subsequently merged, and the finds are housed at the Rutland County Museum.

The Nether Hambleton Excavation

Nether Hambleton lay on clayey soil in the valley bottom at a height of some 75m OD, about 3km to the east of Oakham. The larger village of Great or Upper Hambleton lies about 1km to the north on a spur which now forms a large promontory projecting into Rutland Water, with the subsidiary settlement of Middle Hambleton lying on the hillside between them

The shrunken medieval village site at Nether Hambleton, looking east, in July 1975, showing the green way running between two lines of house platforms; the excavation site is inside the paling fence (Tim Clough)

Tim Clough, Curator of Rutland County Museum (left), and Fred Adams, project leader (right), inspecting an old lemonade bottle found in a well at Nether Hambleton (Stamford Mercury)

The village earthworks were visibly associated with a green way running from east to west, parallel to the lane to Egleton and at right angles to an old track leading to Lax Hill and Manton. An area of apparent tofts or individual properties was bounded on the east by the road from Hambleton to Lyndon and Edith Weston. The south side of the green way showed ridge and furrow, and on the small hill were two dwellings, East View and April Cottage. In the hedge in this area there appeared to be a semi-circular ridge which could have been the tail-post walkway of a windmill but which was not investigated further. Between the green way and Woodbine House was a large pond which at one point exceeded 2m in depth, and there was also an old well nearby, from which was recovered an unopened early twentieth century lemonade bottle – presumably dangled on a string to cool and accidentally dropped!

The most promising of six visible house platforms to the north of the green way was selected for excavation and an area some 15m square was marked out. This was later extended to 17 x 20m to include a section of the green way and signs of an earlier building foundation on the northern side. The excavation proceeded in 1m strips running the full width of the site from the edge of the green way to the northern site boundary. Artefacts were found on the

— 423 —

removal of the first turf in the south-western corner, and the site continued to produce an abundance of pottery sherds – over 4,500 in all – and small finds throughout the three years that followed. Overburden and stone rubble were removed in layers varying from 10 to 15cm. As work progressed across the site, medieval house walls were revealed, with some sections still standing up to six courses in height. It was notable that wall junctions contained, in most cases, very large padstone boulder pebbles up to 70cm in length and up to 40cm in width, possibly providing foundation supports for a timber cruck type of superstructure. The walls in the southern half of the site were substantial and mostly continuous, while the north-west area showed considerable robbing of wall stone. A large number of nails found on the floor of the building suggested where roof beams had collapsed. All the evidence indicated that this was a solid building.

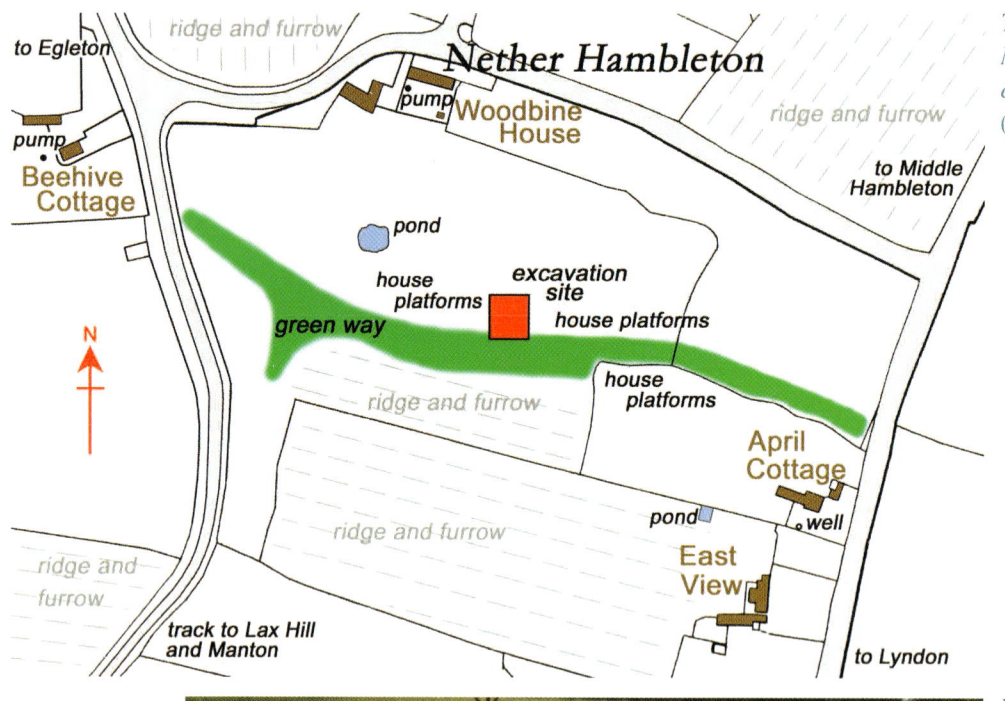

The location of Nether Hambleton excavation site (RO)

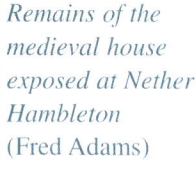

Remains of the medieval house exposed at Nether Hambleton (Fred Adams)

The main rectangular structure appeared to contain two rooms separated by a light-weight partition, near the centre of which was a post-hole, implying a substantial support for the partition and roof. In the smaller northern room a well-paved hearth was revealed, floored with iron ore/limestone blocks, with an adjacent pebble area perhaps for cooking utensils. Two coins found by the hearth proved to be a penny of Edward III (1327-77) and an early fifteenth century Venetian soldino. On the east side of the hearth, close to the main wall and partition, was a raised stone and clay platform suggesting a work area or sleeping bay. In the north-east corner of this smaller room large deposits of ash and charcoal led to the discovery of a substantial corner oven. Although most of the pottery sherds found in the building area were of twelfth and thirteenth century date, they are interpreted as evidence of a phase of occupation earlier than that represented by the remains of the building.

Investigation of a raised stone and clay feature in the south-west corner of the larger room suggested another work area. This contained most of the pieces of a large thirteenth-century Lyveden ware jug decorated with a green and yellow slip pattern. The floors inside the building were mainly of sandy gravel. Outside the main west wall at this point were signs of a substantial eaves drain and a thick deposit of soft grey soapy clay overlying an orange/brown clay floor. This 'west yard' contained an area partly paved with boulder pebbles, and a path from the robbed wall area of the house and stone on the site edge may have led to adjacent buildings. The yard surface contained many larger pot sherds of fourteenth/fifteenth century date.

Above: A medieval hearth found at Nether Hambleton (Fred Adams)

Right: A thirteenth-century Lyveden/Stanion Ware jug found at Nether Hambleton, as reconstructed (RCM)

Towards the northern edge of the site a later wall of poorly bonded stones, possibly a late repair or reconstruction, adjoined the remains of the corner oven. Beyond this wall was a large flat area with foundations of earlier walls containing wide well-worn limestone slabs, but it was not possible to extend the site northwards to investigate what was probably an earlier building.

Following the decision to investigate the southern end of the building and the associated green way or 'street', an earth and stone bank was removed. The main east and west walls were found to continue to the edge of the road metalling and suggested a 'lean-to' extension of the building. A section 1m wide through the edge of the road revealed no wall foundations but showed three levels of road surfacing. A small group of six thirteenth-century Long Cross coins was found by one of the walls.

Besides coins, the many small finds from the site included a large variety of iron objects, mostly in poor condition, some copper alloy artefacts, fragments of lead, and stone artefacts including many whetstones. These and the many animal bones recovered were submitted to specialists for detailed examination.

Medieval Animal Bones

Many animal bones and teeth were found during the excavations at Nether Hambleton, and these were identified by Ian L Baxter. His report shows that they comprised the remains of approximately five cattle, some immature; three small horses, some immature; five or six pigs; and a number of sheep and goats. Butchery marks, evidence of cutting and chopping the carcasses, were found on some of the horse, cattle and sheep/goat bones. At least two domestic fowl were represented, along with probably two geese. Bones from dog, possible wolf, brown hare, cat and rat were also found.

Most medieval occupation sites produce similar selections of bones from animals, birds and fish, providing valuable evidence for the varied diet of their inhabitants. Although wild and farm animals are usually also present, the great majority represent kitchen debris – one area of the Whitwell site too produced cooked butchered bones – but bones were also used productively for making household items and in many other different ways. Worked bone items from Nether Hambleton included an awl from a pig's ulna, a fragment of knife handle, and several circular lathe-turned beads or buttons.

A plan of the late fourteenth/early fifteenth century house excavated at Nether Hambleton (Fred Adams)

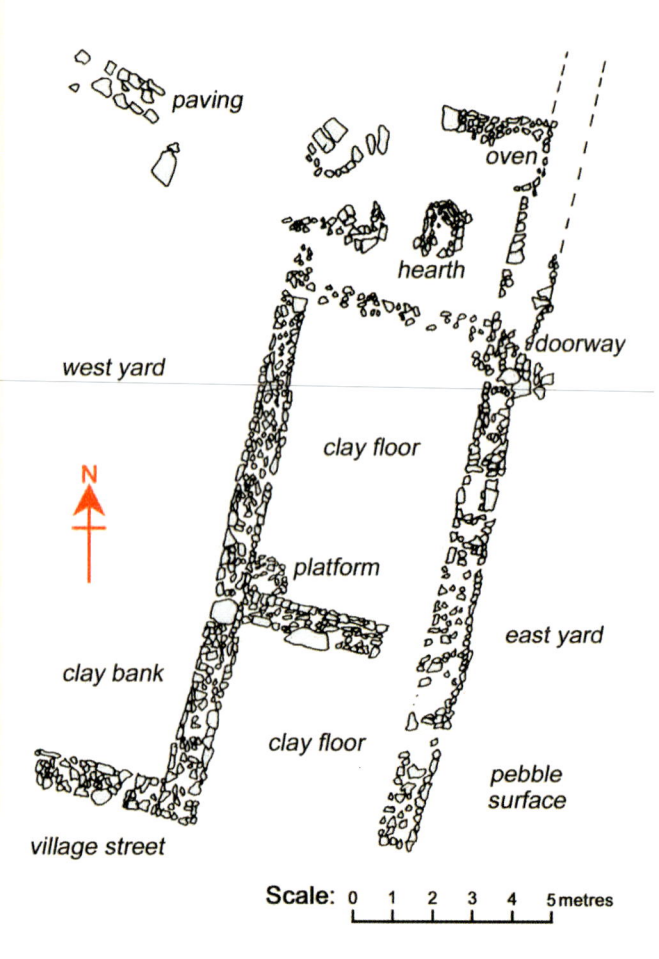

Small Finds from Nether Hambleton

The small finds from Nether Hambleton were examined by Patrick Clay of the then Leicestershire Archaeological Unit. The majority were ferrous nails, hinge pins, pegs and hooks, horseshoe fragments and horseshoe nails; these iron finds were mostly in poor condition. A total of 258 nails were recovered; the most common type was a small variety, the '*brodde*' [brad], a basic headless or lost-head woodworking nail, followed by various sizes of small square-headed carpentry nail and a few large-headed stud nails of the type used to strengthen doors, as well as the horseshoe nails. There were also several buckles including one probably fifteenth century in date, knife blades, a mason's chisel, two hinge pivots used for hanging a door or shutter, an awl fragment, a decorative strip of unknown purpose, fifteenth/sixteenth century heavy horseshoe fragments, and a possible thirteenth-century tanged arrowhead.

Medieval nails from Nether Hambleton. Left to right: stud nail used to strengthen doors; square-headed nail; nail with offset square head; small stud nail; two small square-headed nails; plain nail – a 'brodde' or basic woodworking nail (after Patrick Clay)

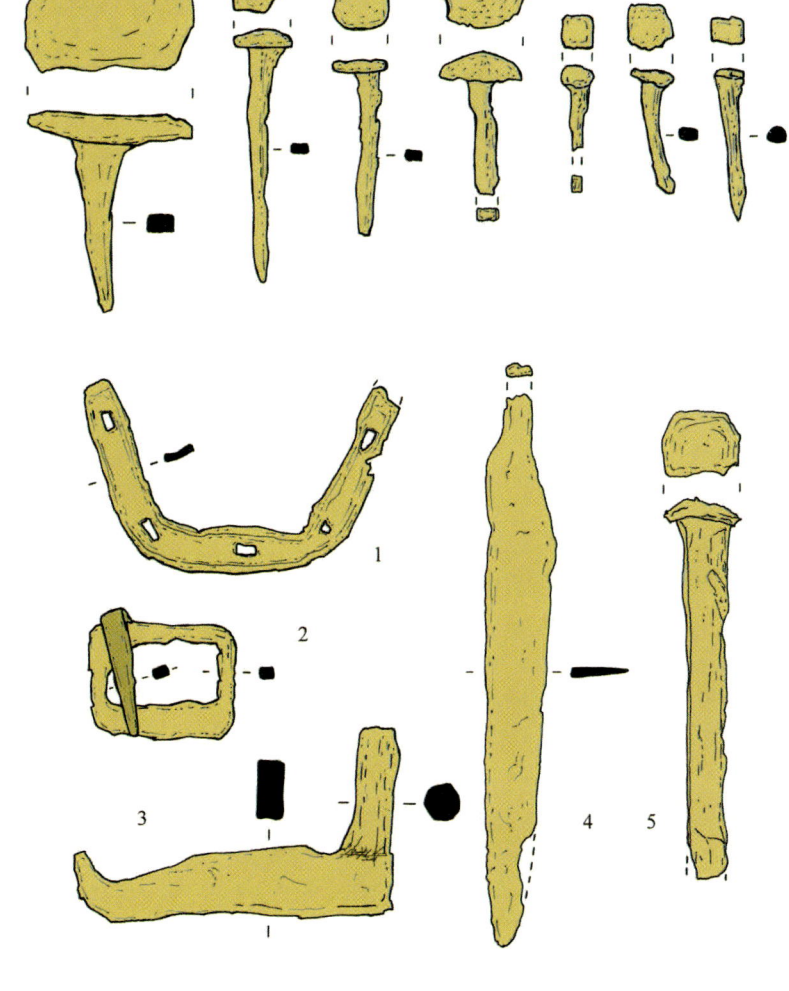

Medieval iron objects from Nether Hambleton. 1: protective or decorative strip, purpose unknown; 2: buckle, perhaps fifteenth century; 3: hinge pivot; 4: knife blade; 5: chisel with burred-over head (after Patrick Clay)

Copper alloy items included several buckles and belt decorations; one of the buckles was of a later fourteenth century type that would have been attached to the name belts in fashion at that time, and a contemporary forked terminal possibly from the same belt was also found. Other copper alloy finds included a finger ring fragment, a twisted wire hairpin, and a cast bowl or skillet fragment encrusted with soot, suggesting its use as a cooking vessel. Most of these are consistent with a fourteenth century date, central to the occupation period of the site. Lead and lead alloy objects included a pewter button, probably post-medieval, a small double-headed decorative lead stud and a small weight.

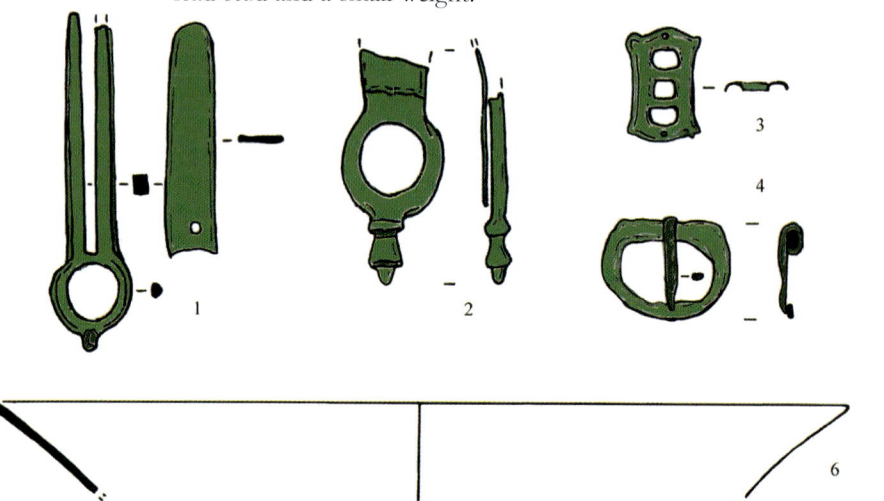

Medieval copper alloy objects from Nether Hambleton. 1: later fourteenth-century pronged buckle and cover plate, pin missing; 2: belt terminal of similar date; 3, 4: small fourteenth/fifteenth-century buckle and small belt plate; 5: hair pin with twisted wire knop; 6: rim fragment from a cast bowl (after Patrick Clay)

Stone objects included small sandstone spindle whorls and a fragment of a small mortar made of Lincolnshire Oolitic limestone. Although samples of gritstone, pebble grinders and iron ore were also collected, the main items of interest were an unusually large group of well-used stone hones or whetstones, mostly either of sandstone, probably originating from the English Coal Measures, or of imported Norwegian Ragstone. There was also one fine-grained siltstone pebble, described as a black cherty stone with vugs of quartz and secondary silica, which, intriguingly, was identified as a possible touchstone, used for testing objects to see if they were gold (Moore & Oddy 1985, 77, no 21, fig. 11d).

Stone Hones from Nether Hambleton

Twenty-six stone hones or whetstones from the Nether Hambleton excavations were examined by microscopic thin section by David Moore of the Natural History Museum. Seven were identified as Norwegian Ragstone, and at least fourteen – mostly coarse muscovite-bearing lithic and/or feldspathic sandstones – probably originated from the English Coal Measures. The others were respectively one muscovite-quartz grit (possibly also from the Coal Measures), one chlorite-biotite-muscovite lithic sandstone, one feldspathic sandstone, one acidic igneous rock (not unlike Mount Sorrel granite from Leicestershire), and one Mesozoic limestone.

All the hones were well used and none was intact. Those made of Norwegian Ragstone, a well-known source of sharpening stones, must have been imported in the medieval period, whilst the typical sandstone examples will have been obtained through more local trade. It is however quite unusual to find so many hones or whetstones in a single building, and this raises questions about the occupations of the people who once lived there and why they appear to have had so many blades that needed sharpening.

Three of the medieval hones found at Nether Hambleton and now in the Rutland County Museum (not to scale) (RO)

Coins Found at Nether Hambleton

Six mid thirteenth century Long Cross coins (so-called because of the long cross which dominates the reverse design) were found close together in heavy clay near the foot of a wall of the excavated house (Archibald & Woodhead 1976, 115, no 452). No purse or other container was found, so we cannot say why or how they came to be there. One of the coins was a complete penny, though broken, but the other five were halfpennies – literally pennies cut in half, common practice at a time when no coins smaller than the penny were issued. As a group the coins must be later than 1256 because one of the moneyers whose names appear on them, Robert of the Canterbury mint, was appointed in that year. The total face value of the coins is 3½d, which might then have paid for three hens and a dozen eggs.

These coins were as follows:

1. Cut halfpenny by the moneyer Nicole of Canterbury.
2. Cut halfpenny by the moneyer Robert of Canterbury (broken into two pieces).
3. Cut halfpenny of the Canterbury mint, moneyer unknown.
4. Complete penny, perhaps by the moneyer Ricard of the Durham mint (broken into five pieces).
5. Cut halfpenny of the London mint, moneyer unknown.
6. Cut halfpenny, illegible (turned over and struck twice between the dies).

Four other medieval coins were found, two by the hearth and one each in the east and west yards:

1. Short Cross cut halfpenny (late twelfth/early thirteenth century), illegible, though the moneyer may be Ricard.
2. Penny of Edward III (1327-77) from the York mint.
3. Soldino or 'galley halfpenny' of Doge Michele Steno of Venice (1400-13).
4. Sterling of Erik VII/XIII of Pomerania (Denmark, Sweden and Norway) (1412-39), minted at Lund in southern Sweden.

The earliest coin is the Short Cross cut halfpenny. Its condition is too poor for it to be identified closely, but the type was current from 1180 to 1240, just before the Long Cross series. The penny of Edward III found by the hearth, again in very poor condition, probably dates from the 1360s, during Archbishop Thoresby's tenancy of the See of York. The two foreign coins, kindly identified by the Department of Coins and Medals, British Museum, are the latest from the site and date from the first half of the fifteenth century. With the other coins, identified by Tim Clough, they suggest that the site was in use at least from the late twelfth to the mid fifteenth century. The presence of foreign coins illustrates the possibility of far-flung contacts, fortuitous and at several removes though they might be, even in small rural communities like Nether Hambleton. Coins of the flourishing trading state of Venice, like the soldino found by the hearth, occur sporadically in England to the extent of having a nickname. They were made of inferior silver and passed as halfpence, but were intrinsically worthless. Scandinavian coins are less common, at least on excavated sites. We may conjecture that the sterling of Erik VII/XIII results from Baltic trade with east coast ports like Boston and Spalding in Lincolnshire or Lynn in Norfolk, all of which would have served merchants for example in the flourishing medieval town of Stamford (Lincolnshire), only a short distance to the east of Hambleton.

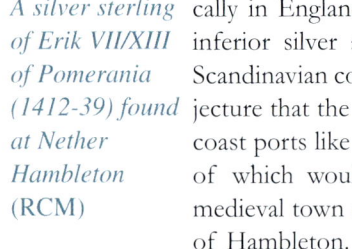

A silver sterling of Erik VII/XIII of Pomerania (1412-39) found at Nether Hambleton (RCM)

A mid thirteenth century Long Cross cut halfpenny by the moneyer Robert of Canterbury found at Nether Hambleton (RCM)

— 430 —

The Whitwell Excavation

This site faced Whitwell Old Hall on the western slope of the Whitwell stream at a height of around 100m OD, and geologically appeared to be below the upper limit of the Upper Lias clay of the Gwash valley. Above the clay were layers of ironstone, soil and turf. The higher valley slopes contain limestone strata much used for building construction and exploited for cement manufacture at nearby Ketton.

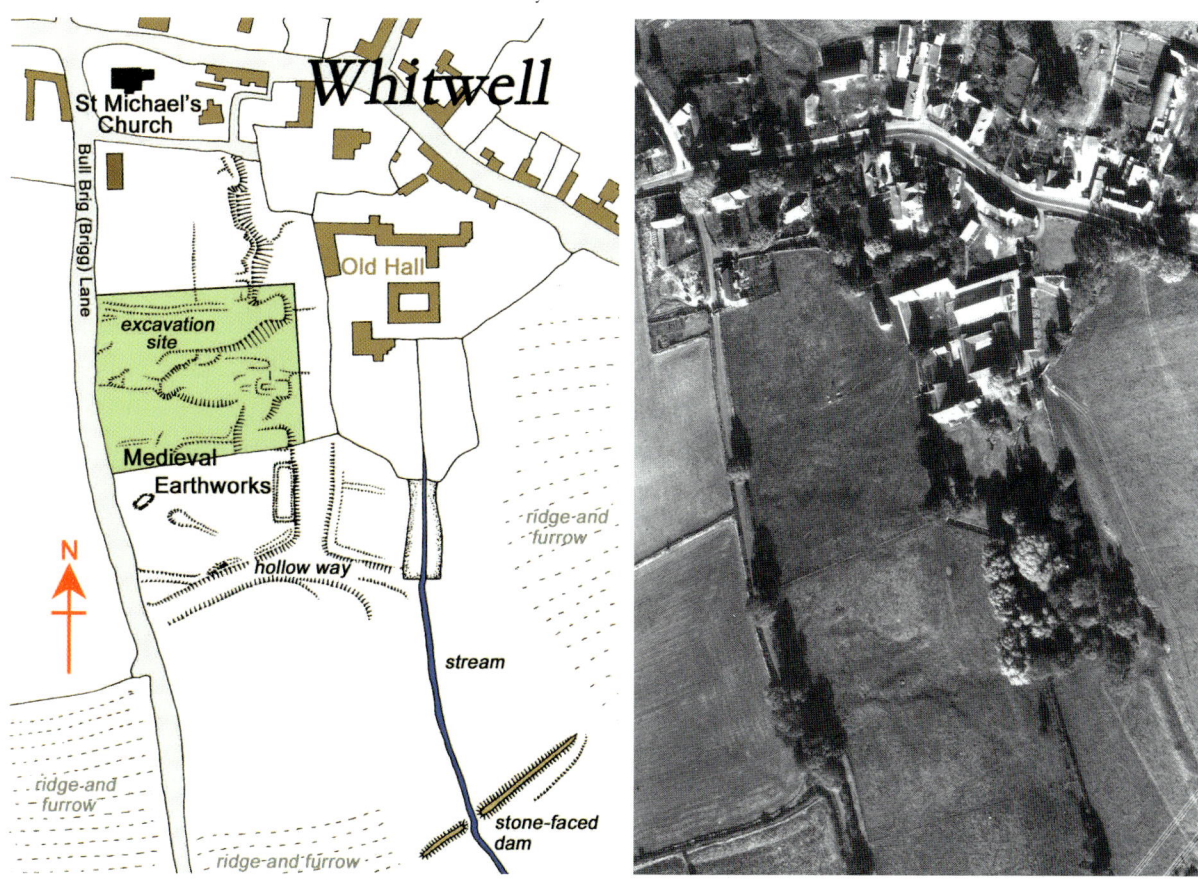

Sketch plan of the village and medieval earthworks of Whitwell (after Hartley 1983, 48)

An aerial view of Whitwell taken in 1968, before Rutland Water works began (Anglian Water)

Material removed by machine before archaeological work began was deposited near the stream to form a substantial bank. A search of this deposit yielded a large collection of pottery which included some Roman material but was mainly twelfth to seventeenth century in date. Traces of charcoal and clinker suggested possible ironworking on the site. The machine-scraped area revealed two charcoal features and indications of a coarsely-built wall and ditch. Following surface examination of the building area and the ground slope to the south, which produced a similarly wide variety of pottery, a flint arrowhead and a number of small finds, work was concentrated on an area some 10 x 30m in extent.

Removal of loose soil and stone debris in approximately 5m strips across the site from north to south revealed what was obviously a stone-spread yard bounded by stone walls on the west and south. To ascertain the size and

— 431 —

construction of these walls a trench 1m deep was dug on what seemed to be the outside; this produced a well-constructed wall face. As the yard was cleared several other features appeared, including a narrow stone drain and a line of large flat stone slabs. These were interpreted as padstones for a short wall. Nearby were an area of large laid pebbles and a line of blue clay running west to east. Crossing the site were the remains of a later surface drain which had been cut through a line of large stone blocks, while further east were another small stone drain and a stone scatter. This work yielded a considerable quantity and variety of pottery, and removal of soil from the late drain produced sherds of Stamford, Midland Purple and other medieval wares.

A paved area in the Whitwell medieval building complex excavated by the Rutland Field Research Group (Fred Adams)

The area further east and at a lower level had been abraded by the levelling machine but many large worked blocks of limestone, up to about 70cm square, were still visible *in situ*. These were found to be covers for a system of stone-lined drains, in which earlier medieval pottery was found; later it became obvious that in most cases the drains formed the foundations of the major walls of the buildings.

Trenches outside the main west wall and the south wall showed that these walls were built above packed Upper Lias clay. The west wall appeared to have been repaired or re-laid at some stage. The lower courses were of larger and heavier material; some of the upper courses had slipped outwards and had been shored up. The southern end proved to form a well-built corner with the south wall, which stood on blue clay for about 13m, at which point a further cross-wall foundation, running northwards, was discovered overlying a stone-lined drain which obviously continued into the adjoining paddock.

The eastern end of the south wall was also built over a stone-lined drain of considerable size, again with limestone covers up to 70cm square, which proceeded in a shallow arc in an easterly direction for over 10m. From this point eastwards and downhill either the drain had been destroyed or the area reverted to natural drainage towards the stream below in the Old Hall garden. It is possible that the stream entered a large millpond – traces of a long dam wall crossed the stream about 100m south of the site and the stream had a well-built stone wall sluice still *in situ* up to the time the reservoir was filled. The sluice walls were about 2m high above the stream bottom but covered by brambles and nettles.

Excavation of the area around the large stone blocks revealed that the underlying drain was misaligned and that the stones were inclined at some 30° to horizontal. The eastern end of the line of blocks ended on a semi-circular block obviously burned brown. The presence of charcoal, ash and brown clay suggested a hearth or burning area. Potsherds found were mostly blackened early Stamford wares.

Clearance of the yard area continued eastwards to a point where the south wall appeared to join the heavy wall-and-drain system. The yard appeared to terminate at this point; the removal of further debris and soil revealed a further wall-and-drain system, overlaid by three courses of wall stone, extending into the site boundary hedge. The underlying 'V' drain consisted of flat limestone slabs approximately 60 x 30cm in size. The junction of this wall-and-drain with the first system revealed a square stone-lined 'socket' some 40cm square, thought to be a support for a large corner upright.

Permission was obtained to extend the excavation into the adjoining paddock, and a second area of some 20 x 40m was enclosed, down to the fence along the Old Hall approach road. Again, this was investigated in strips approximately 5m wide, quite a formidable task as the whole area was covered in deep turf, all of which had to be removed carefully and by hand since it was known that several features passed under the dividing hedge and that early results could be expected. The first strip revealed the possible continuation of the main west wall and a line of large pebbles which continued beyond the limit of excavation, perhaps a boundary line or late pathway from a further house platform to the north-west. This area produced the only coin found during the excavations, a silver circular halfpenny of Edward I[-III]. Coins of this type were introduced in Edward I's great re-coinage of 1279-80, and successive issues continued until the mid-fourteenth century during the reign of Edward III. Iron nails and pegs, fragments of knife blades, sherds of Cistercian, Midland Purple and other wares were also recovered, as well as cooked butchered bones.

Olive Adams inspecting progress at the Whitwell medieval site (Fred Adams)

The stone fall and scatter over the yard area varied in depth from 1m at the western end to about 90cm at the highest point, and contained sherds of twelfth to fifteenth century pottery and several iron nails. Other finds from the new area included bone, nails, a lead strip 100 x 10 x 15mm, a buckle or brooch, sherds of glazed and unglazed gritty ware, Cistercian and Midland Purple ware and a glazed stoneware base.

Further clearance revealed large stones which formed a substantial corner of two walls, one E-W and the other N-S, well laid with several courses surviving above stone rubble foundations. The identification of two other foundation layers suggested rebuilding on at least two occasions, and lines of stone footings containing drainage channels found at a lower level may represent secondary lean-to structures. An area of yard between two of the walls revealed a large burning area dotted with iron lumps up to 2kg in weight, suggesting that if iron had been extracted from local ironstone here the practice had been abandoned, possibly in the Tudor period.

In contrast to Nether Hambleton, a considerable number of medieval ridge tile fragments were recovered. These were mostly of Bourne ware, with some of Lyveden/Stanion ware; all were evidently glazed, often with white slip decoration under the glaze. In the main they date from the thirteenth and fourteenth centuries. Four worn fragments of glazed floor tile were also found, two with white slip decoration and two with white clay inlay. All the evidence suggests that, even though no complete picture could emerge, the buildings on this site were more substantial and to a higher specification than that at Nether Hambleton, and certainly incorporated an unusual technique in placing walls over foundation drains.

Pottery from the Nether Hambleton and Whitwell Excavations

Leaving aside the residual Romano-British pottery from Whitwell, the pottery from the two sites ranged from Saxo-Norman to late post-medieval, but in each case was concentrated in the medieval period. The pottery from Nether Hambleton was examined by Rosemary Woodland, who looked at every sherd using a binocular microscope at x35 magnification to identify the pottery type and build a chronology of the whole assemblage. That from Whitwell was examined by Deborah Sawday using a x20 binocular microscope and catalogued by fabric and context with reference to the University of Leicester Archaeological Services Fabric Series for Leicestershire and Rutland. Vessel form identification was, in most cases, limited to the basic class of vessel, such as jug, bowl or cistern, by the presence of diagnostic features including rims, handles and spouts. Here we record a summary of their findings.

The earliest pieces, from Nether Hambleton, were a single sherd from a light grey hand-made vessel, which would have had a spout and handle and a lug each side, identified as Saxon, perhaps *Ipswich Ware*, with a possible date of AD 650-850, and a fragment perhaps of imported *Pingsdorf/Badorf Ware*, AD 650-1000.

One of the most significant groups of pottery from each site originated from the Saxo-Norman pottery industry of *Stamford*, only some 12km to the east. At Nether Hambleton there were the remains of over 270 wheel-thrown vessels, and there were nearly 900 sherds from Whitwell. Stamford ware was often decorated with incised grooves, rouletting or finger impressions, and some was glazed. Vessel forms ranged from spouted pitchers and collared vessels to bowls and other forms; cooking pots, storage jars and bowls were the most common forms at both sites. The fabric can be divided into three categories, coarse, fine and developed. In the developed Stamford ware from Whitwell, twelve sherds were covered with copper glaze and represent fine table wares. Five of them were also decorated with applied thumbed clay strips under the glaze, all but one with the addition of combing or comb streaking along the strips. These may all represent jugs or tubular spouted pitchers, which were often highly decorated.

Another important medieval production centre from which the inhabitants of both sites obtained pottery was that of *Lyveden and Stanion*, in Northamptonshire, which was especially active throughout the thirteenth and fourteenth centuries. Many examples of this pottery were found, all hand- or coil-built. Three fabric groups, all fairly soft-fired but of different textures, can be identified; all have calcareous inclusions, iron ore, quartz and grog are often present, and one type is often glazed. One fabric, with a smooth, slightly soapy, surface texture and ranging in surface colour from orange/red to buff, was particularly used to produce jugs; these may be decorated with lines of stabbing, applied bands of white slip or incised patterns, and often have a patchy glaze in various shades of green. Applied white clay pads with grid stamps are also commonly found. Stabbed and slashed strap handles and plain, grooved and ribbed rod handles occur, the latter made out of three or four strands of clay twisted together. The handles are generally dowelled into the neck of the vessel; occasionally the lower wall is pushed out into the handle base. The only virtually complete jug recovered, from Hambleton, is of this fabric.

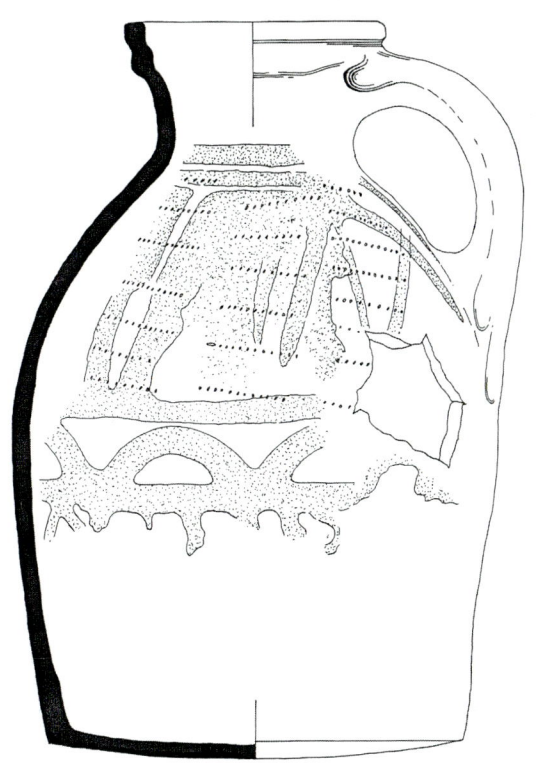

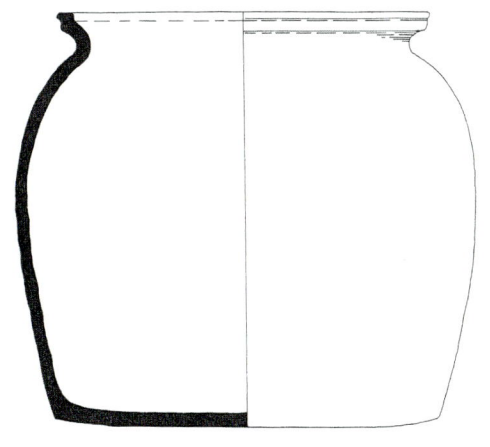

Above: Thirteenth-century Lyveden/Stanion Ware cooking pot from Nether Hambleton (after Rosemary Woodland)

Left: Thirteenth-century Lyveden/Stanion Ware jug from Nether Hambleton (after Rosemary Woodland)

A little later, Bourne in Lincolnshire became an important pottery centre. There were over 900 sherds of *Bourne Ware* at Whitwell and it was also well represented at Nether Hambleton. The fabrics have been divided into two groups, the earlier being a generally wheel-thrown fabric with a rough sandy surface texture and the later a finer sandy wheel-thrown late medieval/early post-medieval fabric which can be paralleled at the kiln site.

Examples of the earlier fabric from Whitwell included internally glazed bowl rims; another vessel, probably a bowl, was decorated with a zigzag pattern in a trailed slip on the exterior, and glazed both internally and externally. Some, but not all, of the eight jugs identified showed evidence of external glazing. The handles were either rod or strap, the latter often being stabbed or slashed. At least some of the jug handles were dowelled into the top of the neck of the vessel. Five cistern rim fragments and a hand-built dripping dish rim were also recorded. At Nether Hambleton, most vessels were too fragmentary to identify form but jugs and bowls were certainly present, including jugs decorated externally with white slip patches, with green glaze over the slip and incised decoration on the neck or body under the glaze, and bowls decorated with rilling on the interior of the rim, covered with green glaze.

Many vessel forms were identified in the later Bourne fabric at Whitwell: a cooking pot/storage jar, bowls, and jug fragments. Many of the jugs were decorated with white slip under the glaze, which varied in colour between an apple green and yellow and brown, and had ridged strap handles. Also present were single rims representing a jar, a bottle and a cistern. Similarly, at Nether Hambleton, this fabric is mostly represented by jug fragments, although again much of the material is too fragmentary to identify vessel type. Decoration on the jugs consists of applied slip patches on the exterior, with dark green glaze over, on both the body and handles, but rare on the base. Two bases have the impression of the rim of another vessel, seemingly a jug, suggesting that the vessels were fired upside-down, since the glaze has run downwards onto the base from the rim of the vessel above.

Several other medieval pottery industries were represented on both sites by smaller numbers of sherds. The most important of these was *Nottingham Ware*, a fairly hard-fired sandy wheel-thrown fabric, often glazed externally, of which there was more at Whitwell than at Nether Hambleton. Most of the sherds probably come from jugs, one or two with decorative rilling, cordons or under-glaze decoration. The underside of one jug base shows evidence of how it was stacked in the kiln. At Whitwell, there was a single sherd of *Lincoln/Lincolnshire Shelly Ware*, a wheel-thrown cooking pot rim, and another in a reduced and wheel-thrown sandy ware in the *Torksey* tradition.

A few shelly ware sherds of uncertain provenance may represent a *Lincolnshire* kiln. Some sherds from Whitwell in oxidised and reduced sandy ware may originate from *Nottingham* or *Bourne*; others may be from sources including *Lincoln* or *Ticknall* in Derbyshire. A few white-bodied sherds in a sandy wheel-thrown fabric, externally glazed olive green, probably came from the *Chilvers Coton* kilns in Warwickshire. At Nether Hambleton, three vessels including a jug, the base and body of which remains, were identified in a fabric described as *Local Sandy Ware*, possibly from a kiln in the *Leicester* area.

Midland Purple, with its rough surface texture and purple or orange colouring, is a well-known late medieval fabric, and there were numerous examples at both sites. Many are highly fired and vitrified, some less so, and they vary considerably in hardness. The softer-fired vessels may reflect a transitional period of manufacture between medieval sandy wares and true Midland Purple wares. Vessels from Whitwell included four wide-mouthed bowl rims, five jugs and some sixteen cisterns, some with evidence of internal glazing, and a range of other forms. At Nether Hambleton too, jugs decorated with cordons or incised parallel lines running around to the neck or shoulder, and cisterns with a variety of decorative techniques were found; one complete cistern profile, no bigger than a cooking pot/storage jar, could be reconstructed. At least two sources are suggested. Many of the vessel forms, and those features associated with the cisterns in particular, can be paralleled at the Austin Friars site in Leicester (Woodland 1981). One likely source for this pottery is *Ticknall* in Derbyshire, but some of the sherds in this group may be very highly fired products of the *Bourne* kilns.

Cistercian Ware is another hard-fired vitrified purple fabric with smooth surface texture, and there is a related ware which is less highly fired and more red than purple in colour. The Nether Hambleton material was fragmentary, but cups, posset pots or jugs may be represented, since one handle was found – this was only patchily glazed, and thus not true Cistercian ware. White applied slip decoration occurs on the exterior of several sherds; this appears yellow when covered with glaze. At Whitwell there were 200 sherds of two more or less indistinguishable fine, glazed, wheel-thrown, sandy fabrics in this tradition. Typologically the identifiable vessels, represented by the fragments of approximately 21 cup rims, all appear to be late medieval in form, and hence may be *Cistercian* rather than *Midland Black Ware*. They may also originate from *Ticknall*.

Two *Tudor Green Ware* vessels were represented at Nether Hambleton; neither is of identifiable form and the kiln source is unknown. From each site there was a little fragmentary sixteenth or possibly seventeenth century *Midland Yellow Ware*, a wheel-thrown, lead-glazed pottery which fires yellow over the pale buff fabric. The vessels included hollow forms such as jug or mugs rather than flat wares such as wide-mouthed bowls. At Whitwell, there were sherds of various post-medieval *earthenwares* or *pancheon wares*, some of which may have replaced Midland Purple during the early post-medieval period, and a few of *brown-glazed stoneware*.

Seventeenth and eighteenth century *stonewares*, characterised by the very fine nature of the fabric, highly fired and in many cases vitrified, derive from a variety of sources. Fragments of three small wheel-thrown and glazed stoneware drinking jugs or mugs in a dark grey body with a glossy brown glaze, imported from the Rhineland and probably originating from either *Raeren* or *Frechen*, were found at Whitwell, while the one imported stoneware vessel at Nether Hambleton is a salt-glazed *Westerwald* jug or mug, which has multiple incised horizontal lines on the neck, with cobalt painted in some of the depressions. Local stonewares are similar in fabric and decoration; the latter consists of incised horizontal or wavy lines on the exterior surface, and the salt glaze appears brown over the fabric. No vessel forms could be identified for these hard-fired totally glazed fabrics; they may be from *Nottingham* or *Derby* or possibly from another more local source. The final group of late stoneware from Nether Hambleton may be from *Staffordshire*; the only vessel form identified is a plate, which has panels of basket-weave decoration interspersed with scrolling and grids on the rim.

The largest group of vessels from amongst the post-medieval pottery from Nether Hambleton was in the fabric termed, perhaps inaccurately, *manganese-glazed earthenware*. The fabric is fairly hard-fired, occasionally vitrified, with smooth surface texture; the core is mainly purple, but streaked with white and orange as a result of bad mixing and preparation of clay. The vessels in this group are thick-walled, with glaze usually on the interior. Two large bowls or pancheons were identified. The source may have been fairly local, although many centres may have been producing such coarse and probably relatively cheap vessels. A seventeenth to nineteenth century date is suggested, although it is possible that production of such vessels began earlier than the seventeenth century.

The remaining fabrics from the site are all seventeenth to nineteenth century in date, and mostly derive from the *Staffordshire* or related industries. They include very hard-fired vitrified white *bone china*, hard-fired smooth white *creamware*, and tin-glazed, slip-decorated cream-glazed and brown-glazed *earthenwares*. In no case do more than six vessels occur in any group; most sherds were too fragmentary to enable identification of form.

Interpretation and Dating of the Sites

Any attempt to understand how sites such as these developed and changed over the centuries relies on the stratigraphy of the excavated structures and on the relationship of finds to those structures, as well as on any historical information that can be brought to bear. At Nether Hambleton, we have the benefit of a well-defined archaeological structure, a series of small finds complemented by a definitive range of pottery, and some relevant documentary sources. At Whitwell, the structures are harder to understand, there are fewer datable small finds, and at present there are no historical pointers; despite the absence of clear chronological grouping of pottery from individual features, it is the pottery from the site which adds most to our knowledge.

Not surprisingly, given that Hambleton and Whitwell are adjacent parishes, the two pottery groups are very similar. The two sites lie so close to Stamford that it would be remarkable if they did not receive at least some of the products of its high-quality pottery industry, which operated from about AD 850-1250 and was one of the most important in the east midlands during this period (Kilmurray 1980, Leach 1987). At Nether Hambleton, the quantity of Stamford ware, the vessel forms and the range of decoration indicate that this connection extended back into the tenth century and continued into the early part of the thirteenth, while at Whitwell the date range of pottery associated with the drains, yard and some of the walls suggests occupation on the site from at least the Saxo-Norman period. Trade in Stamford ware to other sites in Rutland, such as Oakham Castle (Gathercole

1958) and Alstoe Mount (Dunning 1936), is well attested, and the Nether Hambleton and Whitwell assemblages emphasise its importance. The sites are well within the distribution radius of even the largest vessels, the most difficult to transport.

During the twelfth century, however, the status of Stamford as a supplier of pottery evidently declined, with the Lyveden/Stanion industry in north Northamptonshire (22km to the south) becoming a major new source, indicating a shift in supply from the east to the south. This is shown by the appearance of new fabrics, chiefly in the form of bowls and cooking pots or jars. During the thirteenth century, highly decorated Lyveden/Stanion vessels become important amongst the glazed wares, perhaps continuing into the fourteenth and even the fifteenth century. Another shift takes place when the Bourne kilns (also lying some 20km away, but to the north-east in Lincolnshire, not the south) also became a major source of pottery. Cooking pots or jars, jugs, many bowls, a dripping dish and a new later medieval pottery form, the cistern, for storage of liquids and equipped with a bung-hole, occur in this fabric. Later Bourne products such as bottles and jars dating from the fifteenth century are also present.

Previous excavations in the area produced varying quantities of material of the period, and more or less limited ranges of fabrics. At least one Lyveden jug sherd was found at Oakham Castle, and it is possible that more Lyveden type wares were recovered there, but included under St Neots ware, since the existence of the Lyveden kilns was unknown when that report (Gathercole 1958) was published. Bourne ware may also be present but there seems to be a distinct lack of what might be termed medieval sandy fabrics at Oakham Castle, although post-medieval fine and coarse wares were well represented. The range of fabrics at our sites is thus far more complete than that from either Oakham Castle or Alstoe Mount, or indeed Martinsthorpe (Wacher 1963-64), and can therefore be used to fill in gaps in our knowledge of the trade and distribution of pottery during the medieval period.

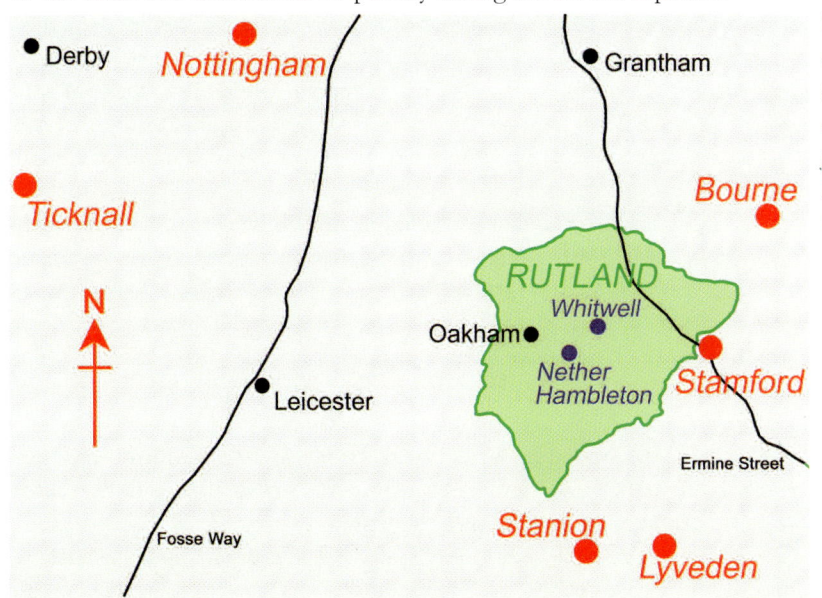

The major sources (shown in red) of pottery found at Nether Hambleton and Whitwell (RO)

Little of the pottery from any of these sites, or indeed from field-walking in the area, derives from sources to the west, certainly in the medieval period, though Nottingham (47km to the north-west) soon becomes a significant source, primarily for jugs. The presence of Nottingham ware is interesting, since it might be thought to be too distant for any of its products to be traded here. However, this is by no means unusual, since it occurs at a number of other sites in the area.

The origins and trade patterns of much of the pottery of the fifteenth and sixteenth centuries, including local sandy wares but notably Midland Purple and Cistercian ware, remain uncertain, though typologically quite a high proportion seems to originate from the Ticknall kilns, 60km to the west, in Derbyshire. Typically, Midland Purple vessel forms are predominantly cisterns, with jugs, bowls, and bottles or jars also occurring. The number of fine cup forms in Cistercian ware is also of interest. The presence of Midland Yellow, perhaps Midland Black ware, and certain earthenware products shows that Ticknall continued as the major supplier of pottery in the early post-medieval period.

At Nether Hambleton, it was possible to show the relationship between pottery groups and the house structure in a way that could not be done at Whitwell. Plans showing the pottery distribution within floor surfaces over the site revealed that most of the Stamford, Lyveden, Nottingham and earlier Bourne wares were randomly distributed over the whole site, both inside and outside the house structure. However, in the case of the later Bourne, Local Sandy and Midland Purple wares, very little was found within the house, the majority being found in fairly specific deposits to its north-west and east; both were located near doorways to the structure, and are suggested as midden areas, where disposal of broken vessels and other household rubbish took place during the occupation of the house. The distinction of these two pottery groups is crucial to our understanding of the history of the site.

The absence from the middens of earlier fabrics, together with their presence in some quantity within the house, as well as over the yard area, is suggestive. It is highly unlikely that the occupants of the house would have allowed so much broken pottery to accumulate on the floor of their dwelling without making some attempt to clear it, especially in view of the small amount of later pottery that is found within the structure. It is more likely that the early fabrics accumulated during the construction of the house platform, either carried here from other parts of the village and spread over the site or, as perhaps in the case of the nearly complete Lyveden ware jug, deriving from an earlier structure on the same site. Thus the Stamford, Lyveden, Nottingham and earlier Bourne wares may reflect pottery usage within the village, and possibly within this area of the settlement, at a period prior to the life and use of the excavated house; the later Bourne, Local Sandy, and Midland Purple wares from the two middens represent vessels in use in the building itself – joining sherds of vessels in both Bourne and Midland Purple occur in both middens.

The Cistercian and later fabrics do not occur within the midden material, but derive mostly from the upper layers of the excavation. Their distribution shows no pattern, the number of vessels is very small, and they are not considered relevant to the dating of the excavated building.

The predominance of early medieval wares at Nether Hambleton suggests that substantial occupation of the settlement as a whole was perhaps more concentrated during the Saxo-Norman and early medieval periods, from *c*1100 or even earlier on the evidence of the Stamford ware, than in the later medieval and post-medieval periods. Before that, mid to late Saxon activity in the vicinity is hinted at by the sherds of possible Ipswich and Pingsdorf/Badorf ware. The importance of Hambleton, with its Saxon place-name, as a manorial and ecclesiastical centre in the Saxo-Norman period – at least as important, it seems, as Oakham – is well attested historically (*see* Chapter 8 – Hambleton: The Settlement on the Crooked Hill), and it seems likely that Nether Hambleton was one of the seven outlying berewicks or hamlets ascribed to it in Domesday Book in 1086 (Phythian-Adams 1977).

It is estimated that the house platform had been occupied from early medieval times until at least the mid fifteenth century – mid thirteenth century activity is attested by the group of Long Cross coins – but the evidence of the groupings of earlier and later pottery types noted above suggests that this occupation may not have been continuous. The lifespan of the excavated structure itself does not seem to have been a long one; a date range centred on *c*1400-1450 is suggested on the evidence of the pottery from the middens, a date which is in accord with what can be adduced from the small finds and coins. Thus the pottery distribution pattern implies that there were two distinct phases of occupation.

If there was indeed such a hiatus, documentary evidence may provide an explanation. In the 1330s the manor of Hambleton was in the hands of Giles de Badlesmere, heir of the Umfraville family. He died in 1337-8, and his *inquisition post mortem* (a report into the affairs of a deceased person) mentions a number of field names in Hambleton, including Sundermedow and Lampolmedow. The former may be the same as Cinder Meadow at the eastern end of the Burley Fishponds, and the latter seems certain to be Lampleys at Nether Hambleton; both field names are well attested in later documents. By the 1340s Hambleton had passed to Giles's sister Elizabeth and her husband William de Bohun, Earl of Northampton. When he died in 1360-61, his *inquisition post mortem* recorded untenanted ruinous buildings and eleven tofts and eleven virgates of land in his hands which had brought an income of £11 yearly 'before the pestilence' – that is to say, the Black Death of 1349-50. Again, the proof of age of one John Basynges of Hambleton in 1362-63 says that he had been eight years old and more at the time of the same pestilence.

The Black Death was not such a significant reason as was once thought for the mass desertion or reduction of medieval villages, major changes in land use such as the introduction of intensive sheep farming being but one other. However, the combination of this documentary evidence with that of the pottery sequence and its relationship with the archaeological stratigraphy does make it more than likely that the excavated house was erected on the site of one which had been rendered vacant by that plague, perhaps after an interval of a generation or so. What we cannot know is whether the large number of hones, the possible touchstone, and the intrusive early fifteenth century foreign coins reflect some commercial activity on the part of its occupants.

This house in its turn then fell into disuse. The presence of iron slag may imply that when this happened it was used as an opportunist source for ironstone. Subsequently, perhaps until the eighteenth century, it may have been used by neighbours as a convenient midden. Although occupation continued nearby, a terminal date for the final desertion of the house is impossible to gauge from the pottery evidence alone in view of the small but significant quantity of later seventeenth century wares. There is no reason to suppose that the whole settlement was deserted at the same time; certainly there is reference to 'le Blynde Lane [perhaps a *cul de sac*] in Nethertowne' in 1549 – perhaps the earliest written mention of Nether Hambleton as such. However, evidence that this particular site was uninhabited by 1797 is found in a sketch map and accompanying list of households in Lower (Nether) Hambleton (ROLLR DG 7/4/27); indeed it appears from this late eighteenth century plan that Nether Hambleton changed little from that date until the arrival of Rutland Water (*see* Chapter 9 – Lower Hambleton in 1797).

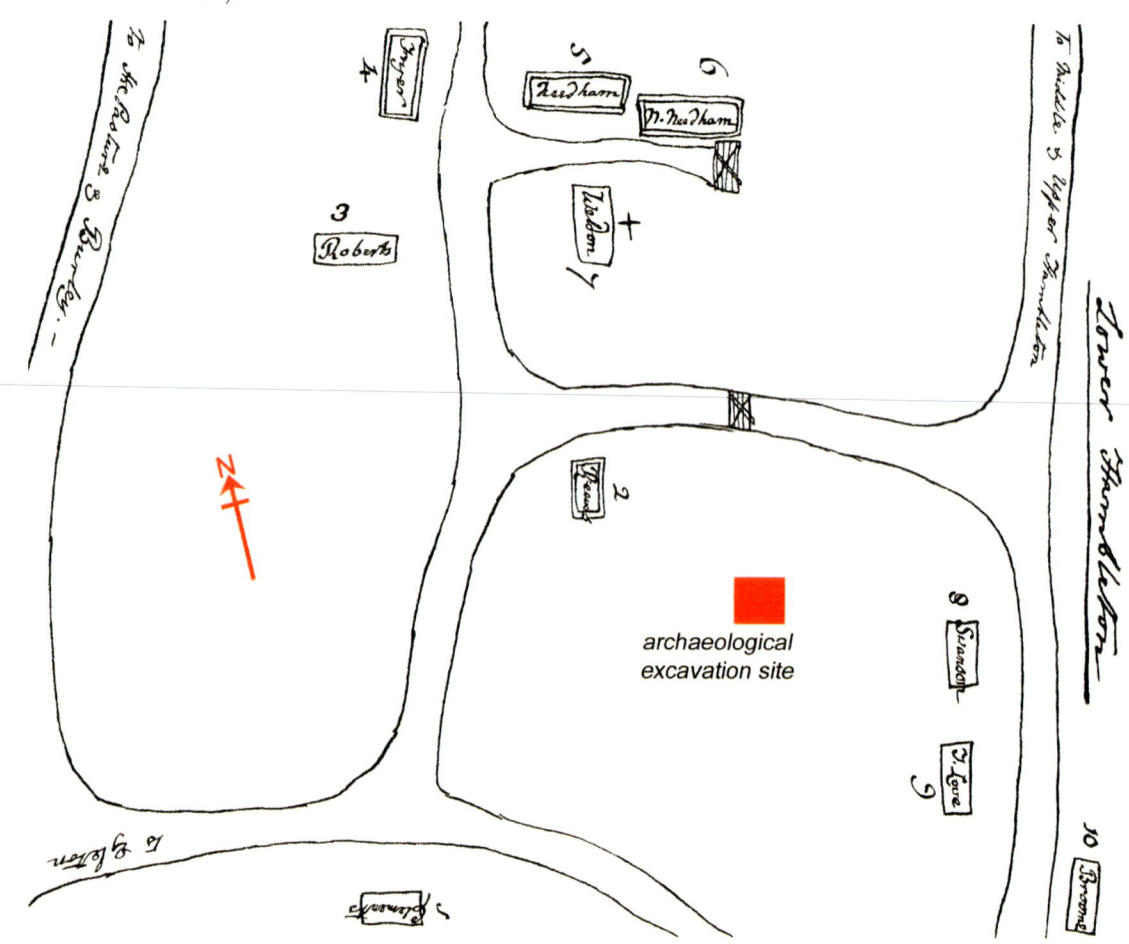

Below: The map of Lower Hambleton in 1797 (ROLLR DG 7/4/27) shows that land in the immediate vicinity of the 1970s archaeological excavation was uninhabited at that time

— 442 —

The position at Whitwell is rather different. Here, whilst there is a significant quantity of Saxo-Norman pottery, including the earliest coarse Stamford fabric dating from the tenth and eleventh centuries, there are relatively higher proportions of the later medieval and early post-medieval fabrics, Midland Purple, Cistercian/Midland Black ware and Midland Yellow. Even the sherds of imported Rhenish ware are not out of place: 'from about 1485 until 1550 the classic type of small Raeren jug was very widely exported and arrived in Britain in such large quantities that it became a type fossil of this period on every site ranging from royal palace to peasant house' (Hurst *et al* 1986). Whilst Whitwell may not have been a site of high status, however, the presence of ridge and floor tile – materials which were absent from Nether Hambleton – suggests that there was at least one building of some quality in the vicinity.

At Whitwell, much of the material covered a wide date range and was clearly residual, suggesting that it had been redeposited, possibly as make-up levels in later phases. The archaeological levels may have been further disturbed by subsequent agricultural activity, such as ploughing, after the abandonment of the site. However, it does seem that occupation continued here into the sixteenth if not the seventeenth century, rather later than can be deduced for the Nether Hambleton house.

Both sites produced pottery assemblages typical of the period and locality in terms of the vessel forms and fabrics present, the latter reflecting the essentially local, or at most regional, nature of most of the medieval and early post-medieval pottery distribution patterns. The pottery is mainly domestic in character, but the predominance of bowls and jugs may reflect the importance of dairy processing in the agrarian economy. The absence of cooking pots or jars in the later wares and the appearance of cisterns reflect not only the introduction of metal cooking vessels during the later medieval period, but also changing drinking fashions.

There is much information still to be obtained, both from new material brought to light through fieldwalking or excavation, and, perhaps just as importantly, from material from earlier sites already examined and described. Many sites which were excavated and written up before the discovery of the Lyveden and Bourne kiln groups may have yielded material from both these sources which has yet to be identified. In this context, therefore, the Nether Hambleton and Whitwell assemblages add considerably to our knowledge of the trade and usage of medieval ceramics in this area of the county in the medieval and early post-medieval periods. Future work will no doubt amplify what has been undertaken so far, and enhance our understanding of the history and development of these two settlements. For the moment, though, if not for always, intriguing questions remain unanswered.

Aspects of Topography

Gibbet Lane

Gibbet Lane, now under Rutland Water, ran in an easterly direction along the south side of the Gwash from Hambleton Bridge, or High Bridge, to Edith Weston. This lane and the nearby Gibbet Gorse take their names from the gibbeting of Richard and William Weldon of Nether Hambleton who were hanged for the murder in 1788 of John Freeman, a baker of Edith Weston, whilst returning this way from Oakham (*see* Chapter 30 – Extra, Extra, Read all about it!). The local name for the lane was 'Cattle Grid Road' (Edna Locke).

Another crime committed here was reported in the *Stamford Mercury* on 18th December 1818:

'On Monday last, as Mr S [Samuel] Suitor, shoemaker, of Hambleton, was returning from Edithweston between 7 and 8 o'clock in the evening, he was met at the end of the lane . . . by two footpads, who knocked him down and otherwise ill treated him and robbed him of 17li.16s.6d, the amount of bills he had received that day.'

A more recent traveller was Sheila Drake (*née* Tibbert) of Nether Hambleton who frequently went this way with her parents on a pony and trap to visit her grandparents in Edith Weston, where a short length of the lane remains today as the access road to Rutland Sailing Club.

High Bridge in 1970, looking north. Gibbet Lane is to the right (Jim Levisohn ARPS)

Above: Gibbet Lane at Edith Weston looking west in 1970 (Jim Levisohn ARPS)

Left: Gibbet Lane highlighted on the OS 2nd ed 1" map 1906

Chapter 21
Lost Homes
Sheila Sleath and Robert Ovens

When over 3,000 acres of land in the Gwash Valley were flooded in order to create Rutland Water, it was inevitable that a great deal would be lost.

A pleasant, rural landscape, containing fertile farmland and natural habitats, disappeared along with a way of life for those who had to forfeit their homes, farms and livelihoods. An entire hamlet, Nether Hambleton, and its connecting network of footpaths and roads to surrounding communities vanished, and these along with other geographical features were erased from the map.

It is difficult to imagine this landscape without water, but fortunately what lay beneath the reservoir is not entirely forgotten. By delving into a vast source of archival material, it is possible to form a picture of what the valley, and life within it, was like in former times. Reports and artefacts from archaeological excavations, historical records, literature, old maps, paintings, photographs and people's memories all help to provide a picture of 'what used to be'. This chapter deals specifically with homes which were demolished to make way for the reservoir. Particular emphasis is given to the houses and former occupants of the lost hamlet of Nether Hambleton.

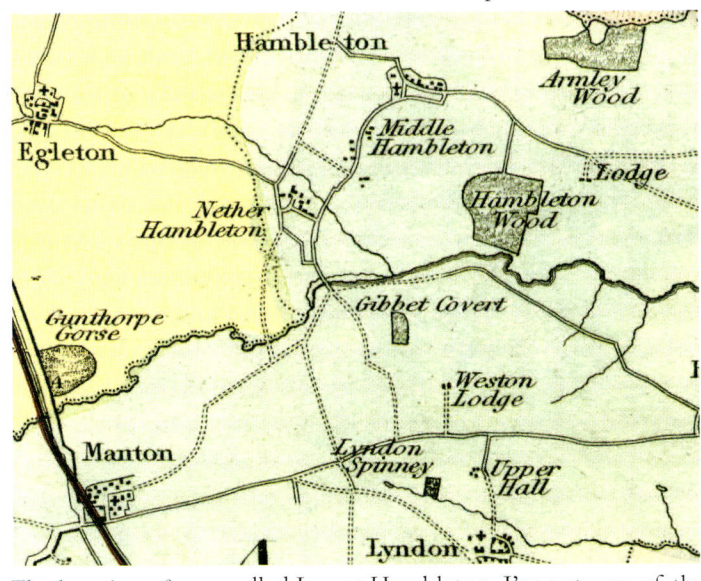

The location of Upper, Middle and Nether Hambleton on J & C Walker's map of 1878

Hambleton originally consisted of three parts, Upper, Middle and Nether, but when Nether Hambleton and part of Middle Hambleton were lost as a result of Rutland Water, what remained became simply 'Hambleton'. The name of Nether, or Lower, Hambleton was always a source of confusion even to those who lived there. Sheila Drake, *née* Tibbert, who was born at East View in 1944, recorded:

'We lived in Nether Hambleton which we always called Lower Hambleton. I'm not sure of the correct term. Our address was always Lower Hambleton all the time that we lived there, but more recently others call it Nether Hambleton. Whether East View and April Cottage [on the Lyndon road from Middle Hambleton] were Lower Hambleton, and Ivydene and Red House round the corner were Nether Hambleton, I don't know.'

Officially the village was Nether Hambleton, as on Ordnance Survey maps dating from 1824. However, due to its geographical position, it is

Sheila Drake moving sheep from Upper Hambleton to East View farm in 1956 (Sheila Drake)

understandable that the hamlet was also referred to as Lower Hambleton. It is interesting to note that a 1797 estate notebook (ROLLR DG 7/4/27) listing the 9th Earl of Winchilsea and 4th Earl of Nottingham's tenants (*see* Chapter 9 – Lower Hambleton in 1797) refers to Lower Hambleton.

In general the Hambleton Parish Registers do not differentiate between the three settlements. There are a few references in the burial records to Lower (from as early as 1859) and Middle Hambleton, but none to Nether Hambleton. For the purposes of this chapter, the hamlet and its outlying cottages on the Lyndon road will be referred to as Lower Hambleton.

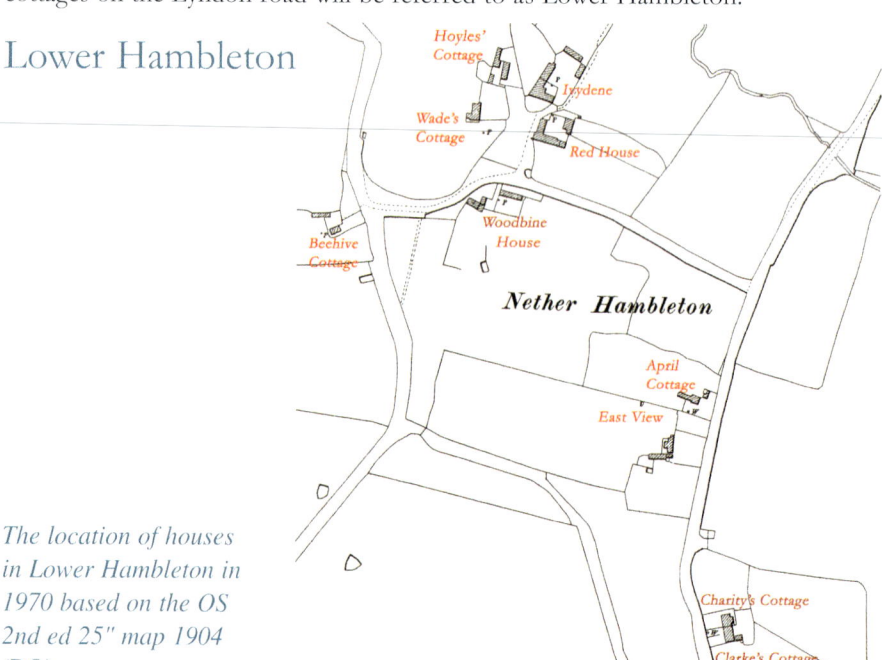

Lower Hambleton

The location of houses in Lower Hambleton in 1970 based on the OS 2nd ed 25" map 1904 (RO)

— 446 —

Beehive Cottage

Prior to being demolished for what was to become Rutland Water, Beehive Cottage was considered to be one of the oldest cottages in Rutland. It was examined in some detail by members of Rutland Field Research Group for Archaeology and History who, from 1973 until 1976, were carrying out an archaeological excavation on the site of a medieval building in a nearby field. They found that Beehive Cottage was of medieval construction, the materials used being stone, wattle and daub. Ideally it should have been dismantled stone by stone and re-erected elsewhere.

It is difficult to identify the early occupants of this cottage. However the 1797 notebook indicates that George Clements, his wife Mary and their six children had just moved into Beehive Cottage. George Clements died in 1829 and later Census Returns indicate that a Hugh Springthorpe took over the tenancy until at least 1851. One of George Clements's daughters, Elizabeth, married Hugh Springthorpe in 1822.

Beehive Cottage from the north-west in the 1960s. In the 1930s the rooms at either end of the cottage were bedrooms, with the kitchen in between. Because of the roof design, the ceilings in these rooms were very low (Jim Levisohn ARPS)

Beehive Cottage in 1970, believed to be the oldest cottage in Rutland (Jim Eaton)

Kemmel Freestone, later of Whissendine, went to live in Beehive Cottage in 1934 when he was 14. He had moved from Trimley Marshes, Suffolk, with his mother and stepfather, Bert West. Bert West and Kemmel both worked for Miss Maud Tryon who farmed at Old Hall, Middle Hambleton. Kemmel recollects:

'Beehive was very old and very, very damp . . . There was no upstairs, it was all on one ground floor. You went in the front door into a room, then you went from one room into the next. There was no back door – as you went in, you had to come out the same way. We had a living room and two bedrooms – one on either side of the main room – and a little kitchenette – you couldn't swing a cat around in it. We always called the kitchenette the "backus" [back-house]. That's where we did the washing up and all that – where we put the water. You see, there was only my stepfather, my mother and myself and we all lived there and I had a little lean-to place for my own room. Of course I wasn't very old when I lived there.

'We got our water from a well in the garden. It had two doors over it which was covered with a large slab of stone. We had to drop a bucket down on a rope to get the water and when it came out the water would be covered with green slime. Sometimes there would be frogs and toads in it.

'We had a coal fire but although the coalman used to come around on the odd times, we rarely got coal, we mostly used wood. I think my mother had a three-[ring] paraffin burner that she cooked on. We had no electricity but used candles and paraffin lamps that had delicate mantles on them. The toilet was in a hovel in the garden – it was really just a bucket that had a wooden seat placed over it. We used to have bits of newspaper on a nail on the back of the door.'

Kemmel and his family left Beehive Cottage in 1938 to live at Normanton. Over the next decade the cottage underwent some modernisation before being sold. On Wednesday 8th September 1948 the outlying portions of the Burley Estates situated in the Vale of Catmose, at Greetham and at Leighfield, were sold by auction under the direction of Major James Hanbury. Beehive Cottage was scheduled to be sold with Hill Top Farm, Upper Hambleton, as Lot 29, and the cottage was described in the following manner:

'THE "BEEHIVE COTTAGE", situate in North [*sic*] Hambleton, is a picturesque Stone-built and Thatched Cottage containing: Sitting Room, Living Room, Bedroom, Bathroom fitted with new bath and "Elsan" Closet: Scullery and Pantry, also outside privy, Coal Store and Kitchen Gardens. Total acreage 31 perches.'

Sheila Drake recalls:

The entrance door to the rear of Beehive Cottage and the inclusion of a bedroom in the roof were possibly a result of improvements carried out in the 1940s (Noel Sharp)

'My first memory of anybody at Beehive Cottage was some people called Hardcastle. When I was at school [in the early 1950s] they were there, because I remember there was a little lad there called Alfie Hardcastle. He must have been about 5 or 6. The road used to get flooded between Beehive Cottage and Hambleton School and I remember helping him to climb along the railings to avoid getting his feet wet. I've been into Beehive. As far as I can remember, as you went into the front door there was only one large room, possibly a little room off there and I think there was a sort of loft bedroom. I can't remember whether you went upstairs or up a ladder. It was when the cottage was empty. I never visited it when there was anybody there. It was a very old cottage.'

Jock Shaw, who lived at the Old Priest House in Upper Hambleton, acquired Beehive Cottage *circa* 1967 and by 1970 had started to modernise it with the idea of living in it himself. However his plans came to nothing due to the construction of the reservoir.

Occupants of Beehive Cottage in the Twentieth Century

It is difficult to determine the occupants of this cottage and their dates of residence. It appears that many of the tenants did not stay for long. Consequently the following is a very incomplete list:

circa 1924-25	Mrs Cumberland
1934-38	Croson family
1938	Mr and Mrs West and Kemmel Freestone
April 1939	Jack Ireland
circa 1950s	Hardcastle family
circa 1960s	Larry and Dawn Hoyles (née Charity)

Watercolour of Beehive by Mary Andrews (Dora Allibone)

Ivydene and Red House

In 1968 Ivydene and Red House were the family homes of Frank and Noel Sharp. Frank lived with his sisters, Ivy and Mary, at Ivydene. Their brother Noel, his wife Dorothy and two daughters, Wendy and Christine, occupied Red House. On hearing of the reservoir proposal, which would swallow up their joint farm, Ivy informed readers of the *Stamford Mercury* (23rd August 1968) that she was stunned by the news, and added, 'It's been our life living here, and I think it will be dreadful if it happens. We are just waiting for the crunch'. Noel Sharp commented, 'It is heartbreaking. I was born on the farm and my father was here before me. I don't know where I shall go'. It was not easy adjusting to the possibility of losing their homes and livelihoods. Noel took an active part in the campaign to oppose the scheme but it was all to no avail.

By 1975 both farmhouses and their adjacent farm buildings, including a cowshed, milking parlour, implement shed, stables, a dutch barn and a huge grain dryer, had been demolished. Two nearby derelict cottages, Wade's and Hoyles', suffered the same fate.

Aerial view of Ivydene and Red House looking south-east. Ivydene farm is in the foreground (Noel Sharp)

Sharp's Friesian cows are taken out to pasture in the 1960s. To the left is Wade's Cottage with Hoyles' Cottage behind (Canon John R H Prophet)

Thomas and Ada Sharp were the parents of Mary, Ivy, Tom, Frank and Noel. Thomas came to Lower Hambleton as a farmer and grazier to live at Ivydene about 1915, taking over the tenancy from his relative Edward Ward. In 1918 Thomas purchased Ivydene and Red House from the Winchilsea Estate, and ran them as one farm. He also acquired the two nearby cottages later known as Wade's and Hoyles'. He built up a thriving business which was carried on by four of his children. On his marriage to Dorothy in 1947, Noel moved into Red House. Frank, Ivy and Mary continued to live at Ivydene after their parents' deaths in the early 1960s.

During the 1920s, Red House had been home to the Shelton family. Mr Shelton was a wheelwright and his wife helped Mrs Sharp at Ivydene. Mr Marriott, who had been a butcher in Nottingham, his wife and daughter Dorothy moved into Red House after the Sheltons. Tom Sharp lived in Red House for a while before his brother Noel and his bride made it their home.

By 1968 the Sharp family was farming a total of 363 acres, much of which was devoted to cereal crops. These were barley, most of which went to Germany for brewing lager, wheat, which was sold to Hovis for breadmaking, and oats. No root crops were grown on the farm. Livestock at this time included 400 sheep whose lambs were sold at Stamford market, 30 milking cows and 150 mixed cattle. All but sister Ivy worked full-time on the farm. She was housekeeper and looked after the poultry.

Red House and Ivydene were demolished in July 1975 and the occupants of both houses moved to North Luffenham.

Ivydene farmyard from the north-east (Bryan Waites)

The Sharp sisters at Ivydene. Ivy, on the left, was housekeeper and looked after the poultry. Mary worked on the farm (Edna Locke)

Above: Mary Sharp feeding a Friesian calf on the farm (Noel Sharp)

Left: The farmyard pump at Ivydene (Noel Sharp)

Ivydene

Ivydene was a large stone-built, L-shaped building, roofed with Collyweston slates. It is possible that it had been two homes at some time during the nineteenth century. In 1970 the main accommodation included nine bedrooms, a kitchen, pantry and two living rooms. There were two staircases in the building. The 'best room' had an Adam fireplace and the adjoining room a tiled fireplace, each tile portraying one of Aesop's fables. Two bedroom windows, looking north, at the east end of Ivydene were barred, suggesting that these rooms were, at some time, used as nurseries. The wing attached to the north and west of the main living accommodation had two cellars.

Although mains water was laid on just before 1954, a nearby well continued to provide water for the dairy cooling system until the 1970s. Electricity was laid on in 1956.

The living room fireplace at Ivydene with tiles portaying Aesop's fables (Jim Levisohn ARPS)

The appropriately named Ivydene just before it was demolished in July 1975, viewed from Red House farmyard (RLHRS)

One of the tiles from the fireplace in the living room at Ivydene. The tile was made by Maw & Co, Benthall Works, Jackson, Shropshire (Noel Sharp)

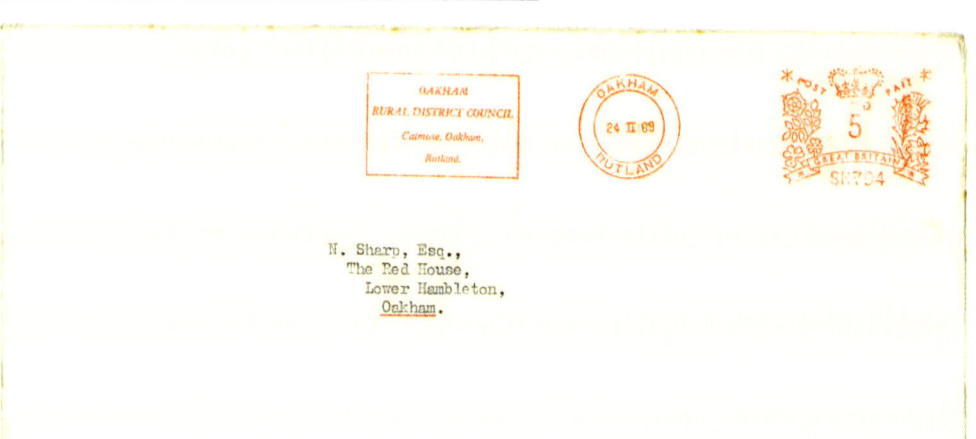

One of the few surviving envelopes addressed to Lower Hambleton (Noel Sharp)

— 452 —

Red House

Right: Red House farm from the south-east (Richard Adams)

Middle Right: Red House in the process of being demolished (Jim Eaton)

Below Right: Lower Hambleton letterbox would now be a collector's item (RO)

This red-brick building with its Collyweston slated roof was built in 1795 according to the date picked out in blue bricks on the south gable. On the ground floor it had a living room, a large kitchen and a utility room. There were six bedrooms, three of which were in the attic. There was a disused well inside immediately in front of the back door. This particular well proved to be an obstacle when the contractors went in to demolish Red House. As the front end of a bulldozer crawled over the well, the cover collapsed and the machine got stuck, an ignominious beginning to its task of razing this farmhouse to the ground.

Stone barns formed two sides of a cobbled yard and those at the eastern end had at some time been used as an abattoir and butcher's shop. A Victorian letterbox was set into the wall of one of the barns which ran alongside the road. It was removed before the building was demolished.

Former Occupants of Ivydene and Red House

The occupants of these two farmhouses in 1797 were Joseph and Nicholas Needham and their families, but it is not known how long they were in residence. Red House may have been a public house, known as The Bull, Nicholas Needham being the publican.

Recent research suggests that the following families were occupants of Ivydene or Red House during the nineteenth century and up to 1915 when Thomas Sharp first went to live at Ivydene. Assuming that the following were occupying one of these two properties, it is still difficult to determine, with absolute certainty, which family lived in which farmhouse. The properties have therefore been labelled A and B. The list is not exhaustive, particularly as Ivydene may, at some time, have housed two families.

A:
circa 1841 – *circa* 1894:
In 1841 Mary Fryer, a widow and farmer, was living here with seven of her children, and a male and a female servant. She was probably the widow of John Fryer, the son of William and Ann Fryer, who in 1797 were living in nearby Hoyles' Cottage.

By 1851 Mary was farming 130 acres and was helped by her son William and daughter Eliza. They had a live-in house servant, Ann Dexter, and Mary employed two men and a boy to work on the farm. Although William had married by 1861 he continued to live at Lower Hambleton with his mother. Mary, aged 77 years, was still head of this household in 1871 and was recorded as farming 136 acres of land and employing one man and two boys.

William Fryer and his wife Mary Ann continued to work the same farm after the death of his mother Mary. By 1881 the total land farmed had increased to 243 acres. Living with William and his wife was a general domestic as well as an agricultural servant. William was still living in Lower Hambleton when he died in 1894. It is not known whether his widow continued to live here.

Ivydene from the south. Note the Victorian letterbox in the barn wall (Sheila Drake)

circa 1898 – *circa* 1915:

Matkin's *Oakham Almanack* records that Edward Bonnie Wilson Ward and his son Edward Ward were resident in Hambleton in 1898. Edward lost his wife the following year. Both men were farmers and in 1901 they appear to be occupying both Ivydene and Red House. Edward, born at Pickworth, was 76 years of age. Living with him was his granddaughter Hannah aged 23 and grandson William aged 19. In the other household was his son Edward, 34 years of age, born at Sproxton, Leicestershire, his wife Lucy, their children Florence and Henry, and Edward's mother-in-law, Sarah Dorman. Although Edward snr, Edward jnr and his wife were buried in Hambleton in 1925, 1949 and 1952 respectively, none was resident in Hambleton at those dates. The Ward family were related to Thomas Sharp who occupied Ivydene about 1915.

A distant view of Ivydene and Red House from the south-west in the early 1970s. Wade's Cottage and Hoyles' Cottage had already been demolished (Tony Traylen)

B:

circa 1841:

In 1841 William and James Hibbitt, both farmers, may have lived in Ivydene or Red House. In the same household were two female members of the family, possibly the wife and daughter of James, and a female servant. The Hibbitts were not born in Rutland. This family does not appear in the Hambleton Census Return for 1851.

circa 1857 – *circa* 1880:

It seems likely that a Richard Healey lived in one of these farmhouses. When two of his children, Francis and Harriet, were baptised in 1857 the parish registers confirmed that they lived in Lower Hambleton. In 1861 Richard, aged 37, was living with his wife Sarah, six children, a governess, a kitchenmaid, a housemaid and a shepherd. At that time Richard farmed 175 acres and he employed two labourers. Although Richard died in 1871 his widow was farming 270 acres and employed three men and two boys. Living with Sarah were six of her children, a housemaid, a general servant and a farm servant.

circa 1898 – *circa* 1915:
Either Edward Ward or his son, Edward, as detailed in farmhouse A.

Ivydene stands isolated in 1975 (Jim Eaton)

Wade's and Hoyles' Cottages

In the 1970s Wade's Cottage and Hoyles' Cottage were owned by the Sharp family, farmers who lived at nearby Ivydene and Red House. The cottages were unoccupied at this time and had been for a number of years. A large grain dryer towered over both cottages, making them unsuitable for habitation.

Although the survey of 1797 gives the names of the occupants of these cottages, it is difficult to determine who lived in them during the nineteenth century. The census returns do not identify individual dwellings, but there is evidence to suggest that on occasion, one or both of the cottages may have been occupied by more than one family.

This photograph, taken by George Henton in 1914 (ROLLR H1009) shows Wade's Cottage from the south-west with its new thatch

Wade's Cottage

When viewed from the south, Wade's Cottage appeared deceptively small. However, there was a large wing to the rear, the thatched roof of which swept down to first floor height. A date stone set into the west elevation of this cottage indicated that it was built in 1729. The Rutland Field Research Group inspected this cottage in 1973 and recorded that the walls were of stone, with wattle and daub partitions. There was also evidence of external bread ovens.

The last known occupants of this cottage were Henry and Mary Ellen Wade and their two daughters who were living there in 1901. Henry was the son of Thomas and Lavinia Wade. In 1871 and 1881 he was living with his parents, possibly at April Cottage. The 1901 Census Return records that Henry was an agricultural labourer, that he was 42 years of age and that his place of birth was Wing. His wife Mary Ellen, who was 41, and their

Wade's Cottage from the south-west (Noel Sharp)

One of the bread ovens at Wade's Cottage (RLHRS)

children Beatrice Mary, aged 12, and Jessica aged 11, were all born at Hambleton. Henry and Mary remained in Wade's Cottage for the rest of their lives. Mary was nursemaid to Mary, Ivy, Tom, Frank and Noel Sharp of Ivydene, and was affectionately known as 'Nanny Wade'. Henry died at Lower Hambleton in 1941 and Mary Ellen in 1949. After the death of her parents, Jessica continued to live, for some time, in Wade's Cottage as sole occupant. In the 1950s she left Lower Hambleton, moving into one of the Thomas Fryer Almshouses at Manton.

A musical photograph album belonging to the Wade family was presented to Rutland County Museum in 1967 (RCM 1967.16). It dates from the mid-nineteenth century. It is a bound volume with ornamentally printed pages. There is a musical box in the back cover, which plays 'Nae Lick Aboot the Hoose' and 'Last Rose of Summer'.

Richard Roberts, a labourer, his wife Mary and their seven daughters lived in Wade's Cottage in 1797. Richard may have occupied this cottage from as early as 1779. Estate records for Burley on the Hill note that he was a good tenant and kept his home well maintained. He died in 1807 and his wife died thirty years later, at the age of 83.

Sarah, daughter of Richard and Mary, married Francis Hill, an agricultural labourer, from Manton, in 1831, and it is highly likely that they lived in Wade's Cottage. Francis, as head of the household, and Sarah lived with their son Richard until their respective deaths in 1855 and *circa* 1871. When widowed in 1855, and up to 1871, Sarah became head of the household. Richard, the son, was a carpenter, and he and his wife Eliza were definitely living in Lower Hambleton when three of their children were baptised in 1863 and one in 1867.

The *Pastures Book 1862* (private collection) records that Richard Hill was regularly employed by the stewards of the Hambleton Cow Pasture. The Pasture had an acreage of 102 acres and was divided into 80 cow commons. Richard's annual bill averaged about £7 from 1863-71 and it appears that this was for fencing. After 1871 and until 1887 he was only employed by the stewards on a few occasions and the work that he did was a fraction of that

Nanny Wade's copper was salvaged before the cottage was demolished. Cleaned and polished, it now makes a fine ornamental feature (private ownership)

done in the 1860s. The Census Returns suggest that this family lived in Wade's Cottage until after 1871. By 1881, due perhaps to the death of Sarah, his mother-in law, and the subsequent termination of the tenancy, Richard Hill and his wife Eliza had moved to live at the Post Office in Upper Hambleton. Thus ended almost a century of the Hill family living in Lower Hambleton, and almost certainly in the same cottage. It is not known who occupied this cottage during the next two decades.

Hoyles' Cottage

This stone-built, thatched cottage had dormer windows at both north and south ends and it appears to have been extended over the years. In 1970 it had three bedrooms, a living room, lounge, kitchen and a utility room.

The occupants of this cottage in 1797, when it was described as a farmhouse, were William Fryer, his wife Ann and their five children. Three more of their children had been baptised by 1803. Exactly how long they lived in this farmhouse is unknown, but it is probable that the family, or their descendants, moved into the adjacent Red House well before 1841.

Hoyles' Cottage from the west. A different stone was used for the south end of the cottage and this may be a later addition (Bryan Waites)

Edward Wadkin may have moved into Hoyles' Cottage, or possibly the adjacent Wade's Cottage, before 1841, and he may have shared one of these houses with another family, but it is difficult to be certain. Edward Wadkin, born *circa* 1786, was a carpenter. In 1841 he lived in Lower Hambleton with his wife Jane, his son, William, daughter-in-law Rebecca and one-year-old grandson Philip. In 1851 Edward was still head of the household and his son shared his father's trade. At this time William and Rebecca had five children. William's mother Jane died in 1847, his father Edward in 1862, and his own wife Rebecca in 1856. His daughter Mary had married David Horn by 1875 and they and their four children were living with William in 1881. Up to this date four generations of the Wadkin family had lived in the same house.

The section of the 1891 Census Return which includes Lower Hambleton appears to be missing; consequently it has been difficult to determine where individual families lived. However, the 1901 Census indicates that William Dolby, an agricultural labourer, his wife and three children may have been living at Hoyles' Cottage.

From about 1936 a Mrs Noble lived in this cottage. A Peter Stewart lodged with her and he married her daughter Violet. Mrs Noble ran a shop in Lower Hambleton and this was located between her cottage and the barns of Red House farm. Kemmel Freestone, who lived in nearby Beehive Cottage remembered:

'It was a small building that was more like an old tin shed . . . we used to go in there to get our stamps and we were able to buy biscuits and sweets . . . the sweets were in jars and they had to be weighed on scales. There was none of this pre-packed stuff then. They didn't sell many provisions.'

During the 1940s, a land girl and Rosie Clements from Upper Hambleton lodged with Mrs Hoyles, the then tenant. In the 1950s Mr and Mrs Laity [Rosie Clements] and their son Barry were the occupants of Hoyles' Cottage.

Woodbine House

Woodbine House

This farmhouse was named Woodbine House because of the Woodbine growing around the front door. On the ground floor from the east end there was a large kitchen, a dairy, a dining room and a lounge. To reach the dairy, which contained several thralls, one had to go down three steps. The brick lean-to at the east end of the farmhouse was a bathroom. At the side of this was a wooden coal shed. The room above the kitchen was used as a storeroom and there were four bedrooms.

Stone-built Woodbine House from the north in the 1960s. The east end of the building on the south side was faced with red brick (Tony Traylen)

Brothers Neville and Winston Gregory and their sister Monica were born at Woodbine House. Neville had taken over the smallholding in 1942 from his father, John Arthur, and it came as a shock when he learned, in 1968, that he was destined to lose his home and 120 acres of land when the reservoir scheme became a reality. The holding was a mixed farm; cattle and sheep were kept and some corn grown for winter fodder. On the site were several small buildings for cattle and implements. At this time of great uncertainty, Woodbine House was also home to Neville's wife Joan and their sons Nicholas and Marcus. Knowing that he was to lose his livelihood, Neville moved and found work as a farm manager outside the area. Joan and her two sons continued to live in the farmhouse for as long as possible but when the farm buildings were being knocked down they knew that they had to vacate the property. They moved to Red House (now The Old Hall Cottage) at Middle Hambleton.

Members of the Gregory family had lived at Woodbine House for more than a century. The time span may be greater for Neville's family had firm links with this farm going back to the eighteenth century. Neville's grandparents, Robert and Mary Gregory, had made Woodbine House their home *circa* 1866. Robert was a grazier. Those living in Woodbine House in 1871 were Robert aged 68, Mary his wife 45, their three sons, Fred, Walter and John, and Sarah Allen, a servant. John, often confusingly referred to as

Arthur, his second name, was Neville's father. When Robert died in 1882 his wife Mary continued to work the smallholding along with her son John Arthur and his wife Olive. Mary and John are described in Matkin's *Oakham Almanack* as graziers and poultry dealers. Mary was buried at Hambleton on 9th April 1921, her son John on 15th July 1942.

Neville was a direct descendant of another Robert Gregory who was baptised at Hambleton in 1766. Robert married Jane, daughter of John and Martha Reeve on 17th November 1796. Jane's parents lived in what became known as Woodbine House and it is almost certain that she was born in this farmhouse. Her father was a tenant of the 9th Earl of Winchilsea. In 1797 John Reeve was a farmer who reared calves for sale.

The smallholding stood on the site of the medieval village of Nether Hambleton and over a three-year period from 1973, the Rutland Field Research Group were able to survey and excavate an area alongside what was identified as an early village street. This was to the south-east of the farm-yard.

It is thought that the ground floor room at the west end of Woodbine House had been licensed to hold church services. Marcus Gregory confirms that a pulpit and various other items of church furniture were stored in one of the first floor storerooms in the 1960s.

Lower Hambleton from the north-east. Woodbine House is left of centre with Red House and Ivydene to the right (Jim Levisohn ARPS)

Below: Woodbine House from the south-east on the left (RLHRS)

Below Right: Looking south-east from the excavation area. East View is to the right, April Cottage to the left (RLHRS)

— 459 —

Clarke's and Charity's Cottages

These picturesque thatched cottages were featured as 'Reservoir Victims' in the *Stamford Mercury* of 19th November 1971. In all, the newspaper produced a series of eight articles describing properties destined to disappear due to the construction of Rutland Water. At this time the two properties were known as Clarke's and Charity's Cottages, named after recent occupants. The brick cottage at the north end of the building had been home to Tom Charity and his wife Emma for over 40 years. As reported in the newspaper article, it was not easy for this elderly couple to accept that they were to lose their home. Tom stated:

Charity's Cottage in the late 1960s. The variety of building materials indicates the extent of additions to the original cottage (Joan Wild)

'Nobody has told us anything and we don't know when – and where we are going . . . I've got used to the idea of moving now, but my wife, Emma, is still very upset. This has been our home now for so many years – it's a great upheaval having to move at our time of life.'

Clarke's and Charity's Cottages from the north-west. The original stone-built cottage is at the southern end (Jim Eaton)

Three years previously, in the *Stamford Mercury* of 23rd August 1968 Emma Charity had forcefully expressed her views on the proposed construction of the reservoir:

'Why they want to build it here I just don't know . . . It's all right for those high-up men who sit behind desks all day: they don't seem to realise they are dealing with human lives. They can't know the suffering they are going to cause and I shouldn't think any of them have seen some of the beautiful land here. The Government tell the farmers they want them to produce more corn. How can they when they are taking all their land for roads, this reservoir and other schemes . . . I am just hoping this won't happen . . . We're going to sit tight as long as we can, but you've got to face the facts. My husband and I are over 70, and I don't think we shall be here when the scheme is finished.'

Mr and Mrs Charity moved into a newly built bungalow, for elderly residents, at Upper Hambleton.

Clarke's and Charity's Cottages were on the Lyndon road below Middle Hambleton. A mid-seventeenth century map of Thomas Barker's estate shows 'Sammons Close and House' at this location. This was almost certainly the original stone-built part of Clarke's and Charity's. By 1797 the building was occupied by two generations of the Broome (Broom) family: Henry and Sarah lived in 'Half the house' and their son John, his wife and family lived 'in the other part'. Whether the brick extension to the north had been built by this time is not known.

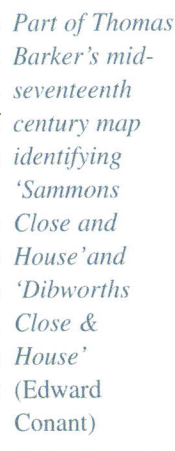

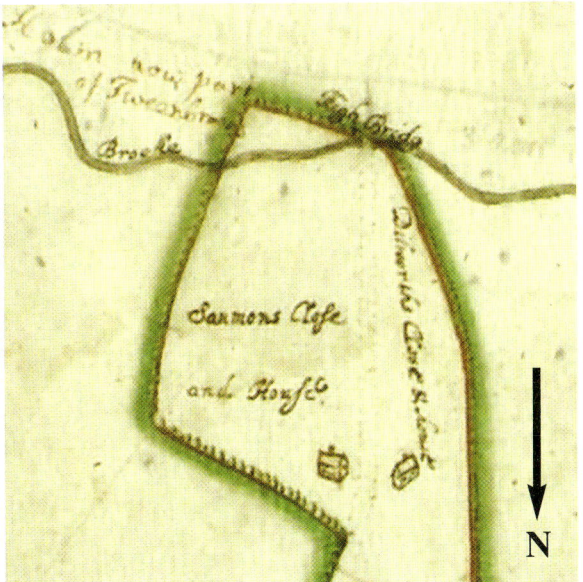

Part of Thomas Barker's mid-seventeenth century map identifying 'Sammons Close and House' and 'Dibworths Close & House' (Edward Conant)

Mary, the daughter of Tom and Emma Charity, at Hambleton School circa 1945. Mary is on the right (Noel Sharp)

Tom Charity in the garden at Lyndon Hall. Before retirement Tom worked on the railway (Sir John Conant)

Thelma Clarke, middle right, at Hambleton School circa 1945. She was the daughter of Harry and Emma Clarke of Clarke's Cottage, Lower Hambleton (Noel Sharp)

The indistinct Census Return of 1841 for Hambleton appears to confirm that there were no members of the Broome family resident in Lower Hambleton at this time. However, by 1851 Henry and Sarah's grandson, Richard, was living at Clarke's or Charity's Cottage. He is recorded as head of the household, and living with him was his wife Ann and three daughters. Richard and Ann were still living there in 1861 and may have remained there until their respective deaths in 1869 and 1866. Richard was an agricultural labourer and in the 1860s the *Pasture Book* records that the stewards employed him on several occasions. He was paid 4s for a day's work. In 1865 the work that he undertook was 'Thistle Mowing', 'Clotknocking', 'Drawing Rails & Cleansing Watering'.

A Coleman Clarke married Richard's daughter Louisa, *circa* 1869. It seems that he continued the tenancy after the death of Louisa's parents. Louisa's brother Robert, sister-in-law Hannah, and their family, had been living in the other cottage prior to 1861 and continued to do so for at least another twenty years. The 1871 Census Return records that Coleman was a shepherd. Ten years later he was described as a cottager. On several occasions during the 1880s and 1890s he was employed to do some fencing by the stewards of the Hambleton Cow Pasture. For each day's work he was paid 2s 6d.

Coleman and Louisa Clarke were still living in Lower Hambleton in 1901, together with three of their daughters and a son, Harry. Harry was baptised at Hambleton on 7th June 1885 and as an adult was often known as 'Stodger'. He continued to live in the stone-built cottage, known in the 1960s as Clarke's Cottage, with his wife Emma and their children, Coleman, Thelma and Mildred. As well as having a small holding, Harry was also the roadman for Lower Hambleton. Kemmel Freestone, who lived at Beehive Cottage from 1934-38, recalled:

'He didn't stand very high – he was more of a dwarf and he was the road sweeper keeping our roads clear and trimmed up. I knew him as Little Harry and he was referred to as 2 foot 2 and a tater [potato].'

Another former resident of Lower Hambleton remembered Harry as being 'the best potato picker in the area. He was nearer to the ground than anyone else so he hadn't so far to bend'.

A Clarence Broome, whose family lived in Leicester, lodged with the Clarke family from about 1937. He was a cobbler and is remembered for selling 'Beaver Boots'. These leather boots had a beaver trade mark on the heel tab and the best boots cost 7s 6d. It is possible, but not confirmed by present research, that Clarence, like 'Little Harry', was related to the Broome family of 1797.

Harry and Emma Clarke left their cottage about two years before the Gwash valley was flooded. They moved to Manton.

By 1901 Charity Cottage, later occupied by Tom and Emma Charity, may have become home to Robert and Emma Smith and their adult children, Alfred, Edwin and Ernest. At this time, Robert was a shepherd, aged 60 years. He was born at Whitwell, and his wife, Emma, and all of their children were born in Hambleton. Robert died at Stamford in 1906 and was buried at Hambleton. His wife Emma died at Lower Hambleton in 1922 at the age of 77.

Hambleton Parish Registers

One of the difficulties for the researcher, when consulting the Hambleton Parish Registers, is that they rarely differentiate between the three settlements of Upper, Middle and Lower Hambleton. However, the following members of the Broome and Clarke families are specifically identified as having lived in Lower Hambleton:

Broome (Broom):
Henry, son of Robert and Hannah, baptised 20th October 1861.
Albert, son of Robert and Hannah, baptised 6th September 1863.
Richard, son of Robert and Hannah, baptised 16th September 1867.
Ann, wife of Richard, buried 6th August 1866 aged 69 years.
Richard, a widower, buried 10th February 1869 aged 72 years.

Clarke:
Coleman, husband of Louisa, buried 2nd February 1920 aged 77 years.
Emma, sister to Harry, buried 8th February 1967 aged 81 years. Emma died at Rutland Nursing Home, Langham.
Coleman, son of Harry and Emma, baptised 24th March 1922.
Thelma, daughter of Harry and Emma, baptised 23rd April 1922.
Mildred Vera, daughter of Harry and Emma, baptised 9th January 1924.

East View in the 1960s when it was home to Harold and Winifred Tibbert.
(Joan Wild)

East View

East View had been bought in the late 1960s by Mr and Mrs Walter Barwell. He was a school groundsman for Rutland County Council and had originally purchased the farm with the intention of spending his retirement at Lower Hambleton. However his plans were thwarted. By 1973 his home was due to be demolished and his 50 acres of grazing land about to be submerged beneath the reservoir. East View was Reservoir Victim No 5 in the series of articles in the *Stamford Mercury*. In the edition for 29th October 1971 Walter Barwell said:

'We had especially chosen to retire in this lovely valley and it is a great pity we won't be able to. This is one of the nicest homes that is going to be demolished for the reservoir. I really can't understand them taking so much land for this scheme. It isn't really justified, as the reservoir will be so shallow at this end – something like five feet of water.'

On leaving East View, Mr and Mrs Barwell moved to a newly built bungalow at Upper Hambleton.

Former Occupants of East View

In 1797 East View was occupied by Thomas Love, who was a butcher, his wife and five children. His descendants continued to live in this seventeenth-century farmhouse for over a hundred years.

In 1841, Amos Love, assumed son or grandson of the above Thomas, was living in Lower Hambleton with his wife Elizabeth and six of their children. Amos was also a butcher. When he died at the age of 49 in 1847, his widow retained the tenancy of East View farm, which had an area of 21 acres. She may have remained here until her death, at the age of 85, in 1887. Living with Elizabeth in 1851 were her children Thomas, another butcher, William, Elizabeth and Harriet. In 1881 Elizabeth was described as a cottager, and the only other occupant in the house was her son William.

The next occupant of East View farm was John Davis, a grazier. He was living here in 1901 with his wife Elizabeth and daughter Laura, who was a teacher. Elizabeth Davis was the daughter of the above Amos and Elizabeth Love. It is not known when this family moved into East View but it may have been as early as 1886 when John is recorded in the accounts of the Hambleton Cow Pasture. He was elected as one of the stewards for seven successive years from 1889. John and his wife were living at Lower Hambleton when they died; Elizabeth was buried in 1915, and John in 1920. Their daughter Laura married Henry Rutherford. Henry went to live in Lower Hambleton *circa* 1913 to work on, and eventually to take over, the smallholding run by his in-laws. Henry and Laura Rutherford had one child, Vera Margaret, who married Ernest Towell of Edith Weston in 1937. In the same year as her marriage Vera found her father, Henry Rutherford, drowned in a nearby pond.

Later occupants of East View were Jack Shaw, Laurie his wife and son Tom, and Jack Ireland. In April 1939, Harold Tibbert and his bride, Winifred, moved into the farmhouse, and it was here that they ran a smallholding and brought up their five children, Peter, Rosemary, Sheila, Richard and Susan. The Tibberts left the farm in 1963, moving to Egleton where Harold worked as a farm labourer.

Harold Tibbert who occupied East View from 1939-63 (Sheila Drake)

Sheila Drake, *née* Tibbert, has many happy memories of her life at East View, Lower Hambleton. She was born in 1944 and can remember her home very clearly:

'I can remember when I was very small, if we went out, when we came back we walked in the front door and had to stop just inside because we hadn't any electricity . . . I would imagine it would be about 1949 . . . we used candles and paraffin lamps. As you went in the front door, on the left hand side were the stairs and then a passage went right through to the back of the house. On the left hand side at the back was the sitting room and on the right hand side was the kitchen and that was the room we virtually lived in; then

— 464 —

on the right hand side of the house was a scullery. You could go through the kitchen into the scullery. The scullery is the bit sticking out at the side of the house. At the back of the kitchen there was a big pantry . . . you went down some steps . . . it was quite cold, almost like a cellar. We had a pump in the kitchen for cold water. It must have pumped the water up from a well. There wasn't piped water at that stage. We didn't get piped water until we had a bathroom built on the back of the scullery. Prior to that we used an outside closet round the back – it was an earth closet. We used a tin bath when I was a child . . . we bathed in front of the kitchen fire. That was the whole of the ground floor. Upstairs there were three bedrooms. Outside at the back there was a big corrugated shed, it wasn't a barn, but a shed that was open fronted where we kept the tractor. On the left-hand side of the house and going away to the back there was the original cowshed and then there was a shed attached beyond that. The cowshed was brick-built with a tiled roof . . . it had piers and mangers at the back of it. Then later, but I can't remember what year, we had a modern cowshed built with a shed at the end where the milking machine was cleaned.'

Winifred Tibbert with her son Peter who was born at East View in 1940 (Sheila Drake)

Harold Tibbert had a small, mixed farm and in his daughter Sheila's words, 'He was a one-man band, he used to do everything'. He reared lambs, calves, pigs and chickens, and these were sold at Melton Mowbray market. Also sold at market were eggs, milk, hay, potatoes and wheat. Hay, peas, mangolds and kale were specifically grown for feeding the animals. The Tibbert children all helped on the farm, particularly during the school holidays.

Lambing time at East View in the 1950s (Sheila Drake)

April Cottage

Susannah Swanson, a widow, and her daughter Mary lived at April Cottage in 1797. They had occupied the cottage for many years but by 1800 Susannah had died and her daughter was in an almshouse. The cottage was built of stone and, at this time, partly thatched.

It is difficult to determine who occupied this dwelling after the Swansons. The Hambleton Census Returns for 1871, 1881 and 1901 indicate that the family of a Thomas Wade may have lived here. Thomas, a stonemason, his wife Lavinia, four sons and one daughter, were occupants in 1871. By 1901 the widowed Lavinia was 79 and head of the household. Living with her were her son Thomas, a grazier, and daughter Lavinia, who were both in their 50s. Thomas, the last surviving member of this branch of the Wade family, died in 1914. It is reported that a Mr and Mrs Smith lived here during the 1920s.

A Miss A Blackwell, housekeeper to Miss Maud Tryon of Old Hall, Middle Hambleton, lived at April Cottage from *circa* 1931. When Miss Tryon retired in 1949 she went to live with Miss Blackwell.

Mrs Smale occupied the cottage during the early 1960s and Edna and Ernie Locke lived there prior to buying Beech Farm, Middle Hambleton, in 1966. April Cottage then became home to Ernie Locke's brother Jack and his family until they moved, in 1968, to the cottage adjoining Beech Farm. April Cottage was then used as a holiday home before it was demolished for the reservoir in August 1975.

Above: April Cottage from the east in the 1960s. The roof on the north side was very low, finishing well below ground floor ceiling height (Richard Adams)

April Cottage in 1975. The semi-circular windows and doors are reminiscent of a chapel (RLHRS)

— 466 —

Residents of Lower Hambleton

Some burial entries in the Hambleton Parish Registers state that the abode of the deceased was Lower Hambleton. The following people (not listed in the main text) were recorded as living in the hamlet:

Edward Billington	buried 29th October 1859 aged 82 years.
Ann Billington	buried 9th February 1860 aged 77 years (wife of Edward).
Herbert Smith	buried 9th March 1916 aged 6 days.
Elsie Mary Smith	buried 7th July 1921 aged 7 years. She died in the Children's Hospital, Great Ormond Street, London.
Mary Jane Smith	buried 25th January 1924 aged 40 years.
Annie Winterton	buried 11th June 1968 aged 89 years (of East View Farm).

Names of people who may have lived in Lower Hambleton according to the Hambleton Census Returns:

1841 & 1851	Edward and Ann Billington (burials noted above).
1851	Henry Tyers, widower, daughter Annie and sons Amos and John.
1861	Robert Watkin, a cottager, his wife Elizabeth and daughters, Ruth and Jane.
1861	William Francis Fryer and his aunt Mary Fryer.
1861	Thomas Cooke and his wife Mary.
1861	George Cunnington, agricultural labourer, his wife Sarah, three sons and a daughter.
1871 & 1861	Robert Watkin, a cottager, his wife Elizabeth.

The Black 'Tin' Hut

Until the early 1970s there was a 'corrugated iron' shed on the south side of the road to the east of Woodbine House. For its last few years it had been used as a storage building by the Rutland Field Research Group, who were carrying out an archaeological rescue excavation in the adjacent field prior to the area being flooded for Rutland Water. Before this the building had been there for at least 30 years and it had an interesting history.

Marcus Gregory, son of Neville, who lived at Woodbine House, remembers this shed quite vividly. Although his father had used it, in the 1960s, as a hen house and for storing corn, it had previously been used as accommodation. Marcus recalls that there was a fence round it, creating a small garden area, and that the entrance was through a gate and a porch on the south side. Inside was a room of reasonable size which served as a living area and kitchen. On the west side of this room there was a wood-burning range. It had a timber floor and the walls were partly covered with wood panelling. An extension on the north side was used as a bedroom.

Winifred Tibbert, who with her new husband Harold, went to live at East View, Lower Hambleton, in 1939, recalls: 'There was a shed next to Gregory's farm that was really meant for accommodation, although it only looked like a shed. A black shed, but there were two rooms and a fireplace in it. Harold said the walls were insulated but I don't know how. Probably double thickness and it was used for accommodation. Old Jack lived there and after he'd gone a temporary school teacher lived in it.'

Winifred's daughter, Sheila Drake, who lived at East View from 1944 until 1963, can also remember this shed:

'I remember a tin hut along that road. We used to call it the hut but it was possibly a little house. I never went into it. It was like a corrugated iron bungalow. I seem to remember it had a chimney so it must have been designed for living in. There was a chap called Jack who used to live there. There was nobody living in the building when we left. The Jack who lived there was a bit of a strange character in a child's mind. I didn't know anything about him and never saw him working anywhere. Whether he went into Oakham to work or whether he worked around Hambleton, I don't know but he seemed to live there quite a while.'

The black 'tin' hut at the side of the road near Woodbine House in Lower Hambleton (RLHRS)

Left: The 'tin' hut from the south in July 1974. By this time it was being used as a site hut for the nearby archaeological excavation (RLHRS)

Middle Hambleton

Whilst all of Lower Hambleton disappeared when Rutland Water was created, Upper Hambleton escaped due to its hilltop location. However some of the houses, farm buildings and land in Middle Hambleton were not so fortunate.

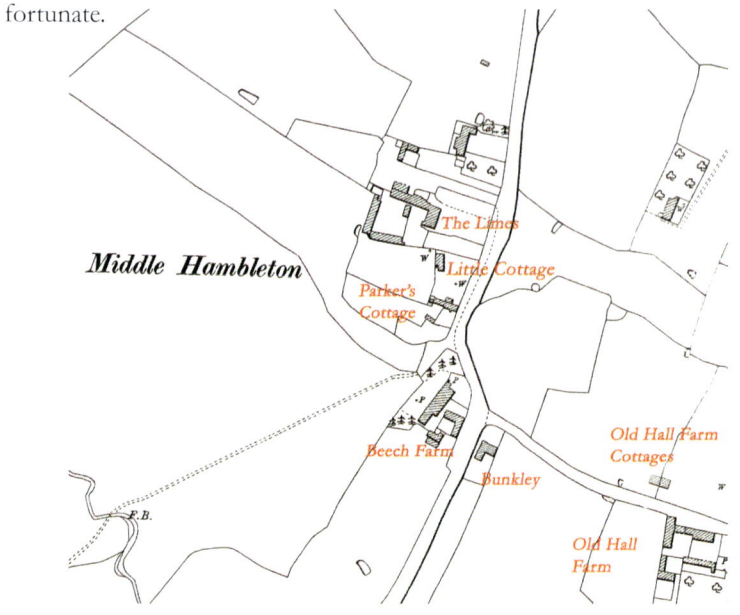

The location of houses demolished in Middle Hambleton during the 1970s added to the OS 2nd ed 25" map 1904

Beech Farm

Beech Farm, Middle Hambleton, was one of two farms in the hamlet which was demolished for Rutland Water.

In 1895 this farm was bought by Thomas Fryer, a grazier from Manton. At this time the farmhouse was unoccupied, but prior to this the tenant had been Thomas' cousin Charles Fryer. This and the following information is taken from documents in the ownership of Sheila Manchester, a descendant of Thomas Fryer.

A Conveyance dated 15th May 1895 states that Thomas Fryer acquired:

'All those closes, pieces or parcels of pasture land and gardens situate in the Parish of Middle Hambleton in the County of Rutland together containing by admeasurements twenty seven acres thirty perches or thereabouts . . . Together with the messuage or farmhouse, yards, barns, stables and other outbuildings adjoining and communicating with the said land . . . .'

Beech Farm, Middle Hambleton in the 1960s (Sheila Manchester)

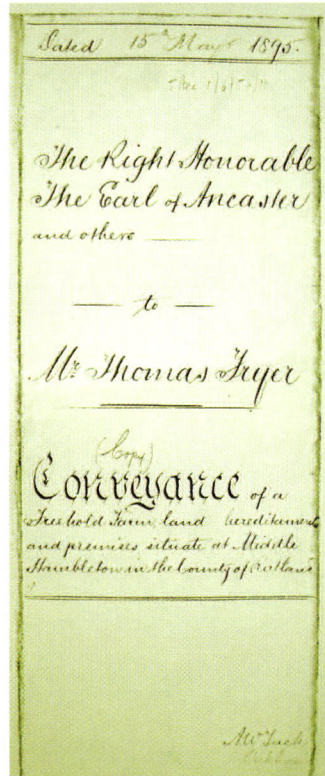

The Conveyance of Beech Farm in 1895 (Sheila Manchester)

The property was sold by Gilbert Henry Heathcote-Drummond-Willoughby, the 1st Earl of Ancaster, for £1,250. The Conveyance indicates that it had been part of the Heathcote estate as early as 1834.

Thomas Fryer had moved into Beech Farm by 1901. At this time he was widowed and living with him was Sarah Emma Brown, his housekeeper. Thomas did not reside at Beech Farm for long for he died 11th November 1902. He is buried, alongside his wife Mary Ann, at Egleton. The main beneficiary of Thomas's will, dated 2nd August 1901, was his second cousin Richard George Fryer of Somerby, Leicestershire. Beech Farm remained in Richard's family until it was sold at auction in 1966.

An Executors' Account of November 1902 gives an insight into the livestock then kept at Beech Farm. Royce of Oakham sold 'lambs, beasts, calves and heifers' for £154 14s and 'sheep & horses' for £151 7s 6d. One of two veterinary surgeons employed by Thomas was G E Gibson of Oakham.

The account also lists local tradesmen and others with whom he did business. Amongst these were: R Draper, an Uppingham wine & spirit merchant, J P Bramley, mineral water manufacturer of Uppingham, C Mould, confectioner of Uppingham, and F W Hart, grocer of Oakham. He obtained personal medicines from Norman & Hewitt of Oakham and he hired a Mrs Wade for nursing. Furley & Hassan of Oakham arranged his funeral at a cost of £27 14s 3d and his solicitor was Ernest W Phillips of Oakham.

The shop of Frederick William Hart, family grocer of Market Place, Oakham. It was on the site of the present Post Office (Hart)

An advertisement for Furley & Hassan, Funeral Furnishers of Oakham, as placed in Matkin's Oakham Almanack of 1916

Left: One of the grindstones used at Beech Farm (Sheila Manchester)

Wheel Bier For Hire.

The great advantage in this Bier is that it overcomes the difficulties in a Church where space is limited, enabling the coffin to be turned completely round upon a revolving platform. The steering is adapted for use at both ends.

Furley & Hassan
Funeral Furnishers.
Phone: 12.   Oakham.

Following the death of Thomas Fryer, Beech Farm was rented by his descendants. From about 1905 it was occupied by John Thomas Williamson, farmer and grazier. Living with John was his wife Edith Annie and their son Cecil. After the death of John and the tragic death of Cecil in 1965, the farm was eventually sold by auction on 11th March 1966. Royce of Oakham were the auctioneers who advertised the farmhouse as 'A very Attractive Freehold GRASS FARM with Stone-Built Farm House and Buildings extending to 27.937 Acres'.

Sheila Manchester, of Brentingby, Leicestershire, whose mother owned Beech Farm, remembers:

'Much earlier than 1954 the very old house had been joined onto the barn, making a very large dwelling. Williamsons only lived in part of the house. The Locke family, who bought the farm at the auction, repaired, divided and modernised the property and two families lived there.'

Edna and Ernie Locke acquired Beech Farm in 1966 and they 'had high hopes for the farm'. They lived here with their five children and Edna's mother, Mrs Nellie Wright. Two years later Ernie's brother, Jack Locke, his wife and mother-in-law moved into the adjoining cottage at the north end of the building. This accommodation was known as Beech Farm Cottage. The two brothers had a drainage contracting business but by 1971 when the reservoir scheme had become a reality, Edna recalls 'this folded, all because of the reservoir'.

Above: Sheila Manchester, whose mother inherited Beech Farm. Sheila has many happy memories of her frequent visits to the farm in the 1950s and 1960s (RO)

Above: Beech Farm Sale Particulars in 1966 (Sheila Manchester)

Left: Beech Farm from the north-west in the 1960s. When Ernie and Edna Locke acquired the farm in 1966 they occupied the farmhouse at the south end of the building (Joan Wild)

Beech Farm, mainly stone-built with a Collyweston slate roof, had three rooms on the ground floor as well as a small kitchen and a store. There were four bedrooms and a bathroom on the first floor. The Lockes had every intention of fully modernising the farmhouse and had firm plans for their future here. In order to realise their dream, they began by repairing the roof and by building a larger kitchen at the rear of the farmhouse. They also built three greenhouses where they grew tomatoes, cucumbers and flowering plants. This produce was marketed by Edna at the door.

Edna Locke in her garden at Beech Farm. Little did she know that her property and Lower Hambleton behind her would be lost to the reservoir. Lax Hill can be seen in the background (Edna Locke)

The Lockes had a herd of 50 cows and Edna recalled:

'We had grazing land at Barnsdale for the Jerseys because they're not like Friesians; they will not feed on any old rough stuff. They'd calve up at Barnsdale and Ern would keep them for three days then bring them to me and I used to do the calf rearing down at Beech Farm.'

The rented land at Barnsdale also included farm buildings which were used for milking the Jersey cows. Most of the milk was sold but Edna retained some so that she could churn butter from the cream. She did not have a dairy so she used the kitchen table in the evening.

They also owned sixteen acres of land in Middle Hambleton where they grew barley which was used to feed the cows, and a large garden and orchard. Edna recalled:

'We were hoping to make many alterations. We were going to have all new windows because the previous farmer had got all these old sash windows and they were getting very rotten. We were going to turn the farm into a market garden and then Frank Knights [Reservoir Engineer] came round

Beech Farm and the nearby bungalow known as Bunkley await demolition in 1975 (Edna Locke)

one day and he said, "I hate to tell you this, Mr and Mrs Locke, but there's a reservoir coming here". Well I blew my top. I said, "You're not going to tell me, Frank, that this hasn't all come about in five minutes. Why didn't we know sooner?" We signed petition after petition, all of us, but it was Government you see and you can't fight Government. We lost out in the end . . . We had to sell up the herd because they took all of our best grazing land at Barnsdale for a new roadway. That's the new roadway from Oakham to Stamford.'

After living at Beech Farm for nine years Edna and Ernie were compelled to move, leaving their home to be demolished. Not only did they lose their home but also their livelihood. However, they both found employment with Anglian Water and grew to enjoy the new landscape and the fishing that the reservoir had to offer.

When they lost Beech Farm Edna and Ernie Locke worked for the Water Authority and Ernie took up fishing as a hobby (Edna Locke)

There were four cowsheds and a pigsty to the east of Beech Farm. When the reservoir is at low water the remains of foundations and concrete floors of some of these buildings can be seen (RO)

Parker's Cottage

This attractive red-brick, thatched cottage in Middle Hambleton, known in the 1970s as Parker's Cottage, was located at the side of the winding road leading down from Upper Hambleton.

John Parker, his wife Lucy and their family were recorded as living in Hambleton from 1871. When their son George, an agricultural worker, was married about 1890, he and his new wife went to live in this brick cottage in Middle Hambleton. George and Elizabeth Parker had seven children, two sons and five daughters, and as these grew up they helped to look after the smallholding that went with the cottage. George kept a few beast, pigs and chickens.

In 1970 it was still home to two of George's offspring, Arthur aged 70 and his sister Ada aged 66. Evidently the cottage had not been altered all the time they had lived in it. Contemporary newspaper cuttings show images of the couple sitting in front of a fire in an old-fashioned range, incorporating an oven and a boiler. Although Arthur was at this time a retired farm worker, having worked for the Sharp family at Lower Hambleton for 36 years, he still

Parker's Cottage, Middle Hambleton (Edna Locke)

— 474 —

enjoyed looking after a few chickens. It was therefore understandable that this elderly couple were unhappy about having to leave their home to make way for the construction of the reservoir. Arthur and Ada moved into one of four new bungalows in Upper Hambleton, specifically built for those who had lost their homes in this way.

Top Left: Arthur Parker and his sister Ada, owners of Parker's Cottage in 1970 (Edna Locke)

Little Cottage

Known as 'Little Cottage' in 1960, this dwelling in Middle Hambleton had been home to William Edward Ludgrove and his wife Elizabeth since about 1924. William died aged 74 in 1933 and Elizabeth aged 93 in 1953. Their daughter Ethel continued to live in this cottage until it was compulsorily purchased and demolished to make way for Rutland Water. Miss Ludgrove moved to another of the new bungalows in Middle Hambleton.

Left: Little Cottage, Middle Hambleton, in the 1960s (Tony Traylen)

The Limes

In 1971 The Limes was occupied by Charles William Wakerley, his wife Catherine and their son Henry. The family home was destined for demolition and Mr Wakerley, known as Bill, was about to lose some 150 acres of good farming land in the Gwash Valley. William's father George Botherway Wakerley and his wife Anne, had farmed at The Limes from about 1909. Four of their children, Tom, Harry, Charles William (Bill) and Grace Bettina were baptised at Hambleton between 1911 and 1914.

Below: The Limes, Middle Hambleton in 1968. The roof of Little Cottage can also be seen at lower left (Henry Wakerley)

Below: Bill and Catherine Wakerley with their three children Steven, Patricia and Henry (Henry Wakerley)

— 475 —

The Limes at Middle Hambleton stands deserted awaiting demolition (Tony Traylen)

Bill Wakerley built a replacement farmhouse on nearby land for which he retained the name of the old house. He and Henry continued to farm from their new home. The reservoir made access to their 30 acres of land on the south side of the valley a more time-consuming exercise. This land, formerly within walking distance, could only be reached by making a seven-mile journey by road, via Egleton and Manton. The main business of the farm was sheep and cattle rearing.

The Limes was L-shaped and possibly built in three phases, with the main elevation facing east. When the house was demolished a date stone was discovered set into this elevation, indicating that this section was built in 1628. The farm had five bedrooms, an upper store room, two large living rooms, a hall and two kitchens. The farm buildings consisted of a four-bay wagon hovel, three stables, four cowsheds, a barn which included a granary, a wash-house and a coal-house. One of the buildings at the south-western corner of the yard was almost certainly a former cottage. It had a staircase and a fireplace.

Although it is known that the farm was occupied by the Robinson family from 1901-08 it is difficult to establish with any degree of certainty who occupied it prior to this.

Old Hall Cottages and Bunkley

Sir John Conant with his family at Lyndon Hall in 1973 (Sir John Conant)

Sir John Conant, owner of Old Hall and its farm at Middle Hambleton (*see* Chapter 8 – Hambleton: The Settlement on the Crooked Hill), was one of the leaders of the 'Don't Dam Rutland' campaign. However, when the Act of Parliament was passed in 1970 sealing the fate of the Gwash Valley, 217 acres of his farmland were submerged. He also lost all his farm buildings as well as a nearby pair of semi-detached farm workers' cottages. Fortunately, the high water level of the new reservoir was just below the seventeenth-century mansion and it was possible to save it by means of a low embankment.

Above: Old Hall at Middle Hambleton survived the inundation but it was necessary to protect it by an embankment (RO)

Above: The bungalow in Middle Hambleton known as Bunkley which was only four years old when it was demolished. This view is from the south-east (Tony Traylen)

Left: Old Hall farm buildings which were to be demolished for the reservoir (Sir John Conant)

A brick bungalow near Beech Farm in Middle Hambleton was built by Lady Periwinkle and Sir John Conant about 1967 to provide accommodation for the foreman of Old Hall Farm. Within four years it had fallen victim to the bulldozers constructing the new reservoir. At the time of demolition this bungalow was known as Bunkley, after an adjacent field known as Bunklins.

Right: The road to Old Hall from Middle Hambleton and the semi-detached farm workers' cottages on the right which were lost when the reservoir was built (Sir John Conant)

Above: The start of the demolition process near Old Hall. Several of the farm buildings have been demolished while others await their fate. The deserted semi-detached farm workers' cottages also await demolition (Jim Levisohn ARPS)

Left: When Rutland Water is at low level the foundations of Bunkley are often revealed. Old Hall, in the background, narrowly escaped demolition (RO)

Other Homes that were Lost
Mow Mires

Mow Mires from the south-east in 1970 (Jim Levisohn ARPS)

The Griffin family owned Mow Mires from about 1930 and in 1971 it was home to farmer John Griffin and his family. In the October of that year they were compelled to move out as the demolition gangs were preparing to clear the site for one of the planned 'borrow pits'. The clay taken from these pits was to be used for constructing the dam.

John Griffin lost all but about fifteen acres of land at Normanton. His crops in the Gwash Valley included wheat and barley but the land around his house was used for grazing.

Mow Mires, built of Ketton Stone, was once part of Normanton Park Estate. It was about a mile south-west of Empingham, just off the private drive through Normanton Park leading to the Hall. Mow Mires was advertised as part of Lot 62 in the Estate auction of 1924. The lot was described as 'A Valuable Little Holding', and comprised The Keeper's House with a large vegetable garden and various outbuildings. At this time the house was divided into three cottages, two having a sitting room, three bedrooms, a kitchen and scullery, the other a sitting room, two bedrooms and a scullery. Outside there was an earth closet and coalhouse serving all three cottages. The outbuildings consisted of a 'Coach House, two stall stable, with loft over, Fowl House, two-bay Cart Shed, Store Room, Large Game Larder,

Mow Mires, the entrance lodges to Normanton Park and part of The Belt on the OS 2nd ed 25" map 1904

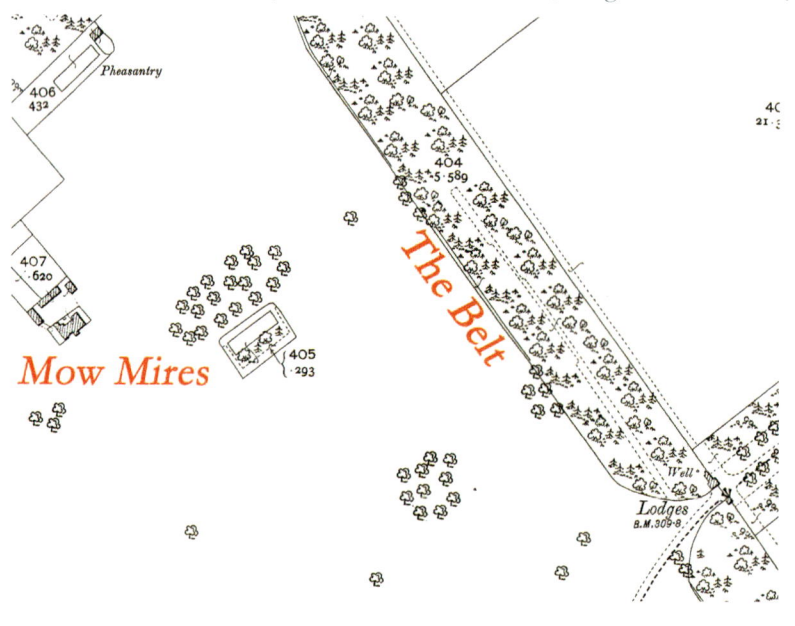

Top Right: The drive leading to Mow Mires in 1972 (Jim Levisohn ARPS)

Middle Right: The location of The Willows and Keeper's Cottage below Barnsdale Hill on the former Oakham to Stamford Road. Taken from the OS 2nd ed 25" map 1904

Bottom Right: From a newspaper cutting, showing David and Irene Goodrick at the gate of their home in 1968. They moved out of The Willows in the spring of 1971 (Stamford Mercury)

The north and east elevations of The Willows circa 1968 (Bryan Waites)

[and] Slaughter House'. There was also a range of 'Off Buildings' including two wood and tile loose-boxes and a stone and slated one-roomed cottage which had formerly been an entrance lodge to Normanton Park. Part of the park and pasture surrounding the Keeper's Cottage, and two wooded areas, Mow Mires Spinney to the north and The Belt to the east, were also included in the sale. In the event, the Lot was withdrawn and later sold privately.

The Willows and Keeper's Cottage, Barnsdale Hill

The Willows and Keeper's Cottage were located at the foot of Barnsdale Hill on the former Oakham to Stamford Road.

Mr David Goodrick and his wife Irene moved into The Willows about 1932. They were understandably upset to hear that their home of nearly 40 years was to be demolished for Rutland Water. Until his retirement in 1960 Mr Goodrick was Works' Supervisor with Rutland County Council.

Keeper's Cottage was on the south side of the road and virtually opposite The Willows. It was built at the beginning of the twentieth century and, on OS maps of that time, called Barnsdale Cottage. In 1968 it was home to Mrs Bernadette Webb and her three children.

Both cottages were vacated and subsequently demolished in 1971. The sites are now covered by up to 30ft of water.

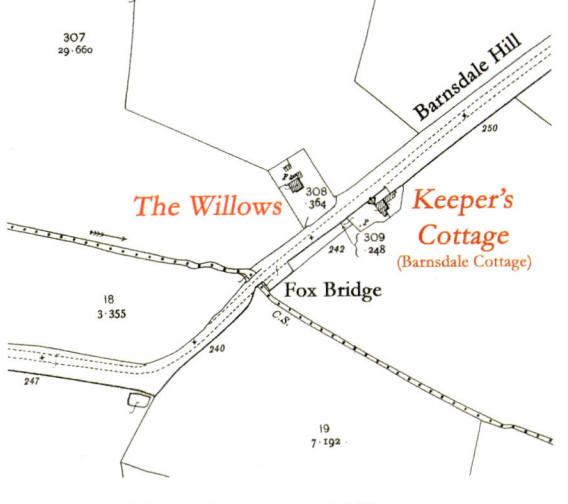

Aspects of Topography

The Stamford to Oakham Turnpike

The turnpike from Scot Gate, Stamford, to Oakham and thence to the Cross Guns inn at Greetham, connecting to the Great North Road at both ends, was first authorised by Act of Parliament in 1794. The Stamford to Oakham section had toll gates at Stamford and Oakham, with toll bars at Stamford Fields (on the county boundary), Tinwell Lodge, Shacklewell, Empingham and Burley Fishponds. This latter bar was known as the Hambleton or Fishpond Bar and was at the turn off the turnpike to Upper Hambleton. Collectors at this bar between 1841 and 1861 were Joseph and William Marriatt, and John Walker. Toll bars were introduced to catch those travellers who attempted to avoid the toll gates by using alternative routes.

Turnpikes were established so that money could be collected from users to pay for their improvement and maintenance. In theory, busier roads, which needed more maintenance, generated more funds to pay for this work. Prior to this, each parish was responsible for the upkeep of its roads, and this still applied to non-turnpike roads. Standards varied considerably and repair methods were primitive in the extreme (*see* Aspects of Topography: Old Barnsdale Hill).

Turnpiking, at first, did not improve matters, but the influence of the great road makers Thomas Telford and John McAdam gradually had such an effect that Royal Mail coaches saw a 40 per cent increase in speed between 1811 and 1835. However, railways were just around the corner by this date, and by 1878 all turnpike trusts in Rutland had ceased to exist, the Stamford to Oakham to Greetham turnpike trust closing in 1871.

FISHPOND TOLL BAR

Toll Receipts	
1820	£177
1825	£159
1830	£206
1835	£252
1840	£360
1845	£451
1850	£251
1855	£226
1860	£326
1865	£359
1870	£346

Right: Fishpond Toll Bar shown on an estate sale map of 1864. The river is the north arm of the Gwash as it passes under the old Stamford Road at Fox Bridge (ROLLR DE 2209/14)

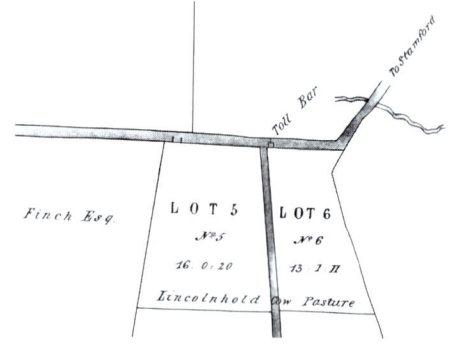

Stamford Road near Burley Fishponds, leading to Barnsdale Hill. The sign post once pointed to Upper Hambleton. This is the former location of Fishpond Toll Bar. This photograph was taken in 1976 as Rutland Water was filling for the first time (Richard Adams)

— 480 —

Chapter 22

Rutland Water: Planning and Developing a Water Supply Reservoir as a World-Class Leisure Venue

David Moore

Planning & Decisions

Today we take the easy access and availability of leisure facilities at water supply reservoirs for granted but planning this into the design of large reservoirs is a relatively new idea. Traditionally reservoirs had relied upon impounding natural watercourses in upland areas where the priority was to keep water treatment processes simple and avoid or restrict public access where possible. Some limited fishing or sailing was frequently provided but usually confined to members of a club and with strict controls. It was only with the construction of major 'pumped storage' reservoirs utilising water from the middle and lower reaches of rivers that recreational use became an important aspect of reservoir design. Early examples include Pitsford Reservoir (Northamptonshire) and Chew Lake (Avon) which were constructed in the 1950s. A later example is Grafham Water (Cambridgeshire) which involved more sophisticated water treatment technology.

The passing of the Water Act in 1973 created the Regional Water Authorities. For the first time the Act integrated the management of rivers, water resources, water supply and sewage treatment within ten such Regional Water Authorities. Prior to this legislation the provision of recreation on reservoirs had been at the discretion of local Water Boards, but now there was a statutory duty to make the best use of water resources and associated land for public recreation.

The timing of 'Empingham Reservoir', as Rutland Water was initially known, coincided with this change in the law and the creation of the new Water Authorities. This enabled a much more progressive approach to providing a balance of recreation and wildlife enhancement as an integral part of its construction. In recognition of this change the Welland & Nene River Authority (W&NRA) established a committee in 1970 to consider these issues. The committee included representatives from the Countryside Commission, the East Midlands Sports Council, the Nature Conservancy Council, Local Authorities and local interest groups. A report was produced in 1971, and what is seen today has developed from the original ideas proposed at this early stage.

David Moore, the new Fisheries Officer to the Welland and Nene River Authority, at Horn Mill hatchery in 1975 (Roy Eaton Photography)

Consultation and Landscape

The overall plan was to develop the shallow western area of the reservoir and its perimeter as a nature reserve and to locate the recreational infrastructure at the deeper eastern end. This decision combined the attraction of good feeding areas for wading birds with the need for easier launching of sailing and fishing boats. Hambleton Peninsula was to be protected as a natural area with a perimeter track for anglers' cars together with parking areas around the peninsula carefully selected so as to screen the cars. Public car parks were to be located at the eastern end of the reservoir, well away from the nature reserve.

The plan recognised the wide-reaching impact that the reservoir would have upon the landscape of the whole valley, and landscape consultant Dame Sylvia Crowe was appointed to ensure that the project would result in the reservoir having the appearance of a natural lake. Today Dame Sylvia's achievement is there for all to see. 'It looks as though it has always been there' is the most common comment by visitors.

Dame Sylvia Crowe

Sylvia Crowe was born on a Surrey farm in 1901. She studied at Swanley Horticultural College in Kent and began her long career in garden and landscape design. In 1935 she was elected a Fellow of the Institute of Landscape Architects, interrupting her work to serve in the Second World War.

Post-war Britain saw an urgent need for new public housing which was partly met by the creation of the New Towns. Sylvia Crowe became involved with a new form of landscape design, involving roads, schools and shopping centres, at Harlow and Basildon in Essex.

With her colleague, Brenda Colvin, Sylvia Crowe was involved as consultant on projects such as the Imperial College development in South Kensington and restoration work in Lincolnshire after the 1953 floods. She also became the first Landscape Architect to the Forestry Commission.

For her work in the United Kingdom, Sylvia Crowe was created a Dame of the British Empire in 1973. By this time she had begun work as Landscape Architect for what was later to become Rutland Water. Although local people feared the loss of a beautiful rural landscape, she was sure that, with careful planning, the expanse of water and surrounding shoreline could ultimately enhance the environment. It was essential that necessary features such as buildings and car parks should be designed to integrate with the landscape.

Left: Bernard Henderson, Chairman of Anglian Water, with Dame Sylvia Crowe at the unveiling of a plaque in recognition of her 21 years as landscape architect for Rutland Water, on 10th June 1992. Behind them is Barnsdale Creek (AW)

To mitigate the effects of 'draw-down', when the water level of the reservoir would drop to reveal barren mud-flats, Dame Sylvia arranged for the planting of varieties of grass, willow and alder which could survive even when submerged, and would help to fill the gap between land and water when levels were low. The excavation of clay to build the dam allowed the car park at Sykes Lane to be built below road level, screened from general view by grassed mounds and tree plantations. Many thousands of trees were planted around the reservoir, and all parking areas were landscaped so that they could scarcely be seen from the water or surrounding roads.

In the 30 years since Rutland Water was completed, Dame Sylvia Crowe's vision has been magnificently fulfilled. This has been due to effective co-operation between the engineers, architects and planners, and the continuing efforts of Rutland County Council and Anglian Water to maintain the beauty and harmony of this largely artificial landscape.

In 1959 Dame Sylvia summed up her philosophy: 'It should be the aim of each of us to leave our chosen corner not more vulgar and submerged, but lovelier and more dignified, after we have gone.' In her nineties, Dame Sylvia unveiled a commemorative plaque in her honour on 10th June 1992 at Sykes Lane, Empingham, overlooking Rutland Water. She died in London on 30th June 1997.

The plaque recognising Dame Sylvia Crowe's achievements (RO)

Working alongside Dame Sylvia was Tony Ford, a highly skilled forester, who converted the plan into reality. Tony established a nursery to supplement young trees brought in from elsewhere, but first he had to improve the 120 acres of poor woodland which contained many diseased elms and few suitable rides for management access. Several hundred young Oak and Birch trees were removed from those parts of Hambleton Wood where they would have been drowned, and replanted above the planned high water level. The rides cleared for managing the woodland were later incorporated into the cycle route around the reservoir. In all, about 175 acres of new woodland was planted although the drought of 1976 took a heavy toll and large areas had to be replanted.

The other big task for Tony was to construct a post and rail fence around much of the perimeter. He also planted 8.5 miles of hedge which was expected to become established within the twenty-year life-span of the fence.

Other key features of the landscaping were the terracing of the car park at Whitwell, re-profiling the contours at Barnsdale, Normanton and Sykes Lane car parks, and the re-aligning of hedgerows towards the waterline. These key features, combined with careful tree-planting, ensured that cars were screened from the opposite side of the reservoir, the main objective being to avoid reflection from windscreens. Further away from the water there were roads and overhead power lines to divert and new sewers to install which would take effluent to the new sewage treatment works downstream of the reservoir, near Empingham.

The reservoir was planned to be filled and opened for recreation in the spring of 1977, and by this time the car parks, toilets, access roads, fencing, Fishing Lodge, harbours, Sailing Club, Information Centre, and water, sewerage and electricity services had to be completed, the boat fleet launched, and the reservoir stocked with Trout. Pick, Everard, Keay & Gimson were the architects appointed to design all the buildings associated with this programme.

Leisure Activities

The initial range of activities to be provided included the traditional pursuits of walking, sailing, fishing and bird watching. Today these are all well established but there are numerous additions and developments which have grown out of the original concept while retaining the theme of peaceful enjoyment in the countryside. One key policy was that all activities should be available to everyone and that it would not be necessary to become a member of any club or exclusive group to enjoy them.

However, clubs were encouraged as part of the community involvement in the project but not with any exclusive use of the water. For example the Leicestershire & Rutland Wildlife Trust has always managed the nature reserve, Rutland Sailing Club, formed in 1975, began sailing in 1976 and built its clubhouse in time for the reservoir's completion, and the Rutland Water Flyfishers Association had been formed by 1977.

The only project which never came to fruition as part of the original concept was the Outdoor Pursuit Centre which was planned by Leicestershire County Council to provide a residential education base similar to that at Grafham Water. Over time, this service has largely been provided by the Sailing Club and the education and training facilities provided by Anglian Water at Egleton and Whitwell.

The Fishery

The reservoir was always expected to be a productive fishery because it is filled with nutrient-rich water from the lower reaches of the Rivers Welland and Nene rather than from the small natural catchment of the River Gwash. However, there was controversy among anglers as to whether it should be a coarse fishery based on the naturally breeding fish populations or a Trout fishery dependent upon frequent stocking with farmed fish, necessary because Trout do not breed in still water. Local anglers were predominantly interested in coarse fish but it was

Left: Roland Field (Chief Scientist, W&NRA) with Peter Tombleson OBE (Chairman of the Welland & Nene Fisheries & Recreation Committee) at Horn Mill Trout hatchery during its construction in 1974 (Roy Eaton Photography)

successfully argued by Peter Tombleson, chairman of the Welland & Nene Fisheries & Recreation Committee, that providing Trout fishing would create a new opportunity and attract visitors rather than more of something already in plentiful local supply.

In February 1974, I was appointed as Fisheries Officer to the W&NRA, working for Roland Field, the Divisional Scientist. The most important part of my job was to establish a Trout hatchery at Horn Mill on the North Brook at Exton, and a rearing farm below the dam at Empingham.

With hatchery manager Colin Harden and assistants Bob Garrett, Doug Cooper, Ziggy Lesiakowski, Jim Britten and head bailiff Keith Bone, we took on the challenge to rear sufficient Trout to stock 3,100 acres of water, the largest area to be stocked over newly flooded land in the United Kingdom. By first reducing the existing coarse fish populations to a minimum it would be possible to stock with young Trout which would grow rapidly without competition. The fishery was planned to open to anglers in the summer of 1977, giving the Trout two years to reach the 2lb to 5lb weight which anglers expected.

Coarse fish were removed from the River Gwash and Burley Fishponds by netting and some large Bream, Carp, Pike, Roach and Tench were transferred to Oakham canal and other local rivers.

Young 'fingerling' Trout were introduced from March 1975 and a total of 360,000 young Rainbow and 272,000 Brown Trout had been released into the reservoir by 1977.

An historic moment – Fisheries Officer David Moore introduces the first of 632,000 Trout into the new reservoir in March 1975 (Trout Fisherman Magazine)

From *Trout Fisherman Magazine,* March 1975:
FIRST TROUT IN AT EMPINGHAM

The giant Empingham Reservoir in Rutland received its first injection of Trout on Tuesday. Around 10,000 yearling Brown Trout – the first of more than 50,000 – went in around the Whitwell Peninsula.

All the fish came from the Welland and Nene River Division's own hatchery on the North Brook – a main tributary of the River Gwash. The hatchery, the most modern ever built by a statutory fishery body, has done its job of providing fish for the 3,100 acre water complex so well that a surplus of several thousand fish has been recorded already. This excess is being sold off to local sport fisheries, and high density reared fish – unsuitable for any stocking – are going to the hotel trade for the table.

The surplus is made up entirely of Rainbow Trout, from nine inches upwards. 'These fish were not needed for Empingham anyway,' said David Moore, who is largely in charge of the development of Empingham as a Trout fishery for the Welland and Nene authority.

Assistant Warden John Clarkson with one of the Trout being stocked in 1977 (AW)

Below: The original Fishing Lodge at Whitwell Harbour in 1978 (AW)

Stocking Trout into newly flooded agricultural land elsewhere had run into problems with de-oxygenation, resulting in a parasitic eyefluke which needs snails and fish to complete its life cycle. By removing topsoil to excavate clay for the construction of the dam in the main bowl of the reservoir the risk of de-oxygenation was reduced. Brown Trout are more resistant than Rainbow Trout to eyefluke infection and by using a high proportion of Brown Trout the risk was successfully reduced.

By the first release of Trout the reservoir had flooded 300 acres of land, and stable water conditions enabled stocking to proceed. Over the next twelve months the area flooded increased to 600 acres and the fish were growing quickly, with the largest already at 2lb. Unfortunately, the winter, spring and summer of 1976 brought little rainfall and pumping from the Rivers Welland and Nene was limited. High summer temperatures aggravated the situation and a drought was declared. In the emergency, water was released from the reservoir into the River Gwash water course, eventually to be taken from the River Welland as a supply to the Etton Water Treatment works near Peterborough (Cambridgeshire). A new pipeline was also installed to transfer raw water to Grantham (Lincolnshire). Many people who doubted that the reservoir was necessary now had reason to be thankful that it was at least part completed!

As a result of the hot weather, lack of rainfall and having to provide emergency supplies to Peterborough and Grantham, the surface area of the reservoir had fallen back to 400 acres by the August of 1976. The high water temperatures resulted in slow growth of both species of Trout. Eyefluke in Rainbow Trout was also prevalent in these conditions. Consequently, they also suffered because of their reduced ability to see their food.

Above: Work goes on throughout the winter at Rutland Water. Here wardens are test-netting to assess over-wintering Trout stocks in 1982 (AW)

Right: Doug Cooper working at the fish-rearing cages about 1983 (AW)

Below: Gordon Griffiths with one of the first big Trout caught at Rutland Water in the early 1980s (AW)

August bank holiday saw the end of the drought with torrential rain throughout the country and this was followed by several very wet months in succession. A combination of maximum pumping from the Rivers Welland and Nene and a flooded River Gwash rapidly filled the reservoir and by May 1977 it was nearly full.

While the fish were growing in the reservoir the erection of the infrastructure for anglers and other reservoir recreational activities was under way. Harry Crowe, Reservoir Manager, and Frank Knights, Reservoir Engineer, had the responsibility of making sure the roads, car parks, toilets, Fishing Lodge, harbour and 50-boat fleet, and tourist information centre were all ready for the May 1977 opening.

The Fishing Lodge was sited on the end of the peninsula at Whitwell, where the shoreline was re-profiled to provide a sheltered harbour to float the pontoon for the fishing dinghies. These 16ft dinghies with inboard diesel engines were an innovative choice at the time, being of a much higher specification than used elsewhere. They were considered necessary because of the conditions expected on such a large exposed reservoir.

Left: Lord Colin Moynihan, Minister of Sport, talks to the competitors at the 1983 International Fishing Championships (AW)

Left: Anglian Water Warden Arthur Chapman starts the 1983 Benson & Hedges Fly Fishing Competition (AW)

Recreation Management

In 1976 Jonathon Inglesant was appointed as Recreation Officer. His team of wardens consisted of Ernie Locke, Arthur Chapman, John Clarkson, Martin Hearth and later John Seaton, and these were ready to manage the thousands of visitors who were already travelling some distance to see the reservoir taking shape.

Capital expenditure on the reservoir's recreational infrastructure had coincided with a period of severe restraint on public expenditure, and although the £1 million budget seemed healthy it represented a cutback on the visitor centres originally envisaged. It has only been in the last decade that the new Normanton Fishing Lodge, Anglian Water Birdwatching Centre and extended Sailing Club have really provided the high quality buildings which the reservoir justifies.

The Rutland Sailing Club was formed in the early stages of the reservoir's construction with its members funding the clubhouse on land leased from the Water Authority. Sailing started at Easter 1976, from which time it has developed into the best inland sailing facility in the country with 2,000 acres of water and a clubhouse, extended in recent times thanks to a lottery grant and support from Anglian Water, to provide world-class facilities for disabled people to sail.

Colin Harder, Fish Farm manager, and John Seaton, Senior Warden, grading fish at the fish farm (AW)

The Rutland Sailing Club clubhouse at Edith Weston, on the south shore of Rutland Water in 2006 (RO)

Rutland Sailing Club from the air in 2006 (John Nowell, Zodiac Publishing)

In 1977 the Fishing Lodge was also the best in the country but other facilities were more basic. For example, a 'Day Sailing Centre' was provided from a Portakabin at Whitwell so that anyone could launch a boat on a casual basis under supervision of a rescue service operated by the Peter Fry Rescue Trust. Whereas the Rutland Sailing Club was responsible for the safety of its own members, the rescue service at Whitwell looked after the 'day sailor' and provided a first aid base for the reservoir.

The Peter Fry Trust was founded by John Fry in memory of his son who drowned in an inland sailing accident in 1972. Rutland Water provided an ideal base for the charity to play a useful role in protecting public safety, and with funding from Anglian Water it operated successfully here until 2003, after which time its role was integrated into the management of Rutland Watersports.

Catering was the least adequately provided service in the early days. At first mobile ice-cream vans were based on the car parks, but, as demand grew, small kiosks were built on each of these and were successfully operated by the Beradi Family of Grantham for many years.

Today, the most popular activity is cycling but there was little thought given to this in the early planning. In 1981 David and Anne Archer, who operated a cycle hire service in the Peak District, approached Peter Langford, the local manager for Anglian Water, with a view to developing a similar business at Rutland Water. Fortunately Frank Knights had appreciated that an off-road access track was essential for efficient operational management of the reservoir and he had already created a route in stages during the construction phase. Although this track was very rough it was adequate, and in 1982 the cycle hire centre opened at Whitwell car park, to be followed by a second centre at Normanton, and then the new building at Whitwell operated by David and Anne's son, Paul Archer.

Reservoir Manager Frank Knights with Jack Charlton at Rutland Water Cycling Centre in 1985 (AW)

Whitwell Cycle Hire Centre (Richard Adams)

Another important development was the launching of *Rutland Belle* in 1986. Again, it was a family business which made the initial approach. Trevor and Joan Broadhead's suggestion wasn't very popular with the existing users and the Rutland Water Users Panel took quite a bit of convincing before agreeing to a two-year trial to test safety, pollution, and wash impact upon fishing and sailing boats. Everyone's fears turned out to be unfounded as the *Rutland Belle* operated without incident in the trial period and has now completed twenty years and given over 500,000 passengers the superb views which can only be fully appreciated from the water.

Mrs Peddler launching Rutland Belle *in November 1985* (AW)

With so much activity, landscaping has been critical in developing and maintaining the natural appearance of the reservoir. Anglian Water's forester, Tony Ford, did a fantastic job in growing 200,000 trees in special nurseries and planting the new woodlands and hedgerows to create the landscape that he and Dame Sylvia Crowe had planned.

With over one million households within a day-trip range of 60 miles, and 400,000 within a half-day trip of 30 miles, the original plan estimated that there could be 17,000 visitors to the reservoir on a busy summer Sunday, based on an average of 3.25 people per car. The reservoir quickly became a regular attraction with 12,000 visitors recorded on a Sunday in 1978, and better facilities were needed to cater for them. In the mid-eighties there was a burst of investment under the initiative of the new Divisional Manager, Ian Ramsden. Cafés were built on each of the four car parks and those at Whitwell, Sykes Lane and Normanton have been extended to meet the standards expected by today's visitors.

Rutland Belle *after twenty years of service, passing Normanton Fishing Lodge in 2006* (RO)

Whitwell peninsula from the air in 2006
(John Nowell, Zodiac Publishing)

The temporary base of the water sports centre at Whitwell moved into a permanent building operated by David Hales as Surface Watersports for many years. The visitor centre was extended into a Tourist Information Centre and an Interpretation Centre was built for the nature reserve at Lyndon. A drought garden was created in 1986 by Tony Ford and television gardening personality, Geoff Hamilton, to show that you could have an attractive garden on a south-facing slope of clay without watering it.

In 1986 there was a major change in the recreational management of the reservoir when the Anglian Water Authority decided to lease its Trout fisheries at Grafham and Rutland Water rather than directly manage them. The Rutland Water fishery was leased for five years to Roger Thom of Northampton who introduced a tackle shop and a small restaurant into the Whitwell Fishing Lodge. During this time the reservoir hosted the 1987 World Fly Fishing Championships, and was fairly successful until the severe blue-green algal bloom in the autumn of 1989 which closed the reservoir to all water-based recreation for two months. This phenomenon was repeated in varying degrees across the country and all of Anglian Water Authority's reservoirs were closed for six weeks until the algae cleared away. Following this the reservoirs were treated with ferric sulphate to reduce the phosphorous content of the water and 'starve' the algae and

A busy day at Whitwell water sports centre (SS)

The Drought Garden at Barnsdale in 2006 (RO)

hence reduce its development. This treatment was successful but could not be continued indefinitely as it might eventually have led to a reduction in the invertebrates, birdlife and fish growth in the reservoir.

The uncertainties over managing fisheries in water supply reservoirs resulted in both Grafham Water and Rutland Water being returned to the direct management of the newly privatised Anglian Water. In 1989 Frank Knights was appointed Recreation Development manager with me as his assistant. The increased customer focus and recognition that reservoir leisure was an important public face of the new Company meant that there were many more improvements. Since 1990, £3 million has been invested by Anglian Water in improved leisure and access infrastructure at Rutland Water.

Normanton Fishing Lodge in 2006 (SS)

— 493 —

The Birdwatching Centre has been built at Egleton and subsequently extended to provide an education service. A new Fishing Lodge was built at Normanton in 1993, complete with a large tackle shop and restaurant, thus freeing up the old building to provide a much needed catering outlet for the water sports and *Rutland Belle* visitors. This was opened by Arthur Lumsden, the actor who played the fictitious angling character J R Hartley, created by Peter Lapsley, himself an enthusiastic angler who had fished Rutland Water on the first press day prior to its opening.

Normanton Fishing Lodge and harbour from the air in 2006 (John Nowell, Zodiac Publishing)

Part of the fishing boat fleet moored at Normanton Fishing Lodge in 2006. The latest boats now have outboard engines (RO)

Also in 1993, the Butterfly and Aquatic Centre was opened at Sykes Lane as a joint venture between Anglian Water and Jack and Sue Harris. This indoor attraction has appealed to all ages, especially schools, for twenty years and is currently run by Jack and Sue's son David.

Normanton Church as a Museum

In the sixteenth century St Matthew's Church at Normanton was described as being 'in a very ruinous condition'. It was rebuilt by the Heathcote family in 1764 and in 1826 Thomas Cundy and his son added the new tower and portico which we see today. Modifications to the west end were completed in 1911 which brought the whole church into the style of the 1826 construction. When Normanton Hall was demolished in 1925-26 it left the church as an isolated feature although it remained in use by the local community until it was deconsecrated in 1970. The high water level for the new reservoir planned for the Gwash Valley was a few feet above the floor of the church and so in 1972 the Normanton Tower Trust was formed to work with Anglian Water to preserve this local landmark.

Inside the tackle shop at Normanton Fishing Lodge (RO)

By the time work on the new reservoir had begun, members of the Normanton Tower Trust had already started fund-raising, and together with Anglian Water a scheme was planned to protect the church from gradual decline. Floors were raised by two metres, walls were repaired and damp-proofed, and an embankment with a causeway to the shore surrounded the entire building to protect it from the waves and provide public access for the future. Work was completed ahead of the rising waters and by 1978 the new landscaping for the church was complete. However, after all the effort put in by so many people, it unfortunately became neglected and vandalised in the few years after the reservoir was completed, although the Normanton Tower Trust had continued to meet and attempt to maintain the building.

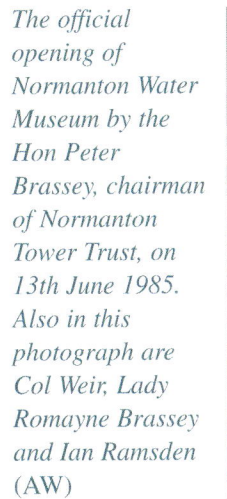

The official opening of Normanton Water Museum by the Hon Peter Brassey, chairman of Normanton Tower Trust, on 13th June 1985. Also in this photograph are Col Weir, Lady Romayne Brassey and Ian Ramsden (AW)

In 1983 Anglian Water took the initiative to refurbish the old church and create Normanton Water Museum, featuring local history and artefacts from the water industry. More extensive repairs were needed to both the exterior and the interior to make the building safe and attractive, but by June 1985 the work had been completed. The museum was officially opened on 13th June by the Hon Peter Brassey, Chairman of the Normanton Tower Trust, and Col Jim Weir, who was the Anglian Water Authority Board member responsible for recreation and conservation at that time. Among the guests was Margaret Plumb of Empingham who, in 1954, was the last bride to be married in the church. The building has become the best known landmark in the county, even featuring in national marketing campaigns by the English Tourist Board.

Above Left: Part of the original display in Normanton Water Museum in June 1985 (AW)

Above Right: Margaret Plumb of Empingham was among the guests at the first opening of the museum. Margaret and Laurence Plumb were the last couple to be married at Normanton Church, in 1954. She is seen here with her father (Margaret Plumb)

Left: Frank Knights, Recreation Manager for Anglian Water, Lady Willoughby d'Eresby and Bernard Henderson, Chairman of Anglian Water, at the re-launch of the museum as Normanton Church on 29th June 1995 (David Moore)

Normanton Church Museum from the Rutland Belle *in 2006* (SS)

Ten years later, in 1995, the Museum was re-launched by Anglian Water as Normanton Church Museum, with a new display featuring the history of the reservoir and its construction. The new display was opened by Lady Jane Willoughby d'Eresby, whose family has been closely associated with Normanton Church since the eighteenth century. Now, 15,000 people visit the museum each year.

Health and Safety

Since 2000, health and safety have been a particular priority for the reservoir management. This can be seen in the massive investment in surfaced car parks. Also, the cycle route from Barnsdale car park, across the dam, through Normanton and to Rutland Sailing Club, has now been resurfaced. This provides an easy route for less able cyclists, walkers, wheelchair-users and those with pushchairs. This leaves a more challenging route around the Hambleton Peninsula for the more adventurous.

Success

In 1994 Rutland Water was entered for the European Union award for Tourism and the Environment. It made the final round, being selected as one of only four finalists in the United Kingdom. It has also won awards from the English Tourist Board, and also from Tourism for All in recognition of the facilities and access it provides for people with disabilities.

Rutland Water wins a top tourist award

RUTLAND WATER has landed a place in Britain's top tourist honours list—the Come To Britain awards.

The giant reservoir, which is developing into an important national centre for sailing, fishing and natural history, gained a certificate of special commendation in the event run by the British Tourist Authority.

The awards are made to organisations and authorities judged to have introduced the year's best new facility, amenity or service for visitors.

Rutland Water's award was presented to Mr. Norman Thompson, chief information officer with the Anglian Water Authority, who run the lake, by Lord Donaldson, Minister of the Arts, at a ceremony in the Royal Festival Hall, London.

prizes of special awards, and Rutland Water came in the next category as one of 20 winners of special commendation certificates, which included places like the new Wimbledon Lawn Tennis Museum.

Said Mr. Thompson: "Great care was taken with the landscaping and architecture at Rutland Water, so as not to detract from the natural beauty of the area.

"And while the lake is there primarily as a major source of public water supply, we are delighted that its attraction as a tourist amenity should also have been recognised in this way."

Delighted

The awards are designed to encourage new areas to develop facilities to attract visitors.

This year's top award, the Come To Britain Trophy, was awarded to the Brighton Centre, a conference, exhibition and entertainment complex in the South Coast resort.

There were four runners-up

An early award for Rutland Water as reported by the Leicester Mercury on 30th May 1978

Today the reservoir has enormous importance in so many people's lives. These include the 500,000 who rely on it for their continuous supply of very high quality drinking water, the local community who enjoy its leisure and sporting facilities throughout the year, and the several hundred people who are employed directly or indirectly by the reservoir and its associated tourist industry.

David Moore, Recreation & Access Manager, and John Seaton, Senior Warden, in 2006. These two men have the overall responsibility for all the public access activities at Rutland Water (RO)

Chapter 23
Fauna and Flora before Rutland Water
Mike Griffin

Introduction

The Rutland Natural History Society (RNHS) was formed by a small group of enthusiasts in February 1965 with William (Dusty) Miller as its first Chairman and Roy Hunter as Secretary. Thus, when the construction of Rutland Water was approved by Parliament in 1970, the RNHS realised the importance of undertaking a detailed survey of fauna and flora in that area of the Gwash Valley to be flooded, before it was lost for ever. The original proposal for a survey was made by Dr Erica Hutton who was a founder member of the RNHS and its Chairperson from 1974-77.

It was recognised that the major influences on fauna and flora would be the earth-moving activities, especially in the vicinity of the dam and the main basin, the clearance of trees and hedges, the demolition of houses and other buildings and, finally, the rising water levels as the reservoir filled. The RNHS's aim was to complete at least one full survey in advance of any of these activities. Over much of the reservoir area, this aim was achieved for birds, insects and plants. Further surveys continued where possible during the construction period.

Vegetation clearance commenced in early autumn 1971 in the dam area close to Empingham, before any surveys began. However, this affected only a relatively small part of the total area covered by the reservoir project. The last areas to be cleared, in early 1974, were the east part of Barnsdale Wood and that part of Burley Wood along the diverted A606.

Looking downstream from Normanton Bridge at Normanton Fishpond before clearance. Note Alder trees in the foreground on both sides (RNHS, 1981)

Vegetation Clearance Programme

Date	Area	Extent
Autumn 1971	Dam area by Empingham	Whole
December 1971 to January 1972	Mow Mires Spinney Cocked Hat Spinney	Whole Whole
November 1972 to March 1973	Hambleton Wood	Part
March 1973 to August 1973	Gibbet Lane area Armley Wood Normanton Fishpond Brake Spinney	Whole Part Whole Whole
October 1973	Barnsdale Wood (Main)	Part
November 1973	Armley Wood Rushpit Wood	Part Part along A606 diversion
February 1974	Barnsdale Wood (East) Burley Wood	Part Part along A606 diversion

Looking downstream at Normanton Fishpond after clearance (RNHS, 1981)

The reservoir took nearly five years to fill. The area flooded rose from ten acres in 1974 to 3,113 acres (1,260 hectares) in April 1979, when it was full for the first time.

Vegetation clearance near Armley Wood (RNHS, 1981)

View downstream of Bull Bridge in 1974 showing an early stage of flooding (RNHS, 1981)

Eastern end of Barnsdale Wood prior to felling, with white stakes showing the future high water line (RNHS, 1981)

Filling the Reservoir

This table shows the approximate water level, the depth and the area covered at various dates from the start of construction until the reservoir was full. Water levels are given as heights above mean sea level, or more correctly, heights above Ordnance Datum (OD).

Date	Water level OD (metres)	Water depth (metres)	Area flooded (acres)
1971	(reservoir empty)	0	0
1974	53	1	10
1975	63	11	330
1976	68	16	720
1977	82	30	2,700
1979	84 (reservoir full)	32	3,113

The dam was closed on 6th February 1975 and the first time that water flooded over the spillway was in April 1979. The exact level at which water starts to flood over the spillway is 83.82m OD.
(RNHS 1981, Map 2 & information provided by David Moore, Recreation & Access Manager, Anglian Water).

The RNHS Survey started in autumn 1971 and continued until autumn 1976, focussing on mammals, birds, insects and plants. However, before the survey started, maps and record cards had to be prepared and permission had to be obtained from farmers for access to their land. Surveys were conducted over nine main areas of land based on parish boundaries. These extended from Normanton and Empingham parishes in the east to the Gunthorpe and Burley parishes in the west. Individual fields were identified and numbered, for example N22 (Normanton) and G9 (Gunthorpe). As work on the clearance of vegetation progressed, inevitably, individual field boundaries became obscured.

The Gwash Valley survey area showing parish boundaries and other key features (RO)

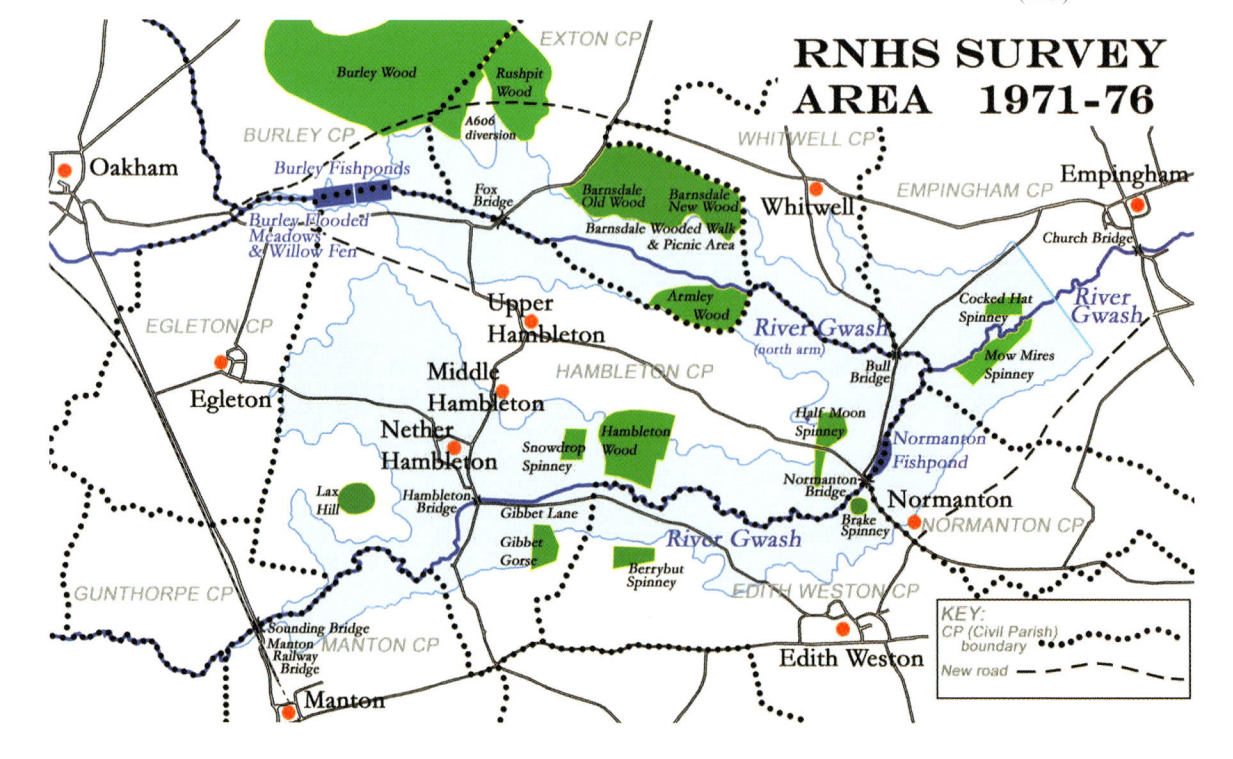

Record card from the bird survey for two fields just upstream of Bull Bridge (Philip Rudkin)

The urgency to start the survey, the limited number of recorders and the enormity of the task meant that survey areas had to be prioritised. The main focus was on the rivers and river banks and ten yards into the fields bordering the rivers, on fishponds and any marshy areas, on woods and spinneys, and on any undisturbed grassy banks. The Carnegie UK Trust gave a grant of £175 towards the cost of the RNHS Survey.

Although not part of the RNHS Survey, a detailed record was made of the resident fish species when they were removed from fishponds, rivers and streams during 1974 (Moore 1982, 179-89). Thus, fish species will be covered in this chapter, along with mammals, birds, insects and plants. Other species not included in the RNHS Survey were reptiles, amphibians, spiders, soil invertebrates, fungi, lichens, mosses and liverworts.

The nomenclature used for some animal and plant species in the RNHS Survey Report (RNHS, 1981) has been superseded. Up-to-date nomenclature is used throughout this chapter.

RNHS survey party standing on a footbridge over the River Gwash south-west of Brake Spinney, looking upstream. From left to right, Betty Eaton, Joan Levisohn and Dr Erica Hutton (Jim Levisohn ARPS)

Mammals

Mammals were recorded at fortnightly intervals from September 1972 to August 1976 along the River Gwash and in the fields bordering the river. However, a year earlier in September 1971, the RNHS was contacted by the Water Board and asked to help with Badger setts in Normanton Park due to be destroyed by earth-moving machinery. Using various Badger-friendly methods, the Badgers were persuaded to vacate their setts before the machinery was moved in.

In 1971, RNHS members persuaded Badgers in Normanton Park to vacate their setts before they were destroyed by heavy machinery (Jim Eaton)

During the five years of the survey led by George Sellars, 22 different species of mammal were recorded (RNHS 1981, 63-66). Rabbits, Brown Hares, Fallow Deer and Foxes were regularly recorded but not so frequently as the Water Vole, sighted on 269 occasions. There were no striking increases or decreases in sightings over the survey period, with the exception of the Water Vole. Sightings dropped from 161 in 1972, to 28 in 1974, and to a mere 12 in 1976. The majority of the 269 sightings were along the main course of the River Gwash; only 16% were along the north arm of the river. The abundance of Water Voles along the River Gwash in 1972 is of particular interest given the dramatic decline of this species since the 1970s. National surveys have shown that Water Voles have been lost from some 90% of the sites they inhabited 60 years ago. The decline has accelerated in the past 20 years and predation by the American Mink is thought to have eradicated many small populations of Water Vole, which is now listed in the UK Action Plan on Biodiversity. They have also been legally protected since 1998 when they were included on Schedule 5, Section 9 (4) a & b of the Wildlife and Countryside Act 1981 (as amended). Clearly, before the site was flooded, the River Gwash between Empingham and Gunthorpe provided an excellent habitat for Water Voles. Tim Appleton, manager of Rutland Water Nature Reserve, has confirmed that the current population of Water Voles in the Rutland Water Nature Reserve is at a very low level with only one or two sightings per year. Also, Linda Biddle, the RNHS mammal recorder, has confirmed occasional recent sightings along the North Brook which runs into the River Gwash at Empingham, about half a mile downstream from the Rutland Water dam.

Mammals recorded during the Survey

Species	Total number of sightings
Hedgehog	2
Mole	72
Common Shrew	4
Pygmy Shrew	4
Water Shrew	1
Noctule Bat	7
Pipistrelle Bat	13
Long-eared Bat	2
Fox	115
Stoat	19
Weasel	26
Badger	72
Fallow Deer	128
Brown Hare	179
Rabbit	189
Grey Squirrel	79
Harvest Mouse	1
Wood Mouse	55
Common Rat	12
Bank Vole	21
Water Vole	269
Field Vole	31

The Water Vole was the most commonly sighted mammal in the RNHS Survey (Wikipedia)

Muntjac were not sighted during the five-year survey from September 1972 to August 1976. This species has now become relatively common (Biddle 1990, 33-36) and is regularly spotted around Rutland Water. Similarly, there was no record of Otters from the Survey but this species has remained absent or very scarce. However, in February 2007, a large male Otter was unfortunately killed crossing the A6003 where the River Gwash flows into Rutland Water by Sounding Bridge near Manton. This was only the second Otter seen around Rutland Water in 31 years. Other recent reports of Otter activity in Rutland (*Fieldfare* May 2007, 18 & 19) are encouraging and consequently there is some hope that breeding pairs might return in the near future.

Tim Appleton with a dead male Otter killed on 17th February 2007 crossing the A6003 road where the River Gwash flows into Rutland Water at Sounding Bridge (Rutland & Stamford Mercury)

Birds

During the five years from 1971/72 to 1975/76, bird surveys, led by Jim Eaton, were undertaken at fortnightly intervals by RNHS members. All sightings were recorded by field number and date, and monthly summaries produced. Data were grouped into winter and summer seasons for the whole area to enable meaningful comparisons for migrant species. The detailed results, for summers and winters, for each of the five survey years, were published in the *Before Rutland Water* report (RNHS 1981, 55-61).

Sightings of Bird Species during the Survey

Species	Total number of sightings	Species	Total number of sightings
Barn Owl	11	Great Crested Grebe	113
Bearded Tit	2	Great Grey Shrike	1
Bewick's Swan	8	Great Spotted Woodpecker	7
Blackbird	567	Great Tit	258
Blackcap	56	Greenfinch	479
Black-headed Gull	1,846	Green Sandpiper	27
Blue Tit	650	Greenshank	4
Brambling	68	Green Woodpecker	95
Bullfinch	300	Grey Heron	97
Buzzard	2	Grey Partridge	112
Canada Goose	32	Grey Wagtail	5
Carrion Crow	230	Herring Gull	49
Chaffinch	894	House Martin	796
Chiffchaff	36	House Sparrow	1,863
Coal Tit	11	Jack Snipe	1
Collared Dove	9	Jackdaw	549
Common Gull	96	Jay	85
Common Sandpiper	47	Kestrel	91
Common Tern	2	Kingfisher	32
Coot	2,402	Lapwing	4,816
Cormorant	25	Lesser Black-backed Gull	50
Corn Bunting	86	Lesser Spotted Woodpecker	5
Cuckoo	29	Lesser Whitethroat	29
Curlew	1	Linnet	1,633
Dunlin	78	Little Grebe	160
Dunnock	330	Little Owl	18
Fieldfare	2,252	Little Ringed Plover	18
Garden Warbler	21	Long-tailed Tit	377
Goldcrest	15	Magpie	41
Golden Plover	38	Mallard	2,754
Goldeneye	34	Marsh Tit	108
Goldfinch	937	Meadow Pipit	194
Goosander	3	Mistle Thrush	26
Grasshopper Warbler	16	Moorhen	386
Great Black-backed Gull	20	Mute Swan	139

Nightingale	4	Song Thrush	202
Nuthatch	13	Spotted Flycatcher	29
Osprey	1	Starling	5,074
Oystercatcher	2	Stock Dove	35
Pheasant	264	Stonechat	30
Pied Wagtail	145	Swallow	612
Pintail	8	Swift	405
Pochard	587	Tawny Owl	39
Red-legged Partridge	98	Teal	862
Redpoll	82	Treecreeper	44
Redshank	38	Tree Pipit	1
Redstart	15	Tree Sparrow	844
Redwing	409	Tufted Duck	1,311
Reed Bunting	756	Turtle Dove	48
Reed Warbler	61	Water Rail	2
Ringed Plover	1	Wheatear	12
Robin	250	Whinchat	21
Rook	1,191	Whitethroat	43
Ruff	11	Wigeon	228
Sand Martin	26	Willow Tit	35
Sedge Warbler	67	Willow Warbler	127
Shelduck	3	Woodcock	18
Short-eared Owl	9	Woodpigeon	3,341
Shoveler	126	Wren	385
Siskin	52	Yellowhammer	648
Skylark	2,136	Yellow Wagtail	70
Snipe	602		

One hundred and twenty-three bird species were sighted during the five survey years from 1971/72 to 1975/76. Eighty-eight species were recorded in 1971/72 and 97 species in 1975/76. The most common species, sighted on more than 2,000 occasions during the five years, were Mallard, Coot, Lapwing, Woodpigeon, Skylark, Fieldfare and Starling. In contrast, species sighted only once included Osprey, Ringed Plover, Jack Snipe, Curlew, Tree Pipit and Great Grey Shrike. For comparison, Terry Mitcham, the RNHS bird recorder, has confirmed that the number of bird species recorded from the Rutland Water Nature Reserve in 2005/06 was 176.

Goldeneye, absent during the first three survey years, first appeared in 1974/75 (Wikipedia)

Tufted Duck, not seen in 1971/72, then increased progressively to 557 sightings by 1975/76 (Wikipedia)

There are many factors which affect annual bird populations and short term trends must be interpreted with caution. However, between 1971/72 and 1975/76, one would have anticipated increases in some wildfowl species as the area of water increased, and decreases in other species due to a combination of disturbance and habitat destruction. This proved to be the case. Ten species of wildfowl showed clear trends towards a progressive increase in numbers over the five years whereas some other species, for example the Robin, showed trends in the opposite direction.

Birds Sightings which increased or decreased during the Survey

Total number of sightings

Species	1971/2	1972/3	1973/4	1974/5	1975/6
Waterfowl					
Great Crested Grebe	0	4	20	50	39
Little Grebe	4	19	18	67	52
Cormorant	0	0	0	6	19
Mallard	235	474	342	357	1,346
Shoveler	0	6	6	10	104
Tufted Duck	0	84	198	472	557
Pochard	0	59	114	239	175
Goldeneye	0	0	0	21	13
Coot	57	133	410	479	1,323
Dunlin	0	10	7	24	37
Other Species					
Cuckoo	17	5	6	1	0
Long-tailed Tit	118	151	64	19	25
Great Tit	115	90	32	12	9
Robin	93	88	36	16	17

Female Shoveler. Absent in the first survey, Shoveler were sighted on 104 occasions by 1975/76 (A Wilson – Wikipedia)

Worthy of mention are a few of the bird species not recorded during the survey. Given the frequency of the surveys over a five-year period, it seems remarkable now that the Sparrowhawk was not recorded. Clearly, populations in the area were at a very low level or even absent during the early 1970s. Terry Mitcham has confirmed that Sparrowhawk sightings are now quite common around the Rutland Water Reserve, as are sightings for other birds of prey either not recorded or not regularly recorded during the survey, namely Red Kite, Common Buzzard, Osprey and Hobby. Also, the Peregrine Falcon is now a regular winter visitor. Another bird of current importance not recorded during the survey is the Gadwall. Since the survey, Gadwall have become established on Rutland Water, and their populations, along with those of Shoveler, are now of international importance and are cited in the Special Protection Area (SPA) designation.

The Sparrowhawk, now commonly seen around Rutland Water, was not recorded during the RNHS surveys from 1971/72 to 1975/76 (Stafford – Fotolia)

Fish

Rutland Water was stocked with Brown Trout and Rainbow Trout in 1975 (*see* Chapter 22 Rutland Water: Planning and Developing a Water Supply Reservoir as a World-Class Leisure Venue). Prior to this, it was necessary to remove resident fish in order to minimise competition with, and predation of, the introduced trout fry. The area within the reservoir's perimeter contained fishponds, farm ponds, ditches, streams and two stretches of the River Gwash including its north arm. Most of these contained species of fish.

The contributory rivers and streams were electrofished during 1974. Burley Fishponds were drained which allowed fish to be netted and transported in tanks for release elsewhere. Final removal was by poisoning the streams with rotenone, a broad spectrum piscicide, to eliminate those fish that had avoided capture. Numerous ditches which contained Sticklebacks were not poisoned as they were too numerous and return of the species was inevitable. Nineteen species of fish were recorded (Moore 1982, 179-89), some of which, such as Carp, Tench and Bream, were mainly or entirely in Burley Fishponds. Most of the species which would be expected from lowland rivers and streams in England were represented. One species not recorded in 1974 but which, according to David Moore, has been present in Rutland Water since the mid-1990s is the Zander, often referred to as the Pike-Perch. It is closely related to the Perch, but not to the Pike and is not native to English waters. It was introduced to the Great Ouse Relief Channel (Norfolk) in 1963 and, since then, has spread rapidly. Zander can now be found in drains, canals, still waters and slow-moving rivers throughout East Anglia and the Midlands.

Fish Species in Watercourses and Ponds which were subsequently flooded by Rutland Water

Bleak
Brown Trout
Bullhead
Chub
Common Bream
Common Carp
Dace
Eel
Grayling
Gudgeon
Minnow
Perch
Pike
Roach
Rudd
Silver Bream
Stickleback
Stone Loach
Tench

Pike were common both in the River Gwash and in Burley Fishponds. This picture shows seventeen Pike weighing a total of 78lb caught at Burley Fishponds on 26th December 1905 by G Welch and J Briggs. The largest fish was nearly 9lb (RCM)

Bullheads were easy to find in the River Gwash, usually hiding under stones (Nick Giles)

Rudd were present in both arms of the River Gwash (John Bailey)

Below: Tench were confined mostly to Burley Fishponds (John Bailey)

Right: A Cormorant which had choked to death trying to swallow too large a Zander was washed up on the shore of Rutland Water by Normanton Church Museum in May 2005 (Mike Griffin)

Insects

The insect survey, led by Maurice (Monty) Tyler, was divided into three periods covering 1971/72, 1973/74 and 1975/76. There were 131 different insect species recorded in the first period, 154 in the second period and 224 in the third period. The areas surveyed in each period were different and so no meaningful comparison can be made between the diversity of species for each period. Light traps for trapping moths were operated in a number of fields. Of the eleven insect groupings, moth species were the most numerous in all three periods, accounting for 48-68% of the species recorded. The butterfly grouping accounted for 8-13% of species recorded. Across the six years of the survey, 368 different insect species were identified. The lists of all species recorded and their locations over the three 2-year periods were published in the *Before Rutland Water* report (RNHS 1981, 35-54).

Insect Species identified during the Survey

Grouping	1971/72	Total number of species 1973/74	1975/76
Mayflies	2	1	2
Dragonflies & Damselflies	8	7	6
Grasshoppers & Crickets	2	2	2
Bugs	2	3	7
Alder Flies & Lacewings	2	2	2
Scorpion Flies	1	1	0
Butterflies	17	15	19
Moths	63	105	149
Beetles	8	5	18
Bees, Wasps & Ants	15	6	8
Flies	11	7	11
Totals	131	154	224

First Insect Survey Period, 1971/72

Right: The Small Copper butterfly reappeared in a field close to Mow Mires Spinney during 1971 (Wikipedia)

The area surveyed during 1971 extended from Church Bridge in Empingham up the Gwash Valley to Bull Bridge. Three species were of special interest, two butterflies and a damselfly. The Common Blue and Small Copper butterflies reappeared in the area after an absence of seven years. The reason for this was thought to be a combination of favourable climatic conditions and an abandoned pasture producing plenty of Bird's-foot Trefoil and Common Sorrel, food plants of Common Blue and Small

Above: The Common Blue butterfly was recorded in 1971 in the same field as the Small Copper (D Zidar – Fotolia)

Below: Poplar Hawkmoth was recorded upstream of Bull Bridge in 1972 (RO)

Copper larvae respectively. The third species to reappear was the Banded Demoiselle damselfly. A combination of the same climatic factors and less spraying was thought to be responsible.

The main areas surveyed in 1972 were Bull Bridge to Armley Wood, Normanton Fishpond to Brake Spinney and Gibbet Lane below Hambleton Wood. A light trap for trapping moths was operated in five fields.

Several fields in the Bull Bridge to Armley Wood section supported a range of butterfly species and Banded Demoiselle, Emerald (recorded as Green Lestes) and Common Blue damselflies thrived by the waterside. Other notable finds were the Poplar Hawkmoth and the Clouded Border moth.

Left: Banded Demoiselle damselflies were found in 1971 in a field close to Mow Mires Spinney (Tim Clough)

In the Normanton Fishpond to above Brake Spinney section, a strong colony of the Common Green Grasshopper was found on the edge of Brake Spinney. Three damselflies, rare in the area, were also found in Brake Spinney, namely the White-legged Damselfly, the Beautiful Demoiselle and the Large Red Damselfly. There were a number of resident butterflies in nearby fields and the Brown Hawker dragonfly was also recorded.

Above: The Brown Hawker dragonfly was seen in 1972 close to Brake Spinney (Wikipedia)

Right: The Speckled Bush-cricket, found on the verge in Gibbet Lane, was a first record for Rutland (M Kosmal – Fotolia)

Above: A colony of Common Green Grasshoppers was found in 1972 on the edge of Brake Spinney (ivp – Fotolia)

Gibbet Lane, the third area surveyed in 1972, had a rich and varied insect population. Butterfly species recorded were Orange Tip, Small Tortoiseshell, Gatekeeper, Meadow Brown, Ringlet, Large and Small Skipper, Brimstone, Peacock and Common Blue. The Speckled Bush-cricket (*Leptophyes punctatissima*), found on the verge of Gibbet Lane, was a first record for Rutland.

Second Insect Survey Period, 1973/74

The main areas covered were: the Gwash Valley from Gibbet Lane to the Manton-Oakham road; land to the south and east of Lax Hill; the lower parts of Hambleton, Barnsdale, Rushpit and Burley Woods; and the Burley Fishponds outflow.

The Gibbet Lane to the Manton-Oakham road section produced several species of butterfly and also several moths including the Narrow-bordered Five-spot Burnet, Mullein, Chimney Sweeper and Common Heath. The larvae of the Narrow-bordered Five-spot Burnet were feeding on Yellow Vetchling and Bird's-foot Trefoil which were growing in the area. Occasional Banded Demoiselle and Common Blue damselflies were seen along the riverside. However, the most interesting find was the Common Field Grasshopper on the roadside verge by Sounding Bridge. Lax Hill and the surrounding fields proved to be a major stronghold of the Meadow Brown butterfly which was counted in the hundreds in 1973. The Large Skipper butterfly and Chimney Sweeper moth were found to be plentiful in a herb-rich meadow to the south-east of Lax Hill.

The woodlands in the survey area proved disappointing for butterflies and no true woodland species were recorded in Burley Wood. Moth trapping proved more successful, with good lists of species from all the woods, especially Hambleton Wood where Red Underwing and Peach Blossom moths were recorded.

The stream down from Burley Fishponds to Fox Bridge was productive with a good range of insect species including a strong colony of Orange Tip butterflies. In 1974, a Brimstone butterfly was observed egg-laying on Buckthorn near Fox Bridge. The larger dragonflies, the Brown Hawker and Southern Hawker, were common in the area of Burley Fishponds in 1973.

Below: In 1973, Lax Hill and the surrounding fields were a stronghold for the Meadow Brown butterfly (S Chushkin – Fotolia)

Right: Large Skipper butterflies were numerous in 1973 in a herb-rich meadow to the south-east of Lax Hill (Wikipedia)

Butterfly Species recorded during the Insect Survey Periods

Species	Number of periods in which recorded	Species	Number of periods in which recorded
Large White	1	Red Admiral	3
Small White	1	Painted Lady	2
Green-veined White	3	Peacock	3
Orange Tip	3	Small Tortoiseshell	3
Brimstone	3	Small Copper	3
Wall Brown	3	Common Blue	3
Meadow Brown	3	Holly Blue	1
Gatekeeper	3	Dingy Skipper	1
Small Heath	3	Small Skipper	3
Ringlet	3	Large Skipper	3

Third Insect Survey Period, 1975/76

By 1975/76, field numbers had to be abandoned as the whole area was cleared of hedges and trees. The reservoir valley became a single large area of grass and herbs. There was, perhaps not surprisingly, a marked increase in those species which prospered in an open wasteland habitat. Butterflies such as the Meadow Brown, Gatekeeper, Wall Brown, Small Tortoiseshell, Peacock, Orange Tip, Small Copper and Large and Small Skipper all showed a marked increase from previous years. The Holly Blue butterfly was recorded for the first time in Snowdrop Spinney in June 1975. Moths showed a similar change with increasing numbers of those species preferring wasteland habitats. Species such as Large Emerald, Gold Spangle, Tissue, Shark, Shoulder-striped Wainscot and Bulrush Wainscot were all first records for the area. The day-flying Chimney Sweeper moth increased noticeably in 1975.

Orange Tip butterflies (seen here on Lady's-smock) were more prevalent during 1975/76 (Wikipedia)

The year 1976 was a record for uninterrupted sunshine, heat and drought favouring the butterfly population, especially the 'Browns'. Meadow Browns, Wall Browns, Gatekeepers and Large and Small Skippers were numerous. Other butterflies which had been quite scarce in the area such as Small Heath, Small Copper and Common Blue became common in areas where they had not previously been recorded. Moth trapping in 1976 was at Nether Hambleton, at Burley Fishponds and on the south bank of the River Gwash below Manton. New records for the Nether Hambleton area were Green Silver-lines, Cinnabar, Bordered White, Knot Grass, Poplar Kitten and Scorched Wing. Records of the Elephant Hawkmoth increased markedly with a maximum of ten recorded on 9th June 1976. Another newcomer to the area was the Mother Shipton moth found at Lax Hill, Nether Hambleton and below Barnsdale Wood.

Above: The Peacock butterfly prospered in the open wasteland habitats of 1975/76 (S Chushkin – Fotolia)

Above: The day-flying Chimney Sweeper moth increased noticeably in 1975 (Wikipedia)

Right: The Green Silver-lines moth was a new record for the Nether Hambleton area in 1976 (Wikipedia)

Damselflies and dragonflies were in similar numbers and areas as in previous years. Grasshoppers seemed to be on the increase in 1975/76 with four new sites being colonised by the Common Field Grasshopper. A Glowworm was recorded in Burley Wood on 24th June 1976, a first record for that area.

Overall Summary – Insect Surveys

The Speckled Bush-cricket (*Leptophyes punctatissima*) found on the verge in Gibbet Lane in 1972 was a first record for Rutland and an interesting find.

Perhaps the most striking change over the six-year survey period was the significant increase in both the numbers and diversity of butterflies and moths during the last two years of the survey. However, there was also a similar trend throughout the countryside during this same period. Thus, it was difficult to say whether the main factor was favourable climatic conditions or the dramatic changes to the habitat in the Gwash Valley. It is likely that both factors played a part.

An interesting discovery was how quickly abandoned fields became colonised by the range of insects associated with the typical herb-rich hay meadows of the pre-1950s. A major mystery was the lack of typical woodland butterfly species in outwardly ideal woods such as Burley, Barnsdale and Hambleton. The authors of the survey report (RNHS, 1981) speculated that, with sympathetic habitat management in the future, the rarer butterflies such as Speckled Wood, Comma, Dark Green Fritillary and Purple Hairstreak, which had disappeared from the Gwash Valley, might return. Their speculation was largely correct; John Wright, of Rutland Water Nature Reserve, has confirmed that Speckled Wood, Comma and Purple Hairstreak are now commonly recorded in the Reserve.

Far Left: Purple Hairstreak, a butterfly not recorded in the 1971-76 Survey, is now commonly seen (Wikipedia)

Left: Comma, another butterfly not seen in the Survey, is now common in the Rutland Water Nature Reserve (Wikipedia)

Flora

The Botanical Survey, led by Janet Buchanan, started in Autumn 1971 and was completed in late 1974. In 1971, the main objective was to record the trees and shrubs in the Empingham to Normanton Bridge section of the River Gwash before they were felled and cleared. Unfortunately, around the area of the dam, some felling and clearing started just ahead of the survey. In 1972, the remaining flora of this area was recorded along with a more thorough survey of the River Gwash as far as Fox Bridge below Barnsdale Wood in the north and Nether Hambleton in the south. Recording included Armley Wood, some thick spinneys at Whitwell and Hambleton and a rough scrubby bank at Edith Weston. During late 1972 and 1973, the remaining areas were recorded, namely to Sounding Bridge near Manton in the south and Burley Fishponds in the north, including the Burley Flooded Meadows and Willow Fen, other marshy areas by Burley Fishponds and at Nether Hambleton, Rushpit Wood, Burley Wood and Barnsdale New Wood. By 1974, the main recording had been completed.

The recording method was to walk all areas being surveyed once a month, ticking off common species on a check list, and listing uncommon species separately. All species were listed by area and field number. During the three survey years from 1971/72 to 1973/74, 412 different plant species were recorded in the Gwash Valley. A full list of all species identified was published in the *Before Rutland Water* report (RNHS 1981, 11-33).

Plants recorded in the Botanical Survey

Group	Number of species recorded
Horsetails and Ferns	11
Grasses, Sedges, Reeds and Rushes	74
Trees and Shrubs	67
Herbaceous Plants	260
Total	412

Horsetails and Ferns

Just three species of the primitive horsetail and eight species of fern were recorded during the Botanical Survey. The ferns were mainly in Hambleton, Armley, Burley and Barnsdale Old Woods. In the north of Hambleton Wood, above the level of felling and against a small waterway, a colony of Hard Shield Fern was found in Spring 1973. Male Fern, Broad Buckler Fern and Lady Fern were all abundant in Armley Wood, and a few plants of Bracken and Scaly Male Fern (listed as Golden Scaled Fern) were also found. Hartstongue was recorded on the parapet of the causeway dividing the two Burley Fishponds and Black Spleenwort on the old brickwork by the railway bridge over the A6003 near Sounding Bridge.

Hard Shield Fern was found in Hambleton Wood in Spring 1973 (Wikipedia)

Grasses, Sedges, Reeds and Rushes

There were 74 species of grasses, sedges, reeds and rushes listed in the *Before Rutland Water* report (RNHS 1981, 11-33). Two of these, Lesser Reedmace (*Typha angustifolia*), listed in the survey as Lesser Bulrush, and Greater Tussock Sedge (*Carex paniculata*), listed as Tussock Sedge, were reported as first records for Rutland. However, there was an earlier record of Lesser Reedmace at Foster's Bridge on the River Chater in 1933 (Messenger 1971, 95).

Lesser Reedmace, recorded in 1972 on the bank of the Gwash in the Edith Weston sector, was a rare find for Rutland (Fotolia)

Greater Tussock Sedge, recorded in Mow Mires Marsh in 1971, was a first record for Rutland (Wikipedia)

Some species recorded in the Empingham to below Edith Weston section of the main river included Greater Tussock Sedge (from Mow Mires in 1971), Greater Pond Sedge, Reed Canary-grass (listed as Reed-grass), Plicate Sweet-grass (listed as Sweet-grass), Reed Sweet-grass (listed as Great Water Grass), Wood Club-rush, Bulrush (Common Club-rush), and Lesser Reedmace. Under the instruction of Janet Buchanan, clumps of Lesser Reedmace were lifted, using a mechanical digger, and transplanted in the upper reaches of the River Gwash near to Gunthorpe. Unfortunately, it did not survive. Some of the Greater Tussock Sedge was also lifted and transplanted near to Burley Fishponds, and did survive.

Lesser Reedmace being excavated for transplanting in the River Gwash near Gunthorpe witnessed by Guy Messenger (left), author of Flora of Rutland *(Jim Eaton)*

The survey continued along the main River Gwash from Edith Weston to Nether Hambleton and Gunthorpe. Species recorded included Wood Meadow-grass, Greater Pond Sedge, Cocksfoot, Bearded Couch, Creeping Soft-grass (in Hambleton Wood), Tufted Hair-grass, Glaucous Sedge, Lesser Pond Sedge, Quaking Grass, Common Sedge, several other Sedge species, Unbranched Bur-reed (listed as Small Bur-reed), Branched Bur-reed, Common Bulrush and Common Reedmace (listed as Greater Reedmace or False Bulrush).

A detailed botanical survey was also conducted along the north arm of the Gwash from Bull Bridge to Burley Fishponds. Species recorded were Greater Pond Sedge, Common Couch, Bearded Couch, Slender Tufted Sedge (recorded as Graceful Sedge), Lesser Pond Sedge, Fern Grass, Common Reed (listed as Reed), Common Reedmace, Branched Bur-reed, Oval Sedge and Sharp-flowered Rush.

Above: Branched Bur-reed was recorded at several locations along the River Gwash (Wikipedia)

Left: The reedbed in the Upper Burley Fishpond, looking from the causeway (RNHS, 1981)

Trees and Shrubs

There were 67 species of trees and shrubs recorded in the Botanical Survey between 1971 and 1974 (RNHS 1981, 11-33). The range of species was much as expected for the habitat type. There were sixteen Willow species/hybrids associated with the River Gwash, including the north arm and Burley Fishponds. Another feature was the presence of Alder trees, which were growing alongside the river in numerous areas either singly, or in belts. A few illustrative excerpts from the RNHS (1981) report are given below.

Willow Species and Hybrids recorded in the Botanical Survey

Bay Willow
White Willow
Weeping Willow
Crack Willow
Salix decipiens
Almond Willow
Purple Willow
Salix x rubra
Common Osier
Salix caprea x viminalis
Salix cinerea x viminalis
Salix calodendron
Pussy Willow (Great Sallow)
Common Sallow
Eared Sallow
Goat Willow

The description for the trees and shrubs on the island in Normanton Fishpond was: 'Among these trees was a Black Poplar, Silver Birch, Wych Elm, several Alder, Sycamore, and a big Grey Poplar making a beautiful colour contrast with its leaves. These big trees were thickly spaced, with a few low shrubs, including Box, Snowberry, Willows and Dogwood . . .'.

Continuing along the river to the south west of Normanton Bridge was 'an almost impenetrable wilderness with very thick scrub, partly planted with young Willows and Poplars, and with a belt of large Alders by the river . . .'. One of the Edith Weston fields below Hambleton Wood 'had a large steep bank down to the river thickly covered with shrubs . . . . There were two Oak trees, Hawthorn, Blackthorn, Ash, one Alder and willows: Crack Willow and Goat Willow'.

The description in the survey report for Hambleton Wood was 'mixed deciduous, the southern edge was thick with Blackthorn and there were numerous Hazels showing yellow in the bare wood in early spring. The trees were mostly Oak, Ash and Maple, with an occasional Willow, thorn and Crab Apple'. In Snowdrop Spinney below Hambleton 'were many well grown trees of Oak, Ash, Wych Elm, Horse Chestnut, Sweet Chestnut, Norway Spruce and Common [European] Larch. On the southern boundary were many bushes of Cherry Plum'.

Armley Wood, alongside the north arm of the River Gwash was described as 'consisting of well grown mixed deciduous trees, three quarters of which fell victim to the reservoir workings, [and] was perhaps the worst casualty amongst the woodland habitats of the survey. The wood came right to the bank of the river . . . and contained Maple, Sycamore, Silver Birch, Beech, Ash, Oak, Horse Chestnut and two kinds of Elm among its trees. Among the smaller trees and bushes were both Hawthorns, Blackthorn, Dogwood, Elder, Wild Plum, Box and Red Currant. Ground cover was very thick with Blackberry . . . .'

A more detailed description of the trees and shrubs recorded in the Botanical Survey can be found in the *Before Rutland Water* report (RNHS 1981, 11-33). Although many trees were lost when the area to be inundated was cleared, thousands of new trees were planted around the perimeter of Rutland Water (Ford 1982, 47-50; Gill 1982, 51).

Herbaceous Plants

Two hundred and sixty species of herbaceous plant were recorded during the 1971 to 1974 Botanical Survey. The number of species was swelled by the rich crop of casuals which invaded abandoned arable fields, felled and cleared woodland and areas of bare ground created by the various construction activities. None of the 260 species was a new record for Rutland although Golden Dock (*Rumex maritimus*) had not been seen since 1900. Another unusual find in 1971 was a large clump of Small Teasel (*Dipsacus pilosus*) under trees in a field just downstream of Bull Bridge. Occasional plants of Small Teasel were also found in nearby fields. The full list of herbaceous plants recorded is given in the *Before Rutland Water* report (RNHS 1981, 11-33). A few typical extracts from this report are given in the paragraphs below.

Yellow Water-lily was recorded in several sections of the River Gwash (J Gil – Fotolia)

The main interest in three Normanton fields was in the River Gwash where there was 'Curled Pondweed and Fennel Pondweed, Yellow Water-lily and, against the low banks Purple Loosestrife, Pink Water Speedwell . . . and common Water Forget-me-not'. On the north bank of the Gwash to the west of Normanton Bridge 'There was a rough bank of varying width most of the way, growing Marsh Woundwort, common Teasel, Hemlock, Hedge Bedstraw, an occasional bright Meadow Cranesbill and quantities of Nettles and rough grass'. Some old grass pastures on the south bank of the river had 'Cowslip, Red Clover and, most interesting of all, Meadow Saxifrage; some of this latter plant was saved for replanting on in the Rutland Water Nature Reserve'.

Above: A clump of Small Teasel was found downstream of Bull Bridge (Wikipedia)

Left: Purple Loosestrife was common along the river banks (S Camp – Fotolia)

In the river below Hambleton Wood, 'Water plants provided the most interest: Curled Pondweed . . . [and] Yellow Water-lily, while on the banks there was the inevitable Water Figwort, Water Chickweed, common Water Forget-me-not and various willow-herb, found everywhere during the survey'. The ground cover in Hambleton Wood 'was Dog's Mercury, Bluebell . . . Tormentil, Barren Strawberry, Primrose, Wood Dog Violet [and] Bugle . . .'. One dead plant of Broad-leaved Helleborine (recorded as Common Helleborine) was seen in a cleared section of Snowdrop Spinney.

One dead plant of Broad-leaved Helleborine was found in Snowdrop Spinney (Wikipedia)

Right: Cowslips were found upstream of Normanton Bridge and elsewhere (Wikipedia)

In the wide rough bank of one of the arable fields in the Hambleton Bridge to Lax Hill section, growing in the shade of some trees, were '. . . Wood Forget-me-not, Moschatel, Wood Goldilocks, Sweet Violet and Common Dog Violet; where it was more sunny . . . there were Cowslips and Hairy St John's Wort. In the river itself were Yellow Water-lily . . . and Curled Pondweed'. In the river just upstream was the only patch in the whole survey of Blue Water Speedwell, the first record of Canadian Waterweed, and Yellow Water-lily.

Bluebells were prolific in Hambleton and Armley Woods (SS)

Orchids were uncommon in the Botanical Survey area. However, in a marshy field by Beehive Cottage in Nether Hambleton, Early Marsh Orchid, Southern Marsh Orchid and their hybrids were recorded. Also found were Yellow Rattle, Pink Water Speedwell and Tufted Forget-me-not. Southern Marsh Orchids were also found in a small marshy area just to the east of Burley Fishponds. The only other location with orchids was Barnsdale New Wood with both Early Purple Orchid and Common Spotted Orchid.

Early Purple Orchid was found in Barnsdale New Wood (K Hewitt – Fotolia)

Southern Marsh Orchids were seen in marshy fields both by Nether Hambleton and by Burley Fishponds (pdtnc – Fotolia)

To the south of Lax Hill, a small dense spinney cleared early in 1973 later revealed some interesting ground cover plants. These included '. . . Dog's Mercury, Moschatel and quantities of Field Forget-me-not making a marvellous blue. On the damp ground was Pink Water Speedwell, Yellow Rattle, Fool's Watercress . . . and Persicaria. Among the plants which immediately came into their own when the bushes had gone, Red Campion was especially common and by 1974 there was a thick crop of Nettles, Teasels and [Greater and Lesser] Burdocks'.

The fields alongside the north arm of the River Gwash from Bull Bridge to Burley Fishponds were also surveyed. In two fields just upstream from Bull Bridge, Creeping Jenny, Field Forget-me-not and Lady's-smock were recorded. Further upstream in a field to the south of Whitwell 'was a pale pink Musk Mallow, the only one of the survey'. Ground cover in the adjacent Armley Wood 'was very thick with . . . Bluebell, Dog's Mercury and Greater Stitchwort. In one corner there was a patch of Moschatel and, where there was a small watercourse . . . Primrose, Yellow Archangel, Wood-sorrel, Water Avens, Wood Speedwell and Common Dog Violet . . .'. The Fox Bridge to Burley Fishponds section supported some interesting species including Germander Speedwell (recorded as Bird's Eye Speedwell), Butterbur, Lady's Bedstraw, Lady's-smock, Marsh Marigold (recorded as Kingcup), Fennel Pondweed, Curled Pondweed, Ragged Robin and Fen Bedstraw.

Marsh Marigold (Kingcup) was found upstream of Fox Bridge (D Freer – Fotolia)

Left: Ragged Robin was recorded between Fox Bridge and Burley Fishponds (C Chushkin – Fotolia)

Below: Golden Dock, growing on disturbed ground near Burley Fishponds, had not been seen in Rutland since 1900 (Wikipedia)

    The final part of the Botanical Survey was the Burley Fishponds to the Burley Flooded Meadows section. Some of the more interesting species recorded were Rue-leaved Saxifrage (listed as Fingered Saxifrage), Cornsalad, Kingcup, Butterbur, Pink Water Speedwell, Amphibious Bistort, Tufted Forget-me-not, Mare's-tail, Nodding Bur-marigold, Lesser Spearwort, Celery-leaved Buttercup, Marsh Ragwort, Marsh Yellow-cress, Many-seeded Goosefoot, Red Goosefoot, Field Penny-cress (recorded as Common Penny-cress), and Common Fumitory. Most interesting of all were three plants of Golden Dock (*Rumex maritimus*) on some disturbed ground, the first record in Rutland for over 70 years.

Botanical Survey – Conclusions

The range of flora found was much as would be expected from a largely agricultural area, with only a few unusual or rare species. The Greater Tussock Sedge (*Carex paniculata*) and Lesser Reedmace (*Typha angustifolia*) were two rarities for Rutland. Small Teasel (*Dipsacus pilosus*) appeared in the Normanton section and Golden Dock (*Rumex maritimus*) was found on some disturbed ground at the Burley Flooded Meadows, having last been recorded in Rutland in 1900. Orchids were relatively scarce and there was just a single dead stem of the Common Helleborine (*Epipactus helleborine*) found in Snowdrop Spinney below Hambleton.

It was concluded that 'Except, therefore, for the lamentable loss of rich woodland habitats, the debit side of the reservoir works is not too serious and perhaps we shall benefit from the increased wetlands in the future'.

Later Surveys

Some selected surveys did continue after the reservoir had filled. Jane Ostler (Ostler 1990, 72-75) led a RNHS devised five-year study (1978-1982) of the Barnsdale Picnic Site and Wooded Walk areas which had remnants of ancient woodland, improved and permanent grassland and a conifer plantation. They were surveyed on the first Sunday of each month from January 1978 to December 1982. During the five years, 232 species of flowering plant and 100 species of bird were recorded. Some of the most interesting species were the indicators of ancient habitat such as Moschatel, Early Purple Orchid, Broad-leaved Helleborine, Small Teasel, Dog's Mercury, Pale Wood Violet, Water Avens and Primrose. By the end of this period, some flowering plants such as Perennial Flax had disappeared. Though Soft Rush and Water Forget-me-not had spread from ditches to the water's edge, no new aquatics had appeared. Butterflies were little affected except that Orange Tip and Common Blue became scarce.

Although liverworts, mosses, fungi and lichens were not included in the 1971-1976 RNHS Survey, they were studied in later RNHS surveys (Jeeves 1990, 68-70).

Aspects of Topography

Old Barnsdale Hill

Before Rutland Water, Barnsdale Hill was a landmark on the A606 road between Oakham and Stamford, a former turnpike (*see* Aspects of Topography: Old Barnsdale Hill). Old Barnsdale Hill still exists, but only as an access road to Barnsdale Hall and a Rutland Water car park.

In 1813, J N Brewer described the state of Barnsdale Hill in *The Beauties of England & Wales*:

'. . . in the course of the last summer, the Editor of these sheets observed a very awkward part of the road on the rise and turn of the hill between Burley and Whitwell, covered for some perches along the centre with immense fragments of ragged stone, thicker and harder than even the heads of the surveyors who had directed them to be laid down, and this without any mixture of sand or gravel to fill up their interstices. Here, it seems, they were laid, in hopes that coaches, carts, and waggons, would gratuitously pulverize them . . . it must have produced a complete system of blockade and non-intercourse between Oakham and Stamford.'

An aerial view of Barnsdale Hill in 1967. The new road from Oakham now joins at X (Anglian Water)

The old Barnsdale Hill milestone no longer serves a useful purpose (RO)

Barnsdale Hill towards Fox Bridge in 1972. Vegetation clearance is well under way (Roland Meadows)

The old road at the foot of Barnsdale Hill is revealed at low water level (RO)

Chapter 24
Tim Appleton MBE – Thirty Years of Rutland Water Nature Reserve
Sue Howlett and Robert Ovens

Background

Tim Appleton is the manager of Rutland Water Nature Reserve, but he is not just the man whose inspiration and dedication have given bird-life a spectacular presence across Rutland Water. He has also become a global conservationist and a driving force in the battle to save wetlands all over the world.

Tim Appleton's achievements were rewarded by an MBE in the 2004 New Year's Honours List for services to wildlife and nature conservation, an award which absolutely stunned him, but one of which he is very proud. He is very keen to make sure that everyone knows about it because he sees it as a reward for all those who have contributed so much in making Rutland Water the wonderful place that it has become.

Tim was born at Westbury-on-Trym, near Bristol, Avon, and attended Wells Cathedral School in Somerset. He studied zoology and botany at Bristol Technical College, and his career in nature conservation began in the late 1960s when he started work at Woburn Abbey, Bedfordshire, where he was involved with deer management. In 1970 he became a deputy curator, working with Sir Peter Scott at The Wildfowl Trust, now known as The Wildfowl and Wetlands Trust, at Slimbridge in Gloucestershire, on the River Severn estuary. After four years he moved to Peakirk, near Peterborough, Cambridgeshire, as warden for what is now Peakirk Wildfowl and Wetlands Trust, but within ten months he was back at Slimbridge and in charge of the whole site. But soon he was ready for an even greater challenge, and it came with the birth of Rutland Water.

Tim Appleton (right) with Bill Oddie (TA)

The shock announcement of a new reservoir to be constructed in the middle of Rutland galvanised nature-lovers across the county into action. The Rutland Natural History Society was founded in February 1965, and its first major project was to record and photograph the flora and fauna of the Gwash Valley, soon to be lost for ever (*see* Chapter 23 – Fauna and Flora before Rutland Water). But plans were in hand to ensure that a wonderful new wildlife sanctuary would compensate for the inevitable loss of a natural habitat. According to the Leicestershire and Rutland Wildlife Trust:

'Rutland Water Nature Reserve is unique in that it was declared a reserve before it existed. The wildlife potential of the proposed reservoir was recognised as early as 1969. Reserve boundaries and the construction of lagoons were formulated in 1972, and in 1975 the Trust signed a management agreement with the Welland and Nene Division of the Anglian Water Authority, later to become Anglian Water.'

A Warden was needed who could bring valuable experience of wetland habitat combined with visionary organisational skills to the new Nature Reserve. The man who fitted the bill, as Warden and later Reserve Manager, was the young Tim Appleton who was appointed in 1975.

The rest of this article is based on a talk given by Tim Appleton to Rutland Natural History Society on 5th January 2006, with additional information provided by Alison Rogers, former Reserve Education Officer.

From Green Fields to Ramsar

In the 30 years since Tim Appleton was appointed to manage the new Rutland Water Nature Reserve, amazing transformations have taken place. Against the backdrop of elm-covered Lax Hill, green fields once lined the old road between Lyndon and Hambleton, divided by flourishing hedgerows. But in the area soon to be covered by water, crops had to be harvested for the last time, buildings demolished, families displaced, trees and hedges removed and the rich, fertile topsoil carried away in lorry-loads. For about six years, it looked like a huge prairie. The droughts of 1975 and 1976 meant that only a small quantity of water accumulated behind the dam, but serious pumping began the following year, and in March 1979 Rutland Water was filled to the top water line for the first time. Even before it flooded, the reservoir began to attract huge varieties of bird species. Amazing sights included two or three hundred Corn Buntings at a single time, coming into roost around the old Burley Fishponds.

Ada and Arthur Parker's cottage at Middle Hambleton was demolished to make way for the reservoir (Edna Locke)

Downstream of Bull Bridge in 1976. The water level is just beginning to rise (Jim Levisohn ARPS)

Left: Lyndon Hill towards Lax Hill in 1975 (TA)

Lax Hill and Manton Bay from Lyndon Hill. The reservoir had reached its top water level by March 1979 (TA)

Above: Corn Buntings could be seen at Burley Fishponds before the reservoir was flooded (John Wright)

In Tim Appleton's words: 'All these things were going on, and it was an extraordinary time to be around the reservoir, and to see history disappearing, and history in a way being made.' Rutland Water was soon brought to international attention by the vast numbers of duck that began to arrive in the years following its completion. Counts of over 20,000 waterfowl were noted, and with the inclusion of gulls there were probably up to forty or fifty thousand birds recorded on some winter nights. The largest number of Great Crested Grebe ever recorded at a single site in England, Scotland or Wales was seen on Rutland Water, when over a thousand were counted at one time. Most of these birds are seen around the Nature Reserve, although large numbers of many species also appear in other areas of the reservoir, including in the main basin by the dam.

Great numbers of two species in particular, Gadwall and Shoveler, led to the site's designation by the European Bird Directive as a Special Protection Area, which has implications for future developments of the reservoir. Up to 900 Shoveler have been recorded, and up to 2,000 Gadwall, making Rutland Water probably the most important site in Britain for these two species. The reservoir was designated a Site of Special Scientific Interest, and by 1992 had become a Ramsar site – a wetland of international importance, named from the Iranian city where the Ramsar Convention was signed in 1971.

Right: The largest number of Great Crested Grebe ever recorded at a single site in England, Scotland or Wales was seen on Rutland Water in the late 1970s (TA)

Great numbers of Gadwall, seen here, and Shoveler led to the site's designation as a Special Protection Area (John Wright)

A male Shoveler at Rutland Water. Its large spatula-shaped bill makes it easy to identify (RO)

Meeting Different Needs

Given the potential disturbance from the one million people per year enjoying Rutland Water's numerous recreational facilities, this great influx of birds is even more remarkable. Some 200,000 cyclists and countless walkers use the perimeter track annually. The reservoir is a national fly-fishing centre, with the World Fly-Fishing Championships held here. The Sailing Club at Edith Weston provides training for some of our Olympic sailors, and now with all the wonderful sailing facilities for disabled people, it is becoming more and more important.

Many anglers come to fish at Rutland Water (TA)

Rutland Water is a world famous sailing venue (Richard Adams)

So why are so many birds able to use this site, alongside these human activities? Even before the reservoir was being flooded, the Reservoir Users' Panel was set up to focus on what people, with their different needs, would actually be wanting from the reservoir. Representatives of different interest groups met. The fishermen said, naturally, 'We'd like to fish everywhere', and the sailors said, 'Well, we'd like to sail in most places, but of course, if we capsize in the shallow end, our masts get stuck!' Nature Reserve representatives said, 'Well, the shallow end is great for us, but of course diving ducks need deeper water'.

So, by agreement, the reservoir was divided up to accommodate different needs in different areas. Sailing would be allowed over about 2,000 acres of water, but beyond a certain point yachts with their bright sails were kept out, so that birds would be undisturbed. Fishing boats, causing less disturbance, could venture further into the shallow ends of the reservoir. However, in the three lagoons near Egleton, neither bank and boat fishing nor sailing and wind surfing were allowed.

In addition to what was achieved at the Nature Reserve, this agreement for shared use of the reservoir proved so successful, that, according to former Reserve Education Officer, Alison Rogers:

'Rutland Water is a world-famous fishery and we have international matches held there. Several members of England's Fly Fishing Teams, both Able-Bodied and Disabled, work at Rutland Water. It is also a world-famous sailing venue, because of the shape of the reservoir. The Hambleton Peninsula comes almost down the centre, making it more or less a horseshoe shape. This means that there are all sorts of different wind conditions, making it challenging sailing for Olympic sailors as well as novices. So Rutland Water has that reputation of marrying those two things together with its primary purpose which, of course, is supplying water.'

Creating the Nature Reserve

In the early 1970s, major construction work was carried out around the eastern end of the reservoir. The great earth dam took about five years to build. Two towers were constructed, one in the north arm and one in the open area near the dam, as well as a complex system of pipes which would take water to the pumping station at Empingham or the treatment works at Wing. Meanwhile at the western end, a very different kind of construction was taking shape. To make a desirable habitat which would attract as many species as possible, specific wetland areas needed to be artificially created. These took the form of lagoons, designed and constructed before the reservoir was filled.

When Tim Appleton was appointed Reserve Warden in 1975, he suddenly found himself obliged to become a temporary construction engineer. With no experience whatsoever, he took charge of building the big clay wall, in order to construct three large lagoons near Egleton. Clay was dug out with huge machines from a massive borrow-pit just below Hambleton, over a period of several weeks. Despite opposition, the new Warden insisted that the lagoons were constructed with curves, bends and extensions out from the main body of the clay wall. These would form what he then called 'Duckling Survival Bays'. Over the years these nooks and crannies have helped to give the lagoons the character which they still have today.

Building the lagoons in October 1975 (TA)

Above: Building the bunds in December 1975 (TA)

Right: May 1976. A water control point in the canalized section for regulating the water levels in the lagoons (TA)

    Clay was built up in three layers into bunds or embankments which would retain water in the shallow areas, even in the driest season. Hardcore from demolished houses was spread on areas over which water was expected to flow, with topsoil on the areas remaining above water level. Much of this stone gradually washed away, and the bunds required later reinforcement by riprap, rocks used as bank protection, along the main water edges. There was a canalized section going back into the village of Egleton, with water control points by which the water levels within the lagoons could be manipulated. After waiting eighteen months, special grasses were planted that would help to stabilise the banks, and then the water was slowly let in, using all the catchment water from the hills at the back of Egleton.

One of the great benefits of having the Warden in place right from the outset was that any waste material which might have been taken off site could be utilised, reducing costs to some extent. Whenever Tim Appleton saw a lorry loaded high with earth or rubble travelling along the old Nether Hambleton to Egleton road he would stop the driver and persuade him to tip his load at the side of the road. It was then used to form the islands that can be seen throughout the Reserve today. One such island was constructed in front of Swan Hide, which is at Gibbet Gorse.

Above: When these houses at Nether Hambleton were demolished in 1975 some of the hardcore was used to form islands in the Nature Reserve (TA)

Right: The island being constructed in front of Swan Hide at Gibbet Gorse in 1975 (TA)

The lagoon islands in 1980, near the old Egleton to Nether Hambleton road (Jim Eaton)

Lagoon I in October 1976 (TA)

Three sanctuary areas were created to form the Nature Reserve: the southern shoreline by the Lyndon Hill Nature Reserve; the old Burley Fishponds in the north arm of the reservoir; and the main reserve area at Egleton. In Tim Appleton's words:

'. . . the shoreline of the Lyndon Hill Nature Reserve, is really underrated. I almost don't want to tell you about it because it's such a good area. It has all the water birds, but it has all the small birds as well. In the Spring, just go down to Gibbet Gorse and listen to the Nightingales, and enjoy the Whitethroats and the Grasshopper Warblers. There is so much to see there. And then we have our main "birdy" area, the Egleton Nature Reserve, and the quieter old Burley Fishponds area in the north arm.'

The sanctuary areas of the Rutland Water Nature Reserve (Shirley Design)

The Burley Fishponds area of the Nature Reserve (RO)

Over the first four winters many thousands of new trees of many different species were planted around the new Nature Reserve. Some of these have now grown to between 30 and 40 feet high, and the Willows have been coppiced twice over the years. The reservoir's Landscape Architect, Dame Sylvia Crowe, provided a great deal of valuable advice. Further advice as well as help with the planting was provided by Guy Messenger. However, most of the tree-planting was completed with the help of the local community. Friends and colleagues were press-ganged by the Warden, along with anyone who happened to go past that looked as though they needed some exercise! Pupils from Oakham and Uppingham Schools, and later the Community Colleges, also became involved. A voluntary warden scheme was also established and this has gone from strength to strength.

The service track near Egleton car park in 1975. It is now lined with tall Ash trees (TA)

It was always important to try to envisage what the Reserve would look like in twenty years' time. By planting different types of Willow together with Poplars or other taller trees to provide varied canopy levels, a mosaic of different habitats was achieved. This is why the Reserve, along with all the other habitats, is so remarkably diverse.

Young Willow trees (Salix) planted with the help of volunteers from the local community (TA)

The Reed Beds

Close to the Warden's Cottage, along the old road to Stamford, were the Burley Fishponds, now part of Rutland Water Nature Reserve. A wonderful avenue of Lime trees once lined the edge of the ponds, which were largely covered with reed. With the coming of the reservoir, it was important to try and save as much as possible. Although the trees were felled, different organisations were involved in moving plants, such as Primroses and Bluebells. Staff at the Nature Reserve were anxious to save some of the reeds to establish a reed bed by the new lagoons. In the 1970s, reed beds were fairly few and far between in Britain. Since the 1980s, up to £22 million has been spent by conservation societies on trying to restore reed beds as habitat for Bitterns. At present this is working out at about half a million pounds a Bittern!

Right: The avenue of Lime trees which were felled at the edge of Burley Fishponds (TA)

Above: Rutland Water at low level in 2005. These tree stumps mark the location of the former avenue of Lime trees at Burley Fishponds (RO)

Right: Digging Phragmites rhizomes at Burley Fishponds for planting in the new reed beds in May 1976 (TA)

The new reed bed, covering almost 35 acres, is one of the biggest reed beds in the East Midlands. It originates from clumps of reed taken from the Burley Fishponds in the summer of 1976. Machinery was used to create the shallow areas in which to plant the reeds. Clumps of reed were put into the lagoon where they needed protecting by volunteers from hordes of Canada Geese! As the reed beds grew bigger and bigger, more money was made available for the project, and now there is a healthy population of Reed Warblers and other species associated with this rich habitat.

Scraping out one of the shallow areas to create the new reed beds in February 1975 (TA)

The new reed beds were established by December 1976 (TA)

Martyn Aspinall, now Head Warden, and Helen Dixon protecting the young reeds from Canada Geese (TA)

A Bittern on its nest. The target is to have these birds staying and breeding at Rutland Water (TA)

Above: A Reed Warbler at nest in one of the new reed beds (TA)

Right: A Reed Bunting seen at the new reed beds (John Wright)

For more than eighteen years and using the same length of nets, a ringing group has operated at the reedbeds recording and ringing up to a 1,000 birds each year. This recording contributes enormously to knowledge of the bird population, the survival rate and the longevity of many resident as well as migratory birds. The target, of course, is to have Bitterns not only coming in during the winter months as they do at present, but staying and breeding. This may not happen for a few years, but things are improving for the Bittern, and hopefully in another five to ten years it might be a bird that is heard booming in Rutland. If so, that might be the first booming Bittern ever heard in Rutland.

Reserve Volunteers

In those early days there was of course much interest from various people. After four years of working on the Reserve it was possible at last to see water actually approaching.

May 1976. The tip of water creeps along the south arm towards Lax Hill, but it still has a long way to go (TA)

It was important to prepare the habitat: preparing the trails, locating the hides and planting trees. At this stage volunteers were again being sought. As there was little funding to spare, everything was done as cheaply as possible. Tim Appleton recalls the day he met David Needham:

'I remember meeting a young man and heard that he was a carpenter. From that day he'll probably regret ever meeting me! Because he then became our head craftsman, and along with one or two other people, was the stalwart of so much of the early work of this Nature Reserve. I'm really grateful to all those people who help and guide me.'

October 1976. Water crosses the Hambleton to Lyndon road for the first time (TA)

Tim Pridmore, the first Assistant Warden, erecting a nest box (TA)

One of the 'kennel' nesting boxes for Barn Owls (TA)

Tim Pridmore was the first Assistant Warden to be appointed and began working at the Nature Reserve as a volunteer, aged about seventeen. He helped to put up huge numbers of nest boxes, right from the beginning. Most of the trees were new, only a few feet tall, but nest boxes were hung wherever there was an old tree or something big enough to hang a nest box on. Years later, other volunteers helped to build 'the world's largest nest box' to encourage Sand Martins to breed at the Reserve. This proved so successful that, in 2005, about 90 pairs successfully bred in it.

A Sand Martin at one of its more traditional nesting sites (TA)

Volunteers, under the direction of Head Warden Martyn Aspinall, building 'the world's largest nest box' to encourage Sand Martins to breed at the Reserve (TA)

The completed Sand Martin wall in 2000. In 2005 about 90 pairs successfully bred in it (TA)

Volunteering on the Nature Reserve can, however, have its less glamorous aspects, as described by Alison Rogers:

'One of my friends came back from the first day of ringing Sand Martin chicks . . . and they came in and they just stood there. They were as lousy as you could possibly be, because some of the parasites on the young Sand Martin chicks, had been transferred to these two macho ringers. They were looking very bedraggled and very miserable about the whole affair. So ringing Sand Martin chicks was not a favourite activity. Nor was ringing the Cormorants, because if Cormorants don't like what you're up to, they will eject foul-smelling oily residue from either end. So if you're coming up in a boat underneath the Cormorant colony, then you might well need an umbrella!'

A Cormorant with young: '. . . if Cormorants don't like what you're up to, they will eject foul-smelling oily residue from either end' (TA)

A group of young volunteers take a break after a hard day coppicing near Lagoon II (TA)

Volunteers, especially those who are ready for any kind of challenge, have always been essential to the work of the Nature Reserve. Many who began as young helpers on the Reserve went on to work in conservation. Volunteer numbers continue to grow steadily – in 2005 more than 365 volunteers helped in one way or another. So many people have worked at Rutland Water over the 30 years of its existence that Tim Appleton and Martyn Aspinall (Head Warden) talked about writing a book to pay tribute to the hundreds remembered only by their first names. It was to be called 'We never knew their last name'!

The Hides

In the 30 years of Rutland Water, some of the hides are now being replaced. One of the earliest, Mallard Hide, was originally built by staff and volunteers from reclaimed telegraph poles and the cheapest possible or donated wood, and with a felt-covered roof. The only access was by a steep ladder! It has recently been rebuilt nearer to the water, with disabled access. In 1979 Fieldfare Hide was donated by Rutland Natural History Society, and that was the very first thirty-foot hide, double the length of the original hides. This meant that, as more visitors flocked to visit the Reserve, more could be accommodated to watch the birds. Today the same hide is still in place, but with raised ramps for wheelchair access.

Above: Tim Appleton working on Mallard Hide near Lagoon I in 1978 (TA)

Left: Opening Fieldfare Hide which was donated by Rutland Natural History Society in 1979 (TA)

One vivid memory of Plover Hide is recalled by Tim Appleton:

'One regular visitor was a lady pharmacist from Oakham, who used to come in her lunch hour to watch birds from Plover Hide. Sadly she died and for a long time her husband couldn't decide what to do with the ashes. In the end, his family told him to take them off the shelf, and bring them down to the Nature Reserve. Her friends and family were all sitting huddled in the hide, on a windy day, wondering what to do. Finally one bird-watching friend, who had popped over from Oakham in his lunch hour, said, "Oh, Dammit!" and threw the ashes out of the window of the hide. It was an easterly wind and it all blew back in, all over us. Believe me, we all went away smiling.'

Building Plover Hide (TA)

After many years it became clear that the hides were getting overcrowded, and pressure was felt to provide more. The result was the largest of all, Lapwing Hide, reached by a great walkway. The first winter following completion of this major project, disaster struck when it was blown down in a storm, and had to be rebuilt using considerably stronger posts! Fortunately most of the materials were salvaged, despite much having blown over the

Lapwing Hide, the largest of all the hides when it was built (TA)

— 550 —

Right: Tim Appleton with Lord Cranbrook at the official opening of Lapwing Hide (TA)

water to Hambleton. The rebuilt hide was opened by Lord Cranbrook, who became Chairman of English Nature, one of many dignitaries who have graced the Reserve over the years. More hides were built, including Swan Hide on the Lyndon Hill Nature Reserve, with attention now being paid to improving access for disabled visitors. These were growing in numbers, and it was essential to give them equal access to the whole of the Reserve. Ramps were built to improve access, and the Rutland Lions Club donated the first wheelchair for visitors' use. Now, with the help of three organisations, Anglian Water, the Leicestershire and Rutland Ornithological Society and the Wildlife Trust, Rutland Water has become the first reserve anywhere in Britain to provide an electric buggy, which can take any less mobile visitors as far as Lax Hill.

Above: Improved access for disabled visitors (TA)

Right: Building Swan Hide on the Lyndon Hill Nature Reserve (TA)

Above: Rutland Water was the first reserve in Britain to provide an electric buggy for less mobile visitors (TA)

— 551 —

Breeding and Diversity

As well as erecting bird boxes in the early years, feeders were regularly provided throughout the year. This policy led to a very healthy population of Tree Sparrows – probably the biggest population in Britain now occurs in the Rutland Water area. As a result of this, Anglian Water, RSPB and English Nature funded a project to investigate the reasons. The project findings, recently published, demonstrate that, as well as nest boxes, all-year-round feeding is vitally important. Because these Tree Sparrows are constantly able to find food, they are always in good condition, so that they are able then to have second and third broods. In the countryside, where there has been a dramatic decline of natural food for such birds, many do not successfully rear even one brood. This has led to almost a 95 per cent reduction in the Tree Sparrow population in less than twenty years.

As the years progressed and more money became available, especially during the 1990s, many improvements took place. With the use of mechanical diggers and scrapers, and some help from visiting children, water was brought closer to some of the hides. Harrier Hide, which was once some distance from the water, now has new 'scrapes' in front of the hide where Little Egrets feed along the edge for much of the summer. Such new and varied habitats mean that birds which in the past rarely nested inland now come to breed at Rutland Water. Three or four pairs of Oystercatchers now breed annually, while Little Ringed Plovers have also become regular breeders. The reed beds have been expanded, and the new wader scrapes are working well, encouraging a wide range of wading birds at almost any time of year. Because nature is very quick at colonising these areas, scrapes are difficult to manage and need regular clearing.

A Rutland Water Tree Sparrow (TA)

Diggers on the scrape at Harrier Hide in October 1982 (TA)

Left: Oystercatcher (TA)

Below: Little Ringed Plover (TA)

Bottom right: Black Tailed Godwit (TA)

Bottom left: Curlew (TA)

The wading bird record was broken in September 2005 when 21 different species were seen on the Reserve in one day, an unusually high number for an inland site. Little Ringed Plovers are already breeding here and Black-tailed Godwits are seen during most of the year. Although they have not yet bred at Rutland Water, it is hoped that improvements in grassland management will encourage this species to start to breed here in the next few years. Curlews are now breeding elsewhere in the UK and unexpectedly over-wintering in Rutland. On the muddy shore at Lyndon two or three thousand Golden Plovers can be seen at times, a wonderful sight when caught by the sun as they rise and circle around.

An unexpected arrival has been that of tree-nesting Cormorants, thought to be of the European Sinensis race. Four arrived in Rutland in about 1977, their rings indicating that they originated from Abberton Reservoir, Essex. The inland appearance of these birds was such an extraordinary sight that local people flocked to see them. In 1994 over 1,200 were seen on one day. Up to 120 pairs of Cormorants now breed at the Burley Fishponds every year, producing very healthy offspring, but they are not very popular with the fishermen.

A cross-eyed Sparrowhawk at nest (TA)

Another arrival, in this case unwelcome to pigeon-fanciers, has been the Sparrowhawk, whose population 30 years ago had been greatly reduced as a result of the use of chemical pesticides. The first recorded Sparrowhawk appeared at Rutland Water in 1979, and since then it has become almost as common as the Kestrel. Similarly, Buzzards were rarely seen before the 1990s, but are now seen almost daily. Red Kites, introduced recently into Rockingham Forest, now circle above the woodlands of Rutland, especially in the spring. In past years, Long-eared Owls have roosted near Gadwall Hide, while Kingfishers have returned to inhabit the banks of the new lagoons.

A Buzzard with its prey (TA)

Far Left: A Kingfisher after a successful fishing expedition (TA)

Left: A Kestrel (TA)

Providing for Visitors

As public awareness and the number of visitors increased, so did the regular arrival of coach parties. Originally the Birdwatching Centre at Egleton was based in a small wooden shack, measuring 8ft by 12ft. This was replaced by a larger Portakabin, in which it became possible to run a shop and provide more support to visitors.

In 1984, a grant was received from the Local Authority and other sources, to start construction of the first purpose-built centre which became the Lyndon Hill Visitors' Centre. The new Centre was opened by Sir David Attenborough, who, as Patron of the Leicestershire and Rutland Wildlife Trust, has played a very active part in the Reserve over the years.

Work started on the Lyndon Hill Visitors' Centre early in 1984 (TA)

The Portakabin which replaced a wooden hut to become the new Birdwatching Centre in Egleton car park (TA)

— 555 —

The Lyndon Hill Visitors' Centre was completed by September 1984 (TA)

Close to the Lyndon Hill Vistors' Centre, where children are encouraged to join a Watch Group, are ponds, with Common and Great Crested Newts. A more recent development is the wild flower meadow, where up to 10,000 Common Spotted Orchids now flourish every summer, with many other wild flowers and all the insects and butterflies that might be expected in a traditional meadow. Since Rutland now has very few traditional meadows remaining, this has proved a very valuable contribution to the environment. The Reserve is also nationally important as a habitat for Dragonflies and Damselflies, with fifteen or sixteen species recorded.

The new Lyndon Hill Visitors' Centre provided an opportunity to hold more public events. These began with Book Fairs and Wildflower Sales, raising money for the Wildlife Trust. There was also the County Bird Race which raised money for various projects and the annual prize-giving ceremony for this national event was hosted by the Centre. The total number of different species seen during bird races within the county of Rutland is now between 150 and 160.

The Bird Race in 1984. Martyn Aspinall (Warden), Chris Park (Assistant Warden) and Terry Mitcham (Rutland Natural History Society) (TA)

The Bird Races started a friendship that began many years ago between Tim Appleton and Bill Oddie, now known locally as the 'Little and Large Show'. Bill Oddie is a good friend to the Nature Reserve who never misses the annual Birdfair, and helps in any way he can. With growing interest in the huge numbers of birds visiting Rutland Water, Terry Mitcham produced a book, published in 1984: *Birds of Rutland and its Reservoirs*. The public launch of this book, with interviews on the shore at Lyndon, was one of the many highlights of Rutland Water's first decade.

The Nature Reserve entered a new era with the construction of yet another Centre. Tim Appleton proudly observes, 'There can't be too many reserves in Britain that have got two centres!' The Anglian Water Birdwatching Centre at Egleton was designed as a facility for all. 'We were already looking at how we could create a Centre for everybody to enjoy, so there would be disabled access, windows at the bottom level and a great gallery at the top where people could get up and watch birds at the start of their birdwatching tour of the Reserve. It does have fantastic views out onto Lagoons I and II where people can see male Smew and other wildfowl. On a nice cold day, what better place to come, putting your backside close to the radiators and enjoying the birds.'

The new Anglian Water Birdwatching Centre was opened by Lady Scott on 4th September 1992, during the Birdwatching Fair.

Bill Oddie never misses the annual Birdfair (TA)

Terry Mitcham being interviewed at the launch of his book Birds of Rutland and its Reservoirs (TA)

The new Anglian Water Birdwatching Centre at Egleton under construction. It was designed as a facility for everybody to enjoy (TA)

The viewing gallery at the Anglian Water Birdwatching Centre just after it was opened (TA)

The reception area at the Anglian Water Birdwatching Centre (TA)

The plaque recording the opening of the new Anglian Water Birdwatching Centre at Egleton (RO)

Alison Rogers remembers a visit to the Centre by the Duke of Edinburgh while the Queen was visiting Oakham. Sixty-four children from Brooke Hill Primary School, Oakham, were also there working on environmental projects and designing posters. Prince Philip, wearing a suit, was accompanied by his aide-de-camp and others wearing smart uniforms. One child pulled the trouser leg of the one not in uniform and said, 'Which one's the Duke of Edinburgh?', to which the response was, 'I am!'

Unwelcome Arrivals

Rutland Water has been fortunate in not, as yet, seeing many of the controversial North American Ruddy Duck. In other regions, their interbreeding has threatened endangered species such as the White-headed Duck. Anglian Water does not allow shooting of birds on its reservoirs, although in other areas of the UK, culling of Ruddy Ducks is now allowed. A more pressing problem at Rutland Water is the large number of Egyptian Geese, which take over many nest boxes and nest-holes, squeezing out Owls and other birds – these geese even nest on the Osprey platforms! However the most unwelcome arrival was the blue-green algae of the late 1980s, which killed up to twenty or thirty sheep and ten dogs. The Reservoir had to be closed for almost a month. Fortunately the algae had no impact on the fish or the birds, but the biggest surprise was that, without any sailing, fishing or cycling, the normal bird population of around 12,500 leapt up within six days to around 19,500.

Egyptian Geese are unwelcome arrivals at Rutland Water (TA)

The Osprey Project

Centuries ago, Ospreys – beautiful fish-eating birds of prey – lived in this area. One of the woods on the Exton Estate is actually called Osprey Wood. But no Ospreys had bred in England since 1850 when the last ones were recorded on the Somerset Levels, although brief visitors were sighted near Burley Fishponds in the late 1800s (*see* Chapter 26 – A New Home for the Osprey).

However, a few years after Rutland Water changed the landscape of the East Midlands, Ospreys were observed flying over the reservoir on their migration to nest sites in Scotland. With plenty of Trout in the water below, it seemed a wonderful hope that one day they might return to Rutland, so in 1982 an artificial nest platform was built on Lax Hill. Finally, one pair arrived in 1994, and stayed throughout the whole summer. This was the impetus for a determined programme to reintroduce the Osprey to Rutland. The translocation programme, only the second ever attempted worldwide, began in 1996, with 64 Osprey chicks taken over several years under licence from sustainable Scottish nests. Roy Dennis was a stalwart in helping with the project, and advising on the various types of monitoring devices used to follow the birds, including satellite tags as they moved south on their migration.

The most unwelcome arrival at Rutland Water was the blue-green algae of the late 1980s, which killed many sheep and ten dogs (TA)

Chris Park, Assistant Warden, inspects an artificial Osprey nest at Lax Hill (TA)

Left: Tim Appleton and Tim Mackrill, who was to become Osprey Project Officer, weigh an Osprey chick (TA)

Osprey chicks relocated from Scotland were reared in these cages (TA)

Three Osprey chicks having just been ringed (TA)

Alison Rogers describes helping to fit a radio monitor and antenna onto a young Osprey which had been found in Norfolk. The bird was held down in a towel to avoid injury from the ferocious talons and beak. Super-glue was used to glue the antenna along the central tail feather. The satellite monitors were put on with little Teflon straps, rather like a jacket, because they needed to be really secure when the bird dived into the water. They were sewn on in the expectation that, after a couple of years, both the battery and the degradable cotton stitching would have failed. But while the equipment lasted, the bird could be tracked, providing valuable information about the migration routes of this endangered species.

The release of the Osprey chicks brought a huge amount of attention to the reservoir, as people flocked to see such rare birds. A recent survey carried out by a student for her MA Dissertation shows that around £600,000 is now being injected into the local economy by 'Osprey Tourism' in Rutland.

The good news is that the translocated Osprey chicks did eventually return to Rutland. They started nest building and reared the first chick in England in 2001. In the years up to 2006, fourteen chicks have been reared and have migrated. The first chick was named, by a children's competition, 'Aqua', but sadly it never returned. Because more male than female adult Ospreys returned to breed in Rutland each summer, steps were taken to redress the imbalance. In the summer of 2005, eleven young Ospreys, nine females and two males, were translocated from Scotland. It is hoped that, when they return in a few years, more breeding nests will be established at Rutland Water.

With funding from a national company in 2005, Tim Mackrill began a three-year full-time contract as Osprey Project Officer. Funds were also donated to install a camera on the nest, so that live pictures can be seen in the Centre. They can also be seen on the project website, which also has all the latest news of the Ospreys as well as the story of the project so far.

In 2006 the first Rutland-born chicks arrived back at Rutland Water – a major milestone in the Osprey translocation project (*see* Chapter 26 – A New Home for the Osprey).

To some addicts, the unfolding story of the relationships and experiences of the Rutland Ospreys can be more riveting than any soap opera!

Egleton Meadows

In the summer months, there are not only Ospreys to observe, but many wonderful things happening on the Reserve. Great pride has been taken in developing the Egleton meadows, which are now some of the finest in Leicestershire and Rutland. Surrounded by beautiful hedgerows, they are ideal for bats flying down to the reservoir to feed, or just feeding along the tops of these tall hedges. Butterflies abound, and the meadows are perfect for the Yellow Wagtails and other birds that arrive in the Spring, because no chemical herbicide or insecticides are put down. The new herd of Dexter Cattle now produce some really healthy cow-pats! Because the Dexters do not require worming, no chemicals pass into the cowpats which can then be broken down by beetles. This not only improves grazing but provides insects for many birds. In particular it has resulted in an ideal habitat for Lapwing, Snipe and Redshank which now breed in this area.

Lapwing now breed in the ideal habitat which resulted from the introduction of the Dexter herd (TA)

Although the meadows look very natural, they have to be actively managed. Almost every day of the year, volunteers and staff are out there doing different types of management work, such as grass cutting or working with a tractor. Some of these volunteers are able to work for NVQ Level II qualification in Conservation Management, with a member of the Reserve staff as assessor. So not only are they doing valuable work baling hay for feeding to the cows during the winter months, but they are learning about Conservation Management and may go on to pursue careers in this profession.

The new herd of Dexter Cattle now produce some really healthy cow-pats which provide insects for many birds (TA)

Managing the meadows. A volunteer mows the hay in one of the meadows (TA)

Volunteers baling the hay for winter cattle feed (TA)

Working with the Community

When the reservoir was being constructed, many thousands of trees were planted by whole groups of people ranging from school children to prisoners, to pensioners. In more recent years, several companies have become involved with the Nature Reserve, paying for employees to have a day out and work together on team-building exercises, such as the erection of a new hide in the wood at Gibbet Gorse. Local companies have provided materials, such as the high-class glass and window frames, so people can enjoy watching the badgers. There are now a number of active badger setts on the Reserve, monitored by the Leicester Badger Group and other volunteers. The joys of badger watching are described by Alison Rogers, former Education Officer at the Reserve:

'We would take groups of people into the badger hide which had an infra-red lamp, and we would sit there watching the badgers in the early evening and sometimes the late evening. And on one memorable occasion, we had put peanuts and molasses out to encourage the badgers to come to the same place where we could see them every evening. A rat arrived to take the easy food we had left out, and then a Barn Owl came and took the rat! So – nature red in tooth and claw, I think!'

Above: A badger emerges from one of the active setts at Rutland Water (TA)

Right: The badger hide at Gibbet Gorse (TA)

For around twenty years the Reserve has also worked with HM Prison at Ashwell. Inmates arrive on their own bicycles, with their many different skills – some more interesting than others! Many of them have learned skills relating to the building trade, and have helped to restore the old Cow Yard by the Burley Fishponds.

Tim Appleton tells of a memorable episode which occurred when staff at the Reserve needed an electric grinder to sharpen tools, rather than using a whetstone which took hours. One of the prisoners offered to help by providing an electric grindstone, which was gratefully accepted. About two days later he returned with a little engine and electric grinder, which worked perfectly. In Tim Appleton's words: 'Anyway, he left, and that winter when I took the tumble dryer out of the shed – I don't use a tumble dryer in the summer – I thought it was pretty light . . . he'd nicked the engine of my tumble drier! And I thought, "Well, there we go!"'

The Burley Hovel

Local thatchers and volunteers from the Reserve restored a wonderful old hovel on the edge of Burley Fishponds in 1992. This rare building is one of the few hovels anywhere in Britain actually built into a dry stone wall. It was in a very poor condition, but local thatchers gave their time free and provided reed for the thatch. Sadly the reed did not come from Burley Fishponds but from Romania!

The Burley Hovel before being restored in 1992 (TA)

The Burley Hovel with its new thatch almost completed (TA)

Managing Woodlands

The Nature Reserve has always worked in very strong partnership with Anglian Water, who recently agreed to allow the Reserve to manage the woodlands around Rutland Water. These areas include Barnsdale Wood, Hambleton Wood and Armley Wood. Tim Appleton comments:

'If you haven't been in Hambleton Wood, shame upon you! If you have, in the Spring, you'll know that it's one of the most wonderful experiences you'll ever have in woodland – the scent of the Bluebells in the evening, the Nightingales singing, and all due to the particular kind of habitat.'

Hambleton Wood in the Spring (TA)

Much of the habitat was changing, and active management was required. Large areas have recently been coppiced. However, most of these coppiced woodlands need to be fenced off, otherwise the new shoots springing from the remaining tree stumps (or stools), get completely eaten down by little Muntjac Deer which are becoming numerous in Britain. Each year following coppicing, the young shoots and Bluebells will do well, with the addition of Primroses and other plants that were lying completely dormant in the wood; they now have space and light to re-emerge.

Muntjac Deer are becoming numerous in Britain (TA)

The intention is to coppice one plot in the woodland every year, and on a 15-20 year rotation the woodland may be restored to the way it was probably managed in the past. Log piles are left to provide habitat for beetles and bugs, as the wood rots down. Some of the logs have also been used in the past to make charcoal. Rutland Water was innovative in being one of the first Reserves in Britain to start producing charcoal. The charcoal was sold, making several thousand pounds each year. This lapsed for a period but is likely to start again in the future.

Pollarding, cutting back branches of a tree to its trunk to encourage denser growth, is also carried out. Tim Appleton is a great believer in pollards, observing, 'I think they look good, they're typical water-edge management, and eventually those large stools up there will provide nests for Mallard and other birds like wintering roosting Wrens.'

Charcoal burning on the Reserve (TA)

The Birdfair

From small beginnings many years ago, Rutland Water's annual Birdfair has become a major part of the life and work of Tim Appleton and his team. It began with a visit to the Game Fair, when Tim Appleton realised that many events were provided for people involved in outside activities such as shooting and fishing. However, there was very little for people who liked nature and birdwatching. This led to the first British Birdwatching Fair, held in a little marquee in the field at Egleton in 1989. It has now grown, under its new name of 'Birdfair', to become one of the biggest tented events in Britain, and the world's largest bird fair. The original idea was for the fair to be a kind of trade fair, to show what this massive industry has to offer. Now, such bird fairs are springing up literally all over the world, as far away as India and Madagascar, with organisers writing to the Rutland Water Nature Reserve asking for support and advice.

Every year, Birdfair at Rutland Water raises huge amounts of money for environmental causes, now totalling nearly one and a half million pounds. It began by supporting European projects, but now money is raised for projects as far away as Ecuador, Burma and Vietnam, where a reserve has been set up to protect the rare Vietnamese Pheasant. Support comes from leading conservationists around the world, and particularly the Reserve's good friend, Sir David Attenborough. The many international guest speakers have included the King of the Cameroon, a very lively character who could have talked for hours. With visitors from Palestine and Israel sharing their love of wildlife, there are no barriers at the Birdfair, just a wonderful opportunity for people to talk about the things that they believe in. All this combines with fun, entertainment and memorable events.

Left: The many international guest speakers at the annual Birdfair have included the King of the Cameroon, a very lively character (TA)

Right: Michael Warren working on his Puffin painting at the 2006 Birdfair (RO)

Above: Anglian Water commissioned Ptolemy Elrington to create a collection of river creature sculptures made entirely out of discarded shopping trolleys. These were exhibited for the first time at the 2006 Birdfair and two examples are shown here (RO)

— 568 —

Colin Woolf puts the final touches to one of his paintings at the 2006 Birdfair (RO)

Ken Smith carves another decoy at the 2006 Birdfair (RO)

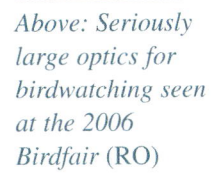

Above: Seriously large optics for birdwatching seen at the 2006 Birdfair (RO)

This aerial photograph shows the extent of the 2006 Birdfair (John Nowell, Zodiac Publishing)

— 569 —

Birdfair Projects – the BirdLife International Partnership

Each year since 1992, money raised by the Rutland Water Birdfair goes towards a special project, enabling some remarkable conservation achievements, including the creation of national parks and helping birds under threat of extinction. Here are details of just some recent projects:

2000 – Saving the Albatross

Up to 300,000 seabirds are ensnared and drowned every year as they scavenge behind fishing vessels trying to snatch bait as the fishing lines are set. Albatrosses are the most threatened and, of the 24 species, 16 are globally threatened. Birdfair 2000 raised £122,000 for this campaign.

Artist John Cox painting a mural to raise funds for the Albatross project in South Africa at the 2000 Birdfair (TA)

2001 – Saving a Unique Caribbean Wilderness

Cuba is the largest island in the Caribbean with more than 350 species of native birds, but the unique habitat is threatened by agriculture, urban development, lumber production and mining. The £135,000 raised at the 2001 Birdfair was used to purchase essential equipment for the project.

2002 – Saving Sumatra's Last Lowland Rainforests

Sumatra's lowland rainforests are rapidly disappearing and many of the spectacular birds that depend on them face extinction. The £147,000 raised by Birdfair 2002 has helped BirdLife Indonesia to undertake surveys and consultations in order to prepare the feasibility study for the Sumatra Initiative.

2003 – Saving Madagascar's Fragile Wetlands

Madagascar has a unique flora and fauna and many of the native bird species are threatened, especially those living in Madagascar's wetlands. The record sum of £157,000 raised at the 2003 British Birdwatching Fair was used by BirdLife International to launch the Madagascar Wetland Conservation Programme.

2004 – Saving Northern Peru's Dry Forests

The geographic complexity of north-western Peru has created a great diversity of habitats, including mangroves, desert, three types of dry forest, as well as subtropical forest. The £164,000 raised at the 2004 Birdfair has been used to initiate a project that focuses on conserving the critically threatened species and their habitats.

2005 – Saving Gurney's Pittas and their Forest Home

By 1980 it was thought that the Gurney's Pitta was extinct as it had not been seen in the wild for half a century, its decline being due to the loss of ninety-five per cent of its home, the rainforest-cloaked Thailand peninsula. Painstaking detective work, however, led to the re-discovery of about 45 pairs at Khao Nor Chuchi, Thailand, in 1986. Money raised at the 2005 Birdfair supported the ongoing conservation work.

2006 – Saving the Pacific's Parrots

In the Pacific Islands, bird species are becoming extinct at a higher rate than anywhere else in the world. The biggest threat is from invasive alien species, notably black rats and cats. Proceeds from the 2006 Birdfair will be used to support a project to address these overall threats.

Ian and Richard Lewington working on the mural at the 2006 Birdfair to raise funds for the Pacific Parrots project (RO)

Rare Birds in Rutland

For Tim Appleton, one of the joys of birding is that you can go every day and see birds such as Mallard or Teal, and get a lot of pleasure: 'But then, suddenly, up might come a lovely male Smew, right in front of you when you least expect it!' In 1977, at the Manton osier bed before it flooded, he identified the first Cetti's Warbler to be seen in Rutland. The appearance of the first White-winged Black Tern caused huge excitement – large numbers of people came down to see this unusual bird collecting insects along the shore, as the water rose up by Normanton Church. Another bird that Tim Appleton will never forget is the first and only Night heron, a juvenile that spent most of the winter at Burley Fishponds, hardly seen until it was forced up by the cold weather. Sadly, it died, despite sprats and other food being thrown to it, and lies in state in Leicester Museum.

The first Cetti's Warbler was found at Manton osier bed before it flooded (TA)

Other memorable events include the Red-throated Pipit seen from Mallard Hide in 1982, probably the only one in Leicestershire and Rutland, and the sight of a Nightjar which spent a day in the Egleton car park. One exciting day, a Great White Egret arrived, one of three different Great White Egrets that have appeared over the years. Every now and again a number of Spoonbills arrive, and perhaps in the future this species may breed at Rutland Water. A rare Bluethroat, the only one ever seen in Rutland, was caught in a net. One spectacular bird, a little Red-footed Falcon, spent several days around Lagoon III, sitting on the posts where it was easily photographed.

What could have been the most spectacular start for Rutland Water occurred when a pair of Avocets arrived, several years ago, the first time they had spread out from their traditional coastal homes. They started breeding here and laid four eggs. At the time, this was the first fresh-water breeding of Avocets anywhere in the world. But the Coot came in and ate their four eggs. They tried laying elsewhere, but once again the Coot took the next set of four eggs. Had these survived, they could well have been the start of a big population at Rutland Water, because the Avocets went on to breed at several sites elsewhere. There was food for them at Rutland Water, they just needed to break the mould, but it never quite happened. Other coastal birds have been unexpected arrivals at this inland site. These include a Guillemot, normally found nesting on steep rocky cliffs, and an even stranger Little Auk, blown inland by storms and washed up on the shore of Rutland Water.

Education Programme

Rutland Water Nature Reserve offers courses for students of all ages. People from this country and abroad come to learn skills such as hedge-laying. Links have been made with a number of organisations and universities from Norway to Southern Spain, whereby students come for two, three or even five weeks a year, to learn English and to work alongside other volunteers.

Over the years, many local children have taken part in a very active Education Programme at the Nature Reserve. In 1997 Alison Rogers began part-time work, assisting the Education Officer as a Teacher Naturalist, employed by Leicestershire and Rutland Wildlife Trust. Two years later she was promoted to become Anglian Water's Education Officer for Rutland Water, as well as Manager of the new Anglian Water Birdwatching Centre at Egleton. This appointment meant that she was heavily involved in the building of the new Centre at the beginning of the millennium.

People from this country and abroad learn skills such as hedge-laying (TA)

Mute Swans and young (John Wright)

2001 was the year in which Foot-and-Mouth disease hit Rutland, and the reservoir was closed for 58 days. The only people allowed on the site were builders doing the construction work. The weather that February was atrocious, cold and wet with a very high water table and mud everywhere. However, when the work was completed there was a new Education Centre and brand new offices overlooking the reservoir. As Alison Rogers remembers:

'One of the things you notice when sitting in an office is things like ice, and the number of times I came into work to find Swans frozen in the lagoon. They had perhaps been there from 4 o'clock in the morning and they waited till 11 o'clock, or 12 o'clock till the ice thawed and they could go off. It didn't seem to bother them at all. We were just amazed to see these Mute Swans sitting still in the ice, just waiting for it to thaw.'

Proposed gardens for wildlife to be made near the Birdwatching Centre (RO)

Among Alison Rogers' most enjoyable jobs was taking groups of children round and showing them things they did not know existed, like looking under leaves and finding butterfly eggs, or looking at flies, beetles and other insects under a microscope or magnifying glass to discover that there were hooks on their feet that gripped.

Students from playgroup to university age regularly visit the Nature Reserve, investigating different aspects related to their curriculum. If they are lucky, this may be followed in the second part of the day by a visit to the Butterfly and Aquatic Centre at Sykes Lane or the Watersports Centre at Whitwell.

The Rewards of Vision, Energy and Enthusiasm

The success of Rutland Water Nature Reserve over the past 30 years has been closely linked to the vision, energy and enthusiasm of Tim Appleton and his team of staff and volunteers. The green fields of the Gwash Valley under the reservoir may be no more, and they are still missed by many. But in their place a unique lake has been created providing pleasure for many thousands of locals and visitors every year, as well as a world-famous sanctuary for some of our most threatened wildlife. For all the varied species that have benefited from Rutland Water, the future is looking good.

Chapter 25
The Birds of Rutland Water
Terry Mitcham

Why does Rutland Water Attract Birds?

The outcry, in the early 1970s, against the development of Empingham Reservoir, as Rutland Water was first called, and enshrined in the slogan 'Don't Dam Rutland', was not shared by the bird watchers of the area. With their experience of Eyebrook Reservoir, then 35 years old, to draw on they knew that they were in for a real treat as the new reservoir would attract a large number of birds of many species. They were not to be disappointed as this review will show, but why does Rutland Water feature so prominently as a bird watching site which attracts ever-increasing numbers of bird watchers?

The answer lies in its large size and unique position. With a surface area, when full, of 3,000 acres and a shoreline of around 26 miles it would be bound to attract birds almost anywhere. Add to this its location within 33 miles of the coast of the Wash and its situation just north of the Welland valley and the planners unwittingly created an ornithological magnet.

Wildfowl arriving on the east coast of England regularly use the north Norfolk coast as a landmark and are thus funnelled into the Wash from where, in good weather, they can probably see Rutland Water glinting invitingly in the distance, drawing them further west. The Welland valley was discovered in 1948 by Eric Simms to be part of an important overland migration route connecting the east and west coasts via the Welland and Avon valleys, the latter leading down to the Bristol Channel and onwards to Ireland. Many small birds – Swallows, Pipits, Wagtails and Finches – use this fly-way, especially in autumn, and reservoirs such as Rutland Water are ideal places for them to rest and feed on their migration.

Yellow Wagtails are regularly seen at the dam on migration (John Wright)

Small numbers of Bramblings arrive in October (John Wright)

Several thousand Wigeon winter at Rutland Water, grazing around the reservoir margins (John Wright)

Another intriguing route by which birds may reach Rutland Water could be along the Humber and the Trent valley, with birds continuing south from the Newark area across the East Midlands. This idea was first suggested by Albert Jolley in 1945. Having arrived at Rutland Water, wildfowl and waders are able to commute between the many reservoirs and gravel pit complexes which are now such a feature of our region – Eyebrook, Pitsford (Northamptonshire), Grafham (Cambridgeshire), and Draycote (Warwickshire) reservoirs and the Titchmarsh and Paxton (Northamptonshire) gravel pits. When flooding forces species such as Wigeon to leave the Ouse Washes many probably relocate at Rutland Water.

Birds before the Reservoir was Created

The ornithological importance of Rutland Water began long before the first drop of water was pumped in during the drought year of 1976. As part of the preparation of the reservoir site the hedgerows and trees which were to be below the top water line were cleared and felled. The valleys which would soon be flooded echoed to the sound of bulldozers and chainsaws and there were huge bonfires of accumulated vegetation.

The resulting landscape resembled a battlefield but was quickly taken over by open-country species such as Sky Larks whilst Turtle Doves, then a common Rutland bird, appreciated the weed seeds now available on the vacated farmland. A run of mild winters in the early 1970s attracted Stonechats in numbers and four or five might be seen on a morning's walk, perched prominently on an exposed tree root or fence post.

As the first water began to accumulate in the borrow pits near the dam, waders appeared on their autumn migration – Ringed Plovers, Ruff, Dunlin and Greenshank. The reservoir attracted its first rarity when a Pectoral Sandpiper from North America was found in September 1973. The rough grassland which developed on the cleared reservoir site was much appreciated by the voles and mice, whose

Ruff appear on autumn migration from July onwards and small numbers now winter at Rutland Water (John Wright)

— 576 —

numbers proliferated, but their day ended when regular pumping began. The slow but relentless advance of the water forced them to move on, often into grass tussocks where they were easy prey for Kestrels and Short-eared Owls. The temporary abundance of small mammals attracted a female Hen Harrier during the winter of 1976-77. It was regularly seen hunting over the area near Lax Hill and is commemorated in Harrier Hide, which now overlooks the very different scene of Lagoon One on the Egleton reserve.

Open Water Birds

A casual glance across the reservoir can, at first sight, appear rather uninteresting but perseverance will be rewarded at any season. Viewing from the dam in winter, the observer may expect to see good numbers of Tufted Ducks and Goldeneye, along with attractive drake Smew and Goosander. A careful search through the Tufted Ducks usually reveals one or two Scaup, close relatives which are normally encountered in coastal waters. Slavonian and Red-necked Grebes are regular visitors and may be seen along either arm of the reservoir, sheltering in the bays. Perhaps the most exciting winter visitors are the divers, which, as their name suggests, spend much time below the surface and can be difficult to find. Strangely, the rarest of the three species which visit Rutland Water is the one which is most common off the Norfolk coast, the Red-throated Diver. The Black-throated Diver and the Great Northern Diver are much more regular and in January 1978 up to three of the latter species could be seen off Sykes Lane.

Any lingering Slavonian or Red-necked Grebes in March are moulting into their stunning breeding plumages. They are joined over the reservoir by the first Sand Martins and Swallows whilst in April flocks of Arctic Terns pass through on their journey north. Local breeding Common Terns mingle with them and pose interesting identification problems. April often sees flocks of Common Scoter calling in as they migrate across the country en route for Scandinavia. These black sea ducks rarely stay long but may occur in sizeable flocks, with 31 off Hambleton in April 2003.

Over 1,000 Great Crested Grebes winter at Rutland Water (John Wright)

Top Right: The open landscape of the reservoir site provides ideal hunting opportunities for Kestrels (John Wright)

Above: Tufted Ducks are one of the most common wildfowl at Rutland Water, with autumn numbers often exceeding five thousand (John Wright)

— 577 —

Nowadays all eyes hope for sightings of fishing Ospreys, usually noted from late March. The north arm at Barnsdale is a likely site to see one of these magnificent birds diving into the water, as is the south arm near Manton (*see* Chapter 26 – A New Home for the Osprey).

An Arctic Tern resting on its northward spring migration (John Wright)

Ospreys may be more obvious in the summer months, especially as in 2005 up to thirteen birds frequented the reservoir area. Common Terns, now feeding young on the Egleton reserve, call raucously as they fish for fry in the more sheltered areas. Thousands of Swifts feed over the reservoir, flying low over the water in overcast conditions. They, and the Swallows and Martins, may fall prey to Hobbies which by now have young to feed in their crow nests on nearby farmland.

House Martins and Sand Martins assemble in their hundreds over sheltered stretches of water in September where, again, they are a target for the Hobbies which will soon be joining them on the journey to Africa. This is also the time when European Black Terns appear, lazily hawking insects from the air or water surface. They are sometimes joined by the rarer White-winged Black Tern, usually as single birds but three were present in September 2005. Rarer autumn visitors have included Great and Arctic Skuas and Little Auk, mostly in October.

Above: The introduction of Ospreys to Rutland Water has been a major conservation success (John Wright)

House Martins collecting mud for nest building (John Wright)

Wildfowl and Waders

A handsome drake Gadwall. Rutland Water supports internationally important numbers of this dabbling duck (John Wright)

Rutland Water's exalted status as a bird reserve is based on the variety and numbers of the wildfowl which it attracts. Careful management has created the shallow lagoons required by the dabbling ducks – Mallard, Teal, Gadwall and Shoveler – and the deeper water where thousands of Tufted Ducks and Pochard can moult safely in August and September. Large counts of Mallard and Teal were typical when the reservoir first flooded as the rising water released countless seeds from the weedy grassland and the fertiliser-rich water encouraged an explosion of aquatic plant and animal life. In December 1976, 2,961 Mallard were counted with 2,038 Teal in the following month. These high totals were not sustained once the initial fertility of the water was lost. Comparable figures for December 2005 and January 2006 recorded 1,123 Mallard and 938 Teal.

One species which can fairly claim a close affinity with Rutland Water is the Gadwall. When the reservoir was filling it was an uncommon autumn and winter visitor in the area with up to 25 birds appearing at Eyebrook Reservoir. A remarkable expansion across eastern England saw increasing numbers visiting Rutland Water in autumn. Gadwall have an interesting feeding relationship with Coot, several thousands of which winter at Rutland Water. Coot dive to reach water plants and bring them to the surface to eat. As they surface they are surrounded by an eager scrum of Gadwall which take fragments of water plants and larger pieces if they can do so. Rutland Water is now the most important site for Gadwall in Britain and has recorded counts exceeding 1,500 birds.

Oystercatchers have nested at Egleton since 1977. The breeding birds usually arrive in March (John Wright)

Another species for which Rutland Water is particularly important is the Shoveler, a specialist feeder of shallow water where it uses its large bill to filter seeds and invertebrates. Autumn counts regularly reach 600 and over 1,100 have occurred (in September 1999). Numbers decline thereafter, especially if the lagoons freeze, but there is often a return spring passage of up to 200 birds, and one or two pairs may remain to breed.

Two other ducks deserve a special mention, the Garganey and the Pintail. The former is a Teal-sized summer visitor from Africa, the drake sporting a distinctive white line above the eye and greyish flanks. It is a rare breeder in Britain – less than 50 pairs annually – but it usually appears as singles or pairs in April and May and again in

A party of elegant Black-tailed Godwits feed on a lagoon as they pause on spring passage (John Wright)

August and September. The drake Pintail is surely our most elegant duck with its long brown and white neck and striking plumage offset by a long tail. Uncommon or absent in summer, numbers increase from August, reaching over 200 by November, when the males have acquired their breeding plumage.

Rutland Water's extensive shoreline and the lagoons have proved to be a magnet for waders, making it the most important inland site for this group of birds in the country. Thirty-seven species have been recorded on migration and over twenty species may be present on a good day in September. The Egleton reserve has attracted a variety of breeding species to its gravel-covered islands and wet meadows, including Little Ringed Plover, Oystercatcher, Lapwing, Snipe and Redshank. The creation of these special habitats has been an important factor in persuading passage birds to stay and breed. Curlew are becoming more regular visitors for longer periods and may soon be added to the list of breeding species.

Passage waders, those which stop to rest and feed on their migrations between northern Europe and Africa, account for much of the interest which the reservoir holds for bird watchers. One literally does not know what may appear during the spring migration in April and May or the more protracted return passage between July and October.

Spring migration brings adults in breeding plumage – Dunlin, Black-tailed and Bar-tailed Godwits, Whimbrel, Wood and Common Sandpipers and tortoise-shell chequered Turnstones, perhaps en route for Greenland or the Russian tundra. Scarcer visitors include Sanderling, Knot, Temminck's Stint and Curlew Sandpiper. Rarely do these birds linger long as they must press on to establish their arctic breeding territories.

Parties of Ruff herald the return migration in late June, some of the males still in their gaudy breeding plumage. They are joined by noisy Greenshanks, Wood, Common and Green Sandpipers and the first flocks of Dunlin, always worth checking for Little Stints or Curlew Sandpipers. Autumn waders are often a challenge with birds in breeding, non-breeding and juvenile plumage often present in the

A migrant Turnstone finds suitable habitat on the Rutland Water shoreline (John Wright)

A juvenile Curlew Sandpiper on its first southerly migration from its arctic birthplace (John Wright)

Middle Right: Many Lapwings from Europe winter at Rutland Water. Increasing numbers breed by the Egleton lagoons (John Wright)

Below Right: The Green Sandpiper is a common autumn migrant and a scarce winter visitor (John Wright)

same flock. Occasionally some real rarities appear. These have included Long-billed Dowitcher (2005), White-rumped Sandpiper (1994, 1995 and 1998) and American Golden Plover (November 1996). These New World waders always attract many visitors. Another species, the Pectoral Sandpiper, has occurred seventeen times.

By November most waders have passed through, to be replaced by large wintering flocks of Golden Plovers and Lapwings. These may number over 4,000 and make a fine sight over the Egleton lagoons as they are harassed by a Peregrine, now a regular winter visitor. Up to 200 Dunlin may remain with perhaps a Little Stint, as in winter 2005-06. One or two Green Sandpipers also frequent the lagoons along with varying numbers of Snipe and Jack Snipe.

Rarely seen in spring or summer, Snipe are regular winter visitors (John Wright)

Woodland Birds

The loss of so much woodland to Rutland Water was a major heartache to naturalists, whatever their interest. The old deciduous woodlands at Barnsdale, Burley and Hambleton, together with Armley Wood, held a marvellous array of wildlife – flowers, insects and mammals as well as birds. Fortunately time has been kind to the woodland which remains, and despite increased levels of disturbance from cyclists, walkers and dogs, much can still be found. Among the birds, many species have maintained their numbers, some have declined or been lost and some have re-colonised the area.

These fine oak woodlands, with their hazel shrub layer and thickets of blackthorn with bramble, support a varied bird community. Nuthatches and Great Spotted Woodpeckers are common and possibly increasing. Treecreepers nest in crevices in the bark of old trees and Tits breed in suitable holes. The Lesser Spotted Woodpecker still occurs but has declined, and favours stands of old timber where the softer wood is easier for the excavation of nest cavities. Woodcock still occur in winter, mainly as continental migrants, but the slow roding flight of the males as they patrol their territories on summer evenings has not been seen for several years – part of a national decline of the species. Another charismatic species which has declined is the Nightingale. From a reservoir woodland population of eight singing males in 1977 only five were found in 2005, all in Hambleton Wood and Gibbet Gorse. Rutland birds seem to favour dense blackthorn scrub from which to sing. Hopefully, recent coppicing in Hambleton Wood will recreate the right habitat and enable their numbers to recover.

Lesser Spotted Woodpecker – most obvious when calling or drumming in March and April (John Wright)

The Redstart used to be a regular summer migrant to Burley Wood, where a population of up to six males remained throughout the 1980s. Then a decline set in and the last confirmed breeding record was in 1995. This colourful and lively bird used nest boxes for several years and a number of broods were ringed. One bird ringed in 1989 was caught by a cat at Redhill in Surrey in August 1990 but was released unharmed and hopefully completed its migration to Africa.

The recovery of birds of prey has been an encouraging feature of the bird watching scene over the last 30 years. Before the reservoir site was flooded Sparrowhawks were virtually unknown in the area, scarce winter and passage visitors. In February 1979 one soaring over Half Moon Spinney proved to be the advance guard of a re-colonisation which has seen all woodlands now occupied and local villages receiving visits from hunting birds. The display flights of breeding pairs can be seen from February to May, especially where there are tall conifers which provide secure nest sites.

Nightingales have declined in recent years but may still be found in Hambleton Wood (John Wright)

The arrival of the Buzzard as a resident has been a more recent event, dating from 1998. Pairs or larger groups soaring over Barnsdale or Burley hark back to the nineteenth century before persecution eliminated this fine raptor. Also returning is the Red Kite, colonising from the population established by releases and breeding in Rockingham Forest. As the Rutland Water woodlands regain their full quota of lost species we may hope for the return of the Raven, which last bred in Rutland in 1840 but has been present in Leicestershire since 2000.

Reedbed Birds

When Burley fishponds were flooded the Phragmites *reedbeds vanished and an important habitat for Reed Warblers was lost* (RO)

A Reed Bunting at the new reedbeds on the nature reserve (John Wright)

Concerns over the fate of birds which rely on reedbeds were expressed as the Rutland Water project evolved as there were important stands of *Phragmites* around Burley Fishponds. They supported the largest population of Reed Warblers in Rutland, some twenty-five pairs, and occasionally attracted small numbers of Bearded Tits in winter and a passing Marsh Harrier in spring. Establishing new reedbeds on the nature reserve was a priority and these now occupy the northern edge of Lagoon Three. They have proved to be a great success, attracting ringed Reed Warblers from the now vanished Fishponds reedbeds along with Cetti's Warblers in winter (1995-96, 1997-98 and 2001-02) and the rare Savi's Warbler. Marsh Harriers are now annual visitors in April and May and could breed – if a male and a female were to arrive at the same time! These new reedbeds have played a major role in attracting Bitterns to the reserve, although they are rarely easy to see. Bitterns have become regular winter visitors since 2001; there had been about five or six previous records, dating back to 1979, including a juvenile which had been fitted with a radio transmitter at the RSPB Minsmere reserve earlier in the summer. The reedbeds support a good winter population of Water Rails, which have bred in recent years.

Migrants

A reservoir as large and popular as Rutland Water was bound to attract rare birds among the large numbers of migrants which pass through in spring and autumn and this has certainly been the case. Early examples, a Collared Pratincole (July 1977) and an Alpine Swift (August 1978) were seen mainly by reserve staff but others have attracted large numbers of admirers; a Red-throated Pipit came in May 1981 and a Bridled Tern in June 1984. A juvenile Night Heron wintered in 1984-85 but unfortunately died, whilst a Cattle Egret stayed for twelve days in April 1993. Little Egrets were first recorded at Rutland Water in 1989 and they are now regular visitors in late summer and autumn. Six were present in 2004. Their larger relative, the Great White Egret, has visited the reservoir on three occasions. Ringing provided the county's first Bluethroat, a female, in April 1996.

Wildfowl have naturally provided a number of rarities including American Wigeon, Blue-winged and Green-winged Teal, Ring-necked Duck and Lesser Scaup, but the rarest of all was a drake Redhead found among a flock of Pochard in February 1997. It was only the second record of this species in the Western Palearctic. Most of the rare waders have already been mentioned but several Purple Sandpipers have occurred and a North American Lesser Yellowlegs was present at Egleton for a week in September 2004. Avocets appear in most years and looked set to breed in 1996 until their nest was predated by a Coot.

A Bearded Tit at Burley Fishponds from Haines' Notes on the Birds of Rutland, published in 1907

One or two Yellow-legged Gulls may be found in the early winter gull roost (John Wright)

Conclusion

This review highlights the changes which have occurred to the bird life as a result of the development of Rutland Water, as habitats have changed or matured or have been deliberately created to attract key species. It has not been possible to mention all of the 256 species which have been recorded at the reservoir but the reader will have gained a good impression of what can be seen, when and where, throughout the year. In a changing world it is difficult to predict what is to come but at Rutland Water the proposed development of lagoons at the western end of the reservoir should mitigate any problems which may arise from increased draw-down, which would affect the feeding opportunities for dabbling ducks and waders. The Osprey introduction project could see a self-sustaining population of these marvellous fish-eating raptors becoming established and further habitat management on the nature reserve may add Curlew or Black-tailed Godwit to the breeding birds. Many would welcome an increase in Nightingales to pre-reservoir days.

An Osprey with its recently caught evening meal – a Pike (John Wright)

Ask any bird watchers what they love about Rutland Water and you will get a range of answers: seeing the first Wheatear of the year flitting across the stonework of the dam on a cold March morning; hearing the Nightingale in a still dawn at Hambleton; or seeing unending streams of gulls coming in to roost on a January afternoon. For most the sight of an Osprey labouring over the water carrying a freshly caught Pike or Rainbow Trout and the huge flocks of winter wildfowl on the lagoons will ensure many more visits to this magical reservoir.

A Mute Swan and chicks at the Rutland Water Nature Reserve (John Wright)

Chapter 26
A New Home for the Osprey
Barrie Galpin, Rutland Ospreys Project Team

(The Rutland Ospreys project is a partnership between Anglian Water and the Leicestershire and Rutland Wildlife Trust)

Soon after the reservoir began to fill with water, a rare and rather special bird of prey, an Osprey, was recorded at Rutland Water for the first time on 4th May 1978. It was viewed with great excitement: sightings of Ospreys in England were very few in the 1970s. Who would have guessed that within 30 years these magnificent birds would be regularly breeding here and that the Rutland Ospreys would attract thousands of people to the county each year to see them? This chapter tells the story of the ground-breaking project based at Rutland Water which has re-introduced the Osprey as a breeding species to central England.

A male Osprey (John Wright)

A Little Osprey History

The Osprey that passed through Rutland in the spring of 1978 was almost certainly making its way north to breed in Scotland. It was one of a very small but growing population of about 40 adult birds that was becoming re-established in the central highlands. Hundreds of years previously, Ospreys had bred commonly throughout Britain. Around the coast, in the wet expanses of the East Anglian fens, near rivers and lakes, wherever there was a plentiful supply of fish, the Osprey thrived. Shakespeare in *Coriolanus* referred to the Osprey, clearly indicating that the bird was common enough for the name to be readily recognised by theatre-goers at the end of the sixteenth century.

However, as a fish-eating bird of prey, the Osprey was not a welcome visitor to fishing lakes and fishponds. As the human population of Britain grew, as wet-land areas were 'improved', as the invention of the gun made it easier to kill wild animals, Osprey numbers fell. By the mid-nineteenth century persecution and habitat loss had become so extreme that there were no Ospreys left breeding in England. In the remoter parts of Scotland a few birds managed to survive for longer but by 1908 the species had probably become extinct in Britain.

An extract from *Notes on the Birds of Rutland*, by C Reginald Haines, published in 1907:

'OSPREY, *Pandion haliaetus*. (Fish hawk.)

An occasional visitor on its spring passage to the Burley and Exton Ponds [see note 1]. One came on the same day, and even almost the same hour, to the Burley Ponds every year from 1878 to 1883, staying thirty hours on each occasion. In 1884 it was shot at Coleorton in Leicestershire [see note 2] and another was not seen till April 2, 1886. Again in the spring of 1894 it was seen at Exton by W. Whittington, park keeper, and again on February 21 and March 5, 1898 [see note 3]. There is a stuffed specimen at Burley House, which was most probably shot at the ponds.

The late Mr. R. Tryon describes the fishing operations of one which he watched at Burley Lower Pond – no doubt one of the above mentioned birds. It dropped like a stone with its wings slightly open, then rose from the water with what might have been a Jack in its claws.'

Notes:

1. The country houses of Burley on the Hill and Exton Hall, both to the north of Rutland Water, had large estates. Their fishponds and lakes were stocked with fish which was an important food supply for both humans and passing Ospreys. Burley Fishponds were incorporated into the reservoir when it was built. They form the area known as Fishponds in the north-west corner of the reservoir. In the twenty-first century it is once again a good place to see Ospreys fishing.

2. Coleorton is in north-west Leicestershire, some 50km from Rutland Water. Haines assumes that this was the same Osprey but he must have had little way of knowing.

3. These are most surprising dates. If Whittington was right in his identification, in 1898 the Ospreys passed through the county on migration nearly a month earlier than their descendants a hundred years later.

Male Osprey eating a Pike (John Wright)

— 588 —

A Revival of Fortunes in Scotland

After an absence of 50 years, a pair of Ospreys began to breed in the 1950s at Loch Garten. Probably of Scandinavian origin, these birds suffered repeated onslaughts from egg-collectors, but with the help of a dedicated team of nest-protectors, the number of Ospreys gradually began to increase. By the time Rutland Water came into existence about 40 Ospreys each year were making their way north each spring and then south again in September, as they made their way back to the wetland areas of West Africa where they spend the winter.

An Osprey nest in a Scots Pine (Rutland Osprey Project)

Osprey Facts and Figures

Found in every continent except Antarctica.
European race migrates to Africa for the winter.
North American race migrates to South America.
Two races do not migrate – one resident in the Caribbean, one in south-east Asia and Australasia.
Wingspan: male 147 to 166cm, female 154 to 170cm.
Length: male 56 to 60cm, female 57 to 62cm.
Weight: male 1,400g, female 1,600g.
Apart from Eagles, they are Britain's largest bird of prey.
Food is almost exclusively live fish, both fresh and salt water species.
Fish are caught near the surface of the water by plunge-diving feet first.
Nest built in prominent position, usually in a tree-top.
Ospreys are semi-colonial, preferring to nest close to other Ospreys.
Males particularly favour a nest site close to where they themselves were raised.
Usually lay three eggs which take 35-42 days to hatch.
Young fly about 53 days after hatching.
Juveniles migrate, entirely on their own, at the age of three months.
They stay in West Africa until they are two or three years of age.
Usually ready to breed at the age of three to five years.
Once established, they use the same nest with the same mate every year.
Average life span about 15 years – maximum about 25 years.

Osprey in flight (Chris Lythall)

An Increase in Osprey Sightings

During the 1980s and early 1990s, as the Scottish population grew and as the habitats around the reservoir developed, more Ospreys were seen each year passing through Rutland. In 1994 a female stayed the whole summer, raising hopes that some might eventually breed. To encourage this, artificial Osprey nests were erected on platforms and in the tops of trees around the reservoir. This work was carried out by staff and volunteers working for the Leicestershire and Rutland Wildlife Trust, the local conservation organisation which, from the very beginning of the reservoir's history, had managed the Nature Reserve at the west end of the reservoir on behalf of Anglian Water.

Right: Erecting a nesting platform at the Burley Fishponds (Rutland Osprey Project)

Above: Building a tree nest (Rutland Osprey Project)

Left: A pole nest is occupied (Rutland Osprey Project)

A Bold Idea: Osprey Translocation

During the early 1990s ornithologists began to experiment with new ways of re-introducing species to areas in which they had become extinct. The technique of translocation had been used successfully with White-tailed Sea Eagles and Red Kite in the UK. Young birds are taken from their parents and moved to a new location where they are fed and cared for until they are self-sufficient. They learn to fly in their new surroundings and when they are old enough they breed there. In the USA similar techniques had been used to help the Osprey population recover in areas where the birds had been hit by the ravages of DDT. No one had yet tried to translocate the European sub-species of Osprey but in 1995 Nature Reserve Manager Tim Appleton and Roy Dennis of the Highland Foundation for Wildlife began to formulate a plan to translocate Scottish Ospreys to Rutland Water.

The idea quickly received the backing of the Leicestershire and Rutland Wildlife Trust. Crucially, Anglian Water pledged financial support, allowing long-term plans to be drawn up. Before licences could be granted, it was necessary to consult national and local organisations on the impact the project might have on landowners, fish farms, fishing clubs and conservation societies. International criteria concerning the translocation of species had to be satisfied. In order to ensure that the Scottish Osprey population was sufficiently stable to allow removal of young without significant impact, an independent population analysis was carried out. A steering group was set up and a detailed proposal submitted to the licensing bodies. Finally, licences were granted to translocate a limited number of young birds from Scottish nests to be released at Rutland Water over a period of six years.

Translocation of Young Ospreys

The first phase of Osprey translocation from Scotland to Rutland Water commenced in 1996 and continued for a further five years. During this period between eight and twelve chicks were moved each year. A total of 64 had been moved by the end of this phase.

Chicks were moved when they were between five and six weeks old. No more than one was selected from each nest, usually where there was a brood of three. They were then transported to Rutland Water by road overnight. On arrival they were placed in special pens built on Lax Hill, overlooking the reservoir. Whilst in captivity, they were fed on fresh trout from the Horn Mill fish farm and progress was constantly monitored by a large volunteer project team. They were released when they were able to fly, by which time they were eight to nine weeks old. From this point on they took ever-longer flights around the reservoir, but they continued to be fed and monitored by the project team. At the age of three months they all migrated south.

Young Ospreys ready for release from Lax Hill (Barrie Galpin)

A young Osprey takes a rest from learning to fly (Rutland Osprey Project)

The Volunteer Force

The translocation captured the public imagination and a growing number of volunteers of all ages and types joined the team helping to care for and monitor the Ospreys. Some were local retired people with a lifetime interest in conservation and wildlife. Others were young people for whom watching the majestic Osprey provided an introduction to a wider delight in the natural world.

Norman Gordon remembers joining the project in 1997, having retired from the Health Service and seeking outdoor activities:

'I was one of a team involved in monitoring the progress of the young birds which had been brought down from Scotland and were being cared for in newly constructed pens on Lax Hill with minimal human contact. We kept them under constant observation during daylight hours and watched them thrive on a generous diet of Rutland trout. After release we kept an eye on them as they gradually increased their range, flying around the reservoir until, at the end of August, they left on migration. It was altogether a very rewarding exercise and was heartening to see these magnificent birds around the reservoir and to share the pleasure with the many visitors.'

Tim Mackrill was just fifteen years old when he joined the volunteer team in 1997:

'I can still vividly remember my first monitoring shift in a rather run-down caravan at the foot of Lax Hill. The eight juveniles translocated to Rutland Water in 1997 had just been released and were enjoying their new-found freedom, making short but increasingly competent flights between their favoured perches. To see up to eight Ospreys in the air together was a truly memorable experience and I was instantly hooked. I still get that same buzz when I see the birds, but I couldn't possibly have guessed where that first monitoring session would lead . . . .'

A decade later in 2006 Tim became the Project Officer, heading a team of nine staff and over 110 volunteers.

Tracking Migration by Satellite

When the young translocated Ospreys left each September it was thought that they probably went to West Africa where Scottish Ospreys were known to spend the winter. However, little was known of the migratory routes of British Ospreys. In 1999 a decision was made to follow some of the young birds as they migrated south, using the latest satellite technology. From 1999 to 2001 fourteen of the Rutland juveniles were tracked and, for comparison, so also were some birds from Scotland (seven adults and two juveniles). Using a harness, small radio transmitters were carefully fitted to the birds. Signals from the radios could be detected by very fast moving satellites on polar orbit around the earth. The system was able to calculate the latitude and longitude of the transmitting radios and, by contacting the processing centre in Toulouse, it was possible to learn the daily positions of the Ospreys during their migration. As the data arrived, maps were constructed showing the routes taken by the Ospreys and reports were published on the project website, creating considerable interest and excitement.

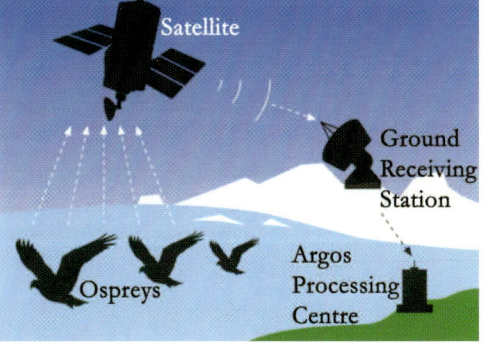

A fairly typical autumn migration: S18 was a young adult male, who was thought to have bred for the first time in 2000 (Rutland Osprey Project)

Data from the Osprey transmitters is detected by satellites and relayed via the ground receiver to the processing centre (Rutland Osprey Project)

Several of the adult birds from Scotland used a fairly direct route to the wintering grounds. They tended to fly south through England, crossing the English Channel into France and continuing south through central or eastern Spain. They crossed into North Africa near, but not necessarily at, Gibraltar, then through the passes of the Atlas Mountains. The adults crossed the Sahara desert in about five days, shortening the distance over the fish-free zone by maintaining a relatively western route. They then settled for the winter in wetland areas in parts of West Africa, particularly Senegal.

The data showed that the birds almost always rested at night and occasionally would break the journey with a stopover for a day or more at a favoured spot along the way. The average total distance travelled was about 4,000km in an average of 29 days (ignoring stopovers).

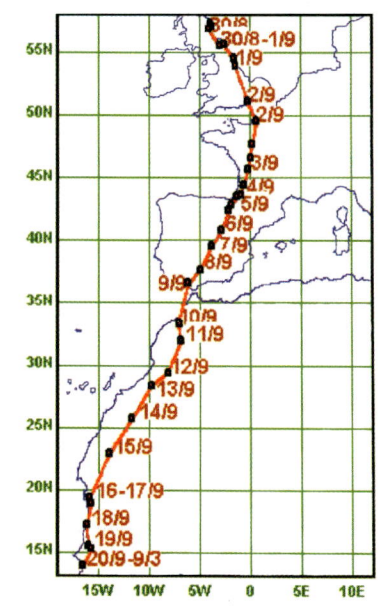

Juvenile Ospreys do not migrate with their parents or with other Ospreys. Their ability to reach the wintering grounds is presumably inherited through the genes of their parents: genes that have been honed through natural selection over many generations. It was known that, like most birds, a very high percentage of young Ospreys do not survive to join the breeding population and the expectation was that the hazards of initial migration would be one of the major causes of early death.

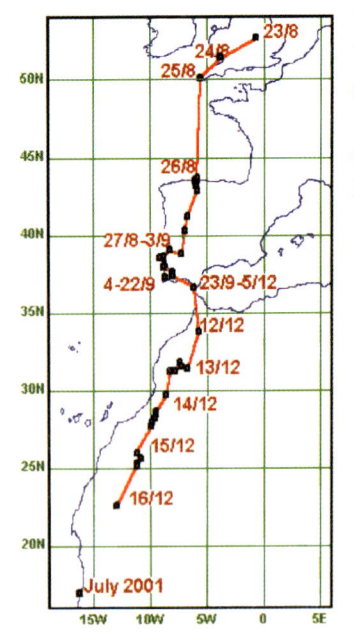

The migration of T03, a juvenile male, from Rutland Water in 2000 (Rutland Osprey Project)

T03, a juvenile male, like the majority of juveniles, started off from Rutland Water in a south-westerly direction. After Land's End, it was soon faced with the largest 'lake' it had ever seen in the form of the Bay of Biscay. Other tracked juveniles did not survive this hazard but T03 made the 716 km crossing in 24 hours. He made his way south with extended stopovers in southern Spain and Portugal until early December. Transmissions ceased as the bird was crossing the Sahara desert, leading us to assume that the bird had perished. However, the transmitter revived seven months later from the West African coast, proving that the bird had certainly completed the crossing of the desert.

The migration maps of all the satellite-tracked birds, together with flight statistics and analysis are displayed on the Rutland Ospreys website (www.ospreys.org.uk).

The Return of the Osprey
– A Series of Milestones

Although it was interesting to learn where the young Ospreys went when they left Rutland, what was crucial was that some of them would return here. It was not until 1999 that the first milestone was reached when the first of the translocated birds was identified back beside the reservoir. He had a white ring with the letters 08 on his left leg, identifying him as one of the 1997 contingent. He arrived on 29th May, stayed for several days, caught fish of various species and was often seen sitting on the artificial nests and perches in Manton Bay, the south-west corner of the reservoir. His return as a two-year-old raised hopes that he might return in future years to breed on the nature reserve. In Scotland, male ospreys do not usually breed until they are at least four years old, but they often establish territories in their second or third year, so the behaviour of 08(97) was certainly encouraging. However, another male from the 1997 translocation also returned later in the summer of 1999 and it was this bird 03(97) who was later to become the first of the Rutland Ospreys to breed.

2000 – Another Milestone

Both 08(97) and 03(97) returned early in 2000 and they were joined by two more males that had been released in 1998. 08 began to entertain crowds of visitors to the Lyndon Nature Reserve by adding sticks to an artificial nest. He then attracted a passing female. It was too late for them to breed but she stayed all summer. She was not a translocated bird, but it was a second milestone for the project: not only were the males returning but Scottish females were noticing, and could perhaps be enticed to see Rutland Water as home in future years.

While 08 and his female were cavorting in the media glare of Manton Bay, 03(97) had quietly begun to build his own nest in the top of a half-dead oak tree on private land in a very secluded corner of the county.

2001 – The First Breeding

The winter passed in hope and anticipation. The four male Ospreys returned in the spring of 2001 but sadly 08's female from the previous year did not return. That year he attracted at least three unknown females for short-term relationships and 08(97) came to be known as Rutland's most eligible bachelor.

Meanwhile, 03(97) was certainly getting it right. He returned early, enlarged the nest he had built for himself the previous year and by the end of April had lured one of 08's females to join him. She laid eggs and by early June it was clear that there was a chick in the nest. For the first time in 150 years there was an Osprey chick in central England and a major milestone of the project had been achieved.

Above: Osprey 08(97) with a female in Manton Bay (John Wright)

The first juvenile Osprey in its nest (Rutland Osprey Project)

Ups and Downs

Since 2001 the male 03(97) has returned to breed in his private nest site every year. By 2007 he had fathered a total of fifteen chicks all of which fledged successfully. In 2003 his original mate did not return, but her place was quickly taken by a three-year-old female, the first translocated female to return to Rutland. She has returned each year and the pair have become excellent, experienced parents.

An Osprey nest at the top of a tree with an adult and three chicks (John Wright)

Every year a close watch is kept over the Osprey nest, particularly during the incubation period. The number of volunteers has grown to over 100 each year and they record fascinating data about the breeding process. For example, the project team has learned when and what species of fish are brought to the nest, the proportion of time that the male and female spend incubating and the number of times that the nesting pair have to defend the nest against other birds, particularly Red Kites, Common Buzzards, other Ospreys and, amazingly, Greylag Geese!

In 2003 another pair of translocated Ospreys bred, once again using a nest away from the reservoir in a remote corner of the county. They produced two chicks in 2003 but the female did not return and the nest has not been used successfully in subsequent years.

And what of 08(97)? Every spring he was returning to Manton Bay. Every spring he was building up an artificial nest. Every spring he was having relationships with at least one female. But every summer he was alone again in Manton Bay. Why should this be? – theories abounded!

Taking Stock in 2005

By 2005 a total of twelve of the Ospreys translocated between 1996 and 2001 had returned to the UK. One female had returned to Scotland, breeding there for several years. Two males, having attracted females, were discovered breeding in Wales in 2004. However, nine Ospreys had returned to Rutland Water. Of these seven were males and two females, reflecting the gender composition of the translocated group. It had been thought that, as with American translocation schemes, males would be more likely to be site faithful and would easily be able to attract breeding females from other populations. However, our experience was showing that translocated females would readily breed here if they returned and the gender imbalance had lessened the chances of more nests being established. Therefore in 2005 a second phase of translocation took place with nine young females and two male birds being moved to Rutland from Scotland in the hope of increasing the rate at which the population would expand.

Each year growing numbers of people were coming to Rutland in the summer hoping to see the Ospreys. Most were successful thanks to 08's exploits in Manton Bay, and thanks to the volunteers and staff who mounted public watch-points to watch him. However, we were disappointed that no pairs of Ospreys were breeding at a nest-site where the public could watch the breeding process from a safe distance without fear of disturbing the birds.

An Osprey cruise on the Rutland Belle (RO)

Ospreys had certainly become a popular part of the Rutland county scene: there were proposals to name roads in their honour; a hotel had an Osprey restaurant; there were regular Osprey cruises on the *Rutland Belle* and the local and national media often ran features about the Rutland Ospreys. A survey in 2005 estimated that £154,000 of visitor spending in the local area was attributable to the presence of the Ospreys here.

Events in 2006

On 24th March 2006 male 03(97) arrived back at his regular breeding nest near Rutland Water. He was just two days later than the previous year, but looking in superb condition after his long flight from the wintering grounds in (presumably) West Africa. Field Officer John Wright was watching and taking photographs less than 24 hours after the breeding male's return. John said, 'The nest is the worst I've ever seen. It's virtually a huge ball of soil and turf without any sticks holding it together'. So there was lots of work for 03 to do before his mate 05(00) also returned. He didn't have to wait long because she arrived on 31st March, although it was time enough for 03(97) to have a brief flirtation with a passing Scottish female.

05(00) produced three eggs and after incubation for 37 days the first egg hatched. Soon it was possible to see three tiny heads above the rim of the nest. Yet again this pair produced a full clutch, bringing their total of chicks to twelve since they first got together in 2003.

On 30th June, with the chicks not yet able to fly but with their legs fully grown, it was safe to take them briefly from the nest and fit the rings that will enable them to be uniquely identified in the future. Getting up to the nest was no easy task but the task was made easier thanks to the loan of a 'cherry picker' by British Telecom. The chicks were gently lowered, one at a time to the ground where they were quickly weighed, measured and ringed. At this stage it was possible to make a very good estimate of their sex – two females and a male. The male was given a maroon ring inscribed AA, the larger female a yellow ring inscribed 7T, and the second female a silver ring, also inscribed AA. There was a very large difference in size – the male weighing just 1,350g and the bigger female a whopping 1,800g.

By 12th July with fresh westerly winds, the chicks had been exercising their wings, beating the air and doing lifted hops on the nest. A few days later all three young birds were flying.

The Next Milestone

Another exciting development in 2006 was the arrival of an unidentified male Osprey in the afternoon of 11th June 2006. The bird was fishing near the fisherman's car park overlooking the north arm of Rutland Water. Through a process of elimination and a sighting elsewhere it was confirmed as 5R, a male who was hatched on 6th June 2004, his parents being 03(97) and 05(00). Prior to this he had intruded briefly at the breeding nest before being chased away by 03(97): not a particularly warm home-coming from his father. He had also been sighted at Coombe Abbey Country Park near Coventry at 5am on 11th June. The distance between Coombe Abbey and Rutland Water is about 56 km as the crow flies, perhaps only an hour's flight for an Osprey.

5R(04) was the first naturally-reared chick to return to England or Wales for 150 years and so it was a real milestone for the project. But four weeks later there was even better news when 5R's twin sister from 2004, 5N, was also identified. The new arrival was first spotted on an artificial nest on Lax Hill. It was clearly a female because of the attention she was receiving from two males displaying above. The newcomer moved off to the Manton Bay area and it was soon possible to glimpse the green ring on her right leg and to read the characters 5N. It was hard to believe but the entire 2004 brood from the Rutland nest had returned as two-year olds.

5N immediately became the focus for 08(97)'s well-honed courting techniques. The young female seemed very impressed by the fish he brought her, by his substantial nest and by its proximity to her own natal site. The pair remained together throughout August 2006 until they migrated. The project team had spent every winter since 2001 hoping that 08's female consort from the previous year would return in the following spring to breed on the publicly viewable nest in Manton Bay. Every year the team and, no doubt, 08 himself had been disappointed. Now at last 08 had attracted a locally bred female who would have no instinct drawing her to breed in a natal site in Scotland. Surely, at long last the spring of 2007 would bring better news for Rutland's famous bachelor-Osprey?

Successes in 2007

The end of March is always an anxious time waiting for Ospreys to arrive back from Africa. In 2007 we were delighted to see the regular breeding pair arrive back at their nest. We were very relieved to see 08 arriving and repairing the Manton Bay nest too. However, we were ecstatic to see 5N join him on 6th April and it immediately became clear that 08's bachelor days were over. The pair of Ospreys bonded immediately and set about creating a truly enormous nest on top of the old structure on a post in the middle of the bay. Eggs were laid, and the inexperienced pair took it in turns to incubate them. Hatching occurred and it soon became clear that there were two chicks in the nest. Through some of the heaviest rain ever seen in Rutland, the adults protected and fed their rapidly growing offspring.

Female 5N and male 08 landing on their Manton Bay nest in early April 2007 (John Wright)

The regular breeding pair was also quietly getting on with raising a family of three chicks so the volunteer force was at full stretch monitoring two nests. At Manton Bay monitoring duties included helping visitors understand what was happening. This was no small task, for news of an easily viewable Osprey nest brought enthusiastic visitors in their thousands from all over the country. By early August about 20,000 visitors had walked from the Lyndon Hill Visitor Centre along to two hides from where breathtaking views of Osprey family life were to be had.

Five healthy youngsters was excellent but there was further good news during the summer of 2007. In 2005 the regular breeding pair had produced three young and two of the three were also recorded back in the county as two-year olds. One of these, a female was courted by another of the translocated males and showed every sign that she too would breed in future years.

Osprey family life on the Manton Bay nest in June 2007. Female 5N feeds the two tiny chicks as male 08 looks on (John Wright)

The Future

New Osprey populations usually take many years to grow to about ten pairs when they become self-sustaining and safe from the impact of disease and natural catastrophe. In Scotland in the 1950s the recolonisation was slowed by the ravages of egg-collectors and in the Forest of Orleans in France the population also hovered at a few pairs for many years before it achieved a critical mass. It remains to be seen whether the same will be true in Rutland.

Here the species has much in its favour: a plentiful fish supply, a wealth of potential nest sites, and an enthusiastic and dedicated team of local people who are determined that there will be no disturbance of the breeding birds. Until recently the survival of the colony has been very dependent on the safe return from migration of a handful of individual birds that were translocated from Scotland. However, we are now seeing their numbers being swelled by young birds that were born and bred in Rutland. It is beginning to look more certain that these very special birds of prey will become an ever more frequent sight in the English Midlands. Rutland Water seems almost certain to go on providing a new home for the Osprey.

The Rutland Ospreys website (www.ospreys.org.uk) has a detailed history of the project together with very regular news and pictures during the summer months.

Chapter 27
A Panorama of Activities at Rutland Water
Robert Ovens and Sheila Sleath

In the previous chapter, David Moore explained how the passing of the Water Act in 1973 created new Regional Water Authorities with a statutory duty to make the best use of water resources and associated land for public recreation. This enabled a progressive approach to providing a balance of recreation and wildlife enhancement as an integral part of the construction of new reservoirs.

Almost 35 years later, the success of this approach is obvious to any visitor to the shores of Rutland Water. In establishing and maintaining the delicate balance between leisure, sport and wildlife conservation, it has gained an international reputation for providing something for everyone.

This chapter offers a selected panorama of activities that can be enjoyed on and around the reservoir.

Left: A wonderful location for artists (RO)

Left: Sunny days in October, when the reservoir is at low level, provide endless opportunities for the photographer (SS)

— 601 —

Rutland Water's many moods make it a photographer's paradise (Richard Adams)

Below: Time for a break at the annual Birdfair, which draws thousands of visitors to the nature reserve (Richard Adams)

Right: Rest and contemplate in peace at the Barnsdale Drought Garden and Arboretum, designed by the late Geoff Hamilton (RO)

Above: The shores of Rutland Water are ideal for picnics. Celebrate your birthday or any other anniversary here (RO)

The cafés at each of the four car parks, known as the Four Foxes, are good stopping-off places on a cycle ride around the reservoir (SS)

Below: Sounding Bridge, near Manton, one of many locations around Rutland Water regularly chosen by birdwatchers (RO)

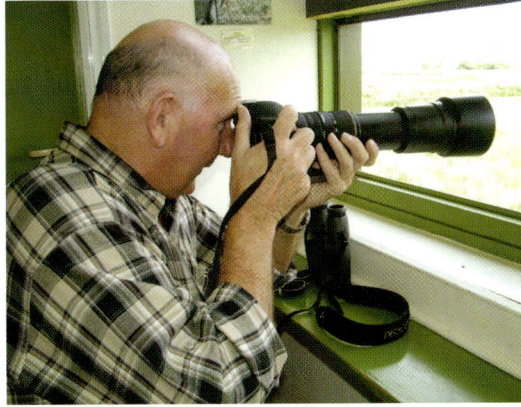

Left: The Birdwatching Centre at Egleton is invariably the starting point for visitors to the internationally famous nature reserve (RO)

Right: The view from Deep Water hide on Lyndon Hill Nature Reserve. Rutland Water has one of the most important wildfowl sanctuaries in Great Britain and with 22 hides the birdwatcher is well catered for (RO)

— 603 —

Competitive sailing with Rutland Sailing Club (Richard Adams)

Below: 'Messing about in boats!' The watersports and training centre at Whitwell Harbour is a wonderful place to windsurf, sail and canoe (RO

Above: Lyndon Hill Visitor Centre is described by Anglian Water as 'the gateway to a quieter, more peaceful place that is rich in flowers and birdsong in spring and summer'. Nesting Ospreys are a big attraction here (SS)

Normanton Church Museum, the reservoir's most famous landmark, tells the story of Rutland Water (RO)

Sailing classes for youngsters are summer favourites (Rutland & Stamford Mercury)

Rutland Water is an ideal place for windsurfers, and for those just watching them (Rutland & Stamford Mercury)

Camping for watersports enthusiasts near Whitwell Harbour (RO)

*The annual 'Dambuster' triathlon is the only opportunity to swim in Rutland Water (David Moore)
Below: The cycle hire centres at Whitwell and Normanton are busy throughout the year (RO)*

*Below: A bicycle made for two. Cycling is one of the most popular activities at Rutland Water and there are plenty of routes to choose from (RO)
Bottom Left: Cycling for the whole family (RO)
Bottom Right: Exercising the dog the easy way! (RO)*

The perimeter track of Rutland Water offers plenty of scope for both casual and serious walkers (SS)

Above: The Heritage of Rutland Water guided historical walk at Normanton Church Museum in September 2006 (RO)

Left: Fundraising for the brass band of the Ancient Order of Foresters (RO)

A cruise on the Rutland Belle *is an excellent way to explore Rutland Water* (RO)

A late afternoon Osprey cruise on the Rutland Belle *usually results in one or more sightings of this bird, recently reintroduced to Rutland* (SS)

Spacious play areas for children of all ages (RO)

The Rockblok climbing centre at Whitwell car park offers activities to suit all ages and abilities. The challenging climbing wall requires a good deal of concentration (RO)

The high-ropes assault course at the climbing centre tests the nerves – and head for heights (RO)

The Butterfly and Aquatic Centre at Sykes Lane car park, Empingham, invites visitors to enter a tropical world (RO)

Above: Trampolining skills being demonstrated at the climbing centre (RO)

Right: Rutland Water fly fishing instructor Dave 'Curly' Doherty (left) prepares to net a fish for Rutland Water's Tackle Shop retail assistant Paul Shaw near Manton Bay (Cliff Waters Design)

Above Left: Reservoir warden Alan Dalton with a 20lb Pike he caught when fly fishing on the north arm of Rutland Water in 2006
(Nigel Savage, Anglian Water)

Above Right: The weigh-in near Normanton Fishing Lodge at the end of a two-day trout fishing competition which attracted anglers from all over the country and abroad (SS)

Below: A family from St Albans, Bedfordshire, enjoying well-earned ice-creams, having just completed a 17-mile cycle ride around the reservoir (SS)

Chapter 28
Rutland Water Fishing
John Wadham

The Lake

Rutland Water, despite being a water supply reservoir, has the appearance of a natural lake. It is a great attraction to anglers and they travel from all over the world to fish here. Local anglers are therefore very lucky to have access to such a beautiful spot on their doorstep.

Right: Rutland Water has the appearance of a natural lake. It attracts anglers from all over the world (John Nowell, Zodiac Publishing)

Below: Yellowstone Bay, on the south shore of Hambleton peninsula, is a popular location for bank fishing (RO)

Ecology

From an angler's point of view, Rutland Water is a lake of many moods. Every bay and open bank has its own ecosystem and consequently they appear to be separate fisheries. As any Rutland Water fisherman knows, if fish are not found in one location, the answer is to move on. The fishing could well be very different a few yards away.

To those used to the smaller fisheries the sheer size of the lake can appear quite daunting. At over 3,000 acres the water in the lake takes a long while to warm up in spring and, conversely, takes a long time to cool down in the autumn. The water temperature in late May is generally around 11°C (52°F) and equates to that in mid-October. This is the optimum temperature for Trout to feed and therefore the most productive time to fish.

The main diet of the Trout is the non-biting midge in its various life stages from larva to adult, as it hatches out at the water's surface. The density of this springtime hatch, the peak of which is generally mid to late May, varies from one season to the next. In some years, the hatches of these insects can be so prolific that in the evening the trees around the lake where the insects gather in swarms can appear like smoking chimneys.

The Sedge, or Caddis Fly, is seldom eaten by the Trout despite the vast number that hatch from June to September. The *Caenis horaria*, a tiny white Mayfly that appears in June, is known as the 'angler's curse'. It hatches in billions, again forming white clouds. With so many to choose from the fish become preoccupied feeding on this source and consequently can prove very difficult to catch.

The other food item particularly important to the Trout is *Daphnia*, probably better known as the water flea, which grazes on various species of algae on overcast days. These tiny crustaceans also bloom in vast clouds and concentrations can make the water appear pink locally. This rich food source,

Rutland Water, near Old Hall, Hambleton at low level. The resulting exposed shore area is quickly colonised by land-borne rather than water-borne insects (RO)

which is available for most of the warmer months, causes the fish to put on weight rapidly.

During the summer months when the water level drops the resulting exposed shore area is quickly colonised by land-living rather than water-borne insects. As the water level rises again the fish are able to take advantage of this harvest and bank fishing becomes particularly rewarding.

Trout in Rutland Water also eat many other things. Examples include Hog Lice, found on the bed of the lake and under stones, *Corixidae*, or Water Boatmen, which are free-swimming, Damselfly larvae, which crawl up reed stems to hatch on sunny days in June and July, and coarse fish fry such as Perch, and Daddy Long Legs, snails, Caddis Fly larvae and other land-living insects that fall onto the water. Close inspection of the stomach contents of Trout will reveal all manner of items in addition to their normal diet including, for example, cigarette ends, Mars Bar wrappers, deflated balloons, sticks, stones, feathers, silver paper, shrews and moles.

Fishing Tales 1

'The hatch of the larger buzzers, which started on the 18th of the month [May], coincided with a temporary *Daphnia* crash. However the *Daphnia* has now bloomed again and the fish are spoilt for choice and appear to be ready to consider anything in the way of food. Typical was a 3lb Rainbow caught from the Old Hall Point, which contained: *Daphnia*, various sizes and colours of buzzers, green & red larvae, larger Bloodworms, snails, Caddis, Ostracods (tiny free swimming mussels the size of Daphnia), amber Sedge pupae and assorted flies. Another fish was found to contain about 300 large buzzers all the same size & colour. This is one of the most interesting parts of the sport which the catch and release anglers miss out on.' (*RWFF Newsletter*, June 2005)

Fly Patterns

Popular fly patterns, or lures, for general use are Gold Ribbed Hares Ear (GRHE), Diawlbach, Cove Nymph and Pheasant Tail Nymph. These lures can represent many different food items including Water Boatmen, Hog Lice, various insect nymphs and even tiny fish.

The angler attempts to imitate the various life stages of the midge with three patterns known as 'bloodworms' (the larval stage), 'buzzers' (the pupal stage) and 'emergers' (the hatching stage on the surface of the water).

To catch Trout feeding on such tiny food items as *Daphnia*, lures that act as attractors will draw fish. In general these are in the colour that roughly represents that of the *Daphnia*. They are available in many different shades and have many different names. Dawson's Olive, Black & Green Tadpole and Orange Blobs are three of the most commonly used patterns. For deep fishing from boats flashy 'sparkler' lures tied on tubes are used.

Popular Lures used by Rutland Water Fly Fishermen

1.

2.

3.

4.

5.

6.

7.

8.

Photographs courtesy of Cliff Waters Design.

1. Black Buzzer
2. Booby Minkie
3. Cove Nymph
4. Cruncher
5. Daddy
6. Damsel
7. Diawl
8. Perch Fry
9. GRHE [Gold Ribbed Hares Ear]
10. Minkie
11. Orange Blob

Stocking

Trout only breed in running water and consequently they do not spawn naturally in Rutland Water. Artificial stocking of both Rainbow and Brown Trout is therefore carried out by Anglian Water.

Young fish with an average weight of 2lb are introduced at regular intervals throughout the season. A good summer's feeding can double their weight. After some time in the lake both species take on a silvery hue and are a joy to behold. Brown Trout live much longer than Rainbows and consequently can reach great weights. Brown Trout of up to 17lb have been found swimming in the margins. Although they have shorter lives, Rainbow Trout tend to grow more quickly and specimens up to 14lb have been taken by fly fishermen. Such fish have probably been in the lake for no more than three years, having prospered on the abundance of food available.

Laurence Ball and Jamie Weston of Gwash Fish Farm delivering good-sized Rainbow Trout to Rutland Water ready for the first day of the fly fishing season (Anglian Water)

Fishing Tales 2

'During the warm spell mid-month [May] the lake fished very well from both boat and bank. Some superb browns were caught. Of particular note was the fish weighing an estimated 14lb caught by Paul Friend on one of his "Friendy" tubes. The fish, which was very deep in shape, was returned unharmed to the water.' (*RWFF Newsletter*, June 2005)

Rainbow Trout (Wikipedia)

Many of these larger specimens are caught from the bank, spring and autumn being the best times. They come in for the buzzer in April and May and in autumn for the fry. In the warmer months fishermen in boats find these fish in deeper water. Trout, particularly Rainbows, tend to feed mainly near the surface and are therefore guided by the wind. They will travel miles in search of food, and fish stocked at Hambleton can swim to Whitwell overnight.

Fishermen are allowed to take their catch away, up to a specified limit. Alternatively a catch and release ticket is available for those who return the fish to the water. In order for Anglian Water to keep track of fishery performance and to be able to calculate future stocking levels, anglers are obliged to submit daily or weekly catch returns.

Above: A fine catch by G Pearson at Rutland Water. Superb specimens of Brown and Rainbow Trout (Anglian Water)

Left: Brown Trout (Wikipedia)

Permits to Fish

Permits for day and season fishing and boating hire, details of the fishery, and rules and safety information are available from the Fishing Lodge at Normanton, where there is a tackle shop as well as catering facilities.

The tackle shop at Normanton Fishing Lodge (RO)

Other Fish Stocks

Rutland Water also supports a head of fish other than Trout. Some notable specimens, especially Pike, Roach, Carp, Bream, Zander, Rudd and Perch, have been caught by fly fishermen. In their early stages, the offspring of these coarse fish, especially Perch, provide an essential part of the Trout's diet. This is particularly so in the early summer soon after they have hatched from eggs to appear as 'pin fry'. They are also consumed in the autumn when they have grown to two inches or so in length and congregate in vast hordes around the bank-side structures. Trout know about this food source and can be seen charging these shoals all day from October onwards.

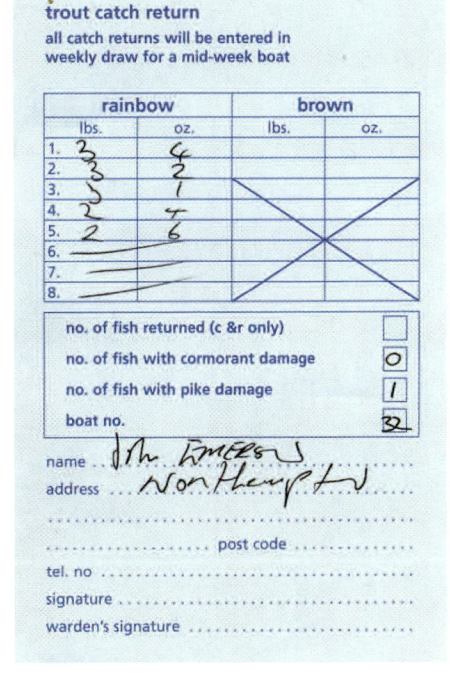

Right: Perch spawn at the end of April or beginning of May, depositing their eggs upon weeds or branches of trees immersed in the water. Perch fry provide an essential part of the Trout's diet (Wikipedia)

Above Right: A typical mature Pike is three feet in length and weighs about 25lb, although specimens twice this size have been caught. Their primary food source is other fish, particularly Roach, Perch and Trout, and other Pike smaller than themselves (Wikipedia)

Above: A typical catch return (RO)

Below: Members of Rutland Water Fly Fishers who took part in the Anglian Water Fly-fishing Challenge in June 2005 (Anglian Water)

Rutland Water Fly Fishers

Rutland Water Fly Fishers is open to all and draws members from as far afield as Orkney. It organises bank and boat matches for members as well as being involved in fund raising activities for various charities. One of the most important annual events at Rutland Water is the Anglian Water Fly-fishing Challenge. The club helps to run this boat-fished competition as well as providing volunteers and ghillies. In 2006 the Challenge raised over £20,000 for Water Aid. Another important activity is an annual litter pick around the lake perimeter every March which is sponsored by Anglian Water. The club also organises out-of-season winter events, and publishes monthly newsletters to keep members in touch with the fishery.

Fishing Tales 3

'Litter Pick Sunday March 5th 2006
. . . we had a record turn out. Some thirty-five members and their families gathered at the Lodge on a sunny but icy March morning for a delicious bacon sandwich and coffee. Before setting off with gloves and bags waving in the wind, the assembled group was photographed. Thirty-five bags of litter were collected . . . At the first event some years ago twenty of us collected 80 bags of litter. Either, we are now well on top of the job, or people are more litter conscious!
RWFF and Anglian Water would like to thank all those who took part. A presentation will in due course be made to the Rutland Memorial Hospital.' (*RWFF Newsletter*, April 2006)

John Seaton, Anglian Water Senior Warden, Mary Ward, Ward Manager at Rutland Memorial Hospital and John Wadham of Rutland Water Fly Fishers after the 2005 sponsored litter pick at Rutland Water (Cliff Waters Design)

Learning to Fly Fish

For those who wish to learn the techniques of fly fishing Anglian Water run frequent fly-fishing day courses at the Normanton Fishing Lodge. Local anglers are also always willing to lend a hand to those newcomers who are struggling to cast or who are looking for fish. Two essential guides are available for the new or visiting angler: *Rutland Water Bank angler's guide* by Henry Lowe & John Wadham and *Rutland Water Boat angler's guide* by Henry Lowe & John Maitland. These are available from Anglian Water fishing lodges or on line at www.hlredseal.co.uk

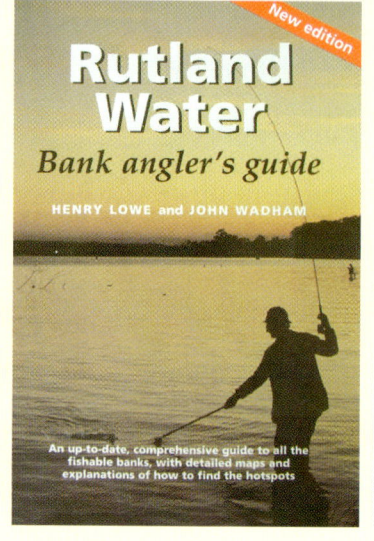

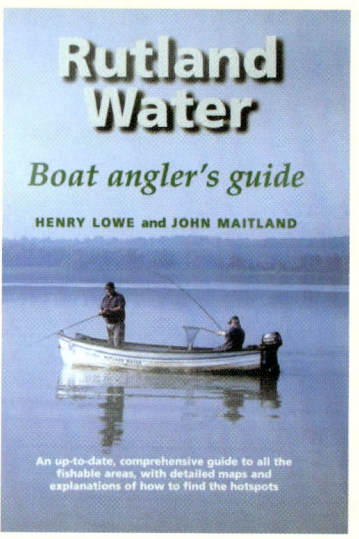

Safety

Safety has to be in the minds of all who fish at all times. Life jackets are compulsory under Anglian Water regulations and must be worn when out in boats and on the boat-dock. Also, fly-fishing rods, which are almost exclusively made from carbon fibre, are extremely efficient lightning conductors. They must be laid down at the least hint of a thunderstorm. Wave action, which results from strong winds occasionally experienced on the lake, has caused some bank erosion over the years. This has resulted in some undermining of the banks and care has to be taken when approaching the water's edge.

Rutland Water on a stormy day. Wave action such as this has caused some bank erosion (Tim Hawkins)

Methods

Fishing is by fly only from the bank, usually with floating fly lines, or from one of the large fleet of motor boats. Many fly-fishing methods are used at Rutland Water and these will vary with weather conditions, the depth at which the fish are feeding and their current diet. Rutland Water has some fifteen miles of bank available for fishermen and local knowledge is invaluable when deciding where to fish. Anglian Water fishery staff and local anglers are always willing to share information with newcomers on location and method of capture of the fish, whether from bank or boat.

Bank Fishing

Fishing on Rutland Water is totally governed by the speed and direction of the wind. The westerly wind can cause the water to become quite turbid in the margins which may limit bank fishing space to just a few hundred yards, whereas a north-easterly wind gives access to most banks. There are, of course, many regular hotspots. Examples include The Mound, Stockie Bay, Fantasy Island, Normanton Blue Pipes, East Creek and New Zealand Point, and on the Hambleton peninsula, The Finches, Barn Hill Creek, Yellowstone, Old Hall Bay, Old Hall Point and Green Bank.

Right: Tony Bokenham enjoying bank fishing at Rutland Water (Anglian Water)

Below: Late evening fishing. Casting from the bank at Rutland Water (Tim Hawkins)

Left: Bank fishing near Armley Wood in the northern arm of Rutland Water in 1979, the first year that the reservoir was full to capacity (Brian & Elizabeth Nicholls Photography)

Below: Basic tackle for fly fishing from the bank at Rutland Water (Cliff Waters Design)

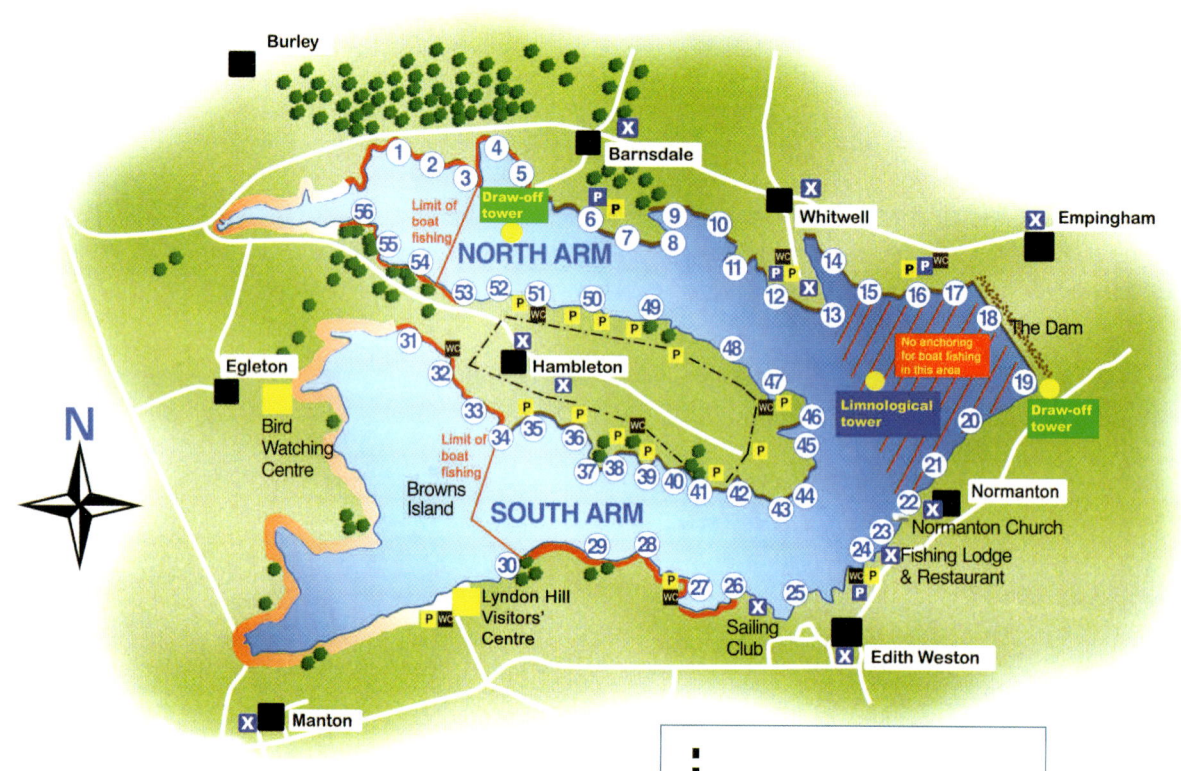

Rutland Water Anglers' Map

- 1-3 Burley Reach
- 3-5 Dickenson's Bay
- 5 Barnsdale Road End
- 6 - 8 Barnsdale Steep Bank
- 8-10 Barnsdale Bay
- 10-11 The Mound
- 12 Willow Bay
- 13 Ernie's Point
- 13-15 Whitwell Creek
- 15 Tombleson's Point
- 15-18 Sykes Lane Bank
- 16 Stockie Bay
- 17 Sykes Lane
- 18-19 The Dam
- 19 Fantasy Island
- 20 Mow Mires Reach
- 21 Three Trees
- 22 Normanton Church
- 23 Normanton Frontage
- 24 Pontoon Bay
- 25 East Creek
- 26 Sailing Club East
- 27 Sailing Club West Bay
- 28 New Zealand Point
- 29 Berrybutt Spinney
- 30 Gibbet Gorse
- 31 Green Bank
- 32 The Stones
- 33 Dalton's Point
- 34 Old Hall Point
- 35 Old Hall Bay
- 36 Old Hall Flats
- 37 Hambleton Wood
- 38 Yellowstone Bay
- 39 Yellowstone Point
- 40 No Wading Bank
- 41 Hinman's Spinney
- 42 Spud Bay
- 43 May Tree Bank
- 44 Half-Moon Spinney
- 45 Barnhill Creek
- 46 Barnhill Point
- 47 Carrot Creek
- 48-49 Armley Wood
- 50 Saville's Travels
- 51 The Finches
- 52 Tree in Water
- 53 Transformer
- 54 The Dead Elms
- 55 North Arm Shallows
- 56 Tim Appleton's (Anglian Water)

Legend:
- Hambleton Perimeter track for anglers cars and cyclists only
- **WC** toilets
- **P** Public car parks (free to anglers)
- **Nature Reserve** – no bank fishing
- **Bank Fishing** – 1 April - 31 October only

Fishing Tales 4

'. . . I had spent an unproductive time up on Old Hall Point and needed a pee, so I cast out, put the rod down and started the rigmarole of taking off jacket and lowering body waders etc before getting down to business. Halfway through, the reel screeched and the rod shot off down the bank and into the water before I could get to it. I saw it disappearing for at least a hundred yards on a course for Gibbets Gorse until it disappeared from sight. We tried to hail some boats for help but none heard us. At this point my fairly new rod and reel and the new line which was making its debut today was feared lost. Some ten minutes later, however, an angler on the right hand side of the Point shouted – he could see a fly line travelling in the direction of Green Bank and parallel to us. He managed to cast out over my line and drew it in so I could wade out to get hold of it – which I did, and, with great aplomb I thought, hand lined first the fish and then my rod in safely. What a relief!!'
(*RWFF Newsletter*, June 2005)

Boat Fishing

In the warmer months fishing from the bank can be difficult because the Trout prefer to retire to cooler water in deeper parts of the lake. Boat fishing then comes into its own.

Floating or sinking lines are used either from a drifting boat or at anchor. From mid-May onwards, there is a tendency for the shallower waters at the Manton end of the south arm to provide the best midge hatches and thus the best fishing. This area can only be fished from a boat.

A number of major boat competitions are held throughout the season and the results of these give a good idea of the performance of the fishery.

Above: The fishing boat fleet moored at the Fishing Lodge jetty (RO)

Left: Fly fishing from one of the motor boat fleet near Rutland Water Sailing Club (Cliff Waters Design)

Left: Early evening boat fishing near Normanton (Tim Hawkins)

Below: Launching the Wheelyboat. This boat enables wheelchair users to enjoy fishing on Rutland Water (Anglian Water)

Conclusion

No two seasons are the same and that makes the fishing at Rutland Water fascinating, challenging and very rewarding. It is a beautiful place to fish. The fishermen are very sociable, environmentally friendly and helpful people and one can make many friends here over the years.

Left: This Rainbow was caught on 31st December 2004, the last day of the fishing season (Anglian Water)

Below: A young angler proudly displays his catch (Anglian Water)

Chapter 29
Sailing on Rutland Water – Rutland Sailing Club
Tony Gray and Mike Barsby

Rutland Sailing Club on a clear summer's day. The slipways, jetties and sheltered creeks with moorings provide excellent access to the water. The founders chose an excellent location for the clubhouse (Martin Hollingshead)

Introduction

Where would you look to find a world-class British sailing club, internationally recognised as a prime sailing location and the home of champions at World, Olympic, European and National level? The Isle of Wight? Cowes? The Solent? The Clyde? Devon and Cornwall? As you're reading *The Heritage of Rutland Water*, you will have realised that the answer lies not in a coastal region but in an unexpected location more than 70 miles from the sea! Yes, it's Rutland Sailing Club on Rutland Water, one of only a handful of venues in the country recognised by the Royal Yachting Association (RYA) as a Championship Club and centre of excellence for sailing at all levels from beginner to world champion.

So how did this remarkable and unusual situation come about? This chapter will answer this question and introduce you to the club, its purpose and its history, illustrating the story with pictures and 'famous facts' from the full span of the Club's 40-year history.

How did it all Begin?

The most amazing single fact about Rutland Sailing Club (RSC) is that it existed a full six years before there were any boats or water to sail them on! Three of the founder members met to discuss the news that the Gwash Valley was to be flooded. A conversation followed, and there and then it was decided to form a sailing club for the benefit of the people of Rutland and its surrounding area.

The date was summer 1969, and the founders demonstrated great foresight, because at the time it was likely that the preferred approach of the then Welland and Nene River Authority would have been to establish a commercial enterprise, rather than to encourage local people to set up and run an independent organisation, open to all and for the benefit of Rutland.

At the beginning of August – just after the County Council had given up its opposition to the development of a resorvior – a press notice appeared in the local papers advertising a public meeting the following week in a side room at the Victoria Hall in Oakham. The day came and, according to one founding member, the room 'was overflowing with interested parties and prospective members'. So full in fact, that there was no room for journalists and the meeting itself was not reported. Discussion amongst those who did manage to squeeze into the room led to an agreement to form the club, and all those attending donated one pound to offset the initial costs of room hire, stationery and so forth. The best and most important inland sailing club in the United Kingdom was on its way.

The decision to set up the club was the easy part, setting in motion years of hard work for all those involved. A committee was formed and negotiations with the Welland and Nene River Authority began. The RYA was also contacted, and they were subsequently surprised to find that they had admitted into affiliation a sailing club without water, premises or boats!

The whole process of getting agreements and support took nearly five years. However, by 1st April 1974, all the vital strategic decisions had been made, agreements were in place, and the Club was established as a Limited Company with a proper Constitution and Governing Council representing the membership. The continuing presence of this structure speaks to the sound nature of those early foundations – the Club Council is still manned by volunteers from the membership, managing the Club for the benefit of its members and local people.

Sailors and Snow

The very first sail on Rutland Water, or Empingham Reservoir as it was then called, took place in 1975. Let the Club magazine of the time speak for itself:

Left: After six long years without water, Rutland Sailing Club finally gets afloat on 31st May 1975 (Richard Adams)

'Saturday May 31st and Sunday June 1st, 1975 have gone down in history. After six long and agonised years of anticipation, Rutland Sailing Club finally got afloat. With remarkably little ceremony, and no pomp at all, the first boats to sail on Rutland Water were launched about midday on the Saturday, and by the time the last Mariner had reluctantly left the water on Sunday evening, some eighty boats had sampled the delights in store.

'Although the reservoir is nowhere near even its low water mark, its size is already impressive. With some 700 acres of the eventual 3,000, even the larger boats were soon little more than white or brightly coloured blobs on a vast expanse of empty water.

'Even the weather was fairly kind, with reasonable wind and some sunshine – one could hardly ask for more. To highlight our good fortune, the next day, being June 2nd, it snowed.'

So nothing new weather-wise there then!

The pictures of this first foray on to the water are instructive. Any dinghy sailor of today looking at the boats will recognise a Mirror, a Laser and an Enterprise, all still present in the club's fleet, particularly the single-handed Laser which still has a very active racing membership at RSC. The water does look limited to our eyes, however, as the hedge line halfway up the far slope represents today's waterline!

And much of the activity is familiar – families enjoying themselves, a range of cars and people. Contrary to popular belief, sailing is not an élite sport. RSC today may have a wider range of boat types, but those early days still chime with today's membership, which also still comes from a wide spectrum of local people.

However, despite the familiarity of the boats and people, one crucial element enjoyed by today's membership is missing from these photographs – the Clubhouse and its shore-side facilities.

Sailing for the Landlubber: Boat Spotting 1
Dinghies

These are the small boats you see all over the lake. They are usually less than 5m long and designed for racing and cruising, generally by one or two people but some larger dinghies can take a family of four. They have one or two sails. The key thing about a dinghy is that the crew have to keep it balanced. A dinghy will tip over in strong winds if the crew are not alert. Each type, or class, of boat has distinctive markings or sail colour, or both, and every boat has its own number for easy identification. Dinghies are great fun to sail, and the vast majority of sailors in the UK sail in dinghies. It is possible to pick up a second-hand dinghy for little outlay, take a few lessons, and be on the water in no time.

Near Right: The Laser Pico dinghy is a small sailing boat designed in the mid-1990s and used primarily for training and day sailing (Tony Gray)

Far Right: The key thing about a dinghy is that the crew have to keep it balanced (Martin Hollingshead)

Sailing for the Landlubber: Boat Spotting 2
Multi-hull Boats

These boats look like nothing else on the water. Instead of having a single hull where the crew sits, they usually have two, or sometimes three long, slim hulls joined together by cross-pieces. Twin-hull boats are catamarans, three-hulled craft being trimarans. They are the smaller cousins of the world-record breaking boats sailed by Ellen MacArthur and her colleagues. Very fast in a straight line, they are exciting to sail and at Rutland, where the multi-hull fleet is large and enthusiastic, they are exclusively used for racing. RSC has boats of the latest high-tech design, built from materials like carbon-fibre, usually associated with Formula 1 racing cars. They are very demanding to sail and require a skilful and agile crew. RSC also has a fleet of trimarans. These single-handed craft have two sails and are used mainly by our disabled sailors, who are amongst the best in the country.

Multi-hulls, like this Laser Dart 16, usually have two or three slim hulls joined by a cross-piece (Tony Gray)

Sailing for the Landlubber: Boat Spotting 3
Keelboats

These look like dinghies but are generally larger, being 6m and more in length, and have two sails. Again, they are designed for racing and family cruising by a crew of up to four people. Unlike a dinghy, a keelboat has a heavy plate or keel hanging down below the boat into the water. This can weigh up to 50 per cent or more of the total weight of the boat and so keeps the craft stable even in quite high winds. A keelboat doesn't have a cabin. RSC has a large keelboat fleet mainly interested in racing, which is exciting, sometimes hard work and often close-run. Rutland keelboats can be any colour and usually have orange-brown sails, but sometimes white. As with some of the dinghies and other boats mentioned here, keelboats can put up a large brightly-coloured sail at the front of the boat, known as a spinnaker. When set, the spinnaker increases the sail area considerably and allows the boat to sail downwind very quickly.

Keelboats can set a large brightly-coloured sail at the front, known as a spinnaker, which allows the boat to sail more quickly downwind (Martin Hollingshead)

— 628 —

Sailing for the Landlubber: Boat Spotting 4
Cruisers

On Rutland Water, cruising boats vary in size from 5.5 to 8 metres. They are generally white with white sails, have a keel and also a cabin with galley and bunks. There is a very active cruising fleet of sailors who take to the water for picnics or quiet enjoyment of our lovely water. And since the lake is more than 3,000 acres, there are many places for these boats to sail, drop anchor and relax. But not all cruisers like to take things so easy. RSC has a group of hard-core racing sailors who enjoy the thrill of pushing these larger boats to the limit. Stripped of bunks, galleys and other comforts, these boats are crewed by up to five, each member of the crew having a specific job to do. Racing a cruiser offers an opportunity for teamwork and the odd white-knuckle ride.

Above Right: Cruising boats have a keel, and a cabin with galley and bunks (Phil Tomaszewski)
Below: The Optimist has become the most popular craft for introducing children to sailing. These young sailors are aged ten to fifteen and some of them will progress to become top-class adult helmsmen (Martin Hollingshead)

Sailing for the Landlubber: Racing

A sailing race can look completely chaotic, and sometimes it even feels that way to those involved! But the concept is just like any other race. You start, you go round the course and you finish after a pre-determined number of laps.

The course is defined by the buoys, known as marks, which can be seen all over the water. The marks have letters or numbers on them, so a course might look like 'Y, R, C3, 17 – 6 Laps'. A board put up by the Race Officer tells the competitors whether a mark has to be passed to their left (port) or to their right (starboard). Courses are aligned according to the direction of the wind. The first leg is into the wind, other legs are usually across or away from the wind, and then the boats sail back into the wind, cross the start line, and start the next lap.

At RSC, the Race Officer is usually stationed on a green and yellow motor boat which displays the course and has lots of flags on one side. These flags give the sailors information about starting and stopping the race. The order in which the boats cross the finish line is recorded, and if all the boats are the same type or class, first past the post wins. If the boats are in different classes the final results are calculated using a handicap system.

Starting a race well is crucial and difficult. This is because, unlike most other types of race which have a standing start, the boats are continuously in motion right up to the time the race begins. Start late and you are miles behind. Start early and you are penalised and have to start after everyone else! How does this work? Well, just prior to the start of the race crews try to manoeuvre their boats so that they cross the start line at exactly the right moment, going at top speed, travelling in the right direction, and not breaking the rules. This is not easy to do when there are thirty, or even a hundred other boats, in several different classes, all trying to do the same thing! Just prior to the start the Race Officer drops a class flag, accompanied by a loud hooter, to indicate to each class that their race is about to start. This is repeated, for each class, at the exact start time. A complicated process for the uninitiated!

A Place to Call our Own

How did RSC come by its clubhouse? And why is the building sited in Edith Weston? In fact, three potential sites were considered for the clubhouse: Whitwell Creek, Normanton former Women's Auxiliary Air Force war-time site, and Gibbet Lane, its final location. The ever-busy founding fathers set about selecting their ideal location. They rejected Whitwell Creek because it was too small and cut off from the prevailing winds and Normanton because of its exposure to south-westerly gales. Gibbet Lane, however, seemed ideal. Access was convenient but away from through traffic, there were large creeks to the east and west for moorings, the site faced north and so provided good visibility and an overview of two-thirds of the lake, and there was a long waterfront with excellent space for dinghy and car parking. The gentle gradient of the site also meant that slipways could be built without resort to major earthworks.

Above: Richard Eberlin's vision of the proposed clubhouse for RSC. This is the view from the lake side (RSC)

Right: Another of Richard Eberlin's original sketches of the proposed clubhouse for RSC. The finished building is remarkably similar (RSC)

Having decided upon a location, a building design was needed. Plans were drawn up at no cost to the club by Richard Eberlin of Nottingham, an architect and club member. The estimated cost of building the clubhouse and associated slipways and roads was also calculated. As is the way of these things, the first estimate of £120,000 quickly climbed to £160,000, and soon reached £240,000, twice the original cost. To put these figures into perspective, the price of an average family house at the time was £7,500 and a weekly wage packet usually contained about £50! Today, we can only admire the spirit of these pioneers who, from a small membership base, with no major sources of revenue and no external support, decided to take on this project.

A Building Committee was formed and the club set about raising the cash required. The first decision was to cap expenditure at £160,000, the equivalent of £1.2 million today, the amount raised by RSC to fund the expansion of the clubhouse in 2004.

From the very beginning, the club was advised by the RYA and the Sports Council to think big, and to plan for a club of a thousand members with five hundred boats. This projected the club's ambitions into a world not necessarily envisaged by the founders, but which gave access to considerable sources of public funding. In the event, £32,000 was offered by the Sports Council, and the membership was faced with finding the rest. A debenture scheme was begun to raise these funds, new members lending the club £100 interest free for ten years on top of their membership and entry fees. Also, grants were made to the club by both Rutland and Leicestershire County Councils, and these, together with gifts from well-wishers and sponsors, enabled the club to finance and finish the entire building programme by the end of 1979. The final bill came to £220,000 thanks to inflation which in the mid-to-late 1970s was running at 17.5 per cent.

Famous Facts 1

In August 1973, the club asked Anglian Water to leave Normanton Church isolated from the shore, half-submerged, so that club sailors could sail round it, and use it as a mark for racing! Sadly this was not agreed!

Famous Facts 2

Ever wondered about the mounds which have to be climbed over to get to the car park from RSC's clubhouse and dinghy park? They are bunds built at the insistence of Dame Sylvia Crowe, the landscape designer for the entire reservoir and to whom we owe a debt for the fabulous scenery we now enjoy. She believed that the mounds would hide the parked vehicles from the Hambleton Peninsula.

They don't, but they still look nice!

The process of building the clubhouse and the associated outbuildings was not straight-forward. Money arrived much as the rain did in the 'heat wave followed by drought followed by torrential rain' summers of the mid-to-late 1970s. And this dictated a 'stop-go' building programme. Fortunately for the club, there was a building recession in 1974, and the builder, another member, agreed to do the work for no profit and at a rate dictated by the erratic flow of funding so that he could keep his workforce together, thereby benefiting everyone. Consequently, the work progressed in fits and starts, but always onwards and upwards as the Building Committee and membership strove to raise finance, bring in new members and battle towards their dream of a place to call their own.

Eventually, much of the groundwork, slipways and other roads were completed, again thanks to generous and flexible attitudes by various benefactors in the local councils and water authority. Bricklaying commenced on the clubhouse in July 1975, and a formal stone-laying ceremony was held on 15th September 1975 when the club President, Colonel Haywood, laid the stone which can still be seen on the west wall of the clubhouse. At a meeting shortly after this happy occasion, RSC was astonished to discover that Anglian Water had plans, and clearly expected to take over the club because they were sure that the members could not continue to raise the necessary finance. They were to learn never to under-estimate the determination of a Rutland Sailor!

The clubhouse was completed in two stages following the laying of this foundation stone. The first stage was completed in 1976, the building being completed in 1979 (Michael Barsby)

Membership now stood at around 450, representing £45,000 of debentures, and a drive to recruit a further 150 members before Easter 1976 was undertaken. This influx would generate the £13,000 required to enable the ground floor of the clubhouse to be completed in time for a 'Grand Opening' at Easter. The floor of the top storey would be used as a temporary roof and left incomplete until funds could be found to finish the work.

And it was done! – despite the fact that Post Office Telephones, East Midlands Electricity Board and Severn-Trent Water Authority all required paying in advance because they mistrusted sailing clubs. And despite a decision by Anglian Water to renege on an agreement to connect the sewage disposal system to the mains at their own cost, thereby requiring £5,000 to be found urgently and meaning that the system only went in twelve hours before the opening ceremony, the clubhouse was ready for the Grand Easter Opening.

On the weekend of 16th to 19th April 1976, Rutland Sailing Club officially opened its new home. The weather was fine and the sailing was excellent. The sight of a 1,200 gallon cold-water tank perched precariously on 'stilts' high in the sky, already occupying what would be its final position in the as yet non-existent roof, provided just the right note of incentive and ambition to tempt the membership to even greater fund-raising efforts during the coming year of 1977.

Eventually, of course, all was well. It took time and dedication. But members were recruited with vigour and relieved of their debentures to feed the seemingly inexhaustible requirement for building funds. The clubhouse was finally completed in 1979 and now, 30 years later, remains one of the best sailing facilities in the country.

Famous Facts 3

In April 1975, the Commodore appealed for members to offer services and labour to help with the building programme and establish the facilities necessary to develop the sailing club. This appeal resulted in the gift of thirty doors for the club house, an Avon Inflatable Rubber Dinghy, and forty 30-gallon aluminium beer barrels, regrettably all empty. But they did come in handy as racing marks.

Famous Facts 4

RSC has a Race Control Box standing on stilts next to the western end of the clubhouse. It commands an excellent view of the water and is fully equipped with sirens, lights, radio and all the paraphernalia dear to the heart of a Race Officer.

Not many people know that this excellent structure was presented as a gift to the club by the builders. A kind gesture, particularly given their forbearance over the piecemeal funding of the main building.

Famous Facts 5

Why are the Club colours green and gold?

In 1974, Rutland disappeared as the smallest county in England, being absorbed into Leicestershire, much to the disgust of local people. As one way of perpetuating the heritage of Rutland before its demise, the County Council granted special dispensation to the Sailing Club to use in its livery the county's horseshoe emblem and green and gold colours.

England's smallest County regained its independence in 1997 after a battle lasting more than twenty years. Once again the determination and pride of Rutlanders resulted in an unlikely victory.

The RSC logo incorporates Rutland's horseshoe device and colours (RSC)

After a ten-year struggle to set up the club and raise the £220,000 needed to build the clubhouse and its associated shore side facilities, RSC was fully operational by 1979 (Brian and Elizabeth Nicholls Photography)

In the Meantime

During the period from 1976 to 1999 the club grew steadily, adding to its stature as a sailing venue, creating a professional-quality highly trained on-the-water safety team, purchasing a fleet of working and committee boats to manage the many racing and other events established in the club's calendar, and putting in around a hundred moorings so that cruising and keelboat members could leave their boats on the water safely and comfortably. In addition, new slipways were built, special facilities for disabled sailors were added, and a professional catering operation opened in 1979 to replace the do-it-yourself bar and sandwich service offered by volunteer members.

However, if the story of RSC is to be told in full, there are three aspects of the club's activities during this period which should be looked at in more detail. The first two relate to our involvement and promotion of sailing for the disabled. The third relates to a special individual – the amazing John Merricks, Olympian, Rutlander and inspiration to us all.

From 1991, the venues for the International Federation of Disabled Sailors (IFDS) World Championships were:

Nyon, Switzerland (1991)
Barcelona, Spain (1992)
Marblehead, USA (1993)
Edith Weston, Rutland (1994)

What was that again?! Edith Weston, Rutland . . . Yes, it's all there on the IFDS web-site so it must be true. But how on earth did the World Championships of disabled sailing come to Rutland of all places, given alternatives such as Sydney (Australia), San Remo (Italy), and Florida?

It all began when the then RSC Commodore and another member who had represented the United Kingdom at the previous IFDS Championships attended a disabled sailing demonstration day at Whitwell Creek in 1993. Sailing back across the lake to the clubhouse, they decided that the next IFDS Worlds would be sailed on Rutland Water. Given the track record of determination showed by RSC, it is no surprise to hear that this is exactly what happened!

The ISDF was persuaded that the club was serious. The club's fleet of National Squibs donated the boats. Sail makers donated free sails. The Sports

In 1994 RSC hosted the IFDS World Championships thanks to the support of the Sports Council, many local businesses and the efforts of many club members. The event was sailed in Squib keelboats loaned from the local fleet (Peter Craven)

Council sponsored the building of a ramp to allow disabled access to the first floor of the clubhouse. Local businesses provided all kinds of goods and services free or at cost, and a new floating jetty suitable for wheel chairs was provided.

Sailors from Armenia, Australia, Belgium, Finland, Germany, Ireland, the Netherlands, Norway, Poland, Spain, Sweden, Switzerland, the United States of America and the United Kingdom were present and the event was attended by Princess Christina of Spain, President of the ISDF.

Typical of the club's approach to this event is the story of one member who saw a huge crane laying water pipes in his village, stopped his car, and persuaded the contractor, Balfour Beatty, to go over to RSC and help position the newly-built pontoon jetty for wheelchairs – for free.

Needless to say, the event was a huge success, and the IFDS Championships came again to RSC in August 2006.

The Jubilee Sailing Trust and Sailability

The IFDS Championships were not RSC's first involvement with sailing for the disabled. The IFDS is a national organisation, set up with assistance from the Queen's Jubilee Fund, whose aim is 'to restore dignity and confidence to disabled people and re-integrate them into able-bodied society. Sailing is, in the Jubilee Sailing Trust's view, one of the most effective and desirable ways of achieving this aim'. This goal appealed strongly to a group of RSC members, who set up a local fund-raising group and arranged for the Jubilee Sailing Trust (JST) to be adopted as RSC's 'special charity' in 1983.

Still enthusiastically run by a team of dedicated supporters, RSC's JST group has become frighteningly professional and creative in finding ways to relieve members and the general public of their cash, and hundreds of disabled sailors have benefited from its efforts over the past 20 years.

Building upon this existing interest in sailing for the disabled, and following on from the success of the RSC organised ISDF event in 1994, the RAF sponsored a boat for use by disabled sailors at Rutland Water. This in turn led to a blossoming of interest from local people with physical disabilities who wanted to give sailing a try. As a result, two club members, sailors of the Challenger trimaran, one able-bodied and one with a physical disability, formed a Committee and founded Rutland Sailability with the full support of RSC.

By 1997, Rutland Sailability had begged and borrowed a variety of boats from all round the country. But this situation was not entirely satisfactory. Boats were needed which could be sailed by people with physical disabilities.

Rutland Sailability enables disabled people to regain their independence (Rutland Sailability)

Other boats were required which could be used to take people sailing who were not physically capable of sailing on their own or who had a learning disability which made it impossible for them to sail without supervision.

The 'Access Dinghy' is a relatively low-cost boat made in Australia. It can't capsize and is specifically designed for disabled people. Initially, RSC's JST group decided to import seven of these boats, and Rutland Sailability now has a fleet of twenty-six. The majority have been provided by very generous sponsors, most notably the local Rotary Clubs.

Rutland Sailability is now a Registered Charity and a Company Limited by Guarantee, and is one of the best and most active Sailability Clubs in the country. Members range in ability from beginners to those among the best in the world. The United Kingdom was represented by a member of RSC and Rutland Sailability at the Paralympics in 2004. It is also likely that the club will again be representing the United Kingdom at the 2008 Paralympics in Beijing.

The following quotation by a member sums up the importance of Rutland Sailability: 'For six days a week I am disabled. But on Saturdays at Rutland Sailability I regain my independence.'

John Merricks

To quote Keith Wheatley of *The Times*, 'John Merricks was a former apprentice electrician, a cheeky chappy who left school at sixteen and was happy to live on his wits'. Taken from us in 1997 at the age of 24, John was one of the finest sailors of his generation, a member of Rutland Sailing Club, and a continuing inspiration.

John began sailing at an early age with his father, starting in a Mirror dinghy on a gravel pit in Syston, Leicestershire. His talent was quickly spotted, and he was advised to seek the challenge of a more significant water. RSC being the natural choice, John joined the club in 1984, aged eleven. Over the next few years, his skills grew, and thanks to the very generous sponsorship of a club member, who also belongs to a long-standing Leicestershire brewing family, John was eventually able to stop work and concentrate on his sailing.

As a result, in 1994 John won the inaugural 'Rutland Challenge for the Tiger Trophy' with Ian Lovering crewing for him in a 420 dinghy, a men's Olympic class. His prize was a terracotta Chinese Tiger. Fifty-six boats attended this first event, the ice flying off the jib every time they tacked reminding them of the temperature. John, who never wore gloves, showed the Race Officer that at one point his hand had actually frozen to the main sheet of his boat!

This steely determination took John to a silver medal in the Atlanta Games, crewed by Ian Walker, and a career in the highest reaches of competitive sailing beckoned. Tragically, John died in a car accident in Italy in 1997 while competing in the European Championships of the Melges 24 keelboat.

His name lives on through the John Merricks Sailing Trust which is now one of the United Kingdom's most important sources of funding for young

Two hundred and fifty of the best young sailors in the world descend on Rutland every February for the John Merricks Tiger Trophy (Sailracer)

talented sailors of limited means. The annual Rutland Challenge for the John Merricks Tiger Trophy is one of the year's most important regattas for young sailors. It is sponsored by RSC and Everards Brewery, and concentrates on the twin attributes close to John's heart: 'Keep it Fast' and 'Keep it Fun'.

John Merricks, a leading Olympic sailor and 1996 Olympic silver medallist, was an example to all through his exceptional skill and down-to-earth good nature.

Rutland Sailing Club Today and Tomorrow

The RSC Committee Boat stranded on ice. Weather-wise, Rutland Water behaves much like an estuary for sailors. They experience gale force winds, extremes of heat and cold, and waves which, although not as large as those at sea, can carry great force. Many coastal sailors have come to Rutland and been caught out by disparagingly thinking of the lake as a mere 'pond' (RSC)

Left: A stormy day on Rutland Water, near Normanton Church Museum (Martin Hollingshead)

The Building Programme – Here we go again!

In the late 1990s the club's facilities and buildings were coming up to 25 years old and the time was ripe for taking stock and deciding how to take the club forward. Equally, new facilities were required, and the club's status had evolved to the extent that many new challenges presented themselves. Sports Clubs all over the country were finding themselves in competition for their members' decreasing amounts of leisure time. The whole nature of dinghy sailing was being changed as large manufacturers came into the sport with new classes and types of boat targeted by skilful marketeers at the owners of the traditional classes of boat, and at new sailors whose needs were different from those of their predecessors.

The Club's Council, aware of these changing needs, began a programme of development, the goal of which was to escalate RSC into a polished professional outfit which could compete and win in the world of the twenty-first century leisure industry. The central plank of this plan was the upgrading of the club's buildings and facilities so that they would meet the requirements of the National Institute of Sport and become an RYA National Centre of Excellence for Sailing. Other aspects of the plan concerned building upon the club's training activities to create a top-class Sailing School with a national reputation. This would link the club more strongly into its Rutland community by developing school and other local links. It was also necessary to ensure that RSC's Safety and Race Management teams could meet the highest national and international standards. A professional approach to the management and promotion of the club was also required.

All this, of course, could only be achieved by raising a considerable amount of money. Consequently, with a strong sense of *déjà vu*, RSC set about finding the £1.2 million needed for the transformation, a sum which was equivalent in modern terms to the £160,000 raised by the club's founders. A second Everest loomed.

With advice from the ever-helpful RYA, the club's main target was the Sport England Lottery Fund. A Lottery Team was established and approaches were made to the club's long-standing friends in the RAF, Sailability and other generous sponsors. To quote from the Lottery application:

'The primary objectives of this plan are to provide the RYA and disabled sailors with upgraded facilities to support the RYA World-Class Performance programme.'

In addition, of course, this would also give the people of Rutland and its surrounding communities an even better facility for themselves, their children and grandchildren.

After several months of intensive work, RSC received a Christmas present in 1999. An 'in principle' award of £720,000 was made to the club by the Sport England Lottery Fund. Delight all round! All the club had to do now was to find the balance of £450,000.

More work, planning, architect's designs, building, delays, frustrations, negotiations, joy and despair, which went on for four years.

In the end, all parts of the club were accessible to persons with disabilities. There was a lift to the first floor, improvements to the pontoons and access ways for wheelchairs, and special lifting equipment to enable sailors in and out of boats.

To meet the requirements of the RYA World Class programme the clubhouse was extended and reconfigured to include new training rooms and equipment. Extended accommodation means that the clubhouse can now accommodate sixty sailors in comfortable rooms, some with en suite facilities. There is also an improved and extended restaurant, a refurbished and comfortable lounge, a clubroom, offices and stores. Even the clubhouse heating, ventilation and catering equipment were brought up to 'world class' standard.

There were also improvements to the water-side components of the operation including stabilising the foreshore and beach, piling the pontoon jetties and providing new inflatable boats and engines for safety cover.

Above: The Clubhouse exterior in 2003. RSC opened its newly refurbished Clubhouse to the great delight of members and relief of the fund-raising team (Michael Barsby)

Left: RSC Clubhouse from the shore of Rutland Water (Tony Gray)

As for the training and youth sailing side of the club's activities, which are essential to secure the future of the club, RSC has grown a Sailing School second to none. It is staffed by a full-time Manager and Chief Instructor, and during the season employs up to fifteen highly qualified instructors capable of offering a full range of teaching from the six-year-olds getting started, through the teenagers who just want to sail faster, to adults and families who want to get afloat safely and enjoy themselves.

RSC Clubhouse interior (Michael Barsby)

The result is that Rutland now has the finest inland sailing club and venue in the United Kingdom on its doorstep.

The Future – Secured?

RSC now employs eight full-time and numerous temporary and part-time staff, and is recognised all over the sailing world as a centre of excellence for training, racing and family sailing.

For many, the only contact with the Club is the sight of members and visitors out on the water during the week and at weekends. What they don't realise is that today more than 20,000 'sailor days' worth of activity take place at RSC each year, almost 7,500 of these being related to visitors from all over the country and even from abroad. This activity generates around 3,000 bed-nights of benefit to the local economy, as well as financial input to Oakham, Uppingham and surrounding villages by the sailors' partners and children, who take advantage of tourism opportunities while their relatives are out sailing on our excellent Water.

Each year RSC holds championships of national and sometimes international importance on behalf of the RYA. And the club is also involved in Britain's Olympic sailing success story. Britain's sailors are our most successful Olympic athletes, winning more medals than any other sport, and RSC plays its part in this venture by providing a training venue for the squad and helping in the selection process which will identify our future champions. Rutland will be very important in the run-up to both the 2012 Olympics and Paralympics.

The club has also produced its own world class sailors, including, for example, John Merricks whose achievements have already been acknowledged. Amongst its membership there are other Olympic, Paralympic, World, European and National medallists and champions.

This has been achieved because, from the very early days of the club, there has been an emphasis on training, particularly for young people. RSC is one of only five Royal Yachting Association World Class Sailing Centres in the United Kingdom, and the only one inland. There is also a very successful RYA accredited Sailing School and RSC is one of only a small number of 'RYA Championship Clubs'. These are dedicated to helping young people and others get afloat, and to this end, there is a sponsored sailing programme for local schools and children, a thriving Disabled Sailing Group, and close links with important Rutland organisations such as the Army, the

Left: Balcony Panorama. The view from the clubhouse balcony is considered to be the best on the lake (Tony Gray)

RAF and the county's large private schools.

All this adds up to a major force for health and environmental care in Rutland. The club actively promotes a sport which burns no fossil fuels, is careful about its environmental responsibility and encourages young people to stretch and challenge themselves in an adventurous and exciting way.

So is all Well with the World? – Well, not Quite.

Recent changes in the water authority's plans for extraction and throughput of water potentially threaten both the club and its environment. As a result, water levels may fall lower than they ever have done since the reservoir was filled. With global warming and changes in weather patterns, who knows what the future will bring. Perhaps members will once again find themselves confined to the small area of water they sailed across on that first day of sailing back in 1975. It is hoped not, but the club cannot be complacent.

As a result, the present Club Council, not unlike its predecessors, is having to prepare to meet yet another set of challenges in fighting for the good of the sport it promotes, the membership whom it serves, and the people of Rutland for whom the club's founders began this sailing adventure in the most unlikely place in England.

We can only wish them well. Do not be surprised if somehow RSC and the people of Rutland overcome these and any other difficulties which might cloud the horizon. Remember the county's motto, '*Multum In Parvo*' – 'Much In Little' – and how, from the seed of a conversation between three enthusiasts, a major presence in the world of sailing has emerged over the past 30 years.

Sunset Lake (Tony Gray)

Aspects of Topography

New Barnsdale Hill

The realignment of the A606 to the north of Rutland Water was necessary because the old Stamford Road between Burley Fishponds and Barnsdale Hill was below the projected high water level of Rutland Water. From the west, the diverted route starts at what is now the Hambleton turn. It passes through the south ride to Burley on the Hill to the north of Burley Fishponds, then through the southern edges of Burley and Rushpit Woods before joining the old road at its junction with Barnsdale Avenue at the top of the hill. Tree clearance started in late 1973 and, as the route crossed a large area of ancient land-slipping, this was followed by a meticulous investigation of the geology. Before road construction could start, a programme of drainage works to stabilize the slope had to be completed. The road opened to traffic in 1976.

Work on the new road is well under way in July 1975 (Richard Adams)

The realigned Barnsdale Hill nearing completion, looking towards Oakham (Richard Adams)

The new Barnsdale Hill in 1976, looking towards Whitwell (Andrew Burns)

Chapter 30
Extra, Extra, Read all about it!
Sheila Sleath and Robert Ovens

The area in and around the Gwash Valley is not short of stories and curiosities which make interesting reading. This chapter brings together a representative sample of notable personalities, place names, extraordinary events, both natural and supernatural, and tragedies including murder most foul!

The selected items cover a period of eight hundred years and are supported by extracts and images from antiquarian sources, documentary records, contemporary reports and memorials.

A Meeting Place for Witches?

The name Witchley originates from the East and West Witchley Hundreds which, in 1086, were part of north Northamptonshire. However, following a boundary change a few years later, they became East Hundred and Wrangdike Hundred in the south-east part of Rutland. Witchley Heath, land lying within an area approximately bounded by Normanton, Empingham and Ketton, was named as a result of this historical association. It is shown on Morden's 1684 map and other seventeenth and eighteenth century maps of Rutland. Witches Heath, a corruption of Witchley Heath, is shown on Kitchin and Jeffery's map of 1751.

Kitchin and Jeffery's map of 1751 showing Witches Heath

The area of heathland adjacent to the villages of Normanton, Ketton and Empingham became known locally as Normanton Heath, Ketton Heath and Empingham Heath. By the nineteenth century the whole area was better known as Empingham Heath. The name Witchley was, however, retained in Witchley Warren, a small area to the south-east of Normanton Park, and shown on Smith's map of 1801. Witchley Warren Farm, halfway along the road from Normanton to Ketton, was named after this area.

Wytchley Warren Farm, Wytchley Warren Long Covert and Wytchley Warren Spinney on today's maps mark the site of Wichele which was within the Forest of Rutland at the end of the thirteenth century. Their names remind us of this link with the past. When Edward I relinquished the eastern part of the forest he retained Wytchley as his personal property, the only royal warren in Rutland.

A warren was an area of land which varied in size from a small field up to a square mile or more. Its purpose was to breed rabbits for food, and it was usually owned by the lord of the manor, who employed a warrener to look after it.

Empingham Heath

The coming of age celebrations of the fourth Sir Gilbert Heathcote of Normanton were held on Empingham Heath in 1794. The heath was also an important venue for horse racing as the following advertisement in the *Stamford Mercury* on 11th June 1724 shows:

'On Thursday, the 25th of this Instant June, will be run for on Empingham Heath, in the county of Rutland, a purse of Thirty Pound or upwards, by Galloways 14 Hands or under, nine Stone the highest, to allow Inch and half-stone. Every Horse, Mare or Gelding, belonging to a Contributor, to pay Two Guineas Entrance. The winning Horse, etc., to be sold for Forty Guineas. Every Horse, etc., that runs for this Plate, to be shewn and entered at the White Horse, in Empingham, on Thursday, the 18th Instant, between the hours of Four and Six in the Afternoon, before William Rowlate, Clerk of the Race, and to be kept in the town of Empingham till the Day of Running. To Run according to Articles.'

J & C Walker's map of 1878. Witchley Warren and Ketton Heath are shown, but not Witchley Heath

Below: Wytchley Warren Farm from the south-west in 2005 (RO)

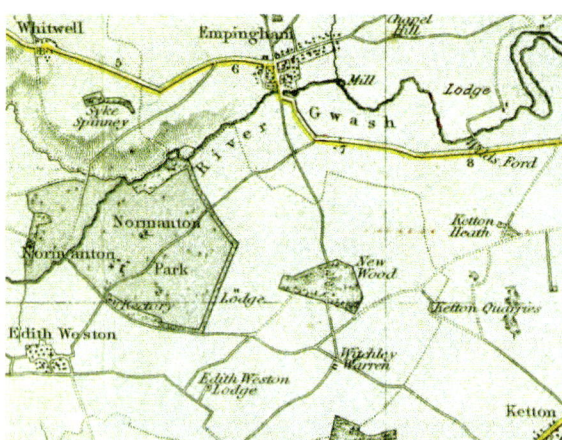

Murderer Pardoned

The Rev E A Irons, Rector of North Luffenham, 1900-23 researched medieval and later church court records and similar documents, from which he prepared his 'Notes'. These cover every parish in Rutland and are well-known to local historians. They provide a fascinating insight into a little known aspect of Rutland's history. One account is of a murder perpetrated in the reign of Edward III. The following is a modern translation of this account:

In January 1375, John, the son of Simon, was charged with killing another John, the son of Henry, at Normanton. Both men lived in Whitwell. It appears that they had been involved in an argument in Whitwell Fields, Normanton, as a result of which John, the son of Henry, struck the other John on the head with a stick causing him to fall to the ground. However, he managed to get up and run 'towards the great water which he could not cross as it was too deep'. The injured man turned on his pursuer and in self defence struck him on the head with a stick. His injuries were so severe that he died. The court found that John, son of Simon, was not guilty of murder, and he was pardoned.

A Cure for Sore Eyes

On the north side of Burley Road, Oakham, about a quarter of a mile east of the Odd House Inn, is the site of Our Lady's Well. It is described in the Rev Thomas Cox's *New Survey of Great Britain,* (1720-31) as follows:

'In ancient Times, before the Reformation, there was a Custom among the devout People of this Nation, and especially of these Parts [Oakham], to go on Pilgrimage in Honour of the blessed Virgin *Mary*, to a Spring in this Parish, about a Quarter of a Mile from the Town, which is still known by the Name of our Lady's Well, near which we may perceive in several Places the Foundations of an House or two remaining; but that which will confirm our Belief of such an Usage, is a Record found in the Firstfruits Office, containing, among other Things these Words, That very many Profits and Advantages belonging and appertaining to the Vicarage of *Okeham* did consist in divers Obventions and Pilgrimages to the Image of the Virgin *Mary* at the Well, and St. *Michael* the Archangel, and diverse other Rites and Oblations, which now are quite abolished, with the Benefits and Advantages which accrued there-from to the Vicar.'

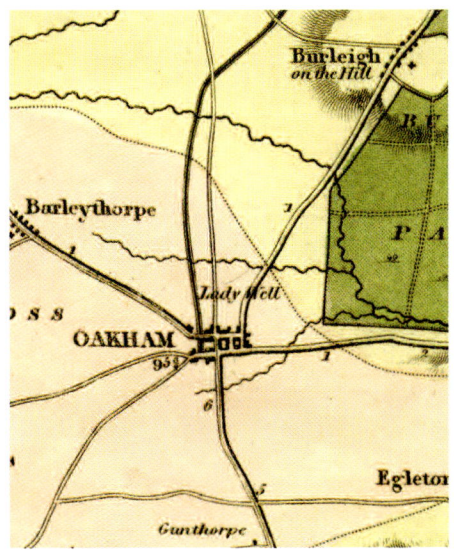

The Rev E A Irons, Rector of North Luffenham Church 1900-23 (Churchwardens of North Luffenham)

A century on, local people still had faith in the healing powers of the spring water. It was considered to be particularly valuable for treating sore eyes, especially if applied after a pin had been thrown in the well.

Although the well is no longer a shrine or visited for its healing powers, the site has been preserved. It is now managed as a nature reserve by Leicestershire and Rutland Wildlife Trust. A nearby road has been named Ladywell as a reminder of the area's historical link with the past.

The location of 'Lady Well' on Murray's map of Rutland dated 1830

Midget Pie

Jeffrey Hudson was born in Oakham to a Roman Catholic family in 1612. His father John, who had been a butcher in the town, was employed by the Duke of Buckingham to work on his estate at Burley on the Hill where he bred bulls for baiting. He presented Jeffrey to the Duchess of Buckingham and she took him into her service in 1628. It is said that she clothed him in satin and appointed two servants to attend to his needs.

Jeffrey is often called a dwarf but this may be an incorrect description. He was illustrated by artists of the day as being a well proportioned young man, thus suggesting that he was a midget. Many accounts have been published about him. Slight variations in the telling are inevitable, but it is apparent that he led an adventurous life. The following is an early account of his life from *New Survey of Great Britain* (1720-31):

'*Jeffrey Hudson* the Dwarf, memorable upon many Accounts; he was the Son of *John Hudson* a Person of a mean Condition, but of a lusty Stature, as were all his other Children . . . At 7 Years old being scarce 18 inches high, he was taken into the Family of the late *Duke of Buckingham*, at *Burley on the Hill* in this County, as a Rarity in Nature; and the Court being then in a Progress, he was put into a cold Pye, and served up to the Table. After the Marriage of King *Charles I.* with the Princess *Henrietta Maria* of *France*, he was presented to that Queen, and became her Dwarf. When the Rebellion broke out, he became a Captain of Horse in the King's

Above: King Charles I and Jeffrey Hudson (Rutland Magazine V opp 21)

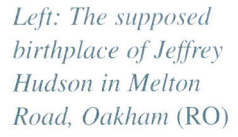

Left: The supposed birthplace of Jeffrey Hudson in Melton Road, Oakham (RO)

Service, till he went over with the Queen into *France*, where having the Misfortune to kill one Mr. *Crofts*, Brother of the Lord *Crofts*, in a Combat on Horseback, he was expelled the Court. Being put now to his Shifts, he went to Sea, and was taken by a *Turkish* Pyrate, who carried him to Barbary, where he was sold, and remained a Slave for many Years. He was at last redeemed, and coming into *England* lived several Years upon certain Pensions allowed him by the Duke of Buckingham, and some other Noblemen; but being a Papist, and going to *London* when the Popish Plot, in 1678, was in Agitation, he was taken up and clapt into the *Gate-house*, and lay there some considerable Time, but was at length enlarged, and died about the Year 1682. It is further observable of this Person, that from the 7th Year of his Age, when . . . he was not above 18 Inches high, till he came to be 30 Years of Age . . . he never grew any Thing considerable; but after it, he shot up in a little Time to the Height he continued to his Death, viz. about 3 Foot and nine Inches, which he attributed to the Hardships he underwent in *Turky*.'

Jeffrey Hudson Memorabilia

There are a number of published drawings and sketches which bear little or no resemblance to Jeffrey Hudson. Paintings by Daniel Mytens commissioned by King Charles I in 1630 are considered to be the most accurate. Today there is much local interest in Jeffrey and many items of memorabilia have been privately collected in commemoration of this local celebrity.

Top Right: A modern stone statue of Jeffrey Hudson (RO)

Centre right: A Jeffrey Hudson weathervane (RO)

Bottom right: Jeffrey Hudson Bitter brewed by a local brewery (RO)

Right: This Rutland Independence teapot depicts Jeffrey Hudson emerging from a pie (RO)

— 647 —

The Last Public Hanging in Rutland

William and Richard Weldon were baptised on 7th August 1763 and 20th April 1766, the sons of Mary and Richard Weldon of Lower Hambleton.

On the evening of 15th November 1788 John Freeman, a baker of Edith Weston, made his return journey home on horseback from Oakham market. Nearing home, he was 'most barbarously murdered' about half a mile distance from Hambleton, his head 'being almost beat to a mummy, and his skull most shockingly fractured' (*Stamford Mercury*, 21st November 1788). The coroner's inquest returned the verdict, 'Wilful murder by some person or persons unknown'. The newspaper article continued:

'The depravity of human nature was never more evinced than in the above horrid murder. It does not appear that the unfortunate man had any ways offended his cruel murderers, or that he in particular was chose out for their victim, but that the first person who came that way was to feel their vengeance, as in order to effect their savage purpose, they had fastened the gate thro' which every horseman must pass.

'A pole was taken from a hay-stack in a close, adjoining, and tines of a fork were found near to the place where the bloody deed was committed, and from which it appears the deceased received his death blows, whilst endeavouring to open the gate. His pockets were rifled of a ten pound Stamford banknote, and eight guineas.'

John Freeman's wife, Mary 'had been deprived of a tender husband, and a young family of an affectionate father'. He was buried at Edith Weston and entry 196 in the Parish Register reads 'John Freeman (Murdered) Nov 16 1788' (ROLLR DE 1937/2).

When suspicion fell on William Weldon of Lower Hambleton, he was immediately apprehended. On the following Tuesday he was escorted to Empingham where he appeared before the magistrate, the Rev Thomas Foster. It was reported that William was filled with remorse and confessed that his brother Richard had committed the murder and had

John Freeman's route from Oakham to Edith Weston would have been via Egleton and Nether Hambleton. It is superimposed on Letts' map of circa 1883

Left: A vivid portrayal of the barbarous murder of John Freeman. This is one of three illustrations, originally drawn by R C Chatburn for the Northampton and County Independent *in 1980. They were presented to Rutland County Museum by the artist* (RCM)

— 648 —

given him a share of the plunder. Richard kept the banknote and through this was traced to Empingham, Stamford in Lincolnshire and Barnack and Elton, Huntingdonshire, where eventually Mr Smith, a butcher, exchanged it for cash. Richard was arrested and on further examination both brothers were committed to Oakham Gaol on the following day, to be tried at the next assize.

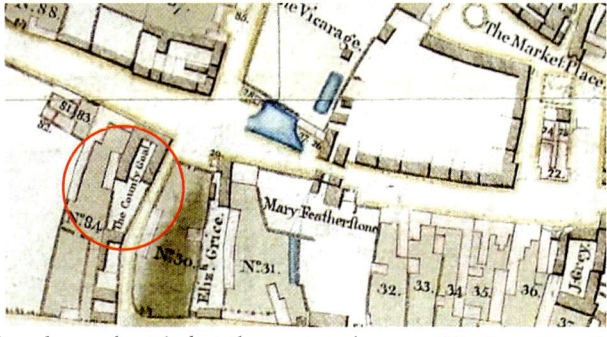

The location of the County Gaol (ringed) on a map of Oakham prepared in 1787 for the Earl of Winchilsea (ROLLR DE 3443 / DG7)

During the afternoon of Sunday 8th February 1789 the gaoler, Henry Lumley, as was his practice, went into the room where Richard Weldon was usually confined in the daytime. He took William, Richard's brother with him in order to pray with them. In a premeditated attack, Richard Weldon struck Mr Lumley on the side of his head with a large faggot stick, fracturing his skull. William knew nothing of his brother's intention and prevented him from striking Lumley again. Richard then left the room, having locked his brother and another prisoner inside, and went to make his escape through the gaoler's house. However Mrs Lumley, on hearing the noise of Richard's ankle irons, looked out of the window and on seeing the prisoner raised the alarm. Local townspeople caught Richard before he could make good his escape.

Mr Lumley did not survive the attack and died the following day. The coroner's inquest brought a verdict of wilful murder against Richard Weldon.

The brothers were brought to trial at the Oakham Assizes before Baron Thompson on Saturday 14th March 1789. An extract from an old newspaper 'kindly lent by Mr. R.L. Healey of Hambleton' was published in Matkin's *Oakham Almanack* (1897) under the heading 'An Account of the Trial and Behaviour of William Weldon & Richard Weldon'. Their parents were described as 'poor people, who seem utterly to have neglected giving their children any education . . . and, excepting their having the human shape, can scarcely be allowed to enjoy any of the faculties with which man in general is endowed'.

Richard Weldon prepares to strike gaoler Henry Lumley (RCM)

The court was crowded. William Weldon pleaded not guilty, Richard pleaded guilty. When all of the evidence had been presented the learned judge exhorted the jury:

'. . . in the most serious manner, not to pay any attention to what they had heard out of court respecting the bloody transaction, nor to Richard

Weldon having pleaded guilty; but to attend only to the evidence that they had heard in court; and if they entertained any doubt of their guilt, to lean on the side of mercy.'

It only took the jury a few minutes to conclude that both prisoners were guilty. When the judge passed sentence 'in the most affecting manner' it 'drew tears from many of the spectators, but seemed to have little effect on the two unhappy men'. Baron Thompson ordered that after both men had been hanged their bodies were 'to be afterwards delivered to the surgeons to be dissected and anatomised'. The brothers were hanged on Monday 16th March 1789 and it was ordered that their bodies were to be suspended in chains near to the place where the murder of John Freeman was perpetrated.

> *This Day is publiſhed*, Price Four-Pence,
> THE TRIAL OF
> **William and Richard Weldon,**
> Before BARON THOMPSON.
> At OAKHAM,
> On SATURDAY the 14th of March, 1789,
> FOR THE MURDER OF
> Mr. JOHN FREEMAN, of Edith-Weſton;
> (AS TAKEN BY A GENTLEMEN IN COURT):
> WITH THEIR CONFESSIONS.
> And an Account of the MURDER of Mr. LUMLEY, Goaler, at Oakham.
> Stamford. Printed by NEWCOMB and PEAT; and ſold by R. NEWCOMB, Stamford; W. Brooke, John Drury, and Joſhua Drewry, Lincoln; Preſton, Boſton; Booth, Caiſtor; Cooke, Uppingham; Horden, Peterboro'; Ellis, Horncaſtle; Allin and Ridge, Newark; Sheardown, and Marſh, Louth; Whaley, and Allen, Grantham; Albin, Spalding; Worley, Alford; Hicks, Oakham; right, and Allen, Melton; and by all Bookſellers and Newſcarriers

This publication of an account of the Weldon trial was advertised in 23rd March 1789 edition of the Stamford Mercury

The Rev Richard Williams, Vicar of Oakham from 1782 to 1805 and chaplain to the gaol, was in attendance at the hangings. The publication continued:

'Before their arrival at the gallows, and when there, they both confessed to the crime for which they suffered. Richard also confessed to having committed a number of petty thefts; and declared it had been his intention to murder Mr. Hippisley, Mr. Stimson, Mr. Freer, Mr. Needham, and Mr. Rott, all of Hambleton. Also Mr. Bunning, of Kilthorpe, and his servant maid.'

Not only was this believed to be the last public hanging at Oakham, it was possibly the last gibbeting to take place in Rutland. Matkin's *Oakham Almanack* (1902) reported that the gibbet post survived for some 50 years until it was sawn down and turned into a gatepost and that it was still 'doing duty as a gate post on some farm premises a short distance away'. Part of the irons at that time were at Hambleton, and the balance at Deeping, Lincolnshire.

Part of Owen and Bowen's map of 1720 showing the site of the gallows near to Mount Pleasant, Oakham

— 650 —

Prosecution and Execution Costs

George Phillips in 'The Annals of Rutland' (*Rutland Magazine* IV, 156) noted the following details in the Quarter Session Records: 'Prosecution of Wm. and Richard Weldon and for twenty nine witnesses Lent Assize 1789 £67 for the murder of Freeman. Prosecution of the said Richard Weldon and for eight witnesses at the said Assizes £12.10.0 for the murder of Gaoler Henry Lumley. John Grant for Gallows £2.8.4. Rev. Mr. Williams for attending Prisoners £10.10.0.'

The bodies of the Weldon brothers hanging from the gibbet near Lower Hambleton (RCM)

Dick Christian

Dick Christian, baptized on 6th March 1779 at Cottesmore, became a horse breaker and was known as 'the Emperor of rough-riders'. He gave the following eyewitness account of the Weldon brothers' execution and gibbeting which is recorded in G Paget's *The Flying Parson and Dick Christian*:

'That's Gibbet Gorse [Hambleton], as fine a cover as ever was seen. I saw those two brothers hanging on the gibbet, with white caps on; they murdered a baker called Freeman. I was only seven when they were hung [at Oakham]; I stood on my father's pony, and looked over his shoulder; I wasn't ten yards off them. The youngest of them, Bill, father had hired him to be a shepherd; he had been at our place only a week before he was took, to settle about coming. Poor fellow, he cried sadly; his brother Dick, he was a regular hardened one – you know what he said about not dying in his shoes: I heard him say it distinct. He could see Appleton [Hambleton], the village he lived at, from the gallows, and he turns his face right towards it, and he says, "Now I'll prove my mother's a liar; she always said I'd die in my shoes". Them were his very words; and away he kicks them among the crowd. I think I see him a-doing it. Father went quite white, and fairly trembled in his saddle. They had chains from the waist down between their legs, and they hung on the gibbet that way. That was a great plum year, but there was no sale for them round Oakham; people wouldn't buy them if a fly had been at them; they had a notion that they'd been at the gibbet, and sucked the flesh. I took no notice of it: I always ate plums when I could get them. They hung [on the gibbet] till they fell down; the good one [Bill] lasted the longest; people watched for that. I never heard of anyone finding bits of their bones; I've seen parts of their clothes lying about when we've been drawing the gorse, but never no bones; they say they're not to be seen. That green field on the left where the sheep's feeding, just on this side of the windmill, is where they were hung.'

Gibbet Gorse and Gibbet Lane

Gibbet Gorse lies on the south shore of Rutland Water, across from Hambleton. On the First Edition OS 1" map of 1824 it is called Gibbet Cover. Prior to this it was called Weldon's Gibbet on a map of 1806.

Before the construction of Rutland Water the lane from Edith Weston to Gibbet Gorse was traditionally known as Gibbet Lane. Although only a short length of this lane remains, residents still refer to it as Gibbet Lane.

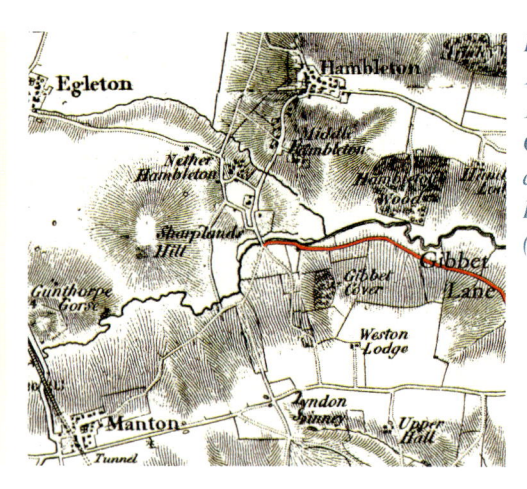

From the OS 1st ed 1" map 1824 showing Gibbet Cover and Gibbet Lane (highlighted)

Crackers Galore!

The 17th April 1789 edition of the *Stamford Mercury* reports on a remarkable firework display at Burley on the Hill in celebration of George III's 'happy recovery' [from porphyria]:

'The right hon. the earl of Winchilsea, lord lieutenant of the county of Rutland, appointed Monday last for a public rejoicing on his majesty's recovery, at his lordship's seat at Burley. An elegant entertainment was given on the occasion to the nobility, gentry, freeholders, and his lordship's tenants, all of whom received a general invitation.

'His lordship having engaged an eminent fire worker from London, a scene beautiful beyond description was exhibited in the large court in front of the house, at night. Amidst a variety of works was a pyramid 15 yards high, and a transparency, representing a medallion of his majesty suspended by two cherubs, bearing a crown, *G. III*. Beneath, "*Long Live the King*". The bust was in a glory; at top of the pyramid was a large crown, and a little

Burley on the Hill, the scene of the firework display in 1789, was built 1694-1708 by Daniel, 2nd Earl of Nottingham (Hart)

below on each side, the letters G. R. which with the corresponding works around, surpassed any thing ever seen in this part of the country. At intervals rounds of cannon were fired, together with repeated shouts of the populace, producing a pleasing awful effect . . . The ballroom was crowded, and the company continued dancing till after 5 o'clock on Tuesday morning.

'The house and court yard was, literally speaking, like a fair, for many hours. It is supposed that near 4,000 people were entertained.

'In the left colonnade, was placed a very large quantity of ale, bread, &c. which was distributed to the populace so liberally, that near two hogsheads of liquor were obliged to be returned again into the cellar.

'The whole entertainment was conducted in that true stile of old English hospitality, which reflects the biggest honor on the noble donor, and will ever be remembered by his guests.

'In the midst of the jollity an ungrateful rascal took an opportunity of stealing three hats and some napkins. It gives us pleasure to add, that he was detected, and likely to be dealt with according to his deserts.'

Burley Hermitage

The Hermitage at Burley was not what its name suggested. It was a wooden structure in Burley Woods used as a summer house by the owners of Burley on the Hill. It was evidently a favourite retreat for the young ladies of the house who would often have their meals there. It was wantonly destroyed by fire in 1965.

The following extract describing the Hermitage is from the *Rutland Magazine* (IV, 124-5):

The Hermitage in Burley Woods circa 1905 (Hart)

'The building, which has a rustic appearance, is constructed almost entirely of wood. The crevices are filled with furze, and the roof is thatched with reeds. The front of the structure is open lattice work. The interior consists of two rooms, one evidently having been used as a sleeping apartment, as it contains a straw bed covered with fibre matting. There is, also, in this room a fire place composed of rough stones, and the smoke is conducted to the outside by means of a chimney, built of similar material, which rises several feet above the roof of the building.

'The front room is furnished with chairs, benches and tables, having a home-made rustic appearance. They are disfigured with the names and initials of visitors, a propensity too much indulged in by English people, whether at home or abroad. It must be an annoyance, and it is certainly an eyesore, not only to the owner, but to all lovers of such relics of the past, to see sprawling letters, large and deep, cut into the trees and on every available place both inside and outside the building. After seeing so many examples of this reprehensible practice, one is forced to the conclusion that there are a large number of people afflicted with a peculiar disposition to revert, in another form, to the claw sharpening propensity of a far distant ancestor.

An artist's impression of the interior of the Hermitage in Burley Woods (David Carlin)

'The floor of the interior is tastefully paved with pebbles, and the knuckle bones of sheep. They are laid in a mosaic pattern and enclose the letter W., supposed to be the initial of the Earl of Winchelsea, a former owner of the property.

'The figures 1807 also appear on the floor, indicating, it may be presumed, the date of the erection.

'There is no authentic record to show how or for what purpose the building was erected, but in all probability it was built for and used as a summer house or picnic lodge.'

Lockjaw and Suicide

On Friday 16th May 1817 Drakard's *Stamford News* reported the following unfortunate accounts. The first concerned the death of Joseph Sutor of Hambleton, who was buried under the authority of the coroner on 30th April. Joseph, the son of Ann Sutor, was baptized at Hambleton on 11th November 1792:

'An inquest was lately held at Hambleton, Rutland, on the body of a poor fellow, who died of a lock-jaw, occasioned by a wound he received in his foot when chopping wood for the Earl of Winchilsea, on the 3rd of April, although surgical assistance was immediately had. He lived a week after the beginning of his lock-jaw [tetanus]. Verdict – accidental death.'

Another inquest was held in Hambleton on the body of Mary Shilaker who drowned herself in a shallow part of the River Gwash. She was buried on 10th May 1817 at Hambleton again under the authority of the Coroner. She was just 20 years of age:

'[An inquest was held] . . . on the body of Mary Shilaker, a servant maid, who drowned herself in a shallow part of the river, for which rash act no cause could be assigned. She went out at six o'clock in the morning to fetch up her master's cows, and having brought three, returned for the others, but was not seen again until her body was found where we have stated. Verdict – lunacy.'

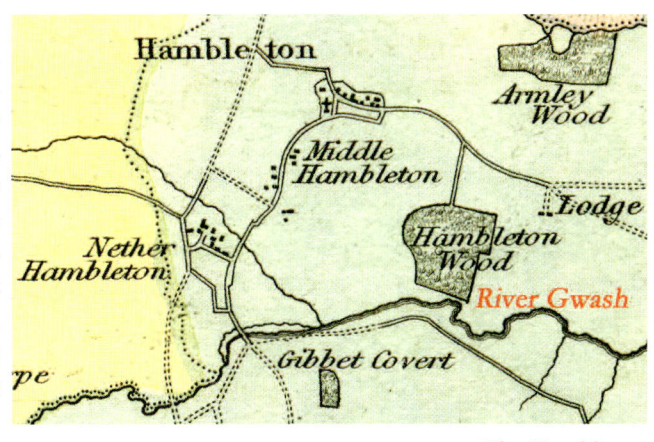

The Hambletons on a map dated 1878 by J & C Walker. Mary Shilaker met her death in the River Gwash below Middle Hambleton

The Wise Woman of Wing

Amelia Woodcock, the daughter of John and Elizabeth Dexter, was born about 1816 at Barleythorpe. In 1841 she was living with her parents, brother James and sister Catherine at Hambleton. In January 1842, she married Matthew Woodcock, a stonemason, who had been born in the village, and they made their home at Egleton. Later that year their first child Mary Ann was born. By 1845 they had moved to Wing where four more children, Lillah, John, Charlotte and Harriet, were born between then and 1854. Another child, Georgiana, was baptised at Egleton in January 1857.

It was at Wing that Amelia acquired the title 'The Wise Woman of Wing'. She was evidently clever in the cure of slight wounds, and villagers always visited her with their ailments. Stories about her ability to treat the sick soon spread to the surrounding district, and by 1851 an extraordinary number of sufferers believed in her healing powers. As a result, her reputation became widespread and hundreds of ailing people were drawn to the once quiet village of Wing. It was difficult for Amelia to cope with this influx. Such a constant and high volume of patients meant that there was no way that she could give immediate consultations. It was therefore of great financial advantage to the local publicans, shopkeepers and cottagers, who were able to accommodate the many visitors. It is difficult to imagine the impact that Amelia's popularity had upon this rural community.

Some people believed that Amelia was either a charlatan or a witch. However it appears that she was guilty of nothing more than possessing a remarkable knowledge for making herbal medicines and salves.

Much of her doctoring was carried out at Wing, but her obituary in 29th May 1863 edition of the *Stamford Mercury* states that:

'The house at Wing becoming too small, she bought a house at Oakham, and established an omnibus to meet the various railway trains. Mrs Woodcock was rather of a retiring disposition but her amount of work was very large, and it is surprising how she was able to get through so much.'

It is not known when Amelia moved to Oakham, but she was living there in 1857. Her house was at Mount Pleasant, on the southern outskirts of the town. Whilst there, Dick Christian, in Paget's *The Flying Parson and Dick*

On 10th September 1852 the *Stamford Mercury* featured two accounts detailing a little of Amelia's life and activities at Wing. One was 'furnished by a respectable correspondent at Oakham' who gave 'one view of her pretensions', the other 'from an equally respectable source at Uppingham':

Oakham correspondent:
'It had been stated in some of the communications to the local papers that only ignorant, vulgar, and poor people visit her, which is quite contrary to the fact, for each day in the week vehicles of every description may be seen in the place, and many people of high respectability daily apply to her. The fact cannot be denied that she has cured and relieved many; and in this neighbourhood cures have been made by her when medical men have given patients up as incurable, or have intimated that a limb must be amputated. She has at the present time the wife of one medical man and the daughter of another under her care. The village is now completely full of lodgers, and respectable people too, – not the "poor, ignorant, and vulgar"; and Wing has the appearance of a small watering place so far as regards the strangers there. Indeed it is quite a common thing for 200 people daily to make application to the woman. Witchcraft has been imputed to her, but she is no more a witch, nor uses what is usually termed witchcraft, than those who make such unfounded statements. It is true the woman has not had a refined education, but where is the person who would not be cured of the "ills which flesh is heir to" because the party administering the remedy has not obtained a diploma? The Midland Railway must be great gainers by the doctress, for scarcely a day passes but 50 or 60 people alight at the Manton station, and no less than three licensed vehicles are generally employed to convey patients from the station to the village and back. People from almost all quarters of England have visited her, and Scotland and Wales have contributed their portion of the poor, ignorant and deluded people.'

Uppingham correspondent:
'We have received other communications showing the extraordinary excitement this woman is causing among invalids. We are assured that last week she had upwards of 300 patients in her books, and that two persons who went to visit her on Thursday had to wait till Saturday before their turn arrived for an interview. The age of the woman is between 30 and 40: she is the wife of a labourer, can neither read nor write, and is very brusque in her manner. It is stated that she has seen something of gypsy life, and thus probably required a knowledge of the properties of herbs. It is also said she gained some experience in Stamford Infirmary, where she was a patient, and afterwards as a nurse. A story is current that having succeeded on curing two patients of cancer, a neighbouring medical practitioner offered a large sum for her recipe to which she replied, "I received the gift of cure from God and I do not barter God's gifts". She has now a secretary, who records the names of her visitors as they call and they are ushered to her presence in the order of their application.'

Extracts from articles about Amelia Woodcock in the *Stamford Mercury*:

17th September 1852:
'It has been understood that the medicine administered by this famous woman to her patients would almost have the effect of raising the dead, but this week there has been an example to the contrary. A patient living in a village not far from Stamford having occasion for the much coveted compound, employed a neighbour to procure it from Wing, and he was supplied with a tolerably large sized bottle. On the road home, the man's curiosity prompted him to "a taste" when to his surprise, he found "it not so bad after all", and continued to take occasional sips until his gait became rather unsteady under its stimulating influence. He, however, not being satisfied with his sipping, took a "strong pull", the effect of which was that he was found by the road side *dead drunk*.'

17th February 1854:
'An inquest was held at Oakham, on Friday last before J. F. Jones, Esq. coroner, on the body of a young man, 20 years of age, named Oliver Epery, who had come from Earith, Hunts., and had been a patient for some weeks in the house of Mrs Woodcock, better known as the "Wise Woman of Wing" and who died suddenly there on the previous Wednesday night. There being no evidence as to the immediate cause of death, the jury returned a verdict that the deceased died from *natural causes*.'

Amelia lived with her family in this cottage in City Yard, Wing. It was here that she began to dispense medicines and salves to those who consulted her about their ailments (Hart)

Christian, described her as 'the doctress lady . . . her that makes the wind pills. I've heard she's got as many as one hundred and fifty patients; she takes two or three days to get once through 'em'.

Amelia died at Mount Pleasant on 24th May 1863 at the young age of 47 years. Perhaps she died of overwork, something she had no medicinal cure for. After Amelia's death, Matthew, her husband, continued to live at Oakham until at least 1871. He died at Egleton in 1877. Both Amelia and her husband chose to be buried at Hambleton.

The headstone of Amelia Woodcock, The Wise Woman of Wing, and her husband Matthew is in the south-east corner of Hambleton churchyard.

The inscription reads:

In
MEMORY
of
MATTHEW WOODCOCK
WHO DIED APRIL 21ST 1877
Aged 58 years
ALSO OF
AMELIA WIFE OF THE ABOVE
WHO DIED MAY 24TH 1863
Aged 47 years

Old Herbal Remedies

The majority of the salves and medicines used by Amelia would have been made from herbs gathered from the fields and woods. The following plants could have been used by Amelia:

Far left: Betony was evidently one of Amelia's favourite herbs. It was used to clear the head from over-imbibing, to alleviate shortness of breath and, when mixed with 'Hogges Lard', to ease wounds (aphotoflora.com)

Left: Dandelion contains a number of bitter ingredients which act as an aid to digestion (aphotoflora.com)

Left: The drug obtained from Herb Robert has been of interest to folk healers for centuries. It has astringent properties and is a mild diuretic (aphotoflora.com)

The narcotic qualities of Field Poppy are legendary (aphotoflora.com)

Left: Celandine is a favourite plant used by healers. It is believed to have powers which sharpen or correct vision (aphotoflora.com)

A Remarkable Escape

In the *Rutland Magazine* (II, 61) Edward Costall, at some time 1st Lieutenant in the Rutland Militia, relates the following tale:

'A man named Knight, of Burley-on-the-Hill, joined the Militia, and after serving for a year volunteered into the Coldstream Guards, and at the outbreak of the War with Russia went with his regiment to the Crimea, and was in the battle of the Alma, which was fought on the 10th of September, 1854. The battle was about over. They had driven the Russians over the river, and were pursuing them – when the Russians turned round and gave them a parting volley. Knight was struck in the breast by a bullet and fell, and at night when the Surgeons went round they found him, and seeing that the bullet had entered his chest – said "Well my poor fellow, you have not many hours for this world – here is some lint to staunch your wound, and a little brandy to comfort you. We can do no more for you, but must go and attend to those that we can be of use to".

'The following morning on the Surgeons going round again they found him still alive, attended to his wound, and found that the bullet had passed through his body (through one lung) and through the blade bone, and completely through his knapsack, and had carried a piece of his shirt front through his body and had left it in his knapsack. He was sent to the Hospital at Scutari, recovered, and in due course got his discharge and was invalided home. He got quite well and offered himself again for the Militia, was passed by the Doctor, and became a very useful man to us, and we made him a Sergeant. I can absolutely vouch for the truth of this statement for I have seen the scar on his chest where the bullet entered, and also the one in his back where it came out. After serving for the time for which he enlisted in the Militia he worked as a farm labourer and was alive until a very few years ago.'

The soldier injured at the Battle of Alma was almost certainly James Knight. He was baptised at Burley on 26th March 1837, the son of William and Elizabeth Knight. He was buried at Burley 26th September 1896, aged 59 years.

Florence Nightingale arrived at the army hospital at Scutari in November 1854. With determination and patience she made much needed changes there. She brought comfort and care to the virtually abandoned men, becoming a true 'ministering angel'. Her arrival at Scutari was just over a month after the Battle of Alma and James Knight was probably one of her patients.

An Extraordinary Event

The following account of an extraordinary event, which took place in the summer of 1880, was recorded by the Rev Benjamin Barratt, Vicar of Hambleton 1879-85, in *Leicestershire and Rutland Notes and Queries* (I, 298-9):

The location of the supernatural appearance on the Oakham to Stamford road, added to Letts' map of 1883

'I once witnessed an appearance which I should hesitate to believe had it been told me by anyone I thought at all accustomed to draw the long bow. It occurred in winter about ten years ago at about half-past six in the evening, at the place where you turn off the Stamford Road for Hambleton, where I then lived. At that time I used very often to drive down to Oakham in the evening to bring up my son from school. Generally speaking, we used to meet the Exton postman (who drove a cart) before we turned off the Stamford Road for Hambleton.

'One night, I and my son will remember as long as we live, for we both saw it, the most extraordinary thing we are ever likely to see. Just as we were in the very act of crossing the road to take the turn to Hambleton, to our horror we saw the Exton postman in his trap close upon us, and as we were already well into the middle of the road, nothing I thought could avert a collision. However, I instantly pulled my left hand rein to try to regain in some measure my proper side of the road, and allow the trap to pass. But lo, in almost less time than I could take to give a sudden pull at my rein, man, cart, horse and all had utterly vanished, and the road was free for us to take

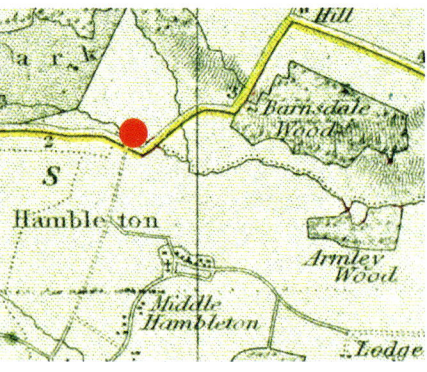

Hambleton Hall in 2006 (RO)

> **The Rev Benjamin Barratt referred to Hambleton Hall in his account of the mirage and he recorded the following information about it in the parish register:**
>
> 'The New Hall called Hambleton House was begun to be built in June 1880. Owner Walter Gore Marshall Esquire. Architect Mr Lee, London. Contractor Messrs Rudd, Grantham. Mr Marshall was High Sheriff for the County of Rutland in the year 1880.' The Hall is now a well known restaurant and hotel.

the turn for Hambleton without let or hindrance. We could both have sworn that it was the Exton postman and his horse and cart that we saw so close upon us, for we generally met him. We could not understand at the moment how he and his horse and trap could have come upon us so quietly, and therefore so suddenly. But it was no man, horse and trap that we saw, as the whole thing no sooner appeared than it suddenly disappeared again. We had scarcely turned the corner into the Hambleton road than we heard the Exton postman's trap coming along the road some two or three hundred yards off. I and my son concluded that it must have been a mirage, for we both saw man horse and cart close upon us as distinctly as ever we saw anything in our lives, and the impression it made upon me remains most vividly printed on my mind at the present moment.

'About that time, it may have been some months earlier or later, but it was about the time Mr. Marshall's house at Hambleton was being built, some workmen going to their work at Hambleton told me that they saw what they described as two suns.

'What I and my son saw, which I have accurately described may appear very extraordinary, but we can both vouch for its being a fact.'

Ghost with Vigorous Knuckles

The *Rutland Magazine* (I, 128) provides an extraordinary account of a Rutland ghost. Much of the information was provided by Mr Vernon Bryan Crowther-Beynon FSA, who lived at Edith Weston 1895-1912. He took a keen interest in archaeology and local history and was a frequent contributor to the *Rutland Magazine*:

'Edith Weston . . . in December, 1896, boasted a genuine ghost, a most active ghost, possessing vigorous knuckles, which it utilized upon the doors, floors, and cupboards of the estate bailiff's house. Mr. Crowther-Beynon, who most kindly provided me with full particulars of case, himself heard the knockings in a manner calculated to remove all suspicion of trickery from the most sceptical mind. The knockings lasted from a Friday night to the following Wednesday, and consisted of four separate knocks in rhythmic succession. At first the knocks were loud enough to be heard at the other end of the street a distance of about a hundred yards, and were of such violence that the family feared the woodwork of the door would be shattered; nevertheless, not a mark or scratch could be observed. Trickery it obviously was not. One day Mr. G., the estate bailiff, and H., the keeper, were standing

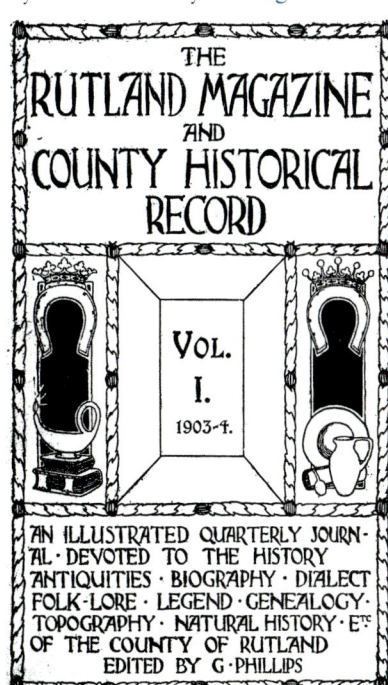

Title page of the first volume of the Rutland Magazine

one inside and the other just outside a room in the house, so that H. obtained a full view of one side of the door, while Mr. G. had a full view of the other. The knocks occurred on the door while they were standing in this position. On another occasion the keeper was examining the cellar to see if there was anything to account for the sounds. He found it empty, except for a few potatoes. He came out, locked the door, and was hanging up the key on the outside, when knocks sounded on the other side of the door with such force and noise that he opened it again, expecting to find the wood splintered. Not a mark was visible. Every sort of suggestion was offered to account for this extraordinary phenomenon, but the affair remains a mystery to this day.'

Horn Fair

In the *Rutland Magazine* (IV, 61-2) there is an article reporting the re-appearance in Rutland of a curious custom known as Horn Fair. It was revived at Edith Weston in 1896, and was described by V B Crowther-Beynon as follows:

'A "Horn Fair" or "Tin-panning" represents the public expression by the villagers of their sense of outraged propriety and decency when some of their fellows have been guilty of a flagrant breach of morality. It takes the form of a series of nocturnal processions round the village with "rough music" produced by means of all kinds of whistles, horns, mouth-organs and trumpets, as well as of "instruments of percussion" in the shape of tin pans, tea-trays and the like. It would appear that the orthodox method in vogue here is to conduct this serenade for three successive nights, finally winding up with the public burning of an effigy of the culprit. In the present instance this closing part of the performance was omitted owing to

A tranquil scene at Edith Weston in 1906 (Hart)

the regrettable interference of an over-zealous member of the County police. I find on inquiry that the last occasion when a "Horn Fair" was carried out in this village was some twenty-five years ago, and that the older inhabitants can recall two or three previous occurrences of a similar kind before that.'

He added:

'However much we may deplore the circumstances which occasioned its revival, we may still admit a feeling of satisfaction in the knowledge that our modern civilisation and progress have not entirely swept away all these old village practices, while we may congratulate the community on the fact that public sentiment – outwardly at any rate – has taken its stand on the side of order and virtue even in these days of laxity . . . This institution, under various names, is, of course, well known and widely distributed over the country, and forms, it must be admitted, a wholesome and useful object lesson to successive generations, as showing that such misdeeds cannot be committed without incurring the odium of respectable citizens. I am glad, for the credit of Edith Weston and the county of Rutland, to record that both the erring parties in this case were persons who have been imported from outside the county in comparatively recent years, and are not members of our local stock.'

A 'Remarkable Meteor'

Thomas Barker, Squire of Lyndon Hall (1759-1809), was well known for his writings and meteorological observations. His journals include many fascinating references to country life at that time. He communicated the following account of a 'remarkable meteor' he had seen in Rutland. The paper was published in the *Philosophical Transactions* of the Royal Society and is reproduced in *The Weather Journals of a Rutland Squire* edited by John Kington:

'*SEPT. 15. 1749.* a remarkable Meteor was seen in *Rutland*, which I suspect to have been of the same kind as Spouts at Sea . . . .

'It was a calm, warm, and cloudy Day, with some Gleams and Showers; the Barometer low and falling, and the Wind South, and small. The Spout came between 5 and 6 in the Evening; at 8 came a Thunder-Shower, and Storm of Wind, which did Mischief in some Places; and then it cleared up with a brisk N.W. Wind.

'The earliest Account I have was from *Seaton*. A great Smoke rose over or near *Gretton*, in *Northamptonshire*, with the Likeness of Fire, either one single Flash, as the Miller said, or several bright Arrows darting down to the Ground, and repeated for some Time, as others say. Yet some who saw it, did not think there was really any Fire in it, but that the bright Breaks in a black Cloud looked like it. However, the Whirling, Breaks, Roar, and Smoke, frightened both Man and Beast. Coming down the Hill, it took up Water from the River *Welland*, and passing over *Seaton* Field, carried away several Shocks of Stubble; and crossing *Glaiston*, and *Morcot* Lordships, at *Pilton* Town's End tore off two Branches, and carried one of them a good way. In a Hedge-row in the Meadow, at

The course of the tornado from Seaton to Hambleton in 1749 shown on Robins' map of 1818

Lyndon Hall in 1910 (Hart)

Right Angles to the Spout's Course, stood an Oak and an Ash 15 Yards asunder; the Oak a young sound one, 16 Inches thick, it split two Yards down, and one Half fell to the Ground, but was not quite parted from the other; the Ash, about 8 Inches thick, was torn off in the Middle, and carried 10 or 12 Yards. Between and on each Side of these Trees were other smaller ones, which were not hurt: I heard of no Harm it did after, but breaking and scattering a few Boughs. I saw it pass from *Pilton* over *Lyndon* Lordship, like a black smoky Cloud, with bright Breaks; an odd whirling Motion, and a roaring Noise, like a distant Wind, or a great Flock of Sheep galloping along on hard Ground; it was divided into two Parts all the Way it went, and tho' there was no Wind, moved apace from S. by W. to N. by E. As it went by a Quarter of a Mile East from me, I saw some Straws fall from it, and a Part, like an inverted Cone of Rain, reached down to the Ground. Some who were milking, said it came all round them like a thick Mist, whirling and parting, and, when that was past, a strong Wind for a very little while, though it was calm both before and after. It then passed off between *Edithweston* and *Hambleton*, but how much further I do not know.'

Bibliography

Adams, A W, *The Excavation of a Medieval Building at Nether Hambleton 1973-1976* (Rutland Field Res Group for Archaeol & Hist, 1990).

Adams, A W, Archaeological reports, *Rutland Record* 1-7 (1980-87).

Adams, A W, Clough, T H McK, Gorin, M S, Reynolds, N M, & Todd, M, Archaeological discoveries at Rutland Water, in Harper & Bullock 1982, 57-66.

Archibald, M M, & Woodhead, P, (eds), Medieval and modern hoards, *Coin Hoards* 2 (1976), 115.

Aston, N, Humphrey Repton and the Burley landscape, *Rutland Record* 9 (1989), 312-17.

Biddle, L, Rutland mammal records 1965-90, *Rutland Natural History Society, 1965-1990* (Spiegl Press, 1990), 33-36.

Bland, R, & Johns, C, A Roman hoard from Whitwell, *Rutland Record* 14 (1994), 151-7.

Bourne, J, & Goode, A, (eds), *Rutland Hearth Tax 1665* (Rutland Loc Hist & Record Soc, 1991).

Braybrooke, Lord, (ed), *The Private Correspondence of Jane Lady Cornwallis* (S & J Bentley, Wilson & Fley, 1842).

Brewer, J N, *Beauties of England & Wales* (Longman, 1813).

Bridle, R C, Vaughan, R C, & Jones, H N, Empingham Dam – Design and Construction, *Proc Inst Civil Engineers* 78.1 (1985), 247-90.

British Museum (Natural History), *British Mesozoic Fossils* (1962).

Broughton, H, The Burley archives, *Rutland Record* 10 (1990), 363.

Brown, A E, *Archaeological Sites and Finds in Rutland: a preliminary list* (Univ Leicester, Dept of Adult Education, 1975).

Buchan, J, *Thatched Village* (Hodder & Stoughton, 1983).

Buckland, P C, An insect fauna from a Roman well at Empingham, Rutland, *Trans Leicestershire Archaeol Hist Soc* 60 (1986), 1-6.

Burke's Genealogical & Heraldic History of the Peerage, Baronetage and Knightage (107th ed, 2003).

Buxton, A, & Martin, B, *Rutland People: The Genuine Article* (Spiegl Press, 2001).

Cambden, W, *A New Survey of Great Britain* (E & R Nutt, 1720-1731).

Cammell, C R, *The Great Duke of Buckingham* (Collins, 1939).

Cantor, L M, The medieval hunting grounds of Rutland, *Rutland Record* 1 (1980), 13-18.

Chandler, R J, The history and stability of two Lias Clay slopes in the Upper Gwash Valley, Rutland, *Phil Trans Roy Soc London*, Ser A, 283 (1976), 463-91.

Childs, J, Queen Mary's final journey, *Leicestershire and Rutland Life* (Leicester Mercury Group, March 2006, 27-29).

Chinnery, A, (ed), *The Oakham Survey of 1305* (Rutland Record Soc, 1989).

Clay, P, An excavation at Burley Road, Oakham, in P Liddle, (ed), Archaeology in Leicestershire and Rutland 1987, *Trans Leicestershire Archaeol Hist Soc* 61 (1987), 87-90.

Clay, P, Oakham, Burley Road in P Liddle, (ed), Archaeology in Leicestershire and Rutland 1988, *Trans Leicestershire Archaeol Hist Soc* 63 (1989), 108.

Clay, P, Neolithic-Early Bronze Age pit circles and their environs at Burley Road, Oakham, *Proc Prehist Soc* 64 (1998), 293-330.

Clay, P, The Neolithic and Bronze Ages of Leicestershire and Rutland, *Trans Leicestershire Archaeol Hist Soc* 73 (1999), 1-17.

Clough, T H McK, (ed), Rutland History in 1996-97, *Rutland Record* 18 (1998), 366.

Clough, T H McK, *Rutland in Old Photographs* (Alan Sutton, 1993).

Clough, T H McK, (ed), *The 1712 Land Tax Assessments* (Rutland Local Hist & Record Soc, for the Village Studies Group for Rutland, 2005).

Clough, T H McK, Dornier, A, & Rutland, R A, *Anglo-Saxon and Viking Leicestershire including Rutland* (Leicestershire Museums, Art Galleries & Records Service, 1975).

Cooper, N J, The Rutland Water Fieldwalking Survey 1990-94, *Rutland Record* 19 (1999), 410.

Cornwall, J, (ed), T*udor Rutland: The County Community under Henry VIII* (Rutland Record Soc, 1980).

Cossons, A, *The Turnpike Roads of Leicestershire and Rutland* (Kairos Press, 2003).

Cox, B, *The Place-Names of Rutland* (English Place-Name Soc 67-69, 1994).

Dickinson, G, (ed), *Rutland Churches before Restoration* (Barrowden Books, 1983).

Dobson, A, (ed), *Diary of John Evelyn (*Macmillan, 1906).

Donnelly, J, Westminster Abbey's Oakham manor 1275-1535, *Rutland Record* 5 (1985), 167-71.

Duckers, N, & Davies, H, *A Place in the Country* (Michael Joseph, 1990).

Dunning, G C, Alstoe Mount, Burley, Rutland, *Antiq Journ* 16 (1936), 396-411.

Ennis, P, *Rutland Rides* I (Spiegl Press, 1979).

Evans, H A, *Highways and Byways in Northamptonshire and Rutland* (Macmillan & Co, 1924).

Evans, I M, (ed), *Before Rutland Water* (Leicestershire Museums, Art Galleries & Records Service, 1981).

Exton Hall Farm, Catalogue of the Entire Herd of Pure-bred Short-horn Cattle (Messrs Royce, 1899).

Finch, P, *History of Burley on the Hill, Rutland* (John Bale, Sons & Danielsson, 1901).

Ford, A, Perimeter forestry and landscape works at Rutland Water, in Harper & Bullock 1982, 47-50.

Fuller, T, *The History of the Worthies of England* (new ed, F C & J Rivington, 1811).

Galitzine, Prince Yuri, *Domesday Book in Rutland* (Rutland Record Soc, 1986).

Gathercole, P W, Excavations at Oakham Castle, Rutland, 1953-54, *Trans Leicestershire Archaeol Hist Soc* **34** (1958), 17-38.

Gentleman's Magazine **64**.2 (John Nichols, 1794).

Gilbert, C, *Thomas Chippendale as Undertaker* (repr from *Journ Furniture Hist Soc* **IX**, 1973).

Gill, C J, Tree pre-planting at Rutland Water, *in* Harper & Bullock 1982, 51.

Goldmark, M, & Traylen, A R, *Maps of Rutland* (Spiegl Press, 1984).

Green, M A E, (ed), *Calendar of State Papers, Domestic* (Longman, 1875-86).

Grimble, I, *The Harington Family* (Jonathan Cape, 1957).

Habakkuk, Sir John, Daniel Finch, 2nd Earl of Nottingham: His House and Estate, *Rutland Record* **10** (1990), 348-52.

Haines, C R, *Notes on the Birds of Rutland* (R H Porter, 1907).

Hall, D, *The Open Fields of Northamptonshire* (Northampton Record Soc **XXXVIII**, 1995).

Harper, D M, & Bullock, J A, (eds), *Rutland Water: Decade of Change. Proceedings of the conference held in Leicester, 1-3 April 1981. Hydrobiologia* **88**.1-2 (1982).

Hartley, R F, *The Mediaeval Earthworks of Rutland, a Survey* (Leicestershire Museums, Art Galleries & Records Service, Archaeol Rep **7**, 1983).

Harvey, A, & Crowther-Beynon, V B, *The Little Guide to Leicestershire and Rutland* (Methuen, 1912).

Henry, D, *Wind and Windmills of Rutland* (Spiegl Press, 1988).

Hill, R, *Burley on the Hill Mansion* (Janet Kirkwood, 2001).

Hollingworth, S E, Taylor, J H, & Kellaway, G A, Large-scale superficial structures in the Northampton Sand ironstone field, *Quarterly Journ Geol Soc London* **100** (1944), 1-44.

Horswill, P, & Horton, A, Cambering and valley bulging in the Gwash Valley at Empingham, Rutland, *Phil Trans Roy Soc London*, Ser A, **283** (1976), 427-62.

Horton, A, & Coleman, B, The lithostratigraphy and micropalaeontology of the Upper Lias at Empingham, Rutland, *Bull Geol Survey GB* **62** (1977), 1-12.

Hoskins, W G, *The Midland Peasant: The Economic and Social History of a Leicestershire Village* (2nd ed, Macmillan, 1965).

Hurst, J G, Neal, D S, & van Beuningen, H J E, *Rotterdam Papers VI: A Contribution to Medieval Archaeology. Pottery produced and traded in north-west Europe 1350-1650* (Museum Boymans-van Beuningen, Rotterdam, 1986).

Illustrated London News, **XXXI**.883, 17 Oct 1857.

Institute of Geological Sciences, *1:50 000 Geological Sheet 157 (Stamford)* (1974).

Irons, The Ven E A, Notes on Rutland (unpublished; Univ Leicester Library Special Collections, MS 80).

Jenkins, A, *Rutland. A Portrait in Old Picture Postcards* (S B Publications, 1993).

Journ House of Commons 7, 1651-1660 (Public Record Office, 1802).

Journ House of Commons 11, 1693-1697 (Public Record Office, 1803).

Judd, J W, *The Geology of Rutland* (Geological Survey GB, 1875).

Kelly, A L, *Directory of the Counties of Leicester and Rutland* (1876, 1900, 1904, 1909, 1925).

Kilmurray, K, *The Pottery Industry of Stamford, Lincolnshire, circa 850-1250*, Brit Archaeol Rep, Brit Ser, **84** (1980).

Kington, J, (ed), *The Weather Journals of a Rutland Squire* (Rutland Record Soc, 1988).

Laird, F C, *Beauties of England. A Topographical and Historical Description of the County of Rutland* (Sherwood, 1818).

Leach, H, Stamford Ware fabrics, *Medieval Ceramics* **11** (1987), 69-74.

Leicestershire & Rutland Notes & Queries **I**, 1889-91 (Elliot Stock, 1891).

Leith-Ross, P, *The John Tradescants* (Owen, 1984).

Liddle, P, *Leicestershire Archaeology: the present state of knowledge: 1: to the end of the Roman period* (Leicestershire Museums, Art Galleries & Records Service, Archaeol Rep **4**, 1982).

Lucas, J, Roman burial at Edith Weston, *Rutland Record* **13** (1993), 144.

McCarthy, M R, The Pottery, *in* Williams, J H, *St Peter's Street, Northampton, Excavations 1973-76* (Northampton Dev Corp Archaeol Monograph **2**, 1979), 151-229.

McKenna, J M, Horswill, P, & Smith, E J, Empingham Reservoir – Seepage Control Measures, *Proc Inst Civil Engineers* **78**.1 (1985), 291-326.

Matkin, C, *Oakham Almanack* (1881-1941).

Matthew, H C G, & Harrison, B, (eds), *New Oxford Dictionary of National Biography* (Online edition, Oxford Univ Press, 2007).

Matthews, B, *The Book of Rutland* (Barracuda Books, 1978).

Mayhew, C, *Lyndon, Rutland* (Rutland Loc Hist & Record Soc, 1999).

Messenger, G, *Flora of Rutland* (Leicester Museums, 1971).

Mills, E, *Empingham Remembered* (privately published, 1984).

Mitchell, A, Rutland elections in the early eighteenth century, *Rutland Record* **15** (1995), 207-12.

Moore, A, *Leicestershire's Stations, an Historical Perspective* (Laurel House Publishing, 1998).

Moore, D E, Establishing and maintaining the trout fishery at Rutland Water, *in* Harper & Bullock 1982, 179-89.

Moore, D T, & Oddy, W A, Touchstones: some aspects of their nomenclature, petrography and provenance, *Journ Archaeol Sci* **12** (1985), 59-80.

Morris, J, (ed), *Domesday Book* **29**, *Rutland* (Phillimore 1980).

Nichols, J, *The Processes, Processions and Magnificent Festivities of King James the First* **I** (1824).

Normanton Estate Sale Catalogue (Duncan B Gray & Partners, 1924).

Normanton Park, Rutland: Catalogue of the Interior and Exterior Fixtures and Fittings (Perry & Phillips, Bridgnorth, 1925).

Ostler, J, The Barnsdale survey, *Rutland Natural History Society 25 Years 1965-1990* (Spiegl Press, 1990), 72-75.

Ovens, R, & Sleath, S, *Time in Rutland* (Rutland Loc Hist &

Record Soc, 2002).

Paget, D, & Irvine, L, *The Flying Parson and Dick Christian* (Backus, 1934).

Palmer, R, *The Folklore of Leicestershire and Rutland* (Sycamore Press, 1985).

Parkinson, R A, *A General View of the Agriculture of the County of Rutland* (1808).

Paul, J A, *3000 Strangers* (Silver Link Publishing, 2003).

Pevsner, N, *The Buildings of England: Leicestershire and Rutland* (2nd ed, Penguin Books, 1984).

Phillips, G, *Cambridge County Geographies: Rutland* (2nd ed., Cambridge University Press, 1920).

Phillips, G, *Rutland and the Great War* (J Padfield & Co, Salford, 1920).

Phillips, G, Some Rutland ghosts, *Rutland Magazine and County Historical Record* **I** (1903-04), 127-29.

Phillips, G, A Rutland man's remarkable escape on the battlefield, *Rutland Magazine* **II** (1905-06), 61.

Phillips, G, Notes on some Edith Weston village institutions, *Rutland Magazine* **II** (1905-06), 176-80.

Phillips, G, "Horn Fair" at Edith Weston, *Rutland Magazine* **IV** (1909-10), 61-62.

Phillips, G, Burley Woods and Hermitage, *Rutland Magazine* **IV** (1909-10), 122-26.

Phillips, G, The annals of Rutland, *Rutland Magazine* **IV** (1909-10), 150-60.

Phillips, G, Sir Jeffrey Hudson, the Oakham dwarf, *Rutland Magazine* **V** (1911-12), 21-24.

Phythian Adams, C, Rutland reconsidered, *in* Dornier, A, (ed), *Mercian Studies* (Leicester Univ Press, 1977), 68-84.

Phythian-Adams, C, The emergence of Rutland and the making of the realm, *Rutland Record* **1** (1980), 5-12.

Return of Owners of Land 1873 (Local Government Board, 1875).

Richardson, N, Uppingham's 1875-77 Typhoid Outbreak: a re-assessment of the social context, *Rutland Record* **26** (2007), 195-213.

Rider Haggard, H, *Rural England* (Longmans, 1902).

Ryder, I E, *Common Right and Private Interest. Rutland's Common Fields and their Enclosure* (Rutland Loc Hist & Record Soc, 2006).

Spelman, J, *Rutland Voices* (Tempus Publishing, 2000).

Squires, A, Jeeves, M, *Leicestershire and Rutland Woodlands Past and Present* (Kairos Press, 1994).

Stock, R, *The Churches Lamentation for the Losse of the Godly* (J Beale, 1614).

Stokes, J & A E, *Just Rutland* (repr S R Publishers, 1969).

Tew, D, *The Melton to Oakham Canal* (Sycamore Press, 1984).

Thomson, E McL, (ed), *Letters of John Chamberlain* (Putnam, New York, 1965).

Timby, Jane, *The AngloSaxon Cemetery at Empingham II, Rutland: excavations carried out between 1974 and 1975* (Oxbow Books, Oxbow Monograph 70, 1996).

Todd, M, *The Iron Age and Roman Settlement at Whitwell, Leicestershire* (Leicestershire Museums, Art Galleries & Records Service, Archaeol Rep **1**, 1981).

Traylen, A R, *The Villages of Rutland*, **1 & 2** (Spiegl Press, nd).

Traylen, A R, *Old Village Schools of Rutland* (Spiegl Press, 1999).

Traylen, A R, *Oakham in Rutland* (Spiegl Press, 1982a).

Traylen, A R, *Turnpikes & Royal Mail of Rutland* (Spiegl Press, 1982b).

Traylen, A R, *Uppingham in Rutland* (Spiegl Press, 1982c).

Traylen, A R, *Notable Citizens of Rutland* (Spiegl Press, 2002).

Twigge, S, & Scott, L, The other other [*sic*] missiles of October: the Thor IRBMs and the Cuban missile crisis, *Electronic Journ Internat Hist* **3** (Internet, 2005).

Uppingham Local History Study Group, *Uppingham at War* (2005).

Victoria County History: Rutland **I** (1908), **II** (1935).

Wacher, J S, Excavations at Martinsthorpe, Rutland, 1960, *Trans Leicestershire Archaeol Hist Soc* **39** (1963-64), 27-28.

Waites, B, (ed), *Who was Who in Rutland: Rutland Record* **8** (1987).

Waites, B, *Normanton Tower, Rutland Water* (Anglian Water, 1984).

Waites, B, *Rutland Water: a Visitors' Practical Guide* (Samuel Walker, 1978).

Waites, B, *Rutland Heritage* (Spiegl Press, 1986).

White, W, *History, Gazetteer, and Directory of Leicestershire and Rutland* (1846, 1863, 1877).

Williams, S, *Grimsthorpe Castle* (Grimsthorpe & Drummond Castle Trust, 2003).

Winder, A J H, Cole, R G, & Bowyer, G E, The Empingham Reservoir Project (Rutland Water), *Proc Inst Civil Engineers* **78**.1 (1985), 219-46.

Woodfield, C, & Woodfield, P, *Lyddington Bede House* (repr English Heritage, 2006).

Woodland, R, Pottery from Nether Hambleton (unpublished, for Rutland Field Res Group for Archaeol & Hist, 1982).

Woodland, R R, The Pottery, *in* Mellor, J E, & Pearce, T, *The Austin Friars, Leicester*, Council Brit Archaeol Res Rep **35** (1981), 81-129.

Wright, G N, *Turnpike Roads* (Shire Publications, Princes Risborough, 1992).

Wright, J, *History and Antiquities of the County of Rutland* (London 1684 and later Additions, repr E P Publishing, 1973).

Index

This index is divided into two sections: Index of Surnames, Organisations and Corporate Bodies, and General Index. In the General section the county is Rutland unless indicated otherwise. Current county status is shown for most places outside Rutland.

Index of Surnames, Organisations and Corporate Bodies

Abbots of Cluny 211
Adams 246, 316, 410, 421-2, 433
Adcock 123, 131, 167
Agnew 327
Albert of Lorraine 149
Alexander 217, 354
Alexandra, Princess of Wales 246-7
Alfred McAlpine 413
Allen 280, 294, 458
American servicemen 187
Ancaster, Earl of 101, 138, 144, 146, 231, 237-9, 250, 261, 272-3, 308
Ancient Order of Foresters 607
Andrews / Andrew / Andres 85, 159, 196, 292, 449
Anglian Water [Authority] / Mid-Northamptonshire Water Board / Welland & Nene River Authority 124, 299-300, 321, 326, 348-9, 351, 355-7, 369-71, 398, 400, 409, 418, 422, 473, 481, 483-4, 488-9, 491-3, 495-7, 530, 551-5, 559, 566, 568, 587, 589, 591, 604, 615-6, 619, 626, 631-2
Anne, Queen 70, 235
Appleton 504-05, 529-530, 532, 535, 537, 545, 548-51, 557, 561, 565-67, 572, 574, 591
Archer 489
Armstrong 66
Army regiments 50, 84-5, 114, 217, 293, 372
Armyn 161
Arnold 100, 183
Aspinall 543, 547-8, 556
Astley Paston Cooper 179-80, 183, 185, 187
Aston 240
Astor 239
Attenborough 555, 568
Atter 310
Audley 164
Auxiliary forces 121, 297
Aveland, Lord 41, 136-8, 237, 245-6, 260-1, 263, 271, 307-09
Aylesford 71
Bach 406

Badeslade 326
Badlesmere 441
Bailey 187
Baines / Bains 25, 208, 306
Baker 41, 309-10
Bakewell 172
Ball 615
Bank of England 133, 235, 239
Baptie 418
Barker 153-71, 173, 175, 290-1, 461, 663
Barnett 313
Barratt / Barrett 280, 660-1
Barsby 625
Barwell 463
Basing / Basynges 233, 441
Batts 198
Baxter 426
Bayliss 183
Beaufort, Duke of 80
Beaumont 281
Beaver / Beavor 131, 327
Bede, Cuthbert 246-7, 319
Bedford, Earl of 57
Beecham 294
Bell 162, 200, 300, 368
Bellamy 224
Belvoir Hunt 48, 85, 178
Bennet 70
Beradi 489
Bernini 66
Berridge 306
Bessow 240
Bettinson 188-9
Biddle 504
Billington 467
Binnie 372
Binns 140, 264
BirdLife International Partnership 570
Blackett 217
Blackwell 183, 466
Bletchley 240
Bliss 107
Bloodworth / Bludworth 234, 265, 280
Blore 134, 221
Blow 240

Board of Health or Nuisance Committee 343
Bohun 441
Bokenham 620
Bone 485
Bonney 100-01
Boot 187
Booth 127
Bottomley 298
Bourgoing 210
Bourne 193, 217
Bowley 188
Bowyer 369
Bradley 246-7, 314, 319, 350
Bradshaw 120
Braithwaite 101
Bramley 470
Branson 295
Brassey 495-6
Breese 239
Bretton 97
Brewer 528
Bricker 107
Bridges 234
Briggs 510
British Museum 237, 284, 430
Britten 485
Broadhead 490
Broadsworth 280
Brocklebank 187
Broom / Broome 125, 205, 209, 461-3
Broughton 31
Brown 75-6, 89, 103, 131, 271, 326, 349, 416-17, 470
Brus 45
Bryan 130
Buchan 319
Buchanan 518, 520
Buckingham, Duchess of 61, 63, 646
Buckingham, Duke of 21, 60-5, 90, 118, 152, 156, 163, 646-7
Buckworth 136
Bunning 280, 650
Burchnell 280
Burghersh, Bishop 322
Burton 151, 156-7
Busby 240

Bushell 181, 183, 188, 240
Cameroon, King of the 568
Campden, Viscount 59, 289-90
Canfield 240
Carausius 407
Carnegie 503
Carpendale 123
Carr 89
Carrington 82
Carter 120, 130
Case 173
Cavenagh 298-9, 422
Cecil 58, 292
Chamberlain 183, 280, 306
Chambers 89, 306
Chantrey 72
Chapman 291, 487-8
Chappell 183
Charity 88, 183, 449, 460-2
Charles I , King 61, 152, 154-5, 158, 646-7
Charles II, King 63, 98, 161, 163, 288
Charles, Prince 58, 61
Charlotte, Queen 72
Charlton 490
Charter 234
Chatburn 648
Childs 210
Chinnery 422
Chippendale 277-80
Chirac 301
Christian 280, 651, 655, 657
Church 299, 301
Church Missionary Society 313
Churchill 82-3
Clarendon, Earl of 63
Clark / Clarke 462-3
Clarkson 486-8
Clavering 173
Clay 412, 427
Clayton 198
Clayton and Shuttleworth 30, 36
Clements 183, 187, 196-7, 205, 447, 458
Clementson, John 267
Clough 410, 415, 421, 423, 430
Codrington 223
Coghill 240
Coldstream Guards 659
Cole 179, 369
Coleman 462
Collier 309-10
Collington 280
Collingwood 130
Colvin 482
Commons Select Committee 351

Conant 156, 166, 177, 184, 189-91, 308-09, 311, 313, 476-7
Cooke 305, 467
Cooper 485, 487
Corby 146
Corner 118
Corston 217
Corus 339
Costall 659
Cottesmore Hunt 29, 48, 178, 189, 237, 262
Cotton 280
Cornwall, Countess of 118
Council for the Preservation / Protection of Rural England 51, 350, 370
Country Landowners Association 350, 370
Countryside Commission 481
Coward 179
Cox 570
Cramp 223
Cranbrook, Lord 551
Crispe 57
Croden 171, 173, 349
Crofts 647
Cromwell 63, 159, 161, 290
Croson 449
Crouch 240
Crowe 353, 400, 482-3, 487, 491, 540, 631
Crowther-Beynon 103, 661-2
Crumbie 254
Crutchley 121
Culpin 267
Cumberland 449
Cundy 495
Cunnington 122, 132, 467
Dalby 97, 420
Dalton 610
Dambusters, The 339
Darnley, Earl of 74
Davies / Davis 240, 464
Dawson 238
Daynes 159
Deacon 372
Dean 403-05, 415
Deere 42
Degremont Laing 398
Denbigh, Earl of 61, 210
Dennis 240, 560, 591
Department of the Environment 403, 417
Deputy Lieutenant of Rutland 162, 169
Derby, Earl 307

Despenser 56
Dewar 240
Dexter 454, 655
Dickins 239
Digby 154
Dimbleby 168
Disraeli 145
Diver 415
Dixon 543
Doble 316
Dodds 421
Dodgson 119
Doherty 609
Dolby 457
Don 403
Dorman 454
Dormer 66
Downes 333
Drake 444-6, 448, 464-5, 467
Drummond-Burrell 239
East India Company 133, 235, 237
East Midlands Electricity Board 632
East Midlands Sports Council 481
East Midlands Young Liberals 356
Eaton 503, 506
Eayre 275
Eberlin 630
Ecgwulf 117
Ecob 421
Edith, Queen 93-4
Edith Weston Parish Council 116
Edward I, King 93-4, 149 433, 643-4
Edward III, King 425, 430, 433, 644
Edward IV, King 56, 59 151
Edward VI, King 97
Edward, Prince of Wales 246-7
Edwards 143, 221
Eisenhower 111
Eldon 239
Eleanor / Elenor, Queen 219, 310
Elizabeth I, Queen 57, 210
Elizabeth II, Queen 372, 559
Elizabeth, Queen, of Bohemia 58-9
Ellicott, Bishop 293-4
Ellingworth 103, 181
Elliott 122-3, 217, 222
Ellis 89
Ellis and Everard 296
Elrington 568
Emma, Queen 94
Emmerson 421
Empingham Parish Council 352, 354
Empingham Sick and Dividend Club 296
English Heritage 332, 338, 404, 415
English Nature 551-2

English Tourist Board 496-7
Ennis 282
Epery 656
Erik VII/XIII of Pomerania 430
Evans 113, 350, 355
Exeter, Lord / Marquis of 73, 75
Exton 131
Fairfax 63
Fancourt 280
Feilding 210
Felton 61
Ferguson 43
Fermor 72
Fernie Hunt 178
Ferrari 112
Ferrers / Ferris 151
Ferrier 30
Field 400, 484-5
Finch 61, 64-7, 69-73, 75, 79-85, 89, 91, 120-1, 123, 166, 177, 185, 193, 198, 202, 206-07, 307, 309-10, 323, 652
Finch-Hatton 79
Fitzwilliam, Earl 48, 50
Flore / Flower 97, 150, 286-8
Forbes 240
Ford 483, 491-2
Forestry Commission 482
Forsyth 30
Foster 48
Fowler 29, 41, 183
Fox Talbot [Museum] 100-01
Fraunchhomme 95
Frederick, Elector Palatine 58
Freeman 205, 444, 648, 650-1
Freer / Freere / Frere 88, 234, 288, 290, 650
Freestone 185-6, 267-8, 447-9, 457, 462
French 240
Friend 616
Fry 489
Fryer 198-200, 207, 215, 223, 225, 453-4, 456-7, 467, 469-70
Fuller 60
Furley & Hassan 470
Gainsborough, Earl of 29, 32, 46, 59, 65, 291, 295, 326-8, 335
Gainsborough, Lady 73, 297
Gallop 240
Galpin 587
Garrett 485
George I, King 70
George II, King 71
George III, King 72, 75, 79, 193, 652
George IV, King 72, 179

George V, King 211, 223
George, Prince of Wales 72, 79
Gibson 470
Gilbert of Ghent 56
Gleeson 381
Gloucester, Bishop of 293
Godwin, Earl of Wessex 94
Goldsmith 135
Goodband 86
Gooding 400
Goodrick 479
Gordon 239, 592
Gorin 415-18, 420
Gourley 372
Grant 280, 651
Gray 625
Greane / Green 162, 219
Gregory 123, 130, 183, 290, 421, 458-9, 467
Grenadier Guards 189
Greneham 232
Grey, Lord 62
Griffin 124, 259, 319, 478, 499
Griffiths 487
Groom of the Stole 79, 193
Guest 82
Guy 122, 136
Hack 223
Hackett 297
Haggard 182
Haggitt 175
Haig 279
Haines 91, 325, 330
Hales 492
Halford / Holford 70, 98-100
Hall 291, 367
Halliday 183
Hamilton 52, 302, 492, 602
Hammond 132
Hanbury 85-8, 448
Harborough, Earl of 225
Hardcastle 448-9
Harden 485
Harder 488
Hardy 101, 103, 418-19
Harington / Harrington / Haryngton 57-60, 62, 151, 154, 156-8, 197-8, 205, 207, 209, 288
Harman 406
Harold 93-4
Harris 267, 495
Harrison 234, 254
Harrison and Dunn 296
Hart 189, 281, 314, 470
Hartley 45, 494
Hartoppe, Lady 234

Harvey 183
Hasley 287
Hatton 64, 69, 79
Hawksley 312, 369, 371-3
Haywood 223, 632
Healey 255, 267, 301, 403-04, 415, 454-5, 649
Hearth 488
Heathcote 100, 133, 135-8, 140-7, 173, 177, 214, 223, 225-6, 231, 233, 235-7, 239-40, 244, 269, 271, 273-4, 273, 277-81, 309, 316, 470, 495, 644
Heathcote-Drummond-Willoughby 239-40, 308, 470
Heaton 234
Henderson 482-96
Henfrey 122
Henrietta Maria, Princess 646
Henrietta Maria, Queen 61
Henry I, King 94, 211
Henry III, King 96
Henry VIII, King 97, 118, 151, 232, 286
Henry, Prince 58-9
Henton 455
Herbert Lapworth 372
Herne 157
Hibbitt 146, 183, 454
Hicks 59, 59, 288
Hill 74, 85, 88, 90, 136, 280, 456-7
Hippisley 166, 173, 650
Hives 131
Hoare 188-9, 356
Holler 156
Horn 457
Horswill 381
Horton 63
Hoskins 19-20, 60
Hospital of St John & St Anne, Oakham 97
Hoston 232
House of Commons 61, 70
Howard 84
Howcraft 68
Howell 400-01
Howlett 45, 55, 93, 149, 283, 529
Hoyles 449, 458
Hozier 82
Hubbard 118, 120
Hudson 61, 162, 239, 646-7
Hunter 499
Hutton 499, 503
Institute of Geological Sciences 380
Institution of Civil Engineers 369
International Federation of Disabled

Sailors (IFDS) 634-5
Ireland 183, 449, 464
Irons 644-5
Isaac 291
Islip 99
James I, King 57-8, 61, 152-3
James II, King 69, 71
Jardine 298
Jenkins 183
Johnson 183, 191
Jolley 576
Jones 47, 359, 656
Judd 332, 360
Judith 13
Justice of the Peace 98, 185
Juxon 220
Kelly 108
Kelso 118
Kelway 57
Kington 663
Kinleside 294
Knight / Knights 37, 39, 41-2, 265, 352, 354-5, 400, 472-3, 487, 489-90, 493, 496, 659
Knights Hospitaller 285
Knights of the Shire 166
Lacy 136
Laird 25
Laity 458
Land 297
Lane 89, 90
Langford 400, 489
Lanscroon 67
Lapsle 494
Laurant 240
Lavender 177
Layfield 62
Leach 276
Lee 133, 661
Legg 327
Leicester Tigers Rugby Football Club 254
Leicester University 95, 411, 421
Leicestershire & Rutland Ornithological Society 551
Leicestershire & Rutland Wildlife Trust 53, 484, 519, 529, 551, 555, 556, 573, 587, 589, 591, 645
Leicestershire Archaeological Unit 427
Leicestershire County Council 484, 631
Leicestershire Museums 284, 415, 422, 572
Leicestershire Yeomanry 217
Lesiakowski 485
Levisohn 503

Lewington 571
Lewis 351, 356, 372
Lincoln Record Office 277
Lisette 295
Lock / Locke 217, 466, 471-3, 488
Longsett / Longfoote 119
Lord 74
Lord Lieutenant of Lincoln 271
Lord Lieutenant of Rutland 75, 162, 169, 193, 223
Lord Mayor of London 133, 235, 239
Love 197, 208, 464
Loveday 153
Lovering 636
Lowe 416, 618
Lucas 97, 99-101, 103
Ludgrove 183, 475
Lumley 66, 205, 649, 651
Lumsden 494
Lustig 356
Lyne 201
McAdam 480
MacArthur 628
McKinn 223
Mackrill 561-2, 592-3
Mackworth 133, 232-4
Macmillan 111
Mahany 410, 415, 421
Maitland 618
Malson 234
Manchester 469, 471
Mandeville 240
Manners 60, 239
Manton Parish Council 115
Marriatt / Marriott 183, 450, 480
Marshall 107, 178, 181-2, 661
Martin 87
Mary, Queen 71, 223
Mary, Queen of Scots 210
Mason 183
Masters 325
Matthews 112-3, 352
Maw 452
May 48, 418-19
Meadows 120, 129, 183
Mellish 88
Melton Mowbray Fire Brigade 83
Members of Parliament, 80-1, 135-6, 161, 155, 233, 235, 237, 239, 307, 351
Merchant Venturers 122, 124, 133
Merricks 634, 636-7, 640
Merritt 356
Meryll 232
Messenger 520, 540
Messing 54

Metropolitan Water Board 389
Mid-Northamptonshire Water Board see Anglian Water
Miller 499
Mills 308, 333
Mitcham 507, 509, 556-7, 575
Mitchell 204, 271
Moles 234
Monck 161
Montgomery 81
Moore 428, 481, 485, 498, 501, 510, 601
Mould 129, 470
Moynihan, Lord 487
Muirhead 240
Musson 154, 165
Mytens 647
Nadir 86
Nailer / Naillour 232, 285
Napoleon 173
Nash 78
National Archives, The 187
National Farmers Union 350, 370
National Institute of Sport 638
Natural History Museum 428
Nature Conservancy Council 481
Naval Brigade 123
Neal / Neale 66, 125, 222
Needham 173, 175, 201-04, 128, 453, 545, 650
Neville 406
Nevinson 311-12
Newhaven 240
Newman 137, 140, 263, 267
Newton 169
New Town Development Corporations 349
Nicholls 136, 267, 278
Nicole of Canterbury 430
Nightingale 659
Nixon 199
Noble 183, 457
Noel 41, 46, 59, 62, 64, 69-70, 161-2, 177, 288-91, 327-8
Noel Edwards 122
Norman 309
Norman & Hewitt 470
Norman Coleman Waterfield and Jarrom 227
Normanton Tower Trust 275, 277, 373, 495-6
Normanville 233
North Atlantic Treaty Organisation (NATO) 105
Nottingham, Earl of 65, 67-9, 71-3, 75, 80

Nourish 35, 42
Novo Castro 269
Nuttall 377, 389
Oakham Rural District Council 307
O'Brien 41
O'Connor 108
Oddie 529, 557
Oglanby 400
Ormond / Ormonde 174-5, 177
Orpin 133
Orr-Ewing 183
Osborn 125, 127
Ostler 527
Oswald 186
Ovens 117, 193, 211, 231, 315, 369, 415, 445, 529, 601, 643
Overseers of the Poor 175, 202, 204
Overton / Ouerton 57, 232
Owen 238
Paget 651, 655
Palmer 71, 161, 167-8, 170-8, 289, 403-04, 420
Park 556, 560
Parker 172, 183, 280-5, 474-5, 530
Parkes 406
Parkinson 27, 31
Parr 97
Peach 136-7
Peakirk Wildfowl and Wetlands Trust, Peterborough 529
Pearson 616
Peat 130
Peddler 491
Peel Shaw 112
Penman 50-1
Perkins 136
Petit 57
Pettifer 131
Petty 157
Pevsner 60
Phillips 185, 217, 470, 651
Phipps 82
Pick, Everard, Keay & Gimson 484
Pile 240
Pinder 292-5
Plumb 275, 281, 314, 496
Polish Air Force 104
Polytoy 223
Poole 159
Pope 133, 233
Postles 95
Poulteney 66
Preston 132, 183
Pridmore 546
Primrose League 145
Prince 240

Prince of Wales 29, 72, 79, 138, 143, 246-7, 260, 262, 314, 319
Prince Philip, Duke of Edinburgh 559
Princess Christina of Spain 635
Princess of Wales 138, 143, 246-7, 260, 262, 314, 319
Prisoners of War 123, 187, 259
Purbeck 64
Pye 157
Quarles 153-4
Queen Mother 39
Quorn Hunt 48, 178
Rainbow 240, 491, 495
Ranze 157
Ratcliffe 300
Rayner 239
Ream 240
Record Office for Leicester, Leicestershire & Rutland 156, 219, 421
Rector of Lyndon 306, 311-13
Reeve / Reeves 197, 217, 240, 303, 459
Renner 267
Repton 75-8, 90-1, 242, 270, 316-9, 323-4, 326-9, 333
Reynolds 287
Ricard of Durham 430
Richard de Whitwell 286
Richard of York 56
Richards 97
Ridlington 167
Rippon 130
Risi 115
Robert of Canterbury 430
Robarts / Roberts 198, 456
Robertson 267
Robinson 183, 226, 351, 476
Rockingham, Marquess of 71
Rogers 530, 534, 559, 564, 573-4
Rogerson 26
Rolfe 240
Ross 157, 240
Rott 650
Rowlate 644
Royal Agricultural Benevolent Institution 313
Royal Air Force 105, 111, 113-5, 635, 639, 641
Royal Air Force Motor Sport Association 111-2
Royal Air Force squadrons 104-5, 107
Royal Canadian Air Force 105, 107-8, 110, 217
Royal Navy 71, 217
Royal Society 169, 663

Royal Society for the Prevention of Cruelty to Birds 552, 584
Royal Yachting Association 625, 631, 638, 640
Royce 29, 144, 176, 470-1
Rudd 661
Ruddle 355
Ruker 108
Rupert, Prince 62
Russell 170, 174
Rutherford 464
Rutland County Council 115, 344, 350, 355, 370, 413, 463, 479, 483, 626, 631, 633
Rutland County Museum 38, 284, 300, 403, 410, 415, 417, 419, 421-3, 429, 456, 648
Rutland District Society of Ratepayers and Residents 356
Rutland, Earl of 60
Rutland Field Research Group for Archaeology and History 152, 286, 410-11, 415, 421-2, 432, 447, 455, 459, 467
Rutland Home Guard 188
Rutland Lions Club 551
Rutland Local History & Record Society 422
Rutland Memorial Hospital 618
Rutland Militia 79, 97-8, 121-2, 129, 659
Rutland Natural History Society 90, 499-527, 529-30, 549, 556
Rutland Sailability 533, 635
Rutland Sailing Club 116, 448, 484, 488-9, 497, 533-5, 604, 623, 625-641
Rutland Sixth Form College 356
Rutland Society for Industry 75, 194
Rutland Water Users Panel 490
Ryder 13
Rysbrack 235
Sandford 419
Sapcote 56-7, 168, 170
Sargent 179
Sawday 434
Saxton 280
Schofield 264
Scott 129, 137, 529, 557
Segrave 56
Seaton 119, 126, 128, 488, 498, 618
Sellars 504
Senior 298, 422
Servante 183
Severn-Trent Water Authority 398, 632

Sharman 405
Sharp / Sharpe 38-9, 130, 183, 187, 449-51, 455-6, 474
Shaw 448, 464, 609
Shelton 122, 130, 265, 450
Sherard, Lord 69, 70, 166, 232, 288
Sheriffs of Rutland 98, 156, 178, 184-5, 219, 233, 661
Sherwood 232
Shilaker 655
Simms 575
Simpson 175
Skellett 183
Skillington 280
Skinner 400
Skirth 84
Sleath 117, 193, 211, 231, 315, 369, 415, 445, 601, 643
Smale 466
Smith / Smyth / Smythe 119, 183, 210, 218-221, 223, 232, 280, 372, 462, 466-7, 569, 649
Soil Mechanics 380, 382
Somerset, Lady 80
South Lincoln militia 271
Spell 159
Spence 255
Springthorpe 291-7, 300, 447
Sports Council 631, 634-5
Stacey 267
Stamp 31
Starkey 113
Stephens 280
Stevyn 232
Stewart 329, 457
Stewarts and Lloyds 329
Stimpson / Stimson 122, 128, 174, 650
Stokes 414
Stone 240
Storey 280
Storges / Sturges 162, 165
Street 223
Strickland 188
Stubbs 280
Suckling 286
Suitor / Sutor 444, 654
Sutons / Sutton 162, 165, 280
Swaffeld 232
Swanson 206-07, 466
Swetbon 232
Switzer 326
Syson 142
Tailor / Taillor / Taylor 144, 209, 217-19, 232, 234
Tallis 310

Tampion 233
Tankerville 94
Telford 216, 332, 341, 480
Thatcher 301
Theobold 191
Thom 492
Thomas 298, 300-01, 418
Thompson / Tomson 120, 122, 129, 649-50
Thoresby 430
Thorpe 229
Thring 335
Throsby 123
Tibbert 102, 113, 444-5, 463-5, 467
Tilton 232
Tindall 400
Tirrell 120
Todd 409, 415, 422
Tollemache 80
Tomlinson 226
Topps 306
Towell 120, 125, 464
Townsend 113
Traylen 98, 144
Trent, Lord 187-8
Trolley 137
Tryon 21, 133, 183-6, 189, 233, 239, 447, 466, 588
Tuxford 26
Tween 183
Tyers 467
Tyler 182, 512
Tymson 119,
Umfraville 150, 233, 441
United Steel Company 32
University of Leicester 415, 434
University of Leicester Archaeological Services (ULAS) 434
University of Nottingham 415
Urmeston 57
Van Dyck 62, 155
Vanbrugh 326
Verrio 67
Victoria, Queen 177
Villiers 59, 60-3, 151, 158, 323
Vine 198, 234
Vulliamy 99-100
Wade 136, 183, 219, 224, 455-6, 466, 470
Wadham 611, 618
Wadkin 457
Waite 62, 158-9, 161
Wakefield 267-8
Wakerley 183, 475-6
Walcott 156
Walker 205, 232, 240, 336-7, 480, 636

Walpole 70
Waltheof, Earl 285
War Agricultural Committee 32
War Office 372
Ward 118, 122, 173, 280, 450, 454-5, 618
Warren 568
Wass 186
Watkin 467
Watson 372, 373
Watson Hawksley 373-2
Watt 273, 277
Weaver 102
Webb 479
Weed 146, 265
Weir 495-6
Welch 510
Weldon 204-5, 209, 444, 648-51
Welland & Nene Fisheries & Recreation Committee 485
Welland & Nene River Authority see Anglian Water
Wellington, Duke of 79
Wentworth-Fitzwilliam 50
West 268, 447, 449
Westland 180, 188
Weston 615
Wheatley 636
Whiston 169
White 169, 239, 291
Whitehouse 306
Whittingham 217
Whittington 588
Wilcox 127
Wild 33-4, 179-81, 183-4, 187-8, 190-1
Wildfowl and Wetlands Trust, Slimbridge Gloucs 529
William I, King 13, 93-4, 150
William II, King 94
William III, King 64-5
William IV, King 72
Williams 650-1
Williamson 183, 471
Willoughby d'Eresby 138, 237, 239, 261, 264, 496-7
Wilson 108
Wimpey 105
Winchilsea, Earl of 71-5, 76-80, 89, 121-2, 128, 173, 193-4, 196-9, 203-5, 207-9, 236, 323, 327, 337, 446, 459, 649, 652, 654
Winder 369, 371-3
Wing 21-2, 63, 241
Winkles 66
Winterton 467
Wise Woman of Wing 655-6

Wolsey 118, 151, 232
Women's Auxiliary Air Force 630
Womens' Land Army 123, 187, 297
Wood 176
Woodard 234
Woodcock 655-7
Woodland 434
Woods 130, 203
Woolf 569

Wortley 41
Wren 66
Wright 55, 60, 93, 220-1, 312, 471, 518, 597-8
Wykley 287
Wyles 280
Yates 264
York, Duke of 79, 151
Yorke 239

General Index

Abberton Reservoir, Essex 554
Abbey of St George de Boscherville 94, 97
Agricultural changes 22, 24-44, 172
Agriculture 13-44
Agriculture, medieval farming systems 13-19, 24, 40, 96, 149-50
Aircraft types 104-08, 110-11, 113-14, 339
Airfields 187
Algae 353, 560
Alien priory cell 94-5
Allexton, Leics 316
Alstoe 56, 439
Amphibian species 556
Ancaster Estate 146-7, 308, 324
Ancaster style 139-40, 147, 264
Anglo-Saxon archaeology 93, 285, 403-05, 407, 415-16, 418-19
Arboretum and drought garden 52, 492-3
Archaeology in the Gwash Valley 284, 402-443
Armley Wood 45, 159, 375, 500-01, 513, 519, 522, 524-5, 566, 582, 621
Ashbourne, Derbys 221
Ashwell 187, 225, 227, 300, 318
Ashwell prison 303, 404, 421, 564
Aylsham, Norfolk 242
Bakewell, Derbys 221
Bark Temple 337-8
Barleythorpe 655
Barnack, Lincs 407, 649
Barnsdale 4, 28, 45-54, 289, 329, 364, 397, 455, 472-3, 514, 578, 583
Barnsdale Creek 482
Barnsdale deer park 45, 52, 289
Barnsdale Drought Garden 492-3, 602
Barnsdale Gardens 45, 52-4, 354
Barnsdale Hall 45-6, 50-2, 528
Barnsdale Hill 46, 50-1, 323, 353, 376, 479-80, 528, 642
Barnsdale houses 479

Barnsdale Lodge 45, 52
Barnsdale Wood 45-9, 53-2, 375, 499-501, 516, 518-19, 524-5, 527, 566, 582
Barrowden 137, 320
Barrowden Church 316
Barrowden pond 346
Barrowden watermill 321
Basildon, Essex 482
Battle of Alma 659
Battle of Britain 106
Battle of Hastings 93-4, 149
Battle of Jutland 123
Battle of Worcester 63
Beaumont Chase 316
Belmesthorpe 317
Belt, The 479
Belton House, Lincs 165
Belton in Rutland 316, 343
Belvoir Castle 58, 60, 154
Benwick Hall, Herts 221
Bird hides 537, 549-52, 554, 572, 603
Bird migration 575-6, 578, 580, 583, 585
Bird Race 556-7
Bird ringing 585
Bird species 91-2, 309, 335, 503, 506-9, 511, 530, 532-3, 538, 541-4, 546-8, 552-5, 559, 562, 566-8, 570-75, 577-86, 589, 591, 596
Bird surveys 503, 506, 508
Birdfair 124, 354, 557, 567-71, 602
Birdwatching Centre 282, 354, 488, 555, 494, 557-9, 573, 603
Birmingham 229
Bishop's Frome, Herefordshire 240
Blagdon, Somerset 240
Blenheim Palace, Oxon 133, 336
Bloodhound missile 110, 112
Boer War 312
Borrow pits 379-81, 383-5, 478, 535
Borth, Wales 345
Boston, Lincs 136, 342, 430

Botanical surveys 518-9, 521-2, 524, 526-7
Bourne, Lincs 146, 404, 410, 436-7, 443
Brake Spinney 192, 317, 359, 375, 459, 500, 503, 513-14
Brampton, Hunts 372
Broadeng bridge, Stamford, Lincs 316
Braunston 317-18, 341, 345-6
Brentingby, Leics 341, 471
Bridges 113, 262, 316-17, 328, 331, 358-9, 368, 414, 444, 480, 499, 501, 503, 505, 512-13, 515, 518-23, 522-6, 528, 531, 603
Bristol, Avon 122, 124, 133, 529, 575
Bronze Age 192, 402, 412-13
Brooke 117, 317-18, 320, 323
Bull Bridge 262, 359, 368, 398, 501, 503, 512-13, 521-3, 525, 531
Bull Brig (Brigg) Lane 22, 283-4, 286, 300, 302, 352, 368
Bulwick, Northants 184-5, 233
Bunkers Hill 314
Burghley House, Stamford, Lincs 58, 75, 221, 290
Burley 20, 55-92, 120, 151-2, 166, 193, 196-7, 303, 306, 310, 323, 337, 501-02, 583, 659
Burley Church 56, 72, 80
Burley cricket team 74, 80
Burley Estate 20, 55, 60, 63-4, 76, 85, 88-9, 121, 124, 198, 204-05, 207, 333, 311, 333, 335, 448, 456
Burley Fishponds 90-2, 183, 220, 317, 323, 325, 333-5, 340, 346-7, 353, 480, 485, 510-11, 514-16, 519-21, 524-6, 530, 532, 538, 541-2, 554, 560, 564-5, 572, 584-5, 590, 642
Burley Hermitage 78, 653-4
Burley houses and farms 78, 84, 89-91, 306, 333, 335
Burley Hovel 565
Burley on the Hill 55, 58-60, 62-8, 70,

— 674 —

72-5, 79-82, 84-8, 90-2, 120, 128, 156, 158, 173, 193, 242, 262, 307, 309, 335, 588, 646, 652-3, 659
Burley on the Hill fire 67, 82-3
Burley on the Hill gates 78, 60, 91, 333, 335
Burley on the Hill, Repton's Red Book 76-8, 91, 333-4
Burley Post Office 89
Burley school 89-90
Burley Vicarage 85, 90
Burley washdyke 346-7
Burley water meadows 335, 519, 526-7
Burley Wood 71, 90-2, 375-6, 499-500, 514-15, 518-19, 582-3, 642, 653-4
Burton Lazars, Leics 132
Burton on Trent, Staffs 210
Bury St Edmunds, Suffolk 242
Butterfly and Aquatic Centre 354, 495, 574, 609
Caldecott 23, 213, 315-16, 320, 339, 344
Cambridge 80, 169, 228
Canterbury, Kent 429-30
Canterbury Mint 29-30
Carsington Reservoir, Derbys 351
Catterick, North Yorks 372
Cattle Grid Road 444
Catton Park, Derbys 242
Caythorpe, Lincs 240
Chantry Act 286
Chartley, Staffs 210
Chatsworth, Derbys 165
Chelmsford, Essex 240
Chelsea, London 240
Chesterfield, Derbys 133, 233, 344
Chew Lake, Avon 481
Chilvers Coton, Warks 436
Chingford, Essex 100
Chipping Campden, Gloucs 59
Church bells 114, 310-111
Church Bridge 317, 378, 512
Churchstanton, Somerset 240
Civil Wars (English) 21, 46, 62, 63-4, 98, 118, 120, 154-5, 158-9, 161-3, 220, 288, 290, 333
Clipsham 66, 337
Coat of arms 141
Cocked Hat Spinney 261, 375, 500
Coggeshall, Essex 161
Colchester, Essex 419
Cold Overton, Leics 318
Cold War 105
Coleorton, Leics 588
Collyweston, Northants 109, 210, 316, 453, 472

Colsterworth, Lincs 378
Coombe Abbey, Warks 57-8, 60, 598
Corby Glen, Lincs 265
Corby, Northants 31, 339, 369
Cottesmore 60, 317, 346-7, 651
Coventry, Warks 43, 97, 217, 268, 598
Cowes, Isle of Wight 625
Crich, Derbys 387
Cricket 74, 300, 312
Crieff, Scotland 240
Crimean War 659
Cuckoo Spinney 317, 336
Cycling 283, 489-90, 497, 606
Daventry, Northants 369
D-Day landings 339
Deeping, Lincs 650
Deserted medieval villages 317-8, 210
Diddington, Cambs 372
Dissolution of Monasteries 97, 286
Domesday Book 13-6, 56, 93, 117, 149-50, 211, 285, 319-20, 441
Don't Dam Rutland campaign 349-57, 575
Dove Water Scheme 345
Draycote Water, Warks 576
Driffield, Derbys 111
Duddington, Northants 316
Earith, Hunts 656
Earthmoving machines 12, 383-5
East Dean, Sussex 240
Easton-on-the-Hill, Northants 136
Edenham, Lincs 238, 240, 273
Eder Dam, Germany 339
Edinburgh, Scotland 240
Edith Weston 93-116, 149, 157, 167, 205, 210, 219, 240, 251, 272, 283-4, 298, 300, 303, 306, 353, 359, 368, 423, 422, 444, 448, 488, 519-22, 533, 630, 634, 648, 652, 661, 663-4
Edith Weston Church 93, 95, 97-8, 114, 235, 273-5, 281, 328
Edith Weston customs 103, 662
Edith Weston fishponds 94-6
Edith Weston Hall 98-99, 101-02
Edith Weston manor 94, 103
Edith Weston parish registers 648
Edith Weston Park 101
Edith Weston population 99, 102, 104
Edith Weston Priory 94-8
Edith Weston public houses 109, 112, 116
Edith Weston school 103-04, 111, 115, 146
Edith Weston village hall 281
Edmondthorpe, Leics 341
Egleton 85, 117-32, 159, 193, 282,

292, 303, 305, 310, 319, 353, 412, 414, 423, 464, 470, 476, 484, 534-8, 572, 579, 585, 648, 655, 657
Egleton Church 117-18, 120, 224
Egleton early taxes 118, 127
Egleton fields 28, 120, 562
Egleton houses and farms 118-132, 305
Egleton manor 65, 69
Egleton Post Office 127, 130
Egleton school 123, 125, 131, 308-9
Egleton surveys 118-19
Egleton toll gate 122
Egleton to Nether Hambleton road 282, 537-8
Egleton village hall 123, 308-9
Egleton windmill 120
Elton, Hunts 649
Empingham 26, 31, 40, 43, 133-48, 175, 238, 241, 244, 251, 255, 261, 264, 295, 303-04, 306, 310, 314, 317, 319-20, 322, 325-6, 343-4, 350, 353, 361, 369-70, 372-3, 375, 383, 385, 389-93, 398, 400-01, 403-04, 409, 417-20, 478, 496, 499, 501-2, 504, 518, 520, 643, 648-9
Empingham archaeology 391, 403, 405-8, 416-17, 419-20
Empingham Audit Hall 142, 144, 146, 420
Empingham cemetery 256, 413
Empingham Chapel 144, 343
Empingham Church 144, 286, 343
Empingham enclosure 134, 136
Empingham Heath 236, 643-4
Empingham houses and farms 27, 134, 139-143, 344, 403, 407, 420
Empingham manor 233
Empingham Post Office 139
Empingham public houses 142, 644, 344
Empingham Pumped Storage Project 352, 369-70, 379
Empingham pumping station 348, 379, 392
Empingham Reading Room / Primrose Hall 144-5
Empingham school 103, 143, 146, 265, 309-10
Empingham tithe barn 18
Empingham village hall 142
Empingham water supplies 144, 343-5
Empingham watermill 317
Enclosure 19-20, 164
Essendine 318
Etton, Cambs 486

European Bird Directive 532
Evacuees 123, 187
Exton 45-7, 54, 57, 59, 65, 151, 159, 175, 197, 288-90, 295, 300-01, 329, 420, 660-1
Exton Avenue 52
Exton Church 59
Exton Hall 59, 289 317, 336-7, 588
Exton Hall Farm 29
Exton Old Hall 59
Exton Park and Estate 31-2, 46, 52, 58, 62, 291, 298, 317-8, 336-7, 340, 560, 588
Exton school 329
Exton water supply 345
Eye Brook 315-16, 318, 320, 339
Eye Brook Reservoir 316, 333, 339-40, 575-6, 579
Falcon Hotel 229
Families displaced 445-479
Farming activities 26, 32-5, 36-7, 40-4, 187, 309-10
Farming equipment 32, 34-9, 41-3, 190
Farming livestock 29, 34, 38, 40, 53, 172, 562-3
Fauna and flora 518, 499-527
Feltwell, Norfolk 111
Fireworks 236, 652
First World War 30-1, 36, 84, 123, 132, 185, 229, 292, 297, 300, 306
Fish species 113, 330, 332, 335, 339, 484-7, 503, 510-1, 560, 586, 588, 592, 610, 612-3, 615-7, 623-4
Fishing competitions 487, 533, 535, 492, 617
Fishing Lodge 339, 489, 492, 618, 623
Fishing, bank fishing 535, 611, 613, 620-1, 622-3
Fishing, boat fishing 535, 623-4, 627-9, 633-6
Fishing, coarse fishing 617
Fishing, fly fishing 113, 484, 613-15, 617-20
Fishing, general 611-624
Fishponds 94-6, 113, 317, 326, 329-34, 353, 358, 499-500, 510-11, 513-16, 519-22, 524-6, 530, 532, 538, 541-2, 560, 564-5, 572, 584-5
Fishponds Bay 348
Flore's Manor, Little Hambleton 152
Folkestone, Kent 372
Fort Henry 317, 336-8
Fort Henry Lakes 317, 333, 336-8
Fosdyke Bridge, Lincs 316
Fossils 365-7, 419

Foster's Bridge 520
Fotheringhay, Northants 210
Fox Bridge 480, 515, 519, 525-6, 528
Fox hunting 30, 48, 152, 178-80, 214, 228
Fungi 90, 527
Gainsborough Estate 298
Geological Ages 360-1, 361, 363, 365
Geological formations 323, 360-7, 369, 374, 377, 380-1, 383-4, 386-7, 389, 391, 398-9, 428-9, 431
Geological surveys / investigations 360-1, 370
Geology 289, 323, 359-367
Gibbet Gorse 375, 446, 514, 537-8, 583, 564, 651-2
Gibbet Lane 444, 500, 513-4, 518, 630, 652
Glaston 192, 212, 346, 663
Gosport, Hants 112
Grafham Water, Cambs 76, 372-3, 481, 484, 492-3, 576
Grantham, Lincs 353, 404, 486, 489, 661
Great Casterton 30, 37, 39, 41, 317, 407, 413
Great North Road (A1) 154, 317, 336, 407-8
Great Ouse, Norfolk 510, 576
Great Stretton, Leics 210
Great Tower, by Alexander 354
Greetham 60, 65, 69, 193, 295, 317, 320, 336, 448, 480
Gretton, Northants 663
Grimsby, Lincs 326
Grimsthorpe Castle, Lincs 138, 146, 237-9, 250-1, 261, 273
Groby, Leics 62
Guildford, Surrey 80
Gunthorpe 20, 219, 222, 303, 317, 501-02, 504, 520-1
Gunthorpe Hall 223
Gwash valley (*also see* River Gwash) 115, 124, 149, 159, 176-8, 182, 231, 242-3, 273, 298, 322, 326, 349, 351-2, 359, 363-5, 367, 403, 413-4, 416, 431, 445, 462, 475-6, 495, 499, 501, 512, 514, 518-9, 529, 574
Gwash valley agriculture 25
Gwash valley archaeology 15-16, 192, 284, 411, 413, 415-16
Gwash valley geology 322, 359-367
Half Moon Spinney 150, 191, 358, 375, 583
Hambleton (*also see* Hambleton, Upper, Middle & Lower) 25, 34,

60, 89, 93, 115, 149-191, 196-9, 201, 203-6, 208-9, 224, 282, 286, 290, 292, 306, 310, 323, 352-3, 356, 423, 430, 449, 454, 456, 462-3, 468, 475, 514, 519, 522, 527, 535, 551, 577, 586, 616, 642, 648, 650-2, 654-5, 657, 660-1, 663-4
Hambleton agriculture 23, 167, 171, 186, 190
Hambleton Bridge 414, 444
Hambleton Church 93, 150, 164, 175, 177-8, 202, 204, 206
Hambleton enclosure 21, 160, 164
Hambleton fields 159, 163, 168, 170-1, 175, 182-3, 196-7, 200, 202, 204, 206, 208-09, 441, 456, 462, 464, 477
Hambleton Hall 168, 177-81, 183-5, 187-9, 660-1
Hambleton manor 65, 69, 149-1, 152-3, 158-9, 164, 166, 183, 211, 441
Hambleton May Day 180-1, 185
Hambleton New Hall 661
Hambleton Old Hall 150, 153-4, 156-7, 160-3, 166-8, 171-2, 174-8, 183-4, 186, 189-91, 612
Hambleton parish registers 173-4, 446, 463, 467
Hambleton Peninsula 23, 26, 97, 149-50, 361, 411-12, 422, 482, 497, 535
Hambleton population and occupations 122, 149, 172, 177, 180-3
Hambleton Post Office 181-3, 188, 457
Hambleton public house 166-7, 183, 187
Hambleton rents, taxes and tithes 151-2, 171, 186, 462, 456
Hambleton schools 178, 180-1, 198, 233, 448, 461-2
Hambleton surveys and valuations 21, 455, 173, 195, 202, 204, 206, 208-9
Hambleton toll bar (Fishpond Bar), 480
Hambleton Wood 317, 500, 513, 515, 518-19, 521-22, 524, 566, 582-3
Hambleton, Little 150, 152
Hambleton, Lower (Nether) 28, 38, 183, 187, 191, 193-209, 282, 323, 360, 375, 403, 410, 414-5, 421, 423, 430, 434, 438-43, 445-468, 516-17, 519, 521, 525, 538, 648
Hambleton, Lower (Nether), archaeology 24, 151-2, 410, 421-43, 447, 468

Hambleton, Lower (Nether), public house 200, 203
Hambleton, Middle 27-8, 196, 445, 469, 474, 477, 176, 178, 191, 323, 376, 414, 423, 446, 461, 463, 468, 472, 475, 475, 476, 530
Hambleton, named houses and farms 27, 33-4, 38, 179, 376, 181, 183-5. 187-9, 191, 193-209, 224, 317, 350, 421, 423, 445-77, 524, 537
Hambleton, Upper 28, 150-1, 153, 163, 180, 188, 191, 193, 196, 199, 202, 204, 209, 304-5, 364, 423, 445-6, 458, 461, 463, 468, 474, 480
Hampton Court, London 67
Hannington Service Reservoir, Northants 325, 348
Harlow, Essex 482
Harringworth, Northants 212
Harrow, Middx 80
Hastings, East Sussex 100
Hearth Taxes 162, 290
Helmsley, Yorks 65
Herbal remedies 658
High Bridge 414, 444
High Bridge Road 414
Highways and byways 60, 91, 119, 123-27, 130, 132, 154, 353, 380
Hobbs Bridge 414
Holywell Hall, Lincs 188
Horn 300, 317-18, 320, 336
Horn Fair / Tin-panning 662-3
Horn Mill fish farm 484-5, 591
Horn watermill 317, 320, 336, 481, 484-5, 591
Houghton on the Hill, Leics 210
Howells Inlet 393, 401
Hudds Mill, Stamford 316
Hungerford, Berks 240
Hunstanton, Norfolk 180
Hunting lodges 48, 50, 214,
Husbands Bosworth, Leics 315
Ice Age 381
Insect species 90-1, 503, 512-18, 527, 556, 562, 574, 612-3, 616
Insect surveys 512, 514, 516
Iron Age 56, 284, 409, 412, 415, 284
Iron smelting 412
Jubilee Lodge, Ridlington 323-4
Kenilworth, Warks 240
Kensington House, London 64
Kettering, Northants 227, 229, 340
Ketton 136, 146, 161, 210, 225, 316-7, 320, 431, 478, 643
Ketton Heath 643-4
Ketton stone 66, 95, 365, 478

Kielder Water, Nthumb 351
Kirby Hall, Northants 64
Knebworth, Herts 240
Knossington, Leics 255
Lacock Abbey, Wilts 101
Lady Ann Harington Dole 197-8, 205, 207, 209
Ladysmith, Siege and Relief 312
Lagoons 348, 376, 530, 535, 538, 541, 548-9, 554, 581, 584, 586
Lamington, Scotland 240
Land Tax 291
Land Utilisation Survey of Great Britain 31
Landscape design 16, 76, 359, 445, 482, 540, 576
Langham 35, 42, 318
Langham Church 117
Langham nursing home 463
Langham Old Hall 257
Launde Abbey, Leics 316
Lax Hill 26, 28, 200, 217, 423, 472, 514-16, 524-5, 530-1, 545, 551, 560, 577, 591-2, 599
Lay Subsidies 150, 232
Leicester 62, 210, 229-9, 308, 393, 418, 436-7, 462
Leigh Lodge, Leighfield 170, 323, 325
Leighfield 316, 448
Leisure pursuits 283, 354, 481, 484, 488-9, 493, 497, 501, 533-5, 567, 575, 586, 601-611
Lesswade, Scotland 240
Leytonstone, Essex 273
Lichfield, Staffs 62
Limnological tower 368, 397-8
Lincoln 271, 286
Little Bytham, Lincs 174
Little Casterton 42, 317
Little Eye 316
Liverpool 108, 240
Loch Garten, Scotland 589
Loddington, Northants 185
London 21-22, 39, 58, 61, 63, 67, 69, 71-2, 74-5, 78, 94, 124, 135, 157, 162, 169, 171, 184, 199, 208, 214, 220-1, 227-8, 229, 240, 298, 337, 372, 407, 467, 483, 652
London cricket grounds 74
London Mint 30
Lord of the Manor 17-8, 319
Lost homes 38, 445-79
Loughborough, Leics 218
Luffenham 93, 137, 146, 260
Luffenham brickyard 138
Lyddington 331-2, 345

Lyddington Bede House 332
Lyddington enclosure 23
Lyddington fishponds 319, 332
Lyddington Little Park 331-2
Lyddington Palace 332
Lyndon 162, 164-7, 170-1, 173-6, 219, 291, 303, 414, 423, 553, 557, 664
Lyndon Church 311
Lyndon earthquake 178, 312
Lyndon Hall 165-70, 175, 184, 189, 191, 308, 311, 313, 461, 476, 663-4
Lyndon Hill Nature Reserve and Visitor Centre 216, 531, 538, 551, 555-6, 595, 599, 603-4
Lyndon parish registers 313
Lyndon to Hambleton road 530, 545
Lyndon Top Hall 165-6
Lyndon village hall 309, 311
Lynn, Norfolk 430
Lyveden, Northants 410, 439, 443
Mammal species 503-05, 564, 566, 576
Manor Court 17-18
Mansfield Woodhouse, Notts 221
Manton 29, 182, 203, 210-30, 240, 303-4, 306, 316, 322-3, 326, 349, 370, 423, 456, 462, 469, 476, 516, 578
Manton Bay 216, 325, 353, 531, 594-7, 599-600, 609
Manton bus 229
Manton Church 216-20
Manton Hall 225-6
Manton houses 213-16, 222-6, 228-9, 456
Manton manor 211, 220-1
Manton public houses 213, 215-16, 227
Manton railway 212, 214, 225-9, 304
Manton Reservoir 216, 321-2, 324-5, 349, 370, 380, 388
Manton school 216, 221-3
Manton village hall 216, 222-3
Market Overton 341
Markfield, Leics 123
Martinsthorpe 19-20, 210, 218-19, 317, 439
Martinsthorpe coaching road 323
Medieval guilds 118
Melton Mowbray, Leics 35, 83, 111, 178, 26, 225-7, 240, 300, 309, 341, 465
Meteorological observations 312, 663
Middle Ages 30, 402
Middle Stone Age 402, 411
Middle Temple, London 220-1
Milford, Hamps 240

Military surveys 57, 151, 232, 287
Milton Keynes, Bucks 71
Milton, Cambs 50
Mohne Dam, Germany 339
Molluscs 366, 612-3
Moneyers 429, 30
Morcott 663
Mortlake, London 67
Moth trapping 515-6
Motorway, M62 372
Mount Sorrel, Leics 428
Mow Mires 241, 314, 351, 375-6, 478, 520
Mow Mires Spinney 262, 317, 375, 479, 500, 513
Murder 204-05, 310, 447, 644, 651
Napoleonic Wars 22
Naseby, Northants 340
Nature Reserve 92, 124, 354, 482, 504, 507, 509, 518, 523, 529-574, 580-1, 584, 586, 589, 594, 602-3
New Forest, Hants 94
New Inn, London 220
New Stone Age 402, 412
Newark, Notts 62, 404, 415, 417, 576
Newbiggin, Northumberland 240
Normanton 25-6, 28, 37, 135, 137-8, 173, 231-81, 283-4, 303, 314, 326, 329-30, 353, 359, 368, 394, 401, 412, 448, 478, 489, 497, 501-02, 523, 527, 630, 643-4
Normanton archaeology 232, 358
Normanton Bridge 113, 330, 328, 331, 358, 499, 518, 522-4
Normanton Church 101, 233, 235, 244, 258-9, 269-8, 275, 278, 280-1, 328-9, 358, 373, 495-7, 572, 631, 638
Normanton Church headstones 275
Normanton Church Museum 231, 269, 274, 276, 354, 365, 393, 419, 495-7, 511, 604, 607
Normanton enclosure 21
Normanton Estate 30-1, 101, 133-6, 138, 142, 146, 150, 231, 237, 251, 258, 262, 265-7, 271, 324, 401, 478
Normanton Estate sale 133-4, 146, 252-3, 256, 263, 478
Normanton farms 36, 264, 266-8
Normanton Fishing Lodge 371, 488, 491, 493-5, 610, 616, 618, 623
Normanton Fishpond 113, 317, 326, 329, 330-1, 358, 499-500, 513, 522
Normanton Gardens 245
Normanton Hall / House 138, 146, 231, 233-4, 237, 239-42, 242-3, 245-61, 265, 270, 272, 275, 308, 314, 326, 328-9, 478, 495
Normanton Hearth Tax Return 234
Normanton Heath, 643
Normanton Park 25, 135, 137, 231, 241-7, 252, 256, 258, 260, 271, 307, 314, 328-9, 358, 376, 478-9, 504, 643
Normanton Park Hotel 258
Normanton Park House 258-9, 281
Normanton Park Road 314
Normanton Park, Repton's Red Book 78, 326, 328-9
Normanton prison camp 187
Normanton Rectory 272-3
Normanton Works 138, 146, 262-7
North Brook 317-8, 336, 485, 504
North Luffenham (*also see* Luffenham) 105-6, 108, 113-14, 110, 219, 316, 450, 644-5
North Luffenham Church 114
Northampton 45, 66, 369, 492
Norwich, Norfolk, 56, 228
Nottingham 69, 187-8, 227-8, 291, 403-4, 415, 419, 440, 422, 630
Nuneaton, Warks 57
Oakham 15, 17, 23, 60, 62, 64-5, 69, 90, 93, 115, 117-18, 120, 122, 142, 150-1, 157, 176, 188, 204, 216, 220, 225, 227, 229, 257, 262, 284, 292, 296, 309-10, 312, 315, 323, 326, 342, 350, 359, 361, 370, 398, 412-13, 416, 421, 423, 438-9, 451, 468, 470-1, 480, 528, 540, 550, 559, 640, 642, 646, 648-50, 656
Oakham Assizes 142
Oakham buildings 122, 151, 185, 221, 286, 645-6
Oakham bypass 412-13
Oakham canal 216, 341, 485
Oakham Castle 62, 262-3, 284, 310, 438-9
Oakham fields 15
Oakham schools 169, 193-4, 288, 301, 307, 540, 559
Oakham Survey 16-17, 23
Oakham Union Workhouse 143, 175, 224, 306-8
Oakham Vicarage 220
Oakham water supply 317, 345
Oakham, Mount Pleasant 655, 657
Oakham, Riding School 122
Oakham to Stamford road (A606) 47, 52, 91, 311, 333, 335, 353, 375-6, 418, 473, 499-500, 541, 642, 660
Occupations 136-7, 146, 183, 197, 215, 265, 304-12
Olympics and Paralympics 533, 535, 634, 636, 640
Order of the Garter 193
Osprey 92, 509, 559-61, 560-1, 586-90, 592, 595-6, 599-600, 607
Osprey cruise 597, 608
Osprey migration 560, 589, 593-4
Osprey Project 560-2, 594, 600
Osprey translocation 560, 591, 596-7, 599-600
Osprey Wood 560
Osprey, persecution of 588
Overton Longville, Hunts 240
Owston, Leics 317
Oxford 73, 220, 372
Pacific Parrots Project 571
Paddington, London 221
Parish roads 306
Parliament 70, 99, 158, 161, 164, 341
Paxton gravel pits, Northants 576
Peckham, London 220
Penshurst, Kent 240
Peterborough 35, 104, 225-6, 228-9, 273, 275, 311, 337, 342, 369, 418, 486
Pickwell, Leics 199
Pickworth 454
Pilton 138, 265, 663-4
Pilton brickworks 138, 265
Pitsford Reservoir, Northants 339, 369, 481, 576
Plagues and epidemics 18-20, 24, 151, 164, 343, 345, 441
Plant species, flowerless 90, 397, 493, 519, 527
Plant species, grasses 519-21, 542, 584
Plant species, herbaceous 53, 90, 244-5, 282, 503, 513, 515-6, 519, 522-7, 541, 556, 566 582, 658
Plant species, trees and shrubs 499, 515, 518-9, 521-2
Plants, reed beds 521, 541-4, 584
Plough Monday 311
PLUTO (pipe line under the ocean) 339
Ponds 346, 510
Poor Law 138, 175
Popish Plot 647
Portsmouth 61
Pottery, distribution of 440-1
Pottery, industry and trade 430, 434, 439-40, 443
Pottery, types of 410, 432-5, 437-43, 425
Pumping stations 322, 324, 379, 388-9,

— 678 —

392-3
Radcliffe on Trent, Notts 416, 418-19
RAF Feltwell, Norfolk 111
RAF Hemswell, Lincs 104, 111
RAF North Luffenham 104-5, 107, 110-122, 187
RAF Woolfox Lodge 105, 112
Ramsar site 530, 532
Ravenstone, Buckinghamshire 64, 71
Redhill, Surrey 583
Red Books by Repton 76-8, 91, 326, 328-9, 333-4
Reservoir clearance works 375, 399, 499-501, 530, 516, 522, 530, 576
Reservoir Act 373
Ridgeway / trackway, ancient 407, 210
Ridlington 13, 41, 93, 316, 323, 340
Ridlington to Ayston road 340
Ridlington to Brooke road 323
River Chater 216, 316-19, 320, 322-3, 325, 340-1, 349, 353, 380, 398, 370, 380, 520
River Eg 319
River Glen 318
River Gwash (also see Gwash Valley) 26-8, 40, 46, 96, 112-13, 115-16, 124, 149, 159, 176, 178, 182, 191, 220, 231, 244, 273, 298, 317-20, 322-3, 325-6, 330, 333, 345, 347, 349, 351-2, 358-60, 363-5, 367, 369-70, 374, 377-8, 395, 403, 406-07, 413, 416, 431, 445, 462, 475-6, 480, 499, 501-05, 510-12, 514, 516, 518-23, 525, 529, 574, 625, 643, 654
River Hlyde 319
River Nene 50, 322, 324-5, 341, 353, 369-70, 388-9, 393, 413
River Seine 301
River Severn 529
River Soar 341
River Trent 318, 576
River Welland 98, 227, 229, 315-16, 317-22, 324-5, 345, 369-70, 339, 341, 345, 353, 388-9, 393, 407, 413, 575
Road construction 314, 412, 642
Robin Hood's Cave 45-6, 228
Rock Blok 283, 609
Rockingham Castle, Northants 67, 156, 315, 554, 583
Romano-British archaeology 284, 405-7, 409, 413, 415, 420
Rushpit Wood 500, 514, 519, 580, 642
Rutland archaeology 402-443
Rutland Belle 283, 302, 419, 490-1, 494, 497, 597

Rutland County Show 86
Rutland Hundreds 221, 643, 643
Rutland independence 353, 633
Rutland Lay Subsidy 95
Rutland Military Survey 97
Rutland Parliamentary enclosure 21-3, 96, 134, 136, 159-60, 163-4, 170, 289
Rutland Ploughing Match 38, 40, 43
Rutland population 303-04
Rutland Quarter Session records 651
Rutland railways 48, 122-3, 178, 212-14, 225-9, 260, 300, 304, 341, 461
Rutland Water 113, 286, 298, 300-01, 359-61, 363-5, 401, 410, 413, 418-9, 423, 431, 444, 460, 467-9, 475, 479, 493, 501, 505, 509-11, 522, 529, 532-5, 548-9, 552-3, 557, 559-60, 562, 566-8, 573-4, 620
Rutland Water aqueducts and pipelines 325, 388-9, 393, 397, 413
Rutland Water car parks 113, 482-3, 491, 497, 528, 606
Rutland Water construction 32, 284, 321-2, 369-401, 415, 421, 481, 499, 535, 626
Rutland Water dam 323, 349, 352, 359-62, 365, 367, 369, 374, 377, 379-81, 382-7, 392, 395, 401, 403, 418, 483, 485-6, 499-500, 502, 504, 518, 530, 532, 535
Rutland Water fishery 484, 488, 492, 615
Rutland Water fishing tackle shop 609
Rutland Water landscaping 482-3, 491
Rutland Water perimeter track 482, 607
Rutland Water planning and construction 32, 321-2, 369-401, 481
Rutland Water planning and development 481 to 498
Rutland Water seepage problems 398-9
Rutland Water Tourist Information Centre 354, 403, 484
Rutland Water, naming of 354, 356
Rutland Water, objections to 191, 349-357, 575
Rutland watercourses 315-347
Ry Gate Lake 317, 336-7
Ryhall 317, 320-1, 346-7, 352
Saddington, Leics 340
St Albans, Beds 610
St George's Barracks, North Luffenham 114, 217, 640

St Paul's Cathedral, London 220
San Remo, Italy 634
Sanctuary areas 539
Sanitary Act 343
Sanitary arrangements, cesspools and drains 343, 510
Sauvey Castle, Leics 316
Saxby, Lincs 146
Scammonden Reservoir, West Yorks 372
Scotland 73, 107, 532, 560, 562, 587-8, 594, 597, 600
Scraptoft, Leics 254
Sculthorpe, Norfolk 93
Seaton 320, 663
Seaton watermill 316
Second World War 31, 34, 39, 43, 74, 86, 105-6, 121, 123, 187, 217, 222, 330, 339, 346, 372, 482
Selborne, Hants 169, 291
Shacklewell 317, 480
Shacklewell Spinney, 317
Sheepdykes and washdykes 346
Shrewsbury, Shrops 372
Site of Special Scientific Interest (SSSI) 47, 339, 532
Skeffington, Leics 316
Skegness, Lincs 180
Skipton, Yorkshire 293
Slimbridge, Gloucs 529
Snowdrop Spinney 375, 516, 522, 524, 527
Somerby, Leics 470
Somerset Levels 560
Sounding Bridge 317, 505, 515, 519, 603
South Kensington, London 482
South Luffenham (see also Luffenham) 166, 225, 316, 320
South Witham, Lincs 146
Spalding, Lincs 316, 337, 430
Spanhoe airfield, Northants 32
Special Protection Area (SPA) 509, 532-3
Springs 342
Sproxton, Leics 454
Stamford Junction Canal 216, 341-2, 415
Stamford, Lincs 58, 75, 80, 93, 98-9, 144, 149, 165, 173, 179, 210, 216, 221, 225-7, 252, 262, 310, 312-17, 337, 341-2, 407, 410, 416, 421, 430, 433, 438-9, 450, 480, 528, 648-9, 656
Stanion, Northants 435, 439
Stapleford Park, Leics 225, 318

— 679 —

Stock Park, Ulverston, Cumbria 101
Stockerston, Leics 156, 316
Stoke Dry 154, 316
Streams 316-18, 336, 485, 504, 510
Stretton 265
Sundew 32
Swanley, Kent 482
Sykes Lane 354, 403, 408, 411-12, 415, 418, 483, 491, 495, 574, 577, 609
Sykes Spinney 231
Syston, Leics 225-6, 229, 636
Tarrant Gunville, Dorset 240
Teigh 176, 341
Temple Newsam House, Leeds 278
Thistleton 14
Thomas Fryer Almshouses 223-5
Thorpe by Water 315-16, 319 20
Tickencote 317, 320
Ticknall, Derbys 436-7, 440
Tilton on the Hill, Leics 210
Tinwell 316, 320, 322, 324, 339, 353, 388-90, 393, 400-01, 480
Titchmarsh gravel pits, Northants 576
Tixover 316
Tolethorpe 39, 100, 317, 320
Toll bars and gates 91, 480
Tree species 244-6, 483, 499, 515, 518-9, 521-2, 540-2, 589
Trimley Marshes, Suffolk 447
Turnpikes 122, 212, 480, 528
Upper Broughton, Notts 310
Upper Palaeolithic period 192, 402
Uppingham 156, 213, 229, 340, 345, 470, 640, 656
Uppingham enclosure 23
Uppingham fair 176
Uppingham schools 169, 288, 340, 345, 540
Uppingham to Oakham road (A6003) 122, 216, 315, 340, 380, 514, 519
Uppingham typhoid outbreaks 345
Uppingham water supplies 345
Vale of Catmose 87, 188, 245, 359, 448
Valley bulge 365, 384, 391, 393
Wales 315, 532, 597
Waltham Abbey, Essex 93
Wansford, Peterborough 322, 324, 337, 353, 388-90, 393, 400-01
Wantage, Oxon 295
War of Austrian Succession 71
Wars of the Roses 56, 151
Wash barrage 350-1
Wash, The 316, 351, 575
Water Act 370, 481, 601
Water Resources Act 321, 349

Water supplies 144, 322, 342, 345, 418
Watercourses 315, 510
Watermills, windmills and sawmills 14-15, 120, 266, 287, 316-7, 319-21, 336, 432-3, 481, 484-5, 591
Weldon, Northants 66
Welham, Leics 98
Welland and Nene (Empingham Reservoir) and Mid-Northants Water Bill 349
Welland Valley viaduct 227, 229
Wellingborough, Northants 339
Wells 168, 211, 285, 342-3, 380, 398-9, 420, 645
Wells, Somerset 529
Wentworth Woodhouse, Yorks 50
West Brook 316
Westbury-on-Trym, Avon 529
Western Flavell, Northants 274
Westminster Abbey, London 17-18, 94
Westminster, London 270, 349, 372
Westminster, St John's Church 270
Westonbirt, Gloucs 100
Whatborough, Leics 316, 353, 359
Wherwell, Hants 94
Whissendine 123, 225, 318, 356
Whissendine Brook 318
Whitehall, London 322
Whitwell 20, 31-2, 45, 47, 115, 161, 175, 283-302, 310, 320, 329, 409-10, 415, 419, 438-9, 440, 442-3, 463, 483-4, 489, 492, 519, 525, 616, 642, 644
Whitwell agriculture 13, 20, 289
Whitwell archaeology 15, 284-7, 289, 409-11, 412-13, 415, 422-43
Whitwell Church 13, 283, 285-6, 288, 294-5, 297, 300
Whitwell Creek 299, 302, 630
Whitwell Domesday Survey 13
Whitwell enclosure 20-1, 289
Whitwell Feast Week 295
Whitwell fields 20, 289
Whitwell Fishing Lodge 421, 492
Whitwell Harbour 486, 604-5
Whitwell Hotel and Conference Centre 291, 299, 300
Whitwell houses and farms 286-7, 295, 297-8, 300
Whitwell manor 20, 288-9, 291
Whitwell occupations and population 15, 285, 291, 295
Whitwell Old Hall 286, 289, 291-5, 298-9, 421-2, 431-3
Whitwell parish conduit 285
Whitwell Peninsula 368, 487, 485, 492

Whitwell Post Office 296
Whitwell public houses 300-01
Whitwell Rectory 285, 291, 299
Whitwell Rescue Centre 421
Whitwell school 295-6
Whitwell twinning ceremony 301-02
Whitwell Water Sports Centre 368, 492, 574
Whitwell watermill 287, 432-3
Whitwell, White Well 285
Wick, Scotland 240
Wigston, Leics 19
Wildlife and Countryside Act 504
Wildlife and nature conservation 418, 529, 603
Winderton, Norfolk 240
Windermere, Cumbria 351, 416
Window Tax 290
Windsor Castle, London 63, 67
Wing 187, 212, 313, 325, 348, 353, 655, 657
Wing to Whatborough pipeline 353
Wing Water Treatment Works 324-5, 348, 353, 369, 378, 395, 398, 413
Witches Heath / Witchley Heath / Witchley Warren 280, 643-4
Withcote, Leics 210, 213, 256, 322, 316, 340
Woburn Abbey, Bedfordshire 529
Woods and spinneys 14, 16, 45-49, 53, 71, 90-2, 150, 159, 191, 200, 231, 261-2, 317, 336, 359, 375-6, 445, 459, 479, 499-501, 503, 513-16, 518-19, 521-2, 524-5, 527, 537-8, 560, 564, 566, 582-3, 621, 643-4, 651-2,
Woolfox 105, 112, 136, 187
Wyfordby, Leics 341
Wytchley Warren Spinney, 643
Yarmouth Norfolk 146
Yarnton, Oxon 220
York 430
York Mint 30